C AND C++ PROGRAMMING CONCEPTS AND DATA STRUCTURES

C AND C++ PROGRAMMING CONCEPTS AND DATA STRUCTURES

Dr. P. S. Subramanyam
M.Tech., Ph.D.
Professor Emeritus
Formerly Professor and HOD in CSE & IT over two decades
Vignana Bharathi Institute of Technology,
Aushapur, Hyderabad - 501 301.

A unit of **BSP Books Pvt., Ltd.**

4-4-309/316, Giriraj Lane, Sultan Bazar,
Hyderabad - 500 095
Phone : 040 - 23445605, 23445688

Published by :

A unit of **BSP Books Pvt., Ltd.**

4-4-309/316, Giriraj Lane, Sultan Bazar,
Hyderabad - 500 095
Phone : 040 - 23445605, 23445688
e-mail : info@bspbooks.net

ISBN : 978-93-85433-41-2 (HB)

Dedicated To

LOTUS FEET

of

Lord

Preface

Gone are the days when students used to think and staff members used to wink over the idea that a good knowledge of computer programming is necessary only for Computer Science students. Now it has been well established that an adequate and sufficient knowledge of computer programming is a must for any student, he or she be, not only from any branch of Engineering or Science but from Humanities, Arts, Commerce Economics, Finance as well. Recognising this fact the Universities particularly J.N.T.U. Hyderabad has made it compulsory for all students other than CSE and IT, study of the subject "C and Data Structures" in addition to having a minimum of four computer oriented subjects in their discipline. Of late the national and international companies prefer students of other branches with a good knowledge of computing skills particularly a knowledge of C and C++ languages and preferably C++ for placements in their organizations, because of their domain knowledge in their chosen areas.

Bearing this in mind, as an author, I have taken the initiative of preparing this book on "**C AND C++ PROGRAMMING CONCEPTS AND DATA STRUCTURES**" for the benefit of young students aspiring for covetted positions in good multinational companies, be they from any discipline.

The algorithms which form the basis of programming, the syntax and their appropriate use at the proper place in programming have been highlighted in this book. The book deals with C programming which forms the much sought after basics of programming at present and a some what object oriented though not fully object oriented language like C++ including the different types of data and Data structures with a comparitive study. Common features are given first, and special feautres separately. A good number of C and C++ programs which are of day to day use are the assets of this book. Also it can be observed that many modules of programming are used repeatedly in the development of different programs. The necessary comments and highlighting of the location and appropriate usage of concerned features are the highlights of the book. In addition the book brings out clearly the comparison between C and C++ programming for any problem.

As such, the author feels that the book caters well to the requirements of first two years of B.Tech. students belonging to any branch, particularly so for C.S.E and I.T students to have a good grip in efficient programming in C and C++.

For better understanding and grasp of the subject, a set of Comprehension Questions and Exercises have been provided at the end of each chapter.

By answering all the questions given in the comprehension at the end of each chapter one can answer any objective type of question easily whatever be the form of the question. Answers for those questions can be obtained by going through the topics in the chapter carefully. It also helps in understanding the subject covered in the chapter thoroughly.

By answering all the questions given in the exercise at the end of each chapter one can answer subjective type of questions easily including programs for different tasks. The programs illustrated in the chapter will help creating confidence in the students in developing efficient programs for any day to day problem in Engineering, Finance, Economics and other disciplines.

I express my gratitude and thanks to the Management of **Vignana Bharathi Institute of Technology, Aushapur, Ghatkesar Mandal, Hyderabad,** who have conferred the status of Professor Emeritus to me and for encouraging me to bring out this book **"C AND C++ PROGRAMMING CONCEPTS AND DATA STRUCTURES".**

My hearty thanks are due to **M/s. B.S. Publications** for bringing out this book in the present pleasant form.

I have to make a special mention of the immense help rendered by M/s. Bharadwaj Solutions (Website : www.bharadwajsolutions.com) and Mr. J. Sudheer for doing the necessary D.T.P. Operations to bring out this book in a nice format.

I thank my family members for their constant encouragement in this work and the patience exhibited by them during the period of authoring this book.

Comments & Suggestions are Welcome to improve the book in subsequent editions.

I wish to dedicate this book to LORD ALMIGHTY who is the first and foremost GURU and the fountain head of all knowledge, to my teachers and to my students with whose inquisitiveness I could learn more and develop the subject, in the true tradition of GURU PARAMPARA.

Dr. Subramanyam S. Pisupati
subramanyamps@gmail.com

Contents

Preface .... (vii)

CHAPTER 1

INTRODUCTION TO COMPUTERS

1.1. INTRODUCTION TO COMPUTERS 1
1.2. HISTORY OF C & C++ 3
1.3. DESIGN, DEVELOPMENT AND EXECUTION OF A PROGRAM 3
1.4 TESTING OF PROGRAMS 4
  1.4.1 White Box Testing 5
  1.4.2 Black Box Testing 5
  1.4.3 Testing Bench Mark Problems 5
1.5 POINTS TO BE CONSIDERED IN PROGRAMMING 5
1.6 DIFFERENT LEVELS OF PROGRAMMING LANGUAGES 5
  1.6.1 Imperative and functional programming languages 6
    1.6.1.1 Imperative programming language 6
  1.6.2 Functional programming language 7
  1.6.3 Interpretation and compilation 8
    1.6.3.1 Interpreted language 7
    1.6.3.2 Compiled language 7
    1.6.3.3 Intermediary languages 8
  1.6.4 Some widely used languages 8
1.7. APPROACHES IN PROGRAMMING 8

1.8 **TOP-DOWN PROGRAMMING AND STEP-WISE REFINEMENT** **10**
1.8.1 (a) Advantages of Top down Programming 11
(b) Disadvantages of Top down programming 11
1.9 **BOTTOM-UP PROGRAMMING** 11
1.9.1 Working of bottom-up programming 11
1.9.2 (a) Advantages of bottom-up programming 12
(b) Disadvantages of bottom up programming 12
1.10 **OPERATING SYSTEMS** **13**
1.10.1 Types of operating systems 13
1.10.2 Examples of operating systems 15
1.10.3 Components Of an Operating System 18
1.10.4 Modes 19
1.10.5 Networking of Computers 22
1.10.6 Computer Security 23
1.10.7 Operating system user interface 24
1.10.8 Diversity of operating systems and portability 25
1.10.9 Black Berry and Black Berry O.S 26
1.10.10 C Programming is a subset of C++ programming 27
COMPREHENSION - 1 .... **28**
EXERCISE - 1 .... **30**

CHAPTER 2

BASICS OF PROGRAMMING

2.1 INTRODUCTION TO BASICS OF PROGRAMMING 31
2.2 LOGIC FOR PROGRAMMING 31
2.3 ALGORITHM 31
2.3.1 Pseudo code 31
2.3.2 Flow Chart **32**
2.4 BASIC CATEGORIES OF OPERATIONS 36
2.5 IMPORTANCE OF 'C' LANGUAGE **37**
2.6 IMPORTANCE OF C++ LANGUAGE 38

2.7 SOME OF THE COMPILERS AVAILABLE FOR C AND C++ 39
2.7.1 List of compilers for C 40
2.7.2 List of compilers available in C++ 40
2.8 STRUCTURE OF A 'C' PROGRAM 40
2.9 PROGRAMMING RULES 43
2.10 EXECUTING THE PROGRAM 43
2.11 STEPS TO EXECUTE A C PROGRAM USING TC++ COMPILER 45
COMPREHENSION - 2 47
EXERCISE - 2 48

CHAPTER 3

DECLARATIONS IN C AND C++

3.1. INTRODUCTION TO C DECLARATIONS 49
3.2. CHARACTER SET 49
3.2.1 Letters 49
3.2.2 Digits 49
3.2.3 Special Characters 50
3.2.4 White spaces 50
3.2.5 Delimiters 50
3.2.6 Escape sequences or back slash character constants 50
3.3. C TOKENS / C++ TOKENS 51
3.3.1 Key Words 51
3.3.2 Identifiers 52
3.3.3 Constants 52
3.3.3.1 Integer Constants 52
3.3.3.2 Real Constants 54
3.4. CHARACTER CONSTANTS 56
3.4.1 Single Character Constants 56
3.4.2 String Constants 56
3.5. SPECIAL SYMBOLS 57
3.6. OPERATORS 57

3.7. VARIABLES **57**
3.7.1 Rules for defining Variables *58*
3.8. DATA TYPES 59
3.8.1 Primary or Basic or Fundamental Data type 59
3.8.1.1 Integer, Float and Char Data types 59
3.8.2 User-defined Data Types 61
3.8.2.1 User defined data 61
3.8.2.2 Enumerated datatypes 62
3.8.2.3 Storage Class Data types 63
3.8.2.4 Derived Data Types 65
3.8.2.5 Empty Data Set or Void data type in C and C++ 66
3.8.2.6 Additional Data Types in C++ 66
3.9. DECLARATION AND INITIALIZATION OF VARIABLES **68**
3.9.1 Type conversion or type cast 69
3.10. CONSTANT AND VOLATILE VARIABLES 69
3.11. DEFINING SYMBOLIC CONSTANTS **70**
3.12. MODIFIABILITY **71**
3.12.1 Overflow and Underflow of Data 72
3.12.2 Constant Qualifier 72
3.12.3 Reading Data from Keyboard 72
COMPREHENSION - 3 .... **74**
EXERCISE- 3 .... **76**

CHAPTER 4

OPERATORS AND EXPRESSIONS

4.1 INTRODUCTION **79**
4.2. PRIORITY OR HIERARCHY OR PRECEDENCE OF OPERATORS **79**
4.2.1 Use of Different Operators 81
4.2.2 Evaluation of expressions using the priorities of operators 87
4.3. TYPE CONVERSIONS IN EXPRESSIONS 89
4.3.1 Operator precedence and associativity 92

4.4 SOME SPECIAL FEATURES OF C++ OVER C : 94
4.5 SOME PROGRAMS IN C 95
4.6 DIFFERENCES BETWEEN OLD AND AND CURRENT VERSIONS OF C++ 109
4.6.1 Scope Resolution Operator 109
4.6.2 Differences in I/O statements 110
4.7. SOME PROGRAMS IN C++ USING TC++ 111
COMPREHENSION - 4 115
EXERCISE - 4 116

CHAPTER 5

INPUT AND OUTPUT OPERATIONS IN C

5.1. INTRODUCTION 121
5.1.1 Formatted Input Functions: (without field width specifications) 123
5.1.2 Inputting Integer Variables 123
5.1.3 Inputting Real Variables 124
5.1.4 Inputting Character / String constants 125
5.1.5 Inputting Mixed Variables 125
5.2. FORMATTED OUTPUT STATEMENTS (WITHOUT FIELD WIDTHS) 126
5.2.1 Outputting Integer Variables 126
5.2.2 Outputting Real variables 127
5.2.3 Outputting Mixed Variables 127
5.3. FORMATTED INPUT STATEMENTS (WITH FIELD WIDTHS) 128
5.3.1 Inputting Integer numbers 129
5.3.2 Inputting Real Numbers 130
5.3.3 Inputting Characters & Strings 130
5.3.4 Reading Mixed Data Type using scanf ( ) 131
5.3.5 Detection of Errors in Input ed 131
5.3.6 Commonly used scanf ( ) format codes 132
5.4. FORMATTED OUTPUT (WITH FIELD WIDTH) 132
5.4.1 Outputting of Integer Numbers 133
5.4.2 Outputting of Real Numbers 134

5.4.3 Outputting of Mixed Variables without field widths 136
5.4.4 Outputting of Strings with field widths 136
5.4.5 Commonly used printf ( ) format codes 137
5.5 ENHANCING THE READABILITY OF OUTPUT 138
5.6 UNFORMATTED INPUT/OUTPUT FUNCTIONS 138
5.6.1 Types of Unformatted Input / Output Functions in C 139
5.7 CHARACTER RECOGNITION USING CODES 143
5.8 COMMONLY USED LIBRARY FUNCTIONS 145
5.9 C LIBRARY FUNCTION 145
5.9.1 The Standard C Library Functions 147
5.10 PARTIAL C/C++ FUNCTION LIST 149
5.10.1 Functions Listed Alphabetically 149
5.11. PROGRAM TO CONVERT DECIMAL NUMBER INTO BINARY NUMBER SYSTEM : DOWNLOAD 150
5.11.1 Logic of This Program 150
5.11.2 Program 150
5.11.3 Flow Chart of sub-routine Convert Decimal to Different Number Base 153
COMPREHENSION - 5 155
EXERCISE - 5 157

CHAPTER 6

DECISION AND LOOP CONTROL STATEMENTS

6.1. INTRODUCTION 163
6.1.1 Conditional Operator 163
6.1.2 The Simple if Statement 164
6.1.3 Block if statement 164
6.1.4 Nested if statements 165
6.1.5 Simple if else statement 166
6.1.6 Block if else statement 166

6.1.7 Nested ifs or Nested else if or if else if ladder 168
6.1.8 Break statement 169
6.1.9 The continue Statement 170
6.1.10 The goto Statement 170
6.1.11 Switch Statement or Switch case statement 170

6.2. THE BREAK STATEMENT 172

6.2.1 Exit ( ) Function 173

6.3. LOOPING 174

6.3.1 for LOOP 174

6.4 NESTED for LOOPS 178

6.5 WHILE-LOOP 181

6.6 DO-WHILE LOOP 183

6.7 The DO-WHILE statement WITH WHILE loop 185

6.8 JUMPS IN LOOPS 185

6.8.1 Jumping Out of a Loop using Break Statement 186

6.9 JUMPING WITHIN AND EXITING FROM THE LOOPS WITH GOTO STATEMENT 187

6.10 SKIPPING A PART OF A LOOP USING CONTINUE STATEMENT 189

COMPREHENSION - 6 191

EXERCISE - 6 193

CHAPTER 7

ARRAYS

7.1 INTRODUCTION 203

7.2 ONE DIMENSIONAL ARRAY 203

7.2.1 Single dimensional Array initialisation 204

7.3 TWO-DIMENSIONAL ARRAY 209

7.3.1 Initialization of Two-dimensional arrays 210
7.3.2 Two-dimensional sorting 215

7.4 MULTIDIMENSIONAL ARRAYS 217

COMPREHENSION - 7 221

EXERCISE - 7 223

CHAPTER 8

FUNCTIONS

8.1 INTRODUCTION 225
8.2 THE RETURN STATEMENT 226
8.2.1 Function with a return statement to return an expression ... 229
8.3 CALLING A FUNCTION AND OBTAINING ITS RESULT 230
8.3.1 Call by Value 232
8.4 CALL BY REFERENCE 233
8.5 CATEGORY OF FUNCTIONS 235
8.6 CALLING A FUNCTION WITH NO ARGUMENTS AND NO RETURN VALUES 235
8.7 CALLING FUNCTIONS WITH ARGUMENTS AND NO RETURN VALUES 237
8.8 CALLING FUNCTION WITH ARGUMENTS AND WITH RETURN VALUE 238
8.9 FUNCTION RETURNING MORE VALUES 239
8.10 LOCAL AND GLOBAL VARIABLES 240
8.11 ARGUMENTS OF A FUNCTION 242
8.12 FUNCTION PROTOTYPES 244
8.13 FUNCTIONS AND DECISION STATEMENTS 244
8.14 FUNCTION AND LOOP STATEMENTS 245
8.15 NESTING OF FUNCTIONS 246
8.16 RECURSION 247
8.17 FUNCTIONS WITH ARRAYS AND POINTERS 249
8.18 SPECIAL FUNCTIONS OF C++ 252
8.18.1 Default Parameters 253
8.18.2 Inline functions 254
8.18.3 atexit ( ) Function 255
8.19 LIBRARY FUNCTIONS 256
COMPREHENSION - 8 257
EXERCISE - 8 262

CHAPTER 9

STORAGE CLASS MODIFIERS

9.1 INTRODUCTION 265

9.2 AUTO VARIABLES OR LOCAL VARIABLES 265

9.3 DYNAMIC STORAGE OR EXTERNAL GLOBAL VARIABLES 266

9.4 STATIC STORAGE OR STATIC VARIABLES 268

9.5 REGISTER VARIABLES 271

COMPREHENSION - 9 272

EXERCISE - 9 274

CHAPTER 10

POINTERS

10.1 INTRODUCTION 275

10.2 WHAT IS A POINTER? 275

10.3 POINTER OPERATORS 276

10.4 HOW TO ACCESS A VARIABLE THROUGH ITS POINTER? 277

10.5 POINTER EXPRESSIONS 279

10.5.1 Pointer Assignments 279

10.5.2 Arithmetic Operations with Pointers 281

10.6 POINTERS AND ARRAYS 283

10.7 ARRAY OF POINTERS 288

10.8 POINTERS TO POINTERS 289

10.9 POINTERS AND CHARACTER STRINGS 289

COMPREHENSION - 10 292

EXERCISE - 10 295

CHAPTER 11

PRE-PROCESSOR DIRECTIVES

11.1 INTRODUCTION 297
11.2 # define DIRECTIVE AND MACRO SUBSTITUTION 297
11.3 UNDEFINING A MACRO 300
11.4 CONDITIONAL COMPILATION USING PRE-PROCESSOR DIRECTIVE 301
11.5 THE #ifndef DIRECTIVE (if not defined) 302
11.6 #if, #else and #elif (else-if) 303
11.7 THE # line DIRECTIVE 304
11.8 THE #error DIRECTIVE 305
11.9 #OPERATOR OR TOKEN PASTING & STRINGIZING 305
11.10 MACRO CONCATENATION WITH THE # # OPERATOR 307
11.11 The # include DIRECTIVE 308
11.12 INLINE DIRECTIVE 308
11.13 THE #pragma SAVEREGS 308
11.14 THE #pragma DIRECTIVE 308
11.15 THE PREDEFINED MACROS IN ANSI AND TURBO-C 310
11.16 STANDARD I/O PREDEFINED STREAMS IN C - stdio.h 311
11.17 THE PREDEFINED MACROS IN ctype.h 312
COMPREHENSION - 11 314
EXERCISE - 11 316

CHAPTER 12

STRUCTURE AND UNION

12.1 INTRODUCTION 319
12.2 FEATURES OF STRUCTURES 319
12.3 DECLARATION AND INITIALIZATION OF STRUCTURES . 320
12.4 STRUCTURE WITHIN STRUCTURE OR NESTED STRUCTURES 324
12.5 ARRAY OF STRUCTURES 328

12.6 STRUCTURES & POINTERS OR POINTER TO STRUCTURE 330
12.7 STRUCTURES AND FUNCTIONS 332
12.8 BIT FIELDS 335
12.9 UNION 337
12.10 ANONYMOUS UNIONS 338
12.11 typedef 339
12.12 ENUMERATED DATA TYPE 340
12.13 CALLING BIOS AND DOS SERVICES 342
12.14 UNION OF STRUCTURES 343
12.15 SCOPE OPERATOR OR SCOPE RESOLUTION OPERATOR :
IN C++ 344
COMPREHENSION - 12 346
EXERCISE - 12 348

CHAPTER 13

FILE OPERATIONS IN C

13.1 INTRODUCTION 351
13.2 STREAMS AND FILE TYPES 351
13.3 STEPS FOR FILE OPERATIONS 351
13.3.1 Opening of a File 352
13.4 FILE I/O OPERATIONS 362
13.5 BINARY MODE - READ AND WRITE 366
13.6 OTHER FILE FUNCTIONS 367
13.7 SEARCHING ERRORS IN READING / WRITING FILES 368
13.8 USE OF MULTIPLE FILES 370
13.9 LOW LEVEL DISK I/O OPERATIONS 374
13.10 COMMAND LINE ARGUMENTS 376
13.11 APPLICATION OF COMMAND LINE ARGUMENTS 378
13.12 ENVIRONMENT VARIABLES 379
13.13 I/O RE DIRECTION 380
COMPREHENSION - 13 381
EXERCISE - 13 383

CHAPTER 14

DYNAMIC MEMORY ALLOCATION - I (LINKED LISTS)

14.1 INTRODUCTION 385

14.1.1 Classification of Data Structures 386

14.2 LINKED LIST 387

14.2.1 Singly Linked List 388

14.2.2 Traversing a singly linked list 392

14.2.3 Addition and Deletion of Elements in a Singly Linked List 394

14.2.4 Insertion in singly linked list 395

14.2.5 Counting of Nodes in a Singly Linked List 407

14.2.6 Deletion of nodes in a Singly linked list 407

14.2.7 Changing the content of an element in a Singly Linked List 412

14.2.8 Reversing of a singly linked list 413

14.3 DOUBLY LINKED LIST (DLL) 415

14.4 MODIFICATION OF DOUBLY LINKED LIST 419

14.4.1 Insertion in a doubly linked list at the beginning 419

14.4.2 Insertion in a doubly linked list at a specified position 419

14.4.3 Deletion of an existing node in a doubly linked list 421

14.5 CIRCULARLY LINKED LIST 423

14.5.1 Singly linked Circular List 423

14.5.2 Doubly linked Circular List 428

14.6. LINKED LIST AS APPLICATIONS OF LINEAR DATA STRUCTURE 429

14.6.1 Polynomial Operation 429

14.6.2 Linked Dictionary 429

COMPREHENSION - 14 430

EXERCISE - 14 431

CHAPTER 15

DYNAMIC MEMORY ALLOCATION - II (STACKS AND QUEUES)

15.1 INTRODUCTION TO STACKS **433**

15.2 IMPLEMENTATION OF STACKS USING LINKED LIST **434**

15.3. STACK RELATED TERMS **435**

15.4 OPERATION ON A STACK **436**

15.5 IMPLEMENTATION OF A STACK **437**

15.6 INTRODUCTION TO QUEUES **445**

15.7 REPRESENTATION OF QUEUE **446**

15.8 INSERTION AND DELETION OPERATIONS IN A QUEUE **450**

15.9 CIRCULAR QUEUES **456**

15.9.1 Deletion and insertion in a full circular queue 461

15.10 PRIORITY QUEUE **462**

15.10.1 Similarity to queues 462

15.10.2 Implementation of priority queue 463

15.10.3 Effect of different data structures on priority queue 463

15.10.4 Equivalence of priority queues and sorting algorithms 464

15.10.5 Applications of priority queue 465

15.11 DEQUE or DEQUEUE (as Noun), Deque (as verb) and Double-ended Queue **470**

15.11.1 Naming conventions of Deque 470

15.11.2 Distinctions and sub-types of Deque 471

15.11.3 Operations of Deque in different languages 471

15.11.4 Implementations of Deque 472

15.11.5 Language support for Deque 472

15.11.6 Complexity of Deque 473

15.11.7 Applications of Deque 473

15.12 REPRESENTATION & OPERATIONS OF ARITHMETIC EXPRESSIONS USING STACK OPERATIONS 473
15.12.1 Infix, prefix, and postfix notations 474
15.12.2 Evaluation of postfix expression 478
15.12.3 Conversion of expression from infix to postfix 480
15.13 RECURSION 493
COMPREHENSION - 15 494
EXERCISE - 15 496

CHAPTER 16

OPERATIONS ON DATA STRUCTURES (SEARCHING AND SORTING)

16.1 INTRODUCTION 499
16.2 SEARCHING 499
16.2.1 Linear Search or Sequential Search 500
16.2.2 Binary Search 501
16.2.2a. Time complexity of binary search 502
16.2.2b. Comparison of binary search with other techniques 502
16.2.3 Features of Binary Search 509
16.2.4 Comparison of Binary Search with other Search Techniques 510
16.3 TREES AND GRAPHS 510
16.3.1 Trees 510
16.3.2 Binary Trees 511
16.3.3 Binary Tree Representation 513
16.3.4 Traversing Binary Trees 514
16.4 MINIMUM SPANNING TREE 528
16.4.1 Algorithms to find a minimum spanning tree 531

16.4.2 MST on complete graphs - calculation of approximative expected size 532
16.4.3 Related problems - Types of spanning trees 533
16.5 AVL TREE 534
16.5.1 Basic Operations on an AVL Tree 535
16.5.2 Comparison of AVL to other structures 540
16.6 GRAPHS 540
16.6.1 Prim's algorithm for Traversal of a Graph 546
16.7 TYPES OF TREE SEARCHES 550
16.7.1 Breadth-First Search 550
16.7.2 Depth-First Search 552
16.8 SORTING 557
16.8.1 Exchange Sort (Bubble Sort) 558
16.8.2 Selection Sort 561
16.8.3 Quick Sort 565
16.8.4 Merge sort 571
16.8.5 K-Way Merge Sort 575
16.8.6 What differentiates a K-Way Merge sort from a regular Merge sort? 576
16.8.7 Heap Sort or Tree Sort 579
16.8.8 Insertion Sort (or Simple Insertion Sort) 585
16.8.9 Shell sort 589
COMPREHENSION - 16 593
EXERCISE - 16 596

CHAPTER 17

CLASSES AND OBJECTS IN C++

17.1 INTRODUCTION 590
17.1.1 Difference between Structures and Class 601
17.1.2 Declaration and definition of a simple class 601

17.1.3 Inline Member Functions (Function declared inside the class or outside a class with scope operator): 605
17.1.4 Array of objects 607
17.1.5 Constructor for initializing an object 608
17.1.6 Parameterized Constructors 610
17.1.7 Explicit Constructor 612
17.2 DESTRUCTOR 614
17.3 FRIEND FUNCTIONS 616
17.4 FRIEND CLASSES 618
17.5 DIFFERENT METHODS OF ACCESSION OF OBJECTS 620
17.5.1 Object Assignment 620
17.5.2 Accessing a Private data member from a different object 621
17.6 DYNAMIC MEMORY ALLOCATION IN C++ USING KEY WORDS 622
17.6.1 Const. member function and const. objects 623
17.6.2 Mutable to change const object instance 624
17.6.3 The size of a Class Object 625
17.6.4 Nested Class (Class within another class) 627
17.6.5 The Copy Constructor 629
17.6.6 This Pointer : (this →) 631
17.6.7 Static Class member, Data member & Member Function of a class 632
17.6.8 Classes and structures 635
COMPREHENSION - 17 637
EXERCISE - 17 639

CHAPTER 18

INHERITANCE

18.1 INTRODUCTION 641
18.2 SINGLE INHERITANCE 641
18.2.1 Derived Classes 642
18.2.2 Access in Inheritance 646
18.2.3 Constructors and Destructors in inheritance 653

18.2.4 Multilevel inheritance 654
18.2.5 Multiple inheritance 658
18.2.6 Virtual base class 661
18.2.7 Passing parameters from derived class constructor to base class constructor 664
COMPREHENSION - 18 .... **667**
EXERCISE - 18 .... **668**

CHAPTER 19

DIFFERENT TYPES OF OVERLOADING IN C++

19.1 INTRODUCTION TO OVERLOADING **669**
19.2 TYPES OF OVERLOADING **669**
19.2.1 Overloading related to functions - Function Overloading 669
19.2.2 Over loading of Function Call Operator ( ) 673
19.2.3 Constructor overloading 674
19.2.4 Operator overloading 676
19.2.4.1 Unary Operator Overloading 678
19.2.4.2 Binary operator overloading 681
19.2.4.3 Overloading Relational Operators 685
19.2.4.4 Overloading Arithmetic Assignment Operators 687
19.2.4.5 Overloading the Assignment Operator 689
19.2.4.6 Overloading Special type of Operator [ ] ( ) 690
19.2.4.7 Overloading conversion operators 692
19.2.4.8 Overloading the exponent operator ^ 692
19.2.5 Overloading String Concatenation 694
19.2.6 Overloading new and delete in memory management 696
19.2.7 Operator Functions as friend for overloaded operator to be commutative : 698
COMPREHENSION - 19 .... **700**
EXERCISE - 19 .... **702**

CHAPTER 20

POLYMORPHISM

20.1 INTRODUCTION **703**

20.2 COMPILE AND RUNTIME POLYMORPHISM **703**

20.3 VIRTUAL FUNCTIONS **706**

20.3.1 Pure virtual functions 707

20.3.2 Abstract class 709

20.4 TYPES OF DESTRUCTORS **711**

20.4.1 Virtual destructor 713

20.4.2 Explicit destructor 714

COMPREHENSION - 20 ..... **716**

EXERCISE - 20 ..... **717**

CHAPTER 21

INPUT-OUTPUT OPERATIONS IN C++

21.1 INTRODUCTION **719**

21.2 STREAM INSERTION & EXTRACTION OPERATORS (<<) & (>>) **720**

21.2.1 Stream Insertion Operator for Output (<<) 720

21.2.2 Stream extraction Operator for Input (>>) 720

21.2.3 Formatting Output using manipulators 723

21.2.4 Constructing our own manipulators 727

COMPREHENSION - 21 729

EXERCISE - 21 ..... **730**

CHAPTER 22

FILE OPERATIONS IN C++

22.1 INTRODUCTION **731**

22.2 FILE INPUT / OUTPUT IN C++ **731**

22.2.1 Explicit function for file Closure 733

22.3 INPUT / OUTPUT OPERATIONS ON FILES **734**
22.3.1 I/O operations on text files 734
22.3.2 I/O operations on Binary files 739
22.3.3 I/O Operations on Random files 743
22.4 COMMAND LINE ARGUMENTS IN C++ **747**
22.5 INDEXING DATABASE AND FILES **748**
22.5.1 Indexing Data Base 748
22.5.2 Index architecture 749
22.5.3 Operations on Indexing 751
22.5.4 Applications and limitations of Indexing 752
22.6 FILE INDEXING **752**
22.6.1 Indexing File Record IDs 752
COMPREHENSION - 22 .... **754**
EXERCISE - 22 .... **756**

CHAPTER 23

SPECIAL FEATURES IN C++

23.1 INTRODUCTION **757**
23.2 NAMESPACE **757**
23.2.1 Avoiding of namespace using scope operator 757
23.2.2 Use of namespace to avoid use of scope operator 757
23.2.3 Creation of separate namespace in C++ program 758
23.2.4 Use of namespace 759
23.2.5 Switching of namespaces 760
23.2.6 Run-time Type Information (RTTI) using '#include<typeinfo>' 760
23.2.7 Type Casting 761
23.2.8 Four methods of type casting operations in C++ 762
23.3 TEMPLATES **766**
23.3.1 Types of Templates 767
23.3.2 Faster templates using inline keywords or functions 769
23.3.3 Differences between Class and Function Templates **779**

23.4 DEFAULT INITIALIZER IN TEMPLATE TO ONLY CLASS TEMPLATES 781
23.5 EXCEPTION HANDLING 782
23.5.1 Actions of Exception Handling 782
23.5.2 Methods of Exception Handling 783
23.5.3 Handling of different types of Exceptions 784
23.5.4 Constructors and Destructors in Exception Handling 790
23.5.5 Other Exception Specifications 791
COMPREHENSION - 23 792
EXERCISE - 23 793

CHAPTER 24

ABSTRACT DATA TYPE (ADT) PROGRAMS

24.1 INTRODUCTION 795
24.2 WHAT IS ADT? 795
24.2.1 Abstract Data Structure 796
24.2.2 Abstract Data Type 796
24.3 SALIENT FEATURES OF ABSTRACT DATA TYPES 798
24.4 WHY ADT? 798
24.5 ADT STACK EXAMPLE 799
24.5.1 Stack ADT 801
24.6 A QUEUE ADT 810
24.7 ADT EMPLOYEE LIST 813
COMPREHENSION - 24 816
EXERCISE - 24 817

REFERENCES 819

CHAPTER - 1
INTRODUCTION TO COMPUTERS

1.1. INTRODUCTION TO COMPUTERS :

Computers have become all pervasive in our day to day life. The advent of computers can be treated as another revolution after industrial revolution. It has led to development of not only computation but also Communication, Internet, Multimedia, Games, Accounting, Artificial Intelligence and virtualisation in all fields of life facilitating non destructive testing, simulation and modelling, mechanization and use of Robots in hazardous fields.

Computers being inanimate and capable of understanding only machine language, consisting of ones and zeros, communication with the computers requires special efforts. *The computer can communicate with outside world only through interfaces between the machine and the person.* **The computer consists of main Central Processing Unit, Memory, Input devices and Output devices.** The basic block diagram of a computer is given in fig. 1.1.

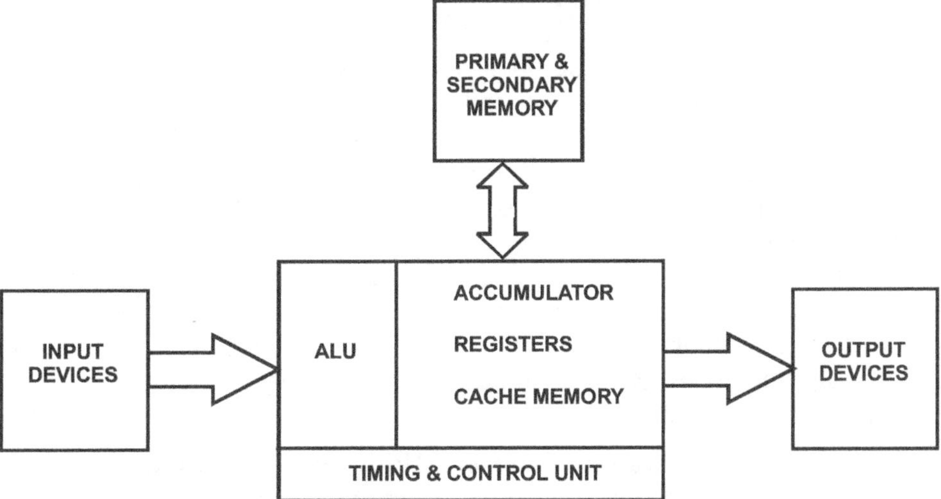

Fig. 1.1 : Block Diagram of a Computer

The **Central Processing Unit** is the Heart and Brain of the computer. It takes data and instructions from the outside world through Input devices, stores them in the memory, does the required processing taking them from memory and stores the results in the memory for future use and also gives the output to the outside world through output devices immediately after processing. The *CPU consists of Arithmetic logic unit,* which does the computations and logic operations, accumulator which is a register used for taking the data and doing the computations, general and special purpose registers for storing the data and instructions inside the CPU on receipt from memory and a timing and control unit which generates timing and control signals required for the execution of instructions and also control the operation of other parts of CPU, Memory and Input, Output devices.

Memory stores the information like program, data results and any other required information. We have a large **Main memory or Primary memory** which is fast and accessible to the computer immediately. We have the **Secondary memory or auxiliary memory** which stores voluminous information including the Operating System. We have also got a small amount of **cache memory** inside the Microprocessor which is a part of the CPU for storing the immediate instructions and necessary data for faster access.

The **Input devices** like the Key board, Card or Tape readers pass on the Input to the CPU as electrical impulses. The **output devices** display the results either on the monitor or screen, or store in the Hard Disc, Floppy Disks, CDs or DVDs or Pen Drives or magnetic disks or magnetic tapes etc.,

The Microprocessor which forms a main component of the CPU, being an electronic device takes electrical impulses and hence it can understand only the machine language consisting of ones and zeros, one being the state of full voltage (5 Volts) and zero being no voltage. These states can also be described as high and low, up and down. This language consisting of only ones and zeros is a Low level language and to program in this **Low level language or machine language** is tedious and susceptible to making mistakes. Hence a slightly Higher level languages known as the **Assembly language** consisting of mnemonics is used in micro-processors. This consists of English abbreviations. To program in assembly language we have to keep track of the memory addresses, register names and their contents etc., which is again difficult. To make communication with the computer easier, **High level languages** like Basic, Fortran, Cobal, Pascal etc., have been designed.

C Language is an Intermediate or Middle level language between the high level language and the Low level language. A program written in C can be carried out at a considerably less time because of its features like few restrictions, compact set of key words, block structures, less documentation, rich set of operators and many built in functions. It consists of features like manipulations of bits, bytes and addresses as in Assembly language. C is highly portable. **Through its functions and structures C language has become very useful in the design of compilers and operating systems** which are essential with features like interface between the user and the computer, controls of the peripherals and other devices to be used by the computer. Compilers translate the High level language program into Low level language understandable by the computer. *High level languages are easy to program by the user but it takes more execution time compared to low level language.*

1.2. HISTORY OF C & C++ :

The most popular programming language C is the result of a development process that started with an older language BASIC COMBINED PROGRAMMING LANGUAGE (BCPL). "Martin Richards" developed BCPL. Ken Thompson developed a language called B, during 1960s. B was modified by Dennis Ritchie which led to the development of C and it was implemented in Bell Laboratories in the 1970s. Since it was developed along with the Unix operating system, for many years C was strongly associated with UNIX. With Micro Computers gaining popularity C gained widespread implementations, under a number of operating systems, including MS-DOS. The source codes accepted by most of these operating systems are highly compatible. C++ is a superset of C.

C and C++ languages being closely related, a compiler for C++, can also work as compiler for C language. There are several types of compilers for C language like Turbo C, Ansy C, Borland C, Unix based C, DOS based C compilers. There are C compilers available for DOS Operating System, OS/2, for Macintosh and also in Microsoft Visual Studio 6.0. Turbo C++ compiler is one of the popular compilers which is used for some of the programs executed in this book. There may be some slight differences between Turbo C compiler and Turbo C++ compiler which will be pointed out in this book as and when required.

1.3. DESIGN, DEVELOPMENT AND EXECUTION OF A PROGRAM :

1. Before developing a program for solving a problem, *the problem has to be understood clearly* as to what are the Inputs, the specifications (and limitations) what is expected to be done and what is the required output and in what form is the output required.
2. *The logic required to meet the constrains and expectations of the problem has to be developed.*
3. After understanding the problem a step by step approach called **algorithm** for solving the problem has to be developed. *The algorithm is a step by step approach for solving the problem without getting into infinite loop.* Infinite loop is a set of steps or instructions that are repeated indefinitely.
4. In the place of Algorithm *a pictorial representation of Algorithms called Flow chart may be developed.*

5. Instead of Flow chart a **Pseudo code** may be developed. *A pseudo code is a program written in any High level language like statements without restricting itself to any particular language using the basic features of a Programming language.*

6. From the Algorithm or a Flow chart or pseudo code a program in the required programming language may be developed. *The program code written by the user in a programming language is called a* **Source Code.** This source program is given a file name in the format **filename .C** or **filename .cpp,** with the extension ".c or .cpp" indicating the compiler to be used for executing the program.

7. For Debugging and testing, this source code is loaded on the computer and *the compiler converts the source code into* **object code** *which is executable* after scanning through all the statements given in the program. ***A compiler is a program which translates all the source code into object code in one go.*** If there are any mistakes it lists out all the syntax errors i.e., errors in the format of the programming statements, errors in defining the identifiers etc., which are said to be **grammatical errors or syntax errors** in programming and displays the error code. After rectifying the mistakes or removing the errors, the program is again fed to the compiler. **The name of the file with a dot (.) extension indicates type of the file.** Ex : **File name .obj** will be the name of the object code file. *An executable file will have the extension* "**.exe**" Instead of using a compiler an interpreter may be used. **An interpreter** *is a program which reads and translates the source program into object code stepwise and any error in that step is pointed out immediately and further translation is stopped.*

8. *After successful compilation of the full program the system links the different library functions and the user define functions, creates a table of symbols assigns the values to the different variables that are defined and used in the program etc.,*

9. *After successful linking the program is executed and the results are displayed or given as outputs in the form required by the user as given in the program.*

10. After obtaining the results the programmer has to analyze the results and see whether he has got the output as desired. Otherwise the program logic will have to be redesigned or it has to be checked whether the inputs have been given proper values or whether any illegal operations like division by zero or overflow or underflow has occurred. In such cases the program has to be revised and fed again.

11. After successful execution of the said program it has to be checked whether the program gives correct results for different values of the data.

1.4 TESTING OF PROGRAMS : There are two types of testing known as **i) White box testing, ii) Black box testing.**

1.4.1 White Box Testing : White box testing is used during the early stages of testing the software to test the internal working of the program. Test cases are provided to verify the proper execution of all independent paths within a module, all logical decisions, and all loops and validate data structures.

1.4.2 Black Box Testing : Knowing the specified functions used in a program, tests can be conducted to demonstrate each function and its operations, simultaneously searching for errors. Black Box tests are used to demonstrate that the software functions are operational, input is correctly accepted, and output is produced correctly and attempts to find errors like, incorrect or missing functions, interface errors, Errors in data structures or data base access, performance errors, initialization/ termination errors.

1.4.3. Testing Bench Mark Problems: *In real time problems it will be a better practice to run the program for bench mark problems, if there are any* as in power systems. **Bench mark problems are standard problems designed by standard institutions like IEEE etc., for which the standard input and outputs are available.** If the program works for different bench mark programs for the same type of problem then it is reasonable to assume that the program developed will work for any other data or any other size of the problem.

1.5 POINTS TO BE CONSIDERED IN PROGRAMMING :

1. For real time problems collection of information, selection of solution, documentation are very important. *Documentation involves developing and writing supporting manuals and on-line assistance or help which the user will need to understand and use the finished program effectively.* Failing to use a good job at this stage can invalidate all the good work done up till now.

2. *It is always better to write a working program first* i.e., a program which works correctly and gives correct results. *Then the program can be refined* to make it more efficient with less coding and requiring less execution time and less memory.

3. **It is also better to write as generic a program as possible by using general variables instead of particular values, template functions** so that the program can work for any values of the variables and data types without a need for rewriting the program steps for different values.

1.6 DIFFERENT LEVELS OF PROGRAMMING LANGUAGES :

A "**programming language**" is a language designed to describe a set of consecutive actions to be executed by a computer. A programming language is therefore a practical way for us (humans) to give instructions to a computer.

On the other hand, the term "natural language" defines a means of communication shared by a group of individuals (for example: English or French)

Languages that computers use to communicate with each other, have nothing to do with programming languages, they are referred to as communication protocols, these are two very different concepts. A programming language is very strict:

EACH instruction corresponds to ONE processor action.

The language used by the processor is called **machine code**. The code that reaches the processor consists of a series of 0s and 1s known as (binary data).

Machine code is therefore difficult for humans to understand, which is why intermediary languages, which can be understood by humans, have been developed. The code written in this type of language is transformed into machine code so that the processor can process it.

The assembler was the first programming language ever used. This is very similar to machine code but can be understood by developers. Nonetheless, such a language is so similar to machine code that it strictly depends on the type of processor used (each processor type may have its own machine code). Thus a program developed for one machine may not be *ported* to another type of machine. The term "**portability**" describes the ability to use a software program on different types of machines. A software program written in assembler code, may sometimes have to be completely rewritten to work on another type of computer!

A programming language has therefore several advantages:

- It is much more understandable than machine code;
- It allows greater portability, i.e. can be easily adapted to run on different types of computers.

1.6.1 Imperative and functional programming languages

Programming languages are generally divided into two major groups according to how their commands are processed:

- Imperative languages;
- Functional languages.

1.6.1.1 Imperative programming language :

An imperative language programs using a series of commands, grouped into blocks and comprising of conditional statements which allow the program to return to a block of commands if the condition is met. These were the first programming languages in use, even today many modern languages still use this principle.

Structured imperative languages suffer, however, from lack of flexibility due to the sequentiality of instructions.

1.6.2 Functional programming language :

A **functional programming language** (often called *procedural language*) is a language which creates programs using functions, returning to a new output state and receiving as input the result of other functions. When a function invokes itself, we refer to this as recursion.

1.6.3 Interpretation and compilation :

Programming languages may be roughly divided into two categories:

- **interpreted languages**
- **compiled languages**

1.6.3.1. Interpreted language :

A programming language is by definition different to machine code This must therefore be translated so that the processor can understand the code. A program written in an interpreted language requires an extra program (the interpreter) which translates the programs commands as needed.

1.6.3.2 Compiled language :

A program written in a "**compiled**" language is translated by an additional program called a **compiler** which in turn creates a new stand-alone file which does not require any other program to execute itself, such a file is called an **executable**.

A program written in a compiled language has the advantage of not requiring an additional program to run it once it has been compiled. Furthermore, as the translation only needs to be done once, at compilation it executes much faster. However, it is not as flexible as a program written in an interpreted language, as each modification of the source file (the file understandable by humans: the file to be compiled) means that the program must be recompiled for the changes to take effect.

On the other hand, a compiled program has the advantage of guaranteeing the security of the source code. In effect, interpreted language, being a directly legible language, means that anyone can find out the secrets of a program and thus copy or even modified the program. There is therefore a risk of copyright violation. On the other hand, certain secure applications need code confidentiality to avoid illegal copying (bank transactions, on-line payments, secure communications...).

1.6.3.3. Intermediary languages :

Some languages belong to both categories (LISP, Java, Python...) as the program written in these languages may in certain cases undergo an intermediary compilation phase, into a file written in a language different to the source file and non-executable (requiring an interpreter). Java applets, small programs, often loaded in web pages, are compiled files, which can only be executed from within a web browser (these are files with the .class extension).

1.6.4. Some widely used languages :

Table 1.1. gives a non-exhaustive list of current programming languages

Table 1.1. List of some current programming languages

Language	Main application area	Compiled/interpreted
ADA	Real-time	Compiled language
BASIC	Programming for educational purposes	Interpreted language
C	System programming	Compiled language
C++	System object programming	Compiled language
Cobol	Management	Compiled language
Fortran	Calculation	Compiled language
Java	Internet oriented programming	Intermediary language
MATLAB	Mathematical calculations	Interpreted language
Mathematica	Mathematical calculations	Interpreted language
LISP	Artificial intelligence	Intermediary language
Pascal	Education	Compiled language
PHP	Dynamic website development	Interpreted language
Prolog	Artificial intelligence	Interpreted language
Perl	Processing character strings	Interpreted language

1.7. APPROACHES IN PROGRAMMING :

There are 3 approaches or methodologies followed in programming.

i) Stepwise Refinement **ii) Modular programming,**
iii) Structured programming.

i) **Stepwise Refinement :** In this method a problem is decomposed into smaller parts or smaller steps and *each step is programmed and analyzed for correctness and refined before going to the next part.*

ii) **Modular programming :** *Large programs are split up into different modules of programming and the modules are programmed separately and are tested separately and all the modules are assembled into a single program* by integrating into a single program. The process of combining the different modules is also known as linking. Different modules can be designed by different programmers. *These modules can be reused in other programs if the modules are programmed in a general manner.*

Conceptually, modules represent a separation of concerns, and improve maintainability by enforcing logical boundaries between components. Modules are typically incorporated into the program through interfaces. A module interface expresses the elements that are provided and required by the module. The elements defined in the interface are detectable by other modules. The implementation contains the working code that corresponds to the elements declared in the interface.

Languages that formally support the module concept include Ada, Algol, BlitzMax, COBOL, Component Pascal, D, Erlang, F, Fortran, Haskell, IBM/360 Assembler, IBM RPG, Java (packages are considered modules in the JLS), MATLAB, ML, Modula-2, Modula-3, Morpho, Oberon, NEWP, OCaml, Pascal, Perl, PL/I, Python, and Ruby. The IBM System i also uses Modules in CL, COBOL, and RPG when programming in the Integrated Language Environment (ILE). Modular programming can be performed even where the programming language lacks explicit syntactic features to support named modules.

Software tools can create modular code units from groups of components. Libraries of components built from separately compiled modules can be combined into a whole by using a linker. modular designed systems, if built correctly, far more reusable than a traditional monolithic design, since all (or many) of these modules may then be reused (without change) in other projects. This also facilitates the "breaking down" of projects (through "divide and conquer") into several smaller projects.

iii) **Structured Programming :** Structured programming was first proposed in the beginning of 1970's by Prof. Edsger Wybe Dijkstra. *Structured programming is a technique for organizing and coding computer programs in which a hierarchy of modules is used, or structures like 'for' structures, 'while' structures etc., each having a single entry point and a single exit point,* and in which control is passed downward through the structure without unconditional branches to other structures, eliminating the use of unconditional branching like 'goto' statement.

> Structured programming (sometimes known as modular programming) is a subset of procedural programming that enforces a logical structure on the program being written to make it more efficient and easier to understand and modify. Certain languages such as Ada, Pascal, and dBASE are designed with features that encourage or enforce a logical program structure.

Structured programming frequently employs a top-down design model, in which developers map out the overall program structure into separate subsections. A defined function or set of similar functions is coded in a separate module or submodule, which means that code can be loaded into memory more efficiently and that modules can be reused in other programs. After a module has been tested individually, it is then integrated with other modules into the overall program structure.

Program flow follows a simple hierarchical model that employs looping constructs such as "for," "repeat," and "while." Use of the "Go To" statement is discouraged.

Object-oriented programming (OOP) can be thought of as a type of structured programming, uses structured programming techniques for program flow, and adds more structure for data to the model.

1.8. TOP-DOWN PROGRAMMING AND STEP-WISE REFINEMENT :

Top-down programming is a style in programming. The mainstay of traditional procedural languages, in which design begins by specifying complex pieces and then dividing them into successively smaller pieces. The technique for writing a program using top–down methods is to write a main procedure that names all the major functions it will need. Later, the programming team looks at the requirements of each of those functions and the process is repeated. These compartmentalized sub-routines eventually will perform actions so simple they can be easily and concisely coded. When all the various sub-routines have been coded the program is ready for testing. By defining how the application comes together at a high level, lower level work can be self-contained. By defining how the lower level abstractions are expected to integrate into higher level ones, interfaces become clearly defined.

Also called "stepwise refinement," it is a software development technique that imposes a hierarchical structure on the design of the program. It starts out by defining the solution at the highest level of functionality and breaking it down further and further into small routines that can be easily documented and coded.

C Languages follows Top-down programming approach with the main function at the top and user defined functions following the main function.

1.8.1 (a) Advantages of Top down Programming:

1. All aspects of the program are know before programming starts
2. Programmers are focused on the task, because they know every aspect of the program.
3. The code should be clean and easy to understand, because it all has purpose.
4. Easier to understand the problem
5. Easier to add a new module
6. Easier to modify a module
7. Easier to test/debug a module
8. Several programmers can work on the same problem/program.
9. Modules can be kept in a library and reused in another program

(b) Disadvantages of Top down programming :

1. Testing is hard until near the end of the project, because no code is written until it is all properly designed.
2. Any mistakes made early on in the development cycle can be hard to fix.

1.9. BOTTOM-UP PROGRAMMING :

Bottom-up programming is the opposite of top-down programming. It refers to a style of programming where an application is constructed starting with existing primitives of the programming language, and constructing gradually more and more complicated features, until the all of the application has been written.

C++ Language follows bottom of approach with objects, classes etc., defined in the beginning and the main programming following after them.

1.9.1 Working of bottom-up programming :

In a language such as C or Java, bottom-up programming takes the form of constructing abstract data types from primitives of the language or from existing abstract data types.

In Common Lisp, in addition to constructing abstract data types, it is common to build *functions* bottom-up from simpler functions, and to use macros to construct new *special forms* from simpler ones.

In a bottom-up approach, the individual base elements of the system are first specified in great detail. These elements are then linked together to form larger subsystems, which then in turn are linked, sometimes in many levels, until a complete top-level system is formed. This strategy often resembles a "seed" model, whereby the beginnings are small, but eventually grow in complexity and completeness. Object-oriented programing (OOP) is a paradigm that uses "objects" to design applications and computer programs. In mechanical engineering with software programs such as Pro/ENGINEER, Solidworks, and Autodesk Inventor users can design products as pieces not part of the whole and later add those pieces together to form assemblies like building LEGO. Engineers call this piece part design.

This bottom-up approach has one weakness. Good intuition is necessary to decide the functionality that is to be provided by the module. If a system is to be built from existing system, this approach is more suitable as it starts from some existing modules. Pro/ENGINEER (as well as other commercial computer-aided design (CAD) programs) does however hold the possibility to create top-down design by the use of so-called *skeletons*. They are generic structures that hold information on the overall layout of the product. Parts can inherit interfaces and parameters from this generic structure. Like parts, skeletons can be put into a hierarchy. Thus, it is possible to build the overall layout of a product before the parts are designed.

1.9.2 (a) Advantages of bottom-up programming :

1. Testing is simplified. The code can be properly tested at any stage in the development cycle.
2. Pieces of programs written bottom-up tend to be more general, and thus more reusable, than pieces of programs written top-down. In fact, one can argue that the purpose bottom-up programming is to create an application-specific language . Such a language is suitable for implementing an entire class of applications, not only the one that is to be written. This fact greatly simplifies maintenance, in particular adding new features to the application. It also makes it possible to delay the final decision concerning the exact functionality of the application. Being able to delay this decision makes it less likely that the client has changed his or her mind between the establishment of the specifications of the application and its implementation.
3. Design flaws can be easily spotted and fixed. Because all design work is done through the code.

(b) Disadvantages of bottom up programming :

1. Programmers may come across many problems during development because they don't have a structured well though out design plan.
2. It can be easy to deviate from the task during development.
3. The code may be messy, because the task was misunderstood early ion development and code has to be changed a lot.

1.10. OPERATING SYSTEMS :

An **operating system (OS)** is a collection of software that manages computer hardware resources and provides common services for computer programs. The operating system is a vital component of the system software in a computer system. Application programs require an operating system to function.

Time-sharing operating systems schedule tasks for efficient use of the system and may also include accounting for cost allocation of processor time, mass storage, printing, and other resources.

For hardware functions such as input and output and memory allocation, the operating system acts as an intermediary between programs and the computer hardware, although the application code is usually executed directly by the hardware and will frequently make a system call to an OS function or be interrupted by it. Operating systems can be found on almost any device that contains a computer—from cellular phones and video game consoles to supercomputers and web servers

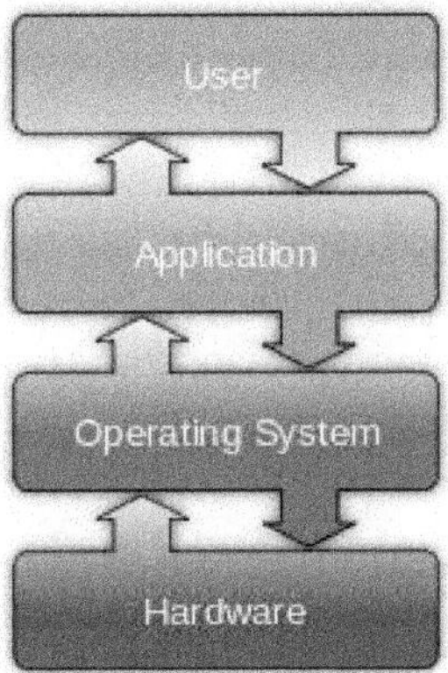

Fig.1.2. An Operating System

Examples of popular modern operating systems include Android, BSD, iOS, Linux, Mac OS X, Microsoft Windows,[3] Windows Phone, and IBM z/OS. All these, except Windows and z/OS, share roots in UNIX.

1.10.1 Types of operating systems :

(i) Real Time Operating System :

Real timeA real-time operating system is a multitasking operating system that aims at executing real-time applications, intended for applications with fixed deadlines (real-time computing). Such applications include some small embedded systems, automobile engine controllers, industrial robots, spacecraft, industrial control, and some large-scale computing systems. Real-time operating systems often use specialized scheduling algorithms so that they can achieve a deterministic nature of behavior. The main objective of real-time operating systems is their quick and predictable response to events. They have an event-driven or time-sharing design and often aspects of both. An event-driven system switches between tasks based on their priorities or external events while time-sharing operating systems switch tasks based on clock interrupts. A real-time operating system (RTOS) is a multitasking operating system

(ii) Multi-user Operating System :

Multi-userA multi-user operating system allows multiple users to access a computer system at the same time. Time-sharing systems and Internet servers can be classified as multi-user systems as they enable multiple-user access to a computer through the sharing of time. Single-user operating systems have only one user but may allow multiple programs to run at the same time.

Multi-tasking vs. single-tasking : A multi-tasking operating system allows more than one program to be running at a time, from the point of view of human time scales. A single-tasking system has only one running program. Multi-tasking can be of two types: pre-emptive or co-operative. In pre-emptive multitasking, the operating system slices the CPU time and dedicates one slot to each of the programs. Unix-like operating systems such as Solaris and Linux support pre-emptive multitasking, as does Amiga OS. Cooperative multitasking is achieved by relying on each process to give time to the other processes in a defined manner. 16-bit versions of Microsoft Windows used cooperative multi-tasking. 32-bit versions, both Windows NT and Win9x, used pre-emptive multi-tasking. Mac OS prior to OS X used to support cooperative multitasking.

(iii) Distributed system :

A distributed operating system manages a group of independent computers and makes them appear to be a single computer. The development of networked computers that could be linked and communicate with each other gave rise to distributed computing. Distributed computations are carried out on more than one machine. When computers in a group work in cooperation, they make a distributed system.

(iv) Embedded operating systems :

Embedded Operating Systems are designed to be used in embedded computer systems. They are designed to operate on small machines like PDAs with less autonomy. They are able to operate with a limited number of resources. They are very compact and extremely efficient by design. Windows CE and Minix 3 are some examples of embedded operating systems.

1.10.2. Examples of operating systems

(i) UNIX and UNIX-like operating systems

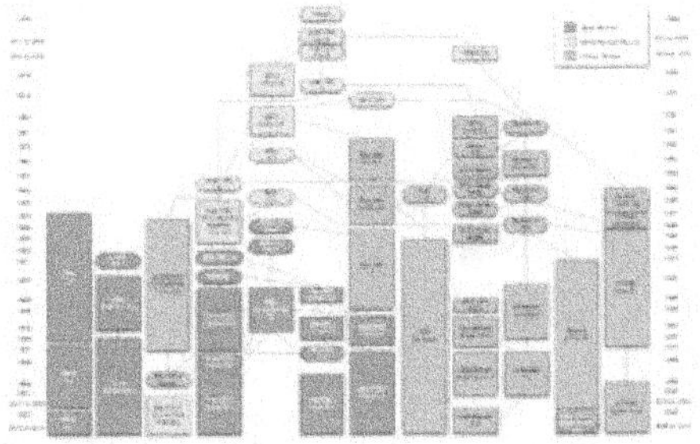

Fig. 1.3. Unix and Unix-like Operating System

Ken Thompson wrote B, mainly based on BCPL, which he used to write Unix, based on his experience in the MULTICS project. B was replaced by C, and Unix developed into a large, complex family of inter-related operating systems which have been influential in every modern operating system The *UNIX-like* family is a diverse group of operating systems, with several major sub-categories including System V, BSD, and Linux. The name "UNIX" is a trademark of The Open Group which licenses it for use with any operating system that has been shown to conform to their definitions. "UNIX-like" is commonly used to refer to the large set of operating systems which resemble the original UNIX.Unix-like systems run on a wide variety of computer architectures. They are used heavily for servers in business, as well as workstations in academic and engineering environments. Free UNIX variants, such as Linux and BSD, are popular in these areas. Four operating systems are certified by the The Open Group (holder of the Unix trademark) as Unix. HP's HP-UX and IBM's AIX are both descendants of the original System V Unix and are designed to run only on their respective vendor's hardware. In contrast, Sun Microsystems's Solaris Operating System can run on multiple types of hardware, including x86 and Sparc servers, and PCs. Apple's Mac OS X, Unix interoperability was sought by establishing the POSIX standard. The POSIX standard can be applied to any operating system, although it was originally created for various Unix variants.

(ii) The standard user interface of Mac OS X :

Fig. 1.4. standard user interface of Mac OS X

Mac OS X is a line of open core graphical operating systems developed, marketed, and sold by Apple Inc., the latest of which is pre-loaded on all currently shipping Macintosh computers. Mac OS X is the successor to the original Mac OS, which had been Apple's primary operating system since 1984.

Six more distinct "client" and "server" editions of Mac OS X have been released, the most recent being OS X 10.8 "Mountain Lion", which was first made available on February 16, 2012 for developers, and was then released to the public on July 25, 2012. Releases of Mac OS X are named after big cats.

The server edition, Mac OS X Server, is architecturally identical to its desktop counterpart but usually runs on Apple's line of Macintosh server hardware. Mac OS X Server includes work group management and administration software tools that provide simplified access to key network services, including a mail transfer agent, a Samba server, an LDAP server, a domain name server, and others. In Mac OS X v10.7 Lion, all server aspects of Mac OS X Server have been integrated into the client version. Mountain lion is the latest version in Mac O.S.

GNU is a Unix-like operating system that is free software—it respects your freedom. You can install Linux-based versions of GNU which are entirely free software. The name "GNU" is a recursive acronym for "GNU's Not Unix!". "GNU" is pronounced *g'noo*, as one syllable, like saying "grew" but replacing the *r* with *n*.

A Unix-like operating system is a software collection of applications, libraries, and developer tools, plus a program to allocate resources and talk to the hardware, known as a kernel.

(iii) GNU, Linux, and Linux kernel :

Fig. 1.5. Screen shot of Linux

Ubuntu, desktop Linux distribution is a very popular Linux Operting System.

(iv) Android :

Fig. 1.6. Android Operating System Model in Mobile Phones

It is a popular mobile operating system using the Linux kernelLinux (or GNU/Linux) is a Unix-like operating system that was developed without any actual Unix code, unlike BSD and its variants. Linux can be used on a wide range of devices from supercomputers to wristwatches. The Linux kernel is released under an open source license, so anyone can read and modify its code. It has been modified to run on a large variety of electronics. Although estimates suggest that Linux is used on 1.82% of all personal computers, it has been widely adopted for use in servers and embedded systems (such as cell phones). Linux has superseded Unix in most places, and is used on the 10 most powerful supercomputers in the world. The Linux kernel is used in some popular distributions, such as Red Hat, Debian, Ubuntu, Linux Mint and Google's Android.

(v) Google Chrome OS :

Chrome is an operating system based on the Linux kernel and designed by Google. Since Chrome OS targets computer users who spend most of their time on the Internet, it is mainly a web browser with no ability to run applications. It relies on Internet applications (or Web apps) used in the web browser to accomplish tasks such as word processing and media viewing, as well as online storage for storing most files.

(vi) Microsoft Windows :

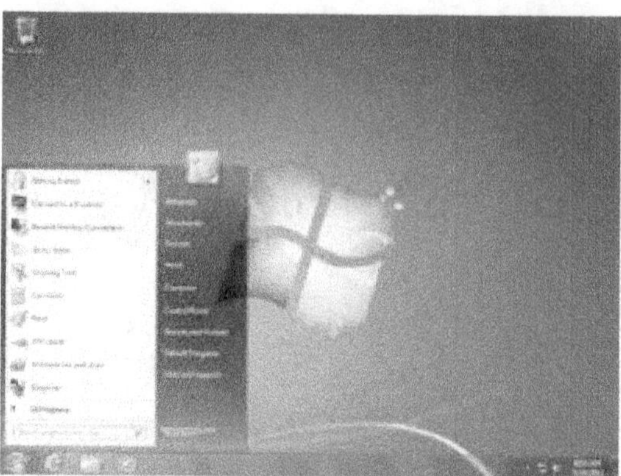

Fig.1.7. Screen shot of MS Windows O.S

Microsoft Windows 7 Desktop. Microsoft has just now released in 2012 its Windows 8 O.S. Still 32 bit Windows XP is very popular.Microsoft Windows is a family of proprietary operating systems designed by Microsoft Corporation and primarily targeted to Intel architecture based computers, with an estimated 88.9 percent total usage share on Web connected computers.[Microsoft Windows originated in 1985 as an operating environment running on top of MS-DOS, which was the standard operating system shipped on most Intel architecture personal computers at the time. In 1995, Windows 95 was released which only used MS-DOS as a bootstrap. For backwards compatibility,The newest version is Windows 8 for workstations and Windows Server 2012 for servers. Windows 7 are new aditions. Win9x could run real-mode MS-DOS and 16 bits Windows 3.x drivers. Windows Me, released in 2000, was the last version in the Win9x family. Later versions have all been based on the Windows NT kernel. Current versions of Windows run on IA-32 and x86-64 microprocessors, although Windows 8 will support ARM architecture. In the past, Windows NT supported non-Intel architectures.

1.10.3. Components Of an Operating System :

The components of an operating system all exist in order to make the different parts of a computer work together. All user software needs to go through the operating system in order to use any of the hardware, whether it be as simple as a mouse or keyboard or complex as an Internet connection.

(i) Kernel :

A kernel connects the application software to the hardware of a computer.Main article: Kernel (computing)With the aid of the firmware and device drivers, the kernel provides the most basic level of control over all of the computer's hardware devices.

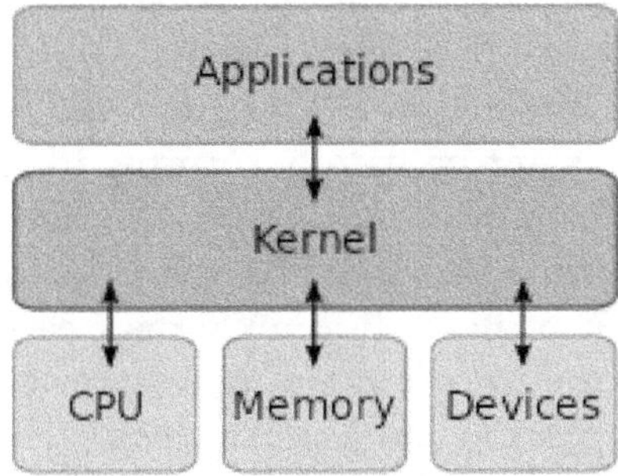

Fig.1.8. Components of Unix/Linus O.S.

Kernel manages memory access for programs in the RAM, it determines which programs get access to which hardware resources, it sets up or resets the CPU's operating states for optimal operation at all times, and it organizes the data for long-term non-volatile storage with file systems on such media as disks, tapes, flash memory, etc.

1.10.4 Modes :

(i) Protected mode and Supervisor mode :

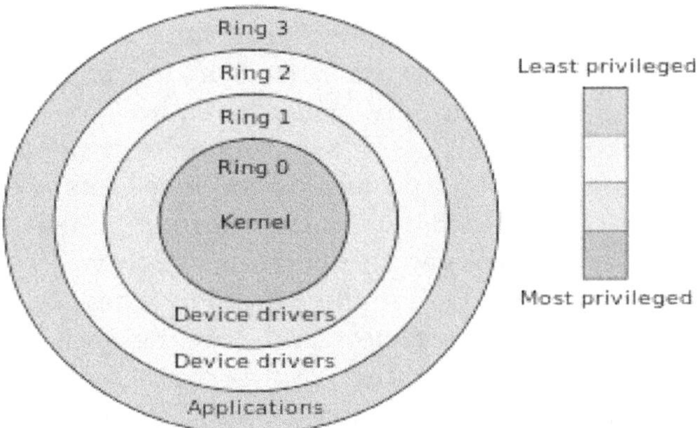

Fig.1.9 Different layers in Unix Operating System

Privilege rings for the x86 available in protected mode. Operating systems determine which processes run in each mode.Modern CPUs support multiple modes of operation. CPUs with this capability use at least two modes: protected mode and supervisor mode. The supervisor mode is used by the operating system's kernel for low level tasks that need unrestricted access to hardware, such as controlling how memory is written and erased, and communication with devices like graphics cards. Protected mode, in contrast, is used for almost everything else. Applications operate within protected mode, and can only use hardware by communicating with the kernel, which controls everything in supervisor mode. CPUs might have other modes similar to protected mode as well, such as the virtual modes in order to emulate older processor types, such as 16-bit processors on a 32-bit one, or 32-bit processors on a 64-bit one.When a computer first starts up, it is automatically running in supervisor mode. The first few programs to run on the computer, being the BIOS or EFI, bootloader, and the operating system have unlimited access to hardware - and this is required because, by definition, initializing a protected environment can only be done outside of one. However, when the operating system passes control to another program, it can place the CPU into protected mode.In protected mode, programs may have access to a more limited set of the CPU's instructions. A user program may leave protected mode only by triggering an interrupt, causing control to be passed back to the kernel. In this way the operating system can maintain exclusive control over things like access to hardware and memory.The term "protected mode resource" generally refers to one or more CPU registers, which contain information that the running program isn't allowed to alter. Attempts to alter these resources generally causes a switch to supervisor mode, where the operating system can deal with the illegal operation the program was attempting (for example, by killing the program).

(ii) Memory management :

Memory protection enables the kernel to limit a process' access to the computer's memory. Various methods of memory protection exist, including memory segmentation and paging. All methods require some level of hardware support (such as the 80286 MMU), which doesn't exist in all computers. In both segmentation and paging, certain protected mode registers specify to the CPU what memory address it should allow a running program to access. Attempts to access other addresses will trigger an interrupt which will cause the CPU to re-enter supervisor mode, placing the kernel in charge. This is called a segmentation violation or Seg-V for short, and since it is both difficult to assign a meaningful result to such an operation, and because it is usually a sign of a misbehaving program, the kernel will generally resort to terminating the offending program, and will report the error.

(iii) Virtual memory :

Virtual memory and Page fault Many operating systems can "trick" programs into using memory scattered around the hard disk and RAM as if it is one continuous chunk of memory, called virtual memory.The use of virtual memory addressing (such as paging or segmentation) means that the kernel can choose what memory each program may use at any given time, allowing the operating system to use the same memory locations for multiple tasks. If a program tries to access memory that isn't in its current range of accessible memory, but nonetheless has been allocated to it, the kernel will be interrupted in the same way as it would if the program were to exceed its allocated memory. (See section on memory management.)

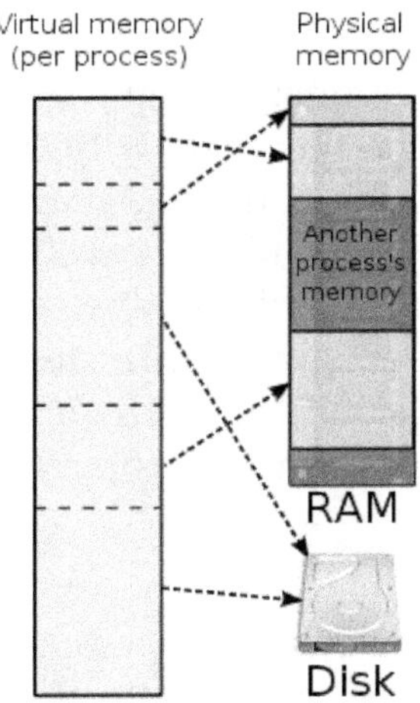

Fig.1.10.Virtual Memory Operations

Under UNIX this kind of interrupt is referred to as a page fault.When the kernel detects a page fault it will generally adjust the virtual memory range of the program which triggered it, granting it access to the memory requested. This gives the kernel discretionary power over where a particular application's memory is stored, or even whether or not it has actually been allocated yet.In modern operating systems, memory which is accessed less frequently can be temporarily stored on disk or other media to make that space available for use by other programs. This is called swapping, as an area of memory can be used by multiple programs, and what that memory area contains can be swapped or exchanged on demand."Virtual memory" provides the programmer or the user with the perception that there is a much larger amount of RAM in the computer than is really there. The philosophy governing preemptive multitasking is that of ensuring that all programs are given regular time on the CPU. This implies that all programs must be limited in how much time they are allowed to spend on the CPU without being interrupted. To accomplish this, modern operating system kernels make use of a timed interrupt. A protected mode timer is set by the kernel which triggers a return to supervisor mode after the specified time has elapsed. (See above sections on Interrupts and Dual Mode Operation.)A virtual file system or VFS. allows the operating system to provide programs with access to an unlimited number of devices with an infinite variety of file systems installed on them, through the use of specific device drivers and file system drivers.A connected storage device, such as a hard drive, is accessed through a device driver. The device driver understands the specific language of the drive and is able to translate that language into a standard language used by the operating system to access all disk drives. On UNIX, this is the language of block devices.When the kernel has an appropriate device driver in place, it can then access the contents of the disk drive in raw format, which may contain one or more file systems. A file system driver is used to translate the commands used to access each specific file system into a standard set of commands that the operating system can use to talk to all file systems. Programs can then deal with these file systems on the basis of filenames, and directories/folders, contained within a hierarchical structure. They can create, delete, open, and close files, as well as gather various information about them, including access permissions, size, free space, and creation and modification dates.Unlike other operating systems, Linux and UNIX allow any file system to be used regardless of the media it is stored in, whether it is a hard drive, a disc (CD,DVD...), a USB flash drive, or even contained within a file located on another file system.

1.10.5 Networking of Computers :

Computer networkCurrently most operating systems support a variety of networking protocols, hardware, and applications for using them. This means that computers running dissimilar operating systems can participate in a common network for sharing resources such as computing, files, printers, and scanners using either wired or wireless connections. Networks can essentially allow a computer's operating system to access the resources of a remote computer to support the same functions as it could if those resources were connected directly to the local computer. This includes everything from simple communication, to using networked file systems or even sharing another computer's graphics or sound hardware. Some network services allow the resources of a computer to be accessed transparently, such as SSH which allows networked users direct access to a computer's command line interface.

(i) Client/server Configuration :

Client/server networking allows a program on a computer, called a client, to connect via a network to another computer, called a server. Servers offer (or host) various services to other network computers and users. These services are usually provided through ports or numbered access points beyond the server's network address. Each port number is usually associated with a maximum of one running program, which is responsible for handling requests to that port. A daemon, being a user program, can in turn access the local hardware resources of that computer by passing requests to the operating system kernel.Many operating systems support one or more vendor-specific or open networking protocols as well, for example, SNA on IBM systems, DECnet on systems from Digital Equipment Corporation, and Microsoft-specific protocols (SMB) on Windows. Specific protocols for specific tasks may also be supported such as NFS for file access. Protocols like ESound, or esd can be easily extended over the network to provide sound from local applications, on a remote system's sound hardware.

1.10.6. Computer Security :

A computer being secure depends on a number of technologies working properly. A modern operating system provides access to a number of resources, which are available to software running on the system, and to external devices like networks via the kernel.The operating system must be capable of distinguishing between requests which should be allowed to be processed, and others which should not be processed. While some systems may simply distinguish between "privileged" and "non-privileged", systems commonly have a form of requester *identity*, such as a user name. To establish identity there may be a process of *authentication*. Often a username must be quoted, and each username may have a password. Other methods of authentication, such as magnetic cards or biometric data, might be used instead. In some cases, especially connections from the network, resources may be accessed with no authentication at all (such as reading files over a network share). Also covered by the concept of requester **identity** is *authorization*; the particular services and resources accessible by the requester once logged into a system are tied to either the requester's user account or to the variously configured groups of users to which the requester belongs. In addition to the allow/disallow model of security, a system with a high level of security will also offer auditing options. These would allow tracking of requests for access to resources (such as, "who has been reading this file?"). Internal security, or security from an already running program is only possible if all possibly harmful requests must be carried out through interrupts to the operating system kernel. If programs can directly access hardware and resources, they cannot be secured. External security involves a request from outside the computer, such as a login at a connected console or some kind of network connection. External requests are often passed through device drivers to the operating system's kernel, where they can be passed onto applications, or carried out directly. Security of operating systems has long been a concern because of highly sensitive data held on computers, both of a commercial and military nature. The United States Government Department of Defense (DoD) created the *Trusted Computer System Evaluation Criteria* (TCSEC) which is a standard that sets basic requirements for assessing the effectiveness of security. This became of vital importance to operating system makers, because the TCSEC was used to evaluate, classify and select trusted operating systems being considered for the processing, storage and retrieval of sensitive or classified information. Network services include offerings such as file sharing, print services, email, web sites, and file transfer protocols (FTP), most of which can have compromised security. Internal security is especially relevant for multi-user systems; it allows each user of the system to have private files that the other users cannot tamper with or read. Internal security is also vital if auditing is to be of any use, since a program can potentially bypass the operating system, inclusive of bypassing auditing.

1.10.7. Operating system user interface :

(i) A screenshot of the Bourne Again Shell command line :

Each command is typed out after the 'prompt', and then its output appears below, working its way down the screen. The current command prompt is at the bottom.

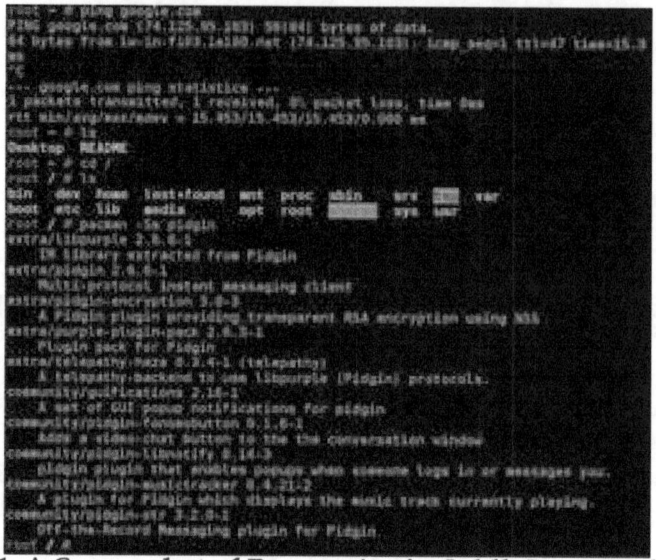

Fig.1.11. A Screen shot of Bourne Again Sehll Command Lines.

Every computer that is to be operated by an individual requires a user interface. The user interface is usually referred to as a shell and is essential if human interaction is to be supported. The user interface views the directory structure and requests services from the operating system that will acquire data from input hardware devices, such as a keyboard, mouse or credit card reader, and requests operating system services to display prompts, status messages and such on output hardware devices, such as a video monitor or printer. The two most common forms of a user interface have historically been the command-line interface, where computer commands are typed out line-by-line, and the graphical user interface, where a visual environment (most commonly a WIMP) is present.

(ii) Graphical user interfaces :

Most of the modern computer systems support graphical user interfaces (GUI), and often include them. In some computer systems, such as the original implementation of Mac OS, the GUI is integrated into the kernel.A screenshot of the KDE Plasma Desktop graphical user interface. Programs take the form of images on the screen, and the files, folders (directories), and applications take the form of icons and symbols. A mouse is used to navigate the computer.Graphical user interfaces evolve over time.

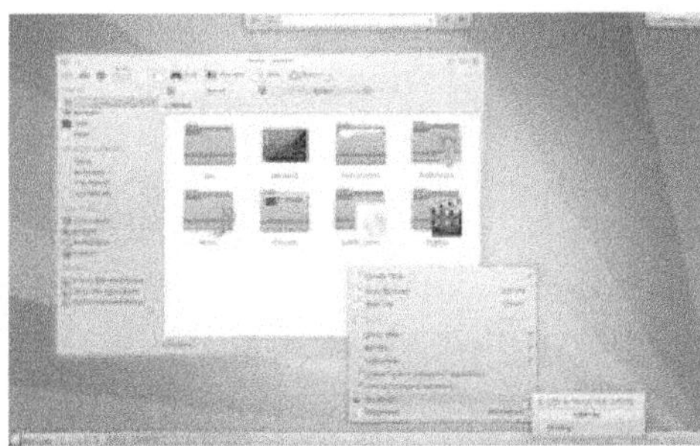

Fig. 1.12. A Screenshot of the KDE Plasma Desktop graphical user interface

For example, Windows has modified its user interface almost every time a new major version of Windows is released, and the Mac OS GUI changed dramatically with the introduction of Mac OS X in 1999.

1.10.8. Diversity of operating systems and portability :

Application software is generally written for use on a specific operating system, and sometimes even for specific hardware. When porting the application to run on another OS, the functionality required by that application may be implemented differently by that OS (the names of functions, meaning of arguments, etc.) requiring the application to be adapted, changed, or otherwise maintained.This cost in supporting operating systems diversity can be avoided by instead writing applications against software platforms like Java or Qt. These abstractions have already borne the cost of adaptation to specific operating systems and their system libraries.

(i) **Java :**

Java is a programming language originally developed by James Gosling at Sun Microsystems (which has since merged into Oracle Corporation) and released in 1995 as a core component of Sun Microsystems' Java platform. The language derives much of its syntax from C and C++, but it has fewer low-level facilities than either of them. Java applications are typically compiled to bytecode (class file) that can run on any Java virtual machine (JVM) regardless of computer architecture. Java is a general-purpose, concurrent, class-based, object-oriented language that is specifically designed to have as few implementation dependencies as possible. It is intended to let application developers "write once, run anywhere" (WORA), meaning that code that runs on one platform does not need to be recompiled to run on another. Java is as of 2012 one of the most popular programming languages in use, particularly for client-server web applications, with a reported 10 million users.

(ii) Java platform :

One characteristic of Java is portability, which means that computer programs written in the Java language must run similarly on any hardware/

operating-system platform. This is achieved by compiling the Java language code to an intermediate representation called Java bytecode, instead of directly to platform-specific machine code. Java bytecode instructions are analogous to machine code, but they are intended to be interpreted by a virtual machine (VM) written specifically for the host hardware. End-users commonly use a Java Runtime Environment (JRE) installed on their own machine for standalone Java applications, or in a Web browser for Java applets.

Standardized libraries provide a generic way to access host-specific features such as graphics, threading, and networking.

A major benefit of using bytecode is porting. However, the overhead of interpretation means that interpreted programs almost always run more slowly than programs compiled to native executables would. Just-in-Time (JIT) compilers were introduced from an early stage that compile bytecodes to machine code during runtime.

Another approach is for operating system vendors to adopt standards. For example, POSIX and OS abstraction layers provide commonalities that reduce porting costs.

1.10.9. Black Berry and Black Berry O.S :

Most BlackBerry devices are smartphones and are primarily known for their ability to send and receive push email and instant messages, mobile telephone, text messaging, Internet faxing, Web browsing and other wireless information services. It is an example of a convergent device.while maintaining a high level of security through on-device message encryption. They are also designed to function as personal digital assistants, portable media players, internet browsers, gaming devices, cameras and more. BlackBerry devices support a large variety of instant messaging features, with the most popular being the proprietary BlackBerry Messenger service. The BlackBerry PlayBook is a tablet computer offered by RIM.

The operating system used by BlackBerry devices is a proprietary multitasking environment developed by RIM. The operating system is designed for use of input devices such as the track wheel, track ball, and track pad. The OS provides support for Java MIDP 1.0 and WAP 1.2. Previous versions allowed wireless synchronization with Microsoft Exchange Server email and calendar, as well as with Lotus Domino email. OS 5.0 provides a subset of MIDP 2.0, and allows complete wireless activation and synchronization with Exchange email, calendar, tasks, notes and contacts, and adds support for Novell GroupWise and Lotus Notes. The BlackBerry Curve 9360, BlackBerry Torch 9810, Bold 9900/9930, Curve 9310/9320 and Torch 9850/9860 feature the most recent BlackBerry OS 7 (launched in 2011).

Third-party developers can write software using these APIs, and proprietary BlackBerry APIs as well. Any application that makes use of certain restricted functionality must be digitally signed so that it can be associated to a developer account at RIM..

A new OS, BlackBerry 10, is slated for release on new BlackBerry models on January 30, 2013, RIM CEO Thorsten Heins announced. At BlackBerry World 2012, RIM CEO Thorsten Heins showed off a few new features of the upcoming OS, including a camera which is able to go back in time to ensure a perfect shot, an intelligent, predictive, and adapting keyboard, and a user interface designed around the idea of "flow".

1.10.10. C Programming is a subset of C++ programming :

C Programming is a subset of C++ programming and most of the character sets, keywords, operations, data structure etc., are common to both the languages and hence it has been proposed to club C and C++ and also to treat the data structures in the two languages comparing them and make a comprehensive study of both the languages and data structures in this book. It is also felt that a comparative study of both C and C++ will enable comprehension of both the languages.

A modest effort has been made in this book to elucidate the salient features of both the languages and the use of data structures in both the languages with the help of adequate background theory and working programs.

* * *

COMPREHENSION - 1

Note : By answering all the questions given in this comprehension one can answer any objective type of questions easily whatever be the form of the question. Answers for these questions can be obtained by going through the topics in this chapter carefully.

1. What are the different blocks of a computer?
2. What are the different components of each block?
3. What are Primary and Secondary Memories?
4. Mention different Input and output devices.
5. What constitutes CPU?
6. What are meant by Registers?
7. How many types of Registers are there?
8. What is the function of ALU?
9. What is the function of Cache Memory?
10. What does Timing and controls unit do?
11. What are the different levels of computer languages?
12. What does Assembly language do?
13. What level is C language?
14. What is the specialty of C language?
15. What is meant by an operating System?
16. What are the different phases of Programming? Explain.
17. What is a Flow Chart? What purpose does it serve?
18. What is meant by Pseudo code? In what way is it different from Source code?
19. What is the process of executing a program?
20. What are the points to be remembered in Programming? What is meant by Modular and Structured Programs?
21. What are the different types of Testing? Explain.
22. What is meant by Bench mark Problems? What purpose do they serve?
23. What is Documentation? What purpose does it serve?
24. Why should we write a Generic program?
25. What is meant by file extensions? How is the file extensions represented?
26. What are Top-down and Bottom-up approaches in programming?
27. What type of programming do C and C++ follow?

28. What are the different approaches followed in programming?
29. What is an operating system?
30. What are the different popular operating systems?
31. What is meant by open source operating systems? What are its advantages? Give examples.
32. What is proprietory operating system? What are its advantages and disadvantages? give examples.
33. Explain multi-user operating system? How does it work?
34. What is Real time operating system? How does it work?
35. What are the different types of Unix-based operating systems?
36. Where do we use Android operating system?
37. What is meant by Kernel in Unix operating system?
38. What are the different layers of Unix operating system and what are their functions?
39. What are the components of operating system?
40. What are the different modes of operating system?
41. What is meant by Memory Management?
42. What is Virtual Memory? What is its purpose?
43. What is meant by Networking of Computers?
44. What is Client-server configuration? explain.
45. What is meant by computer security?
46. Explain GUI.
47. What is meant by portability of operating systems?
48. Explain Java and Java platform. How does it work?
49. What is meant by Black Berry?
50. What is Black berry operating system?

* * *

EXERCISE - 1

Note : By answering all the questions given in this exercise one can answer subjective type of questions easily including problems. The worked examples in the chapter may help in solving these questions.

1. (a) Draw the Block diagram of a Computer and explain its functioning?
   (b) Mention the different devices used in different blocks.
2. (a) Define Algorithm.
   (b) What is the use of flow chart ?
   (c) Explain the steps followed in program development and its execution?
3. (a) What is the difference between a Micro Processor and Micro Computer?
   (b) Explain about different types of memories used in a computer.
4. (a) Explain Flow chart, Pseudo code, Source code, and Machine code.
   (b) How do you conclude that the results obtained from the Computer are correct?
5. (a) Explain the different types of testing a program.
   (b) Explain the importance of documentation while Programming.
6. (a) Explain the different approaches to programming.
   (b) Explain about File Extensions.
7. (a) What is meant by Compilation of a Program?
   (b) What is the difference between a compiler and an interpreter?
8. (a) What is meant by different levels of languages? At what level does C language belong to?
   (b) Why are C and C++ languages considered to be closely related?
9. (a) What is the importance of C Programming?
   (b) Explain about Linking in execution of a Program.
10. Discuss about Top-down programming, its advantages and disadvantages.
11. Discuss about Bottom-up programming, its advantages and disadvantages.
12. Explain the necessity and functions of an Operating system?
13. What are the different components of Operating system?
14. Explain Unix Operating system and its varients?
15. Explain distributed Operating systems.
16. Explain portability of Operating system.
17. Explain Memory management.
18. Explain Networking of computer systems.

* * *

CHAPTER - 2
BASICS OF PROGRAMMING

2.1. INTRODUCTION TO BASICS OF PROGRAMMING :

As indicated in the previous chapter on Introduction of Computers, programming consists of the first basic feature like Algorithm or Pseudo Code or Flow chart and then writing the actual Source code in the given programming language. In addition it can also be stated that a proper logic is to be used for solving a particular problem. This logic forms the basis for developing the algorithm for proper programming and obtaining correct results. One should be good in formulating proper logic and it is this logic that leads to real success.

2.2. LOGIC FOR PROGRAMMING :

A good logic for solving a problem is essential for effective programming. For example ;

To write a given number in reverse order, we know that a modular division of two integer numbers (x % y) gives the remainder of (x / y). Hence the modular division of the given number by 10 will give the first digit of the reverse number. Modular division of the quotient gives the second digit of the reverse number and so on. This process is repeated as many times as the number of digits of the original number.

Eg. let the given number be 8642. first digit of the reverse number will be the modular division 8642% /10 = 2. First two digits of reverse number is obtained as 2 x 10 + 864 % 10 = 24. First 3 digits of the reverse number is obtained as 24 x 10 + 86 % 10 = 246. The Four digits of the reverse number equals 246 x 10 + 8% 10 equals 2468.

2.3. ALGORITHM : Algorithm is a set of step by step instructions for performing a task. Algorithm may also be defined as a set of finite number of steps which provides a chain of actions for solving a definite nature of task. In designing the algorithm one should be very careful to see that one does not get involved into an infinite loop leading to execution of the same set of instructions again and again indefinitely.

2.3.1 Pseudo code : Pseudo code is also an algorithm to solve the problem step by step. But the statements in pseudo algorithm are given in a programming like language but not in an exact programming language. The statements are different from English language statements. Some authors use the words Algorithm and Pseudo code synonymously giving the statements in programming like language as algorithm.

2.3.2. Flow Chart :

A Flow chart can be defined as a pictorial representation of the step by step instructions for solving a problem which is called an algorithm. It gives a visual representation of different tasks or different steps each step corresponding to a process. It also indicates the direction of flow of action in solving the problem. The different processes are represented by different blocks. (given in Fig. 2.1) The different blocks are connected by straight lines with an arrow indicating the direction of flow of operations.

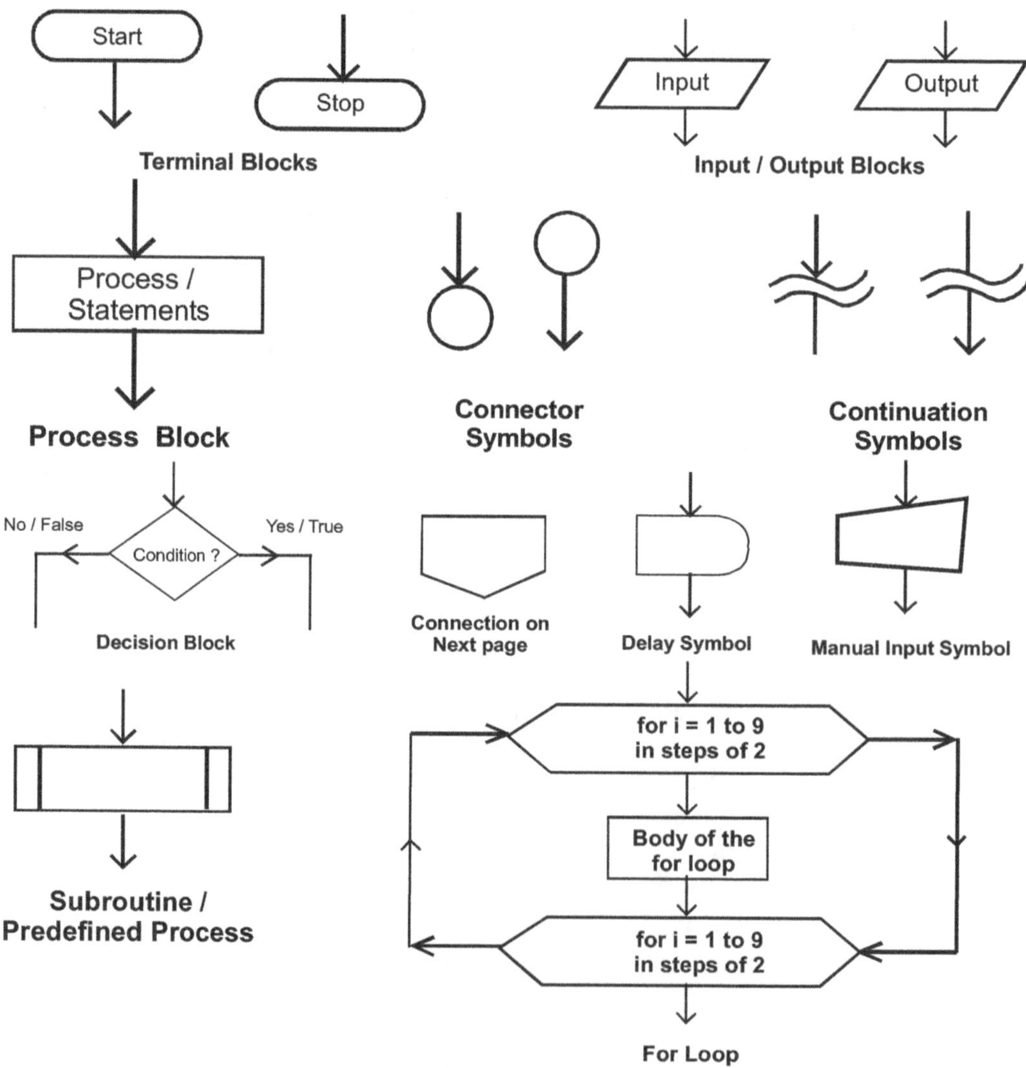

Fig. 2.1 : Symbols / Blocks of a Flow Chart

All the three above items like algorithm, pseudocode and flow chart are the essentials of programming in any language. Any of the above three items fully represents the solution for a problem in any computer programming language. The required programming language the source program for solving the problem can be developed using any of these three items.

Example : 1

The problem of going to the College can be described by the algorithm or flow chart or pseudocode given below.

Algorithm to go to College :

The 6 steps constituting the algorithm can be i) start from the house, ii) walk to the bus stop, iii) wait for the arrival of a bus, iv) if the correct bus has arrived go to the college by bus, v) if the correct bus has not arrived within a specified time go to the college by auto and vi) reach the college.

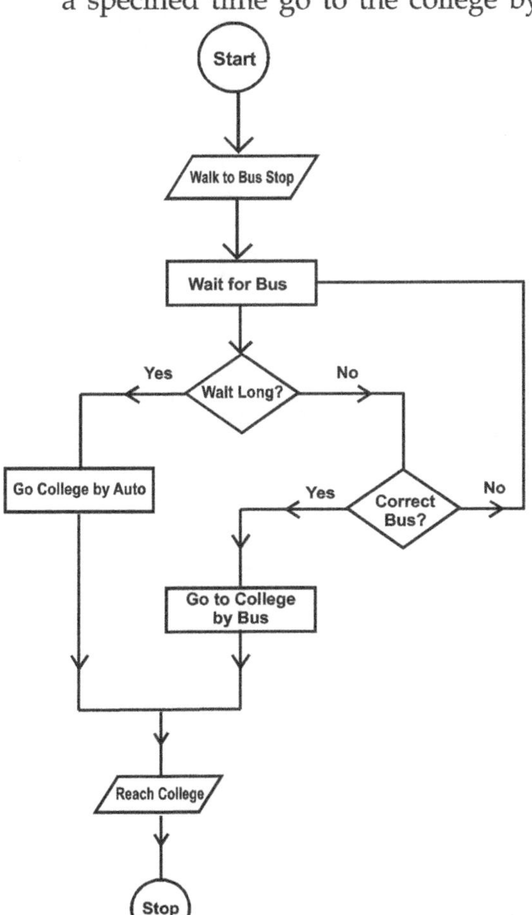

Fig 2.2. Flow Chart to go to College

There can be modifications of these tasks like waiting for a long time and returning back home or hiring a taxi and going to the college if auto is not available.

In such cases the original algorithm has to be modified accordingly. The flow chart for the problem of going to the college is given in figure 2.2. The Pseudo code is given by the side of the figure.

Pseudo Code to go to college :

i) walk to bus stop
ii) wait for bus
iii) if correct bus has arrived go to college by bus.
else wait for bus
iv) if wait is long go to college by auto.
v) reach college

Example 2 :

Given two integer numbers A, B, develop an algorithm and write a flow chart to write the numbers in ascending order. If they are equal write A = B.

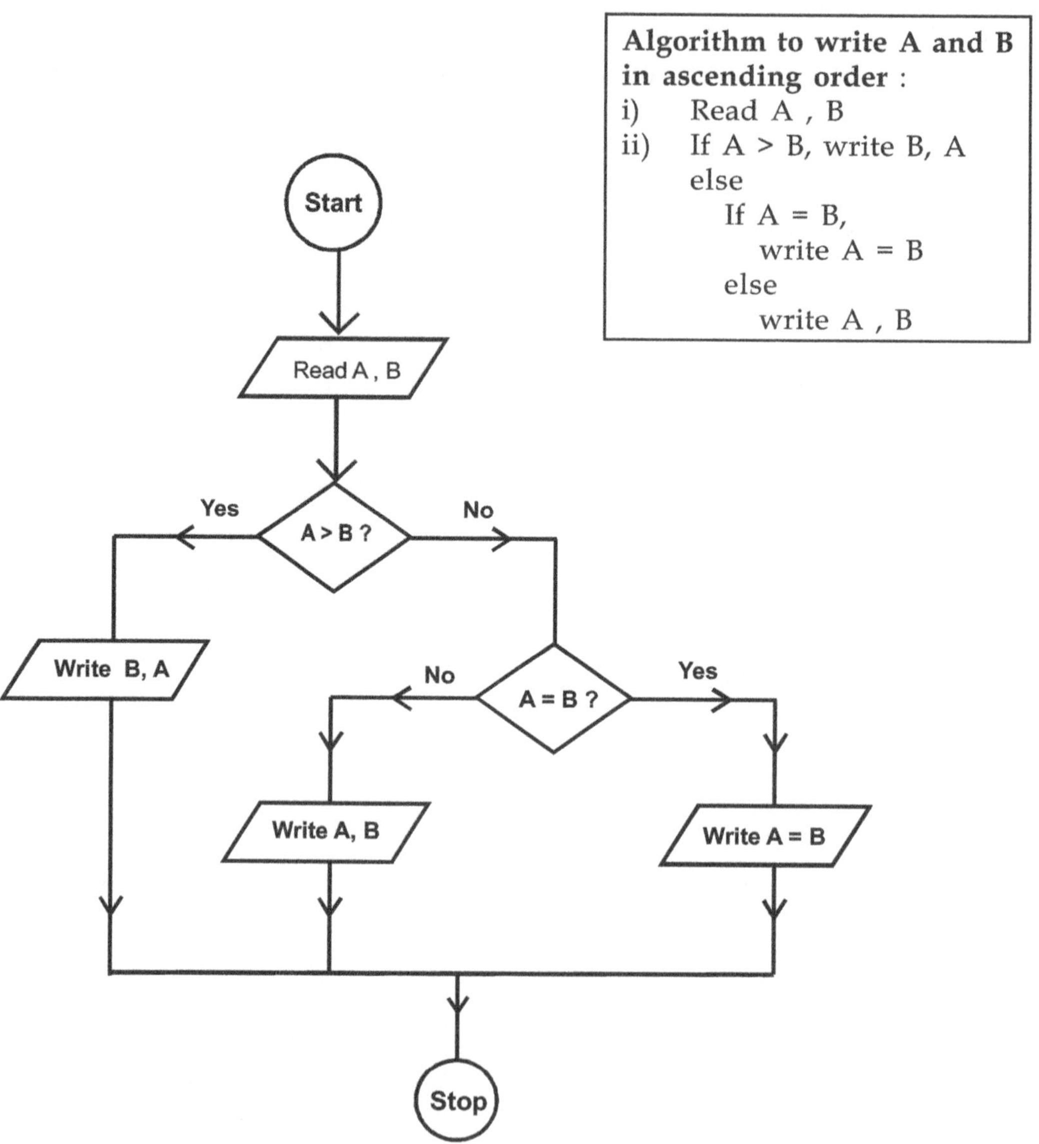

Fig 2.3. Flow chart to write A and B in ascending order

Example 3 :

Give an algorithm to write 3 different integer numbers in descending order.

Solution :

Algorithm to write 3 integer numbers a, b, c in descending order.

i) Start

ii) Read a, b, c

iii) If a > b

```
                and if b > c
                max. = a
                    mid. = b;  min. = c
                    go to step iv          ........ (descending order : a,b,c)
                    else
                    max = a
                    mid = c; min = b
                    go to step iv          ........ (descending order : a,c,b)
    else (i.e., if b > a)
                if a > c
                    max = b
                    mid = a; min = c
                    go to step iv          ........ (descending order : b,a,c)
                    else
                    max = b
                    mid = c, min = a
                    go to step iv          ........ (descending order : b,c,a)
    if c > a
                if a>b
                    max = c,
                    mid = a; min = b
                    go to step iv          ........ (descending order : c,a,b)
                    else
                    max = c
                    mid = b; min = a       ........ (descending order : c,b,a)
```

iv) Print max, mid, min.

v) Stop

On similar lines we can write an algorithm and flow chart to write the 3 numbers a, b, c in ascending order by changing the relationship to if a < b instead of a > b and so on.

Alternately following a different logic, the program of writing a, b, c in descending order can be modified with a set of less number of executable statements. The first set of 3 different blocks of inputs in cyclic order like a, b, c ; b, c, a and c, a, b.

Example 4 :

Alternative logic : Write a generic pseudocode program, using the above principle **to write a, b, c in ascending order**

Solution :

i) Start

ii) Read a, b, c

iii) x_1 = a, x_2 = b, x_3 = c

iv) if $x_1 > x_2$ and $x_2 > x_3$

Max. = x_1

Mid = x_2 ; Min. = x_3

else

Max = x_1

Mid = x_3, Min. = x_2

Go to step vii

v) x_1 = b, x_2 = c, x_3 = a

goto step iv

vi) x_1 = c, x_2 = a, x_3 = b

goto step iv

vii) print Min, Mid, Max

viii) stop

Note : in this program the conditional statements (if else) are repeated 3 times with 3 different steps of inputs a, b, c ; b, c, a ; and c, a, b given in cyclic order.

2.4. BASIC CATEGORIES OF OPERATIONS :

The steps in an algorithm can be divided into 3 basic categories of operation. They are *i) sequence ii) selection and iii) iteration.*

i) ***Sequence :*** In Van Neuman architecture the programming steps are given one after another and will be executed successfully in the same order, without skipping any step. This can be called a sequential operation of the statements. It is simple and easy but in cases where there is a need for selection or multiple selections of different tasks, this sequence operation is not suitable. An example of sequential statements is given below.

a) get ready in the morning

b) go to the college

c) after return from college play

d) after play, study

e) go to bed

ii) ***Selection :*** Where there is a need to test for a certain condition and execute two different programs one for successful selection when the testing condition is true and the other for the testing condition to be false, the sequential algorithm is not suitable. Then we have two sets of sequential algorithms one set for the successful condition and the other set for unsuccessful condition, resulting in branching to the concerned set based on test condition. There can be multiple selections also i.e., selection for different conditions. An example of single selection :

a) go to the bus stop
b) if the correct bus arrives, go by that else go to the college by auto

An example of multiple selections :

a) go to the bus stop
b) if the college bus arrives go to college by it else if a correct route bus arrives go to the college by it else go by auto.
c) if auto is also not available go home.

iii) Iteration : If a certain set of sequential statements are to be executed repeatedly then we call it Iteration. For performing the iterations we may open an iteration counter with an index varying from initial value to final value in steps of increase or decrease of the index. The set of iterative statements is called a loop or an iteration. The statements in an iteration can be sequential or may include selections also. While executing iterative statements one should be careful to see that the iterative statements are not executed indefinitely which may be called an infinite loop.

An example of iteration :

a) dial a phone number
b) if the number is busy, redial
c) repeat steps a and b for a certain number of times till the ring goes.

An example of infinite loop :

a) dial a phone number
b) if the ring does not go at all, then the dialing has to be ended after dialing a certain number of times or after a certain time elapses. Otherwise the process of dialing will fall into an infinite loop.

To guard against infinite loop we can fix up a maximum number of times the iteration can be performed or a maximum time may be prescribed for reiteration process to end which is done in batch processing of programs.

2.5. IMPORTANCE OF 'C' LANGUAGE :

C language has become very popular and important because

i) with its rich set of operators and built in functions any complex program can be written in C language. It is a robust language.

ii) the C compiler as a capabilities of low level assembly language, and a high level language. Hence it is often called a middle level language or an intermediate level language

iii) a good number of compilers are available for C language in the market.

iv) programs in C are efficient and fast compared to other high level languages.

v) c is highly portable. A program written in C for one computer can be executed in another computer with little of no modification.

vi) the key words in C language are less only 32 in Turbo C and 39 in Borland C.

vii) C language is a structured language and is well suited for modular programming

viii) C being a collection of library functions and having provisions for different types of data structures, user defined functions, pointers, structures and union etc., and with provision for calling by reference and calling by values the arguments for different functions is well suited for design of operating systems.

2.6. IMPORTANCE OF C++ LANGUAGE :

C++ is an object oriented programming language. With successful development of Smalltalk complete object oriented language developed at Xerox Corporation's PARC (Palo Alto Research Centre. In 1979, Bjarne Stroustrup from Bell labs brought out, the initial version of C++ called "C with classes". Later the name C++ was suggested by Rick Mascitti and it was used in December 1983. The first commercial version of the language C++ along with the manual was released in October 1985. While languages like Smalltalk-80 are said to be "truly" object oriented, C++ is often called a "hybrid" language because C++ retains its ancestral resemblance to C from which it emerged. The reason for this is that two major goals in developing C++ were to retain both the same performance as, and upward-compatibility with, natural C.

C++ has become an important systems programming language because

i) C++ is an ensemble of different data types and related functions. It provides basic objects and a collection of objects and instances called classes.

ii) C++ provides *good protection* for data and functions. It has provision for providing 3 levels of protection for data members and member functions within a class, viz., private, public and protected security. The default production level is private. The least level of protection is public which provides access to members and functions of that class to any other functions of other classes. A protected data members or members function is accessible to other members of the functions of that class or from classes derived from that class. Also permission can be granted to access to private or protected parts of the classes through 'friend' functions. This is known as *encapsulation.*

iii) C++ provides *data abstraction.* It has provision to provide implementation of set of operations on data elements in addition to organizing the data items into structures leading to *data abstraction.* Data abstraction provides the foundation for Object Oriented Programming.

iv) C++ provides *short and efficient coding* compared to other languages. It provides reusability which is the basic technic behind inheritance. For ex. : a child inherits resemblance or some characteristics of the parent. Where there is a common instances, variables and methods for different objects instead of defining the objects separately, if it is sufficient if we declare the first object which contains common fields of both the objects and then the fields pertaining to the objects alone are declared separately. A sub-class or derived class can inherit the features of the base class or super class from which it is derived.

v) C++ has the property of *polymorphism.* It has the ability to take more than one form. This ability to take different forms is known as 'polymorphism'. The two types of polymorphism are compile time polymorphism and runtime polymorphism whereby member functions defined in classes to be overridden with member functions having the same names (function overloading) and also allowing more features to existing operators (except few) using operator-overloading technique.

vi) C++ has a larger standard library functions which provides standard input, output, strings containers (such as sort, search and merge), and support for numeric computationing.

vii) C++ has the ability to simulate real-world event much more effectively.

viii) Data Becomes active in C++.

ix) C++ has the ability to create graphical user interface (GUI) applications.

2.7. SOME OF THE COMPILERS AVAILABLE FOR C AND C++ :

A few compilers that are popular and available for C & C++ are given here :

2.7.1. List of compilers for C :

- GNU C compiler is freely available under the Free Software Foundation
- Borland C (BC) and Turbo C (TC) are available from Borland Int'l. It is available for DOS and Windows.
- Zorland C, Zortech C (ZTC) is available from Zortech Int'l. DOS and
- OS/2, OS/2.1 C Compilers
- Mac OS X doesn't install the gcc compiler. gcc is typically the compiler of choice.

2.7.2. List of compilers available in C++ :

There are plenty of compiler available for C++, here is a list of few C++ compilers.

- GNU C++ is freely available under the Free Software Foundation 'copy left', a fun on 'copy right'. Usually called g++, it is available via anonymous ftp prep.ai.mit.edu.
- Borland C++ (BC++) and Turbo C++ (TC++) are available from Borland Int'l. It is available for DOS ; an OS/2 2.0 product has been announced.
- Zortech C++ (ZTC++) is available from Zortech Int'l. DOS and
- Microsoft Visual Studio 6.0 - Visual C++.
- OS/2. Semantic's Think-C for Macintosh (5.0 support many of the features of C++)

2.8. STRUCTURE OF A 'C' PROGRAM :

Every C Program has a number of building blocks called functions. Each function performs an independent task. A function is a sub routine or a sub program which may consist of one or more statements.

C Program consists of a number of sections.

i) **Header files section :** There are a number of pre-processor directives some of which providing the necessary standard library functions are included in this section. One of the important pre processor directives is

include <file name> or # include "file name".

There are number of standard file names which are include in this section for different purposes like # include <stdio.h> which will make available the standard input, output library functions for handling the input and output devices for the program at the time of linking. "conio.h" is another console Input Output function which is used for providing formatted input and output statements or any function to operate on the console like clearing the screen clrscr ( ) ;

"math.h" is another function for providing mathematical functions.

There are other such functions also which will be explained as and when we come across.

ii) **Global declaration :** This section declares the variables which are common for both the main function and other functions. This saves memory and repetitive declaration of the variables in different functions can be avoided.

iii) **Main function :** main ( ). This is a necessary section because each C program should contain atleast one main function which does the main work calling others functions if necessary. The main function indicates where to start execution of the program. For any function or for any block the required statements are to be enclosed within braces { }

iv) **Declaration part :** This includes the variables that are local to that particular function. In this section the local variables are declared and initialized.

v) **Executable part :** This contains the statements that are to be executed, sequentially or in selection or by iteration and also the required output statements.

vi) **User defined functions :** These functions are optional and are included if and only if they are required. The main function makes use of these user defined functions calling them by name or by address to do any repetitive task or special task.

vii) **Comments :** Comments are useful in any program to make it understandable to all. Important points can be mentioned in the comments. In C language the comments are given in the form /*..... */.

Any statement inside the comments section will be ignored at the time of execution, but they will be exhibited. There can be nested comments also i.e., comments within comments. In C++ the comments will be in the form //...... till the end of the line. A comment continuing in next line should also be started with //.

The structure of a C program and C++ program are more or less similar except for some slight differences, the main difference being that the output in C++ program is not displayed on the screen but directed into an output file which has to be read for getting the output. The input also can be taken into an input file and read. The inputs can also be given in the form of a read function. The outputs can also be given in the form of functions. Also there will be a return statement in the function programs.

The structure or format of a C program is given below :

```
/*    Name of the program    */
                 Header file section
           Global declaration of variables if any
               /* comments if required */
                  main ( )    Function name
               {
                     /* comments */
         Declaration and initialisation of variables
                    {
                         Executive statements
                    }
                  User-defined function ( )
               {
            Statements of user defined function
               }
```

Fig. 2.4. Format for a 'C' program

The structure of a C++program is slightly different from C Program

The structure of a C++ program is given below.

```
// Name of the Program
Header file section
Global declaration of variables if any
        Main (    ) Function name
{
        Comments if required
        Declaration and initialisation of variables
        {
                Executive statements including
                cin >> input statements ;
        }
        cout << output statements          ;
        return 0
}
        User defined function name ( )
{
  Statements of user defined function
}
```

Fig 2.5. Format for C++ program

In the above structures user defined functions are optional and are used only if they are called in the main function. A user defined function can also be called by another user defined function.

The important differences between the formats for C and C++ program are

1. The format for comments
2. The header file in C++ can be in different forms depending upon the compiler. In TC++ compiler the header file section will be as follows.

```
# include <iostream.h>
# include  <conio.h>        etc.,
```

In ANSI C++ the header file section will be as follows.

```
#include <iostream>
using namespace std;
```

In ANSI C++ the above two statements are used together in the place of the statement # include<iostream.h> #include <stdlib.h> etc.,

3. The statement using namespace std; in ANSI C++ causes use of definition of all the classes, objects and functions of the standard C++. They are defined within namespace Std. indicating that all the functions used in this program belong to the standard library.

2.9. PROGRAMMING RULES :

The programmer should follow the following rules while writing a program.

i) All statements should be written in lowercase letters. Uppercase letters are only used for symbolic constants.

ii) Blank spaces may be inserted between the words. This improves the readability of the statements.

iii) It is not necessary to fix the position of statements in the program, that is, the programmer can write the statement anywhere between the two braces following the declaration part. The user can also write two or more statements in one line separating them with a semicolon(;) *Hence, C is often called a free-form language.*

iv) **Note that there are no blank spaces between the angled brackets and iostream.** If we insert any blanks inside most of the compilers consider it as a serious error and the program won't compile.

2.10. EXECUTING THE PROGRAM :

The following steps are essential in executing a program in C.

a) **Creation of program :** The program should be written in '.C' editor. The file name does not necessarily include the extension '.C'. The default extension is '.C'. The user can also specify his / her own extension.

b) **Compilation and linking a program :** The source program statements should be translated into the object program, which is suitable for execution by the computer. The translation is done after compiling each statement. If there is no error, compilation proceeds and the translated program is stored in another file with the same file name with extension '.obj'. If there are errors programmer should correct them. After compiling linking is also an essential process. It puts together all other program files and functions that are required by the program. For example, if the programmer is using the pow ( ) function, then the object code of this function should be brought from *math.h* library of the system and linked to the main ( ) program.

c) **Executing the Program :** After the compilation, the executable object code will be loaded in the computer's main memory and the program is executed.

All the above steps can be performed using menu options of the editor.

Program 2.10.1

An example of a C program using TC++ compiler is given below :

```
      /* C program to print a text */
#include <stdio.h> // header file section - for i/o
#include <conio.h> // header file section - for console
  void main ( )        /* function name */
{
     clrscr ( ) ;
     printf ("\n Let us see 'C'.") ;
     printf ("\n Welcome to the wonderful world of 'C' ! ");
     printf ("\n If you practise well, C programming is a child's play");
}
```

OUTPUT (From output file)

Let us see 'C'.

Welcome to the wonderful world of 'C' !
If you practise well, C programming is a child's play"

Program 2.10.2

The same program in C++ using TC++ is given below.

```
// program to print a text
# include <iostream.h>
#include <conio.h>
  int main( )
{
  clrscr ( ) ;
```

```
        cout <<("\n Let us see 'C'.") ;
        cout <<("\n Welcome to the wonderful world of 'C' ! ");
        cout <<("\n If you practise well, C programming is a child's play");
        getche ( ) ;
        return 0;       /* statement since no int. output of function */
    }
```

Note : Since the function getche ( ) is used the output will be displayed on the screen itself.

Program 2.10.3

Alternatively the same program using Ansi C++ is given below.

```
// program to print a text
  # include <iostream>
  using namespace std;
    int main( )
  {
    cout <<("\n Let us see 'C'.") ;
    cout <<("\n Welcome to the wonderful world of 'C' ! ");
    cout <<("\n If you practise well, C programming is a child's play");
    return 0;
  }
```

Note : There are no blank spaces between the angular brackets and io streams. The names defined in the C++ standard library, such as cout, cannot be used in our program unless we follow the pre-processor directive

#include <iostream>   and also the statement
using namespace std;

This statement is called a using directive statement. The names in the C++ standard library are declared in a namespace called namespace std and are not visible in our program text file unless we explicitly make them visible.

2.11. STEPS TO EXECUTE A C PROGRAM USING TC++ COMPILER :

1. Switch on the Computer and wait until a windows dialog box appears.
2. The windows dialog box will have two fields.

   User
   Password
   Enter user id and password, press **Enter** Button on Keyboard and wait for desktop to appear. If there is no password simply press enter.

3. On the Desktop there will be an icon for **C or C++,** Click on the icon
4. The C Editor will appear. Now click **File, New** option. An empty file is opened.
5. Now type the program and finally save the file / program by pressing **F2** on keyboard. (Note : File name should compulsorily end with **.C**) or clicking on "save as" in file drop down menu on the screen.
6. Now press **Alt + F9** to compile the program.
7. If no error, press **Ctrl + F9** to execute the program.
8. To see output of the program press **Alt + F5.** Always execute the program and then see the output file by pressing Alt + F5 keys. *Otherwise the output file will display the results of the previous execution.*
9. After execution and display of results press Esc button to go to the program.
10. To exit from the editor press **Alt + X** buttons or Exit option in the dropdown menu of the file.
11. As in the case of a.out file in which the output will be stored in unix, the output file in C++ (using Turbo C++ compiler) can be accessed by pressing Alt + F5 button.
12. Save the program frequently because the program will disappear when the power goes off or even when the power fluctuates, if the program is not saved necessitating re-entry of the same statements again.

* * *

COMPREHENSION - 2

Note : By answering all the questions given in this comprehension one can answer any objective type of questions easily whatever be the form of the question. Answers for these questions can be obtained by going through the topics in this chapter carefully.

1. What is the importance of Logic in Programming?
2. Write a logic for writing a set of give numbers in reverse order.
3. What is a Flow Chart?
4. Write the different types of Symbols used in Flow chart and explain their action.
5. Write a flow chart for writing three numbers in Descending order.
6. Write a flow chart for writing a set of numbers in reverse order.
7. What is pseudo code? What is its importance?
8. Write a pseudo code for writing three numbers in ascending order.
9. What are the basic types of operations used in writing a flow chart or program?
10. Give examples of the basic types of programming.
11. What is the importance of C Language?
12. What is the importance of C++ Language?
13. Mention some C and also C++ Compilers.
14. What is the structure of a C program?
15. Mention the different sections of a C program.
16. What is the structure of a C ++ program?
17. Mention the different sections of a C ++ program.
18. State the rules to be followed while writing a C program.
19. State the process of executing a C program.
20. Where can you see the output of a C program after successful execution of the program?

* * *

EXERCISE - 2

Note : By answering all the questions given in this exercise one can answer subjective type of questions easily including problems. The worked examples in the chapter may help in solving these questions.

1. Write a flow chart and pseudo code to find the maximum of three numbers.
2. Write a flow chart and pseudo code to write three numbers in descending order.
3. Give the structure of a C program fully and explain.
4. Give the structure of a C ++ program fully and explain
5. (a) What is the advantage of using header files in 'C' ?

   (b) Write a program to generate Fibonacci series using recursion.

* * *

CHAPTER - 3
DECLARATIONS IN C AND C++

3.1. INTRODUCTION TO C DECLARATIONS :

A Natural language has alphabets, words, sentences and grammar similarly any computer programming language has also got characterset, identifiers, variables, statements and grammar called Syntax. C and C++ languages have also got all these features. Also they are case sensitive i.e., upper case (Capital letters and lower case (small letters) of the same alphabet are treated as different. A statement is similar to a sentence in natural language. Statements may also be called instructions. Statements are formed using certain words and symbols according to the rules known as syntax rules or grammar of the language. Every program must follow accurately the syntax rules supported by the language. In this chapter, concepts of constants, variables and data types are explained in detail for C and C++. **All these features are more or less common to C and C++. Any deviations will be pointed out later.**

3.2. CHARACTER SET :

The characters used to form variables, numbers and expressions depend upon the computer on which the program runs. *The characters in C and C++ are classified in the following categories.*

1) Letters
2) Digits
3) White spaces
4) Special characters
5) Delimiters
6) Escape sequences or back slash character constants :

Together these are called *literals.*

The characters are used to form words variables, numbers and expressions, in any programming language. These depend upon individual style of each programming language. *In C and C++ the characters are grouped as :*

3.2.1. Letters :

Consisting of uppercase letters A to Z and lowercase letters a to z. It shall be noted that upper and lower case letters are not interchangeable. Like C, C++ is also a strongly case sensitive language.

3.2.2. Digits : Consists of numbers from 0 to 9

3.2.3. Special Characters are given as below :

,	Comma	&	ampersand
;	semicolon	^	caret (Circumflex or crown or hat)
:	colon	*	asterisk (star)
?	question mark	+	plus sign
'	single quote	-	minus sign
"	double quote	<	less than sign
!	exclamation mark	>	greater than sign
@	at the rate of	=	equal to sign
|	vertical bar	( )	left & right parentheses (or round)
/	slash	[ ]	left & right brackets (square brackets)
\	backslash	{ }	left & right braces (or flower brackets)
~	tilde	#	hash or number sign (or sharp)
_	underscore	$	Dollar sign
%	percent sign		

3.2.4. White spaces : Consist of

	blank space
\n	new line
\f	form feed
\r	carriage return
/t	horizontal tab
/v	vertical tab

White spaces are ignored by the compiler unless they are part of string constants. White spaces may be used to separate words but are prohibited between the characters of key words and identifiers. They cannot be represented on the paper.

3.2.5. Delimiters :

:	colon	useful for label
;	semicolon	terminates statements
( )	parenthesis	used in expression and function
[ ]	square bracket	used for array declaration
{ }	curly brace	scope or block of statements
#	hash	preprocessor directive
,	comma	variable separator

3.2.6. Escape sequences or back slash character constants :

\a	audible alert (bell)	\\	backslash
\b	backspace	\?	question mark
\f	form feed	\'	single quote

\n	new line	\"	double quote
\r	carriage return	\ooo	octal number
\t	horizontal tab	\xhh	hexadecimal number
\v	vertical tab		
'\0'	null		

The above escape sequences are used in output functions. Each of them represents a single character though they consists of two characters.

3.3. C TOKENS / C++ TOKENS :

In a sentence in Natural Language individual words, punctuation marks are called tokens. Similarly in **C / C++** program the smallest individual units are known as **C / C++** tokens. **C** has six types of tokens.

1. Key words eg. int, for, while etc.,
2. Identifiers eg. temp, ht (height), apple etc.,
3. Constants eg. 108, -12.6, 3.14152 etc.,
4. Literals / Strings eg. "welcome", "spring", "good" etc.,
5. Special symbols eg. { }, [ ], $, & etc.,
6. Operators eg. +, -, etc.,
7. White spaces eg. blank space, new line, form feed, carriage return, horizontal tab etc.,

3.3.1. Key Words :

In C as also in C++ every word is is classified as either a *keyword* or an *identifier.* **Certain reserved words are known as key words by the compiler. Each key word has a specific meaning.** While naming a variable or identifier we should not use any of these keywords as names, otherwise an error will be indicated since there will be a confusion between the identifiers and keywords for the compiler. In Ansi C compiler we have 32 key words as given in table 3.1.

Table 3.1 : Keywords in C / ANSI C Key Words)

auto	double	int	struct
break	else	long	switch
case	enum	register	typedef
char	extern	return	union
const	float	short	unsigned
continue	for	signed	void
default	goto	sizeof	volatile
do	if	static	while

Borland C has the following additional key words.

asm cdecl far huge interrupt near pascal

C++ has 62 keywords compared to 32 in C. *The additional key words in C++ which are not found in C are given in Table 3.2*

Table 3.2 : Additional Key words in C++

asm	bool	catch	class	const_cast
delete	explicit	export	false	friend
inline	mutable	namespace	new	operator
private	protected	public	reinterpret_cast	static_char
template	this	throw	true	try
typeid	typename	using	virtual	wchar_t

3.3.2. Identifiers :

Identifiers are names of variables, functions, and arrays. They are user-defined names, consisting of sequence of letters and digits, with a letter as the first character. Both Upper case and Lower case letters are permitted to define Identifiers, but lower case letters are preferred. However, the upper case letters are also permitted. The under score symbol '_' can be used as an identifier. In general under score is used as a link between two words in long identifiers.

Examples : User-defined identifiers are as follows.

i) # define PI 3.14159

ii) # define a 27

Here, 'PI' and 'a' are user-defined identifiers. They are also known as symbolic constants. *Symbolic constants* are defined when those constants appeared repeatedly in a number of places in the program to change their values at one place instead of repeatedly, if required.

3.3.3. Constants :

Constants have fixed values and do not change. In C as also in C++ there are several types of constants. Constants are classified mainly as numeric constants and character constants. Numeric constants again in turn are classified as integer constants having no decimal or fractional part and real constants having decimal or fractional parts. Character constants in turn are classified as single character constants and string constants.

3.3.3.1. Integer Constants :

An integer consists a sequence of digits. It may be a signed constant with '+' sign or '-' sign. *Generally for a positive integer the + sign is not used. The + sign is also called Unary +.*

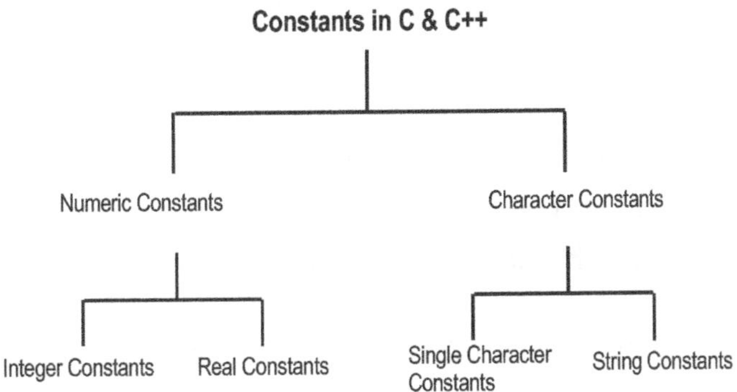

Fig. 3.1. Constants in C and C++

The integer constants can be either decimal integer constants (to the base of 10), or Octal integer constants (to the base of 8) or hexadecimal integer constants (to the base of 16). In decimal integers the digits are 0, 1, 2, 3, 4, 5, 6, 7, 8, 9. The next number will be 10 corresponding to decimal number 10 ; 11 corresponding to decimal number 11 etc.,) In octal integers the digits are 0, 1, 2, 3, 4, 5, 6, 7 The next number will be 10 corresponding to decimal number 8 ; 11 corresponding to decimal number 9 etc.,). In hexadecimal integers the digits are 0, 1, 2, 3, 4, 5, 6, 7, 8, 9, a, b, c, d, e, f (a corresponding to 10, b corresponding to 11 .... f corresponding to 15) etc., The next number will be 10 corresponding to decimal number 16 ; 11 corresponding to decimal number 17 etc., In hexadecimal numbers the digits a, b, c, d, e, f can also be given as upper case letters, A, B, C, D, E, F.

Examples : Decimal integers

478 ; -282 ; 22518 etc.,

Note : Spaces, commas non digit characters like $, Rs., etc., should not be used while writing any integer number let it be decimal or octal or hexadecimal number.

Octal integers consist of any combination of digits from the set 0 through 7 with a leading 0 (zero)

1232 ; -6245 ; 354545 etc.,

The Hexadecimal numbers are : 0 1 2 . . . . . 9 A B C D E F. The hexadecimal integers consists of any combination of digits from the set 0 through F with a leading 0x (zero x) or 0X (zero X, if upper case letters A through F are used).

0x345 ; -0x56B ; 0x65067 etc.

In decimal numbers the different digits 0 to 9 have different values depending upon their places like Ones digit, Tens digit etc.,

For ex:

bit no.	b_2	b_1	b_0
given no.	6	8	9

will have a value = $6 \times 10^2 + 8 \times 10 + 9 \times 10^{-0} = 689$

Similarly the octal number 0345 will have a value $3 \times 8^2 + 4 \times 8 + 5 \times 8^0 = 229$.

The Hexa decimal number 0x34e will have a value $3 \times 16^2 + 4 \times 16 + 14 \times 16^{-0} = 590$.

In binary numbers or machine language we have only two numbers 0 and 1 to be given in each digit.

For ex.: 01 for decimal 1 ; 10 for decimal number 2 ; 11 for decimal number 3

The decimal number 0 will be represented as 000 if we represent the number with 3 digits. The decimal number 1 will be represented as 001. The decimal number 2 will be represented as 010. The decimal number 3 will be represented as 011. Thus with a 3 digit binary number the maximum number that can be represented will be 111 i.e., 7 ($1 \times 2^2 + 1 \times 2 + 1 \times 2^0$)

The octal numbers are generally used in digital electronics indicating sets of eight. The hexadecimal numbers are used in micro processors, computers etc., so that with less number of digits bigger numbers can be represented, increasing the capacity of the data of numbers. In programming octal or hexadecimal numbers are not generally used. The largest integer value that can be stored in a machine is machine dependent. For a 16 bit machine the largest number that can be represented is 32767. For a 32 bit machine the largest number that can be represented is 214,74,83,647. It is also possible to store larger integer constants, with more number of bytes (1 byte = 8 bits) on these machines by appending *qualifiers* _ such as U, L and UL to the constants. With 2 bytes bigger numbers can be stored compared to the storage of numbers with 1 byte. For example :

39494U or 39494u (unsigned integer)
485713848ULor 485713848ul (unsigned long integer)
8492304L or 84923041 (long integer)

The concepts of long, unsigned, and long unsigned integers are discussed in detail later.

3.3.3.2. Real Constants :

To represent quantities which vary continuously the integer numbers are not sufficient and hence we use decimal numbers. The decimal numbers are known as Real numbers or *Real constants* or *Floating point constants*. For ex : the height can be represented as 1.76 meters, weight can be expressed as 5.64 kgs.

etc., The real numbers also can have '+' or '-' sign and usually the + sign is not mentioned. Some examples of Real constants are

0.4567 or .4567 ; -493.48 ; 384.245, 36 or 36.0 ; etc

While representing a real constant the decimal point is a must like-

0.4567 or .4567 ; 36.0 or 36. etc

A real number may also be expressed in exponential (or scientific) notation. For example, the value 215.65 may be written as 2.1565e2 in exponential notation. e2 means multiply by 10^2. *The general form is :*

mantissa e exponent

The *mantissa* is either a real number expressed in *decimal notation* or an integer. The *exponent* is an integer number with an optional plus of minus sign. The letter e separating the mantissa and the exponent can be written in either lower case or upper case. *For a given number of digits a larger number can be expressed if the number is given in exponent form when compared to giving the number in decimal form.* Since the exponent causes the decimal point to "float", this notation is said to represent a real number in *floating point form.* Examples of legal floating point constants are :

0.65e4 to represent the number 6500 (0.65×10^4)

43.45e-2 to represents the number 0.4345 (43.45×10^{-2}. The exponent (e-2) need not be written as e(-2).

-12e-2 to represent the number -0.12 (-12×10^{-2})

-2843E-2 to represent the number -28.43 (-2843×10^{-2})

7500000000 may be written as 7.5E9 or 75E8. Similarly -0.000000368 is equivalent ot -3.68E-7 or -36.8E-6.

Note : A blank space (embedded white space) between the numbers are the decimal point or the digits *mantissa* or exponent value or e should not be given.

Floating point constants are normally represented as double-precision quantities. However, the suffixes for f or F may be used to force single-precision and l or L to extend double-precision further like lf or LF etc.,

There is one another kind of constant, the enumeration constant. An enumeration is a list of constant integer values, as in

enum color { RED, GREEN, BLUE }

The first name in the enum has the value 0 and the next 1 and so on unless explicit values are specified.

enum months { JAN = 1, FEB, MAR, ... DEC}

where the value of FEB is 2 and MAR is 3 and so on.

Some examples of valid and invalid numeric constants are given in table 3.3.

Table 3.3 : Some valid and invalid Numeric Constants

Constant	Valid ?	Reason
986534L	Yes	Represents long integer
36,385	No	Comma is not allowed
+4.0E4	Yes	(ANSI C supports unary plus)
3.6e-3	Yes	
76.8 e4	No	No white space is permitted
-4.5e-02	Yes	
4.8 x 3.6E+3.8	No	Exponent must be an integer
$ 384	No	$ symbol is not permitted
0XFE	Yes	Hexadecimal integer

3.4. CHARACTER CONSTANTS :

Under Character Constants we have a single character constant or a string of characters representing a constant.

3.4.1 Single Character Constants :

A single character constant (or simply character constant) contains a single-character enclosed within a pair of single quote marks. Examples of character constants are :

'5' ; 'X' ; '-' ; ' ' (blank character) etc.,

Note that the character constant '5' is not the same as the number 5. The last constant is a blank space.

Character constants have integer values known as ASCII values. For example, the statements

printf("%d", 'A');

will print the number 65, the ASCII value of the letter a.

Similarly, the statement

printf("%c",66);

will print the letter 'B'. ASCII values for all characters are given in the 5th chapter. (Table 5.5)

Since each character constant represents an integer value it is also possible to perform arithmetic operations on character constants. These are discussed later.

3.4.2. String Constants :

A string constant is a sequence of character enclosed in *double quotes.* The characters may be letters, digits or special characters or combinations of these.

Example of string constants :

"Welcome"
"Good!"
"2004"
"\n ...!"
"6+3"
"A=B+5" etc.,

It may be noted that the single character constant 'X' is different from the string constant "X". Further, a single character string constant does not have an equivalent integer called ASCII code while a character constant has an integer ASCII value. Character strings are often used in programs to build meaningful programs. handling of character strings are considered in detail later.

The computer can identify numbers only and not characters. Hence the characters are coded with numbers. There are two types of codes 1, ASCI code (American Standard Code for Information Interchange) which is a very popular one and EBDIC code. (Extended Binary Coded Decimal Interchange Code) In these codes each character is given a specific number. For example in ASCI code the character 'A' is represented by the number 65. 'B' by 66, 'a' by No.97 and small 'b' by 98, number 47 represents '/ ', 48 represents '0', 52 represents '4' and so on.

3.5. SPECIAL SYMBOLS :

Examples of special symbols used in C and C++ are [ ] ; { } ; ( ) etc.,

List of special characters, delimiters etc., have already been discussed earlier in section 3.2.

3.6. OPERATORS :

In C and C++ we have different type of operators such as arithmetic operators like + ; - ; * ; / ; % , relational operators like > ; < etc., logical operators like && ; | | etc. *They are discussed in greater detail later in chapter 4.*

3.7. VARIABLES :

So far we have discussed the constants whose values do not change before, during, or after execution of a program whereas we may be needing to change the values of the data during execution of the program. During execution of a program many operations are performed on the data. To represent a data which changes its value during execution we represents the data by means of variables instead of constants, So that the variables can be assigned different values at different times.

A variable is a data name which is used for storing a data value. Unlike constants the value of the variable will change and can take any value of the given data type like

integer or real or single character or string. The variables value can change during execution of the program which means a variable can be assigned different values at different times during the execution of the program. A variable can be defined by any name subject to certain rules prescribed by the particular programming language, but it will be better to give a meaningful name for the variable which can be easily understood by the programmer and also by others.

Ex : height or ht, weight or wt, temp (for temperature) or tmp, total, marks, marks1 (for marks in subject 1) class_avg (for average marks of the class) etc.,

3.7.1 Rules for defining Variables :

A variable name should observe the following rules in C and C++.

i) They must begin with a letter. It may include underscore between the characters of the name preferably between two connecting parts of a variable name like marks_s1 (for marks in subject 1). Some systems permit underscore as the first character.

ii) ANSI standard recognizes a length of 31 characters. However, the length should not be normally more than eight characters, since only the first eight characters are treated as significant by many compilers if more characters are given then the compiler will cut-off the variable name to the prescribed (eight) characters and if there is a change in the ninth or more character to distinguish two different variables then the compiler cannot distinguish these 2 variables as separate variables and will treat them as a single variable which will lead to mistakes in calculations. For ex: average_marks and average_grade will be treated as a single variable average_. They can be recast as avg_mrks and avg_grad to treat them as two different variables.

iii) Uppercase and lower case are significant. That is, thc variable **Total** is not the same as **total** or **TOTAL.** The variables temp, temp, teMP or TEmp are all different variables and they do not refer to the same variable because of the differences in Upper case and lower case letters. It will always be better to use the lower case letters for naming a variable which will be easier for entering also.

iv) The variable name should not be a keyword in C or C++.

v) The variable name should not start with a digit.

vi) White space like blank, horizontal tab etc., are not allowed.

Some valid variable names are Tom, harry, marks_1, rad, p1, a etc.,

Examples of valid and invalid Variable names are given in Table 3.4.

Table 3.4. : Some valid and invalid variable names with reasons

Variable name	Valid ?	Reason
Average	Valid	
char	Not valid	Char is a keyword
float	Not valid	Float is a key word
price$	Not valid	Dollar sign is illegal
avg_ht	Valid	
int_pages	Valid	a keyword can be part of a name

3.8. DATA TYPES :

C and C++ have rich data types. The different data types help the programmer to select appropriate data type required for the applications while programming. For ex. : to represent the names the *char data type* consisting of characters, to represent marks integer data type, to represent average marks, float data type etc., can be used. In addition we have provision for user defined data types like enumerated data type, derived data type such as arrays, structures, union etc.,

The Data types in C and C++ can be divided mainly into 4 classes. 1. Primary or Fundamental Data types, 2. User defined Data types, 3. Derived Data types, 4. Empty Data set or Void Data type.

3.8.1 Primary or Basic or Fundamental Data type :

All C and C++ compilers support 4 fundamental data types.

i) Integer data type - key word : int
ii) Floating point data type - key word : float
iii) Character data type - key word : char
iv) Double precision - key word : double

There is provision by many compilers to extend the integer and double precision data type into long integer (key word - long int) and long double (keyword - long double, unsigned char, unsigned long etc.,)

3.8.1.1 Integer, Float and Char Data types :

i) Integer Data type : (keyword : int) This can be divided into signed type or unsigned data types. Signed and Unsigned Integer data type occupies by 2 bytes of 8 bits memory in the case of a 16 bit machine, *short integer* data type and integer data type are both one and the same except for the keywords. Short integer data type also occupies 2 bytes for a 16 bit machine. Some compilers treat **short** as 8 bit or 1 byte data.

In order to provide some control over the range of numbers and storage space, C has three classes of integer storage, namely **short int, int,** and **long int,** in both **signed** and **unsiged** forms. For examples, **short int** represents fairly small integer values and require half the amount of storage as a regular **int** number uses. Unlike signed integers, unsigned integers use all the bits for the magnitude of the number and are always positive. Therefore, for a 16 bit machine, the range of unsiged integer numbers will be from 0 to 65,535

We declare **long** and **unsigned** integers to increase the range of values. The use of qualifier **signed** on integers is optional because the default declaration assumes a signed number.

ii) Float data type : (keyword : float)

Floating point (or real) numbers are stored in 32 bits (on all 16 bits and 32 bit machines), with 6 digits or precision. Floating point numbers are defined in C by the keyword **float.** When the accuracy provided by a **float** number is not sufficient, the type **double** can be used to define the number.

iii) Character data type : (Keyword : char)

A single character can be defined as a character **(char)** type data. Characters are usually stored in 8 bits (one byte) of internal storage. The qualifier **signed** or **unsigned** may be explicitly applied to **char.** While **unsigned chars** have values between 0 to 255, **signed char** have values from -128 to 127.

iv) Double precision : (Keyword : double)

A double data type number uses 64 bits giving a precision of 14 digits. These are known as double precision numbers. Remember that **double** type represents the same data type that **float** represents, but with a greater precision. To extend the precision further, we may use **long double** which uses 80 bits.

The control string given in input and output statements indicates the type of data to be inputted or outputted.

CHAR DATA TYPE *both signed and unsigned occupies single byte in the case of 16 bit machine.*

LONG INTEGER *both signed and unsigned occupies 4 bytes in the case of 16 bit machine.*

DOUBLE *occupies 8 bytes for floating type data leading to greater precision in the case of 16 bit machine.*

LONG DOUBLE *occupies 10 bytes for floating type data leading to still greater precision in the case of 16 bit machine.*

Data types and their control strings in the case of a 16 bit machine are given in table 3.5.

Table 3.5 : Different Numeric Data Type with Size and Range

Key word	Size (in bits)	Range	Control String
char or signed char	8 bits (1 byte)	-128 to 127 (-2^7 to 2^7-1)	%C
unsigned char	8 bits	0 to 255 (0 to 2^8-1)	%C
signed int (or int)	16 bits (2 bytes)	-32,768 to 32767 (-2^{15} to 2^{15}-1)	%i or %d
short int (or short or signed short int)	16 bits	-32,768 to 32767	%i or %d
signed long int (or long int or long)	32 bits (4 bytes)	-2147483648 to 2147483647 (-2^{31} to 2^{31} - 1)	%ld
unsigned long int (or unsigned long)	32 bits (4 bytes)	0 to 4294967295 (0 to 2^{32} - 1)	%lu
float	32 bits	3.4E - 38 to 3.4E + 38	%f or %g
double	64 bits (8 bytes)	1.7E - 308 to 1.7E +308	%lf
long double	80 bits (10 bytes)	3.4E - 4932 to 1.1E+4932	%lf

3.8.2. User-defined Data Types :

There are several data types in C and C++ which are defined by the user for convenience. This feature enables these language to be very rich in data handling with speed and less memory requirements.

3.8.2.1 User defined data :

C and C++ support a special feature known as "type definition" which allows users to define a different identifier to represent a particular data type that would *represent an existing data type.* The user-defined data type identifier can later be used to declare variables. *The syntax for type definition will be*

typedef type dataname or identifier ;

Where type refers to an existing data type and "identifier" refers to the "new" name given to the data type. The existing data type may belong to any class of type, including the user-defined ones. It may be noted that the new type is 'new' only in name, but not the data type. **typedef** does not create a new type. But this helps increasing the readability of the program.

Some examples of type definition are :

i) **typedef int** unit;
unit batch1, batch2;

These declarations cause the new declaration unit for batch1, batch2 to be integers.

This is in the place of the usual statement

int marks1, marks2;

The advantage of typedef is that typedef can be given earlier and the user data type can be given later. Similarly

ii) **typedef float** avgmarks;
avgmarks marks1, marks2, marks3

These statements caused marks in subject 1 called marks 1, marks in subject 2 called marks2 to be of float type.

iii) **typedef int** hours ;
hours hrs;

3.8.2.2 Enumerated datatype :

Another useful user-defined data type is Enumerated data type. *The syntax for enumerated data type will be*

enum identifier {value1, value2, ...valuen};

The identifier **enum** is a user-defined enumerated data type which can be used to declare variables that can have one of the values enclosed within the braces (known as enumeration constants). After this definition, we can declare variables to be of this 'new' type as below. Example :

enum identifier v1, v2, ...vn;

The enumerated variables v1, v2,... vn can only have one of the values value 1, value2, ... valuen. The assignments of the following types are valid :

v1 = value3;
v5 = value 1;

For example : On seeing the statement

i) **enum month {Jan, Feb, Mar, Apr, ..., Nov, Dec} ;**

the compiler automatically assigns integer digits beginning with 0 to all the enumeration constants. That is, the enumeration constant **value1** is assigned 0, **value 2** is assigned 1, and so on. However, the automatic assignments can be overridden by assigning values explicitly to the enumeration constants.

The given statement causes Jan = 0 meaning January is zeroth month. Feb = 1, meaning February is the first month etc. which is not the convention. So to make January as first month we can declare

ia)**enum month** {Jan =1, Feb, Mar, Apr, ..., Nov, Dec} ;

Now January will be the first month .... and December will be the12th month.

ii) **enum day** (Monday, Tuesday, ... Sunday);
iii) enum day week_st, week_end;

```
        week_st = Monday;
week_end = Friday
if(week_st ==Tuesday)
week_end = Saturday;
```

iv) **enum day** (Monday = 1, Tuesday, ... Sunday);

Here, the constant Monday is assigned the value of 1. The remaining constants are assigned values that increase successively by 1.

v) The identification and declaration of enumerated variables can be combined in one statement. Ex :

enum day (Monday, ... Sunday) week_st, week_end ;

3.8.2.3. Storage Class Data types :

Variables in C can have not only data type but also storage class that provides information about their location and visibility. The storage class decides the portion of the program within which the variables are recognized. Consider the following example :

```
  /* Example of storage classes */
int m;
main()
{
  int i;
  float balance;
  ....
  function1( );
}
function1( )
{
  int i;
  float sum;
  .....
  ....
}
```

The variable **m** which has been declared before the **main** is called global variable. *The global variable can be used in all the functions in the program.* Here **int m** is common to both **main** ( ) and **function1** ( ) It need not be declared in other functions. *A global variable is also known as an external variable and is called by the keyword* **extern**.

The variables int i and balance are local variables to **main** ( ) in the above example.

The variables **i** and **sum** are called local variables to **function1** ( ). because they are declared inside the **function1** ( ). *Local variables are visible and meaningful only inside the functions in which they are declared and are called* **auto variables.** *They are not known to other functions.* Note that the local variable int i has been declared in both the functions, main ( ) and function1 ( ) in the above example. Any change in the value of **i** in one function does not affect its value in the other.

C provides a variety of storage class specifiers that can be used to declare explicitly the scope and lifetime or variables. The concepts of scope and lifetime are important only in multifunction and multiple file programs and therefore the storage classes are considered in detail later when, functions are discussed. For now, it can be remembered that there are four storage class specifiers (**auto, register, static,** and **extern)** whose meanings are given table 3.6

Table 3.6 : Storage Classes and Their Meaning

Storage class	Meaning
auto	Local variable known to only to the function in which it is declared. Default is *auto*
static	Local variable which exists and retains its value even after the control is transferred to the calling function.
extern	Global variable known to all functions in the file.
register	Local variable which is stored in the register.

The storage class is another qualifier (like **long** or **unsigned**) that can be added to a variable declaration as shown below :

auto int count;
register char ch ;
static int x a;
extern long total;

Static and external (extern) variables are automatically initialized to zero. Automatic (auto) variables contain undefined values (known as 'garbage') unless they are initialized explicitly.

The **register** variables are stored in the CPU registers instead of in memory. Access of data from registers inside CPU is much faster than access from memory but the number of registers in CPU are limited. We cannot declare more variables with register variables. However, compiler automatically converts register variables to non-register variables once the limit for register variables is reached. The user cannot determine the success or failure of register variables. We cannot use register class for all types of variables.

There are some more types of user defined data types called **'Derived data types'** in C and C++ like arrays, structure, union and also pointer type of data.

3.8.2.4 Derived Data Types : C and C++ have provision for different types of derived data types like i) arrays, ii) structure, iii) union, iv) pointer.

i) Derived data type - Arrays :

A simple variable or a single variable can have a single value for the variable of one particular data type only whereas there are instances like having more values of the same data type requiring more number of variables to be declared which is inefficient. For example the marks of different students in a particular subject. If there are 60 students we will be having marks for each of the 60 students in the same subject. So to economise the memory and to minimize the variable names we have a user defined derived data type called arrays. *An array has a single variable name which can accommodate more number of values of the same data type stored sequentially in the memory.* All the array elements will be of the same data type stored one after another. The memory size will usually be 8 bits. Hence for one integer data type of 16 bits we need two memory locations. The second integer variable of the array will be stored in the third and fourth memory locations from the beginning of the first element storage. There are single dimensional, two dimensional and multi dimensional arrays we shall discuss them in detail later.

ii) Derived Data Type - Structure :

Another derived data type is called **structure** (keyword ; **struct**) *which will be defined data type by which we can have different data of different types for the same variable name.* For example the payroll for employees consists of employee's identification number which is an integer, employee's name which is char type, employee's pay which is of float type. Thus for each employee we have three different data types. These three data for an employee can be called the record for that employee's payroll. *For each data type appropriate* *memory is allocated.* This collection of three different types of data for an employee is called a structure payroll for an employee. Structure is discussed in detail later.

iii) **Derived Data Type - Union :**

Like structure union also has different data of different data types for the same variable name, but has memory allocation for only any one of the above data types at a time. Hence the size of the memory allocated for union will have to be the largest of the size of different data types used in the union. The union is discussed in detail later.

iv) **Derived Data Type - Pointer :**

*A pointer is a memory variable, which stores a memory address, Pointer can have any name that is legal for any variable and it is declared in the same fashion like other variables but it is always denoted by * operator (star or asterisk operator). For example a pointer is declared as int *a; float *b; etc.,*

*Here the variables a and p refer to the address of the variables where the values are stored. * a, * p referred to the actual values of the pointer variables.* Pointer variables are discussed in detail later.

These different user defined data types are discussed in greater detail in the subsequent chapters.

3.8.2.5 Empty Data Set or Void data type in C and C++ :

Void data type is value less, It has two uses ; one to explicitly declare a function as returning no value; second to create generic pointers. Void data type is discussed in detail later while dealing with functions and pointers.

3.8.2.6 Additional Data Types in C++ :

All the data types discussed above are common to C and C++. In addition to the above data types of C, the language C++ is equipped with some more data types namely bool, wchar_t etc., We will see one by one with suitable examples.

1. **Boolean Data Type :**

In C, any number except Zero is considered as true and Zero is considered as false. In C++, the value true and false are called as Boolean literals and belong to type **bool**. Like with other standard data types, we can declare a variable of type bool for the purpose of storing Boolean values. *Bool will have only two values, true or false.* Consider the following statements :

bool result = false;

The above statement declares and defines the variable result as Boolean, with the initial value as false.

2. **Wchar_t Data Type :**

Most of the legacy languages required only one byte to store character constants and it is enough to hold ASCII or EBCDIC character set. To accommodate some of the important universal languages. Unicode representation is followed in C++ through **wchar_t.** The size of variables of type wchar_t is varies with the compiler in use. Most compilers require 2 bytes to store and it can be also be 4 bytes in some compilers, *By using these Unicode representation it is possible to store 65,536 different character codes.*

Consider the following declaration :

wchar_t wx = L 'y' ; here L stands for long. The single character is enclosed within single quotes.

The above statement declares and defines 'wx' to be of type wchar_t, and initializes it to the wide character representation for 'y'.

3. **Additional String Data Type in C++ :**

The C language style of character strings can be of 0 length and therefore treated as empty in one of two ways, the character pointer can be set to zero and therefore point to no object; alternatively the pointer can be set but the array it refers to contains only the null character. For example :

```
/* pc1 addresses no array object */
char pcl = 0;
/* pc2 addresses the null character */
const char *pc2 = "  " ;
```

C-style strings generally prove error-prone with the novice of C or C++ programmer because of the low-level nature of its representation.

To overcome this error and other errors in string data type found in C language, the C++ standard library provides a common implementation of a string class abstraction. This will be studied in greater detail when we deal with strings.

4. **Reference Data types in C++ :**

A reference, sometimes referred to as an alias, serves as an alternative name for an object. A reference allows for the indirect manipulation of an object in a manner similar to the use of a pointer but without requiring use of pointer syntax. In real-world programs, references are primarily used as formal parameters to a function - usually to pass class objects into a function. This will be studied in detail later when we deal with classes and functions.

5. **Vector Container Type in C++ :**

The vector class provides an alternative representation to the built-in-array. The vector class, like the string class, is part of the standard library introduced with

Standard C++. There are two very different forms of using a vector, what we called the *array idiom* and the *STL idiom*. They will be discussed in detail later.

6. **Complex Number Types in C++ :**

In C language the complex numbers have to be treated separately with their real and imaginary parts or magnitude and phase. C++ provides a convenient way of dealing with complex numbers types. *The complex number class ia a part of the standard library.*

7. **The Pair Type in C++ :**

The pair class, part of the standard library, allows us to associate two values of either the same or different types within a single object. To use the pair class, we must include the following header file.

```
#include <utility>
```

This will be discussed later.

8. **The Class Types in C++ :**

The class mechanism supports the design of new types, such as the object-based string vector, complex, and pair class types discussed in this chapter, as well as the object-oriented iostream class hierarchy. The underlined concepts and mechanisms supporting object-based and object-oriented class design through the implementation and evolution of an Array class abstraction etc., will be discussed separately later.

3.9. DECLARATION AND INITIALIZATION OF VARIABLES :

After designing the suitable names for different variables the compiler should be informed as to what are the variables, what are their types and what are the initial values if necessary for the variables etc., Declaration is done by the declaration part of the program. *The syntax for variable declaration will be*

data-type variable1, variable2,....., variablen;

where variable1, variable2 etc., are the names of variables. A declaration statement must end with a semicolon. For example, valid declarations are :

```
int count;
int number, total;
double ratio;
```

int and **double** are the keywords to represent integer type and real type data values respectively.

Initial values for the different variables can be given separately by assignment using assignment operator = . More variables can also be initialized in the same statement.

Syntax variable_name = constant

or

data_type variable_name = constant

Example: int x = 2 ; where x is an integer variable.

Example: float y = 2.4; or float z = 3. ;

Example: int x=y=z=1;

The third example of initialization is also a valid statement where more than one variables can be iniatilized with the same value using such a format.

3.9.1. Type conversion or type cast :

Sometimes it becomes necessary to have results in certain data type, other than what is available from the given statement. Division of two integer numbers gives the results in integer number only in which case the fractional or decimal part of the quotient will be cut off. To get the correct results we will have to give the quotient in real format or float type. **This is achieved by forcing one of the integer numbers into float, thus and converting the expression into mixed more or division with integer and real numbers. The result will be of float type giving the correct value with decimals.** *For example the statements*

```
int a, b, c ;
c = a/b ;
```

give the result in integer form.

If a = 5, b = 2, then c= a/b will be equal to 2 and not 2.5 if a and b are both integers.

To overcome this problems we can give the statements as

```
int a, b ;
float c ;
c = (float) a/b ;
```

The third statement of type cast converts the integer ***a*** *into float and the results will be division of float with integer resulting in quotient in float giving a value of 2,500000.* **Note :** If the third statement is given as c = a/b then the result will be c = 2.000000 and not 2.500000.

3.10. CONSTANT AND VOLATILE VARIABLES :

i) Constant Variable : If we want that the value of certain variable remains the same or remains unchanged during the execution of a program then, it can be done only by declaring the variable as a constant. The keyword constant is then added before the declaration. It tells the compiler that the variable is constant. Thus *constant declared variables are protected from modification.*

Example 3.1 :

const int m = 10 ;

Where, const is a keyword, m is a variable name and 10 is a constant value

The compiler protects the value of **const int m** *from modification. The user cannot assign any value to m, but using scanf ( ) statement the value can be replaced.*

ii) Volatile variable : *The volatile variables are those variables that are changed at any time by other external program or the same program. The syntax is*

Volatile int d ;

If the value of a variable in the current program is to be maintained constant and desired not to be changed by any other external operation, then the declaration of variable will be as follows.

volatile const d=10 ;

3.11. DEFINING SYMBOLIC CONSTANTS :

We often use certain standard or unique constants in a program like calculation of area and perimeter of a circle. These constants may appear repeatedly in a number of places in the program. One example of such a constant is 3.142, representing the value of the mathematical constant **pi**. Another example is the total number of students whose mark sheets are analyzed by a 'test analysis program'. The number of students, say 50, may be used for calculating the class total, class average, standard deviation, etc. We face two problems in the subsequent use of such programs.

1. Problem in modification of the program.
2. Problem in understanding the program.

To facilitate modification of the symbolic constant we can redefine using **#define** statement as follows :

#define PI 3.14159

Some other define statements are

```
#define PASS_MARK      50
#define  MAX - MARKS   100
#define STRENGTH       90
```

Note : *The define statements should not be ended with ;*

Symbolic names are sometimes called constant identifiers, The following rules apply to a #define statement which define a symbolic constant.

1) Symbolic names have the same form as variable names. (Symbolic names are written in CAPITALS to visually distinguish them from the normal

variable names which are written in lowercase letters. This is only a convention, not a rule.)

2) No blank space between the harsh or pound sign '#' and the word **define** is permitted. Some compilers allow space between # and the word **define** in which case the spacing is optional.

3) '#' must be the first character in the line.

4) A blank space is required between **#define** and symbolic name and between the symbolic name and the constant.

5. **#define** statements must not end with a semicolon.

6. After definition, the symbolic name should not be assigned any other value within the program by using an assignment statement. For example, after having defined the statement # define PI 3.14159 we cannot reassign the value of PI to be different by the statement PI = 3.142. If we want to reassign the value then we have to give a new statement # define PI 3.142 deleting the statement # define PI 3.14159.

7. Symbolic names are NOT declared for data types. Its data type depends on the type of constants.

8. **#define** statements may appear anywhere in the program but before it is referenced in the program (the usual practice is to place them in the beginning of the program). Some valid and invalid define statements are given in table 3.7.

Table 3.7 : Some Invalid #define Statements

Statement	Validity	Remark
#define PI 3.14159	Valid	
# define PI 3.14159	Valid	only with some compilers
#define X = A+B	Invalid	signs like=and+are not allowed
#define MAX100	Invalid	No white space between Max and 100 define
#define N 25;	Invalid	No semicolon at the end
#define A 8, B 10	Invalid	Only one name is allowed
#Define ARRAY 11 #DEFINE ARRAY 14	Invalid	define should be in a lower case letters
#define PRICE$ 100	Invalid	$ symbol is not permitted in name

3.12. MODIFIABILITY :

We may like to change the value of "pi" from 3.142 to 3.14159 to improve the accuracy of calculations or the number 50 to 40, to redefine the minimum marks for Pass. In both the cases, we will have to search throughout the program and explicitly change the value of the constant wherever it has been used. If any value is left unchanged, the program may produce disastrous outputs. *To avoid these problems we can redefine the said symbolic constant with the new value deleting the definition of the old symbolic constant statement.*

3.12.1.Overflow and Underflow of Data :

The largest value that a variable can hold also depends on the machine. Problem of data overflow and underflow occur when the value of a variable is either too big or too small for the data type to hold. *However since floating point values are rounded off to the number of significant digits allowed (or specified), an overflow normally results in the largest possible real value, whereas an underflow results in zero.*

Integers are always exact within the limits of the range of the integral data types used. *Overflow which is a serious problem may occur if the data type does not match the value of the constant. C does not provide any warning or indication of integer overflow. It simply gives incorrect results. (Overflow normally produces a negative number).* We should therefore exercise a greater care to define correct data types for handling the input/output values.

3.12.2. Constant Qualifier :

Consider the following loop statements

```
for ( int index = 0 ; index < 512; ++index )
    ................ ;
```

Instead of using the constant value for index to terminate the loop we can use a variable name to determine the termination of the loop.

For example

```
for ( int index = 0; index < bufsize; ++index )
    ................ ;
```

and this variable **bufsize** should be initialized before the occurrence of the statement using **bufsize**. This variable is said to be localised. The constant type Qualifier transforms an object into a constant and in the above example it ensures unalteration of buff-size even if it encounters a statement in the middle of the loop like

```
if ( bufsize = 1 )
.......... ;
```

3.12.3. Reading Data from Keyboard :

In interactive presentation of data and results we input data through key board using the **Scanf( )** function. We get the output on the screen using the function **printf ( )** function. The general format of **scanf** is as follows :

scanf ("control string", & variable 1, & variable2.....) :

The control string contains the format of data being received. The ampersand symbol before each variable name is an operator that specifies the address of the variable. *We must always use this ampersand operator for the input data, otherwise unexpected results may occur.* Let us see how the scanf ( ) is implemented by the user.

When the statement **scanf("%d", &number);** is encountered by the computer, the execution stops and waits for the value of the variable **number** to be typed in. Since the control string "%d" specifies that an integer value is to be read from the terminal, we have to type in the value in integer form. Once the number is typed in, the 'Return' Key is pressed, the computer then proceeds to the next statement. Thus, the use of **scanf** provides an interactive feature and makes the program 'user friendly'. **The symbol ampersand indicates that the data entered is to be stored in an address for retrieval later.**

In interactive programming to indicate the place and the type of data to be given we can use an input **printf** ( ) statement like

printf ("\n Enter an integer number ..... ") ; before the scanf ( ) statement. This printf ( ) statement indicates in printout that we have to give an integer number at this place. The control string \ indicates next line.

Some compilers permit the use of the 'prompt message' as a part of the control string in scanf, like **scanf("Enter a number %d", &number);**

The **Scanf ( )** and **Printf ( )** functions come under formatted input/ output functions, the former for input and the latter for output.

* * *

COMPREHENSION - 3

Note : By answering all the questions given in this comprehension one can answer any objetive type of questions easily whatever be the form of the question. Answers for these questions can be obtained by going through the topics in this chapter carefully.

1. What is meant by Syntax and Syntax Rules for a Programming Language?
2. Mention the different categories of characters with examples.
3. What is meant by Literals?
4. What are Special Characters and their uses?
5. Mention White Spaces and their uses.
6. What are Delimiters and what functions do they do?
7. Give Escape Sequences and their uses.
8. What is a token? Mention the different tokens of C and C++.
9. What is a Keyword? How many key words are there in ANSI C and Borland C?
10. Mention the key words in C and C++
11. What are Identifiers? Give the rules to coin Identifiers.
12. What are Constants in C or C++?
13. What are the different types of Constants? How are they represented?
14. What are the different methods of writing any number? Explain how they are represented in different bases and how they are converted from one base to another base?
15. What is E format of writing a number? Explain the conversion of E format and Decimal numbers from one another? What is the advantage of E format number?
16. What is meant by Enumerated Constants? Explain.
17. Explain how Character Constants are represented.
18. Explain how String Constants are represented.
19. What is a variable? How does it take different values?
20. What are the rules to name a Variable?
21. What is meant by Data Type? What are the different classes of Data Types?
22. Give examples for different Data Types .
23. What are Volatile Variables? How are they defined?
24. Explain User defined Data Types with examples.

25. Explain Enumerated Data Types with examples.
26. What are Storage Data Types? State with examples.
27. Mention the meaning of different Storage Data Types.
28. What are Fundamental Data Types?
29. What are Derived Data Types?
30. Explain Arrays, Structures, Union and Pointers.
31. What is Empty Set or Void Data Type? Explain.
32. Mention the additional Data Types in C++.
33. Give examples of different additional Data Types in C++.
34. Why is initialization of Variables required?
35. How are the Variables declared and initialized?
36. Explain Type Conversion or Type Cast.
37. Explain the difference between Constants and Volatiles.
38. What is Symbolic constant? What is its use?
39. How are Symbolic Constants defined?
40. What is the Syntax for DEFINE statement? Why and where is it used?
41. What is meant by MODIFIABILITY of Symbolic Constants? How is it done?
42. Explain Overflow and Underflow.
43. What is meant by Constant Qualifier? Explain
44. What is meant by void declaration? If it is used in a function declaration what does it mean?
45. What is the use of declaration void? Can it be used to create Generic Pointers?

* * *

EXERCISE - 3

Note : By answering all the questions given in this exercise one can answer subjective type of questions easily including problems. The worked examples in the chapter may help in solving these questions.

1. What is meant by declarations?
2. Write briefly about Character sets, and Special Characters.
3. Explain about Delimiters and Back Slashes.
4. What are White Characters? What are their functions?
5. What are Key Words? Give the Key Words of C and C++.
6. What are C or C++ Tokens?
7. What are Identifiers or Variable names? What are the rules for forming Identifiers?
8. (a) Mention whether the following variable names are correct or not. Give reasons.

   i) Average ii) char iii) float iv) price$ v) avg_ht vi) int_page vii) Temp. .viii) Temp ix) temP x) " Wren & Martin "

   (b) Do the two Variable names 'temp' and 'temP' refer to the same variable? Give Reason.
9. Mention the different methods of representing Constants and their initializations with examples, in C and C++. Represent the same number in different forms.
10. How are Character and Character stings represented in C. Give examples,
11. Explain different types of Data types, their representation, word length ,their ranges and their control strings etc.
12. Explain the difference between type definition and typecast with examples.
13. Explain with examples the difference between Enumeration constants and Enumerated Data Type? How do you change the enumeration constant value? Give examples.
14. Explain with examples Storage class data and their meaning.
15. Explain with examples the different types of Derived Data types.
16. What is the difference between %f and %g ?
17. What are the ASCII CODES and what is their use?

18. What is the difference between %d and %i ? Explain with examples.
19. What is the difference between %c and %s ? Explain with examples
20. How does Character Constant differ from String Constant
21. What is the difference between double and long double? Is there any difference between their Control Strings? Explain with examples.
22. What are the differences between signed and unsigned data types?
23. What are Symbolic Constants? When are they used? How do you modify Symbolic Constants?
24. Are the following statements correct? What do they do?

    Printf (" %d ",'A');

    Printf ("%c", 66);
25. What are Octal and Hexadecimal numbers? How do you indicate their type in the program?

* * *

CHAPTER - 4
OPERATORS AND EXPRESSIONS

4.1 INTRODUCTION :

In C and C++ action is referred to by an expression. An expression consists of number of operands and operators. An operand can also be an expression. Every expression is terminated by a semicolon. An expression ending with a semicolon is known as a statement. A statement can be small or big occupying a space within a line or extending beyond one line. If the statements are small, if we choose, instead of giving one statement in every line, more than one statement can also be given in same line each statement ending with a semicolon. The smallest independent unit in a program is a statement similar to a sentence in Natural Language.

Both C and C++ support a rich set of operators. *An **operator** is a symbol that tells the computer to perform certain mathematical or logical manipulations. Operators are used in programs to manipulate data and variables. They usually form a part of the mathematical or logical expressions.*

C and C++ operators can be classified into a number of categories. The different classes of operators and their symbolic representation are given in Table 4.1

Table 4.1 Types of Operators

<table>
<tr><td>Arithmetic operators</td><td>+, -, *, / and %</td></tr>
<tr><td>Relational operators</td><td>>, <, = =, <=, >= and ! =</td></tr>
<tr><td>Logical operators</td><td>&&, | | and !</td></tr>
<tr><td>Increment and decrement operator</td><td>+ + and - -</td></tr>
<tr><td>Assignment operators</td><td>=</td></tr>
<tr><td>Bitwise operator</td><td>&, |, >>, <<, ^ and ~</td></tr>
<tr><td>Comma operators</td><td>,</td></tr>
<tr><td>Conditional operators</td><td>? :</td></tr>
<tr><td>Special operators</td><td>( ), [ ], { }, . , →</td></tr>
</table>

4.2. PRIORITY OR HIERARCHY OR PRECEDENCE OF OPERATORS :

Various relational operators have different priorities. If an arithmetic expression contains more than one operator then the execution will be performed according to their priorities. The precedence is set for different operators in C and C++. Among operators of the same priorities generally the corresponding operations are done from left to right except in some special cases as given in Table 4.2 (operators with different priorities (hierarchy)

Table 4.2 Priority and Grouping of Operators

Operators	Operation	Clubbing	Priority
1. Special Operators of Top priority :			
( )	Function call	Left to right	1st
[ ]	Array expression or square bracket		
->	Structure Memory Operator		
-	Structure Member Operator		
2. Special Operators of Second priority :			
+	Unary plus	Right to left	2nd
-	Unary minus		
+ +	Increment		
- -	Decrement		
!	Not operator		
~	Ones complement		
*	Pointer Operator		
&	Address Operator		
size of	Size of an object		
Type	Type cast		
3. Arithmetic Operators of First priority :			
*	Multiplication		3rd
/	Division		
%	Modular division		
4. Arithmetic Operators of Lower priority :			
+	Addition	Left to right	4th
-	Subtraction		
5. Bitwise Operators of Higher priority :			
<<	Left shift	Left to right	5th
>>	Right shift		
6. Relational Operators of Higher priority :			
<	Less than	Left to right	6th
<=	Less than or equal to		
>	Greater than		
>=	Greater than or equal to		
7. Relatinoal Operators of Lower priority :			
= =	Equality	Left to right	7th
! =	Inequality		
8. Bitwise Operators of Different Lower priorities :			
&	Bitwise AND	Left to right	8th
^	Bitwise XOR	Left to right	9th
|	Bitwise OR	Left to right	10th
9. Logical Operators of Different priorities :			
&&	Logical AND	Left to right	11th
| |	Logical OR	Left to right	12th
10. Ternary Operator pair or the Conditional Operator :			
? :	Conditional operator	Right to left	13th
11. Assignment Operators of Equal priorities :			
=, +=, - =, *=, / =, & = , | =, ^ =, <<=, >>=	Assignment Operators	Right to left	14th
12. Special Operator of Least priority :			
,	Comma operator	Left to right	15th

4.2.1. Use of Different Operators :

1) Special Operators :

i) The Special Operator ( ) is used in functions to specify the arguments of the function. Also this operator is used to over ride the priorities of different operators like arithmetic operators in expressions.

ii) The square brackets are used in array expressions to indicate the size of the array or the index of the array also. Arrays is called matrix in mathematics.

iii) The braces { } are used to enclose the function statements or statements of any block like 'true block' or 'false block' which enclose the statements for condition to be true or condition to be false for conditional statements etc.,

iii) The structure memory operator or arrow operator is used to denote the memory address of the members or elements of the derived data type structures.

iv) The member operator or the dot operator **.** is used to denote the elements or members of the derived data type structures.

2) Special Operators of Lower Priorities :

i) The unary plus + operator or unary minus - operators are used to indicate the sign of the data.

ii) Increment operators + + and the decrement operator - - when attached to a variable indicates increment or decrement of the variable by one. Here again we have pre increment operation and post increment operation like + + x or x + + etc.,. In pre increment the value of the variable is increased by one before the execution of the expression whereas in post increment the value of the variable is increased by one only after executing the given statement with the previous value of the variable. So is the case with decrement operators also. Ex :

int a = 3, b = 4, c,d ;

c = + + a * 4 ;

d = 5 * b + +

After execution of these statements we will have c = 16, because a is pre-incremented and hence becomes (3 + 1) before multiplication and a = 4.

After execution of these statements we will have d = 20, because b is post-incremented and hence b will be equal to 4 only before multiplication and after multiplication b will be = 4 + 1.

iii) The Not Operator ! is used to negate the operation. For example ! = indicates the not =. Another example ; the statement ! a && b means the logical operation of not a and b i.e., absence of a and presence of b .

iv) The bitwise not operator or ones complement operator ~ is used in binary operations to **flip** the bits. The operator ~ is called tilde. ~1 is 0 and ~ 0 is 1. This operation is done on individual bits of the binary number. For example if x = 1001 then ~x = 0110.

v) The pointer operator * before a variable or a structure indicates the the address of the variable or address of the structure. This facility helps in quick retrieval of the data from memory particularly when arrays, structures etc., are used as arguments of any function.

vi) The address operator & indicates the address of the variable so that the variable can be accessed later at any time when required.

vii) The size of an object operator 'sizeof' indicates the size of the particular data object. For ex. sizeof an array or size of a structure gives the total memory address required for storing the members of the array or the structure. The size is expressed in bytes.

viii) The type operator or type cast operation indicates the data type of the variable in the case of type definition or type conversion which is used to forcibly change the type of the given data from one type to another type.

3) Arithmetic Operators of Higher priority :

i) The binary arithmetic operator - multiplication operator * is used for multiplication. For ex : the statement for 4x2 will be 4 * 2. A binary operator is an operator which operates on only two operands. An operand can be a simple variable or an expression. For example in the expression c = a+b, a and b are the two operands and + is the binary operator for addition. Either a or b or both can be expressions also.

ii) There are two Division operators, / and Modular division % . The modular division % gives the remainder and not the actual quotient. For ex : 7 % 4 gives 3 as the result ; 1 % 2 will be 1 and not 0 or 0.5 because only the remainder will be given as result in modular division.

iii) The division operator is / and not. The division of two integer numbers using the symbol / gives only the integer part of the quotient cutting off the decimal part. The division of two real numbers gives the quotient as real with decimals. To get the correct value of the integer division we should change one of the integer numbers to act as a real number using type cast. For example to get the correct result 4.5 instead of 4 for the expression 9/2 we use type cast as (float) 9/2.

4. Arithmetic Operators of Lower priority :

i) The binary arithmetic operators of lower priority + and - have the usual addition and subtraction operations used in arithmetic.

5) Bitwise Operators of Higher Priority :

i) The left shift operator << implies shifting of the given binary number left by one digit and is used to multiply the given number by 2. Let us consider a decimal number 89. If it is left shifted by one digit we get 890 (i.e.89 x 10). Similarly any binary number when left shifted by one digit will amount to multiplication of the number by 2. For example the given binary number 101 used to represent the decimal number 5 when left shifted by one digit becomes 1010 which will represent the decimal number 10 i.e., multiplication of the given number 5 with 2.

ii) The right shift operator >> implies shifting of the given binary number right by one digit and is used to divide the given number by 2. Let us consider a decimal number 89. If it is right shifted by one digit we get 8.9 (i.e.89 ¸10). Similarly any binary number when right shifted by one digit will amount to division of the number by 2. For example the given binary number 1000 used to represent the decimal number 8 when right shifted by one digit becomes 0100 which will represent the decimal number 4 i.e., division of the given number 8 with 2.

In bitwise shift operations the operand's excess bits are discarded.

6. Relational Operators of Higher priority :

The Relational operators of Higher priority like < is used for less than operation. For ex. the statement a < b ? means if the condition a < b is true. The Less than or equal to operator will be <= ; greater than or equal to operator be will be >=. The greater than operator will be >. Not equal to operator will be ! =. Ex : 8 > 5 ? will be true returning a value 1 and 8 < = ? will be false giving a returning value of 0.

7. Relational Operators of Lower Priority :

The equality operator will be = =. The inequality will be ! =. The normal mathematical equality sign = does not have the same meaning in C and C++ where the = sign represents an assignment operator. For example a = 5 ; means the value 5 is assigned to the variable a. a = b + c ; means the value (b+c) is assigned to the variable a.

8. Bitwise Operators of Different Lower priorities :

In general AND operator will given output only if both the operands are present. If either one or both of the operands are absent the output will be zero. This is expressed in truth table 4.3.

Bitwise operation is a speciality in C and C++ languages wherein the logical operations like OR, AND, XOR (i.e., Exclusive OR) are done on the individual bits of the number in binary form.

The OR operation will give the output if either of the 2 inputs or both the inputs are present. This is given in table 4.4.

The exclusive OR (XOR) operation will give the output only if either of the 2 inputs are present and no output when both the inputs are present or when both the inputs are absent. This is given in truth table 4.5.

Table 4.3 : Truth table for AND operation

S.No.	Input A	Input B	Output
1.	0 or false (F)	0 or false (F)	0 or False (F)
2.	0 or false (F)	1 or true (T)	0 or false (F)
3.	1 or true (T)	0 or false (F)	0 or false (F)
4.	1 or true (T)	1 or true (T)	1 or true (T)

Table 4.4 : Truth table for OR operation

S.No.	Input A	Input B	Output
1.	0 or false (F)	0 or false (F)	0 or False (F)
2.	0 or false (F)	1 or true (T)	1 or true (T)
3.	1 or true (T)	0 or false (F)	1 or true (T)
4.	1 or true (T)	1 or true (T)	1 or true (T)

Table 4.5 : Truth table for XOR operation

S.No.	Input A	Input B	Output
1.	0 or false (F)	0 or false (F)	0 or False (F)
2.	0 or false (F)	1 or true (T)	1 or true (T)
3.	1 or true (T)	0 or false (F)	1 or true (T)
4.	1 or true (T)	1 or true (T)	0 or flase (F)

For example : A = 10 (decimal number). In binary form A = 1010
B = 12 (decimal number). In binary form B = 1100

i) Bitwise AND operation of A and B (A & B) = 8 = 1000

ii) Bitwise OR operation of A and B (A | B) = 14 = 1110

iii) Bitwise exclusive OR operation of A and B(A^B) = 6 = 0110

Here for simplicity only 4 digit binary numbers are used. For any number of digits the bitwise operations will be similar.

9. Logical Operators :

The bitwise logical operations are done on the corresponding individual bits whereas the logical operations are done on the words as a whole i.e., for the entire individual numbers. The truth table for the logical operations AND, OR, operations will be the same as given in tables 4.3 & 4.4. But instead of the inputs A and B being individual bits, they are the numbers A and B each represented by a series of bits. All the bits of a word put together represents the number A or B. Logical and operations. The logical NOT operation gives an output true i.e., 1 if the given condition is not true and an output False i.e, 0 if the given condition is fulfilled. For ex :

i) The Logical AND operation A>B & & x = = 10 will be true only if the two conditions A is greater than B and B is equal to 10 are true. In case the logical operation is true it returns true value i.e., 1. If these 2 conditions are not fulfil the output will be false i.e., 0.

ii) The Logical OR operation A>B | | x < 10 will be true if either A is greater than B or B is less than 10 or if A is greater than B and also B is less than 10. In case the logical operation is true it returns a value 1 for true. If A is not greater than B and if B is greater than or equal to 10 then the output will be False i.e., 0.

iii) The Logical NOT operation gives output true returning a value 1 if the not condition is fulfilled and output false i.e. 0, if the not condition is not fulfilled. For ex : A != B (Condition A is not equal to B) gives output 1 if A and B are different and gives output 0 if A and B are equal. The condition 8 ! = 8 gives an output 0 ; 8 ! = 6 gives an output 1, since 8 and 6 are not equal.

10. Ternary Operator pair " ?: " or the Conditional Operator :

The conditional operator contains a condition followed by two statements or values with a colon in between. If the condition is true the first statement is executed otherwise the second statement is executed.

The syntax or format for conditional operation will be

Condition ? (expression1 for true) ; (expression 2 for false) ;

The expressions 1 and 2 are separated by a colon. If the condition is true expression1 gets evaluated otherwise expression 2 gets evaluated. The condition is always written before question mark. For example

i) The statement 3 = = 8 ? 4 : 6 gives an output of 6. Since the condition is false.

ii) The statement 3 ! = 8 ? 4 : 6 gives an output of 4. Since the condition is true.

iii) The three statements together a = 10 ; b = 15 ; max = (a>b)? a : b; give an output max = 15

iv) The statements a = 10 ; b = 15 ; min = (a < = b)? a : b ; give an output min = 10

11. Assignment operators of equal priorities :

Unlike the sign = in mathematics, in programming the sign = denotes the assignment operator. That means the value given in the right side of the assignment operator = is assigned to the variable given on the left side of the assignment operator. For ex: The statement a = b ; in programming means the value of the variable b is assigned to the variable a. The assignments operators are used in three different forms

For ex :

i) simple assignment a=12 ; value 12 is assigned to a

ii) multiple assignment a=b=c=12 ; value 12 is assigned to a,b & c
iii) compound assignment a+=12 ; value (a+12) is assigned to the variable a.

Similarly the **short hand assignment operators** are - =, *=, &=, =, |=,<<=, >>= etc. In these operations the operations given on the left hand side of the assignment operator = is performed on the variable given to the left of the compound assignment operators. For ex. the 2 statements : a = 4 ; a* = 3 ; gives the value of 4 x 3 (=12) to a. Now the new value of a will be 12.

The left hand side of an assignment operator in an expression has to be a variable and not an expression. For ex : the assignment statement a = b + c ; is correct but the assignment statement b + c = a ; is not correct.

12. Special Operator of the least priority (Comma Operator) :

The comma operator is used to separate two or more expressions. The comma operator has the lowest priority among all the operators. It is not essential to enclose the expressions with comma operators within the parenthesis. For example the statements given below are valid.

Example :

int a=2, b=4, c=a+b ;

the above statements assign the value 2 to a, the value 4 to b and the value 6. (i.e.2+4) to c and a, b and c are integers.
int (a=2, b=4, c=a+b;) is also the same as the above statement but the parenthesis is unnecessary here.

It may be noted that the statements are separated by ; and not,

13. Cast or Type Cast Operator :

The process of local conversion is called casting a value. The general form of a cast is,

(type-name) expression

(e.g.)

```
float a=5.5;          int a=5;
int b;                float b;
if b = (int) a        if b= (float) a
then b = 5                then b = 5.0
```

In C++, the following method is also used to convert its type, for example,

```
int i=5;
float f;
f=float(i);
```

the above statement makes the cast look like a function call.

4.2.2. Evaluation of expressions using the priorities of operators :

In programs the expressions given in any statement are evaluated keeping the priorities of the different operators as given earlier in table 4.2 in view. The expression is scanned repeatedly from left to right and between the operators of the same priority or equal priority again the rule left to right. Operations with operators of higher priorities are executed first in each scan from left to right and between operators of the same priority the operations are done from left to right or right to left as the case may be.operators is followed as given in the table 4.2. The parenthesis ( ) over rules the rule of priority of operators. For example consider the statements

i) x = a + b * c ;

In this statement, the right hand side of the expression is scanned from left to right. Even though the + operator comes first the * operator has a higher priority compared to + operator. Hence the expression b * c is evaluated first and the product is added to a and the resulting value is assigned to x. With a = 3, b = 4 and c = 5, this statement gives x = 3 + 4 x 5 = 3 + 20 = 23.

ii) x = (a+b) * c ;

In this statement, the right hand side of the expression is scanned from left to right. Even though the + operator comes first the * operator has a higher priority compared to + operator. But since a + b is enclosed within the parenthesis, parenthesis over ruling the priority of operators the expression a + b is done first. The sum is multiplied by c and the resulting value is assigned to x. With a = 3, b = 4 and c = 5, this statement gives x = (3 + 4) x 5 = 7 x 5 = 35.

iii) x = 4 * 5 + 8 / 2 ;

x = 20 + 4 = 24.

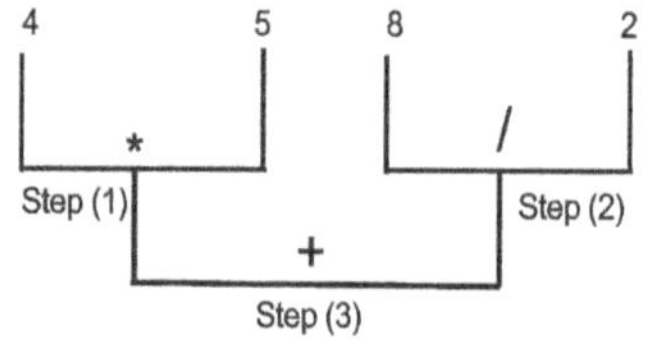

Note : the operations are performed as per the priority of the operators and the operations are numbered in the order they are being performed by the computer.

4 5 8 2
* /
Step (1) Step (2)
+
Step (3)

iv) x = 24 - 6/3 + 4*(8 + 2) ;

First pass : Scanning the operators from left to right of the right hand side of the expression, we have the operator / and the operator * which are of higher priority compared to the operators - and +. But (8+2) over rules the priority rule since 8+2 is enclosed within parenthesis. Performing this operation first we have

x = 24 - 6/3 + 4 * 10

Second pass : Among the two operators / and *, the / operator / occurs first from left. Hence the division operation 6/3 is performed first resulting in 2. Next the operation 4 * 10 is performed resulting in 40. Then we have

x = 24 - 2 + 4 * 10 = 24 - 2 + 40

Third pass : Among the two operators - and +, the operator - occurs first from left. Hence the expression 24 - 2 is evaluated first resulting in 22. Then the plus operation is done resulting in 22 + 40 = 62. Thus x = 62

4.3. TYPE CONVERSIONS IN EXPRESSIONS :

i) Automatic Type Conversion :

C permits mixing of constants and variables of different types in an expression, but during evaluation it adheres to very strict rules of type conversion. We know that the computer, considers one operator at a time, involving two operands.

If the operands are of different types, the 'lower' type is automatically converted to the 'higher' type before the operation proceeds. The result is of the higher type. A typical example of type conversion process is illustrated in Fig 4.7 for the expression x = l / j + i * f - d.

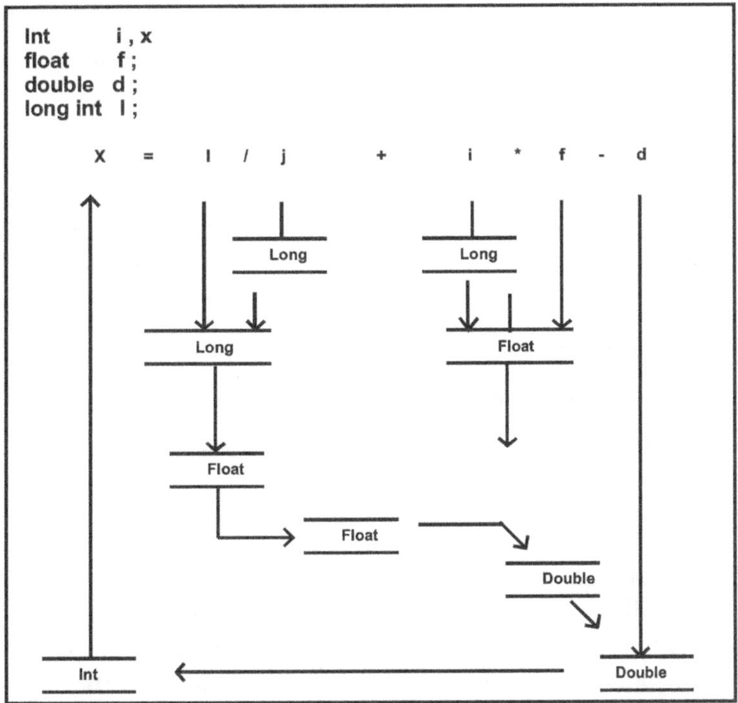

Fig. 4.1 : Process of automatical type conversion

Given below is the sequence of rules that are applied while evaluation of an expression.

1. All **short** and **char** are automatically converted to **int;** then
2. If one of the operands in **long double,** the other will be converted to **long double** and the results will be **long double :**
3. else, if one of the operands is **double,** the other will be converted to **double** and the result will be **double.**
4. else if one of the operand is **float,** the other will converted to **float** and the results will be **float.**
5. else, if one of the operands is **unsigned long int,** the other will be converted to **unsigned long int** and the result will be **unsigned long int;**
6. else, if one of the operands is **long int** and the other is **unsigned int,** then,
   a) if **unsigned int** can be converted to **long int,** the unsigned int operand will be converted into long int and the result will be **long int;**
   b) else, both operands will be converted to **unsigned long int** and the result will be **unsigned long int;**
7. else, if one of the operands is **long int**, the other will be converted to **long int** and the results will be **long int ;**
8. else, if one of the operands is **unsigned int,** the other will be converted to **unsigned int** and the result will be **unsigned int.**

   Note : Some versions of C automatically convert all floating points operands to double precision.

   The final result of an expression is converted to the type of the variable on the left of the assignment sign before assigning the value to it. However, the following changes are introduced during the final assignment.

   1. **float** to **int** occurs truncation of the fractional part.
   2. **double** to **float** causes rounding of digits.
   3. **long int** to **int** causes dropping of the excess higher order bits which causes a serious error.

ii) Casting a Value :

As stated above, we have discussed how C performs type conversions automatically, also, if we want, we can force a type conversion in a way we want to which is different from the automatic conversion. Consider, for example, the calculation of ratio of females to males in a town.

ratio = female_number/male_numb

Since **female_number** and **male_number** are to be declared as integers in the program, the result will be an integer with decimal part of the result of division lost and **ratio** would represent a wrong figure. This problem can be solved by converting locally one of the variables to the floating point as shown below :

ratio = (float) female_number/male_number

The operator **(float)** converts the **female_number** to floating point for the purpose of evaluation of the expression. Then using the rule of automatic conversion, the division is performed in floating point mode, thus retaining the fractional part of result.

If the ratio is declared as float and the type conversion (float) female is not made, then the result will be in float but will not be correct because the integer quotient will be given in decimal form, with the decimal digits as 0s, but not the actual decimal figure.

Note that in no way does the operator (**float**) affect the value of the variable **female_number** And also, the type of **female_number** remains as **int** in the other parts of the program.

The process of such a local conversion is known as casting a value. *The syntax for typecast is*

(type-name) expression

Where type-name is one of the standard C data types. The expression may be a constant, variable or an expression. Some examples of casts and their actions are shown in Table 4.6.

Table 4.6 Use of Casts

Example	Action
x = (int) 8.6	8.6 is converted into integer 8 by truncation.
a = (int) 36.9 / (Int) 4.8	Evaluated as 36/4 and the resulting in 9.
b = (double) sum/n	Division is done in floating point mode.
y = (int) (a+b)	The result of a + b is converted to integer.
z = (Int) a + b	a is converted to integer and then added to b.
p = cost ((double) x)	Converts x to double before using it.

In some of the programs given below the usual header files are assumed and not specified separately.

Program 4.3.1

Write a program in to explain the use of cast operator.

```
/* Example for use of cast */
      main()
{
      float sum;
      int n;
```

```
    sum = 0 ;
    for (n = 1; n <= 10; ++n)
    {
      sum = sum + 1/(float)n; /* int n converted into float n */
      printf("%2d %6.4\n", n, sum);
    }
}
```

OUTPUT :

```
1. 1.0000
2. 1.5000
3. 1.8333
4. 2.0833
5. 2.2833
6. 2.4500
7. 2.5929
8. 2.7179
9. 2.8290
10.2.9290
```

Consider the expression x = (int) (y + 0.5);

If y is 27.6 y + 0.5 is 28.1 and on casting, the result becomes 28, the value that is assigned to **x.** Of curse, the expression, being cast is not changed. This program shows using typecast to evaluate the equation.

$$\text{sum} = \sum_{i=1}^{n} (1/i)$$

When combining two different types of variables in an expression, never assume the values of automatic conversion. It is always a good practice to explicitly force the conversion. It is more safer and more portable. For example, when **y** and **p** are **double** and **m** is **int,** the following two statements are equivalent.

y = p + m;
y = p + (double)m;

However, the second statement is preferable. It will work the same way on all machines and is more readable.

4.3.1. Operator precedence and associativity :

Each operator in C has a precedence associated with it. This precedence is used to determine how an expression involving more than one operator is evaluated. There are distance *levels of precedence* and an operator may belong to one of the levels. The operators at the higher level of precedence are evaluated first. The operators of the same precedence are evaluated either from left to right or from right to left, depending on the level. This is known as the associativity property of an operator. Table 4.8 provides a complete list of operators, their precedence levels, and their rules of association. The groups are listed in the order of decreasing precedence (rank 1 indicates the highest precedence level and 15 the lowest). The list also includes those operators which we have not yet discussed.

It is very important to note carefully, the order of precedence and associativity of operators. Consider the following conditional statement :

If (x == 10 + 15 && y < 10)

The precedence rules say that the addition operator has a higher priority than the logical operator (&&) and the relational operators (= = and <). Therefore, the addition of 10 and 15 is executed first. This is equivalent to :

if (x == 25 && y <10)

The precedence rules say that the addition operator has a higher priority than the logical operator (&&) and the relational operators (== and <). Therefore, the addition of 10 and 15 is executed first, This is equivalent to :

if (x == 25 && y < 10)

The next step is to determine whether x is equal to 25 and y is less than 10. If we assume a value of 20 for x and 5 for y, then

x == 25 is FALSE (0)
y < 10 is TRUE (1)

Note that since the operator < enjoys a higher priority compared to ==, y < 10 is tested first and then x == 25 is tested.

Finally we get ;

if (FALSE && TRUE)

Because one of the conditions is FALSE, the complex condition is FALSE.

In the case of &&, it is guaranteed that the second operand will not be evaluated if the first is zero and in the case of the second operand will not be evaluated if the first is non-zero.

Program 4.3.2

Write a Program in C to calculate salesman's salary using the formula

Gross salary=base salary+(quantity *bonus rate)+(quanityt *Price)* Commission

/* Program to calculate a salesman's salary */

```
#define BASE_SALARY     3000.00
#define BONUS_RATE       400.00 per unit sold
#define COMMISSION         0.02
          main ( )
{
     int  quantity;
     float  gross_salary,price, bonus, commission;
     printf ("\n input number sold and price \n");
     scanf (%d %f", &quantity, &price);
     bonus           = BONUS_RATE *quantity;
     commission      = COMMISSION *quantity *price;
     gross_salary    = BASE_SALARY + bonus + commission;

     printf("\n");
     printf (*Bonus            = %6.2f\n",bonus);
     print(*Commission         = %6.2f\n",commission);
     printf(*Gross  salary     = %6.2f\n", gross-salary);
}
```

OUTPUT :

```
input number sold and price
5     20450.00
Bonus          = 2000.00
Commission     = 2045.00
Gross salary   = 7045.00
```

4.4. SOME SPECIAL FEATURES OF C++ OVER C :

The relationship between the algorithms and collection of data against which the algorithms are written is known as *programming paradigm.*

In procedural programming paradigm a problem is directly modelled by a set of algorithms and the statements are executed sequentially unless some exemptions are made like branching as in the case of Fortran, Pascal, C Languages. C++ also supports procedural programming. In 1970's the programming design shifted from the procedural paradigm to that of *abstract data types* (now generally referred to as *object-based* programming). *In this paradigm, a problem is modeled by a set of data abstractions. In C++ we refer to these abstractions as classes.*

C++ provides several other powerful extensions to the C programming language. Among these are :

1. Constructors and destructors, which are used to create, initialize and destroy class objects.

2. Overloaded functions and operators, which let you extend the operations a function or operator can perform on different data types.
3. Inline functions, which make programs more efficient.
4. References, which allow a function to modify its arguments in the calling function.
5. Template functions and classes, which allow the definition of generic classes and functions.
6. Object-Oriented Exception handling, which provides transfer of control and recovery from errors and other exceptional circumstances.

Benefits of Object-Oriented programming include :

a) Ability to simulate real-world event much more effectively.
b) Code is reusable unless code may have to be written using inheritance.
c) Data becomes active
d) To create graphical user interface (GUI) applications.
e) Programmers are able o reach their goals faster
f) Programmers are able to produce faster, more accurate and better-written applications.

Some programs in C to illustrate the use of operators and control strings are given here.

4.5. SOME PROGRAMS IN C :

Program : 4.5.1 :

Write a program in C to illustrate the use of Arithmetic Operators using Formatted Input Out Statements without Field Widths - Addition, Subtraction, Multiplication and Division.

```
/*arithmetic operators*/
# include <stdio.h>
# include <conio.h>
void main( )
{
int a,b,c,d,sum,diff,prod,intdiv,mod_div;
float div;
sum=0;diff=0;prod=0;div=0;intdiv=0;mod_div=0;
clrscr( );
printf("\n Enter integer values a b, c, d.....");
scanf("\n  %d\t %d\t %d\t %d",&a,&b,&c,&d);
sum=a+b+c+d;
diff=a+b-(c+d);
prod=a*b;
```

```
intdiv=a/b;
mod_div=a%b;
div=(float)a/b;/* type cast-int"a" converted into float to get float div*/
printf("\n  a= %d  \t b= %d  \t c= %d  \t d= %d ",a,b,c,d);
printf("\n");
printf("\n (a+b-(c+d)) (a-b) intdiv(a/b) mod_div(a%b) fdiv(a/b) (a*b)");
printf("\n");
printf("\n  %d      %d      %d      %d      %f      %d  ",
sum,diff,intdiv,mod_div,div,prod);
getche( );
}
```

OUTPUT :

```
Enter integer values a b, c, d.....10 25 18 74
a= 10      b= 25      c= 18      d= 74
 (a+b-(c+d)) (a-b) intdiv(a/b) mod_div(a%b) fdiv(a/b) (a*b)
127     -57     0     10     0.400000     250*/
```

Program : 4.5.2 :

Write a program in C to find Sum and Average of 3 Integer numbers using Formatted Input Out Statements Without Field Widths

```
/ * sum and average of three integer numbers * /
#include<stdio.h>
#include<conio.h>

void main()
{
int num1,num2,num3,sum=0;
float avg;
clrscr( );
printf("\n\n Enter three integer numbers:");
scanf("\n\n%d%d%d",&num1,&num2,&num3);
sum=num1+num2+num3;
avg=sum/3;
printf ("num1=%d\tnum2=%d\tnum3=%d\tsum=%d\tavg=%f",num1,num2,num3,sum,avg);
getche();
}
```

OUTPUT :

```
enter the three integer numbers:num1,num2,num3...
3 33 333
number1 is =3
number2 is =33
```

```
number3 is =333
sum    is =369
Average is =123.000000
```

Program :4.5.3 :

Write a program in C to find Sum and Average of 3 Real Numbers using Formatted I/O without Field Widths

```
/* sum and average of three float numbers */
#include<stdio.h>
#include<conio.h>
void main()
{
float num1,num2,num3,sum=0, avg;
clrscr( );
printf("\n\n Enter three integer numbers:");
scanf("\n\n%f%f%f",&num1,&num2,&num3);
sum=num1+num2+num3;
avg=sum/3.0;
printf("\n");
printf("\nnum1=%f\num2=%f\num3=%f\sum=%f\tavg=%f",num1,num2,num3,sum,avg);
getche();
}
```

OUTPUT :

```
enter the three real decimal numbers:num1,num2,num3...
33.1  56.7  897.727
number1 is =33.099998
number2 is =56.700001
number3 is =897.726990
sum    is =987.526978
Average is =329.175659
```

Program : 4.5.4 :

Write a program in C to find the Sum and Average using Formatted I/O and also to give the Sum and Average of 3 Integer Numbers in tabular form using Formatted I/O with Field Widths

```
/*arithmetic sum and average of three integer numbers*/
#include<stdio.h>      /*header files- for scanf & printf*/
#include<conio.h>      /*header files- for use of control strings or*/
                        /*conversion factors*/
void main()    /*main function- void: no parameters*/
               /*beginning of main function*/
{
int num1,num2,num3,sum=0; /* type  declaration & initialization of variables*/
```

```
float avg;          /* type declaration*/
clrscr();           /* clears screen to avoid garbage display*/
printf("\nEnter three 2 digit integer numbers:"); /* request to enter data*/
scanf("\n%d%d%d",&num1,&num2,&num3); /* reading and & for storing of data*/
sum=num1+num2+num3; /*calculation of expression using assignment operator*/
avg=float(sum)/3; /*type cast to convert int sum to float sum*/                /
*calculation & assignment*/
printf("\nnum1\tnum2\tnum3\tsum\tavg");
printf("\n%3d\t%3d\t%3d\t%4d\t%8.6f",
         num1,num2,num3,sum,avg);//formatted
                              /*output for results*/
getche( ); /* to display entered data */
}
```

```
/*OUTPUT :
enter three 2 digit integer numbers:num1,num2,num3...
33 45 59
number1 is =33
number2 is =45
number3 is =59
num1  num2  num3  sum   avg
 33    45    59   137   45.666668
```

Program 4.5.5 :

Write a program in C to illustrate the Use of the Pre & Post Increment Operators

/* PRE OPERATOR AND POST OPERATORS PROGRAM */

```
/*usage of post increment & preincrement of a variable */
#include<stdio.h>
#include<conio.h>
void main( )
{
int k=8,b,k1=8,c,d;
clrscr( );
printf("\n\n k is %d and k1 is %d",k,k1);
b=(k++ - k++);
/*evaluates b to 0 with k=8, then with k=9 (right k++) then with k=10 (left k++) */
printf("\n\n b is = %d and \n\n k is = %d",b,k);
k=(k++ - k++);/*with k=10 evaluates to 0 then *k=1 and k=2 (right & left k++) */
printf("\n\n k is %d",k);
c = (k1++ -k1++-k1++ +k1++);//c = 0 with k1=8, k1 becomes 9,10,11 and 12
printf("\n\n k=%d\tb=%d",k,c);
```

```
b=8;c=9;//more than one statement in same line each is separated by ";"
d=b++ + c--;//d=(8+9);b=(8+1);c=(9-1)
printf("\n\n d,b,and c are   %d \t %d \t %d",d,b,c);
d=++b - --c;//b=(9+1);c=(8-1);d=(10-7)
printf("\n\n d,b,and c are   %d \t %d \t% d",d,b,c);
getche ();
}
```

OUTPUT :

```
k is 8 and k1 is 8
b is = 0 and
k is = 10
k is 2
k=2   b=0
d,b,and c are  17     9     8
d,b,and c are  3     10     7
```

Program 4.5.6 :

Write a program in C to explain the use of Pre Operator for array elements with Arrays :

```
/* pre-operator  with array elements ++ */
#include<stdio.h>
#include<conio.h>
void main ()
{
int b,a[ ]={0,0,0,0,0,};/*initialises array;max dimension optional*/
clrscr ();
for (b=0;b<=4;b++)
        { printf("\n\n b is %d and a[b] is %d before first pre incr.",b,a[b]);
          /*a[b] without preincrement */
          ++a[b];/*a[b] is increased by 1 before processing*/
          printf("\n\n b is %d and a[b] is %d in first pre incr.",b,a[b]);
          /*a[b] increased by 1 before processing */
         printf("\n\n b is %d and a[b] is %d in 2nd pre incr.",b,++a[b]);
        /*a[b] is further increased by 1 before processing*/
         printf("\n\n");
        }; /*Semicolon is optional here.Works even without it */
}
```

OUTPUT :

```
b is 0 and a[b] is 0 before first pre incr.
b is 0 and a[b] is 1 in first pre incr.
b is 0 and a[b] is 2 in 2nd pre incr.
```

```
b is 1 and a[b] is 0 before first pre incr.
b is 1 and a[b] is 1 in first pre incr.
b is 1 and a[b] is 2 in 2nd pre incr.
b is 2 and a[b] is 0 before first pre incr.
b is 2 and a[b] is 1 in first pre incr.
b is 2 and a[b] is 2 in 2nd pre incr.
b is 3 and a[b] is 0 before first pre incr.
b is 3 and a[b] is 1 in first pre incr.
b is 3 and a[b] is 2 in 2nd pre incr.
b is 4 and a[b] is 0 before first pre incr.
b is 4 and a[b] is 1 in first pre incr.
b is 4 and a[b] is 2 in 2nd pre incr.
```

Program : 4.5.7 :

Write a program in C to explain the Precendence of Operators with Post Increment Operator :

```
/*Precedence or Hierarchy of different types of operators */
# include <stdio.h>
# include <conio.h>
        void main ( )
{
  int a,b,c,d,e;
  a=b=c=d=e=0;
clrscr( );
printf("\n Enter four int values a,b,c,d with space between them...");
scanf("\n\n %d %d %d %d",&a,&b,&c,&d);
printf("\n\n a= %d; b= %d; c= %d; d= %d; e= %d",a,b,c,d,e);
            /* overall: 2nd priority;among them right to left priority */
e=a+b*c++ -d; /*unary"-" for d;e is executed with old value of c
            and later c is increased by one*/
printf("\n\n e=a+b*c++ -d is %d and c after execution is %d",e,c);
getche( );
}
```

OUTPUT :

```
Enter four int values a,b,c,d, with space between them....
9 8 6 4
a= 9; b= 8; c=6; d=4; e=0
e=a+b*c++ -d is 53 and c after execution is 7
```

Program 4.5.8 :

Write a program in C to explain the use of Precedence of Operators for Arithmetic Operators

```
/* Precedence or Priority of arithmetic operators */
/* arithmetic operators- (*;/;%)-1st among arithmetic oprtrs - among them */
/* left to right;(addn.'+',sub '-')2nd among arith.optrs ; between them left to right*/
/* Parenthesis : higher priority. Evaluates exprn. inside paranthesis first */
/* WHEN IN DOUBT USE PARANTHESIS */
# include <stdio.h>
 # include <conio.h>
   void main( )
{
     float a,b,c,d,e,f,x; //all values in float to avoid int divn
                                 //which truncates decimal part
clrscr( );
printf("Enter float nos. a,b,c,d,e,f with space between them .... ");
printf("\n\n a,b,c,d,e,f (all the six float values)  are : ");/*if int values*/
    /* are given- mixed mode gives wrong results */
    /* eg. float of int 9 is 9.0 or atleast 9.  Decimal pt. is must */
      scanf("\n\n  %f%f%f%f%f%f",&a,&b,&c,&d,&e,&f);
x=a+b/c*d-e/f;
printf("\n\n a+b/c*d-e/f = %f",x);
x=(a+b)/c*d-e/f;
printf("\n\n (a+b)/c*d-e/f= %f",x);
x=(a+b)/c*(d-e)/f;
printf("\n\n (a+b)/c*(d-e)/f= %f",x);
x=(a+b/c)*d-e/f;
printf("\n\n (a+b/c)*d-e/f= %f",x);
x=a*(b/c*(d-e)/f);//inner most paranthesis evaluated first;no. of
                         //opening and closing paranthesis should match
printf("\n\n a*(b/c*(d-e)/f= %f",x);
 getche( );
}
```

/***INPUT:**

Enter float nos. a,b,c,d,e,f with space between them ....
a,b,c,d,e,f (all the six float values) are :
1.2 2.3 3.4 5.2 2.3 1.6 */

OUTPUT :

```
(a+b/c)*d-e/f= 8.320147    a+b/c*d-e/f = 3.280147
 a*(b/c*(d-e)/f= 1.471323  (a+b)/c*d-e/f= 3.915441
 a+b/c*d-e/f = 3.280147    (a+b)/c*d-e/f= 3.915441
(a+b)/c*(d-e)/f= 1.865809  (a+b/c)*d-e/f= 8.320147
 a*(b/c*(d-e)/f= 1.471323
```

Program : 4.5.9

Write a program in C to explain the use of Post and Pre Increments of a Variables Addition & Subtraction Sum and Difference

```
/* usage of post increment & preincrement of a variable */
#include<stdio.h>
#include<conio.h>
void main()
{
int k=8,b,k1=8,c,d;
clrscr();
printf("\n k is %d",k);
b=(k++-k++);
/*evaluates b to 0with k=8,then with k=9 (right k++) then with k=10 (left k++)*/
printf("\n bis =%dand\n kis=%d",b,k);
k=(k++-k++); //with k=10 evaluates to 0 then k=1 and k=2(right&left k++)
printf("\n k is %d",k);
c=(k1++-k1++-k1+++k1++);//c=0 with k1=8,k1 becomes 9,10,11,and12
printf("\n k1=%d\tb=%d",k1,c);
b=8;c=9;/*more than one statement in same line separated by ";" */
d=b++ +c—;//d=(8+9);b=(8+1);c=(9-1)
printf("\n d,b,and c are %d\t %d\t %d",d,b,c);
d=++b - —c;//b=(9+1);c=(8-1);d=(10-7)
printf("\n d,b,and c are %d\t %d\t %d",d,b,c);
getche( );
```

OUTPUT :

```
k is 8 and k1 is 8
b is = 0 and
k is = 10
k is 2
k=2   b=0
d,b,and c are 17   9   8
d,b,and c are 3   10   7
```

Program 4.5.10 :

Write a program in C to explain the use of Pre & Post Increments in Multiplication

```
/* using product with post/pre increments of a variable */

#include<stdio.h>
#include<conio.h>
```

```
void main()
int x,y,z;
clrscr( );
x=0;
y=4;
printf("\n  x=%d  y=%d",x,y);
x=2*(y++)+3;//x=(2*4) +3;y=(4+1)
printf("\n  x=%d  y=%d",x,y);//product with y++
x=2*(++y)+3;//y=(5+1);x=(2*6)+3
printf("\n  x=%d  y=%d",x,y);//product with++y
getche( );
}
```

OUTPUT :

```
x=0  y=4
x=11  y=5
x15  y=6
```

Program 4.5.11 :

Write a program in C to illustrate the Arithmetic Operators with Different types of Division :

```
/* arithmetic operators */
# include <stdio.h>
# include <conio.h>
void main( )
{
int a,b,c,d,sum,diff,prod,intdiv,mod_div;
float div;
sum=0;diff=0;prod=0;div=0;intdiv=0;mod_div=0;
clrscr( );
printf("\n Enter integer values a b, c, d.....");
scanf("\n  %d\t %d\t %d\t %d",&a,&b,&c,&d);
sum=a+b+c+d;
diff=a+b-(c+d);
prod=a*b;
intdiv=a/b;
mod_div=a%b;
div=(float)a/b;/* type cast-int"a" converted into float to get float div*/
printf("\n  a= %d  \t b= %d  \t c= %d  \t d= %d ",a,b,c,d);
printf("\n");
printf("\n  (a+b-(c+d)) (a-b) intdiv(a/b)  mod_div(a%b)  fdiv(a/b)  (a*b)");
```

```
printf("\n");
printf("\n  %d      %d      %d      %d      %f      %d  ",
           sum,diff,intdiv,mod_div,div,prod);
getche( );
```

OUTPUT :

```
Enter integer values a b, c, d.....10 25 18 74
  a= 10      b= 25       c= 18       d= 74
(a+b-(c+d)) (a-b) intdiv(a/b) mod_div(a%b) fdiv(a/b) (a*b)
   127      -57      0      10      0.400000      250*/
```

Program 4.5.12 :

Write a program in C to illustrate the use of formatted I/O statements and control strings

```
    /* Formatted I/O functions and control strings */
# include <stdio.h>
# include <conio.h>
void main( )
{
int intnum;
float realnum;
char a,word[10];
clrscr( );
printf("\n\n Enter an integer number ....");
scanf("%d",&intnum);/*some compilers allow textprompt*/
             /* in scanf( ) as in printf( )*/
if(intnum<100)
printf("\n The entered number is = %d", intnum);
else
printf("\n The entered integer number is greater than 100");
printf("\n");/*printing a blank line*/
printf("\n\n Enter a decimal number ....");
scanf("%f",&realnum);
  if (realnum>100.) /*for float atleast decimal point must*/
   printf("\n The entered real number is =%f", realnum);
  else
   printf("\n The entered real number is <100.0");
printf("\n");
printf("\n\n Enter a single character....");
scanf("%s",&a);/* cntrl string should be %s not %c since it is
```

```
in the middle of a program*/
printf("\n The entered character is : %c",a);
printf("\n");
printf("\n\n Enter a word with less than 9 characters....");
scanf("%s",&word);
printf("\n The entered word is : %s", word);
getche( );
}
```

OUTPUT :

```
Enter an integer number ....369
The entered integer number is greater than 100
Enter a decimal number ....468.6
The entered real number is =468.600006
Enter a single character....P
The entered character is : P

Enter a word with less than 9 characters....GoodWork
The entered word is : GoodWork
```

Program 4.5.13 :

Write a program in C to explain the Mismatch of control strings for Characters

```
/*Use of proper and other mismatched control strings for Character*/
# include <stdio.h>
# include <conio.h>
void main( )
{
char ch,a;
int b=0;
clrscr( );
printf("\n\n\n Enter any single character....");
        /*matching ctrl ch.for scanf & printf */
scanf("%c",&ch);/*cntrl string is %c not %s since in top of prgrm*/
printf("\n\n The entered character is : %c",ch);
  /*mismatched control strings for characters:%d for scanf %c for printf*/
printf("\n\n Ascii code for the entered character is =%d ;",ch);
printf("\n\n\n Enter any integer code for b which is less than  256...");
scanf("%d",&b);
printf("\n character for the int b is = %c",b);
printf("\n\n\n Enter any int code for b greater than 256....");
scanf("%d",&b);
printf("\n character for int is =%c",b );
```

```
        /*mismatch of control strings-%c for scanf and %d for printf*/
printf("\n\n\n enter any integer < 256....");
scanf("%c",&a);
printf("\n\n The entered int is =%d",a);
printf("\n\n\n Enter any integer > 256....");
scanf("%c",&a);
printf("\n The entered int is =%d",a);
printf("\n NOTE:Integer input with char control in scanf");
printf("\n leads to garbage in input and output");
getche( );
}
```

OUTPUT :

```
Enter any single character....P
The entered character is : P
Ascii code for the entered character is =80 ;
Enter any integer code for b which is less than  256...75
character for the int b is = K
Enter any int code for b greater than 256....258
character for int is =?
enter any integer < 256....
The entered int is =10
NOTE:Integer input with char control in scan
 leads to garbage in input and output
```

Program 4.5.14 :

Write a program in C to explain the proper use of Control strings

```
/* Use of proper and other mismatched control strings for Charector */
# include <stdio.h>
# include <conio.h>
 void main( )
{
char ch,a;
int b=0;
clrscr( );
   /* Matching control strings : %c for scanf and printf functions */
printf("\n\n Matching ctrl string c for scanf and printf functions");
printf("\n\n\n Enter any single character....");
scanf(" %c",&ch);/*cntrl string should be %s not %c in scanf if it is not
            in the beginning  of the program*/
printf("\n The entered character is : %c",ch);
```

```
  /* Mismatched control strings for characters : %d for scanf %c for printf */
printf("\n\n\n ctrl c in scanf and d in printf functions");
printf("\n\n Ascii code for the entered character is =%d ;",ch);
printf("\n\n\n ctrl d in scanf and c in printf functions");
printf("\n\n Enter any integer code for b which is less than  256...");
scanf("%d",&b);
printf("\n character for the int b is = %c",b);
printf("\n\n\n If no. >256 the number less 256 will be the ascii code for ch")
printf("\n\n Enter any int code for b greater than 256....");
scanf("%d",&b);
printf("\n character for int is =%c",b );
  /* Mismatch of control strings : %c for scanf and %d for printf */
printf("\n\n\n ctrl c for integer in scanf and d in printf functions");
printf("\n\n enter any integer < 256....");
scanf("%c",&a);
printf("\n\n The entered int is =%d",a);
printf("\n\n Enter any integer > 256....");
scanf("%c",&a);
printf("\n The entered int is =%d",a);
printf("\n\n\n NOTE:Integer input with char control in scanf");
printf("\n\n leads to garbage output");
getche( );
}
```

OUTPUT :

```
Matching ctrl string c for scanf and printf functions
Enter any single character....P
The entered character is : P
ctrl c in scanf and d in printf functions
Ascii code for the entered character is =80 ;
ctrl d in scanf and c in printf functions
Enter any integer code for b which is less than  256...80
character for the int b is = P
If no. >256 the number less 256 will be the ascii code for ch
Enter any int code for b greater than 256....336
character for int is =P
ctrl c for integer in scanf and d in printf functions
enter any integer < 256....
The entered int is =10
Enter any integer > 256....336
The entered int is =51
NOTE:Integer input with char control in scanf
leads to garbage in output
```

Program 4.5.15

Write a program in C to convert Celsius temperature into Fahrenheit temperature?

```
#include<stdio.h>
#include<conio.h>
main()
{
float c,f;
clrscr();
print("enter Celsius temp\n");
scanf("%f",&c);
f=1.8*c+32;
printf("Equivalent of ", c "⁰Centigrade in Fahren heat degrees %f=",f);
getch();
)
```

OUTPUT :

Equivalent of 25⁰ Centigrade in Fahrenheit degrees = 77);

Program 4.5.16.

Write a program in C to Find Simple interest and Compound interest

```
#include<conio.h>
#include<stdio.h>
#include<math.h>
int main()
{
float p,t,r,si,ci;
clrscr();
printf("Enter values of p,t,r\n");
scanf("%f%f%f",7p,&t,&r);
si=p*t*r/100;
ci=p*pow((1+r/100),t)-p;
printf("simple interest =%.2f/n",si);
printf("compound interest=%2f\n",ci);
getch( );
}
```

OUTPUT :

```
Enter values of p,t,r
10000, 2, 10
Simple interest = 2000
Compound interest = 2100
```

4.6. DIFFERENCES BETWEEN OLD AND AND CURRENT VERSIONS OF C++ :

In the older version of C++, the inclusion of header file is as follows.

#include <iostream.h>

Since now classes and functions of the standard libraries are located within the std namespace we must use the C++ using directive so that these become usable in the same way they were in pre standard code. For example, to use all the standard classes of iostream we would have to include something similar to this :

```
#include<iostream>
using namespace std;
```

that would be equivalent to the old expression

```
#include<iostream.h>
```

previous to the standard.

The difference between above two is that we have included the header file without the .h extension in new version. If we include the library this way all the classes, objects and functions of it will no longer be directly in the global scope, but under the namespace std, and therefore to use new version, we will have to use either the scope resolution operator : : or to include a using namespace directive.

4.6.1. Scope Resolution Operator :

In C all variables must be declared and defined before it is involved in any computation, whereas in C++ we can declare variable dynamically. In C, once a variable is defined as global in the beginning of the program its value remains constant throughout the program without changing. Global variable cannot be change in the middle of the progrm. In C++ the global variable need not necessarily be in the beginning of the program. The scope resolution operator is denoted as : :

For example :

```
#include <iostream>
void main ( )
{
   std : : cout <<"Hello world";
}
```

by eliminating scope resolution operator and introducing 'namespace std', the above program can be changed into,

```
#include <iostream>
using namespace std;
```

```
void main ( )
{
   cout <<"Hello world"'
}
```

Both of the above programs produce same results and we have followed second method throughout this book.

4.6.2. Differences in I/O statements :

Unlike other programming languages, C++ does not have any built-in Input / Output (I/O) statements or standard functions as a part of its syntax. *All I/O operations in C++ are carried out through streams. The streams is nothing but a flow of data.* When we want to output some data, we put into an output stream through **cout**. Similarly, to get input data from user we get in from an input stream through **cin.** The standard input and output streams available in C++ are **cin** and **cout.** The cin refers keyboard and cout refers display screen respectively. *In C++ we use two operators namely extraction operator (>>) and insertion operator (<<) for input and output purposes.* That's why *our first program consists insertion operator to display the message **"Hello world".*** The header file iostream consists of all necessary definition for the operators cin and cout. Hence it is essential to include the header file iostream in all the program requiring input and output operations.

For example, if we want to enter 5,7,9 for a, b, c and all belong to int type then the declaration and input statements might look like this,

```
int a, b, c;
   cin >>a>>b>>c
```

and this way of giving input is called cascading of input, then we have to enter data as follows.

5 7 9

Note that there is a space between two values.

Similarly, when we want to display message we use the following form;

```
cout << "Welcome to C++" ;
```

to display the message along with its value we use another form as follows,

```
cout << "welcome" ;
cout << "welcome again" ;
```

The effect of these statements is the message "welcome" and "welcome again" displayed on same line. If we want to display on different lines, the escape sequence \n has to be used.

Example :

```
cout << "welcome to Turbo C++ \n" ;
cout << "C++ is an object oriented programming language" ;
```

The output for these two statements will be

welcome to Turbo C++
C++ is an object oriented programming language

4.7. SOME PROGRAMS IN C++ USING TC++ :

Program 4.7.1 :

Write a program in C++ to have simple Text Print Program

```
//welcome to C++ program
include <iostream.h>
#include <conio.h>// This header file is must to clear the screen.
 int main( )
{
clrscr( );
cout<<"\n\n Welcome to the wonderful world of C++ !";
return 0;
}
```

OUTPUT :

Welcome to the wonderful world of C++ !

Program 4.7.2 :

Write a program in C++ for calculation of Interest amount

```
// Calculation of interest
 # include <iostream.h>
 # include <conio.h>
  int main( )
{
 float prncpl,yrs,intrate,intrst;
 clrscr( );
 cout << "\n Enter Principal amount\n";
 cin >> prncpl;
 cout << "\n Enter Number of years\n";
 cin >> yrs;
 cout <<"\n EnterRate of interest\n";
 cin >> intrate;
 intrst=(prncpl *intrate * yrs)/100;
cout <<"\n Principal amount is:"<<prncpl<<"\n";
 cout <<"\n Rate of interest is:"<<intrate<<"\n";
 cout <<"\n Number of years is:"<<yrs<<"\n";
 cout <<"\n Interest amount is:"<<intrst<<"\n";
 return 0;
}
```

OUT PUT :

Enter Principal amount
10000

Enter Number of years
6.0

EnterRate of interest
8.0

Principal amount is : 10000
Rate of interest is : 8.0

Number of years is : 6.0
Interest amount is : 4800.00

Program 4.7.3 :

Write a program in C++ to illustrate the use of Scope Resolution Operator in CPP : Global and Local variables

```
//Example Program for scope resolution operator

#include <iostream.h>
#include <conio.h>
int a=200; //global variable common to all blocks 'a' initialized to value 200
  int main ( )
{
  int a=400; //global variable: a is redefined locally in main fn.to value 00
  int b=500; //local variable b: initialised to value 500
clrscr( );
cout<<"\n\n The value of a (local in main fn.) is :"<<a<<"\n";
cout<<"\n The value of b (local in main fn.) is :"<<b<<"\n";
cout<<"\n The value of a (global) is:"<< : : a<<"\n";
{
int a=600; //global variable a is again redefined in this block
int b=800; //b is again redefined in this block
  cout <<"\n\n The value of a in this block is : "<<a<<"\n";
  cout <<"\n The value of b in this block is : "<<b<<"\n";
  cout <<"\n The value of a (global) in this block is : "<< : : a<<"\n";
              //note operator : : for global variable
}
 cout <<"\n\n The value of a (global) out of the block is : "<< : : a<<"\n";
 cout <<"\n The value of b out of the block is : "<<b<<"\n";
 return 0;
 }
```

OUTPUT :

```
The value of a (local in main fn.) is : 400
The value of b (local in main fn.) is : 500
The value of a (global) is: 200
The value of a in this block is : 600
The value of b in this block is : 800
The value of a (global) in this block is : 200
The value of a (global) out of the block is : 200
The value of b out of the block is : 800
```

Program : 4.7.4 :

Write a program in C++ for Conversion of Fahrenheit Temperature to Centigrade Temperature using ANSI C++

```
//Program to convert fahrenheit to centigrade temperature
#include <iostream>
using namespace std;
    int main ( )
{
    float centi,fahren;
    cout <<"enter Fahrenheit temperature \n";
    cin>>fahren;
    centi = 5.0/9.0* (fahren-32);
    cout <<"\n the centigrade temp is : "<<centi<<"\n";
    return 0;
}
```

OUTPUT :

```
enter fahrenheit temperature
120
the centigrade temp is 48.8888
```

Program 4.7.5 :

Write a program in C++ to calculate simple interest using ANSI C++

```
#include <iostream>
using namespace std;
    int main ( )
{
    float prin.noy.roi,intrst;
    cout <<"enter principal amount \n";
    cin >>print;
    cout <<"enter number of years \n";
    cin >>noy;
    cout <<"enter rate of interest \n";
    cin >>roi;
```

```
    intrst=(prin *noy*roi)/100;
    cout <<"\n interest : "<<intrst <<"\n";
    return 0;
}
```

OUTPUT :

enter principal amount
10000
enter number of years
5
enter rate of interest
15
interest : 7500

Program 4.7.6 :

Write a program in C++ to reverse a 5 digit number less than 32768

Logic :

1. Modular division of the number gives the remainder
2. Number/10 gives the left side 4 digits
3. Number/100 gives the left side 3 digits
4. Number/1000 gives the left side 2 digits
5. Number/10000 gives the left side 1 digit

```
//program to reverse a given 5 digit number
//numbers for reversal should be < 32768
#include <iostream.h>
#include <conio.h>
  void main ( )
{
  int a,b,c,d,e,no;
  clrscr ( );
  cout<< "\n Enter number to reverse \n";
  cin>>no;
  a=no%10;
  b=(no/10)%10;
  c=(no/100)%10;
  d=(no/1000)%10;
  e=no/10000;
  cout<<"\n Reversed number";
  cout <<a<<b<<c<<d<<e;
}
```

OUTPUT :

Enter number to reverse
12345
Reversed number54321

* * *

COMPREHENSION - 4

Note : By answering all the questions given in this comprehension one can answer any objective type of questions easily whatever be the form of the question. Answers for these questions can be obtained by going through the topics in this chapter carefully.

1. What is an Operator?
2. Mention the different types of Operators.
3. What is priority of Operators? Why is priority required?
4. Give the different Groups of Operators, the priority of the Groups and Priority of the Operators in each Group.
5. Explain Special Operators and Special Operators of lower Priority.
6. What are the different Arithmetic Operators of Higher and Lower Priority.
7. Explain Bit wise Operators of Higher and Lower Priority and their use.
8. Give the Truth Tables for AND, OR, XOR Operations.
9. Explain the Logical Operators.
10. Explain Relational Operators of Higher and Lower Priorities.
11. What is Conditional Operator and Ternary Operator Pair? Explain the use.
12. What is the difference between Equality Operator and Assignment Operator? Explain.
13. What are Shorthand Assignment Operators? Explain with examples.
14. What is the Special Operator of Least Priority? Where is it used?
15. Explain Cast or Type Cast Operator.
16. Explain the evaluation of an Expression using Priorities of Operators.
17. What is meant by Type Conversions used in an Expression?
18. How many types of Type Conversions are there? What are they?
19. Explain Automatic Type Conversion.
20. How can we force a Type Conversion different from Automatic Type Conversion?
21. Explain the use of Type Casts with Examples.
22. What is meant by Programming Paradigm?
23. Mention some special features of C++ over C regarding Programming Paradigms.
24. What is Object Oriented Programming?
25. What are the benefits of Object Oriented Programming? Mention some of the Object Oriented Programming Languages. Is C++ an Object Oriented Programming Language?

* * *

EXERCISE - 4

Note : By answering all the questions given in this exercise one can answer subjective type of questions easily including problems. The worked examples in the chapter may help in solving these questions.

1. Explain the different types of Operators and their Heirarchy with examples.
2. What are Unary Operators and their Use?
3. What is Modular Division? In what way is it different from Ordinary Division? Explain with examples.
4. What is the difference between & and && Operators? Explain with examples.
5. Explain with examples prefix and postfix auto increment/decrement operators in C?
6. Determine the value of each of the following Arithmetic Expressions if the integers a=5, b=3, c= - 8

   i) a+b+c ii) a*2+58(b-c) iii) b/a iv) b%a v)a%b+c vi) a+b*a/b vii) a+b*(a/b) viii) A+b/c ix) a*b++ x) a*++b
7. Determine the value of each of the following Arithmetic Expressions if the integers a=5.5, b=3,.3 c= - 8.8

   i) a+b+c ii) a*2+58* (b-c) iii) b/a iv) b%a v)a%b+c vi)a+b*a/b vii) a+b*(a/b) viii) A+b/c ix) a*b++ x)a*++b
8. Determine the value of each of the following expressions if integers a=5, b=3, c= - 8
9. i) << ii) c>>=2 iii) a>b || a>c iv)A==b || c<a v) A>b && a>c vi) C != (a+b)
10. A C program contains the following declaration

    int a,b; short st; char ch;

    long ab; float x; double dx;

    Determine the data type of each of the following expressions.

i) a+ch	ii) x + ch	iii) dx + x	iv) (int) dx + ab
v) a+x	vi) st + h	vii) ab + b	viii) ab + b
ix) xt + ch	x) ab + ch		
11. Which of the following arithmetic expressions are valid? If valid, give the value of the expression, otherwise give reason.

a) 25/3% 2	b) + 9/4 + 5	c) 7.5 % 3
d) 14% 3 + 7 % 2	e) –14 % 3	f) 15.25 + –5.0
g) (5/3) * 3 + 5 % 3	h) 21 % (int) 4.5	

12. Write C assignment statements to evaluate the following equations :

a) Area = $\pi r^2 + 2\pi rh$ b) $Torque = \frac{2m_1m_2}{m_1 + m_2} - g$

c) $Side = \sqrt{a^2 + b^2 - 2ab\cos(x)}$

d) Energy = mass $\left[acceleration \times height + \frac{(velocity)^2}{2} \right]$

13. Identify unnecessary parentheses in the following arithmetic expressions.
    a) ((x-(y/5)+z)%88) + 25 b) ((x-y) * p)+q
    c) (m*n) + (-x/y) d) x/(3*y)
14. Find errors, if any, in the following assignment statements and rectify them.
    a) x = y = z= 0.5, 2.0. - 5.75; b) m = ++a * 5;
    c) y = sqrt(100); d) p * = x/y;
    e) s = /5; f) a = b ++ -c * 2
15. Determine the value of each of the following logical expressions if a = 5, b = 10 and c = -6.
    a) a> b && a < c b) a < b && a > c
    c) a == c | b > a d) b > 15 && c < 0 | a > 0
16. The straight-line method of computing the yearly depreciation of the value of an item is given by

$$Depreciation = \frac{Purchase - Salvage\ Value}{Years\ of\ Service}$$

Write a program to determine the salvage value of an item when the purchase price, years of service, and the annual depreciation are given.

17. Write a program that will read a real number from the keyboard and print the following output in one line:

Smallest integer not less than the number	The given number	Largest integer not greater than the number

18. The total distance travelled by a vehicle in t seconds is given by

$$distance = ut + (at^2)/2$$

Where u is the initial velocity (meters per second), a is the acceleration (meters per second^2). Write a program to evaluate the distance travelled at regular intervals of time, given the values of u and a. The program should provide the flexibility to the user to select his own time intervals and repeat the calculations for different values of u and a.

19. In inventory management, the Economic Order Quantity for a single item is given by

$$\text{EOQ} = \sqrt{\frac{2 \times demand\ rate \times setup\ \cos ts}{holding\ \cos t\ per\ item\ per\ unit\ time}}$$

and the optimal Time Between Orders

$$\text{TBO} = \sqrt{\frac{2 \times setup\ \cos ts}{demand\ rate \times holding\ \cos t\ per\ item\ per\ unit\ time}}$$

Write a program to compute EOQ and TBO, given demand rate (items per unit time), setup costs (per order), and the holding cost (per item per unit time).

20. For certain electrical circuit with an inductance L and resistance R, the damped natural frequency is given by

$$Frequency = \sqrt{\frac{1}{LC} - \frac{R^2}{4C^2}}$$

It is desired to study the variation of this frequency with C (capacitance). Write a progrma to calculate the frequency for different values of C starting from 0.01 to 0.1 in steps of 0.01.

21. Determine the value of each of the following arithmetic expressions, where the integer variables are assign the values as a=5, b=3, c=-8

i) a+b+c ii) a* 2+5* (b-c) iii) b/a

iv) b/c v) a/c vi) a%b+c vii) a+b* (a/b)

22. In the above problem if the variables are assigned the following floating values, determine the value of each of the arithmetic expression as in problem (12) a=5.5, b=3.3, c=-8.8

23. Determine the value of the following expression, if

a=5, b=3, c=-8

i) a>b ||a>c ii) a==b ||c <a

iii) a>b && a>c iv) c! = (a+b)

24. Determine the data type of each of the following expressions.

i) a+ch ii) x+ch iii) dx+x iv)((int) dx + ab

v) a+x vi) st +h vii) ab+b viii) ab+b

ix) st + ch x) ab + ch

25. Assuming temp is 1, find the value of the exrpession temp = (temp<<.1%2)
    a) 2   b) 0   c) 1   d) not an expression
26. a) Write a program in C to shift the entered number by three bits left and display the result and run the program.
    b) Write a program in C to shift the entered number by five bits right and display the result and run the program.
27. Write a program to enter a number and carry out modular division operation by 2, 3 and 4 and display the remainders.
28. Write a program in C to convert hexadecimal to decimal numbers. Enter the numbers such as 0 × 1c, **0 × 18, 0 ×cd** etc.
29. Write a program to enter two numbers. Make the comparison between them with conditional operator. If the first number is greater than second perform multiplication otherwise division operation.
30. Write a program in C to enter a four-digit number. Display the digits of the number in the reverse order using modular division and division operation. Perform addition and multiplication of digits.
31. Write a program in C to evaluate the following expression and display their results.
    a) $x^2 + 2\ x^3 * (2*x)$
    b) $x^1 + y^2 + z^3$
    where x, y and z are integers.
32. Explain how the expression x=24-6/3+48(8+2) will be evaluated using Priority of operators.
33. Explain how automatic type conversion is carried on if different types of numerical data are used in the same expression.
34. Write a program to calculate the total cost of the vehicle by adding basic cost with a) excise duty (15%) b) Sales tax (10%) c) Octroi (5%) and d) Road tax (1%). Input the basic cost.
35. Write a program to display ASCII equivalents of
    a) 'A', 'B', 'C' and 'a', 'b', 'c'
    b) 'a' - 'C', 'b' - 'A' and 'c' - 'B'
    c) 'a' + 'c', 'b' * 'a' and 'c' +12

* * *

CHAPTER - 5
INPUT AND OUTPUT OPERATIONS IN C

5.1. INTRODUCTION :

The essential functions of computer programs are reading, processing and writing the data. The data can be read and inputted through various input devices and the output can be exhibited or placed on various output devices.

Unlike other high level languages, like BASIC and COBOL which have built in statement for performing input and output operations C does not have any built-in input/ output statements as part of its syntax. All input/output operations are carried out through function calls such as **scanf** ( ) and **printf** ( ). There exist several functions that have more or less become standard for input and output operations in C. These functions are collectively known as the *standard I/O library*. In this chapter we shall discuss some common I/O functions used in C which can be used on many machines without any change. However, one should consult the system reference manual for exact details of these functions and also to see what other functions are available. **The I/O operations in C++ are different from I/O operations in C and hence they are discussed later separately.**

Each program in C uses a standard input / output function. The use of standard input and output function is given by the statement

#include <stdio.h>

at the beginning. However, there might be exceptions. For example, this is not necessary for the functions **printf** and **scanf** which have been defined as a part of the C language.

The file name **stdio.h** is an abbreviation for *standard input-output header* file. The instructions **#include <stdio.h>** tells the compiler to search for a file named *stdio.h* and place its contents at this point in the program. The contents of the header file become part of the source code when it is compiled.

Inclusion of another standard library functions useful in mathematics for calculation of sin x, cos x etc., which is given by the statement.

#include <math.h>

There are other # include statements. These types of statements are known as **pre processor directives** which are always drafted and made available at the beginning of the program for carrying out different types of tasks. They are discussed in detail later. *Pre-processor is a program that processes the source program before it is passed on to the compiler and the necessary functions are made available for execution of the program by these pre-processor statements.*

The basic input, output statements in C are discussed now so as to run simple programs initially.

The input and output functions can be classified mainly into two groups. 1) Formatted input, output functions, and 2) Unformatted input, output functions. The classification of different types of formatted and unformatted input and output functions are given in Fig. 5.1.

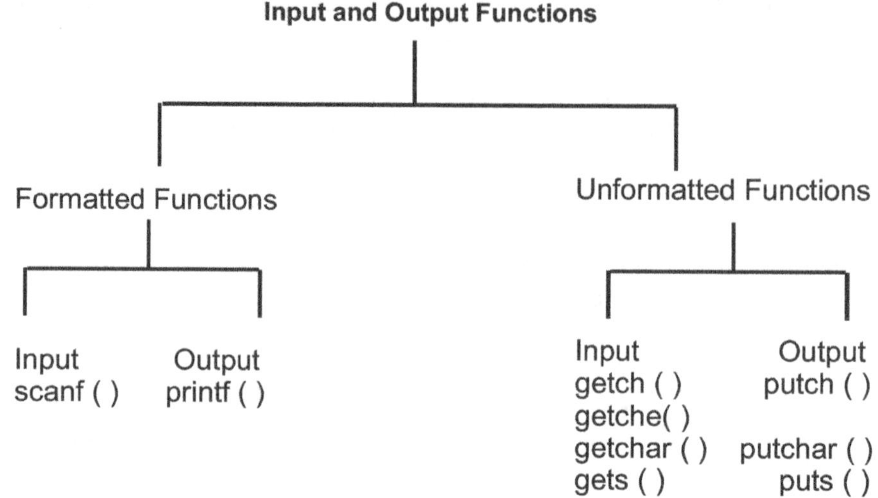

Fig. 5.1 : Formatted and Unformatted Input and Output functions

a) **Formatted I/O functions :**

The formatted input / output functions read and write all types of data values. They require conversion symbol to identify the data type. Hence, they can be used for both reading and writing of all data values. The formatted functions return the values after execution. The return value is equal to the number of variables successfully read / written. Using this value the user can find out the errors occurring during reading or writing the data. *The formatted I/O statements can be given with field width specifications or without field width specifications. The field width specification gives the number of digits and the number of decimal places for the given data.*

b) **Unformatted I/O functions :**

The unformatted input / output functions only work with the character data type. *They do not require conversion symbol for identification of data types because they work only with character data type.* There is no need to convert the data. *In case values of other data types are passed to these functions, they are treated as the character data.* The unformatted functions also return values, but the return value of unformatted functions is always the same.

5.1.1. Formatted Input Functions : (without field width specifications)

For all the formatted input functions there should always be a declaration of the data type given in the Declaration part of the program like

```
int     a, b, c ;
float   x, y=3.4, ;
char    p, q, r ;
char    name [30], string1 [25] ;
```

Formatted input refers to an input data that has been arranged in a particular format. For example, consider the following data :

4860 689.4 'a' "sum"

This line contains four pieces of data, arranged in a particular form. Such data has to be read conforming to the format of its appearance. For example, the first part of the data should be read into a variable **int,** the second into **float,** and the third part into **char** and the fourth into **string.** This is possible in C using the **scanf** function.

The syntax or format of **scanf** is

scanf ("control strings", arg1, arg2, ... , argn) ;

The control string specifies the field format in which the data is to be entered and the arguments arg 1, arg 2..... argn specify the address of locations where the data is stored. Control string and arguments are separated by commas. **The control strings and the corresponding data are to be given in the same order.**

Control string contains field specifications which direct the interpretation of input data. It may include :

* Field (or format) specifications, consisting of the conversion character %, together with a data type character (or type specifier), and an optional number, specifying the field width.
* Blanks, tabs, or new lines.

Blanks, tabs and newlines are ignored. The data type character indicates the type of data which is to be assigned to the variable associated with the corresponding arguments. *The field width specifier is optional.* The formats that follow will clarify these concepts. For ex : with no field width specifications.

5.1.2. Inputting Integer Variables :

The format for Inputting Integer Variables without field width specification will be as follows :

Declaration Part :

Int a, b, c ;

Input Function for Integer Variables :

scanf ("%d %d %d", &a, &b, &c) ;

The **scanf ( )** *statement requires '&' operator called address operator. The address operator points the memory location of the variable.* Here, in the **scanf** ( ) statement the role of '&' operator is to indicate the insertion of the given data in a memory location for the specified variable, so that the value read would be placed at that location.

The scanf ( ) statement also returns values. The return value will be exactly equal to the number of values correctly read. In case of any mismatch, error will be indicated. Otherwise if the read the value is converted to the given format.

The reading of data continues until a character that is not valid for the value being read is encountered. In the case of integers, valid characters are an optionally signed sequence of digits.

An input field may be skipped by specifying %*f or %*d in the place of field width. For example, the statement will assign the data

scanf("%d % *d %d", &a, &b, &c) ;

will assign data only for the first and third control characters and not for second because of the * between % and d.

The assignment of data for the above scanf statement with keyed in data as given

4860 484 8 will allot input

4860 to variable a
484 skipped (because of * in control string)
8 to variable c

*The control character **d** may be preceded by "1" (letter ell) to read long integers.*

If necessary the field width of integer numbers (i.e., the number of digits) for the data can be specified with a different format which will be discussed later.

5.1.3. Inputting Real Variables :

The field width of real numbers need not to be specified and therefore **scanf** reads real numbers using the simple specification **%f** for both the notations, namely, decimal point notation and exponential notation. For example, the statement

scanf ("%f %f %f", &x, &y, &z) ;

with the input data

4860.484 36.39E-1 789

will assign the value 4860.484 to x, 3.639 to y, and 789.0 to z. *Even though the number given is 789 it is treated as 789.0 because of the control character* %f. The input field specifications may be separated by any arbitrary blank spaces.

If the number to be read is of **double** type, then the specifications should be % **lf** instead of simple **%f.** A number may be skipped using **%*f** specification.

5.1.4. Inputting Character / String constants :

We can have single character inputs given within single quotes like 'p' or a set of characters called strings given within double quotes like "student1" etc.,

The formatted input statement for character input like

scanf ("%c %c %c", &ch1, &ch2, &ch3) ;

has to be given single character inputs with space between them like 'p' 'q' 'r'.

Then the character p will be assigned to the character variable ch1, then the character q will be assigned to the character variable ch2, and the character r will be assigned to the character variable ch3.

The formatted input statement for string constants like

scanf ("%s %s %s", name1, name2, name3) ;

has to be given string inputs with space between them like "Jack" "Jill" "Jim".

Note : for string constants the ampersand (&) is not given before the variable names for the string constants because they are string constants. Instead, the strings are given within double quotes like ".........."

To avoid unnecessary confusion that may arise when we use formatted I/O statements with field widths, it will be preferable to use always formatted I/O statements without field width specifications. Only if necessary, to have the result in the requisite form as to the number of decimal digits etc., we can go for output statements with field width specifications.

5.1.5. Inputting Mixed Variables :

Scanf ("%d %f %c %s", &a, &b, &c, "string") ; where a is an integer variable, f is a real variable and c is a character and s is a a set of characters including numerals called string variable.

The input statement for mixed variables should also contain the different types of the input variables in the declaration part. For ex. :

Declaration Part :

```
Int a;
float b;
char c ;
char d [15];
```

Input Function for Mixed Variables :

Scanf ("%d %f %c %s", &a, &b, &c, "string") ;

The Scanf statement will read through the keyboard the integer variable a, the real variable b, the single character variable c and the string variable d with less than or equal to 15 characters because of the declaration char [15];

5.2. FORMATTED OUTPUT STATEMENTS (WITHOUT FIELD WIDTHS) :

The Printf( ) statement The printf ( ) function prints all types of data values to the console. It requires conversion symbol and variable names to print the data. The conversion symbol and variable names should be same in number. The data to be printed will be given inside the parenthesis after the double quotes of control strings end followed by a comma and each variable separated by commas. *There will be no ampersand address of operator for the variables in* printf ( ) *statements.* The syntax for printf ( ) will be as follows :

printf ("control variable1 ctrl var 2 ctrl var3",variable1, var2, var3);

eg : printf ("%d %f %c %s", a,b,c,d); where a is int, b is float, c is char and d is string.

5.2.1. Outputting Integer Variables :

Before using the Formatted Output Statement without field width specifications, the type of the variable like integer should have been declared in the declaration part as in the case of inputting the integer variables. In addition the input variable should have been given a value either by formatted input statement or by assignment of value to the given variable. For ex :

declaration part :

int num1, num2;

inputting part :

scanf ("%d %d", &num1, &num2);

Outputting part :

printf("%d %d", num1, num2);

or

printf("\n The value of variable1 = %d", num1);
printf("\n The value of variable2 = %d", num2);

The first printf ( ) statement will print the values of num1 and num2 in integer form in a single line.

The second set of printf ( ) statements will print the value of variable1 and variable 2 viz., num1 and num2 in integer form, in two separate lines leaving one blank line alongwith the text given inside the quotes. Any space given inside the double quotes or \t will give blank space equal to the blank space given within the quotes or horizontal tab \t will give the printout leaving a blank space of one field width of a table in the same line before printing the next variable.

5.2.2. Outputting Real variables :

Before using the Formatted Output Statement without field width specifications, the type of the variable like real variable should have been declared in the declaration part as in the case of inputting the real variable. In addition the input variable should have been given a value either by formatted input statement or by assignment of value to the given variable. For eg:

declaration part :

```
float  num1, num2;
```

inputting part :

```
scanf ("%f %f", &num1, &num2);
```

Outputting part :

```
printf("% f % f", num1, num2);
```

or

```
printf("\n The value of variable1 = % f",  num1);
printf("\n The value of variable2 = % f ",  num2);
```

5.2.3. Outputting Mixed Variables :

The mixed variables include integer variable, real variable, single character variable and string variable. The difference will be only in the type declaration and control strings for the concerned variables.

For eg :

```
main( )
{
int x=2;
float y=4.2;
char z=' A' , strg = "Delhi" ;
printf ("%d  %f  %c   %s" ,x,y,z,strg);
}
```

OUTPUT;

2   4.2000   C   Delhi

Since the character sets are governed by ASCII code of characters with ASCII values from -128 to 127 or 0 to 255, totalling 256 characters including zero, as a text character each of these numbers having one byte, it is economical and efficient to use the control string %c for integers -128 to 127. The corresponding ASCII code number will represents integer data in that range, taking one byte only to represent the integer number. On the other hand if the control character %d is used for each integer number it will take two bytes of memory for each integer number.

This type of deliberate mismatch of data types is helpful.

For eg :

i)

```
    {
    int a ;
    clrscr ( ) ;
    printf("Enter value of 'A' :");
    scanf(" %c", &a);
    printf("A=%c",a);
}
```

OUTPUT :

Enter value of 'A': 8

A=8

ii)

```
    {
    char a;
        clrscr( ) ;
        printf("Entervalue of 'A':");
        scanf("%d",&a);
        printf("A=%d",a);
    }
```

OUTPUT :

Enter value of 'A' : 255

A = 255

Enter value of 'A' : 256

A = 0

Note : Since the characters have 0 to 255 as ASCII code for unsigned char, the number 256 given for A leads to the output A=0.

5.3. FORMATTED INPUT STATEMENTS (WITH FIELD WIDTHS) :

The generally used formatted input statement without field width specification allots the standard field width like 8/16 digits for integer variables, 32 digits for float or real variables, single byte for single character variable and the number of characters specified inside the square brackets for string variables. On the other hand the formatted input statements with field width specification gives us the freedom to use as many digits or as many decimals or as many characters in required form as desired by us.

5.3.1. Inputting Integer numbers :

The field specification for reading an integer or real number is :

% w d or % w f

The per cent sign (%) indicates that a conversion specification follows. w is an integer number that specifies the field width of the number in terms of the number of digits, including decimal or exponents in the case of float, to be read and d or f, known as data type character, indicates that the number to be read is in integer mode or real mode. *When using mixed numbers with field widths specified we have to be careful as explained below.* Consider the following example :

scanf("%2d %5d", &num1, &num2);

Data line :

50 31426

The value 50 is assigned to **num1** and 31426 to **num2.** Suppose the input data is as follows.

31426 50

The variable **num1** will be assigned 31 (because of %2d) and **num2** will be assigned 426 (unreal part of 31426. The value 50 that is unread will be assigned to the first variable in the next **scanf** call. *This kind of errors may be eliminated if we use the field specifications without the field with specifications.* That is, the statement

scanf ("%d %d", &num1, &num2);

will read the data

31426 50

correctly and assign 31426 to **num1** and 50 to **num2.**

Input data items must be separated by spaces, tabs or new lines. Punctuation marks do not count as separators. When the **scanf** function searches the input data line for a value to be read, it will always bypass any white space characters.

What happens if we enter a floating point number instead of an integer? The fractional part may be stripped away! Also, **scanf** *may skip reading further input.*

When the **scanf** reads a particular value, reading of the value will terminate as soon as the number of characters specified by the field width is reached (if specified) or until a character that is not valid for the value being read is encountered. In the case of integers, valid characters are an optionally signed sequence of digits.

An input field may be skipped by specifying *in the place of field width. For example, the statement

scanf ("%d %*d %d", &a, &b) ;

will assign the data

321 654 987

as follows :

321 to **a**
654 skipped (because of *)
987 to **b**

5.3.2 Inputting Real Numbers :

The field width of real numbers need not to be specified and therefore **scanf** reads real numbers using the simple specification **%f** for both the notations, namely, decimal point notation and exponential notation. For example, the statement

scanf ("%f %f %f", &x, &y, &z) ;

with the input data

4860.484 36.39E-1 789

will assign the value 4860.484 to x, 3.639 to y, and 789.0 to z. Even though the number given is 789 it is treated as 789.0 because of the control character %f. The input field specifications may be separated by any arbitrary blank spaces.

If the number to be read is of **double** type, then the specifications should be **% lf** instead of simple **%f.** A number may be skipped using **%*f** specification.

5.3.3 Inputting Characters & Strings:

The **scanf** function can input strings containing more than one character. Following are the specifications for reading character strings :

% ws or %wc

The corresponding argument should be a pointer to a character array. However, %c may be used to read a single character when the argument is a pointer to a **char** variable.

When we use **%wc** *for reading a string, the system will wait until the* w^{th} *character is keyed in.*

The specification **%s** *terminates reading at the encounter of a blank space.*

Some versions of **scanf** *support the following conversion specifications for strings :*

%[characters] and %[characters]

The specification % **[characters]** means that only the characters specified within the brackets are permissible in the input string. If the input string contains any other character, the string will be terminated at the first encounter of such a character. Eg. %[abcd^] The specification **%[characters]** does exactly the reverse. That is, the characters specified after the circumflex (^) are not permitted in the input string. The reading of the string will be terminated at the encounter of one of these characters.

We have just seen that %s specifier cannot be used to read strings with blank spaces. But this can be done with the help of % [ ] specification. Blank spaces may be included within the brackets, thus enabling the **scanf** to read strings with spaces. Remember that the lowercase and uppercase letters are distinct.

5.3.4.Reading Mixed Data Type using scanf ( ) :

It is possible to use one scanf statement to input a datga line containing mixed mode data. In such cases, care should be exercised to ensure that the input data items match the control specifications in the same order and the same type. *When an attempt is made to read an item that does not match the type expected, the scanf function does not read any further and immediately returns the values read.* The statement

scanf ("%d %c %f %s", &count, &code, &ratio, name);

will read the data correctly if the following data is entered.

15 p 1.575 coffee

and assign the values to the variables in the order in which they appear. Some systems accept integers in the place of real numbers and vice-versa, and the input data is converted to the type specified in the control string.

5.3.5. Detection of Errors in Input :

When a scanf ( ) function completes its list, it returns the value of number of items that are successfully read. This values can be used to test whether any errors occurred in reading the input. For example, the statement

scanf("%d %f %s", &a, &b, name);

will return the value 3 if the following data is typed in :

330 18.025 apple .... (three correct variables)

and will return the value 1 if the following line is entered

330 apple 18.025 ...... (indicating 1 variable is correct)

This is because the function would encounter a string when it was expecting a floating point value, and would therefore terminate its scan after reading the first value.

5.3.6. Commonly used scanf ( ) format codes :

The control strings for different data types used in scanf functions are given in table 5.1.

Table 5.1 Scanf Format Codes

Code	Meaning
%c	read a single character
%d	read a decimal integer
%e	read a floating point value
%f	read a floating point value
%g	read a floating point value
%h	read a short integer
%i	read a decimal, hexadecimal, or octal integer
% o	read an octal integer
% s	read a string
% u	read a unsigned decimal integer
% x	read a hexadecimal integer
%[..]	read a string of word(s)

An Important Note : *Scanf statements are used for interactive inputting of the data.* To indicate the information as to how many data, the type of the data, in what format and where the data are to be given, we normally give a printf statement giving all the information like

printf ("Enter two integer data, one real data, two characters, one string ....") ;

Then immediately after that we have to give the corresponding scanf statement.

scanf (" % d % d %f %c %c %s", & i1, & i2, & f1, &f2, &f3, 'c1', 'c2', "string") ;

where i1, i2 are the two integer numbers

f1, is the a real number

c1, c2 are the two characters and

string is the word in character string.

5.4. FORMATTED OUTPUT (WITH FIELD WIDTH) :

We have seen the use of **printf** function for printing captions and numerical results. It is highly desirable that the outputs are produced in such a way that they are understandable and are in an easy-to-use form. It is therefore necessary for the programmer to give careful consideration to the appearance and clarify of the output produced by this program.

The **printf** statement provides certain features that can be effectively exploited to control the alignment and spacing of print-outs on the terminals. The general form of **printf** statement is

printf ("control string", arg1, arg2, ... argn);

Control string consists of three types of items :

1. Characters that will be printed on the screen as they appear.
2. Format specifications that define the output format for display of each item.
3. *Escape sequence* characters such as \n, \t, and \b.

The control string indicates how many arguments follow and what their types are. The arguments *argl, arg2, ... argn* are the variable whose values are formatted and printed according to the specifications of the control string. The arguments should match in number, order and type with the format specifications.

A simple format specification has the following form :

% w.p type-specifier

where w is an integer number that specifies the total number of columns for the output value and p is another integer number that specifies the number of digits to the right of the decimal point (of a real number) or the number of characters to be printed from a string. Both w and p are optional. Some examples of **printf** statements are :

```
printf("Programming in C language");
printf(" ");
printf("\n");
printf("%d",x);
printf("a=%f\n b=%f", a, b);
printf("sum=%d", 5678);
printf("\n\n");
```

printf *never supplies a new line automatically and therefore multiple* ***printf*** *statements may be used to build more than one line of output.* A new line can be introduced by the help of a newline character "\n" as shows is some of the examples above.

5.4.1. Outputting of Integer Numbers

The format specification for printing an integer number is

% w d

Output Format	Output
printf("%d", 6789)	|6|7|8|9|
printf("%5d", 3456)	| |3|4|5|6|
printf("%2d", 6789)	|6|7|8|9|
printf("%-6d", 6789)	|6|7|8|9| | |
printf("%06d", 6789)	|0|0|6|7|8|9|

where *w specifies the minimum field width for the output. However, if a number is greater than the specified field width, it will be printed in full, overriding the minimum specification,* **d** specifies that the value to be printed is an integer. The number is written *right-justified* in the given field width. Leading blanks will appear as necessary. The following examples illustrate the output of the number 6789 under different formats :

It is possible to force the printing to be left-justified by placing a minus sign directly after the % character as shown in the fourth example above. It is also possible to pad with zeros the leading blanks by placing a 0 (zero) before the field width specifier as shown in the last item above.

Long integers may be printed by specifying **ld** in the place of **d** in the format specification.

5.4.2. Outputting of Real Numbers

The output of a real number may be displayed in decimal notation using the following format specification.

% w.p.f

The integers w indicates the minimum number of positions that are to be used for the display of the value and the integer p indicates the number of digits to be displayed after the decimal point (precision). *The value, when displayed, is rounded to p decimal places and printed right-justified in the field of w columns.* Leading blanks and trailing zeros will appear as necessary. *The default precision is 6 decimal places.* The negative numbers will be printed with the minus sign. The number will be displayed in the form [-] mmm . nnn.

We can also display a real number in exponential notation by using the specification.

% w.p e

The display takes the form

[-] m.nnnne [±] xx

where the length of the string of n's is specified by the precision p. The default precision is 6. The field width w should satisfy the condition.

$$w \geq p+7$$

The value will be rounded off and printed right justified in the field of w columns.

Padding the leading blanks with zeros and printing with left-justification is also possible by introducing 0 or - before the field width specifier w.

The following examples illustrate the output of the number y = 98.7654 under different format specifications :

Format	**Output**										
printf("%7.4f".y)	9	8	.	7	6	5	4				
printf("%7.21".y)			9	8	.	7	7				
printf("%-7.2f".y)	9	8	.	7	7						
printf("%f",y)	9	8	.	7	6	5	4				
printf("%10.2e'.y)			9	.	8	8	e	+	0	1	
printf("%10.2e".y)	-	9	.	8	7	6	5	e	+	0	1
printf("% - 10.2e".y)	9		8	8	e	+	0	1			
printf("%e".y)	9		8	7	6	5	4	0	e+	0	1

Some systems also support a special field specification character that lets the user define the field size at run-time. This takes the following form :

printf("%, "f", width, precision, number);

In this case, both the field width and the precision are given as arguments which will supply the values for w and p. For example,

printf("%*.*f", 7,2, number);

is equivalent to

print("%7.2f", number);

The advantage of this format is that the values for width and precision may be supplied at run-time, thus making the format a dynamic one. For example, the above statement can be used as follows :

```
int width = 7;
int precision = 2 ;
............
............
printf("%*.*f", width, precision, number);
```

5.4.3. Outputting of Mixed Variables without field widths :

It is allowed to mix data types in one printf statement. For example, the statement of the type

printf("%d %f %s %c", a,b,c,d);

is valid. As pointed ou earlier, printf uses its control string to decide how many variables to be printed and what their types are. Therefore, *the format specifications should match the variables in number, order, and type.* If there are not enough variables or if they are of the wrong type. incorrect results will be the output.

If the format of the control string and the data do no match then a number which is equal to the number of correct control strings and corresponding data will be printed, indicating an error in the i/o statement.

5.4.4. Outputting of Strings with field widths :

The format specification for outputting strings is similar to that of real numbers. It is of the form

% w.ps

where *w* specifies the field width for display and p instructs that only the first p characters of the string are to be displayed. The display is right-justified.

The following examples show the effect of a variety of specifications to printing a string "NEW DELHI 110001", containing 16 characters (including blanks).

Specification	*Output*																			
	1	2	3	4	5	6	7	8	9	0	1	2	3	4	5	6	7	8	9	0
% s	N	E	W		D	E	L	H	I		1	1	0	0	0	1				
%20s					N	E	W		D	E	L	H	I		1	1	0	0	0	1
%20.10s											N	E	W		D	E	L	H	I	
%5s	N	E	W		D															
%-20.10s	N	E	W		D	E	L	H	I											
%5s	N	E	W		D	E	L	H	I		1	1	0	0	0	1				

Note :

As seen above it can be observed that providing the input and output statements with field widths specified is cumbersum and is likely to lead to clumsy results at times if the field width specifications are not proper. Hence it is always better to give the input and output statements without specifying the field widths in which case the specified fieldwidths as specified for the control characters will be followed and this will not lead to any clumsy results and also it will be easier to use these formats without mentioning field widths.

5.4.5. Commonly used printf ( ) format codes :

The control strings for different data types used in printf functions are given in table 5.2

The following letters may be used as prefix for certain conversion characters.

Table 5.2. Commonly used printf Format Codes

Code	Meaning
%c	print a single character
%d	print a decimal integer
%e	print a floating point value in exponent form
%f	print a floating point value without exponent
%g	print a floating point value either e-type or f-type depending on value
%i	print a signed decimal integer
% o	print an octal integer, wihtout leading zero
% s	print a string
% u	print an unsigned decimal integer
% x	print a hexadecimal integer, without leading 0x

h for short integers

l (character l) for long integers or double

L for long double

A table of output format flags is given in Table 5.3.

Table 5.3 Output Format Flags

Code	Meaning
–	Output is left-justified within the field. Remaining field will be blank.
+	Causes leading zeros to appear.
0	Causes leading zeros to appear.
# (with o or x)	Causes octal and hex items to be preceded by O and Ox, respectively.
# (with e, f or g)	Causes a decimal point to be present in all floating point numbers, even if it is whole number. Also prevents the truncation of tralling zeros in g-type conversion.

5.5. ENHANCING THE READABILITY OF OUTPUT :

Computer outputs are used as information for analyzing certain relationships between variables and for making decisions. Therefore the corrections and clarity of outputs is of utmost importance. While the correctness depends on the solution procedure, the clarity depends on the way the output is presented, Following are some of the steps we can take to improve the clarity and hence the readability and understandability of outputs.

1. *Provide enough blank space between two numbers.*
2. *Introduce appropriate headings and variable names in the output.*
3. *Print special messages whenever a peculiar condition occurs in the output.*
4. *Introduce blank lines between the important sections of the output.*

The system usually provides two blank spaces between the numbers. However, this can be increased by selecting a suitable field width for the numbers or introducing a 'tab' character between the specifications. For example, the statement

```
printf("a=%d\t b = %d", a,b);
```

will provide four blank spaces between the two fields. We can also print them on two separate lines by using the statement.

```
printf("a=%d\n b = %d", a, b);
```

Messages and headings can be printed by using the character strings directly in the **printf** statement. Examples :

```
printf("\n OUTPUT RESULTS \n");
printf("code\t Name\t Age\n);
printf("Error in input data\n");
printf(Enter your name\n");
```

5.6. UNFORMATTED INPUT/OUTPUT FUNCTIONS :

The formatted input / output functions read and write all types of data values. They require conversion symbol to identify the data type. Hence they can be used for both reading and writing of all data values. The formatted functions return the values after execution. The return value is equal to the number of variables successfully read / written. Using this value the user can find out the errors occurring during reading or writing the data.

On the other hand the unformatted intput / output functions only work with character data type. They do not require conversion symbol for identification of data types. Because they work only with character datat type. There is no need to convert the data. In case values of other data types are passed to these functions, they are also treated as the character data. The unformatted functions also return values, but the return value of unformatted functions is always the same.

5.6.1. Types of Unformatted Input / Output Functions in C :

C has three types of unformatted I/O functions

1. Character Input / Output Functions
2. String Input / Output Functions
3. File Input / Output Functions

1. Character Input /Output Functions :

a) **Character Input functions :**

i) **getch( )** This functions reads any alphanumerical character on the standard input device. *The character entered through getch ( ) is not displayed by this function on the screen.*

ii) **getche ( )** This functions reads any alphanumerical character on the standard input device. *But the character entered through getche ( ) is displayed by this function on the screen. It is better to use getche ( ) in interactive input for us to know the inputted data.*

The program using getch( ) and getche ( ) will look like :

```
..........................
..........................
void main ()
{
clrscr ( );
printf ("Enter any two alphanumerics");
        getch( ) ;
        getche ( ) ;
}
```

iii) **getchar ( )** This function needs character type data from the standard input. *It reads one character at a time till the user presses the enter key.* The simplest of all input / output operations is reading a character from the standard input unit (usually the keyboard) and writing it to the standard output unit (usually the screen). Reading a single character can be done by using the function **getchar.** (This can also be done with the help of the **scanf** functions which had been discussed in Section 5.1) The **getchar** takes the following form :

variable_name = **getchar( ) ;**

variable_name is a valid C name that has been declared as **char** type. When this statement is encountered, the computer waits until a key is pressed and then assigns this character as a value to **getchar** function. Since **getchar** is used on the right-hand side of an assignment statement, the character value of **getchar** is in turn assigned to the variable name on the left.

For example :

char name :
name = getchar ( ) ;

will assign the character 'H' to the variable **name** when we press the key H on the keyboard. Since **getchar** is a function, it requires a set of parenthesis as shown. The **getchar** function may be called successively to read the characters contained in a line of text. For example, the following program segment read characters from keyboard one after another until the 'Return' key is pressed. The program using getchar will look like :

```
..........................

..........................
char character;
character = ' ';

{
while (character ! = '\n')
character = getchar() ;
}
..........................

..........................
```

Warning : The **getchar ( )** function accepts any character keyed in. This includes RETURN and TAB. This means that when we enter single character input, the newline character is waiting in the input queue after **getchar ( )** returns. This could create problem when we use **getchar ( )** interactively in a loop. A dummy **getchar ( )** may be used to 'eat' the unwanted new line character. By getchar the program receives a character types from the keyboard and tests whether it is a letter or digit and prints out a message accordingly. These tests are done with the help of the following functions :

isalpha(character)
isdigit(character)

For example, **isalpha** assumes a value non-zero (TRUE) if the argument **character** contains an alphabet ; otherwise it assumes ( ) (FALSE). Similar is the case with the function **isdigit.**

C supports many other similar functions which are given in Table 5.4

Table. 5.4 : Character Test Functions

Code	Meaning
isalnum(c)	Is c an alphanujmeric character?
isalpha(c)	Is c an alphabetic character?
isdigit(c)	Is c a digit?
islower(c)	Is c a lower case letter?
isprint(c)	Is c a printable character
ispunct(c)	Is c a punctuation mark?
isspace(c)	Is c a white space character?
isupper(c)	Is c an upper case letter?

b. Character Output functions : These functions write a character or a string on the screen.

i) **putch ( )** This function prints any alphanumeric, character taken by the standard input device. *The putch displays the character pressed on the keyboard. It is preceded by* **getch ( ).** In the program we should have input statements for the character/string before asking the output of the character/string to be printed. The appearance of the programs for inputting character / string will be as shown earlier. For the output we will have the statement using this output function putch ( ) The program will look like

```
{
........................
........................
char ch;
clrscr ( ) ;
printf("Press any key to continue");
ch=getch( );
printf ("\n You Pressed :");
putch(ch) ;
}
```

ii) **putchar ( )** Like **getchar** for inputting a character we have **putchar** for outputting the entered character. *This function prints one character on the screen at a time which is read by the standard input. The syntax is putchar(variable_name);*

Program 5.6.1.

Write a program in C to illustrate the use of putchar ( ) function

```
# include <stdio.h>
void main ( )
```

```
{
char ch [20];
int c=( );
clrscr ( );
printf("\n Enter Text Here :");
scanf("% c" ,ch);
printf("\n The Entered Text is :");
while(ch[c] != '\0')
   {
   putchar (ch[c]);
   c++;
   }
}
```

OUTPUT :

Enter Text here : Welcome to C programming !

The entered text is : Welcome to C programming !

2) String Input /Output :

a) **String inputs ;** A string consists of a set of alphanumerics. Each set can be treated as a separate string variable and is entered using the function gets ( ) function.

i) **gets** ( ) This gets function is used for accepting any string through stdin (keyboard) until enter key is pressed. *The header file stdio.h is needed for implementing the above function.* Also when using gets function we should give in the declaration part an indication that the string constant is a char variable, (variable consisting of characters) The program looks like

```
..........................

..........................
char a [20];
clrscr ( ) ;
{
   printf ("Enter the string within double quotes");
        gets(a) ;
        getche ( ) ;
   printf ("The entered string is : %s", a ) ;
}
..........................

..........................
```

ii) **cgets** ( ) This function reads string from the console. The syntax is as given below.

Syntax for cgets( )

cgets (char *st);

It requires character pointer as an argument. The strings begins from st [2]

b) String output : The string output is obtained by using the function

i) **puts ( ).** *This function prints the string or character array.*

The syntax for printing a string output will be

puts( );

Program 5.6.2.

Write a program in C to explain the use of puts ( )

```
# include <stdio.h>
main ( )
{
char a[20] ;
clrscr( ) ;
printf("Enter the String:");
gets(a);
puts ("The entered String is :");
puts(a);
}
```

OUTPUT :

Enter the string is : Welcome to C !
The entered string is :
Welcome to C !

ii) **cputs ( )** This function displays string on the console. *The syntax is as given below.*

*cputs (char *st) :*

This requires character pointer as an argument.

3. **File Input / Output Functions :** These are treated in the chapter 13, **"File operatioins in C"**

5.7. CHARACTER RECOGNITION USING CODES :

There are 2 types of codes popularly used to recognise the characters from numerical codes.

i) ASCII code or American Standard Code for Information Interchange which is an industry (and government) standard code developed in the early 1960s.

ii) EBCDIC , or Extended Binary Coded Decimal Interchange Code, which is used in most large computers, particularly those made by IBM and Burroughs.

ASCII code for characters which is a popular one based on which the key board characters are recognised and operations on strings are performed is given in Table 5.5.

Table. 5.5 : ASCII Values of Characters

ASCII Value	Character	ASCII Value	Character	ASCII Value	Character	ASCII Value	Character
000	NUL	032	blank	064	@	096	‘
001	SOH	033	!	065	A	097	a
002	STX	034	"	066	B	098	b
003	ETX	035	#	067	C	099	c
004	EOT	036	$	068	D	100	d
005	ENQ	037	%	069	E	101	e
006	ACK	038	&	070	F	102	f
007	BEL	039	’	071	G	103	g
008	BS	040	(	072	H	104	h
009	HT	041	)	073	I	105	i
010	LF	042	"	074	J	106	j
011	VT	043	+	075	K	107	k
012	FF	044	‘	076	L	108	l
013	CR	045	-	077	M	109	m
014	SO	046	.	078	N	110	n
015	SI	047	/	079	O	111	o
016	DLE	048	0	080	P	112	p
017	DC1	049	1	081	Q	113	q
018	DC2	050	2	082	R	114	r
019	DC3	051	3	083	S	115	s
020	DCA	052	4	064	T	116	t
021	NAK	053	5	085	U	117	u
022	SYN	054	6	086	V	118	v
023	ETB	055	7	087	W	119	w
024	CAN	056	8	088	X	120	x
025	EM	057	9	089	Y	121	y
026	SUB	058	:	090	Z	122	z
027	ESC	059	;	091	[	123	{
028	FS	060	<	092	\	124	|
029	GS	061	=	093	]	125	}
030	RS	062	>	094	†	126	~
031	US	063	?	095	-	127	DEL

Note : The first 32 characters and the last character are control characters, they cannot be printed.

5.8. COMMONLY USED LIBRARY FUNCTIONS :

1. **clrscr ( ) :**

   It is always better to use clrscr ( ) function after the declaration and before starting the other statements.

2. **exit ( )** This function terminates the program. It is defined in **process.h** header file. To use exit function the header

   #include <process.h> has to be included in the program.
   The syntax is as follows.

   exit ( ) ;

3. **sleep ( )**
   This function pauses the execution of the program for a given number of seconds. The number of seconds is to be enclosed between the parenthesis. It is defined in **dos. h** header file. Example of syntax is as follows.
   Syntax

   sleep (1) :

4. **system ( )** This function is helpful in executing the different **dos** Commands. It returns 0 on success and -1 on failure. Example of the syntax the syntax is as follows.

Syntax

system ("dir");

The command should be enclosed within the double quotation marks.

There are many other ANSI C library functions, some of which like header functions, determination of whether the argument is alpha numeric isalnum(c) etc., have already been discussed earlier. Some functions which are under the different headings of header functions have not been discussed here. For example acos(d), log(d), log10(d), sinh(d) etc., come under the header file <math.h>

For reference of those functions which are not discussed in this book may be obtained from other sources which give ANSI C library function in detail.

5.9. C LIBRARY FUNCTIONS :

The C language is accompanied by a number of standard *library functions* which carry out various useful tasks. In particular, all input and output operations (*e.g.*, writing to the terminal) and all math operations (*e.g.*, evaluation of sines and cosines) are implemented by library functions.

In order to use a library function, it is necessary to call the appropriate *header file* at the beginning of the program. The header file informs the program of the name, type, and number and type of arguments, of all of the functions contained in the library in question. A header file is called via the preprocessor statement

#include <filename>

where filename represents the name of the header file.

A library function is accessed by simply writing the function name, followed by a list of *arguments*, which represent the information being passed to the function. The arguments must be enclosed in parentheses, and separated by commas: they can be constants, variables, or more complex expressions. Note that the parentheses must be present even when there are no arguments.

The C *math library* has the header file math.h, and contains the following useful functions as shown in Table 5.6.

Table 5.6 : C Math Library Functions

Function	Type	Purpose
acos(d)	double	Return arc cosine of d (in range 0 to pi)
asin(d	double	Return arc sine of d (in range -pi/2 to pi/2)
atan(d)	double	Return arc tangent of d (in range -pi/2 to pi/2)
atan2(d1, d2)	double	Return arc tangent of d1/d2 (in range -pi to pi)
cbrt(d)	double	Return cube root of d
cos(d)	double	Return cosine of d
cosh(d)	double	Return hyperbolic cosine of d
exp(d)	double	Return exponential of d
fabs(d)	double	Return absolute value of d
hypot(d1, d2)	double	Return sqrt(d1 * d1 + d2 * d2)
log(d)	double	Return natural logarithm of d
log10(d)	double	Return logarithm (base 10) of d
pow(d1, d2)	double	Return d1 raised to the power d2
sin(d)	double	Return sine of d
sinh(d)	double	Return hyperbolic sine of d
sqrt(d)	double	Return square root of d
tan(d)	double	Return tangent of d
tanh(d)	double	Return hyperbolic tangent of d

Here, Type refers to the data type of the quantity that is returned by the function. Moreover, d, d1, *etc.* indicate arguments of type double.

A program that makes use of the C math library would contain the statement

#include <math.h>

close to its start. In the body of the program, a statement like

```
x = cos(y);
```

would cause the variable x to be assigned a value which is the cosine of the value of the variable y (both x and y should be of type double).

Note that math library functions tend to be *extremely expensive* in terms of CPU time, and should, therefore, only be employed when absolutely necessary. The classic illustration of this point is the use of the pow() function. This function assumes that, in general, it will be called with a *fractional* power, and, therefore, implements a full-blown (and very expensive) series expansion. Clearly, it is not computationally efficient to use this function to square or cube a quantity. In other words, if a quantity needs to be raised to a small, positive integer power then this should be implemented *directly,* instead of using the pow() function: *i.e.,* we should write x * x rather than pow(x, 2), and x * x * x rather than pow(x, 3), *etc.* (Of course, a properly designed exponentiation function would realize that it is more efficient to evaluate small positive integer powers by the direct method. Unfortunately, the pow() function was written by computer scientists!)

The C math library comes with a useful set of predefined mathematical constants as shown in Table 5.7.

5.7. C Math Library Constants

Name	Description
M_PI	Pi, the ratio of a circle's circumference to its diameter
M_PI_2	Pi divided by two
M_PI_4	Pi divided by four
M_1_PI	The reciprocal of pi (1/pi)
M_SQRT2	The square root of two
M_SQRT1_2	The reciprocal of the square root of two (also the square root of 1/2).
M_E	The base of natural logarithms

5.9.1. The Standard C Library Functions :

Some of the "commands" in C are not really "commands" at all but are functions. For example, we have been using **printf** and **scanf** to do input and output, and we have used **rand** to generate random numbers - all three are functions.

There are a great many standard functions that are included with C compilers and while these are not really part of the language, in the sense that you can re-write them if you really want to, most C programmers think of them as fixtures and fittings. Later in the course we will look into the mysteries of how C gains access to these standard functions and how we can extend the range of the standard library. But for now a list of the most common libraries and a brief description of the most useful functions they contain follows:

1. **stdio.h: I/O functions:**
   1. **getchar()** returns the next character typed on the keyboard.
   2. **putchar()** outputs a single character to the screen.
   3. **printf()** as previously described
   4. **scanf()** as previously described
2. **string.h: String functions**
   1. **strcat()** concatenates a copy of str2 to str1
   2. **strcmp()** compares two strings
   3. **strcpy()** copys contents of str2 to str1
3. **ctype.h: Character functions**
   1. **isdigit()** returns non-0 if arg is digit 0 to 9
   2. **isalpha()** returns non-0 if arg is a letter of the alphabet
   3. **isalnum()** returns non-0 if arg is a letter or digit
   4. **islower()** returns non-0 if arg is lowercase letter
   5. **isupper()** returns non-0 if arg is uppercase letter
4. **math.h: Mathematics functions**
   1. **acos()** returns arc cosine of arg
   2. **asin()** returns arc sine of arg
   3. **atan()** returns arc tangent of arg
   4. **cos()** returns cosine of arg
   5. **exp()** returns natural logarithim e
   6. **fabs()** returns absolute value of num
   7. **sqrt()** returns square root of num
5. **time.h: Time and Date functions**
   1. **time()** returns current calender time of system
   2. **difftime()** returns difference in secs between two times
   3. **clock()** returns number of system clock cycles since program execution
6. **stdlib.h:Miscellaneous functions**
   1. **malloc()** provides dynamic memory allocation, covered in future sections
   2. **rand()** as already described previously
   3. **srand()** used to set the starting point for rand()

5.10. PARTIAL C/C++ FUNCTION LIST

All the important functions of C and C++ have been given at the appropriate places. However they have been given again for ready reference. This list of functions is incomplete.

A note about C Vs. C++

Note that header files from the C standard library should have the form headername.h when used in a C program, and the form cheadername when used in C++ programs (note the c as a prefix). For instance, in a C program the stdlib header file would be included as follows

#include <stdlib.h>

whereas in a C++ program it would be included like this:

#include <cstdlib>

5.10.1. Functions Listed Alphabetically :

- abort()
- abs()
- acos()
- asin()
- atan()
- atexit()
- atof()
- atoi()
- atol()
- ceil()
- clock()
- cosh()
- ctime()
- div()
- exit()
- fabs()
- floor()
- fmod()
- getchar()
- getenv()
- isalnum()
- isalpha()
- isdigit()
- isgraph()
- ispunct()
- isspace()
- isupper()
- kbhit()
- log10()
- log2()
- log()
- memcmp()
- modf()
- pow()
- putchar()
- putenv()
- puts()
- rand()
- remove()
- rename()
- sinh()
- sqrt()
- srand()
- strcat()
- strcmp()
- strerror()
- time()
- tolower()
- toupper()

5.11. PROGRAM TO CONVERT DECIMAL NUMBER INTO BINARY NUMBER SYSTEM : DOWNLOAD

5.11.1 Logic of This Program :

1. Accept Number from User
2. As we are dividing number by 2, we have only remainders 0,1 etc
3. Take an array of remainder i. rem[20];
4. Let ,Initial elements in rem[] be Zero
5. In each iteration Store Remainder in the Array & Divide original number by 2
6. Also Count the number of remainders stored
7. To Convert into Binary Just Reverse Remainder array

5.11.2 Program :

```
#include<stdio.h>
#include<conio.h>
#include<math.h>
void dec_bin(long int num)   // Function Definition
{
long int rem[50],i=0,length=0;
while(num>0)
{
rem[i]=num%2;
num=num/2;
i++;
length++;
}
printf("\nBinary number : ");
   for(i=length-1;i>=0;i–)
        printf("%ld",rem[i]);
}
```

```
//=============================================================
void main()
{
long int num;
clrscr();

 printf("Enter the decimal number : ");
 scanf("%ld",&num);

   dec_bin(num);  // Calling function

 getch();
}
```

Output :

Enter the decimal number : 7

Binary number : 111

Conversion from decimal number system to another number system.

Example :

Convert decimal number 512,125 to numerical system with two digits, known as Binary system.

$(512{,}125)_{(} = (\ ?\ )$

1. Separate Integral part from Fractal part of number. (Integral = 512, Fractal = 0,125)
2. Divide Integral part of number with Base of number system that you want to convert number in.

   Binary number system Base is two.

   Integral / Base = Result Of Division

   512 : 2 = 256,0
3. Separate Integral part of Result Of Division, Integral Of Division Result = 256
4. Multiply Integral Of Division Result with Base

   Integral Of Division Result * Base = Result

   256 * 2 = 512
5. Subtract Integral and Result and remember result as a sequence of Ciphers
   512 – 512 = 0

6. New Integral = 256 (Integral = Integral Of Division Result)
7. If Integral not equal zero go to step 2 (condition for stopping process of conversion)
8. Read Cipher sequence in oposit direction and get Binary number.

   The result of conversion is 512 = 1000000000

   The whole process is better understandable trough this table, just follow the header of the table.

Table 5.8. Conversion of Decimal Number 512 into Binary Number - Integer part

A	B	C	D	E	F
Integral part of number	Base to convert in (2)	Integral part of result of division Integral / Base A / B	Result of multiplication Integral * Base C * B	Result of subtraction Cipher sequence A - D	Read Cipher sequence in opposite direction and get Binary number Converted Integral part of number to binary number system $512_{(10)}$ = $1000000000_{(2)}$
512	2	256	512	0	1
256	2	128	256	0	0
128	2	64	128	0	0
64	2	32	64	0	0
32	2	16	32	0	0
16	2	8	16	0	0
8	2	4	8	0	0
4	2	2	4	0	0
2	2	1	2	0	0
1	2	0	0	1	0

Process of converting Fractal part of number 0,125(is shown below in table .

Table 5.9. Conversion of Decimal Number 512 into Binary Number - Fractional part

A	B	C	D	E
Fractal part of number	Base to convert in	Result of multiplication Fractal *Base A * B	Integral part of result of multiplication Cipher sequence	Converted Integral part of number to binary number system$0{,}125_{(10)}$ = $0{,}001_{(2)}$
0,125	2	0,250	0	0
0,250	2	0,5	0	0
0,5	2	1,0	1	1

1. Separate Fractal part of number (Fractal = 0,125)

2. Multiply Fractal and Base number

   Result Of Multiplication = Fractal * Base

   0,125 * 2 = 0,250

3. Separate Integral part of result of multiplication and remember it as Cipher sequence

   Integral part of result = 0

4. New Fractal = 0,250

5. If Fractal is not equal 0 go to step 2 (condition for stopping process of conversion)

9. Read Cipher sequence and get Binary number (the direction of reading ciphers is the same as Cipher sequence)

10. The result of conversion is $0,125_{(10)} = 0,001_{(2)}$

    Now we have converted Integral and Fractal part of number and when we join them together we get exact result :

    $(512,125)_{(10)} = (1000000000,001)_{(2)}$

    If we want to check if the result is correct, we shall use the conversion method from any to decimal number system :

    $(1000000000,001)_{(2)} =$

    $= 1{*}2^{(9)}+0{*}2^{(8)}+0{*}2^{(7)}+0{*}2^{(6)}+0{*}2^{(5)}+0{*}2^{(4)}+0{*}2^{(3)}+0{*}2^{(2)}+0{*}2^{(1)}+0{*}2^{(0)}+0{*}2^{(-1)}+0{*}2^{(-2)}+1{*}2^{(-3)} = (512,125)_{(10)}$

5.11.3 Flow Chart of sub-routine Convert Decimal to Different Number Base :

Subroutine Convert Decimal To Different Number Base. It also has two parts that needs to be worked out based on the pseudo code : Convert Integral part of number and Convert Fractal part of number.

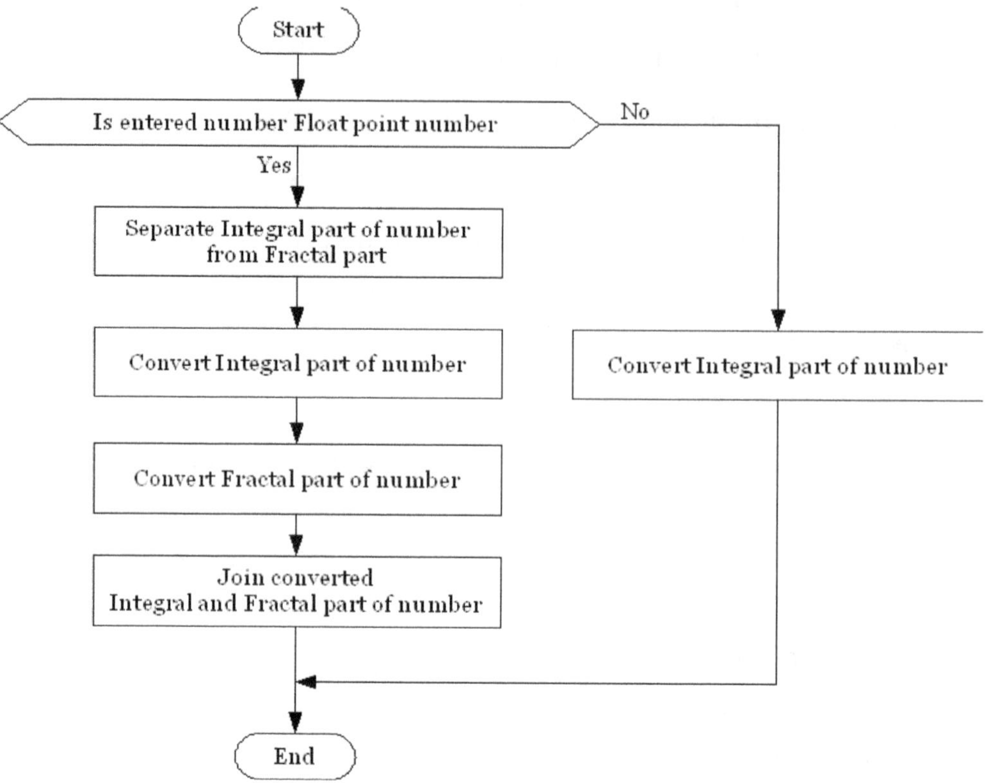

Fig. 5.2. Flow Chart of sub-routine Convert Decimal to Different Number Base

Similarly any number to any base can be converted into its equivalent number to any other base by considering the integral and fractral parts separately as had been done above.

* * *

COMPREHENSION - 5

Note : By answering all the questions given in this comprehension one can answer any objective type of questions easily whatever be the form of the question. Answers for these questions can be obtained by going through the topics in this chapter carefully.

1. What are the essential functions of Computer Programs?
2. Does C have Input/output Syntax? How are inputs and outputs handled in C ?
3. What is Standard I/O Library in C ?
4. Do C and C++ have the same type of I/O Operations?
5. What is the Header function that gives standard I/O functions to C Program?
6. Mention some other standard headers and their uses in C Programs.
7. What is a Pre Processor function? What are Preprocessor directives?
8. Give the different types of I/O functions of C. Also give them in the form of a Chart.
9. What are Formatted and unformatted I/O functions?
10. What does scanf ( ) function do? Give its Syntax.
11. Give the scanf() statement to take any integer, float, character and string Data.
12. What is a control string? Give some control strings and state what for they are used. What are the methods of giving control strings and corresponding data input?
13. What is an address operator? What purpose does it serve? Explain the use of an address operator in an input function.
14. How many data will be read by a scanf() function?
15. If there is any mismatch between the control strings and data what will happen? Explain with example.
16. What will be done by the following input statement?
    scanf("%d % *d %d", &a, &b, &c) ;
17. What is method of giving input data to a scanf() function and when is it given? What is the way o giving the input data?
18. What does the following input function do when the following data are given?
    scanf ("%f %f %f", &x, &y, &z) ;
    with the input data 4860.484 36.39E-1 789
19. Give an example of providing mixed variables of input data statement.
20. If a data 097 is given as input to %f or %d or %c control strings what will happen?

21. Explain formatted and unformatted output statements with examples?
22. State what should be the nature of the output data type for the output statement

    printf ("%d %f %c %s", a,b,c,d);

23. It is economical to use for values -128 to +127 int data the control variable %c instead of control var %d ? Why? Explain with example.
24. For the following statements of statements if the data given to the variable A are 212, 255, and 256 are given as data what will be the output values for A and why?

```
    printf("Entervalue of 'A':");
   scanf("%d",&a);
 printf("A=%d",a);
```

25. Explain input/output statements wit field widths giving examples.
26. What is the problem in giving field widths to I/O statements? Explain with example. When do you use it?
27. How do you detect that errors have occurred in input?
28. Give formatted input codes or control characters used with scanf( ) with meanings?
29. Give formatted output codes or control characters used with printf( ) with meanings?
30. How to enhance the Readability of the output?
31. What are unformatted input/output functions? When do they work?
32. What are the Character input functions? Give their Syntax and explain with examples.
33. What is the difference between getch() and getche() functions?
34. What is problem in using getchar() function interactively in a loop? How do you overcome it?
35. What are Character test functions? Mention them and their meanings.
36. Give different string input functions and their Syntax. Explain with examples.
37. What are the Character output functions? Give their Syntax and explain with examples.
38. Give different string output functions and their Syntax. Explain with examples.
39. What are two popular Character Recognition Codes? Which is used normally in C?
40. Mention some of the commonly used C Library functions and state what they do?
41. What are the different types of number systems and their conversion?

* * *

EXERCISE - 5

Note : By answering all the questions given in this exercise one can answer subjective type of questions easily including problems. The worked examples in the chapter may help in solving these questions.

1. List out the Formatted and Unformatted Input/Output Functions? Give their Syntax and explain with examples.
2. What are Escape List Sequences? List any five Escape Sequences with their uses.
3. What are Conversion Symbols or control constants or control strings? Explain the use of some of them with examples.
4. How is the function ' cgets ' different from the fn. 'gets'. Explain.
5. What is the difference between puts ( ) different from putch ( ) ? Explain.
6. What does exit ( ) do?
7. i) What is the purpose of the scanf and printf functions?

   ii) Write a scanf call to accept a as integer, b as float, c as char and s as string.

   iii) If ij are integer; ch as character. Write a prinft call to display the same.

   iv) Which of the following scanf statement are valid; if invalid, explain why?

      a. scanf (" % d", &f);

      b. scanf ("enter value %f", &g);

      c. scanf(" %f %d",a,b);

   v) What is the purpose of escape sequences?
8. i) Find the output for the following program.

```
main ( )
{
int p = 200, q=100;
printf ("value = %d \n",p - - - q);
}
```

   The value printed is

   a) 99   b) 101   c) 100   d) 300   e) error

   ii) What is the output of the following program segment.

```
n = 7;
printf (" %d  %d  %d", n++, n, n - -);
```

   a) 7 8 7   b) 6 6 7   c) 7 7 8   d) 8 8 7

iii) The code

```
int i = 7;
printf ("%d\n", i++ *i++);
```

a) prints49 b) prints56

c) is compiler dependent d) expression i++ * i++ is undefined.

iv) Find the output for the following program.

```
main ()
{
int i = 010, j = 05, r= 0 × 209;
printf ("value = %d \n", i+j * r);
}
```

when the program is run, it prints.

a) 10 b) 170 c) 300 d) 168

v) Consider the program given below:

```
int num;
main ()
{
int j;
j=num ++;
printf (" the value of j = %d \n", j);
}
```

what is the value printed?

a) 2 b) 1 c) 0 d) unpredictable

9. i) Consider the following program

```
main ()
{
        int var;
        var = 256;
        {
                float var;
                var = 2.35;
        }
        printf ("%d \n", var) ;
}
```

Which of the following statements about the function presented above is TRUE?

a) Will not complete as the variable var is declared twice
b) Will print out 2.35 as the result
c) Will print out 256 as the result
d) Will not compile as the declaration float var follows the executable statment var = 256 .

ii) What is wrong in the following piece of code

```
main ()
{
        {
                9++;
        }
}
```

a) C language does not allow nested blocks of code

b) the main program must contain at least one assignment statement

c) The post-increment operator requires as value

d) The main program is defined without arguments

iii) Consider the following program

```
main ()
{
        double d;
        int i, j = 2;
        i = (j=3/2)* 2;
}
```

The value of i will be

a) 3 b) 2 c) 1 d) none

10. i) Find the output for the following program.

```
main ()
{
        int =7;
        printf ("value = %d \n", ++i + ++i);
}
```

ii) Find the output for the following program.

```
main ()
{
        int a = 10, b=20;
        a= a^b;
        b=b^a;
        a= a^b;
        printf ("n values of a and b = %d %d ",a,b);
}
```

11. A motorcycle covers a distance of 45 km per litre of petrol consumption. The cost of petrol is 30.00 per litre. Write a program in C to calculate the cost of petrol to travel a distance of 120 km verify by the running program.

12. If field widths % w d are specified give the output for the statement
    Scanf('%2d %5d",&num1,&num2);
    If the data line is 31426 50
13. For the statement
    Scanf('%2d %5d",&num1,&num2);
    What will be the output with the input 123 456 789
14. State errors, if any, in the following input statements.
    i) scanf("%c%f%d",city, &price, &year);
    ii) scanf("%s%d",city, amount);
    iii) scanf("%f,%d,& amount, &year);
    iv) scanf(\n"%f",root);
    v) scanf("%c ^d ^Id", "code, &count, Root);
15. What will be the values stored in the variables **year** and **code** when the data 1988, x is keyed in as a response to the following statements:
    i) scanf("%d %c", &year, &code);
    ii) scanf("%c %d", &year, &code);
    iii) scanf("%d %c", &code, &year);
    iv) scanf("%s %c", &year, &code);
16. The variables **count, price,** and **city** have the following values:

    count ← 1275
    price ← -235.74
    city ← Cambridge

    Show the exact output that the following output statements will produce:
    i) printf("%d %f", count, price);
    ii) printf("%2d\n%f", count, price);
    iii) printf("%d %f", price, count)
    iv) printf("%10dxxxx%5.2f", count, price);
    v) print ("%s", city);
    vi) printf ("%-10d%-15s", count, city);
17. State what (if anything) is wrong with each of the following output statements:
    i) printf (%d 7.2%f, year, amount);
    ii) printf ("%_s, %c"\n, city, code);
    iii) printf(%f, %^d, %s, price, count, city);
    iv) printf("%c%d%f\n", amount, code, year);

18. In response to the input statement

    scanf("%4d% "%d", &year, &code, &count);

    the following data is keyed in:

    19883745

    What values does the computer assign to the variables **year, code,** and **count?**
19. Given the string "WORDPROCESSING", write a program to read the string from the terminal and display the same in the following formats:
    i) WORD PROCESSING
    ii) WORD
        PROCESSING
    iii) W.P.
20. Write a program to read the values of x and y and print the results of the following expressions in one line, verify when i) x = 4, y = 2j when x = 5, y =6; ii) x=y=8 by running the program.

    i) $\frac{x+y}{x-y}$ ii) $\frac{x+y}{2}$ iii) $(x+y)(x-y)$
21. Write a program to read the following numbers, round them off to the nearest integers and print out the results in integer form : Run the program

    i) 35.7 ii) 50.21 iii) –23.73 iv) –46.45
22 Write a C Program to reverse a 6 digit number and verify by executing the program.
23. Write a C Program to find the time taken by a car running at 80 km /hr to cover a distance of 630 Km and execute the program.
24. Write a C Program to show that the difference between any 2 digit number and its reverse is always a multiple of 9 and run the program.
25. Write a C program to convert temperature in Fahrenheit into Centigrade and convert it back into Fahrenheit and test the program by running it.
26. Give some important C Library functions which are common to C++ library functions also.
27. How are the Common Statndard Library Functions used in C and C++?
28. Explain about the different types of number systems with their bases?
29. Write an algorithm to convert number of any base system to its equivalent number of a different base system.
30. Write a flow chart to to convert number of any base system to its equivalent number of a different base system.

* * *

CHAPTER - 6
DECISION AND LOOP CONTROL STATEMENTS

6.1. INTRODUCTION :

The decision and Loop Control Statements have the same syntax in C and C++. The Decision Statements are used to take a decision regarding the flow of the program, based on certain condition or conditions being fulfilled. These decision statements may also be called Control Statements. Without any decision or control statement there can practically be no program. PASCAL, C and C++are also considered as structured languages, and one of the reasons for calling them so is that they have rich and varied program control statements. The control statements can be branched as Conditional and Unconditional control statements. Under conditional control statements it has **if** and **switch.** The Unconditional statement is **goto.** The loop constructs are **while, for,** and **do-while.** *The control statements or decision statements are widely used to support decision-making processes. They largely rely upon a conditional test that determines the decision.*

The decision making statements or the control statements have to perform three operations. i) change the flow of the program, ii) test logical condition and iii) control the flow of execution as per the selection made depending on the fulfillment of the logical condition. One of the simplest control statements we have already studied is the use of control operator under the heading operators and their precedences.

6.1.1. Conditional Operator :

The conditional operator contains a condition followed by two statements or values. If the condition is true the first statement is executed otherwise the second statement. The conditional operator (?) and (:) are sometimes calls ternary operators because they take three arguments. The syntax of conditional operator is as given below.

Syntax for condition statement is :

Condition? (expression 1) : (expression 2) ;

Two expressions are separated by a colon. If the condition is true expressional gets evaluated otherwise expression 2 is evaluated. The condition is always written before the question mark.

Ex : printf ("Result is %s" marks >= 50 ? "Pass" : "Fail");

This conditional control statement prints the word "Pass" if marks are greater than or equal to 50 and prints "Fail" if marks are less than 50.

In addition to the use of conditional operator, the different types of conditional statements we have are

i) the **simple if** statement
ii) **block if** statement
iii) **nested if** statement
iv) **simple if-else** statement
v) **block if-else** statement
vi) **nested ifs** statement or **nested else if** statements or **if else if** ladder statement
vii) **break statement**
viii) **continue statement**
ix) **goto statement**
x) the **switch or switch case** statement

The decision-making statement checks the given condition and then executes its sub-block. The decision statement decides the statement to be executed after the success or failure of a given condition.

The conditional statements use relational operators, which have been explained in the third chapter. The relational operators are useful for comparing the two values. They can be used to check whether they are equal to each other unequal or which one is smaller / greater than the other.

6.1.2 The Simple if Statement :

C uses the keyword if to execute a set of command line or one command line when the logical condition is true. It has only one option. The set of command lines or command lines are executed only when the logical condition is true.

Syntax for simple if statement is :

```
if (condition)
statement s1;
```

ex : i)

```
if (sales > 1000 && sales <= 2000)
comn = sales  *0.03;
```

ii)

```
if (x > y)
        printf ("\n x is greater than y");
```

6.1.3 Block if Statement :

Here a block or a group of statements follow the test expression.

Syntax for block if statement is :

```
if(test expression)
  {
    statement s1;
```

```
        statement s2;
        ......................
        ......................
    }
```

Ex : i)
```
if (x >=y)
{
num++;
marks+=num;
}
```

Here if x is greater than or equal to y then num is incremented by one, and the resultant value is added together with marks by the statement marks+=num;

ii)
```
if (physics >=50 && chemistry >=50 && biology >=50)
{
printf ("\n pass in group");
tot=physics+chemistry+biology;
ave = (float) tot/3.0;
printf ("\n total marks is %d", tot);
printf ("\n average marks is %f", ave);
}
```

In this case, if marks in all the three subjects are greater than or equal to 50 then the sequence of statements within the braces are executed. In both the cases i) and ii). if the test expression returns false then the control is transferred to next statement.

6.1.4 Nested if statements :

This is the most important aspect of "if" statement in the sense it may lead to number of test conditions after passing each test. The syntax is

```
if (condition1)
{
  statement s1;
    if (condition2)
    {
      statements s2;
      if (condition3)
            {
                  statement s3; .....
            }
    }
}
```

```
ex :  if (marks > 50 &&marks <60)
      {
         printf ("\n result is pass in second class") ;
            if (marks > 60 )
            {
               printf ("\n result is first class");
                     {
                           if marks > 70;
                           printf ("\n result is distinction");
                     }
            }
      }
```

6.1.5 : Simple if else statement :

Here an optional clause 'else' is used along with the simple if statement.

The Syntax for if else statement is :

```
if(test expression)
   statement;
else
   statement;
(e.g)
   if (total >= 250)
      printf ("\n result is pass");
   else
      printf ("\n result is fail");
```

6.1.6. Block if else statement :

This is similar to the form as in simple "if" except a block (or) group of statements follows the test expression. The general form is,

The Syntax for block if else statement is :

```
if (test expression)
{
   statements
}
   else
   {
      statements;
   }
}
```

```
(e.g.)
  if (sales >= 30000)
    {
      commission = sales * 0.08;
      incentive = commission *0.20;
    }
  else
    {
        commission = sales *0.05;
        incentive = commission *0.015;
    }
```

Here the test expression is tested if it returns true then the sequence of statements followed by if are executed, if it returns false then the sequence of statements followed by else part are executed. Here is a complete program to display total marks, result and class obtained by the student by using block-if construct ;

Program 6.1.1.

Write a program in C to illustrate the use of multiple block-if else constructs.

```
    /* Example program to illustrate Block-if construct */
    #include <stdio.h>
    #include <conio.h>
    int main ( )
{
      int maths, physics, chemistry, total;
      float avg;
      clrscr ( ) ;
      printf (“enter marks for maths, physics and chemistry”);
      scanf (“%d  %d   %d”,&maths, &physics, &chemistry);
      total=maths, physics, chemistry;
      avg=total/3.0;
      if (maths >=50 && physics >=50 && chemistry >= 50)
        {
          printf (“\n Pass in exam”);
          printf (“\n Total marks are %d”,total);
          printf (“\n average is %f”,avg);
        }
          if (total >=180)
            printf (“\n Pass in first class”);
          else
            printf (“\n Pass in second class”);
          else
```

```
        {
            printf ("\n fail");
            printf ("\n Total is %d",total);
            printf ("\n average is %f",avg);
        }
    return 0;
    getche ( );
}
```

OUTPUT :

enter marks for maths, physics and chemistry
55 77 88

Fail in exam
Total marks are 220
Average is 73.3333
enter marks for maths, physics and chemistry
47 65 61
Pass in exam
Total marks are 173
Average is 57.6667
Passed in Second Class

6.1.7 : Nested ifs or **Nested else if** or **if else if ladder :**

This is the most important aspect of "if' statement in the sense it may lead to confusion if not properly used. The 'nested if' is a statement that is the object of either 'if' or 'else'.

The Syntax for nested 'if' or **Nested else if** or **if else if ladder :**

```
if (test expression1)
{
statements;
}
   else if (test expression2)
   {
   statements ;
   }
      else
   {
      statements;
   }
```

In this kind of statements number of logical conditions are checked for executing various statements. Here, if any logical condition is true the compiler executes the block followed by **if** condition otherwise it skips and executes **else** block. In **if... else** statement **else** block is executed by default after failure of condition. In order to execute the **else** block depending upon certain condition we can add repetitively **if** statements in **else** block. This kind of nesting will be unlimited.

The above syntax can also be stated as given below:

```
if (condition1)
{
statement 1;              /* if block */
statement 2;
}
    else if (condition2)
  {
    statement 3;          /* else block */
    statement 4;
  }
      else
      {
      statement 5;        / *default block */
      statement 6;
      }
```

A careful understanding is required to know which **else** associates with which **if**.

From the above block following rules can be described for applying nested if - else - if statement.

1. Nested **if...else** can be chained with one another.
2. If the condition is false control passes to else block when condition is again checked with the **if** statement. This process continuous if there is no **if** statement in the last **else** block.
3. If one of the **if** statement satisfies the condition, other nested **else ... if** will not be executed.

6.1.8 Break Statement :

The keyword **break** allows the programmers to terminate the loop. The **break** skips from the loop or block in which it is defined. The control then automatically goes to the first statement after the loop or block. The **Break** can be associated with all conditional statements.

We can also use **break** statements in the nested loops. *If we use **break** statement in the innermost loop then the control of the program is terminated only from the innermost loop.* This will be explained later.

6.1.9 The continue Statement :

The Continue statement is exactly opposite to break. *The continue statement is used for continuing next iteration of loop statements. When it occurs in the loop it does not terminate, but it skips the statements after this statement.* It is useful when we want to continue the program without executing any part of the program. This will be explained later.

6.1.10. The goto Statement :

This unconditional statement does not require any condition. This statement is to exit from several layers of nesting. *The goto requires a lable for operation and the label must be in the same function as the goto that uses.*

The syntax is

```
goto label;
.......
label;
statement;
```

It is advisable not to use goto statement as far as possible to avoid confusion.

6.1.11. Switch Statement or Switch case statement :

Switch statement is a multiple branching control statement, and this one is very useful for decision making when more than one decision case is involved.

The Syntax for the switch statement is :

```
switch (variable or expression)
{
case constant 1 :
        statements sequence;       /*case constant 1 and break*/
        break;                     /*act as beginning and end of block */

case constant 2 :
        statement sequence;
        break;

case constant 3 :

        statement sequence ;
        break;

default          :
        statement sequence;
}
statement x;
```

Switch statement differs from an 'if' statement in that 'switch' can only test for equality where as 'if' can evaluate for entire given range. Switch case is a multiple branching control statement, and this one is very useful for decision making when more than one case is involved.

When the switch is executed, the value of expression is compared against the 'constant 1', 'constant 2', 'constant 3' etc., If a case is found whose value matches with the expression, then the sequence of statements that follows the concerned case constant is executed.

The 'break' statement at the end of the each block indicates the end of the particular case and causes an exit from the particular 'switch' statement and transferring the control outside switch to statement-x.

The 'default' statement is executed if no matches are found and is optional.

Program 6.1.2.

Write a program in C using switch case to decide the grade of a student based on his marks.

```
    #include <stdio.h>
    #include <conio.h>
    void main ( )
{
      int total, index;
      printf ("enter total marks for maths, physics and chemistry");
      scanf ("%d", &total);
      printf ("\n total marks for maths, physics and chemistry are %d", total);
      index = marks/30;          /* float index is converted to int */
      switch (index)
    {
      case 10:
      case 9 :
      case 8 :
            grade = "Distinction";       /* cases 10, 9, 8 correspond >=70% */
                      break;
      case 7 :
      case 6 :
            grade = "First class";
                      break;
      case 5 :
            grade = "Second class";
                      break;
      case 4 :
            grade = "Pass class";
                      break;
      default:
            grade = "Fail";
```

```
            break;
      }
      printf ("\n Grade is : %s",grade);
}
```

OUTPUT :

enter total marks for maths, physics and chemistry
245
total marks for maths, physics and chemistry are 245

Grade is : Distinction

6.2. THE BREAK STATEMENT :

The keyword **break** allows the programmers to terminate the loop. The **Break** skips from the loop or block in which it is defined. The control then automatically goes to the first statement after the loop or block. The **Break** can be associated with all conditional statements.

We can also use **break** statements in the nested loops. If we use **break** statement in the innermost loop then the control of the program is terminated only from the innermost loop.

An early exist from the loop is possible by a 'break' statement. When a break statement is encountered, the loop is immediately exited and the program continues with the statement immediately following the loop. The general form is,

```
while (test expression)
{
   if (condition)
   statements
   break;
}
```

For example, if we want to add only positive integers, and when the negative number is entered the loop should be terminated and print only the sum of the all the entered positive integer values.

Program 6.2.1.

Write a program in C++ to illustrate the use of break statement.

```
// Example program to illustrate break

#include <iostream>
using namespace std;
```

```
int main ( )
{
   int no,sum=0;
   cout <<"\n Enter number and negative number to exit \n";
   while (true)
{
   cin >> no;
   if (no < 0)
      break;
   else
      sum+=no;
   }
   cout << "\n the sum is "<<sum;
   return 0;
   }
```

OUTPUT :

Enter number and negative number to exit

3 4 5 6 -1

Sum is 18

Here break will terminate the loop when the entered number is less than 0 and print the value of sum.

6.2.1. Exit ( ) Function

The exit function cause immediate termination of the entire program. This function stops the program execution and causes a force return to the operating system. Because of this property this is used only for specific purposes and not commonly used in C++ program. When this is used a program will look like,

```
    int main ( )
{
    if something exit (0);
    ................
    ...............
    return 0;
}
```

Here if 'something' is true, then the program terminates, here exit with a return value of 0 or constant EXIT_SUCCESS indicates success and any other value or constant EXIT_FAILURE is used to indicate an error or an abnormal program termination.

Following is a program to illustrate the exit function. In this example program if the entered number is prime then after displaying the message 'Given number is not prime' the program comes to a halt.

Program 6.2.2.

Write a program in C++ to illustrate the use of exit function.

```
/* Example for exit function to check whether the given number is prime or not */
#include <iostream>
using namespace std;
int main ( )
{
    int no,i,m;
    cout <<"\n Enter number to check ";
    cin >>no;
    for(i=2;i<no;++i)
      {
      m=no%i;
        if (m==0)
        {
          cout <<"\n Given number is not prime *;
          exit(0);
        }
      }
    cout <<"\n Given number is prime \n";
    return 0;
}
```

OUTPUT :

Enter number to check 13
Given number is prime
Enter number to check 12
Given number is not prime

6.3. LOOPING :

C and C++ both have three looping constructs. They are, (i) for (ii)while and (iii) do-while.

6.3.1. for LOOP :

The for loop allows to execute a set of instructions until a certain condition is satisfied. Condition may be predefined or open-ended.

Syntax of for loop

```
for (initialize condition; test condition and re-evaluation parameter)
{
   statement ;
   ..................
   statement ;
}
```

Table 6.1 Various Formats of 'for' loop

	Syntax	Output	Remarks
1)	for (; ;)	Infinite loop	No arguments
2)	for (a=0); a<=20;)	Infinite loop	'a' is neither increased nor decreased.
3)	for (a =0; a<=10;a++) printf ("%d", a);	Displays value from 1 to 10	'a' is increased from 0 to 10 Curly braces are not necessary. Default scope of for loop is one statement after for loop;
4)	for (a = 10;a>0;a--)	Displays value from 10 to 0	'a' is decreased from 10 to 0

for (a=10; a<10; a- -)
printf ("%d", a);

The above program will never execute because the test condition is not proper at the beginning. *Flow chart of 'for' loop is given here along with syntax.*

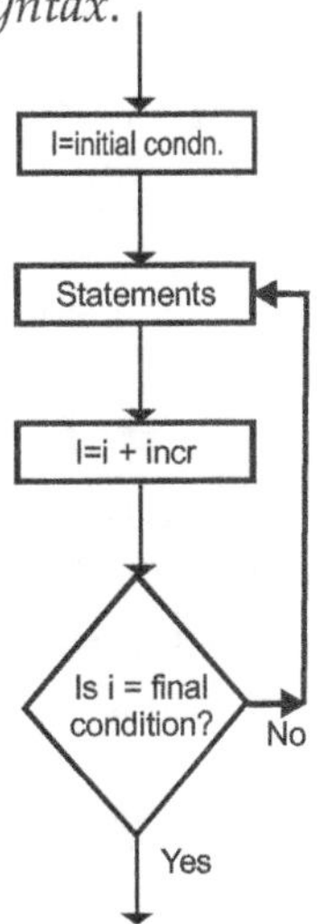

The general form of a for loop can also be stated as

```
for (expression 1; expression 2; expression 3)
{
   sequence of statements;
}
```

Here,

expression 1 is the initial value
expression 2 is the testing value
expression 3 is the increment (step) value

(e.g.)

```
sum =0;
for (i=0;i<=100; i++)
sum +=i;
```

The following steps are involved, namely

1. Initialisation
2. Condition checking
3. Body of the loop
4. Increment
5. (Again) Conditional

Please note that there is no semicolon after for loop; if there is a semicolon after the for loop then the loop is said to be a 'time delay loop' or 'software delay' and the construct is given below;

```
for (i=0;i<100;++i);
```

Also *by using the comma operator, more than one variable can be initialized as seen below;*

```
fir ( fact=1, i=1; i<10; i++)
   fact *=i;
```

Here both **fact** and **i** are variables that are initialized to one. *Similarly we can also have two action statements in an expression used to increment the value as given below.*

```
for(fact=i=1; i<=5; fact*=i,++);
```

Without the comma operator, the same will be seen as,

```
fact = 1;
for (i=1;i<=5;i++)
      fact * = i;
```

Thus using the comma operator reduces the coding.

Instead of initializing the value inside the loop, if we have the option to initialize it before, then the construct will take the following form ;

```
fact=i=1;
   for ( ; i <=5; i++)
      {
      fact * = i;
      i++;
      }
```

Here the index value gets incremented inside the for loop as said before. Consider the last form of for construct in which the initial value, final value and also increment value is not given

```
for ( ; ; )
{
   statements;
}
```

The above for loop executes infinitely, and only way to exit the for loop is by using the abnormal exit (such as goto) in the inside the for loop.

Program 6.3.1

Write a program in C to print the first five numbers starting from 2 alongwith their squares.

```
# include <stdio.h>
# include <conio.h>
main ( )
{
int i;
clrscr ( ) ;
for (i=2;i<=6;i++)
printf ("\number: %5d  it's square : %8d", I, i*i);
}
```

OUTPUT :

```
Number : 2  it's Square : 4
Number : 3  it's Square : 9
Number : 4  it's Square : 16
Number : 5  it's Square : 25
Number : 6  it's Square : 36
```

Explanation : Let us now examine how the program executes.

1) The value of **i** sets to one for the first time when the program execution starts in the for loop.

2) The condition i>=5 is specified and tested in each iteration. Initially the condition is true since the value of **i** is 1. The statements following the **for** loop executes.

3) Upon execution of **printf** statement compiler sends control back to the **for** loop where the value of **i** is increased by one. This is repeated till the value of 'i' is less than or equal to 5.

4) The new updated value of **i** if exceeds 5, the control exists from the loop.

5. The **printf** statement executes as long as the value of **i** reaches to 5.

Consider the following statement

The **for** loop can be used by different ways. Various examples using **for** loops are given below.

Program 6.3.2.

Write a program in C to display numbers from 3 to 18 using the for loop. Use i++.

```
# include <stdio.h>
# include <conio.h>
void man ( )
{
int i;
clrscr ( );
for (i=3;i<=18,i++)
printf (" %5d",i);
}
```

OUTPUT :

3 4 5 6 7 8 9 10 11 12 13 14 15 16 17 18

Explanation : Instead of i ++, if i = i + 1 is used in the **for** statement, the same result can be observed. The increase in a counter can be done anywhere in the body of **for** loop and for infinite times.

6.4.. NESTED for LOOPS :

Both in C and C++ we can also use loop within loops allowing multiple **for** loops in the nested forms. *The numbers of iterations in this type of structure will be equal to the number of iterations in the outer loop multiplied by the number of iterations in the inner loop.*

Program 6.4.1

Write a program in C to perform subtraction of two loop variables. Use nested for loops.

```
# include <stdio.h>
# include <conio.h>
void main
{
int a,b, sub;
clrscr ( );
    for (a=5;a>=5;a--)
    {
      for (b=1;b<=2;b++)
      {
      sub=a-b;
      printf ("a=%d  b=%d  a-b = %d\n", a,b,sub);
      }
    }
}
```

OUTPUT :

```
a=5  b=1  a-b=4
a=5  b=2  a-b=3
a=4  b=1  a-b=3
a=4  b=2  a-b=2
a=3  b=1  a-b=2
a=3  b=2  a-b=1
```

Explanation :

In the above program the outer loop variable and inner loop variables are 'a' and 'b' respectively. For each value of 'a' the inner loop is executed two times. The inner loop terminates when the value of 'b' exceeds 2 and the outer loop terminates when the value of 'a' is 2. Thus, the outer loop executes 3 times and for each outer loop the inner loop executes two times. Thus, the total iterations are 3 x 2 = 6 and 6 output lines are shown in the output.

Program : 6.4.2.

Write another program in C to illustrate an example based on nested for loops

```
# include <stdio.h>
# include <conio.h>
{
int i,j;
clrscr( ) ;
      for (i=1<=3;i++)              /* outer loop block */
      {
         for (i=1;j<=2;j++)        /* inner loop */)
         printf ("\n i+j; %d", i+j);       /* single statement. Hence no block */
      }
}
```

OUTPUT :

```
i+j = 2
i+j = 3
i+j = 3
i+j = 4
i+j = 4
i+j = 5
```

Explanation : Here in the above example for each value of 'i' the inner loop's j value varies from 1 to 2. Outer loop executes three times whereas the inner loop executes six times. The inner loops terminates when the value of j=2 and the outer loop terminates when the value of i = 3. The total number of iterations = outer loop iterations (3) *inner loop iterations (2) = 6.

Program : 6.4.3

Write a program in C using nested for loops to print values and messages when any loop ends.

```
# include <stdio.h>
# include <conio.h>
void main ( )
{
int a,b,c;
clrscr ( ) ;
    for (a=1;a<2;a++)          /* outer loop */
    {
        for (b=1;b<=2,x++)  /* inner loop */
        {
          for (c=1;c<=2;c++)    /* middle loop */
          printf ("\n a=% d+b =%d + c=%d: %d", a,b,c,a+b+c);
          printf ("\n Inner Loop is Over,");
        }
    printf ("\n Middle Loop is Over.");
    }
printf ("\n Outer Loop is Over,");
}
```

Explanation : The execution of the above program will be done by C compiler in sequence as follows : For the first value of the variable in the outer loop all the values of the middle loop variables will be executed with all the variables of the inner most loop being executed for each value of the middle loop.

The total number of iterations are equal to 2 * 2 *2 = 8. The final output provides 8 results.

Program 6.4.4

Write a program in C to find perfect cubes up to given number.

```
/* 1,8,27,64 are perfect cubes of 1,2,3 and 4 */
# include<math.h>
main ( )
{
int i, j, k;
clrscr ( ) ;
printf ("Enter a Number :");
scarf ("%d", &k);
    for (i=1;i<k;i++)
   {
      for (j=1;j<=i;j++)
```

```
    {
if (i==pow(i,3))
printf ("\nNumber : %d & it's Cube :%d",j,i);
    }
getche ( );
}
```

6.5. WHILE-LOOP :

In both C and C++ "While" is an entry controlled loop statement i.e., the test condition is evaluated and if it is true the body of the loop is evaluated. This process is repeated until the test condition becomes false; then the control is transferred out of loop.

The general form of 'while' is

```
while (test expression)
{
    sequence of statements;
}
```

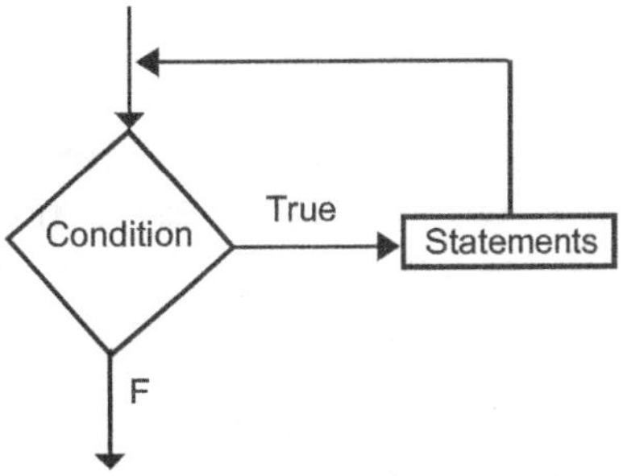

Condition
True
Statements
F

Flow chart for while loop is given here.

The following while loop helps us to sum the numbers between 1 and 100.

```
sum = 0;
  i = 1;
  while ( i <=100)
  {
    sum+=i;
    i++;
  }
```

Here the 'sum' and 'i' are initialised before entering the loop, first test expression is evaluated if it returns true then the statements within braces will execute. Note that 'i' gets incremented inside the loop; *if 'i' is missing then the loop is infinite one as 'i' is always less than 100.*

Consider the following while - loop construct in which the loop is executed infinitely

```
while (true)
{
    statements;
}
```

Again when we want to exit from such a loop, we have to use some unconditional statement, and the above form is similar to the for loop where we have all the 3 expressions are missing.'

Another example of **while** statement which uses the keyboard input is shown before ;

```
.....................
.....................
character = ' ';
while(character f= 'Y')
      (character = getchar( );
xxxxxxxx;
................
...............
```

First the **character** is initialised to ' '. The **while** statement then begins by testing whether **character** is not equal to Y. Since the **character** was initialised to ' '. the test is true and the loop statement

character = getchar( ) ;

is executed. Each ime a letter is keyed in, the test is carried out and the loop statement is executed until the letter Y is pressed. When Y is pressed, the condition becomes false because **Character** equals Y, and the loop terminates, thus transferring the control in the statement xxxxxxx;

Program 6.5.1

Write a program in C calculate factorial of a given number. Use while loop.

```
# include <stdio.h>
# include <conio.h>
  main ( )
{
  int a, factorl
  clrscr ( ) ;
  printf ("\n Enter The Number :");
  scanf("%d", &a);
     while (a>=1)
     {
     printf ("%d*",a);
     factorl=factorl*a;
     a- -;
     }
```

```
    printf ("= %d",factorl);
    printf("\n Factorial of Given number is %d", factorl);
}
```

OUTPUT :

Enter the Number : 6
6* 5 * 4* 3* 2* 1* = 720
Factorial of Given number is 720

6.6. DO-WHILE LOOP :

On some occasions, it may be necessary to execute the body of the loop, before the test is performed. Such an occasion can be handled using 'do-while'.

The do-while loop executes the body of the loop at least once regardless of the logical condition. Flow chart for Do-while loop is also given here.

The Syntax for do while loop is :

```
do
{
   sequence of statements;

} while (test expression);
```

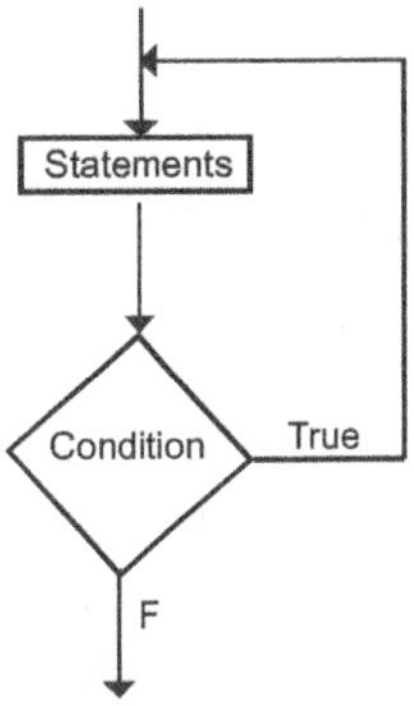

Statements
Condition
True
F

Program 6.6.1

Write a program in C to find the sum of odd numbers that are lying between 1 and 100.

```
# include <stdio.h>
# include <conio.h>
void (main)
{
   int sum, i;
   sum = 0;
   i = 1;
      do
   {
      sum+=i;
      i+=2;
   } while (i<=100);
      printf ("\n sum of odd numbers between 1 and 100 =%d", sum);
   }
```

Here the statements within the braces are executed first and then, the test condition is evaluated. Thus *the statements are executed at least once, in do while loop even if the test expression returns false. This is the fundamental difference between while and do-while construct.*

Program 6.6.2

Write a program to print the entered number in reverse order. Use do-while loop. Also perform Sum and Multiplication with their digits.

```
main ( )
{
int n,d,x=1,mul=1, num=0;
int i;
clrscr ( ) ;
printf("Enter the number of digits :");
scanf("%d", &n);
printf("\n Reversed Number :-");
        do
        {
        i=n%10;
        printf("%d",i);
        sum=sum+i;
        mul=mul*i;
        n=n/10;
        x++;
        } while (x<=d);
printf ("\n Addition of digits : %",sum);
printf("\n Multiplication of digits :%dd", mul);
getche( ) ;
}
```

OUTPUT :

Enter the number of digits : 4
Enter the number which is to be reversed : 4 5 6 8
Reversed Number : 8654
Addition of digits : 23
Multiplication of digits : 960

Explanation : In the above program length of the number and a number are entered. Using repetitive mod operations digits are separated and displayed.

The separated digits are repeatedly added and multiplied with the variable 'sum' and 'nul' respectively. Initially 'sum' is 0 and '\nul' is 1. After termination of loop 'sum' and 'nul' displays addition and multiplication of individual digits of the entered number.

6.7. The DO-WHILE statement WITH WHILE loop :

The syntax for do-while loop with multiple while loops is :

do while (condition)
{
statement/s;
}
while (condition);

Program 6.7.1

Write a program in C to use while statement in do-while loop and print values from 1 to 9.

```
# include <stdio.h>
# include <conio.h>
void main ( )
{
    int x=0;
    clrscr ( );
        do while (x<9)
        {
            x++;
            printf("\t%d",x);
        } while(x<1);
}
```

OUTPUT :

1 2 3 4 5 6 7 8 9

Explanation : The speciality of using the second while loop in the above program is to know that the programme can take second while loop. Though the above program can run with the single while statement.

6.8. JUMPS IN LOOPS :

Care should be taken while getting out of the loop from the middle of a loop. *As far as possible jumping into or jumping out from the middle of the loop should be avoided.*

6.8.1. Jumping Out of a Loop using Break Statement :

An early exit from a loop can be accomplished by using the **break** statement or the **goto** statement. We have already seen the use of the **break** in the **switch** statement and **goto** in the **if ... else** construct. These statements can also be used within **while. do or for** loops.

By using a statement

if (condition)
break;

in the middle of the loop. Control exits from the loop if the given condition is fulfilled. This type of exit from the middle of the loop can be used in **for loop, while loop and do-while loop**. This is explained by the program given below with the use of break statement in C program.

The program reads a list of positive values and calculates their average. The **for** loop is written to read 1000 values. However, if we want the program to calculate the average of any set of values less than 1000, then we must enter a negative number after the last in the list, to mark the end of input.

Each value, when it is read, is tested to see whether it is a positive number or not. If it is positive, the value is added to the **sum;** otherwise, the loop terminates. On exit, the average of the values read is calculated and the results are printed out;

Program 6.8.1

Write a program in C to illustrate use of break in a for loop.

```
/* use of break in a for loop program */
main( )
{
   int m;
   float x, sum, average;
   printf("This program computes the average of a
              set of numbers");
   printf("Enter values one after another\n")
   printf("Enter a NEGATIVE number at the end\n\n");
   sum = 0;
   for (m=1 ; m<=1000 ; ++m)
   {
      scanf(%"d",&x);
      if (x<0)
        break
      sum += x;
   }
```

```
    average =sum/(float)(m-1);
    printf("\n");
    printf("\Number of values = %d\n",m-1);
    printf("Sum              = %f\n",sum);
    prinf("Average           = %f\n",average);
}
```

OUTPUT :

This program computes the average of a set of numbers
Enter values one after another
Enter a NEGATIVE number at the end;

```
15    18    21    24    27    30    -1
Number of values   = 6
Sum                = 135.000000
Average            = 22.500000
```

6.9. JUMPING WITHIN AND EXITING FROM THE LOOPS WITH GOTO STATEMENT :

The format for **jumping from while loop** is given below. This method can also be used for all types of loops like **for, while** and **do while**.

```
while (condition 1)
{
    if (error)
        goto stop;
    if (condition 2)
        goto abc;
        .............
        ............
        abc:
}
    stop:
    ................
    ................
```

Example :

A program to evaluate the series

$$\frac{1}{1-x} = 1 + x + x^2 + x^3 + ... + x^n$$

for -1 < x < 1 to evaluate statement to perform the repeated addition of each of the terms in the series. Since it is an infinite series, the evaluation of the function is terminated when the term x^n reaches the desired accuracy. The value of n that decides the number of loops operations is not known and therefore we have decided arbitrarily a value of 100, which may or may not result in the desired level of accuracy. If the desired accuracy is not achieved within 100 iterations the statement

Program 6.9.1

Write a program in C to illustrate exiting from a loop using goto statement.

```
/* EXAMPLE OF exit WITH goto STATEMENT */
#define    LOOP          100
#define    ACCURACY      0.0001
main( )
{
   int n;
   float x, term, sum;

   printf("\input value of x :");
   scanf("%d%f",&n,&x);

   sum = 0;
   for (term = 1, n=1;n<=LOOP; ++n)
   {
      sum += term;
      if (term <= ACCURACY)
         goto output; /* EXIT FROM THE LOOP */
      term *=x;
   }
      printf("\nFINAL VALUE OF N IS NOT SUFFICIENT\n");
      printf("TO ACHIEVE DESIRED ACCURACY\n");
      goto end;
      output:
      printf("\nEXIT FROM LOOP\n");
      printf("Sum = %f, No. of terms = %d\n", sum, n);
      end:
      ;
   }
```

OUTPUT :

```
input value of x: 0.21
EXIT FROM LOOP
Sum = 1.265800; No. of terms = 7

input value of x : 0.75
```

EXIT FROM LOOP
Sum = 3.999774; No. of terms = 34

input value of x : .99
FINAL VALUE OF N IS NOT SUFFICIENT
TO ACHIEVE DESIRED ACCURACY

Note :

1) break statement is not convenient to use here because both normal exit and break exit will transfer the control to the same statement which appears after the loop. In this problem the normal exit prints this message.

   "FINAL VALUE OF N IS NOT SUFFICIENT
   TO ACHIEVE DESIRED ACCURACY"

2) The use of null statement given by the semicolon at the end is necessary because the program should not end with a label.

6.10. SKIPPING A PART OF A LOOP USING CONTINUE STATEMENT :

During loop operations, it may be necessary to skip a part of the body of a loop under certain conditions. For example, if processing of applications for some job, we might like to exclude he processing data of applicants belonging to a certain category. On reading the category code of an applicant, a test is made to see whether this application should be considered or not. If it is not to be considered, the part of the program loop that processes the application details is skipped by the **continue** statement and the execution continues with the next loop operations.

Continue statements can be used in any type of loop statements and it causes the control to go directly to the test condition skipping the remaining statements and then to continue the iteration process. Continue is the opposite of break statement.

The general format for use of continue statement in **do while** loop is given below.

```
do
{
    ...........
    if ( ........... )
       continue;
       ..............
       .............
} while (test-condition);
```

The general format of **continue** statement inside **for** statement :

```
for (expression 1 ; expression 2; expressein 3)
{
  if condition for something continue;
}
```

Program 6.10.1

Write a program in C++ to explain use of continue statement in for structure

```
//Example program to illustrate "continue" in if else structure
#include <iostream>
using namespace std;
   int main ( )
{
   int i,no,sum=0;
   cout <<"\n enter 10 numbers \n";
   for (i=0;i<10;i++)
   {
      cin>>no;
      if (no < 0)
         continue;
      else
      sum +=no;
   }
   cout <<"\n sum of positive numbers is : "<<sum;
   return 0;
}
```

OUTPUT :

```
enter 9 numbers
1
2
3
4
5
6
-1
7
8
sum of positive numbers is : 21
```

* * *

COMPREHENSION - 6

Note : By answering all the questions given in this comprehension one can answer any objective type of questions easily whatever be the form of the question. Answers for these questions can be obtained by going through the topics in this chapter carefully.

1. What is Decision Statement? What does it do?
2. Give the Syntax of o Decision statement. Explain with an example.
3. What is meant by control statements? How many types of Control Statements are there? Explain their action.
4. What is Control Operator? Give the Syntax and explain the action of a Conditional statement.
5. Give the syntax of Simple if Statement and explain its action.
6. Give the syntax of Block if Statement and explain its action.
7. Give the syntax of Nested if Statement and explain its action.
8. Give the syntax of Simple if- else Statement and explain its action.
9. Give the syntax of Block if- else Statement and explain its action.
10. Give the syntax of Nested ifs or Nested else ifs or if else if Statement and explain its action.
11. Give the syntax of break Statement and explain its action.
12. Give the syntax of continue Statement and explain its action.
13. Give the Syntax of switch or switch case Statement.
14. Explain the action of exit Function.
15. What is meant by Looping?
16. What is infinite loop? How do you avoid infinite loop?
17. What is for loop? Give the Syntax of the popular for loop. What are the parameters of for loop?
18. Can the parameters of for loop be an expression or statement or auto incremented? Explain with statements of for loop with arguments.
19. Give the flow chart of a for loop and explain.
20. Can you enter into the middle of a for loop? State with reason.
21. Can you leave from the middle of a for loop? State with reason.
22. Explain the action of Nested for loops with syntax and example.

23. How many types of while loop are there? Give Syntax.
24. Explain with Syntax the while loop. Also give a flow chart for it and explain.
25. Explain with Syntax the do while loop. Also give a flow chart for it and explain.
26. Explain with Syntax the do while loop with while statement. Also give a flow chart for it and explain.
27. Discuss about jumping in the case of loops.
28. How can you skip a part of a loop. Explain the statements used for the purpose.
29. Differentiate between nested if and switch Statements.
30. What is the difference between continue and break Statements?

* * *

EXERCISE - 6

Note : By answering all the questions given in this exercise one can answer subjective type of questions easily including problems. The worked examples in the chapter may help in solving these questions.

1. (a) Explain the Conditional Operator and Condition Statement with Syntax.

   (b) Write a Condition Statement to write PASS if the marks are 50% and above or FAIL otherwise.

2. Write the Syntax and explain different kinds of Control Statements.

3. Determine whether the following are true or false:

   a) When **if** statements are nested, the **else** gets associated with the nearest **if** without an **else.**

   b) One **if** can have more than one **else** clause.

   c) A **switch** statement can always be replaced by a series of **if.....else** statements.

   d) A **switch** expression can be of any type.

   e) A program stops its execution when a **break** statement is encountered.

4. The following is a segment of a program:

```
x = 1;
y = 1;
if (n > 0)
        x = x +1;
        y = y-1;
        printf(%d",x,y);
```

   What will be the values of x and y if n assumes a value of i) 1 and ii) 0.

5. Find errors, if any, in each of the following segments.

   i)
```
if (x + y = z && y > 0)
        printf(" ");
```

   ii)
```
if (code > 1);
        a = b + c
else
        a = 0
```

   iii)
```
if (p < 0) | (q < 0)
printf ("sign is negative");
```

6. Explain the various forms of **if** construct.

7 How does nested if differ from switch statement?

8 How can a time delay program be written using for loop? Write a program and test.

9. How can you keep track of the number of iterations performed in a numerical solution? How can you stop the loop from going ito an infinite loop/ Write a program and test.

10. Find the output of the following program.

```
a = 3
switch (a)
    {
        case 1:     printf("the value is 1");
                    break;
        case 2:     printf ("the value is 2");
                    break;
        case 3 :    printf ("the vlaue is 3");
        case 4 :    printf ("the value is 4");
    }
```

11. Construct a SINE TABLE showing value of sin of given angles 0 to 90 in steps of 0.01 degree.

12. Assuming i=0 and j=0, what will be the print out from the following statements?

```
if ( i > 0)
if  ( j > 0)
    printf (" i > 0, j > 0 \n");
else
if (i = = 0)
    printf ("i=0  \n");
else
    printf ("i < 0 \n");
```

a) i>0. j> 0 b) i=0 c) i<0 d) None of these

13. The following program will print the message "hello sir" as its output. How many times this message will be printed out.

```
main ()
    {
        int i;
        for (i = 0;  i < 10;  i ++)
        {
            printf ("hellow sir \n");
            i=i-1;
        }
    }
```

14. for (i=0;;i++)
    for (j = 0; ; j++)
        if (j > 100)
        break ;
        printf (" %d %d ",i,j);
        print-out will be

    a) 0 100 b) 0 101 c) 1 100 d) None of these

15. Consider the following program

```
main ( )
    {
        int i=5;
        if (i = 7)
            printf (" the value of i is 7:);
        else
            printf (" the value of i is 5) ;
    }
```

What isll be the output for the above program

a) Compile time error b) The value of i is 7

c) The vlaue of i is 5 d) Run time error

16. The statement which prints out the vlaue 1 to 10 on separate lines, is

    a) for (count=1; count<=10, count=count+1)
       printf("%d\n",count);

    b) for (count=1; count<=10, count=count+1)
       printf("%d\n",count);

    c.) for (count=1; count<=9, count=count+1)
       printf("%d",count);

    d) for (count=1; count<>=10, count=count+1)
       printf("%d\n",count);

17. The statement which sums all values between 10 and 100 into a variable called total is, assuming that total is NOT been initialized to zero.

    a) for (a=10; a<=100; a=a+1)
       total=total+a;

    b) for (a=10; a<100; a=a+1.total,=0)
       total=total+a;

    c) for (a=10; a<100; total=0;a=a+1)
       total=total+a;

    d) for(a=10,total=0; a<=100;a=a+1)
       total = total+a.

18. The statements that tests to see if sum is equal to 10 and total is less than 20, and if so, prints the text string "incorrect", is

    a) if ((sum=10) && (total<20))
    printf("incorrect.");

    b) if ((sum==10) && (total<20))
    printf("incorrect.");

    c) if ((sum==10) | | (total<20))
    printf("incorrect.");

    d) none of the above

19. Write a program to find odd numbers lying between 10 and 100 that are divisible by 5 and test using (a) if (b) while and (c) do . . . .while loop.

20. A set of two linear equations with two unknown x_1 and x_2 is given below :

$$ax_1 + bx_2 = m$$

$$cx_1 + dx_2 = n$$

The set has a unique solution

$$x_1 = \frac{md - bn}{ad - cb} \qquad x_1 = \frac{na - mc}{ad - cb}$$

21. Given a list of marks ranging from 0 to 100, wirte a program to compute and print the number of students.

    i) who have obtained more than 80 marks,
    ii) who have obtained more than 60 marks,
    iii) who have obtained more than 40 marks,
    iv) who have obtained 40 or less marks,
    v) in the range 81 to 100,
    vi) in the range 61 to 80,
    vii) in the range 41 to 60, and
    viii) in the range of 0 to 40

    The program should use a minimum number of **if** statements.

22. Admission to a professional course is subject to the following conditions :

    (i) Marks in mathematics > = 60
    (ii) Marks in physics > = 50
    (iii) Marks in chemistry > = 40
    (iv) Total in all three subjects > = 200

    or

    (v) Total in mathematics and physics > = 150

    Given the marks in the three subjects, write a program to process the applications to list the eligible candidates.

23. Admissions to a professional course is subject to the following conditions.
    a) Marks in mathematics > =60
    b) Marks in physics > = 50
    c) Marks in chemistry > = 40
    d) Total in all three subjects > = 200

    or

    Total in mathematics and physics > = 150

    Given the marks in the three subjects, write a program to process the application to list the eligible candidates.
24. Shown below is a Floyd's triangle

```
1
2 3
4 5 6
7 8 9 10
11 . . . . . . 15
.
.
.
79 . . . . . . . . . . . 91
```

    i) Write a program to print this triangle.
    ii) Modify the program to produce the following form of Floyd's triangle.

```
1
0 1
1 0 1
0 1 0 1
1 0 1 0 1
```

25. A cloth show room has announced the following seasonal discounts on purchase of items:

Purchase amount	Discount	
	Mill cloth	Handloom items
0 - 100	–	5%
101 - 200	5%	7.5%
201 - 300	7.5%	10.0%
Above 300	10.0%	15.0%

Write a program using **switch** and **if** statements to compute the net amount to be paid by a customer.

26. Construct a SINE Table for values of angles 0 to 90 in steps of 10 degrees.
27. Analyze each of the program segments that follows and determine how many times the body of each loop will be executed.

i)
```
x = 5;
y = 50;
while (x <=y)
{
        x=y/x;
        ---------
        ---------
}
```

ii)
```
m = 1;
do
{
        --------
        --------
        m = m+2;
}
while (m < 10);
```

iii)
```
int m = 10;
int n = 7;
while (m % n > =0)
{
---------
m = m + 1;
n = n + 2 ;
---------
}
```

28. Find errors, if any, in each of the following looping segments. Assume that all the variables have been declared and assigned values.

i)
```
while (count !=10);
{
        count = 1;
        sum = sum + x;
        count = count + 1;
}
```

ii)
```
name = 0;
do (name = name + 1;
printf("My name is John\n");}
while (name = 1)
```

iii) do :

```
total = total + value;
scanf(" %f, &value);
while (value !=999);
```

iv)

```
for (x = 1, x > 10; x = x + 1)
{
    ----------
    ----------
    ----------
}
```

v)

```
m = f
n = 0
for (m + n < 19; ++n);
printf("Hello\n");
m = m+10
```

vi)

```
for (p = 10; p > 0;)
p = p - 1;
printf (" %f", p);
```

29. The factorial of an integer m is the product of consecutive integers from 1 to m. That is,

    factorial m = m ! = m x (m – 1) x .... x 1.

    Write a program that computes and prints a table of factorials for any given m.
30. Write a program to compute the sum of the digits of a given integer number.
31. The numbers in the sequence

    1 1 2 3 5 8 13 21 ....

    are called Fibonacci numbers. Write a program using a **do.... while** loop to calculate and print the first m Fibonacci numbers.

    (Hint: After the first two numbers in the series, each number is the sum of the two preceeding numbers).
32. Rewrite the program of the Example 7.1 using the **for** statement.
33. Write a program to evaluate the follwoing investment; equation

    $$V = P(I + r)^n$$

    and print the tables which would give the value of V for various combination of the following values of P, r, and n.

    P : 1000, 2000, 3000, ... 10,000

    r : 0, 10, 0, 11, 0, 12, ... 0.20

    n : 1, 2, 3 10

(Hint : P is the principal amount and V is the value of money at the end of a n years. The equation can be recursively written as

$$V = P(1 + r)$$

$$P = V$$

That is, the value of money at the end of first year becomes the principal amount for the next year and so on.)

34. Write program to print the following outputs using for loops.

i)
```
1
2 2
3 3 3
4 4 4 4
5 5 5 5
```

ii)
```
* * * * *
  * * * *
    * * *
      * *
        *
```

iii)
```
        1
      2   2
    3   3   3
  4   4   4   4
5   5   5   5   5
```

35. Write a program to print a table of values of the function

$$y - \exp(-x)$$

for x varying from 0.0 to 10.0 in steps of 0.10. The table should appear as follows :

Table for Y = EXP (–X)

x	0.1	0.2	0.3	....	0.9
0.0					
1.0					
2.0					
3.0					
*					
*					
*					
9.0					

36. Write a program that will read a positive integer and determine and print its binary equivalent.

(Hint : The bits of the binary representation of an integer can be generated by repeatedly dividing the number and the successive quotients by 2 and saving the remainder, which is either 0 or 1, after each division.)

37. Select the correct answer

```
int   a = 0,      b = 5;
for ( 1 = 0; 1 < 10; 1 - -)
a + =b;
```

a) Value of a will be 45 after coming out of for loop.
b) Value of a will be 50 after coming out of for loop.
c) Value of a will be 55 after coming out of for loop.
d) for loop will never terminate.

38. The statement which reproduces the following output, is

1
22
333
4444
55555

a)
```
a = 1
while ( a < = 5)
  {
     while (b < = a)
     {
        printf ("% d \n",a);
        b = b + 1;
     }
        a=a+1;
```

b)
```
a = 1;
while (a < =5)
{ b = 1;
   while ( b < = a)
   {
      printf ("%d", a);
      b = b + 1;
}
      printf ("\n");
      a = a + 1;
```

c)
```
a = 1
while (a < =5)
 {
 printf ("%", a);
 b = b + 1;
}
     a=a+1;
     printf ("\n");
}
```

d)
```
a = 1;
while (a < = 5)
     printf ("\n");
     {
     while (a <=b)
       printf ("%d", a);
       b = b+1;
     }
       a=a+1;
     }
```

```
{    int i;
     for (i = 0;  1 <10;  i++)
     { printf ("Welcome \n"} ; i = i-1;  }
}
```

which of the following statements is TRUE about the above program

a) will not compile properly
b) will print-out "welcome' 5 times
c) will print-out 'welcome' 10 times
d) will loop indefinitely

39. What is the value of variable "l' prior to termination in the following program segment

```
main ()
    (   int i = 1/2/3;
        int j, k, l = 0;
        for (j = 0; k = 0; j < i; j++
        ++ k;
        l=k;
        printf ("%d", l);
    }
```

a) divide by 0 error occurs b) 1 c) 0 d) 2

40. Consider the following program

```
main ()
    unsigned int a;
    a = -8;
    if (a > 0)
        printf ("positive");
    else
        printf ("negative");
    }
```

The output will be

a) Prints "negative" b) prints "positive"

c) prints NULL d) Error in the program

* * *

CHAPTER - 7
ARRAYS

7.1 INTRODUCTION :

Normally variables can store only one value at a time and it is possible to store a new value only after erasing the previous one. But in real life situations, while computing, we would like to store more than one value at a time for the same variable, and this could be achieved through ARRAYS.

An array is a collection of variables of same data type that are referenced by a common name. Consider the classroom example in which we want to have 10 values for the variable 'english'. Here the marks obtained by the 10 students are different but since all of them come under the variable 'english', our declaration takes the form as

int english (10);

On encountering the above statement, the system will allocate 10 memory locations for the identifier 'english' and the orientation may be as follows :

In C and C++ the index starts from 0 and goes upto 9.

Since the origin starts from 0 we can also call this as **'Zero origin subscripting'.**

While the complete collections or **set of variables is called an array, the individual values are called elements.** A specific value in an array is the value of the array variable for the said array index or subscript.

Arrays may have one to several dimensions. We shall discuss in detail, how arrays are used in C and C++.

7.2. ONE DIMENSIONAL ARRAY :

This is also called as "List". This means that just giving one subscript can access an item in an array. The general form of a single-dimension array is,

type specifier identifier-name [size];

e.g. int a[5];

We are declaring an integer array having 5 elements, a[0] thro' a[4], as explained below

A[0]	A[1]	A[2]	A[3]	A[4]

Several examples indicating the one- dimensional array declaration are given below :

i. **int age[10]** : declares the age as an array to contain maximum of 10 integer constants.

ii. **float marks[20]** : declares the marks as an array containing a maximum of 20 real elements.

iii. **char name[30] :** declares the name as a character array [string]; the size in a character string (here it is 30) represents the maximum number of characters it can hold. Each character of the string is treated as an elements of the array name.

7.2.1. Single dimensional Array initialisation :

C and C++ permit the initialisation of global and static local arrays at the time of declaration itself. The general form of array initiation is,

type-specifier array-name[size]=[value list];

The value list is a comma-separated list of constants whose type is compatible with type specifier.

(e.g)

i. int i[5] = {1,2,3,4,5};
ii. float a[5] = { 1,1,2,3,5,5,6,7,7,0};
iii. int b[ ] = { 1,1,2,2 };

In the third example the size has been omitted (it can be!) and have been declared as an array with 4 elements having 1,1,2 and 2 as initial values.

iv. float sum[5] = {2.2, 3.3, 4.4};

Here the first three elements are initialized to the respective values given and the remaining two elements will set to zero automatically. That is, *if the numbers of values in the list are less than the size, then that many elements corresponding to value list only will be initialised, and the remaining elements will be set to zero automatically.*

Character arrays that hold strings allow a shortcut initialisation of the form :

char array-name[size]="string"

For example :

char messg[8]= {'w','e','i','c','o','m','e', '\0'};

The last character '\0' called NULL character indicates end of the array elements and is a must if the char is declared element by element. If the char elements are declared within double quotes then the null character is not necessary or not to be given at the end.

It may be noticed that in C and C++ array initialisation becomes difficult with larger array sites, as all the array elements have to be initialised, without exemption. Further there is no easy or convenient way to initialize only selected elements. To know about number of elements in an array, the sizeof() operator is used. For example an array 'xxx' will have declaration like this :

int xxx={56,78,44,23,765};

Now,

int no=sizeof(xxx)/sizeof(xxx[0]);

Since, the array 'xxx' is having 5 elements and each one occupying 2 bytes resulting 10 bytes to hold the entire array. Where it is divided by the **sizeof** int, we will get 5 to the variable no i.e., (10 bytes / 2 bytes = 5)

Let us see what we have discussed thro' examples :

Program 7.2.1 :

Write a program in C to add even and odd numbers from 1 to 10. Store them and display their results in two separate arrays.

```
# include <stdio.h>
# include <conio.h>
    void main ( )
{
int oddsum=0, evensum=0, i=0, odd [5], even [5], a=-1 b=-1;
clrscr ( );
    for (i=1;i<=10;i++)
    {
    if (i%2==0)      /*mod division by 2 gives remainder 1 if number is odd*/
    even [++a]=i;
    else
    odd [++b]=i;
    }
printf ("\n\tEven \t\tOdd");
    for (i=0;i<5;i++)
    {
    printf ("\n\t %d\t\t %d",even[i],odd[i]);
    evensum=evensum+even[i];
    oddsum=oddsum+odd[i]);
    }
printf ("\n\t=================== \n");
printf ("sum: %d %14d", evensum,oddsum);
}
```

OUTPUT :

```
            Even    Odd
             2       1
             4       3
             6       5
             8       7
            10       9
         =================
Sum :       30      25
         =================
```

Explanation : i modulo 2 (i %2) gives the reminder of i divided by 2 and if the reminder is 0 then i is even and is allotted to even array. If the reminder is not zero i is odd and is allotted to odd array. The for loop executes 10 times. The index of the odd and even arrays vary from 0 to 4 each.

Program 7.2.2 :

Write a program in C++ to find the maximum number in an array.

Solution :

```
//Example program to find maximum number in an array
#include <iostream>
using namespace std;
int main ()
    {
    int a[5],i,max;
    cout <<"enter 5 numbers one by one in";
    for(i=0;i<5;i++)
        cin >>a[i];
        max=a[0];
        for(i=1;i<5;i++)
            if(max < a[i]) max = a[i];
        cout <<"\n the maximum no in the array is "<<max;
        return 0;
    }
```

OUTPUT :

The output for the above program looks like this :
enter 5 numbers one by one
2
8
6
9
3
the maximum no in the array is 9

Explanation :

First we get 5 elements and store them in an array name a. The first value in the array i.e. a [0] the element is assumed as the maximum number and it is stored in an identifier max. This number is then compared with a [1] the element (number) array. If the number is found to be greater than the number stores in max, then max is reinitialised with this number. This process is repeated for the remaining elements of the array, until the identifier **max** holds the maximum number in the array.

Another good example for one-dimensional array is SORTING. Sorting is a process to arrange a list of quantities in the required manner. For example if we want to arrange 10 marks in an ascending order then we need sorting algorithm. At present many algorithms are available for sorting purposes and the popular ones are Quick Sort, Bubble Sort, Selection Sort, Insertion Sort, Merge Sort, etc.,

Initially we must understand swapping or how values can be exchanged between two variables. For example, if

m = 5 and n = 7
and if we want our output as,
m = 7 and n = 5

Let us use a temporary variable called 't', and then following will be the line of coding to change the values between the two said variables

```
t = m
m = n
n = t
```

The first line of coding will assign the value of n=5 to the temporary location 't'. The second line of coding will assign the value of n=7 to m after erasing the previous value of 'm' i.e. 5. The third line of coding will assign the temporary value (t=5) to 'n' after erasing the previous value of 'n' i.e. 7. The result will be m=7 and n=5. Thus, we interchange the values between the variables.

Let us arrange the given 5 numbers in ascending order by using the popular 'Bubble sort' method which is one of the popular sorting methods.

Program : 7.2.3

Write a program in C to sort numbers in ascending order using bubble sort method.

```
/* Example program to sort numbers*/
# include <stdio.h>
# include <conio.h>
```

```
void main ( )
{
      int a [5], i, j, t ;
      printf ("Enter 5 numbers one by one \n");
      for (i=0; i<5; i++)
      scanf (" %d", &a [i] );
      for (i = 0; i< 4; i++)
      for (j = i+1; j<5; j++)
      if (a [i] > a [j] )
      {
            t = a [i];
            a [i] = a [j];
            a [j] = t;
      }
      printf ("\n The sorted numbers are : \n");
      for (i = 0; i < 5; i++)
      printedf (" %d \n",a [i] );
}
```

OUTPUT :

```
Enter 5 numbers one by one

10
102
09
24
12
The sorted numbers are :
09
10
12
24
102
```

Explanation :

For the input numbers given above viz., 10, 102, 9, 24, 12, the given program does the task of arranging these elements in the ascending order, to get the output as

9 10 12 24 102

The **'for'** and **'if'** statements (in the program) does the job of sorting i.e., the first number is compared with the immediate second number. The number that has the lower value then occupies the first place and the second number is the compared with third number. This process of sorting is done until the ascending list is completed. The pictorial representation of this swapping and sorting is shown below :

The initial values are :

a[0]	a[1]	a[2]	a[3]	a[4]
10	102	9	24	12

First pass

i=0, j=1

10	102	9	24	12

i=0,j=2

10	102	9	24	12

i=0,j=3

9	102	10	24	12

i=0,j=4

9	102	10	24	12

i=1,j=2

9	102	10	24	12

i=1,j=3

9	10	102	24	12

i=1,j=4

9	10	102	24	12

i=2,j=3

9	10	102	24	12

i=2,j=4

9	10	24	102	12

i=3,j=4

9	10	12	102	24

Final output

9	10	12	24	102

7.3. TWO-DIMENSIONAL ARRAY :

A two dimensional array in fact, is an array of one-dimensional arrays. A single dimensional array can store a list of values; where as a two-dimensional array can store a table of values. *The general format is*

type-specifier array-name [row-size][column-size];

In two-dimensional array also, element declaration (both in row and column) is done with 'zero origin subscripting".

Thus an array, int a [3][3] will have element as :

a[0][0] a[0}[1] a[0][2]
a[1][0] a[1][1] a[1][2]
a[2][0] a[2][1] a[2][2]

In the light of the above, we can state that **a two-dimensional array is a 'table', as they store a table of values.**

7.3.1. Initialization of Two-dimensional arrays :

Similar, to one-dimensional arrays two-dimensional arrays can also be initialised by following their declaration with a list of initial values enclosed in braces.

e.g int a[2][3] = {1,1,1,2,2,2};

Here, the first row elements are initialised to 1 and second row to 2. The initialisation is done row by row. This can also be written as,

int a[2][3] = {1,1,1},{2,2,2]

In the syntax, it would be noted that commas are required after each brace that closes off a row except for the last row.

The elements of a two dimensional array are given row wise and each row of elements are given within braces and with a comma between braces of two rows of elements.

Now let us consider the following programming example, which illustrates all the fundamental array manipulations.

Program 7.3.1 :

Write a program in C using two-dimensional array to compute and print the following information for sales in a shop which is given in a table below to find a) Total value of sales by each girl, b) Total value of each item stored, c) Grand total of sales of all item by all girls.

Rows : Sales girl No. i = \ Columns : Item No. j =	0	1	2
0	275	310	365
1	210	325	190
2	340	405	235
3	300	380	260

The formula used for calculations of the above items are given below.

i) Total sales by ith girl for total (j= 0 to 2) items = $\sum_{j=0}^{2} value\,[i]\,[j]$

ii) Total value for jth item sold by (i=0 to 3) sales girls = $\sum_{i=0}^{3} value\,[i]\,[j]$

iii) Grand total sales by (i= 0 to 3) sales girls over items j= (0 to **2**) =

$$\sum_{i=0}^{3} \sum_{j=0}^{2} value\,[i]\,[j]$$

Program 7.3.2

/* Program part showing sales by 4 sales girls for 3 items */

```
#define MAXGIRLS 4
#define MAXITEMS 3
main( )

{
        int    value[MAXGIRLS][MAX ITEMS];
        int    girl_total[MAXGIRLS],item_total[MAXITEMS];
        int    i, j, grand_total;
/*  ......... READING OF VALUES AND COMPUTING girl_total .....*/
        printf("input data\n");
        printf("Enter values, one at a time, row-wise\n\n");
        for (i =0; j < MAXGIRLS ; i++)
          {
          girl_total[i]=0;
          for(j = 0;) < MAXITEMS ; j++)
              {
              scanf("%d",&value[i] [j]);
              girl_total[i] = girl_total[i] + value[i][j];
              }
          }
/*      ............................ COMPUTING item_total ........................ */
        for (j = 0; j < MAXITEMS : j++)
          {
              item_total[j]=0;
              for (i = 0; i < MAXGIRLS; i++)
                    item_total[j] = item_total[j]+value[i][j];
          }
```

```
/*      ......................... COMPUTING grand_total ..................... */
        grand_total=0;
        for (i=0;) < MAXGIRLS; i++)
          grand_total=grand_total+girl_total[i];
/*      ..................... PRINTING OF RESULTS ........................... */
        printf("\n GIRLS TOTALS\n\n");

        for (i=0; i<MAXGIRLS ; i++)
          printf("Salesgirl[%d]=%d\n",i+1,girl_total[i]);
          printf("\n Grand_Total is GIRLS TOTALS=%d\n\n",grand_total);
        printf("\n ITEM TOTALS\n\n");
        for (j=0 ; j < MAXITEMS ; j++)
          printf("\item[%d]=%d\n",j+1,item_total[j]);
          printf("\n c=%d\n\n",grand_total);
          prinf("\n Grand Total is Rs. %d\n", grand_total);
}
```

OUTPUT :

```
input data
Enter values, one at a time, row_value
275     310     365
210     325     190
340     405     235
300     380     260
GIRLS TOTALS
Salesgirl[1] =  950
Salesgirl[2] =  725
Salesgirl[3] =  980
Salesgirl[4] =  940
Grand_Total is GIRLS TOTALS = 3595
ITEM TOTALS
item[1] = 1125
item[2] = 1420
item[3] = 1050
Grand_Total is GIRLS TOTALS = 3495
Grand Total is Rs.3495
```

Program 7.3.3

Write a program in C++ to find the following for a two dimensional array of 4 x 4.

1. Sum all the elements
2. Row wise sum

3. Column wise sum
4. Sum of main diagonal elements
5. Sum of off diagonal elements

```
//Example program for array handling
#include <iostream>
using namespace std;
int main()
{
    int a(10)(10),i,j,sum,n1,n,rowsum,colsum,diasum;
    printf("Enter Order [row][col] of matrix \n");
    cin >>n>>n1;
        cout <<"enter "<<n1*n<<" elements \n";
            for(i=0;j<n;i++)
                for(j=0;j<n1;j++)
                    cin >>a[i][j];
//Program module to sum all elements
    sum=0;
        for(i=0;j<n;i++)
            for(j=0;j<n1;j++)
                sum *= a[i] [j];
    cout <<"sum of all elements "<<sum<<"\n";;

//Program module to sum row wise
    for(i=0;i<n,i++)
    {
        rowsum=0;
            for(j=0;j<n1;i++)
                rowsum += a[i] [j];
        cout <<"row no = "<<i<<" sum = "<<rowsum<<"\n";
    }
    //Program module to sum columnwise
    for (i=0;i<n;i++)
    {
        colsum=0;
        for(j=0;j<n;j++)
        colsum += a[j][i];
        cout<<"col no = "<<j<<" sum = "<<colsum<<"\n";
    }
```

```
// Program module to sum principal diagonal
    diasum=0;

    for (i=0;j<n;i++)
        for(j=0;j<n1;j++)
            if(i==j) diasum += a[i][j];
            cout<<"principal diagonal "<<diasum<<"\n;
// Program module to sum off diagonal
    diasum=0;
    for (i=0;j<n;j++)
    {
        j=--n1;
        diasum += a[i] [j]
    }
    cout <<"off diagonal sum "<<diasum<<"\n";
    return 0;
}
```

OUTPUT :

```
Enter Order [row][col] of matrix
3 3
enter 9 elements
11
22
33
44
55
66
77
88
99
sum of all elements 495
row no = 0 sum = 66
row no = 1 sum = 165
row no = 2 sum = 264
col no  = 0 sum = 132
col no  = 1 sum  = 165
col no  = 2 sum  = 198
principal diagonal sum 165
off diagonal sum 330
```

Explanation

The algorithmic approach is given below;

1. Read the order of Matrix
2. Read the elements row wise
3. Initialise sum as 0
4. Repeat step 5 until i>n and j>n
5. sum=sum+a[i][i];
6. Print sum
7. Repeat step 8 to step 11 until i>n
8. Initialise rowsum=0
9. Repeat step 10 to step 11 until i>n
10. rowsum=rowsum+a[i][j]
11. print rowsum
12. Repeat step 13 to step 16 until i>n1
13. Initialise colsum as 0
14. Repeat step 15 until j>n
15. colsum =colsum+a[j][i]
16. print colsum
17. Initialise diasum as 0
18. Repeat step 19 until i>n and j>n]
19. if i=j then diasum =diasum+a[i][j]
20. print diasum
21. Initialise diasum as 0
22. Repeat step 23 until i>n
23. decrement n1 by 1 store it in j
    diasum=diasum+a[i][j]
24. print diasum

7.3.2. Two-dimensional sorting :

Similar, to the case of single dimensional sorting we can also have 2-dimensional sorting. Let us get more used to this technique through the practical example explained below:

Program 7.3.4

Write a C program for row-wise sorting of a square matrix

```
/* Program for rowwise sort for a square matrix */

# include <stdio.h>
# include <conio.h>
void main()
{
    int a[10][10],i,j,k,order,temp;
```

```
printf ("\n enter order of the matrix \n")
scanf ("%d", &order);
printf ("enter %d elements \n",order * order) ;
for(i=0;i<order;i++)
      for(i=0;j<order;j++)
      scanf ("%d", &a [i] [j] );
      printf ("the given matrix is \n");
      for (i=0;j<order;i++)
            {
                  for(j=0;j<order;j++)
                  printf ("%5d", a [i] [j] );
                  printf ("\n");
            }
      /* Sorting the numbers rowwise */
      for(i=0;i<order,i++)
            for(j=0;j<order-1;j++)
                  for(k=j+1;k<order;k++)
                  if(a[i][j]>a[i][k])
                  {
                        temp=a[i][j];
                        a[i][j]=a[i][k];
                        a[i][k]=temp;
                  }
      printf (" sorted matrix is \n");
      for(i=0;i<order;i++)
            {
                  for(j=0;j<order;j++)
                  printf ("%5d", a [i] [j] );
                  prinf ("\n");
            }
      }
```

The output for the above program looks like this :

OUTPUT :

```
enter order of the matrix
3
enter 9 elements
6
4
3
1
5
8
```

9
7
2
the given matrix is

6	4	3
1	5	8
9	7	2

sorted matrix is

1	2	3
4	5	6
7	8	9

Explanation :

The steps followed to sort two-dimensional square matrix in row wise as follows :

1. Read the order of matrix (order)
2. Read the elements of the matrix
3. Print the given matrix
4. Repeat step 5 to step 7 varying i from 1 to order
5. Repeat step 6 to step 7 varying j from 1 to order-1
6. Repeat step 7 varying k from j+1 to order
7. If a[i][j]>a[i][k]then interchange a[i][j],a[i][k]
8. Print the rowwise sorted matrix A.

7.4. MULTIDIMENSIONAL ARRAYS :

Like other languages C and C++ allow more than two dimensions. The compiler under use determines the exact limit. The general form of a multidimensional array is

type-specifier array-name[a][b]......[k];

Arrays of three or more dimensions are used, depending upon the situation, and also these arrays occupy more amount of memory space.

In the following program we consider a case where there are two semesters, sem1 and sem 2. Sem1 has got four subjects and sem2 has got four subjects. The mark of each subject in a semester is the sum of the three test results, i.e., each subject (in a semester) will have three tests for consideration. This is a suitable case for a three dimensional array.

With 2 semesters,

4 subjects / semester

And Three tests / subjects.

If represented as a mark array it will be as mark [2][4][3]

Program 7.4.1 :

Write a program in C for entering marks for three tests each in different papers 1 to 4 for semester 1 and semester 2 and find the total marks in each semester using multi-dimensional array.

```
/* Example program for three dimensional array */
#include <stdio.h>
#include <conio.h>
void main()
{
    int mark[2][4][3],i,j,k;
    int totalmark,semsum,papersum;

    for (i=0;i<2;i++)
    {
            printf ("for the %d semester \n", i+1);
            for(j=0;j<4;j++)
            {
                printf ("enter 3 marks for paper %d \n", j+1);
                for(k=0;k<3;k++)
                scanf ("%d", &mark [i] [j] [k] );
            }
    }
            totalmark=0;
for (i=0;i<2;i++)
    {
        semsum=0;
        printf ("\n semester %d \n", i+1);
        printf ("paper marks \n");
        for(j=0;j<4;j++)
            {
                papersum = 0;
                for(k=0;k<3;k++)
                papersum += mark[i][j][k];
                printf ("%d  %d  \n", j+1,papersum);
                semsum += papersum;
            }
```

```
                printf ("total makrs in %d semester = %d
                        \n", i+1, semsum);
                total mark +=semsum;
        }
    printf ("\n grand total = ",totalmark);
    }
```

OUTPUT :

```
for the 1 semester
enter 3 marks for paper 1
54
65
76
enter 3 marks for paper 2
77
68
89
enter 3 marks for paper 3
63
74
56
enter 3 marks for paper 4
60
73
85
for the 2 semester
enter 3 marks for paper 1
61
71
82
enter 3 marks for paper 2
73
69
62
enter 3 marks for paper 3
66
67
73
```

```
enter 3 marks for paper 4
92
88
77
semester 1
paper   marks
1       195
2       234
3       193
4       218
total marks in 1 semester = 840
semester 2
paper   marks
1       214
2       204
3       206
4       257
total marks in 2 semester = 881
grand total = 1721
```

* * *

COMPREHENSION - 7

Note : **By answering all the questions given in this comprehension one can answer any objective type of questions easily whatever be the form of the question. Answers for these questions can be obtained by going through the topics in this chapter carefully.**

1. What is an Array? In what way is it different from a Variable?
2. How is an array stored in memory if it is a single dimensional array and if it is a multi dimensional array?
3. How is an array declared in a program? How is an array element referred to? How is an array element retrieved from memory?
4. How is the starting address of an array got if it is a single dimensional array and if it is a multi dimensional array?
5. Give the syntax and examples of Array declarations for different data types for single and multi dimensional arrays.
6. Show the representation of array elements pictorially for single and multi dimensional arrays.
7. Can the array index be zero?
8. If the number of elements initialized in an array is less than the size of the array what happens?
9. Give examples of one dimensional and multi dimensional arrays.
10. What are the different methods of initializing an array? Can an array be used without initializing the array? If done so what happens?
11. Can the array index or subscript be a variable? Can it be an expression?
12. Write a C Program to initialize an array.
13. Explain the need for Array Variables.
14. Write a for loop to total the contents of the multidimensional float array balances.

    i)
    ```
    for (row=0,total=0;row<3;row++)
    for(column=0),total=0;column<column++)
    total=total + balances[row][column];
    ```
    ii)
    ```
    for(row=0,total=0;row<3;row++)
    for(column=0;column<5;column++)
    total = total + balances[row][column];
    ```
    iii)
    ```
    for (row=0,total=0;row<3;row++)
    for (column=0;column<row;column++)
    total = total + balances[row][column];
    ```
    iv) None of the above

15. Identify errors, if any, in each of the following array declaration statements.
    a) int score (100);
    b) float values [10,15];
    c) float average[ROW],[COLUMN];
    d) char name[15];
    e) int sum[ ];
16. Identify errors, if any, in each of the following initialization statements.
    a) static int number[ ] = (0,0,0,0,0);
    b) static float item[3][2] = {0,1,2,3,4,5};
    c) static char word [ ] = ('A','R', 'R','A','Y');
    d) static int m[2,4] = {(0,0,0,0)(1,1,1,1)};
    e) static float result[10] = 0;
17. Assume that the arrays a and B are declared as follows:

    int A[5][4];

    float B [4]

    Find the errors (if any) in the following program segments.

    (a)
    ```
    for (i=1; i<=5; i++)
            for(j=1; j<=4; i++)
                    A[i][j] = 0;
    ```
    (b)
    ```
    for (i=1; i<4; i++)
            scanf("%f" , B[i]);
    ```
    (c)
    ```
    for (i=0; i<=4; i++)
            B[i] = B[i]+i;
    ```
    (d)
    ```
    for (i=4; j>=0; 4; j--)
            for (j=0; j < 4; j ++)
                    A[i][j] = B[j] + 1 0;
    ```
18. Write C Statements to initialize the diagonal elements as 1.0 and the non diagonal elements as zeros for a Square Matrix.
19. Write a small C Program to find the sum of all the elements of a matrix.
20. For the above program should the variable used for sum be initialized? If it is to be initialized to what value should it be initialized? In which part of the program should the initialization be done?

* * *

EXERCISE - 7

Note : By answering all the questions given in this exercise one can answer subjective type of questions easily including problems. The worked examples in the chapter may help in solving these questions.

1. (a) What is the need for an Array? In what way does it differ from an ordinary variable?
   (b) Declare and initialize a single, two and three dimensional arrays.
   (c) Write a C Program to find the sum of all the elements of a two dimensional matrix.
2. (a) Write a C Program to find the transpose of a 3 x 3 matrix.
   (b) If A and B are two 3 x 3 matrices write a C Program find the matrix C = A + B
   (c) If A and B are two 3 x 3 matrices write a C Program find the matrix C = A * B
3. If A is a 3 x 3 float matrix write a program in C to find the
   i. The sum of all the elements of the matrix
   ii. The sum of all the row-wise elements of the matrix.
   iii. The sum of all the column wise elements of the matrix.
   iv The sum of all the diagonal elements of the matrix.
   v The sum of all the non- diagonal elements of the matrix.
4. There are 10 students in a section. Each student has to take 3 Elective subjects. Write a C Program to enter their marks in each Elective subject, the total marks and the average marks obtained by each student, the total and average marks obtained by all the students of the section in each subject, and the overall average for the section in all the elective subjects put together.
5. The following set of numbers is popularly known as Pascal's triangle.

```
1
1   1
1   2   1
1   3   3   1
1   4   6   4   1
1   5   10  10  5   1
*   *   *   *   *   *   *
*   *   *   *   *   *   *
```

6. An election is contested by 5 candidates. The candidates are numbered 1 to 5 and and the voting is done by marking the candidate number on the ballot paper. Write a program to read the ballots and count the vote cast for each candidate using an array variable count. In case, a number read is outside the range 1 to 5, the ballot should be considered a 'spoilt ballot' and the program should also count the number of spoilt ballots.
7. Given two one-dimensional arrays A and B which are sorted in ascending order, write a program to merge them into a single sortd array C that contains every item for arrays A and B in ascending order.
8. Write a program for fitting a straight line through a set of points (x_i, y_i), i = 1, ..., n. The straight line equation is

   and the values on m and c are given by

$$m = \frac{n\Sigma(x_i y_i) - (\Sigma x_i)(\Sigma y_i)}{n(\Sigma x_i^2) - (\Sigma x_i)^2}$$

$$c = \frac{1}{n}(\Sigma y_i - m\Sigma x_i)$$

   All summations are from i = 1 to n.
9. Fibonacci series is 0, 1, 1, 2, 3, 5, ... following the rule.

   x (n+1)=x (n) + x (n-1).

   Write a program in C to give 10 terms of Fibonacci series.
10. Assume that there are two lists A containing M items and B containing N items, M and N not necessarily being equal. Write a Program to merge the two lists into a single list C containing all the elements of both the lists. (list B after list A)

* * *

CHAPTER - 8
FUNCTIONS

8.1 INTRODUCTION :

The C language and also the C++ language are rich in functions and they depend on functions. The C or C++ programs are nothing but combination of one or more functions. Every program starts with user defined function **main ( ).** Each time when a new program is started, **main ( )** function must be defined. The main ( ) function may call other functions to share the work.

The C and C++ languages support two types of functions **1) Library functions 2) User defined functions.** *The Library functions are pre-defined set of functions.* Their task is limited. A user can not understand the internal working of these functions. The user can only use the functions but can't change or modify them. For example **sqrt (81)** gives result **9.** Here, the user need not worry about its source code, but the result will be provided by the function when it is invoked.

The User defined functions are totally different. *The functions defined by the user according to his/her requirement are called as User-defined functions.* The user can modify the function according to the requirement. The user certainly understand the internal working of the function because it is formed by the user. The user has full scope to implement his/her own ideas in the function. Thus the sets of such user-defined functions can be useful to another programmer. One should include the file in which the user-defined functions are stored in the called functions of the program. Example, let **square (9)** is a user-defined function, that gives the result **81.** Here the user knows the internal working of the **square** ( ) function, as its source code is visible. *The major difference between the two types of function is that the user can modify the user defined function.*

It has been mentioned earlier that one of the main strong factors of C and C++ is the use of user-defined function. The C and C++ functions are not only very easy to use but are also very versatile. The usage of several functions like sin ( ) and log ( ) are already discussed. These are called 'library' functions. *The library functions are not required to be developed and written by the user, but a user defined function has to be developed and written by the user.*

These user defined functions can also at a later stage become a part of C or C++ program library.

In this chapter, we shall discuss how a C or C++ functions is defined, designed and how to use them on different occasions.

What is a C or C++ function :

A Function in C or C++ is considered as a fundamental building block of the language. In order to avoid the complexity of a program while coding, debugging and testing, the program is divided into functional parts or subprograms. Thus, each module is considered as a function and functions do everything in C or C++.

The syntax or general form of a C or C++ function is

type-specifier function-name (argument declaration)

```
{
        body of the function (statements);
        return (expression);
}
```

The function 'type-specifier' specifies the type of value (or) data type that the 'return' statement of the function returns. **In C, when the type-specifier is not specified then the function returns integer value by default. In C++, there is no such default to int. Hence it must be explicitly mentioned in the function header.**

(e.g)

(i) int i, marks ( );
here the function marks ( ) returns integer value

(ii) float a,b,sum( );
here the function sum ( ) returns the float value.

The argument is a comma-separated list of variable names that receive the values, when the function is called. Even if there are no arguments, the parentheses are still required in order to differentiate the function from variable.

8.2. THE RETURN STATEMENT :

This statement (i) causes an immediate exit from the function and (ii) to return the value.

The form of return statement can be
return (expression);

The 'simple' **return** statement with no follow up does not return any value and it acts as the closing brace of the function. When it is encountered, the control is immediately passed back to the calling function. **When the function is declared as a void function then there is no need to include a return statement.** This is valid for both C and C++.

Example of void functions :

Program 8.2.1

Write a program in C to define user-defined void function. Call them at different places.

```
/*  example for void function */
# include <stdio.h>
# include <conio.h>
void y ( ) ;                          /* global void functions */
void y ( )
{
printf ("y");
}
void main ( )
{
void  a( ),b( ),c( ),d( );            /* local void functions */
clrscr ( ) ;
      y( ) ;                          /* calling function */
      a( ) ;
      b( ) ;
      c( ) ;
      d( ) ;
}
void a ( )                            /* called function */
{
printf ("A") ;
y ( );
}
void b ( )
{
      printf ("B");
      a ( );
}
void c ( )
{
      a ( ) ;
      b ( ) ;
        printf ("C");
}

void d ( )
{
printf ("D");
c ( ) ;
b ( ) ;
a ( ) ;
}
```

OUTPUT :

Y A Y B A Y A Y B A Y C D A Y B A Y C B A Y A Y

Explanation : From the above program we understand the following :

1) The **main** ( ) function can call any other function defined before or after **main** ( ) function.

2) Any other user defined function can call the **main** ( ) function.

3) The user-defined function can call only those user-defined functions which are defined before and can not call functions defined after that user defined function. Functions c ( ) and d ( ) cannot be called by void (a) and void (b) functions. The function d ( ) can call all the functions because it is the last function and all other functions are defined earlier than function d ( ).

Program 8.2.2

Write a program in C++ using return (expression) to print whether a number is bigger or smaller compared to another number using user-defined void function.

```
//Example for void function
# include <iostream>
using namespace std;
int main ( )
{
      int a,b;
      void small(int,int);
      cout<<"enter 2 numbers \n";
      cin >>a>>b;
      small(a,b);
      return 0;
}
void small (int x,int y)
{
      if(x<y)
            cout<<"a is less than b";
      else
            cout <<"b is less than a";
}
```

OUTPUT :

enter 2 numbers
32 24
b is less than a

Note : In the preceeding the function small is declared as void in the function main ( ) itself. In C there is no need to declare the functions returning int or void in the main ( ). **C++ is a strongly typed language and all the functions calling from main ( ) should be declared in main ( ) itself.**

Here the values of 'x' and 'y' are compared; if 'x' is found to be less than 'y', then after printing the message "a is less than b "the control returns to main ( ). If 'y' is found to be less than 'x', after printing the message "b is less than a" control is transferred to main ().

8.2.1. Function with a return statement to return an expression :

This returns the value of the expression.

Program 8.2.3

Write a program in C to illustrate the use of return of an expression.

```
main ( )
{
        int x=6,y=3, z ;
        z=add (x,y) ;                   /*function call*/
        printf ("sum z = %d",z) ;
}
/*   FUNCTION DEFINITION  */
add (a,b)                               /* function name */
{
return (a+b);
}
```

OUTPUT :

sum z = 9

Program 8.2.4

Write a program in C++ to illustrate the use of return of an expression.

```
    //Example to illustrate the uses of return( )
    #include <iostream>
    #include <cmath>
    using namespace std;
    int main( )
    {
          float x,y,cuberoot(float);
          cout<<"enter number to find cube root \n";
          cin >>x;
          y=cuberoot(x);
          cout <<"the cuberoot of the given number is "<<y,
          return 0;
    }
```

```
        float cuberoot(float a)
    {
        return(exp(1.0/3.0*log(a)));
    }
```

OUTPUT :

enter number to find cube root
125
the cuberoot of the given number is 5

Here return statement returns cuberoot for the given value of x. We are using functions such as log(), and exp() and these two functions are present in the header file "cmath". So, it is necessary for us to include a file "cmath" before main (). The detailed discussion of these file inclusions will be dealt in subsequent chapters. In C the function cuberoot() may also written in the following fashion;

```
float a;
float cuberoot (a)
{
    retunr(exp(1.0/3.0*log(a)));
}
```

In the first line the data type for the variable 'a' is given. The function declaration, along with the function name with only one argument is given in the next line. This method of function definition is obsolete in C++ and hence this way of function definition should be avoided in C++.

8.3. CALLING A FUNCTION AND OBTAINING ITS RESULT :

a) Calling a function :

Both in C and C++, we can call a function in three ways

i. **Call by value**
ii. **Call by reference**
iii. **Call by pointer**

The first two types are discussed here and third one will be discussed after getting some knowledge on pointers. The first method is also called as calling by value of parameter and the next two methods are called as calling by variable parameter respectively.

b) Obtaining the results of a called function :

We can invoke the function in three ways. i) we can place it as the part of an expression. ii) by including the function in cout, iii) giving the output of the called function in the function itself after executing it without passing it on to anywhere or without storing it .

i) example for call by value :

In calculating the amount to be repaid for a loan taken the statement using call by value will be :

repay_amount = loan (p, i, t);

where repay_amount is the amount to be repaid for the loan taken,. Loan is the name of the function which calculates the amount to be repaid,

The arguments p1, i, t, are the arguments that of past from the calling program to the called program which is the user defined function

loan (principal, interest, time_period)

The function by its statements calculates the amount to be repaid and passes on the result to the variable repay_amount, making use of p as the principal amount, i as the interest rate and t as the time period of interest.

(ii) another example for call by value :

we can include the function from the cout. Consider the following example.

cout <<"the maximum number is"<<max(num1, num2, num3);
here the function max is evaluated and its value is given as the output for the variable max using cout statement.

iii) giving the output of a called function in the called function itself :

now we examine the following function call

volume(r);

The above function volume (r); will compute the result and vanish since it does not know (nor has been instructed) where to store the computed result or to which variable to pass on the results. And *this type of function calls are used where we do not want to get any values from functions such as to display error messages or print some information.*

8.3.1 . Call by Value :

Program 8.3.1

Write a program in C to illustrate sending values of a function using call by value.

```
# include <stdio.h>
# include <conio.h>

main ( )
{
int x,y,swaping (int, int) ;
clrscr ( );
printf ("\n Enter values of X and Y :");
scanf ("%d %d",&x, &y);
swaping(x,y);
printf ("\n In main( ) before swaping X=%d Y=%d",x,y);
return 0;
}

swaping(int a, int b)      /* value x passed to a, value y passed to b */
{
int k;
k=a;
a=b;
b=k;
printf ("\n after swaping ( ) X=%d Y=%d",a,b);
}
```

OUTPUT :

```
Enter Values of X and Y : 6  9
In main( ) before swaping X = 6 Y = 9
After swapping x = 9 Y = 6
```

Program 8.3.2.

Write a program in C++ to illustrate calling a function by value

```
//Example program for call by value
    #include <iostream>
    using namespace std;
    main( )
    {
        int a,b;
            void fun1(int,int); //prototype of fun1 in main, must in C++
        cout<<"enter values for p and q\n";
        cin >>p>>q;
```

```
        fun1 (p,q);
        cout<<" \n the value of p and q after executing";
        cout <<" the function is "<p<<"  "<<q;
            return 0;
    }
    void fun1 (int r, int s)
    {
        r=r*6;
        s=s*8;
        cout <<"\n the value of a and b inside the function is
        "<<r<<"  "<<s;
    }
```

OUTPUT :

enter values for p and q
2 3
the value of p and q inside the function is 12 24
the value of p and q after executing the function is 2 3

In this example when the fun ( ) is called, the value of 'p' and 'q' are passed to 'r' and 's' respectively. The result of the execution of **fun1 (p,q)** is not passed on to the main function, because in the main function the function **fun1 (p,q)**is called but its results are not used in the main program. In such cases, the changes inside the function cannot affect the main program. This type of function is called "call by value" or "value parameter", Also **note that there is a semicolon in the function call, and there is no semicolon in the function declaration.**

8.4. CALL BY REFERENCE :

When a function is called by reference, the changes inside the function affect the main program also. In C, this effect can be achieved only by introducing pointers, whereas in C++ this method can be accomplished by using call by reference method. As we know a reference is an alias for another variable and when we specify a function argument as a reference type, the function will use the pass-by-reference technique for passing the variables. When the function is called, the argument corresponding to a reference parameter is not copied. The reason for this is, because the parameter name simply becomes an alias for the argument value in the calling program. And whenever the variable name is used in the body of the function, it will access he argument value in the calling function directly.

Program 8.4.1

Write a program in C to send value by reference to the user defined function swapping.

```
# include <stdio.h>
# include <conio.h>
main ( )
{
int x,y,swapping(int*, int*);    /* the arguments are passed by giving addresses*/
clrscr ( );
printf ("\s Enter Values of X & Y;");
scanf (" %d %d",&x,&y);
swapping (&x,&y);
printf ("\n In main ( )  X=%d Y=%d",x,y);
return 0;
}
swapping (int *a int*b)
{
int *k;
*k=*a;
*a=*b;
*b=*k;
printf ("\n In the user defined function Change ( ) X=%d Y=%d",*a,*b);
}
```

OUTPUT :

```
Enter Values of X & Y : 83, 96
In swapping ( )  X = 96  Y = 83
In main ( )      X = 83  Y = 96
```

Note : *X, *Y etc., are values of variables taken from their addresses which are given. In the function swapping ( ) no return statement is given and it is not necessary also in this type of call.

Program 8.4.2

Write a program in C++to illustrate the use of function with "call by reference"

```
//Example program for call by reference
#include <iostream>
using namespace std;
main( )
{
    int a,b;
```

```
        void fun(int &,int &)   //& is used to refer the addressed parameters
        cout <<"enter values for a and b \n";
        cin >>a>>b;
        fun(a,b);
        cout <<" \n the value of a and b in main after executing";
        cout <<"the function is" <<a<<" "<<b;
        return 0;
    }
    void fun(int&d,int &e)
    {
        d=d*6;
        e=e*8;
        cout <<"\n the value of a and b inside the function is "<<d<<" " <<e;
    }
```

OUTPUT :

enter values for a and b
3 4
the values of a and b inside the function is 18 32
the value of a ad b in main after executing the function is 18 32

Note : The points to remember while using call by reference method is, **we must add '&' after the type name.** To specify as 'reference to int' for example we can write the type as int &;

8.5. CATEGORY OF FUNCTIONS :

(i) A function can be used to a variable by assignment the value returned by the called function. eg. a = sum1 ( )

(ii) A function can be called by simply using the function name in an independent statement or in an expression. For example if the statement contains the name of the function then the called function (user defined function) will be executed in that place and the output of the called function will be placed in that location.

(iii) When the function name is used in an expression the value returned by the said function will be used in the place of function name in the expression.

8.6. CALLING A FUNCTION WITH NO ARGUMENTS AND NO RETURN VALUES :

This kind of function is peculiar in two aspects :

(i) A function, which does not have any argument, receives no data from the calling function.

(ii) With no return value, in the called function the calling function does not receive any data.

Thus, *no data communication takes place with this type of function. Therefore this function cannot be used as an expression. It can only be used as an independent statement.*

Program : 8.6.1

Write a program in C++ to enter only values between 1 and 5 and if it exceeds 5 then the program should inform the user to re-enter the choice.

```
#include <iostream>
using namespace std;
int main( )
{
      int ch;
      void error(void);
      cout <<"enter 1 to add records \n";
      cout <<"        2 to delete records \n";
      cout <<"        3 to delete records \n";
      cout <<"        4 to display records \n";
      cout <<"        5 to exit program \n";
      cout <<" Your choice between 1 & 5 \n";
      cout <<" Your choice between 1 & 5 is"<<ch;
      cin >>ch;
      if (ch > 5)
      error ( );
      return 0;
}
void error( )
{
      cout <<"invalid option, enter correct choice\n";
}
```

OUTPUT :

```
enter 1 To add records
      2 To delete records
      3 To edit records
      4 To display records
      5 To exit program
7
Your choice between 1 & 5 is 7
invalid option, enter correct choice
3
Your choice between 1 & 5 is 3
```

Here when the user inputs a value greater than 5 then the function error ( ) is called to display the error message.

Similarly in C also we can have a calling function with no arguments and no return values just like the one described above in C++.

8.7. CALLING FUNCTIONS WITH ARGUMENTS AND NO RETURN VALUES :

This is another type where one-way communication is possible between the calling and called function. That is, *the called function will receive data from the calling function, but will not transfer any data to it.*

Program 8.7.1 :

Write a program in C++ to illustrate the principle of using calling functions with arguments but no return values.

```
#include <iostream>
using namespace std;
int main ( )
{
    int a,b,c;
    void big(int,int,int);
    cout<<"\n enter 3 numbers";
    cin >>a>>b>>c;
    big(a,b,c);
    return 0;
}
void big(int x,int y,int z)
{
    if (x > y && x > z)
        cout <<"\n a is the biggest";
    else if (y > z && y>x)
        cout <<" \n b is the biggest";
    else
        cout <<"\n c is the biggest";
    }
```

OUTPUT :

enter 3 numbers 4 9 1
b is the biggest

In the given program, the function big is invoked with three arguments. The identifiers inside the function are compared and the result is then displayed. The function big does not return any value to the main.

Similarly in C also we can have a calling function with arguments and no return values just like the one described above in C++.

8.8. CALLING FUNCTION WITH ARGUMENTS AND WITH RETURN VALUE :

Unlike the two categories discussed earlier, in this type, two-way data communication takes place. That is, *both the called and calling function receive and transfer data from each other.* The following illustration will be useful to understand this feature.

Program 8.8.1

Write a program in C to send values to user-defined function and receive and display the returned value.

```
# include <stdio.h>
# include <conio.h>
main ( )
{
int sum (int, int, int), a,b,c,s;
clrscr ( );
printf ("Enter Three Numbers :");
scanf ("%d %d %d",&a,&b,&c);
s=sum(a,b,c);
printf ("Sum = %d",s);
return 0;
}
sum (int x, int y, int z)
{
return (x+y+z);
}
```

OUTPUT :

```
Enter Three Numbers : 12  18  20
Sum = 50
```

Note : *The above program can also be modified to return the address of the result from the user defined function instead of returning the value executed by the user defined function.*

Program 8.8.2 :

Write a program in C++ to illustrate the use of calling function with argument and return value to find the area of a triangle.

```
#include <iostream>
using namespace std;
```

```
int main ( )
{
    float x,y,c, area(float,float);
    cout <<"\n enter base and height";
    cin >>x>>y;
    c=area(x,y);
    cout <<"\n the area is"<<c;
    return 0;
}
float area (float b, float h)
{
    return (0.5*b*h);
}
```

OUTPUT :

enter base and height 10 15
the area is 75

In this example the float function area is called with two arguments. The values get substituted inside the function, and finally return to the main. Since, the function area ( ) contains expression having decimal value the function is declared as float. **Even though the values returned by the user function are float, still the output of the main function is integer because of the declaration int main ( )**

The Before we switch over to next topic, let us **consider the following function declaration ;**

int test( );

In C++, this function declaration means that the function takes no arguments. But, in ANSI/ISO C, it could take any number of arguments and of any type. Hence, in C++ we cannot pass arguments when the function prototype has no argument in it.

8.9. FUNCTION RETURNING MORE VALUES :

The called function can return more than one value instead of a single value. This is valid for both C and C++.

Program 8.9.1

Write a program in C to return more than one value from user defined function.

```
# include <stdio.h>
# include <conio.h>
main ( )
{
int x,y add,sub,change (int*, int*, int*, int* );
```

```
clrscr ( );
printf ("\n Enter Values of X & Y :");
scanf ("%d %d" &x,&y);
change (&x,&y,&add,&sub);
printf("\n Addition :%d",add);
printf("\n Subtraction :%d",sub);
return 0:
}
change (int* a, int* b, int* c, int* d)
{
*c= *a+*b;
*d=*a-*b;
}
```

OUTPUT :

```
Enter Values of X & Y : 8  3
Addition : 11
Subtraction : 5
```

Explanation :

i) *In this program the starred variables are pointer variables.*

ii) In this program return statement is not used. Still function returns more than one value. *Actually no values are returned. Once the addresses of the variables are available, we can directly access then and modify their contents. Hence in he call by reference method, it is possible to directly modify the contents of the variable.* The memory addresses of the variables are unique. There is no scope for memory address. If we declare the same variable for actual and formal arguments their memory addresses will be different from each other.

8.10. LOCAL AND GLOBAL VARIABLES :

i) Local Variables :

The local variables are defined within the body of the function or the block. The variable defined is local to that function or block only. Other functions can not access these variables. The compiler shows errors in case other functions try to access the variables.

Example :

```
value ( int k, int m)
{
int r,t;
}
```

Here 'r' & 't' are the local variables, which are defined within the body of the function value ( ). The same variable names may be defined in different functions. They are local to those particular functions.

ii) **Global Variables :**

Global variables are defined outside the main ( ) function. Multiple functions can use them and any function that uses them will be getting the same values for those variables which are declared as global variables.

Global variables are used to reduce the number of variables and also to reduce the storage space. But special care should be taken when using global variables because if any function changes the value of a global variable then the changed value of the global variable will be passed on subsequently to all other functions also. *Value of a global variable should not be changed in any function using that global variable.*

Program 8.10.1

Write a program in C to show the effect of global and local variables on different functions.

```
# include <stdio.h>
# include <conio.h>
int b=10,c=5;        /* b and c are global variables common to all functions*/
main ( )
{
int D,F;             /* D and F are local variables to main ( ) */
clrscr ( );
printf ("\n In main ( ) b=%d c=%d",b,c);
fun ( );
b++;
c-;
D=b+c;
F=b-c;
printf ("\n Again In main ( ) b=%d c=%d D=%d F",b,c,D,F);
}
fun ( )
{
int D, G;  /* D & G are local variables to fun ( ). Non global D is redefined */
b++;
c--;
D=b+c;
G=b-c;
printf ("\n In fun ( ) b=%d c=%d D=%d G=%d",b,c,D,G);
}
```

OUTPUT :

In main ( ) b=10 c=5 D=15 F=5
In fun ( ) b=11 c=4 D=15 G=7
Again In main ( ) b=12 c=3 D=15 F=9

Explanation :

In the above program variables 'b' & 'c' are defined outside the main ( ) hence they are global. They can be called by any other function. The same variables 'b' & 'c' are used throughout the program. In main ( ), values of 'b' & 'c' are printed.

In main D is a local variable and is applicable only for that main ( ).

When the function fun ( ) is called 'b' is increased and 'c' is decreased. The values of 'b' & 'c' are printed in fun ( ) itself. The Control then returns to the main ( ).

Again in main ( ) 'b' is increased and 'c' is decreased. The values of 'b' & 'c' are printed again in main ( ). Here both the functions use the same variables.

In function fun ( ) D and G are local variables and are applicable only for fun ( ).

Note : The same variable names can be used in different functions if they are local variables since the scope of these variables are the respective functions only. We can also use different variables as local variables in different functions whereas in the case of global variables the same variable names as that of global variables have to be used in different functions which use those global variables.

8.11. ARGUMENTS OF A FUNCTION :

i) The arguments of a calling function are called actual arguments. The arguments of a called function are called formal arguments.

ii) Arguments / parameter list means variable names included within the parenthesis of the function. They must be separated by a comma. The arguments can be variables, addresses of the variables, elements of arrays or arrays themselves.

iii) The passing of array elements as arguments is cumbersome as it involves passing of a large set of numbers, hence array itself is used as parameter to be passed. This will be explained in detail later.

iv) In C the total number of actual arguments of the calling function and the total number of formal arguments of the called function should be the same and should be in the same order. The first actual value of calling function is passed on to the first formal argument of the called function and so on.

v) In the case of C++ total number of arguments in calling function and called function need not be the same which will be explained later.

vi) Addresses can also be arguments as in the case of 'Call by Reference'

vii) Not only the variables but functions can also be arguments of a function

viii) Arguments of a function can also be one or more functions.

An example of function as an argument is given below.

Program 8.11.1 :

Write a program in C to pass a user-defined function as an argument to another function.

```
# include (stdio.h>
# include (conio.h>
main ( )
{
    int y=3, x;
        x=double (square)(y)); /* function square is arg. of fun. double
*/
printf ("x=%d",x);
}
double (m)
{
return (m*4);
}
square (k)
{
return (k*k);
}
```

OUTPUT :

x= 36

Explanation :

In the above example instead of passing a variable or its address a function is passed in an argument. The innermost function square ( ) is executed first and completed. Its returns values is collected by the double ( ) function. The double function uses the square ( ) function as an argument. Repeates on the return value of square ( ) function and makes he returned value double and returns to the main ( ) function.

8.12. FUNCTION PROTOTYPES :

We use many built-in-functions. The Prototypes of these functions are given in the respective header files. Those we include using # include directive. *In C and C++ while defining user-defined functions it is a must to declare its prototype. A prototype statement helps the compiler to check the return type and argument type of the function.*

i) A function prototype declaration consists of the funciton's type, name and types of arguments list. The type declaration before the function name represents the type of the output. The type declarations inside the arguments list refer to the types of the variables used in the function.

ii) Instead of giving only the types of the arguments, the type and the name of the argument both may be given in the arguments list.

iii) When the programmer defines the funciton, the definition of the function must be same like the prototype declarations.

iv) The function prototype must be declared before the use of the concerned function.

v) If the programmer makes any mistake, the compiler flags an error message.

vi) The funciton prototype declaration statement is always terminated with semi-colon.

The statements given below are examples of function prototypes.

a) float sum (float, int);
b) float sum (float x, int y);

In the statement (a) the prototype of function sum ( ) is declared. Its return value is float and arguments are float and integer type respectively. It tells the compiler the return value of the function is float and type of arguments used by this function.

In the example (b) with argument type, argument names are also declared. It is optional and also not compulsory to use the same variable name in the program.

8.13. FUNCTIONS AND DECISION STATEMENTS :

i) Functions can be used in decision statements like **if else statement** and switch case statement. The table below explains if else using fun().

If else without function	**If else with function**
if (condition)	if (fun ( ))
statement 1;	statement 1;
else	else
statement 2;	statement 2;

when function is used in if else decision structure as a condition we are passing the function directly as a condition for the decision statement. When if fun ( ) statement executes control is passed in the function fun ( ). The return value of the function is used for condition.

ii) **Switch case :** The switch ( ) case statement also makes decision at run time in the program. It has multiple choice or multiple decisions. The switch ( ) requires one argument and its body contains various case statements like branch. Depending upon the value of the switch ( ) argument matched case statement is executed. The table below expalains switch case using fun()

Switch case with function

Switch case without function	**Switch case with function**
swith (x)	switch (fun1 ( ))
{	{
case 1;	case 1;
....	....
break;	break;
case 2:	case 2:
....	....
break;	break;
default:	default:
}	}
Where 'x' is an argument of any data type.	where, fun1( ) is a function

8.14. FUNCTION AND LOOP STATEMENTS :

Loop statements are used to repeat program code repetitively for given number of times or based on certain conditions.

i) **Syntax for using function in for loop :**

for (fun ( ) ; fun1 ( ) ; fun2 ( ));

where, fun ( ), fun1 () and fun 2 ( ) are user defined functions representing initial, final and increament step of the for loop. In the above example at every step of the for loop we are using user-defined function i.e., when such statement executes iterations are completed calling the functions.

ii) **Syntax for using function in while loop :**

```
while (fun ( ) )
{
............;
............;
}
```

Where, fun () is a user defined function.

In the above example in place of condition, we are passing a function. The while checks the returned value of function.

iii) Syntax for using function in do while loop :

```
do
{
............ ;
............ ;
} while (fun () )
```

where, fun ( ) is a user defined functions.

In the above example in place of condition, we are passing a function. The while checks the returned value of function.

8.15. NESTING OF FUNCTIONS :

One important advantages of C and C++ function is that they allow nesting of functions in that they can be called from and within another function. Consider the following illustration in C++.

Program : 8.15.1

Write a program in C++ to illustrate the use of nesting of functions.

```
        #include <iostream>
        using namespace std;
        int main( )
{
        void fun1();      //fun1( ) prototype
        cout <<"\n I am main";
        fun1( );
        cout <<"\n Again I am in main returning from fun2( ) thro' fun1( )";
            return 0;
}
void fun1( )
{
        void fun2( );
        cout <<"\n I am in fun1( ) coming from main( )";
        fun2( );
}
void fun2( )
{
        cout<<"\n I am in fun2( ) coming from fun1( )";
}
```

OUTPUT :

I am in main
I am in fun1( ) coming from main( )
I am in fun2( ) coming from fun1( )
Again I am in main returning from fun2( ) thro' fun1( )

It may be appreciated here, that it is possible to call a function from and within another function. *All the called and calling functions transfer and receive data with each other and this is called "Nesting of functions".*

This technique becomes more useful when a complicated software is developed involving different aspects and to bring their outputs together for useful result.

8.16. RECURSION :

Another interesting feature of the function in C and C++ is Recursion. *Recursion is nothing but a function, which calls by itself.*

Program 8.16.1

Write a program in C to call main ( ) functions recursively and perform sum of five numbers from 2 to 6.

```
# include <stdio.h>
# include <process.h>      /* <process.h> used for recursion */

int x=2,s=0;
void main (int);           /* function prototype */

void main (x)
{
    s=s+x;
    printf ("\n x = %d a = %d", x,s);

    if (x==6)
    exit (0);
    main (++x);    /* main( ) is used as recursion with different arg. */
}
```

OUTPUT :

x = 2 s = 2
x = 3 s = 5
x = 4 s = 9
x = 5 s = 14
x = 6 s = 20

Program 8.16.2

Write a program in C++ to illustrate the nesting or arrays

```
//Example program for recursion technique
#include <iostream>
using namespace std;
int main ( )
{
    int n,m;
    int fact(int);
    cout <<"\n Enter number to find the factorial ";
    cin >>n;
    m=fact(n);
    cout <<"\n The factorial of the given number is "<<m;
    return 0;
}
int fact (int x)
{
    if (x==1)
        return(1);
    else
        return(x*fact(x-1));
}
```

OUTPUT :

Enter number to find the factorial 6
The factorial of the given number is 720

Recursion process is also called as "back substitution". Let us see how this process works. The above example is a function to evaluate factorial of n.

Let us assume n=4.

Since the value of n is not equal to 1, the function call

fact = x *fact(x-1)

Will be executed as,

fact = 4 *fact(3)

Subsequently,

fact(3)=3*fact(2)
fact(2)=2*fact(1)

and when n=1, the function returns the value as 1.

and, therefore

fact = 4 * 3* 2*1= 24

Thus recursion works effectively to solve problems, where the result is expressed in terms of successfully applying the same solution to subsets of the problem. **A recursive function must have a 'if' statement to force it to return without the call being executed, as otherwise, the function will never return.** *In C++, main ( ) cannot be called recursively and cannot have its address taken whereas in ANSI/ISO C allows recursive calls and allows pointers to hold the address of main ( ).*

8.17. FUNCTIONS WITH ARRAYS AND POINTERS :

i) Arrays using Functions :

Many times the user initializes the array using statement like int d [ ] = {1, 2, 3, 4, 5}. Instead of this, **functions can also be directly called to initialize the array.** The program given below illustrates this point.

Program 8.17.1

Write a program in C to initialize an array using functions.

```
# include <stdio.h>
# include <conio.h>
main ( )
{
int k,c ( ), d [ ] = {c ( ), c ( ), c ( ), c ( ), c ( )}
clrscr ( );
printf ("\n Array d[ ] elements are :");
for (k=1;k<=5;k++)
printf ("%2d",d[k]);
return (NULL);
}
    c( )
{
    static int m,n;
    m++;      /* m is initialized to zero automatically before the stmt*/
    printf ("\n Enter Number d[%d];",m);
    scanf("%d",&n);
    return(n);
}
```

OUTPUT :

```
Enter Number d[1] : 35
Enter Number d[2] : 36
Enter Number d[3] : 37
Enter Number d[4] : 38
Enter Number d[5] : 39
Array d[ ] elements are : 35  36  37  38  39
```

Program 8.17.2

Write a program in C++ to pass the values of an array to a function using for loop which is an effective way of passing elements of the array.

```
//Program to find maximum number in an array
#include <iostream>
using namespace std;
int main( )
{
        int i,n,m,a(100);
        int big(int [ ],int);
        cout <<"\n Enter how many numbers you are going to feed";
        cin>>n;
        cout <<"Enter "<<n<<" elements \n";
        for (i=0;i<n;i++)
        cin>>a[i];
        m=big(a,n);
        cout <<"\n The maximum number in the array is "<<m;
        return 0;
}
        int big (int x[  ], int y)
{
        int j,max;
        max = x[0];
        for (j=1;j<y;j++)
            if (max < x[i])
                max=x[i];
        return(max);
}
```

OUTPUT :

```
Enter how many numbers you are going to feed 5
Enter 5 elements
381
265
481
399
122
The maximum number in the array is 481
```

Explanation :

Initially the user has enter the numbers for which he wants to find the maximum. Then the statement m=big(a,n) will transfer 'n' elements of an array 'a' to function big ( ). Inside the function big ( ), maximum number is found by using the method, which we have seen in the previous example. The value of max is returned to the main and the same is displayed. Note that, in the main ( ) function the big ( ) receives integer array as first argument and second argument is number of elements in the array hence the declaration of this function is given as big (int[ ], int).

ii) Arrays using Pointers :

Earlier we have seen how array elements can be passed to a function by value. Array elements can also be passed to a function by reference (using pointers)

Program 8.17.3.

Write a program in C to pass array elements to the function using call by reference.

```
# include <stdio.h>
# include <conio.h>
        void main ( )
{
        void show (int*);      /* function prototype for show using pointer */
        int array1[ ] = {68,74,34,48,76};
        clrscr ( );
        show(array1);  /*array name gives address of 1st element of 1 diml.array*/
}
        void show(int *u)      /*pointer *u contains base addr. of array array1[ ]*/
{
        int m=0;
        printf ("\n array1[5]={");
        while (m != 5)
            {
                printf ("%2d,"*(u++));
                m++;
            }
        printf ("\b }");
}
```

OUTPUT :

array1[5]={68,74,34,48,76}

Explanation : In the above program base address of 0th element is passed to function show { }. The pointer *u contains base address of array1[ ]. The pointer notation prints the elements.

Program 8.17.4.

Write a program in C to display array elements in reverse order using the following logic : *instead of giving the address of first element of array, give the address of the last element of array and instead of increasing the address to access next element decrease the address to get the previous element of the array in order to reverse the array.*

```
# include <stdio.h>
# include <conio.h>

void main ( )
{
        int show(int*);
        int array2 [ ]= {89, 34, 58, 38, 44};
        clrscr ( );
        show (&array2[5]);    /* address of last element of array2 given */
}

        show(int*v)
{
        int m=5;
        while (m != -1)
              {
                    printf("\rev_array2[%d]=%d",m,*v);
                    v--;
                    m--;
              }
        return (NULL);
}
```

OUTPUT :

```
array2[4]=44
array2[3]=38
array2[2]=58
array2[1]=34
array2[0]=89
```

8.18. SPECIAL FUNCTIONS OF C++ :

C++ has got some additional special functions compare to C and other languages. They are explained below.

8.18.1 Default Parameters :

In C and in other languages, the number of formal parameters should coincide with the number of actual parameters. Whereas in C++ there is no such restriction we call the function with the lesser arguments than the actual arguments.

Let us consider the following function prototype;

float calculate (float princpl, int years=5, float roi=10.5);

Now, consider the following function call

float intamt = calculate (5000.0);

Here the interest amount calculated for Rs.5000 with 5 as number of years and 10.5 as the rate of interest. These two last parameters can be taken from default values defined in the function declaration.

In the subsequent call,

float intamt=calculate(5000.0,10);

In the above case, principal will be Rs.5000 and number of years will be 10, the third parameter is assumed default value i.e. 10.5.

Note : *To use default function parameters the first declaration of the function should contain the required number of parameters. Subsequently the same function name with lesser number of parameters will take the remaining parameters by default to be the same as those parameters of the first function. If any of the function parameters of the first function changes then the new parameter value has to be necessarily given for the next function with the same name. for eg. :*

float intamt=calculate(5000.0, 10,12,5);

Here the principle amount is Rs.5000.00 and the remaining two parameters are 10 and 12.5 by replacing two parameters defined in the function declaration.

This feature can be best illustrated in the following program.

Program 8.18.1

Write a program in C++ to calculate the interest on a sum of Rs.10,000/- over six years to illustrate the aspect of calling a function with lesser arguments than the actual arguments using default parameters.

```
#include <iostream>
#include <iomanip>
using namespace std;
float proceeds (float princpl, int years=6, float roi=7.5)
```

```
{
    return (princpl*years*roi/100);
}
void main ( )
{
    float intamt;
    cout<<setprecision(2);
    cout<<fixed;
    intamt=proceeds(10000.0);
    cout <<"\n Interest amount by passing principal only; "<<intamt;
    intamt=proceeds(10000.0,9);
    cout <<"\n Interest amount by passing principal and years : "<<intamt;
    intamt=proceeds(12000.0,12,10.5)
    cout<<"\n Interest amt passing principal, yrs and interest rate:"<<intamt;
    cout <<endl;
}
```

OUTPUT :

```
Interest amount by passing principal only                 : 4500.00
Interest amount by passing principal and years            : 6750.00
Interest amt passing principal, yrs and interest rate     : 15120.00
```

8.18.2. Inline functions :

Inline function is another additional, special and powerful facility in C++. The statement in C given below:

```
#define min (a,b) (a<b) ? a : b);
```

saves the overhead of a function call by simply replacing the expression min (a,b) (a < b ? a : b) textually in the program. Since it is being a string replacement, the compiler does not know anything about the function min and therefore its error messages may be confusing when there is an error involving it. Now, let us consider the expression min (++a,++b); here a gets incremented twice if ++a is less than ++b. To overcome this difficulty, **C++ provides an inline function where the compiler writes the code for the function directly in the place where it is invoked, rather than generating the target function for a function and invoking it every time it is needed.** This is similar to the use of macro where all the statements of macro are inserted when the macro name is invoked.

Program 8.18.2

Write a program in C++ to illustrate the principle of inline functions.

```
#include <iostream>
using namespace std;
inline float area(float x)
{
        return (x*x);
}
void main ( )
{
        float side;
        cout <<"\n Enter side : ";
        cout <<"\n Area of square is : "<<area(side);
        cout<<endl;
}
```

OUTPUT :
Enter side : 30
Area of square is : 900
at exit( )

8.18.3. atexit ( ) Function :

Earlier we have used the function exit( ) to terminate program at any part of the program without executing the remaining statements if any, depending on our requirement. **By using the function atexit ( ) we can specify a function to be executed at the time of exit.** The function pointed by function parameter (function name) is called when the program terminates normally. *If more than one atexit( ) function is specified calling this, they are all executed in reverse order, that is, the last function specified is the first to be executed upon exit.* Also note that these **atexit ( ) functions will not receive any parameter when called and also do not return any value.**

Program 8.18.3

Write a program in C++ to illustrate the use of atexit ( ) function.

```
#include <iostream>
#include <cstdlib>
using namespace std;
void display(void);  // function prototype for atexit ( )
```

```
void main ( )
{
    int choice;
    atexit(display); // declaration of atexit ( ) in main ( )
    cout <<"\n Enter 1 for exit program normally";
    cout <<"\n Enter 2 for exit program with function exit :";
    cin>>choice;
    if (choice ==1)
        {
        cout<< "\n Normal exit ";
        cout <<endl;
        }
    else
        {
        cout <<"\n Exiting program with function exit";
        cout <<endl;
        exit(EXIT_SUCCESS);
        }
}
    void display( )
{
    cout <<"\n Always display this message invariable of choice value \n";
}
```

OUTPUT :

```
Enter 1 for exit program normally
Enter 2 for exit program with function exit : 1
Normal exit
Always display this message invariable of choice value
Enter 1 for exit program normally
Enter 2 for exit program with function exit : 2
Exiting program with function exit
Always display this message invariable of choice value
```

8.19. LIBRARY FUNCTIONS :

C++ also has built in library functions, primarily defined to execute specific operations. All the C library functions are also part of it. We have several other library functions also.

* * *

COMPREHENSION - 8

Note : By answering all the questions given in this comprehension one can answer any objective type of questions easily whatever be the form of the question. Answers for these questions can be obtained by going through the topics in this chapter carefully.

1. How many types of functions are there? What are they? What are the differences and similarities between them?
2. What type of function is main ( ) ? What is its syntax? What does it do?
3. Can main( ) include other functions? How are other functions invoked? What happens then?
4. What is meant by function prototype? What is its syntax? Where is it given in the program?
5. Can function prototype be combined with function declaration? How do you do it? Explain with example.
6. What does the function return? How is the return obtained?
7. Should a function always return a value?
8. When does a function not return a value?
9. If no value is to be returned by a function what are the ways of indicating no value return?
10. By default what type of return will be made by a function?
11. What is type-specifier and what is its relationship with the data type?
12. When the return statement is not found in a function what does the function do?
13. What is a void function? What does it do?
14. What is meant by function parameters or arguments of a function?
15. What are the rules governing function parameters?
16. Can the parameters of a function be expressions?
17. Can the return of a function be an expression?
18. Can the parameters of a function be functions ?
19. Can the parameters of a function be Arrays?
20. Can the return of a function be functions or arrays?
21. Can the return of a function be functions ?
22. What are the rules governing naming of a function?
23. What is a calling function and what is a called function?
24. Where is the calling of a function done? What happens when a function call is made?

25. In a program where do you place a user defined function?
26. Is there any limit for the number of functions to be called by a function?
27. How do you call a user defined function?
28. Is there any condition to call a user defined function?
29. What does the user defined function do? After execution of the user defined function what does it do?
30. Can a user defined function call the main function?
31. Give some examples of user defined functions.
32. Give some examples of library functions.
33. Give the syntax for a C or C++ function.
34. What are the different ways of calling other functions by a calling function?
35. Can a function be used as part of an expression?
36. Can a function be used as part of an output expression?
37. Can the results of a function be invoked without passing it anywhere or without storing?
38. What is the difference between a function and a Macro?
39. In C is it necessary to declare functions returning int or void in the main () itself?
40. In C++ is it necessary to declare functions returning int or void in the main ( ) itself? Why?
41. Can a function have more than one return statement?
42. Is it absolutely necessary to place a yser defined function only after main ( ) ?
43. When more functions are to be used should they all be placed in calling order?
44. If nested what it is better to place the functions in calling order. Why?
45. If a function calls itself what do you call such a function?
46. Is a Factorial function a Recursive function? Why?
47. In C how are you passing the values of an array to a user defined function?
48. What is the difference between user defined function and library function?
49. What is the scope of a local variable and global variable in user defined variable?
50. Can a function be defined inside another function? Why?
51. When do you use a calling of a function to give its output in the calling function itself?
52. What happens to such a function? Why?
53. Give examples of such a disappearing function.

54. What is calling a function by reference? What is the difference between C and C++?
55. What are the different categories of function with regard to arguments and return? Give examples.
56. Can a function return more values? What will be the nature of such a return? What condition should be fulfilled in such a case?
57. Can functions be given in Decision Statements? Give example.
58. Can functions be given in Loop Statements? Give example.
59. State about nesting of functions.
60. How do you use functions for initializing Arrays? Give example.
61. What are formal and actual parameters of a function?
62. Can the formal parameters be more than the actual parameters in C and C++?
63. When is atexit ( ) function do?
64. What does atexit ( ) function do?
65. What are inline functions? What do they do?
66. Consider the program

```
main ()
{
        float f;
        f=func ();
        printf ("%f\n",f);
}
```

The function func() is separately compiled with source as follows:

```
        double func ()
        {
                return (2.0123456789);
        }
```

What will be the value printed out by the program?

a) 2.0123456789 b) 2.012345

c) 2 d) Unpredictable

67. Consider the following program

```
main ()
{
        int a [ 5], b;
        for (b=0; b <5; b++)
                a [b] = b * 2;
                b = 0;
        update (a, b);
```

```
        printf ("%d  %d  %d \n", b, a[1], a [3] );
}
update (a, b)
int a [ ], b;
{
        for (; b<5; b++)
                a [ b] = b+1 ;
}
```

The values printed out will be :

a) 0 2 4 b) 6 2 6 c) 0 2 6 d) 6 2 4

66. Comment on the following code:

```
main ( )
{
        int i=0;
        for (i=1; i<4500; i++)
        donothing ( );
}
        void donothing ( )
{
}
```

a) This program will not compile.

b) This program may be used for introducing a delay.

c) There is a runtime error since it is not correct to call a function having an empty body.

d) The number of times donothing funciton is called is unpredictable.

69. Find the output of the following program.

```
main ( )
{
        int x;
        x=maxint (56, 75);
        printf ("value of x = %d \n", x);
}
        maxint ( x,y)
        int x,y;
        {
                retunr (x>y?x:y);
        }
```

70. What is the data type of variable m

```
void main ( )
{
int x=2;
gr (x);
}
sqr (m)
{retunr (m*m); }
```

a) int b) float c) char d) void

71. Arrays are passed as arguments to a function by:

a) Value b) Reference c) Both (a) and (b) d) None of these

72. Is it necessary to declare the type of a function in the calling program if

i) The function returns a non-integer value

ii) The function returns an integer

iii) The funciton is not defined in the same file

iv) None of the above

73. By default the function returns

a) Integer value b) Float value c) Char value d) None of these

74. The meaning of keyword void before the function name means

a) function should not return any value

b) Function should return any value

c) No arguments are passed

d) None of the above

75. The function name itself is:

a) An address b) Value c) Definition d) None of these

* * *

EXERCISE - 8

Note : By answering all the questions given in this exercise one can answer subjective type of questions easily including problems. The worked examples in the chapter may help in solving these questions.

1. (a) Define a function. How many types of functions are there? Explain with examples.

   (b) Explain the action of return ( ) statement. When a function is called by reference why is return ( ) statement not necessary?

2. (a) What are function parameters? Explain the different types of function parameters.

   (b) How can the parameters be passed from calling function to called function?

3. (a) Explain the function prototype and function with examples.

   (b) What type of function is main ( ) function? Why is main ( ) function necessary?

4. (a) What are formal and actual arguments of a function? Explain with examples.

   (b) What should be the relationship between formal and actual arguments in C & C++ ?

5. (a) What is a recursive function? Explain with a program using recursive function.

   (b) Is it possible to call library functions recursively?

6. (a) State the important points to be noted while using a function.

   (b) What are the methods of using the returns of a function?

7. (a) Why is it be possible to use the same variable names for actual and formal arguments?

   (b) Explain clearly as to what happens when a function is called at the time of run?

8. (a) Explain with structure and example the use of nested functions.

   (b) How are arrays and functions passed on as arguments to a function? Explain.

9. (a) What are the different ways of calling a function? Explain with examples.

   (b) Explain clrscr ( ) function and exit ( ) function.

10. Write a program to display "Hello" 10 times. Creat user-defined function message( ).

11. Write a user-defined function for performing the following tasks.
    i) Clearing the screen.
    ii) Display character at specified row and column number.
    iii) Display horizontal line with given symbol.
12. Write a user-defined function for performing the following tasks.
    i) Square of a number
    ii) Area of a square
    iii) Conversion of decimal number to binary
    iv) Reverse the number
13. Write a program to add return values of three functions
14. Write a prorgram to find prime factors of entered number. For example prime factors of 32 are 2, 2, 2, 2 and 2.
15. Write a program to find highest and lowest common factors of the two numbers. For example the highest and lowest common factors for 50 and are 5 and 2 respectively.
16. Write a program to compute the total amount payable with annual interest for given number of years. The inputs are principle amount, rate of interest and number of years. Attempt the program with and without recursion method.
17. A student takes seven tests, on which the scores range from 0 to 100. His final grade is the average of the six highest test score. Write a function to print the student's final grade.
18. Write a C function to perform the following functions for the given 'n' numbers
    i) To count number of odd numbers
    ii) To count number of even numbers
    iii) Find the sum of the odd numbers
    iv) Find the sum of the even numbers
    v) Find the number of positive, negative and zero numbers.
19. A function to produce the following output

```
1
2  2
3  3  3
4  4  4  4
5  5  5  5  5
```

20, Write a progrm to sum integer numbers between 1-N using recursion technique.

* * *

CHAPTER - 9
STORAGE CLASS MODIFIERS

9.1. INTRODUCTION :

Storage Class Variables are applicable to C and C++. Storage class modifiers assume a very important role in C++. **Effective use of Storage class modifiers will lead to economization of variables. These are used to tell the compiler how the variable that follows should be stored.** The general declaration form is storage-specifier type variable-name;

There are four different kinds of storage class specifiers supported by C and C++ and they are :

i) Automatic storage or Automatic variables
ii) Static storage or Static variables
iii) Dynamic storage or External variables
iv) Register variables

In the following sections we will discuss each specifier.

9.2. AUTO VARIABLES OR LOCAL VARIABLES :

The variables generally declared inside any function without storage class name are called automatic variables. The variable that we have declared so far within a block - that is between a pair of braces falls only in this category. Even if the storage class is not specified they become auto by default. **The scope of auto variables is that they are active only within the function (or block) in which they are declared.** That is these variables are created upon entry into their function concerned and are destroyed (or) lose their lives upon exit from that function. It is because of this, **they are also called local variables (or) plain variables.**

For example, inside a function

```
int a,b,c ;
```

is equivalent to

```
auto int a,b,c;
```

Program 9.2.1

Write a program in C to show the working of auto variables in different blocks.

```
# include <stdio.h>
# include <conio.h>
void main ( )
{
int a=10;        /* int a = 10 assigns 10 to auto variable a */
clrscr ( );
```

```
printf ("\n A=%d",a);
{
int x=20;        /*value of auto variable x is changed to 20 inside this block */
printf ("\n A=%d",a);
}
printf ("\n A=%d",a); /* modified value of x=20 is valid only for the above block*/
}
```

OUTPUT :

```
A=10
A=20
A=10
```

9.3. DYNAMIC STORAGE OR EXTERNAL GLOBAL VARIABLES :

Global variables refer to external variables, which are declared outside the function or block in which it is used. Global variables which exist for all parts of the program. We can create global variables by declaring variables above main or outside of any function definition. A variable which is declared by this way is considered to be global to all functions declared after it and, upon exit from a block of a function, the external variable continues to remain in existence. In addition to global variables in C and C++ have a class of variables called external variables which can be declared inside a function by declaring the variable as 'extern'. The sample declarations are,

```
extern int a,b,c;
extern float x;
```

Program : 9.3.1

Write a program in C to declare external variables using key word extern.

```
# include <stdio.h>
# include <conio.h>
int m=88;
void main ( )
{
extern int m;
clrscr ( );
printf ("\n m=%d",m);
}
```

OUTPUT :

```
m = 88
```

Explanation :

In the above program variable 'm' is declared and initialized with 88 before main ( ) function. By declaring 'extern int m' inside the main function the externally declared value m=88 is treated as global variable and is made valid inside the main ( ). The variable 'm' is re-defined with extern keyword. This redefinition as extern int m is optional and is a sort of repetition for the global variable m. Without this statement also the program will work as it done now.

Program 9.3.2

Write a program in C++ to explain the usage of global variables and external variables.

```
#include <iostream>
using namespace std;
extern double base=0,ht=0,area=0;
void main ( )
{
    void area (void);
    cout <<"\n Enter base :";
    cin>>base;
    cout <<"\n Enter height : ";
    cin>>ht;
    area( );
    cout<<"\n Area : "<<area;
    cout<<endl;
}
    void area( )
{
    area=0.5*base*ht;
}
```

OUTPUT :

Enter base : 48.5
Enter height : 16.5
Area : 400.125

Note : By default, global variable and function names are considered external identifiers and they take on the storage class of extern and the function main ( ) has the storage class extern and a return type of int but it can also be declared to return void.

Also the global variable if redefined in any user defined function, the redefined value for the global variable will be applicable only to that function and the original global value for that global variable gets returned as soon as as it leaves the function which redefined the global variable.

Program 9.3.3

Write a program in C to show the use of auto and global variables with the same name.

```
# include <stdio.h>
# include <conio.h>
int z=20;
void main ( )
{
clrscr ( );
callA ( );
callB ( );
printf ("\n In main ( ) Z=%d",z);
}

callA ( )
{
int z=40   /* the same global var name v is redefined as local in callA( )*/
printf ("\n callA ( ) Z=%d"z);
}

callB ( )
{
printf ("\n In callB ( )Z=%d",z);
}
```

OUTPUT :

```
In callA ( ) Z = 40
In callB ( ) Z = 20
In main ( ) Z = 20
```

Explanation : In the above program an external variable and global variables are declared with he same name. In such a case, when callA ( ) function is called, The local variables 'z' of callA ( ) hides the global variable 'z'. As soon as the control returns back from the callA ( ) function the local variable 'z' will be destroyed and the global variables 'z' appears.

9.4. STATIC STORAGE OR STATIC VARIABLES :

In the earlier section we have seen that the scope of a variable is only within a block or a function (in which it is declared), and **the values of auto variables cannot persist after the block or function ceases. But there is special way to retain the value of the variable even after the block or function ceases, by declaring them as 'static'.** So, the 'static' variables will retain their previous values, when subsequently called. The static variable may be of an internal or external type depending on where it is declared. If declared the outside the function of the body it will be static global. If it is declared inside the body or block. It will be auto variable. When a variable is declared as static its garbage value is removed and it is initialised to null value. The contents stores in these variables remain constant throughout the program execution. A static variable is initialised only once and it is never reinitialized. The value of static variable persists at each call and the last change made in the value of the static variable remains throughout the program. Using this property of static variable we can count how many times a function is called. This facility is common to both C and C++.

Program 9.4.1

Write a program in C++ to illustrate the importance of the static variable class.

```
#include <iostream>
using namespace std;
int main( )
{
        void fun1 ( );
        fun1 ( );
        fun1 ( );
                fun1 ( );
                return 0;
}
void fun1 ( )
{

        int fun1 ( )
        {
                int a=0;    //int a is not static it is reinitialized in every call//
                a++;
                cout <<a<<"\n";
        }
}
```

OUTPUT :

1
1
1

In the above program now let us see a function where the variables are declared as static.

```
        void fun1( )
        {
            static int a=0;     //int a is static hence not reinitialized in each call
            a++;
            cout <<a<<"\n";
        }
```

OUTPUT :

here the program output will be

1
2
3

Program 9.4.2

Write a program in C to illustrate the use of static variable.

```
# include <stdio.h>
# include <conio.h>
void main ( )
{
    int a;
    clrscr ( );
    for ( i=1; i<=3;i++; )
    statvar ( );
}
int statvar (int i, int m)
{
int static m;           /* static m is automatically initialised to zero */
printf ("\n Before m=8 loop i=%d\t m=%d",i,m);
m=8;                    /* static m is not reinitialized in subsequent loops*/
m++;
printf("\n After  m++ loop i=%d"\t ,m=%d",i,m);
if (i==3)
exit (1);
}
```

OUTPUT :

```
loop i=1
Before m=8 loop i=1     m=0
After   m++ loop i=1    m=8
Before m=8 loop i=2     m=9
After  m++ loop i=2     m=9
Before m=8 loop i=3     m=10
After  m++ loop i=3     m=10
```

9.5. REGISTER VARIABLES :

The register variables are common to C and C++. **There are two types of modifiers which can be applied to register variables when we declare it and they are register and volatile.** Let us discuss register type first : Usually accessing a data is faster in the hard disk than in the floppy disk. Imaging the speed if the same would be accessed from registers. For example 8088 has about 14 registers. So, the variable can also be placed in them, if they are vacant. **In normal operation, there will be some unused registers, and they can be used with this storage specifier of register variables to access the register variables faster.**

The syntax will be
register int k;

Thus, the specifier "register" requests the C or C++ compiler to keep the value of variables declared with this modifier in the register of micro processor rather than in memory, where normal variables are stored. This means that operation on 'register' variables can occur much faster, as they are actually held in the microprocessor. **This makes 'register' variables ideal for loop control. The storage class is declared as**

register int a,b,c ;

For example, **if we declare more number of variables as registers than the vacant registers, the compiler will take care to declare the extra variables as auto by default.**

Program 9.5.1

Write a program in C to illustrate the use of register class variables.

```
# include <stdio.h>
# include <conio.h>
void main ( )
{
    register int m=8;
    clrscr ( );
    for ( ; m<=12;m++) /* blank initial space since value of m is already given */
    printf ("\t%d",m);
}
```

OUTPUT :

8 9 10 11 12

Explanation : In the above program variable 'm' is declared and initialized to 1. The for loop display values form 8 to 12. The register class variable is used as loop variable.

* * *

COMPREHENSION - 9

Note : By answering all the questions given in this comprehension one can answer any objective type of questions easily whatever be the form of the question. Answers for these questions can be obtained by going through the topics in this chapter carefully.

1. What is the need for Storage Class Modifiers?
2. How many types of storage class modifiers? What are they?
3. What are auto variables or local variables? What is their scope? Give example.
4. What are Dynamic storage variables? What are the other names for them? What is their scope?
5. How do you declare Global Variables? Give examples.
6. What happens if the value of a global variable is changed in the middle of a program or in a function? Is it allowed?
7. Why is it that you can use the same variable name for local variables in different functions?
8. To retain the values of auto variables after the block or function is over what do you do?
9. How do you declare static variables? Give examples. What is their special property?
10. What are Register Variables? Explain the methods of modifying Register Variables?
11. What registers do you use for Register Variable? What is the advantage of it?
12. Explain the use of volatile constants.
13. For what purpose use of Register Variables suitable? Why?
14. If we declare more register variables than the number of vacant registers what happens?
15. Give the syntax for use of different types of storage variables.
16. What is the difference between declaration of global variables and extern variables?
17. Distinguish between static and external variables?
18. List the limitations of register variables.
19. Why register storage class does not support all data types?
20. Can we declare a variable in different scopes with different data types? Explain in detail.

21. A static variable is one that
    a) Retains its value throughout the life of the program
    b) Cannot be initialized.
    c) Is initialized once at the commencement of the execution and cannot be changed at the run time.
    d) Is same as an automatic variable but is placed at the head of the program.
22. An external variable is one
    a) Which is globally accessible by all functions
    b) Which is declared outside the body of any function.
    c) Which resides in the memory till the end of the program
    d) All of the above
23. If a storage class is not mentioned in the declaration then default storage class is:
    a) automatic b) static c) external d) register
24. If the CPU fails to keep the variables in CPU registers, in that case the variables are assumed.
    a) automatic b) static c) external d) none of the above
25. What will be the value of variable 'x' on execution of the following program.

```
#include <stdio.h>
# include <conio.h>
int x;
void main ()
{
clrscr ( );
x++;
printf ("\n %d",x);
}
```

    a) x = 1 b) x=0 c) garbage value d) none of the above

* * *

EXERCISE - 9

Note : **By answering all the questions given in this exercise one can answer subjective type of questions easily including problems. The worked examples in the chapter may help in solving these questions.**

1. Write a program to calculate the sum of digits of the entered number. Create user-defined function **sumd ( )**. Use static variable and calculate the sum of digits.
2. Write a program to call function **main( )** recursively. The program should be terminated when the **main ( )** function is called during 5th time. Take help to static variable.
3. Write a program to calculate triangular number. Use static variable with user defined function.
4. Write a program to create the for loop from 1 to 10000. Declare the loop variable of class register and auto. Observe the time reuired for completing the loop for both the type of variables. Find out in which class the extention time is minimum.
5. Write a program in C to find the area of a triangle declaring an external float function **area ( )** and also without using the float function **area ( )** as extern.
6. Write a note and explain with examples the different types of storage class variables and modifiers.

* * *

CHAPTER - 10
POINTERS

10.1 INTRODUCTION :

Pointers are one of the most important features of C and C++ languages. Any variable that is used in a program will have its address in the memory. In other languages we do not take strain to know the variable address. However, **in C and C++ pointers are used to know the variable addresses** and it has its own benefits. While discussing about functions we have seen that function may be called in three ways a) Call by value b) Call by reference and c) Call by Pointer. We have already discussed several examples to illustrate the uses of Call by value. To fulfill the topic we have to analyze Call by pointer also and this is possible only after knowing about pointers. To underline the importance of pointers, it is often said that if pointers are effectively used, pointers will make the program more efficient. Pointers are useful in many ways.

a) **Pointers provide the means by which function can modify their calling arguments.**

b) **To improve the efficiency of the program.**

The real strength of C++ lies in the proper use of pointers. It is because of the high potential they have that they must be used carefully. Incorrect use or abuse of pointers can cause system crash.

10.2 WHAT IS A POINTER ?

Pointer is a variable, which stores the address of another variable. In other words, if one variable contain the address of another, then the first variable is said to point to the second. Consider the statement to assign value:

eg : int A = 88;

This statement instructs the system to locate for the integer variable "A" and assign the value 88 in that location. Let us assume that the system has chosen the address 500 for "A". This situation is figuratively represented as :

A	→ Variable name
88	→ Value
500	→ Address

Let us assign the address of "A" to a variable "b", and assume the address of "b" is 900. The link between the variable "a" and "b" can be represented as

variable	value	memory address
A	88	500
b	500	900

Since the value of variable "b" is the address of variable "A", we may access the value of "A" whose address is obtained using the value of "b". Hence "b" gets the name "pointer". 900 is the address of the "Pointer". The pointer value is 500.

10.3. POINTER OPERATORS :

To determine the address of a variable or the content of a variable, C permits, the use of two special operators, & and * Here

'&' is "address of" operator
' * ' is "content of" operator
Considering the above example, the statement
b = &a
And, * is "content of" operator
Considering the above example, the statement
b=&a

Would assign 500 (location of A) to variable b. **Thus & operator can be remembered as "address of".**

Let us see how a pointer a pointer variable is declared in C or C++. **The general declaration of pointer form is,**

data-type * var-name;

In this declaration form, three aspects are being conveyed to the compiler.

a) *The "*" operator tells that var-name is a pointer variable.*

b) *The pointer variable needs a memory location*

c) *The pointer variable points to a variable of type "data-type" which can be any fundamental "C" or "C++" data-type or a derived data type.*

Examples :

int *a ; declares "a" as a pointer variable that points to an integer data type. Similarly.

float *b; declares the pointer variable b to a float variable.

Some more examples of Pointers of different data types :

```
int   *x;
float *f;
char  *y;
```

i) In the first statement 'x' is an integer pointer and it tells to the compiler that it holds the address of any integer variable. In the same way 'f' is a float pointer which stores the address of any float variable and 'y' is a character pointer that stores the address of any character variable.

ii) **The indirection operator (*) is also called the deference or deference operator.** When a pointer is dereferenced, the value at that address stored by the pointer is retrieved.

iii) Normal variable provides direct access to their own values whereas a pointer provides indirect access to the values of the variable whose address it stores.

iv) The indirection operator (*) is used in two distinct ways with pointers, declaration and deference.

v) When a pointer is declared, the star indicates that it is a pointer, not a normal variable.

vi) When the pointer is dereferenced, the indirection operator indicates that the value at that memory location stored in the pointer is to be accessed rather than the address itself.

vii) Also note that * is the same operator that can be used as the multiplication operator. The compiler knows which operator to call, based on the context.

viii) The '&' is the address operator and it represents the address of the variable. **The control character %u is is used with printf ( ) function for printing the address of a variable.** The address of any variable is a whole number. The operator '&' immediately preceding the variable returns the address of the variable. In the given below example '&' is immediately proceeded by the variable 'num' which provides the address of the variable.

10.4. HOW TO ACCESS A VARIABLE THROUGH ITS POINTER? :

We have seen the use of "&" and "*" operators. The "&" operator is called as "direction" operator and "*" is called as "indirection" operator.

Let us see how to access the value of a variable using the pointer, once the pointer has been assigned the address of a variable. This is possible by using "*" operator. Consider the following statements :

```
int t, b, *a;
t=5;
a=&t;
b=*a;
```

Here the first statement declares "t" and "b" as integer variable and "*a" as a pointer variable pointing to an integer.

The second statement assigns the value of 5 to the variable "t";

The third statement assigns the address of variable "t", to the pointer variable "a";

In the fourth statement "content of" the pointer variable "a" is assigned to b. Hence the value of b is 5.

Program No.10.4.1

Write a program in C to display the address of a variable without use of the pointer and also with the use of pointer.

```
# include <stdio.h>
# include <conio.h>

main ( )
{
    int a,b,*p;
    clrscr ( );
    /* display of address without use of pointer */
    printf ("\n Display of address without use of pointer\n");
    printf ("Enter a Number a=15");
    scanf ("%d",&a);
    printf ("Value of int a=%d\n",a);
    printf ("Address of int a=%u\n",&a); /*control string u for address*/
    /* display of address with use of pointer */
    printf ("\n Display of address with use of pointer\n");
    p=&b;
    printf ("\n Address of b = %u",p);
    printf ("\n value of b = %d",*p);
    printf ("\n Address of p = %u",&p);
    getche ( );
}
```

OUTPUT :

```
Display of address without use of pointer

Enter a Number a = 15
Value of int a = 15
Address of int a = 4080

Display of address with use of pointer

Address of b = 4082
value of b = 256
Address of p = 4084
```

Explanation for the program data :

Without Pointer **With Pointer**

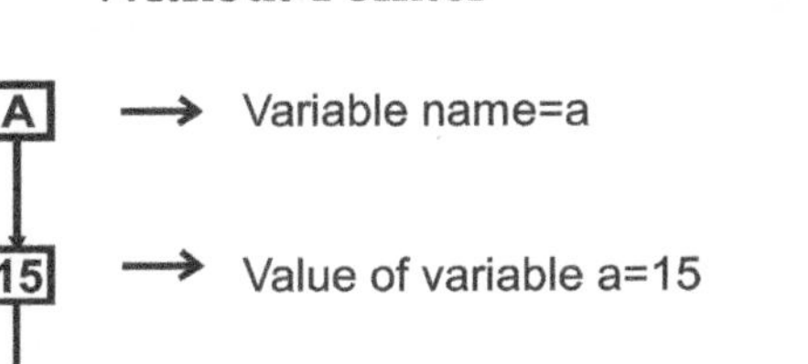

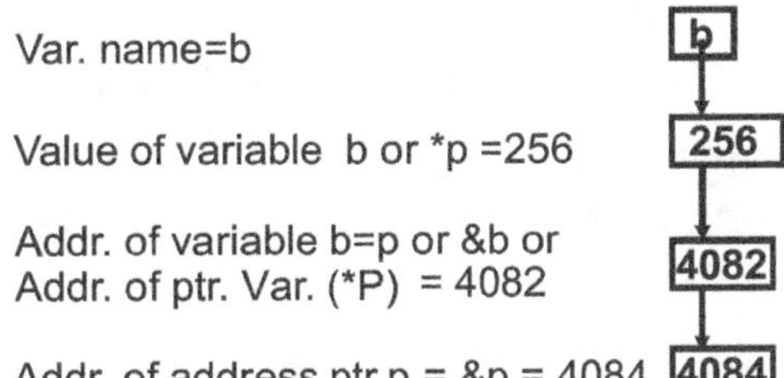

10.5. POINTER EXPRESSIONS :

Like all other C and C++ variables, pointer variables also conform to the same rules when used in an expression. Several valid expressions using pointer variables are :

x=x+ *a; (the content of "a" is added to "x")
c = *a * *b; (the contents of "a" and "b" are multiplied and stored in "c")
y= *a + x; (the content of "a" is added to "x" and stored in "y")

At this point, we must discuss a few special aspects of pointer expressions.

10.5.1.Pointer Assignments :

A pointer may be used in the right hand side of an assignment statement to assign its value to another pointer. For example,

```
swap(a,b)
int *a, *b;
{
        int c;
        c = *a;
        *a =*b;
        *b=c;
}
```

Explanation :

Inside the function swap we first assign the content of "a" into the variable "c". Then the content of "a" is replaced by the content of "b". Finally the content of "b" is replaced with the values of "c". This can be further illustrated thro' the following program in C++ which brings out clearly the use of pointers in the process of calling a function by reference.

Program 10.5.1

Write a program in C++ to illustrate the calling of a function by reference using pointer.

```
//Program to illustrate call by reference
# include <iostream>
using namespace std;
int main ( )
{
    int x,y;
    void swap (int *,int *);    //function prototype; int* means ptr. variable
    cout <<"Enter any two numbers \n";
    cin >>x>>y;
    cout <<"The values of x and y before entering function swap\n";
    cout <<x<<" "<<y"<<"\n";
    swap (&x,&y);           //addr. of x and y arg. passed on to swap ( )
    cout <<"The values of x and y after return from the function swap\n";
    cout <<x<<" "<<y<<"\n";
    return 0;
}
    void swap(int *a, int*b)     //call function includes function prototype
    {
        int c;
        cout <<"\n Input x and y to the function swap( ) \n";
        c = *a;
        *a =*b;
        *b=c;

        cout <<*a<<"\t"<<*b<<"\n";
    }
```

OUTPUT :

```
Enter any two numbers
66  88
The values of x and y before entering function swap
66  88
Input x and y to the function swap( )
88  66
The values of a and b after return from the function swap
88     66
```

10.5.2 Arithmetic Operations with Pointers :

There are the only four arithmetic operators that can be used with pointers. They are +, –, ++ and – –

Let us see what happens in pointer arithmetic:

If "p"is a pointer to an integer with a current value of 1000, then the address of p is 1000 and after the expression

p++;

"p" will contain 1004 (and not 1001 !), because the length of integer is 4 bytes. The same holds good for decrement also.

After the expression

p – –;

"p" will have the value of 996 because "p – – " is a post operator.

A pointer when incremented or decremented is always relative to its base type. That is, its value is increased or decreased by the length of the data type, which is known as the scale factor. The various scale factors are :

character	1 byte
short	2 bytes
integer	4 bytes
float	4 bytes
double	8 bytes

The number of bytes required to store various data types could be found using sizeof ( ) operator. For example if "a" is a variable, then, sizeof (a) returns the number of bytes required to store the variable "a".

The different types of permissible arithmetic operations with pointers are given in Table No.10.1

Table 10.1

Data Type	Initial Address (p or &(*p))	Operation		Address After Operation		Required Bytes
				p++	p - -	
int i=99	4046 (& (*i))	++	- -	4048	4044	2
char c='q'	4053 (& (*c))	++	- -	4054	4052	1
float f=77.6	4058 (& (*f))	++	- -	4062	4054	4
long l=6	4060 (& (*l))	++	- -	4064	4056	4

The following arithmetic operations on addresses of pointers are NOT ALLOWED in pointer operations.

1. *Addition of two address (pointers) : eg. p1 + p2*
2. *Multiplication of addresses or multiplication of address with a constant. p1 * p2 or (k) x (p)*
3. *Division of addresses or Division of address with a constant. eg. p1 / p2 or p1 / k.*

Program : 10.5.2

Write a program in C to show the effect of increment and decrement operator used as prefix and suffix to pointer variable.

```
# include <stdio.h>
# include <conio.h>
void main ( )
    {
        int i *ii;
        puts ("Enter Value of i");
        scanf (" %d",&i);
        ii=&i;
        clrscr ( );
        printf ("The entered value i=%d\n",i);
        printf ("Address ii=&i=%u\n",ii);  /* Ctrl. ch.%u is for address*/
        printf ("After ++ii, address of i=%u\n",++ii);
        printf ("After i++, address of i=%u\n",ii++);
        printf ("After - -i, address of i=%u\n",- -ii);
        printf ("After i- -, address of i=%u\n",ii- -);
        printf ("Now address of i=%u\n",ii);
    }
```

OUTPUT :

```
Enter Value of i=
8
The entered value of i=8
Address ii=&i=4060
After ++ii address of i=4062
After i++ address of i=4064
After - -i address of i=4062
After i- - address of i=4060
Now address of i=4060
```

Program 10.5.3 :

Write a program in C to perform different arithmetic operations using pointers.

```
# include <stdio.h>
# include <conio.h>

void main ( )
{
int a=30,b=20,*p,*j;

p=&a;                /*  p is address of address of a, *p is value of a  */
j=&b;

clrscr ( );
print ("\n Addition a+b=%d",*p+b);
print ("\n Substraction a-b=%d",*p-b);
print ("\n Product a*b=%d",*p**j);
print ("\n Division a/b=%d",*p /*j);   /*integer division gives quotient*/
print ("\n a Mod b = %d",*p % *j);     /*modular division gives remainder*/
}
```

OUTPUT :

```
Addition  a+b  =  50
Substraction a-b = 10
Product   a*b  = 600
Division  a/b  = 1.5
a mod b        = 10
```

Explanation :

For arithmetic, operations the values of the pointer variables are used.

10.6. POINTERS AND ARRAYS :

i) Array name by itself is an address or pointer. **In the case of single dimensional array, the name of the array without dimension points to the address of the first element (zeroth element of the single dimensional array)**

ii) The elements of the array together with their addresses can be displayed by using array name itself. **Array elements are stored in contiguous memory locations.**

iii) **In the case of multi-dimensional arrays the address of the first element of the multi-dimensional array has to be referred by the pointer.**

Program 10.6.1 :

Write a program in C to illustrate the use of array name as pointer to array and access of array elements through different ways using pointer.

```
# include <stdio.h>
# include <conio.h>
void main ( )
    {
      int arr[5] = {1,2,3,4,5},p=0;
    clrscr ( );
    for (p=0;p<5;p++)
      {
      printf ("Value of arr[%d]=",p);
      printf ("%d | ",arr[p]);
      printf ("%d | ",*(arr+p);
      printf ("%d | ",*(p+arr));
      printf ("%d | ", p[arr]);
      printf (" address of arr[%d]=%u\n",p,&arr[p]);
      }
    }
```

OUTPUT :

```
Value of arr[0] = 1 | 1 | 1 | 1 | address of arr[0]=6250
Value of arr[1] = 2 | 2 | 2 | 2 | address of arr[1]=6252
Value of arr[2] = 3 | 3 | 3 | 3 | address of arr[2]=6254
Value of arr[3] = 4 | 4 | 4 | 4 | address of arr[3]=6256
Value of arr[4] = 5 | 5 | 5 | 5 | address of arr[4]=6258
```

Explanation :

i) As arr (p) is a single dimensional array, the array name itself points to the address of the first element of the single dimensional array. p refers to the array element number.

ii) All the above operations on array pointer results in increase of the address by 2 bytes.

iii) *(p+arr refers to the same as arr [p]

iv) p [arr] This statement is same as p the array address.

Program 10.6.2

Write a program in C to display a two dimensional array element and their addresses using pointers.

```
# include <stdio.h>
# include <conio.h>
```

```
void main ( )
{
int i j=1,*p;
int q[3] [3] = {{11,22,33}, {44,55,66}, {77,88,99}};
clrscr ( );
printf ("\Elements of An array with their addresses\n\n");
p=&q[0][0]; /* Pointer p points to address of the first element of an array*/
for (i=0;i<9;i++,j++)
    {
    printf ("%5d[%5u]",*(p),p);
    p++;
    if (j==3);
      {
      printf ("\n");
      j=0;
      }
    }
}
```

OUTPUT :

```
Elements of An Array with their addresses.
11 [5022]  22 [5024]  33 [5026]
44 [5028]  55 [5030]  66 [5032]
77 [5034]  88 [5036]  99 [5038]
```

Explanation :

Since A is a two-dimensional array the pointer is made to point to the address of the first element of the two-dimensional array.

Program 10.6.3

Write a program in C++ to illustrate use of arrays with pointers in user defined function.

```
//To illustrate uses of pointers for single dimensional array
    #include <iostream>
    using namespace std;
    int main ( )
    {
        int b[4],i;
        void multiply(int *);
        cout <<"Enter 4 numbers \n";
```

```
        for(i=0;i<4;i++)
            cin>>b[i];
        multiply (a);
        cout <<"The values in array b after executing function is \n";
            for(i=0;i<4;i++)
                cout <<a[i]<<"\n";
            return 0;
    }
    void multiply(int *p)
    {
        for (int i=0;i<4;i++)
        {
            *p = *p * 2;
            *p++;
        }
    }
```

OUTPUT :

```
Enter 4 numbers
88
66
33
22
The values in array b after executing function is
176
132
66
44
```

Explanation :

After receiving the 5 elements for the array '' is passed to a function multiply(). Now the base address of the array i.e. "&b[0]" is passed to the function. Inside the function multiply (), the base address is received thro' the integer pointer variable "p". The content of base address i.e., "*p" is multiplied by 2, and it is stored in the same address itself. The integer pointer variable is incremented, so as to move the next address. It is repeated for the entire array.

Program 10.6.4

Write a program in C++ for conversion of a two-dimensional array into single dimensional array using pointers.

```
    //Program to convert a table (2 dim. array) into list  (1 dim. array)
    #include <iostream>
    using namespace std;
```

```
int main()
{
        int a[2][2],b[4],i,j,*c;
        cout <<"Enter 4 nos one in each row\n";
        for(i=0;i<2;i++)
                for(j=0;j<2;j++)
                        cin>>a[i][j];
                cout <<"The output in two dimensional array is\n";
        for(i=0;i<2;i++)
                {
                        for(j=0;j<2;j++)
                        cout <<setw(5)<<a[i][j];
                        cout <<"\n";
                }
        c=&a[0][0];        //addr. of 1st element is given to pointer c
        for(i=0;i<4;i++)
                b[i]=*c++;
cout <<"The output is one dimension \n";
        for(i=0;i<4;i++)
                cout <<b[i]<<" ";
        return 0;
}
```

OUTPUT :

```
Enter 4 nos one in each row
45
56
68
79
The output in two dimensional array is
45   56
68   79
The output in one dimension
45 56 68 79
```

Explanation :

In this case the two dimensional array is assigned to a integer pointer variable 'c'. The content of the integer pointer variable 'c' is then assigned to a one dimensional array variable 'b'. The increment for the one-dimensional array is taken care by the "for" loop while the increment operator is used to increment the pointer variable by its scale factor.

10.7. ARRAY OF POINTERS :

So far we have studied array of different standard data types such as array of int, float characters etc., In the same way the 'C' and 'C++ languages also support array of pointers. **Array of pointers is nothing but a collection of addresses. Here, we store address of variables for which we have to declare an array as a pointer.**

Program 10.7.1

Write a program in C to store address of different elements of an array-using array of pointers.

```
# include <stdio.h>
# include <conio.h>
void main ( )
 {
     int *arrp[3];
     int arr1[3]={2,4,6},k;
     for (k=0;k<3;k++)
       arrp[k]=arr1+k;      /*arr1 refers to base addr. of array of pointers*/
     clrscr ( );
     printf("\n\tAddress Element\n");
     for(k=0;k<3;k++)
       {
           printf ("\t"%u",arrp[k]);              /*array of pointers*/
           printf ("\t"%7d\n",*(arrp[k]));   /* array of values from array of ptrs*/
       }
 }
```

OUTPUT :

Address	**Element**
4080	2
4082	4
4084	6

Explanation :

i) *arrp [3] is declared as an array of pointers. Each element of this array of pointers points to the address of the element of the given array of values.

ii)

Array of pointer	**Array Address**	**Element of array**	**Value of element**
arrp[0]	4080	arr1[0]	2
arrp[1]	4082	arr1[1]	4
arrp[2]	4084	arr1[2]	6

10.8. POINTERS TO POINTERS :

This facility is also available both in C and C++. The pointer variables also have an address. **The pointer variable containing address of another pointer variable is called a pointer to pointer.** The chain can be continued to any extent. Thus we can have a pointer of a pointer which points to another point and so on.

The syntax for pointer to pointer is :
**** (variable name)**

Program 10.8.1

Write a program in C to print value of a variable through pointer and through pointer to pointer.

```
# include <stdio.h>
# include <conio.h>
void main ( )
 {
     int b=2,*p,* *q;
     p=&c;
     q=&p;
     clrscr ( );
     printf ("\n        Value of b=%d Address of b=%u",b,&b);
     printf ("\nThrough  *p Value of b=%d Address of b=%u",*p,p);
     printf ("\nThrough  **q Value of b=%d Address of b=%u",**q,*q);
 }
```

OUTPUT :

```
                 Value of b=2 Address of b=4056
Through  *p      Value of b=2 Address of b=4056
Through  * *q    Value of b=2 Address of b=4056
```

Explanation :

b is a variable and b=2
p is address of variable 'b'; p=&b;
*p is the value of the pointer variable where p is the address of 'b' (&b)
* *q is * (*q) and is the pointer to pointer variable *p; q=&p;

10.9. POINTERS AND CHARACTER STRINGS :

A string is nothing but an array of characters, terminated by a null character, as said in the previous sections. **A pointer can be used to point not only int or float variables but character or string variables also. String variables can also be expressed as an array of characters.**

Program 10.9.1

Write a program in C to illustrate the use of pointer to a string.

```
# include <stdio.h>
# include <conio.h>
main ( )
 {
     char name [15], *ch;
     printf ("Enter Your String :");
     gets(name);
     ch=name;
     /* store base address of string name */
          while (*ch != "\0")
     {
          printf (" %c,*ch);
          ch++;
     }
 }
```

OUTPUT :

Enter Your String : **WELCOME TO C**
WELCOME TO C

Program 10.9.2

Write a program in C++ to find the length of the given string by using pointers.

```
//string length using pointers
#include <iostream>
using namespace std;
int main()
{
     char str1[30], *a;
     int i=0;
     cout <<"Enter string str1\n";
     cin.getline(str1,80);
     a=str1 ;
     while (*a != '\0')
     {
          i++;
          a++;
     }
     cout <<"The length of a given string str1 is "<<i<<"\n";
          return 0;
}
```

OUTPUT :

Enter string str1
Hello ! How do you do?
the length of a given string is 22

We can use pointers to access the individual characters in a string. For example.

```
char *City ;
City = "Chennai";
```

Here, "City" is declared as a pointer to character and we assign the string constant "Chennai" to City.

Let us take another example;

```
char *Cities[3] = { "Kolkata", "Delhi", "Hyderabad");
```

Here "City" is declared to be an array of three pointers each pointer pointing to the respective City as shown :

City[0] is : Kolkata
City[1] is : Delhi
City[2] is : Hyderabad

* * *

COMPREHENSION - 10

Note : **By answering all the questions given in this comprehension one can answer any objective type of questions easily whatever be the form of the question. Answers for these questions can be obtained by going through the topics in this chapter carefully.**

1. What for Pointers are used in C and C++?
2. In what way Pointers are useful?
3. What is a Pointer? Explain clearly with figures the address and value of Pointer Variable.
4. How do you distinguish the address and value of a Pointer Variable?
5. What is the difference between the address operator and pointer operator? Explain with examples.
6. What are the rules governing the Pointer arithmetic P and arithmetic for values of Pointer variables?
7. How do you declare a Pointer Variable and initialize it? Explain with syntax and examples.
8. How do you declare an ordinary Variable and initialize it? Explain with syntax and examples.
9. How do you input and retrieve an ordinary variable? Explain with syntax and examples.
10. How do you input and retrieve a Pointer variable? Explain with syntax and examples.
11. What is an indirection or deference or deference operator? Why is it called so?
12. How do you access a variable through its pointer? Explain.
13. Explain pointer assignments using a C Program to swap two integer numbers.
14. Explain with examples pointer expressions.
15. Explain how to call a function by reference using pointer
16. Give in the form of a table the permissible arithmetic operations with pointers.
17. What are the arithmetic operations on the addresses of pointer variables that are not allowed? Why?
18. Explain with examples how you can access the array elements of single and multi dimensional arrays with pointers.
19. What is an array of pointers? Explain with examples.

20. What is Pointer to pointers or pointer of pointers? Explain with examples.
21. Can you use pointer to character or strings? Explain.
22. Explain the effects of the following statements:
    i) int a, *b = &a;
    ii) int p, *p;
    iii) char *s;
    iv) a = (float *) & x;
    v) double (*f) ( );
23. If **m** and **n** have been declared as integers and **p1** and **p2** as pointers to integers, then state errors, if any, in the following statements:
    i) p1 = &m;
    ii) p2 = n;
    iii) *p1 = &n
    iv) p2 = &*&m;
    v) m = p2 = p1;
    vi) p1 = &p2;
    vii) m = *p1 + *p2++
24. Distinguish between (*m) [5] and *m[5].
25. State whether each of the following statements is true or false. Give reasons.
    i) An integer can be added to a pointer.
    ii) A pointer can never be subtracted from another pointer.
    iii) When an array is passed as an argument to a function, a pointer is passed.
    iv) Pointers cannot be used as formal parameters in headers to function definitions.
    v) Value of a local variable in a funciton can be changed by another function.
26. What is meant by Void Pointers? Explain.
27. Which of the following statements is true after execution of following program?

    int a[5]=[2,3],*c;

    c=a;

    (*c) --;

    a) The value of a[0] will be 1; b) The value of a[0] will be 2;

    c) a) The value of a[1] will be 1; d) None of the above

28. The fastest way to exchange two rows in a two-dimensional array is
    a) Exchange the addresses of each element in the two rows.
    b) Exchange the elements of the two rows
    c) Store the address of the rows in an array of pointers and exchange the pointers.
    d) None of the above
29. Which is the correct way to declare a pointer?
    a) int *ptr; b) * int ptr;
    c) int ptr*; d) int _ptr x;
30. What will be the result of the following program?

```
void main ( )
{
int a=8, b=2, c, *p;
c= (a=a+b, b=a/b, a=a*b,b=a-b);
p=&c;
clrscr ( );
printf ("\n %d",++*p);
}
```

31. What will be the value of x after execution of the following program?

```
# include <stdio.h>
# include <conio.h>
void main ( )
{
int x, *p;
p = &x;
*p=2;
clrscr ( );
printf ("\nValue of x=%d",x);
}
```

    a) x=2 b) x=( )
    c) x=65504 d) None of the above

* * *

EXERCISE - 10

Note: By answering all the questions given in this exercise one can answer subjective type of questions easily including problems. The worked examples in the chapter may help in solving these questions.

1. How are pointers helpful in programming when we have a set of data like arrays, strings etc.?

2. Explain the difference between 'call by reference' and 'call by value'.

   In what way pointer will be helpful for the above tasks?

3. Write a program using pointers to read in an array of integers and print its elements in reverse order.

4. We know that the roots of a quadratic equation of the form

   $$ax^2 + bx + c = 0$$

   are given by the following equations;

   $$x_1 = \frac{-b + square\ root\,(b^2 - 4ac)}{2a}$$

   $$x_2 = \frac{-b - square\ root\,(b^2 - 4ac)}{2a}$$

   write a function to calculate the roots. The function must use two pointer parameters, one to receive the coefficients a, b, and c, and the other to send the roots to the calling function.

5. Write a function that receives a sorted array of integers and an integer value, and inserts the value in its correct place.

6. Write a function using pointers to add two matrices and to return the resultant matrix to the calling function.

7. Using pointers, write a function that receives a character string and a character as arguments and deletes all occurrences of this character in the string. The function should return the corrected string with no holes.

8. Write a function **day_name** that receives a number **n** and returns a pointer to a character string containing the name of the corresponding day . The day names should be kept in a **static** table of character strings local to the function.

9 Write a program for extraction of a string using pointers.

10 Write a program for string comparison using pointers.

11 Write a program for writing numbers in ascending order using pointers.

12 Write a program to calculate the square and cube of an entered number using pointer of a variable containing the entered number.

* * *

CHAPTER 11
PRE-PROCESSOR DIRECTIVES

11.1 INTRODUCTION :

We are now aware of the execution of C and C++ programs. Any program execution needs certain steps. They are (a) the C or C++ program is written in the editor, (b) compilation, (c) linking and (d) the executable code is generated. In between these stages there also involves one more stage i.e., preprocessing stage. **The preprocessor is a program that processes the source program before it is passed on to the compiler.**

The program typed in the editor is the source code to the preprocessor. The preprocessor then passes the source code to the compiler. It is also not essential to write the program with preprocessor facility. But it is a good practice to use it preferably at the beginning.

One of the most important features of C and C++ languages is to offer preprocessor directives. **The preprocessor directives are always initialized at the beginning of the program. It begins with a # (hash) symbol.**

Preprocessor is one of the special features in C and C++. It helps to include many information to the Compiler as incorporated in the main program. In other words, it provides definitions, informations and instructions to the main program. The preprocessors, as the name implies, processes the main program before it passes through the compiler. It is a program that contains a set of directives, which are translated into valid C or C++ codes by the compiler. Preprocessor operates under the control of directives (or command lines), which follow a special syntax different from the normal C grammar.

The Pre-processor Directive begins with a symbol # (hash). It can be placed anywhere but quite often it is declared at the beginning before the main ( ) function or any particular function.

11.2. # define DIRECTIVE AND MACRO SUBSTITUTION :

The syntax of #define directive and macro substitution is as follows.

 # define identifier <substitute text>

OR

#define identifier (argument 1.. argument N) substitute text

Example of Definition of the constant π :

define PI 3.14

This statement defines macro templates. During preprocessing the preprocessor replaces every occurrence of PI (identifier) with 3.14 (substitute value). *Here, PI is a macro template and 3.14 is its macro expansion.*

i) The macro templates are generally declared with capital letters for quick identification. One can also define macros with small letters.

ii) The macro templates and its expansions must be separated with at least one blank space.

iii) It is not necessary to provide space between # and **define.** It is optional to the programmer ;

iv) The macro definition can be terminated with semi-colon and it is optional. The programmer can try the macro definitions with and without semi-colons. The words followed by # are not keywords. The programmer can use these words for variable names.

v) With #define, the statement does no have semicolon; however when the macro is used later, it should have a semicolon.

vi) A macro can also include expression as shown below.

vii) Also a macro once defined can be used as part of the definition of other macros.

viii) A macro may also have an argument.

ix) It is important to note that the comma is the delimeter that separates arguments in a macro. A comma can be included as a part of an argument only.

x) Macros can also be used as parameters of other macros, and the other macro calls can be nested in the same way as function calls.

xi) The statement **'#ifdef name'** is a macro for conditional compilation. It allows a part of a program to be compiled only if the defined constant that is specified as parameter has been defined, independently of its value.

The Preprocessor accepts macro definition with the keyword #define. A macro is an identifier for a substitution string that is placed in the main program and the string gets substituted for the identifier in the main program. For example,

i) if the value of A is 5 then the macro definition is

#define A 5

This will cause the compiler to substitute 5, for each A encountered in the main program. By definition, all macros (or) identifiers are written in capital letters. Some other macro examples are,

```
#define LENGTH 165
#define CONAME   INFOSYS
```

ii) A macro can also include expression as shown below.

```
#define A (80-10)
#define B (80 * 3+10)
#define TOTAL P + Q + 2000
#define VOLUME 5*2.67*22
```

iii) Also a macro once defined can be used as part of the definition of other macros. For example

```
#define A 100
#define B A-60
#define C A-B/5
```

iv) A macro may also have an argument. Calculate the following definition.

```
#define AREA(a) (a*a)
```

if,

```
p=AREA(side);
```

the preprocessor expands 'p' as p=(side*side);

Suppose a program consists of the statements,

```
    if (a>0) a-=1;
and if (b>0) b-=1;
```

Here, apart from the different variables, the statements are identical in the form. It would be convenient to have a single macro that can represent both the statements. The preprocessor permits macro's to save arguments just as functions do, with the difference that the arguments (in preprocessor directive) are strings rather than values. The statement,

```
#DEFINE decrement (x) if (x>0) x-=1
```

when expanded, the string passes the argument x replacing all occurrences of x.

Thus the statement DECREMENT(a) is expanded as

```
if(a>0) b-=1; and
DECREMENT(b); to
if(b>0) b-=1;
```

it must be noted here when the macro name "DECREMENT" is used with #define, the statement does no have semicolon; however when the macro is used later, it should have a semicolon.

DECREMENT(a);

v) It is important to note that the comma is the delimeter that separates arguments in a macro. A comma can be included as a part of an argument only.

(a) When it is located between the quotation marks; and (b) when it is used within the parentheses. For example,

```
# define ITER (a,b,c) for (a;b;c)
ITER((i=0,j=1),(i<10,(i++,j++))
```

This can be expanded as,

```
for ((i=0,j=1);i<10;(i++,j++))
```

vi) Macros can also be used as parameters of other macros, and the other macro calls can be nested in the same way as function calls.

```
e.g  #define MAX ((a)/3.0)
     # define A MAX (MAX(a))
```

Program 11.2.1

Write a Program in C to define and use the value of the identifier PI = 3.14

```
# include <stdio.h>
# include <conio.h>
# define PI 3.14
void main ( )
{
    float r, area, circmf;
    printf ("\n Enter radius of circle in cms.");
    scanf ("%f"&r);
    area=PI*r*r;
    circmf = 2.0* PI* r;
    printf ("Area of a Circle = %.2f  cm2  ",area);
    printf ("\n circumference of circle in cm", circmf);
    getche ( );
    }
```

OUTPUT :

```
Enter radius of circle in cms : 7
Area of a Circle =153.86 cm2
Circumference of Circle in cm = 43.96
```

11.3. UNDEFINING A MACRO :

A macro defined with # define directives can be undefined with # undef directive.

Syntax for #undef

#undef identifier

It is useful when we do not want to allow the use of macros in any portion of the program.

#undef fulfills the inverse functionality of #define. What it does is to eliminate from the list of defined constants the one that has the name passed as parameter to #undef:

```
#define WIDTH 100
int s1[WIDTH];
#undef WIDTH
#if def
```

These directives allow us to discard part of the code of a program if a certain condition is not fulfilled.

vi) Conditional #define : The statement **'#ifdef name'** is a macro for conditional compilation. It allows a part of a program to be compiled only if the defined constant that is specified as parameter has been defined, independently of its value. The general form of #ifdef is as follows :

```
#ifdef name
    ............................
    ............................
    #endif
```

For example :

```
    #ifdef WIDTH
        int num[WIDTH];
    #endif
```

In this case, their line int num [WIDTH]; is only considered by the compiler if the defined constant WIDTH has been previously defined independently of the value. On the other hand, if it has not been defined, then the line will not be included in the program.

11.4. CONDITIONAL COMPILATION USING PRE-PROCESSOR DIRECTIVE :

This feature is common to both C and C++. **The most frequently used conditional compilation directives are #if, #else, #elif (else-if), #endif etc. These directives allow the programmer to include the portions of the codes based on the conditions.** The compiler compiles selected portion of the source codes based on the conditions. The syntax of the #ifdef directives is given below.

Syntax

```
# ifdef <identifier>
            statement1;
            statement2;
}
# else
{
            statement3;
            statement4;
}
#endif
```

11.5. THE #ifndef DIRECTIVE (if not defined):

#ifndef is the complimentary of **#ifdef.** *The code between the #ifndef directive and the #endif directive is only compiled if the constant name that is specified has not been defined previously.* For example consider the following.

```
#ifndef WIDTH
#define WIDTH 100
#endif
int num[WIDTH];
```

In this case, if the defined constant WIDTH has not been defined, it would be defined with a value of 100 first. Then the statements after #endif is executed. If the constant WIDTH is already defined it would maintain the value skipping the statements between #infdef and #endif.

The syntax of the #ifndef directive is given below.

Syntax

```
# ifndef <identifier>
            {
            statement1;
            statement2;
            }
#else
            {
            statement3;
            statement4;
            }
#endif
```

The #ifndef works exactly opposite to that of # ifdef. The #ifndef preprocessor tests whether the identifier has defined substitute text or not. If the identifier is defined then #else blocks is compiled and executed and the compiler ignores. # if block even if errors are intentionally made. Error Messages will not be displayed. If identifier is not defined then #if block is compiled and executed.

Program 11.5.1

Write a program in C to use conditional compilation statement as to whether the identifier is defined or not.

```
# include <stdio.h>
# include <conio.h>
# define LINE 5
void main ( )
{
    clrscr ( );
    #ifdef LINE
    printf ("This is line number five,");
    #else
    printf ("This is not line number five");
    #endif
    getche( );
}
```

OUTPUT :

This is line number five.

11.6. #if, #else and #elif (else-if) :

The #if, #else and #elif directives serve for that the portion of code that follows is compiled only if the specified condition is satisfied. **Like any other logical expression this directive is also executed but it can only serve to evaluate constant expressions.**

For example :

```
#if LENGTH>200
    #undef LENGTH
    #define LENGTH 120
#elseif LENGTH <100
    #undef LENGTH
        #define LENGTH 150
    #endif
int num[LENGTH];
```

11.7 THE # line DIRECTIVE

The syntax of the line directive is as follows.

#line <constant> [<identifier>]

Causes the compiler to imagine -the line number of the next source line as given by <constant>, and <identifier> gives the current input file. If <identifier> is absent, then the current file name remains unchanged.

Example #line 15 pragma.c

We can use #line control directives to make the compiler provide more meaningful error messages.

Program 11.7.1

Write a program in C++ to use # line control directive

```
#include <iostream>
#define LINE 200 200
using namespace std;
void main(void)
{
        void func1(),func2();
        func1();
        func2();
        cout<<endl;
}
        #line 100
        void func1()
}
        cout <<"\n function 1 - the current line number is "<<__LINE__;
}
#line LINE200
        void func2()
        {
        cout <<"\n function 2 - the current line number is "<<...LINE...;
        }
```

OUTPUT :

function 1 - the current line number is 102
function 2 - the current line number is 202

11.8. THE #error DIRECTIVE :

The # error is used to display user defined message during compilation of the program.

The syntax for #error directive is given below.

```
# if !defined (identifier)
# error <ERROR MESSAGE>
# endif
```

Program 11.8.1

Write a Program in C to display user define error message using #error directive

```
# include <stdio.h>
# include <conio.h>
# define B 1
void main ( )
{
clrscr ( );
#define A
#if !defined (A)
#error MACRO A IS NOT DEFINED.
#else
printf("Macro A is found,");
#endif
}
```

OUTPUT :

Macro A is found

Tip : The # defined directive will work exactly opposite to # ! defined directive. The syntax is as given below.

```
# if defined (identifier)
{
      ......... ;
      ........ ;
}
#else
# error <ERROR MESSAGE>
# endif
```

11.9 # OPERATOR OR TOKEN PASTING & STRINGIZING :

Stringizing operation :

In this operation macro argument is converted to string. The sing # carries the operation. It is placed before the argument.

The # (single sharp sign) operator converts a parameter of a function-like macro into a character string literal. For example, if macro ABC is defined using the following directive :

#define XYZ(x) #x

For ex :

Macro call	Result of Macro Expansion
XYZ (1)	"1"
XYZ(Hello there)	"Hello there

We can use the '#' operator in a function-like macro definition according to the following rules :

- A parameter following # operator in a function-like macro is converted into a character string literal containing the argument passed to the macro.
- White-space characters that appear before or after the argument passed to the macro are deleted.
- Multiple white-space characters embedded within the argument passed to the macro is replaced by a single space character.
- If the argument passed to the macro contains a string literal and if a \ (backslash) character appears within the liberal, a second \character is inserted before the original \when the macro is expanded.
- If the argument passed to the macro contains a"(double quotation mark) character, a\ character is inserted before the "when the macro is expanded.
- If he argument passed to the macro contains a '(single quotation mark) character, a \ character is inserted before the 'when the macro is expanded.
- The conversion of an argument into a string literal occurs before macro expansion on that argument.
- If more has on ## operator or # operator appears in the replacement list of a macro definition, the order of evaluation of the operators is not defined.
- If the result of the macro expansion is not a valid character string literal, the behaviour is undefined.

Program 11.9.1

Write a program in C to carry out stringizing operation

```
# include <stdio.h>
# include <conio.h>
# define say(m) printf (#m)
```

```
void main ( )
{
clrscr ( );
say (Hello);
}
```

OUTPUT :

Hello

Explanation : In the above program after conversion the statement **say(Hello)** is treated as **printf ("Hello"). It is not essential to enclose the text in quotation in the stringizing operator.**

11.10. MACRO CONCATENATION WITH THE # # OPERATOR :

The ## (double sharp sign) operator concatenates two tokens in a macro invocation (text and/or arguments) given in a macro definition.

If a macro AB was defined using the following directive:

```
#define AB (a,b)        a##b
```

the last token of the argument for x is concatenated with the first token of the argument for y.

For example :

Macro call	Result of Macro Expansion
AB(1, 2)	12
AB(Object,Oriented)	Object Oriented

We can use ## operator according to the following rules :

- The ## Operator cannot be the very first or very last item in the replacement list of a macro-definition.
- The last token of the item in front of the ## operator is concatenated with first token of the item following the ## operator.
- Concatenation takes place before any macros in arguments are expanded.
- If the result of a concatenation is a valid macro name it is available for further replacement even if it appears in a context in which it would not normally be available.
- If more than on ## operator and/or # operator appears in the replacement list of a macro definition, the order of evaluation of the operators is not defined.

11.11 The # include DIRECTIVE :

We are very familiar with this # include statement.

The # include directive loads specified file in the current program. The macros and functions of loaded file can be called in the current program. The included file is also compiled with current program. The syntax is as given below.

a) # include "file name"
b) # include <filename>

Where # is a symbol used with directives.

a) **The file name is included in the double quotation marks which indicates that the search for the file is made in the current directory and in the standard directories.**

Example : # include "stdio.h"

b) **When the file name included without double quotation marks, the search for file is made only in the standard directives.**

Example :

```
# include <stdio.h>
# include <conio.h>
# include "udf.c"
# include <udf.h>
```

Explanation : *The udf.c is a user defined function file which is compiled before the main program is compiled.*

11.12. INLINE DIRECTIVE :

Reports the compiler that the source code has in line **asm** statements. It is important to know previously that the source code contains assembly code.

11.13 THE #pragma SAVEREGS :

The #pragma SAVEREGS guarantees that a huge function will not modify the value of any of the registers when it is entered. Place this directive immediately preceding the function definition.

11.14. THE #pragma DIRECTIVE :

The ANSI-C and TURBO-C provide pragma directives. The #pragma directives are defined with # (hash) and these are the preprocessor directives. **These pragma directives deal with formatting source listing and placing components in the object file generated by the compiler. It sets / resets certain warning and errors during compilation of C program.** Table 10.1, 10.2, 10.3 and 10.4 describe the different pragma names with error messages.

Syntax

pragma warn + xxx

pragma warn - xxx

Where the first statement turns on the warning message and the second statements sets off the warning message.

Table 11.1 ANSI Violations and #pragma

#pragma name	Warning On	Warning Off
Hexadecimal or octal constant too large	+big	-big
Redefinition not identical	+dup	-dup
Both return and return of a value used	+ret	-ret
Not part of structure	+str	-str
Undefined structure	+stu	-stu
Suspicious pointer conversion	+sus	-sus
Void functions cannot return a value	+voi	-voi
Zero length structure	+zst	-zst

Table 11.2 Common Errors and #pragma

#Pragma name	Warning on	Warning Off
Assigned a value but never used	+sus	-sus
Possible use before definition	+def	-def
Code has no effect	+eff	-eff
Parameter never used	+par	-par
Possibly incorrect assignment	+pia	-pia
Unreachable code	+rch	-rch
Function should return a value	+rvl	-rvl
Ambiguous operators need parenthesis	+amb	-amb

Table 11.3 Less Common Errors and #pragma

# pragma name	Warning On	Warning Off
Superfluous & with function or array	+amp	-amp
No declaration for function	+nod	-nod
Call to function with no prototype	+pro	-pro
Structure passed by value	+stv	-stv
Declared but never used	+use	-use

Table 11.4. Portability Warnings and **#pragma**

# pragma name	Warning On	Warning Off
Non portable pointer assignment	+apt	-apt
Constant is long	+cln	-cln
Non-portable pointer comparison	+cpt	-cpt
Constant out of range in comparison	+rng	-rng
Non-portable pointer conversion	+rpt	-rpt
Conversion can lose significant digits	+sig	-sig
Mixing pointers to signed and unsigned char	+ucp	-ucp

The display of these warning messages can be made on or off by setting the pragma options.

11.15. THE PREDEFINED MACROS IN ANSI AND TURBO-C :

a) ANSI C Predefined Macros

The lists of pre-defined macros according to ANSI standard are as per the Table 11.5. There are five pre-defined macros and are always available to the programmer for use. They can not be undefined. Every macro name is defined with two underscores as prefix and suffix. These macros are useful for finding system information such as date, time, and file name and line number.

Table 11.5 Predefined Macros in ANSI-C

Predefined Macros	Function
Date	Display system date in string format
Time	Displays system time in string format
Line	Displays line number as an integer
File	Displays current file name in string format
Stdc	In ANSI 'C' the value returned will be non-zero.

b) Turbo C predefined Macros : The pre-defined macros in Turbo C are listed in the table. The programmer can use the macro ...TURBOC.... to find the version of Turbo. By setting option of code generation in option menu one can test next two macros. For more information the user is advised to view options in option menu.

Table 11.6 : Pre-defined Macros in Turbo C

Predefined Macros	Function
Turbo-C	Displays current turbo C version
Pascal	1 if "Calling convention...Pascal option is chosen, otherwise undefined.
Cdecl	1 if "Calling convention....C" option is chosen, otherwise undefined.
MSDOS	The integer constant 1.

c) **Memory Model Macros :** The following six macros are defined based on the memory models chosen by the user. There are six memory models and only one is defined which is currently in use and remaining all are undefined. To change the memory model user is advised to select option menu->compiler -> model.

Table 11.7 : Memory Model Predefined Macros :

Tiny	_Small_	_Medium_
Compact	_Large_	_Huge_

11.16. STANDARD I/O PREDEFINED STREAMS IN C - stdio.h

The Predefined streams automatically opens when the program is started. The Table 11.8 describes their macro expansion defined in stdio.h header file.

Table 11.8. Standard I/O Predefined Macros in stdio.h

Macros	Function	Definition in stdio.h
stdin	Standard input device	#define stdin (&_streams [0])
stdout	Standard output device	#define stdiout (&_streams [1])
stderr	Standard error output device	#define stderr (&_streams[2])
stdaux	Standard auxiliary device	#define stdaux (&_streams[3])
stdprn	Standard Printer	#define stdprn (&_streams[4])

11.17. THE PREDEFINED MACROS IN ctype.h

The header file "ctype.h" contains a set of macros that checks character. The Table 11.9 describes all the macros. These macros take an argument of integer type and return an integer.

Table 11.9 Predefined Macros in ctype.h.

Sr. No.	Macro	Returns true (!0) value if
01	isalpha (d)	d is a letter
02	isupper (d)	d is a capital letter
03	islower (d)	d is small letter
04	isdigit (d)	d is a digit
05	isalnum (d)	d is a letter or digit
06	isxdigit (d)	d is a hexadecimal digit
07	isspace (d)	d is a space
08	ispunct (d)	d is a punctuation symbol
09	isprint (d)	d is a printable character
10	isgraph (d)	d is printable, but not be a space
11.	iscntrl (d)	d is a control character
12.	isascii (d)	d is an ASCII code

Program 11.17.1 : Write a program in C to identify whether the entered character is letter or digit and capital or small using predefined macros.

```
# include <stdio.h>
# include <conio.h>
# include <ctype.h>        /*header to check character type*/
void main ( )
{
char d;
int f;
clrscr ( );
printf("\nEnter any character :");
d=getche( );

    f=isalpha(d);
    if(f != 0)
    {
        printf"\n%c is letter in",d);
        f=isupper(d);
            if (f != 0)
            printf ("Capital Case");
            else
        printf (" Small Case");
    }
```

```
        else
       {
       f=isdigit(d);

            if (f != 0)
            printf ("\n %c is a digit",d);
            else
            {
            f=ispunct(d);
            if (f != 0)
            printf ("\n %c is a punctuation symbol",d);
            }
       }
            getche( );
}
```

OUTPUT :

Enter my character : a
a is a letter in Small Case

* * *

COMPREHENSION - 11

Note : By answering all the questions given in this comprehension one can answer any objective type of questions easily whatever be the form of the question. Answers for these questions can be obtained by going through the topics in this chapter carefully.

1. What is a Preprocessor? What does it do?
2. How is a Preprocessor directive stated? Give the syntax and four important examples of Preprocessor directives. State when these directives are used.
3. What is define directive? Why is it used?
4. What is meant by a Macro and Macro Template?
5. What is the relationship between a Macro and a define statement?
6. Is it necessary to provide a space between # and define ?
7. Should a define statement be terminated with a semicolon?
8. Should a semicolon be used when a Macro is used after its definition?
9. Are the Macro names or names used for the define statements Key Words?
10. Can you use variable names for define statements?
11. Can a macro use expressions?
12. Can a macro use arguments?
13. How are Macro arguments separated?
14. What is # include directives? What purpose do they serve? Give examples.
15. Give the syntax for conditional compilation and examples.
16. Can Macros use arguments of other Macros?
17. Can a Macro be used as part of other Macros? If so when?
18. Can Macros be used as parameters of other Macros?
19. Is # define a Key Word? What happens when it is seen?
20. When the Macro name is used subsequent to its definition what is done?
21. What should be the type of Preprocessor arguments?
22. In what way arguments of Preprocessor different from arguments of functions?
23. Give an example of Preprocessor directive and explain how it works.
24. How do you undefine a Macro that had been defined earlier? Explain with example.
25. Explain the syntax of if not defined DIRECTIVE.

26. By definition what should be the case of alphabets used for Macro or identifier definitions?
27. Can Macro calls be nested like nested function calls?
28. Explain #if #else and #elif (else-if)
29. Explain #line DIRECTIVE
30. What is error directive? Explain with error directives.
31. What does # (single sharp sign) operator do?
32. What is Stringization or Token Pasting?
33. What are the rules for # operator in a function like Macro definition?
34. Explain Macro Concatenation with # # operators.
35. What are the rules governing Macro Concatenation?
36. Explain with examples and syntax the use of # include directives.
37. What are inline directives? Explain.
38. Explain #pragma DIRECTIVE
39. What does #pragma SAVEREGS do?
40. What are Predefined Macros? State some of them defined in ANSI C and Turbo C.

* * *

EXERCISE - 11

Note : By answering all the questions given in this exercise one can answer subjective type of questions easily including problems. The worked examples in the chapter may help in solving these questions.

1. Define Preprocessor and its functions?
2. Distinguish between # define directive and # include directives with examples.
3. Define #define directive and Macro substitution with examples.
4. What are Macros and the rules governing Macro templates? Explain.
5. Distinguish between functions and Preprocessor directives.
6. Explain token pasting and stringizing operations.
7. How do you undefine a predefined macro? Explain with examples.
8. What are Pragma directives? How do you set them on and off
9. Consider the following C code

```
#define prod (a,b)    (a * b)
main ( )
{
        printf (" %d\n",prod(1+25, 2)) ;
}
```

   The value printed out will be :

   a) 52 b) 51 c) 50 d) Unpredictable

10.
```
#define max (a,b)  (a>b? a  : b)
main ( )
{
        int m;
        m=max (1 2 3,  4 5 6);
        /* some more code */
}
```

   The above program

   a) Assigns 456 to m b) Assigns 123 to m
   c) Assigns the string "(a,b)" to m d) 0 Contains a compilation error

11. What will be the value of y after execution of the following program?

```
# include <stdio.h>
# include <conio.h>
# define plus (x) x;
# define minus (x)  -- x+ plus (x);
```

```
void main ( )
{
int x=8,y;
clrscr ( );
y=minus(x)
printf ("\n y = %d", y);
}
```

a) y=14 b) y=15
c) y=13 d) none of the above

12. What will the values of variables x and y after execution of the following program?

```
# include <stdio.h>
# include <conio.h>
# define P  x++;
# define plus (x)  P

void main ( )
{
int x=2,y;
clrscr ( );
y=plus(x)
printf ("\nx = %d y = %d", x,y);
}
```

a) x=3 y=2 b) x=3 y=3
c) x=2 y=2 d) none of the above

13. In the following example whether macro is treated as

```
# include <stdio.h>
# include <conio.h>
# define S   "This Book Teaches C and C++"

void main ( )
{
printf ("\n  %s", S);
}
```

a) macro as well as array b) only macro
c) only array d) none of the above

14. What will be the output after execution of the following program?

```
# include <stdio.h>
# include <conio.h>
# define S   "This Book Teaches C and C++"
```

```
void main ( )
{
clrscr ( );
printf ("\n %c", * (S+3) );
}
```

a) s b) h c) i d) T

15. The following program will display

```
# include <stdio.h>
# include <conio.h>
# define P &x
void main ( )
{
int x=2;
clrscr ( );
printf ("\t %u", P);
}
```

a) address b) value

c) error message d) none of the above

16. Write a program to check whether the entered character is digit or letter. Display appropriate messages. Use macros defined in "ctype.h" header file.
17. Write a program to define macros for opening and closing curly braces with BEGIN and END respectively. Use these macros in C program in place of opening and closing curly braces.
18. Write a program to explain conditional compilation.
19. Write a program to find the smallest and the largest out of the three numbers using macros with arguments.
20. Write programs to use macros as an array and as pointer.

* * *

CHAPTER 12
STRUCTURES AND UNION

12.1. INTRODUCTION :

C and C++ provide a special type of data structure called structures wherein data of different types pertaining to a single entity like roll numbers and names of students of a class, their marks in different subjects, their fee structure etc., under a single variable name. A variable stores a single value of a data type. Arrays can store many values of similar data type. Data in the array is of the same composition in nature as far as type is concerned. In real life we need to have different data types for example to maintain employees information we should have information such as name, age, qualification, salary etc. Here, to maintain the information of employees dissimilar data types are required. Name and qualification of the employee are char data type, age is integer, and salary is float. All these data types can not be expressed in a single array. One may think to declare different arrays for each data type. But there will be huge increase in source codes of the program. Hence, arrays can not be useful here. For tackling such mixed data types, a special feature is provided by C. It is known as structure.

A structure is a collection of one or more variables of different data types, grouped together under a single name. By using structures we can make a group of variables, arrays, pointers etc.

12.2. FEATURES OF STRUCTURES :

1. To copy elements of one array to another array of same data type elements are copied one by one. It is not possible to copy all the elements at a time. Whereas in structure it is possible to copy the contents of all structure elements of different data types to another structure variable its type using assignment (=) operator. It is possible because the structure elements are stored in successive memory locations.
2. Nesting of structures is possible i.e., one can create structure within the structure. Using this feature one can handle complex data types.
3. It is also possible to pass structure elements to a function. This is similar to passing an ordinary variable to a function.
4. One can pass individual structure elements or entire structure by value or address.
5. It is also possible to create structure pointers. In the pointer we have studied pointing a pointer to an integer, pointing to a float and pointing to a char. In a similar way we can create a pointer pointing to structure elements. For this it requires → operator.

12.3. DECLARATION AND INITIALIZATION OF STRUCTURES :

The syntax of a structure :

```
struct    struct_type
{
type variable1;
type variable2;
};
```

Structure declaration always starts with a struct keyword. **Here, struct_type is known as tag.** The **struct** declaration is enclosed within a pair of curly braces. Using **struct** and **tag** user can declare structure variables like **variable1, variable2** and so on. These are the members of the structure.

After defining structure we can create variables as given below.

struct struct_type v1, v2, v3

Here, **v1, v2,** and **v3** are variables of structure **struct**_type. This is similar to declaring variable of any data type.

int v1, v2, v3

Here, v1, v2, and v3 are variables of integer data type.

The declaration defines the structure but this process doesn't allocate memory. The memory allocation takes places only when variables are declared.

```
struct book1
{
char book [30];
int     pages;
float price ;
};
struct    book1    bk1;
```

In the above example a structure of type **book1** is created. It consists of these members book [30] of **char** data type, pages of **int** type and price of **float** data type. Figure 13.1 explains various members of a structure.

struct book1 bk1;

The above line creates variable bk1 of type book1 and it reserves total 36 bytes (30 bytes for book [30], 2 bytes for integer and 4 bytes for float). Through bk1 all the three members of structure can be accessed. In order to initialize structure elements with certain values following statement is used.

Struct book1

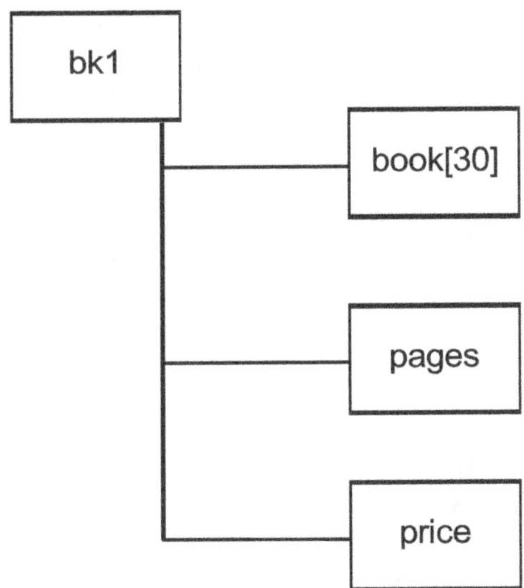

Fig. 12.1 Block Diagram of a Structure

struct book1 bk1 = {*shrinivas*,500,385,00};

All the members of structure are related to variable bk1.

structure_variable.member or bk1.book

The syntax for a member of a structure is :

Structure_variable.member

The period (.) sign is used to access the structure members.

We can directly assign values to members as given below.

```
bk1.book =*shrinivas*;
bk1.pages=500;
bk1.price=385.00;
```

Alternatively the structure can also be defined as follows :

```
struct book
    {
        char book [30];
        int   pages;
        float price ;
    } bk1, bk2;
```

Here bk1 and bk2 are structure variables representing 2 books of structure book.

Program 12.3.1

Write a program in C to display size of structure elements. Use sizeof ( ) of operator.

```
main ( )
{
struct book1
{
char book [30];
int  pages;
float price;
};
struct book1  bk1;
clrscr ( );
printf ("\n Size of Structure Elements");
printf ("\n Book : %d",sizeof(bk1.book));
printf("\n Pages :%d",sizeof(bk1.pages));
printf ("\n Price :%d",sizeof(bk1.price));
printf ("\n Total Bytes :%d",sizeof(bk1));
}
```

OUTPUT :

```
Size of Structure Elements
Book  : 30
Pages : 2
Price  : 4
Total Bytes : 36
```

Program 12.3.2

Write a program in C++ using Structure to enter marks in 3 subjects of a student.

```
# include <iostream>
using namespace std;
int main ( )
   {
        struct stdrec
        {
             char name[15];
             char examno[10];
             int maths,physics,chemistry,
        };
```

```
        stdrec markrec;
        int tot;
        cout <<"Enter name \n";
        cin getline(markrec.name,15);
        cout <<"Enter examno \n";
        cin getline/markrec.examno,12);
        cout <<Enter 3 subjects marks \n";
        cin >>markrec.maths>>markerc.physics>>markrec;chemistry;
        tot = markrec.maths + markrec.physics + markrec.chemistry;
        cout <<"Name : "<<markrec,name<<"\n";
        cout <<"Total marks = "<<tot;
        return 0;
    }
```

OUTPUT :

```
Enter name
Sundar
Enter examno
1201
Enter 3 subjects marks
50
60
70
Name : Sundar
Total Marks = 180
```

Alternatively the initialization of structure variables can be given in structure declaration itself instead of assigning values to the different members of the structure variables defined by the period. eg.

```
main ( )
{
struct book1
{
char book [30];
int     pages;
float price ;
};
struct book1 bk1 = {"C++",300,285};
......
......
```

```
}
```

Another example of initialization

```
        main ( )
    {
        struct st.record
        {
            int weight;
            float height;
        };
        static struct st_record student1 = {60,180.75};
        static struct st_record student2 = [53,170.60};
        ......
        ......
    }
```

12.4. STRUCTURE WITHIN STRUCTURE OR NESTED STRUCTURES :

We can take any data type for declaring members like int, float, char etc. In the same way we can also take object of one structure as member in another structure. Thus, structure within structure can be used to create complex data applications. *When a structure is an element of another structure, it is called a structure within structure or a nested structure. There can be more than two nested structures also whose members will be denoted as s.s1.s2.s3 etc.,*

The syntax of the structure within the structure is as follows.

```
struct    time
{
int   second;
int   minute;
int   hour;
};
struct   t
{
int cerno;
struct time st;
struct time et;
};
struct t player;
```

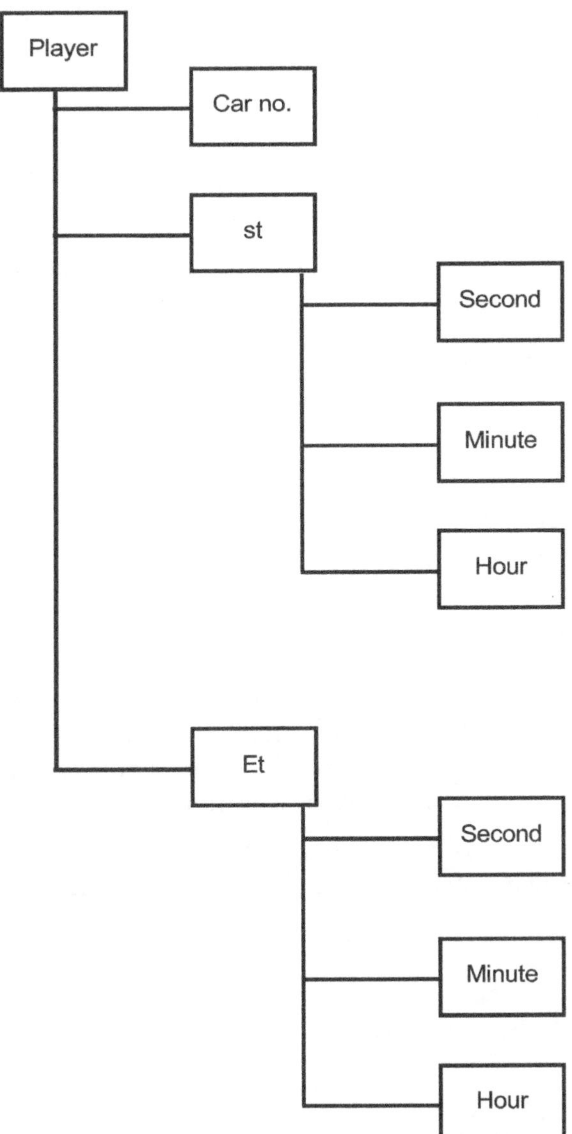

Fig.12.2. Structure within structure

Program 12.4.1. Write a program in C to enter full name and date of birth of a person and display the same. Use nested structure.

```
# include <stdio.h>
# include <conio.h>

void main ( )
{
```

```
struct name
    {
    char first [10];
    char second [10];
    char last [10];
    {;
struct b_date
    {
    int day;
    int month;
    int year;
    };
struct data
    {
    struct name  nm;
    struct b_date bt;
    };
    struct data r1;
    clrscr ();
    printf ("\n Enter Name (First / Second / Last)\n");
    scanf ("%s %s %s",r1.nm.first,r1.nm.second,r1.nm.last);
    printf("\n Enter Birth Data Day / Month / Year \n");
    scanf ("%d %d %d",&r1.bt.day,&r1.bt.month,&r1.bt.year);
    printf ("Name    : %s %s %s\n",r1.nm.first,r1.nm.second,r1.nm.last);
    printf ("Birth Date : %d %d %d",r1.bt.day,r1.bt.month,r1.bt.year);
}
```

OUTPUT :

```
Enter Name (First / Second / Last)
Ram Sham Pande

Enter Birth Date Day / Month / Year
12  12  1980
```

Program 12.4.2 Write a program in C++ using Nested Structure to enter student name, exam number, internal, external and total marks.

```
# include <iostream>
using namespace std;
int main ()
```

```
{
    struct mark
    {
        int inter,exter;
    };
    struct stdrec
    }
        char name[20];
        int regno;
        mark markrec;
    };
    stdrec exam;
    int tot;
    cout <<"Enter student name \n";
    cin.getline(exam.name,20);
    cout<<"Enter examno \n";
    cin>>exam.regno;
    cout <<"Internal mark \n";
    cin>>exam.markrec.inter;
    cout<"\n External mark \n";
    cin>>exam.markrec;exter;
    tot=exam.markrec.inter+exam.markrec.exter;
    cout<<"\n Name : "<<exam.name;
    cout <<"\n total; "<<tot;
    return 0;
}
```

OUTPUT :

```
Enter student name
Kishore
Enter Examno
5
Internal mark
22
External mark
67
Name : Kishore
regno : 5
total : 89
```

12.5. ARRAY OF STRUCTURES :

As we know array is a collection of similar data types. In the same way we can also define array of structure. **In array of structures every element is of structure type.** Array of structures can be declared as follow :

```
struct    time
{
int second;
int minute;
int hour;
} t[3] ;
```

In the above example t [3] is an array of 3 elements containing three objects of time structure. Each element of t [3] has structure of time with 3 members that are second, minute & hour. A program is explained as given below.

12.5.1. Write a program in C to create array of structure objects :

```
main ( )
{
int k;

struct  time
{
int second;
int minute;
int hour;
};

struct  t
{
int carno;
struct time st;
struct time rt;
};

struct  tt r1[3] ;
clrscr ( );
printf ("\nCar No. Starting Time Reaching Time :\n\n");
printf ("\t hh;mm;ss\t hh.mm.ss \n");
for (k=0;k<3;k++)
{
scanf ("%d",&r1[k],carno);
scanf ("%d %d %d",&r1[k],st.hour,&r1[k],st.minute,&r1[k],st.second);
```

```
canf ("%d %d %d",&r1[k],rt.hour,&r1[k].rt.minute.&r1[k].rt.second);
}
printf ("\n\tCar No. \tStarting Time \tReaching Time\n");
for (k=0;k<3;k++)
{
printf ("\nt%d\t" ,r1[k],carno);
printf ("\f%d%d,%d;\t\t",r1[k],st.hour,r1[k],st.second);
printf ("\r%d;%d:%d",r1[k],rt.hour,r1[k],rt.minute,r1[k],rt.second);
}
}
```

OUTPUT :

Car No.	Starting Time	Reaching Time :
	hh:mm:ss	hh:mm:ss
120	2 20 25	3 25 58
121	3 25 40	4 40 25
122	4 30 52	5 40 10

Car No.	Starting Time	Reaching Time :
120	2 : 20 : 25	3 : 25 : 58
121	3 : 25 : 40	4 : 40 : 25
122	4 : 30 : 52	5 : 40 : 10

Program 12.5.2 : Write a program in C++ to explain how arrays are used within a structure and display the marks of a candidate in 2 subjects.

```
# include <iostream>
using namespace std;
int main()
{
    struct mark
    {
        char name [20];
        int s[2];
    };
    mark sem;
    int j;
    cout <<"Enter name \n";
    cin.getline(sem.name80);
    cout<<"Enter 2 marks \n";
    for(j=0;j<2;j++)
```

```
            cin>>sem.s[j];
      cout <<"Name "<<sem.name;
      cout <<"\n Marks are \n";
      for(j=0;j<2;j++)
            cout<<sem.s[j]<<"\n";
      return 0;
}
```

OUTPUT :

```
Enter name
rajan
Enter 2 marks
78
90
Name rajan
Marks are
78
90
```

12.6. STRUCTURES & POINTERS OR POINTER TO STRUCTURE :

We know that pointer is a variable that holds the address of another data variable. The variable may be of any data type **int, float or double.** In the same way we can also define pointer to structure. Here, starting address of the member variables can be accessed. Thus, such pointers are called structure points. **C and C++ permits pointers to structures just as they are allowed to any other type of variable. Structure pointers are declared by placing "*" in front of a structure variable's name** like

```
emp *emprec;
```

Here emp is the name of the structure and "*emprec" declares 'emprec' as a pointer to data of that type.

Program 12.6.1

Write a Program in C to declare a pointer variable as a structure member.

```
# include <stdio.h>
# include <conio.h>

void main ()
{
      struct book
            {     char name [25]
                   char author [25];
```

```
            int pages;
        };}
struct book b1* (*JAVA COMPLETE REFERENCE", "P. NAUGHTON", 886);
struct book *ptr;

ptr=&b1;
clrscr ();
printf("\n %s by %s of %d pages",b1.name,b1.authro,b1.pages);
/* use of pointer to member of a structure follows */
printf("\n %s by %s of %d pages",ptr->name,ptr->author,ptr->pages);
}
```

OUTPUT :

```
JAVA COMPLETE REFERENCE by PNAUGHTON of 886 pages
JAVA COMPLETE REFERENCE by PNAUGHTON of 886 pages
```

in the above example *ptr is pointer to structure book. The syntax for using pointer with member is as given below.

1) ptr->name 2) ptr ->author 3) ptr ->pages

By executing these three statements starting address of each member can be estimated.

Program 12.6.2

Write a program in C++ to explain the use of pointer to structure

```
//Example program to pass structure to a function

#include <iostream>
using namespace std;
struct book
{
    char title[30];author[20];
    int pages;
    int price;
};
int main ()
{
    book bookrec,"bookrec1;
    void recpass (book *);
    bookrec1=&bookrec;
    strcpy(bookrec; little,"Java 2 Complete Reference");
    strcpy(bookrec.author,"Herbert Schildt");
    bookrec.pages=1108;
```

```
    bookrec.price=400;
    recpass(bookrec1);
    return 0;
}
void recpass(book "bookrec1)
{
    cout<<"\n inside the function";
    cout<<"\n Book little "<<bookrec1->title;
    cout<<"\n Author ;"<<bookrec1->author;
    cout <<"\n No of Pages "<<bookrec1->pages;
    cout <<"\n Price   :"<<bookrec1->price;
}
```

OUTPUT :

```
Inside the function
Book title        :    Jave 2 Complete Reference
Author            :    Herbert Schildt
No. of Pages      :    1108
price             :    400
```

12.7. STRUCTURES AND FUNCTIONS :

Like variables of standard data type structure variables also can be passed to the function by value or address. The syntax is as follows.

```
struct book
{
char name [35];
char author [35];
int pages;
} b1;
    void main ( )
    {
    ----------------
    ----------------
    show(&b1); /*address of struct b1 as argument of calling function show*/
    ----------------
    ----------------
    }
    show (struct book *b2)/*type and address of function parameter*/
    {
    --------------------
    --------------------
    }
```

Whenever a structure element is to be passed to any other function, it is essential to declare the structure outside the **main** ( ) function i.e. global.

In the above example structure book is declared before **main ( ).** It is a global structure. Its member elements are **char name [35]** and **int** pages. They can be accessed by all other functions.

Program 12.7.1

Write a program in C to pass address of structure variable

```
/* passing address of structure variable */

# include <stdio.h>
# include <conio.h>

struct book {
char name [35];
char author [35];
int pages;
};

void main ( )
{
/* initialization of struct book b1*/
struct book b1= ("JAVA COMPLETE REFERENCE", "P.NAUGHTON", 886};
show (&b1);
}
show (struct book *b2)
{
clrscr ();
printf ("\n %s by %s of pages",b2->author,b2->pages);

}
```

OUTPUT :

JAVA COMPLETE REFERENCE by P. NAUGHTON of 886 pages.

Note : In the function show ( ) the address is assigned to pointer *b2 which is a pointer to the structure book. Using -> operator contents of structure elements are displayed.

Just as we pass on address of structure variable to user defined function **we can pass on structure elements to user defined function.**

We can also pass on entire structure to user defined function.

All these features are common to C and C++.

Program 12.7.2

Write a program in C to illustrate passing of structure elements and structure as a whole to user defined function.

```
/* passing structure elements to function */

# include <stdio.h>
# include <conio.h>

struct boy      /* struct boy as global structure */
{
char name[25];
int age;
int wt;
};

void main ( )

{

struct boy b1={"Amit",20,25);

print (b1.name,b1.age,b1.wt);  /* structure element to function */
struct boy b2={"Ramesh",19,30);

print(b1);
print1 (b2.name,b2.age,b2.wt);
}

print (struct boy b) /* passing structure as a whole to function print */
{
clrscr ( );
printf("\n %s %d %d",b.name,b.age,b.wt);
return 0;
}
print1 (char *s, int t, int n) /* structure element to function print1 */
{clrscr ( );
printf ("\n %s %d %d",s,t,n);
return 0;
}
```

OUTPUT :

```
Amit 20 25
Ramesh 19 30
```

12.8. BIT FIELDS :

Bit field provides exact amount of bits required for storage of values. If a variable values is 1 or 0 we need a single bit to store it. In the same way if the variable is expressed between 0 and 3, then the two bits are sufficient for storing these values. Similarly if a variable assumes values between 0 and 7 then three bits will be sufficient to hold the variable and so on. The number of bits required for a variable is specified by non-negative integer followed by colon.

To hold the information we use the variables. The variables occupy a minimum of one byte for char and two bytes for integer. Instead of using complete integer if bits are used, space of memory can be saved. For example, to know the information about the vehicles, following information has to be stored in the memory.

1. Petrol Vehicle
2. Diesel Vehicle
3. Two Wheeler Vehicle
4. Four Wheeler Vehicle
5. Old Model
6. New Model

In order to store the status of the above information we may need two bits for types of fuel as to whether the vehicle is of petrol or diesel type. Three bits for its type as to whether the vehicle is to or four-wheeler. Similarly, three bits for model of the vehicle. Total bits required for storing the information would be 8 bits i.e. 1 byte. It means that the total information can be packed into a single byte. Eventually bit fields are used for conserving the memory. The amount of memory saved by using bit fields will be substantial which is proved from the above example.

However there are restrictions on bit fields when arrays are used. Arrays of bit fields are not permitted. Also the pointer cannot be used for addressing the bit field directly, although the use of the member access operator (->) is acceptable.

The unnamed bit fields could be used for padding as well as for alignment purposes.

The structure for the above problem would be as follows.

```
struct vehicle
{
unsigned type : 3;
unsigned fule : 2;
unsigned model : 3;
};
```

The colon (:) in the above declaration tells to the compiler that bit fields are used in the structure and the number after it indicates how many bits are required to allot to the field. Simple programs are illustrated below.

Program 12.8.1

Write a program in C to display the examination result of the student using bit fields.

```
# include <stdio.h>
# include <conio.h>

# define PASS      1
# define FAIL      0
# define A         0
# define B         1
# define C         2

void main ( )
{
      struct  student
      {
      char *name;
      unsigned result     :     1;
      unsigned grade      :     2;
      };
      struct student V;

      v.name="Sachin";
      v.result=PASS;
      v.grade =C;

      clrscr ( );

      printf ("\n Name    : %s",n.name);
      printf ("\n Result : %s",n.name);
      printf ("\n Grade : %d",n.grade);
}
```

OUTPUT :

```
Name    :   Sachin
Result  :   1
Grade   :   2
```

12.9. UNION :

Union is a variable, which is similar to the structure. It contains number of members like structure but it holds only one object at a time. In other words, union is a memory location which is used by several variables of different data types but holding only one data type in that memory at any time. In the structure each member has its own memory locations. It can accommodate one member at a time in a single area of storage. Union also contains members of types int, float, long arrays, pointers etc. It allocates fixed specific bytes of memory for access of data types irrespective of any data type.

The union requires bytes that are equal to the number of bytes required for the largest members. For example the union contains char, integer & long integer then the number of bytes reserved in the memory for the unions is 4 bytes. An example is illustrated below for understanding. **The data type union is common to both C and C++.**

Program 12.9.1

Write a program in C to find the size of the Union and No. of bytes reserved for it.

```
# include <stdio.h>
# include <conio.h>
main ( )
{
union result
{
int marks;
char grade;
};

struct res
{
char name[15];
int age;
union result perf;
} data;
clrscr ();
printf ("Size of union :%d\n"size of(data.perf));
printf ("Size of Structure :%d\n"size of(data));
}
```

OUTPUT :

```
Size of union   :    2
Size of Structure  : 19
```

Explanation :

Union contains two variables of data type int & char respectively. The int & char requires 2 & 1 bytes respectively for storage. According o the theory the union reserves two bytes because int takes more space than char data type.

The structure res are defined immediately after union, which contains data type char, int, & union variable. The size of structure is printed which are nothing but sum of 15 bytes of char array, two bytes of int and two bytes of union variable perf. Thus, the total size of structure is 19.

12.10. ANONYMOUS UNIONS :

C++ can have Anonymous union without union variable name.

For example consider the following union declaration within a structure.

```
struct {
        char empname[20];
        int empno;
        union {
                float dollars;
                int pounds;
              } mode;
    } employee;
```

We use the following statement to access dollars inside the union, employee mode dollars.

Let us consider the above declaration but without union variable name (mode); now the union is said to be anonymous.

```
struct {
    char empname[20];
    int empno;
    union {
        float dollars;
        int pounds;
    };
} employee;
```

Now we can access the elements inside the union directly just specifying its name. To access pounds inside the union we have the following statement.

employee pounds

As we know, the fields 'dollars' and 'pounds' occupy the same space in memory we can access only one value at a time but not both.

12.11.typedef :

We have studied earlier that by using **typedef** we can create new data type. The statement typedef is to be used while defining the new data type. The syntax is as given undef.

typedef type dataname;

Here, **type** is the data type and **dataname** is the user defined name for that typ.ef

C and C++ have provisions to provide typedef in structure form as given below.

```
struct stdrec
{
        char name[20]
        int eamno;
                float ave;
};
```

By having declaration like this

```
        typedef struct stdrec markrec;
```

We may use 'markrec' instead of 'struct stdrec' in structure declaration, So

markrec iyear,iiyear;

Will be converted to

```
        struct stdrec iyear,iiyear;
```

Program 12.11.1

Write in a Program in C to create user defined data type hours on int data type and use it in the program

```
# define H 60
main ( )
{
        typedef int hours;
        hours hrs;
        clrscr ( );
        printf ("Enter Hours;");
        scanf("%d",&hrs);
        printf ("\n Minutes=%d",hrs*H);
        printf ("\n Seconds=%d",hrs*H*H);
}
```

OUTPUT :

Enter Hours : 2
Minutes = 120
Seconds = 7200

Program 12.11.2

Write a program in C to illustrate use of typedef in structure form.

```
main ( )
{
    typedef struct
        {
            char name [20];
            char sex[2];
            int acno;
        } info;
    info employee={"Sanjay',"M",125};
    clrscr ();
    printf("\n Name\t Sex\tA/c No.\n");
    printf("%s\t",employee.sex);
    printf("%d\n",employee.acno);
}
```

OUTPUT :

```
Name     Sex     A/c No.
Sanjay   M       125
```

12.12. ENUMERATED DATA TYPE :

The enum is a keyword. It is used for declaring enumeration types. The programmer can create his/her own data type and define what values the variables of these data types can hold. This enumeration data type helps in reading the program. Earlier we have studied the use of enumerated data type.

Consider the example of 12 months of a year.

enum month {Jan, Feb, Mar, Apr, May, Jun, Jul, Aug, Sep, Oct, Nov, Dec);

This statement creates a user-defined data type. The keyword enum is followed by the tag name month. The enumerators are the identifiers **Jan, Feb, Mar, Apr, May** and so on. Their values are constant unsigned integers and start from 0. The identifier Jan refers to 0, Feb to 1 and so on. The identifiers are not to be enclosed with in quotations marks. Please also note that integer constants are also not permitted.

C and C++ have provisions to provide enumerated data in structure form as given below.

```
enum dept
{
    physics,chemistry,zoology;
};
enum dept dept1dept2;
```

The value in the list stars from 0 to n-1, where 'n' is the total number of items given in the list. In the above case, we have 3 items in the list. Each item in the list can be accessed by subtracting one from the positional value of an identifier. Hence, physics can have 0 as its value, chemistry can have 1 and zoology takes 2 as is value.

Now we can assign values to these variables as shown below.

```
dept1=physics;
dept2=zoology;
```

So, by using enumerated type one can understand flow of the program very easily.

Program 12.12.1

Write a program in C to use enumerated data type.

```
# include <stdio.h>
# include <conio.h>
# include <string.h>

void main ( )
{
    enum capital
        {
            Mumbai, Hyderabad, Bangalore
        };

    struct state
        {
            char name [15];
            enum capital c;
        };
    struct state s;
    strcpy (s.name,"Andhra Pradesh");
    s.c=Hyderabad;
    clrscr ( );
```

```
    printf("\n State :%s",s.name);
    printf("\n Capital :%d",s.c);
    if (s.c==Hyderabad)
        printf("\n Hyderabad is Capital of %s",s.name);
}
```

OUTPUT :

State : Andhra Pradesh
Capital : 1
Hyderabad is Capital of Andhra Pradesh

12.13. CALLING BIOS AND DOS SERVICES :

We can access BIOS and DOS services through C language. Few simple examples are illustrated by making use of BIOS and DOS services. The programmer does not have direct access to the CPU registers. However, the C language provides an interface that allows the programmer to access any BIOS or DOS service. The C language defines a union type called "REGS" and structure type called "SREGS" in the file "DOS.H" which escorts the C compiler. These data types are used to pass parameters to the CPU registers. In order to have access to these definitions the programmer has to include "dos.h" header file.

The union type **"REGS"** contains the CPLI registers. These registers are used for holding the data temporarily. The microprocessors 8086, 8088, 80186, 80286 and 803386 use a variety of registers for arithmetic and logical operations. Also they are used to receive instructions and pass data to and from memory.

The CPU registers are 16 bits in size. They are AX, BX, CX, DX, SI, DI, and CFLAG, which is carry flag. The size of CFLAG is also 16 bits. The structure that defines these 16 bits registers is called 'x'. The 'x' stands for a register pair. Size of each register is 8 bits. Thus, the size of pair registers 'x' is 16 bits.

The union also allows us to refer 8 bit registers of above type processors. These 8 bits registers are AL, AH, BL, BH, CL, CH, DL and DH. The structure that defines these 8 bit registers is called 'h'. Here, 'h' stands for a half register i.e. 8 bit register.

There are also segment registers in the above processors. The size of segment registers is 16 bits. These segment registers DS, ES, CS an SS. The structure type "SEEGS" defines these segment registers.

The C language provides the functions such as **intdos ( ), intdox** ( ) and **segread** ( ) to access **dos** services. The **intdos** ( ) is used for calling dos interrupt. The **intdos** ( ) invokes a **DOS** function by issuing software interrupt INT 21H.

We can also invoke BIOS services by using C functions such as **int86** ( ) and int86x ( ). The **int86** ( ) stands for 8086 interrupt. The **int86** ( ) functions invoke a BIOS function by issuing a software interrupt. The **int86** ( ) function can be invoked with the following three arguments.

Interrupt type number corresponding to ROM-BIOS service.

Two arguments of UNION type REGS. They are 'x' and 'h'.

The int86 ( ) function takes the values of iput registers from one "REGS" union and returns the output registers in another. The int86x ( ) function is similar to int86 ( ). The difference is int86x ( ) requires an input argument in DS or ES register. Given below are few examples of int86 ( ) functions.

Program 12.13.1

Write a program in C to find a memory size of the computer

```
# include <stdio.h>
# include <conio.h>
# include <dos.h>
/* Finding Memory Size */
void main ( )
{
union REGS in,out;
int86 (18,&in,&out);
clrscr ( );
printf("\n Total Memory=%dKB",out.x.ax);
}
```

OUTPUT :

Total Memory = 640 KB

12.14. UNION OF STRUCTURES :

We have noticed that a structure can be defined as a number within another structure resulting in nested structure or structure within structure.

In the same way a union can also be nested within another union.

Similarly we can create structure within a union or a union within a structure.

Program 12.14.1

Write a program in C to use structure within union or union of structure.

```
# include <stdio.h>
# include <conio.h>
```

```
void main ( )
{
        struct a
                {
                        float b;
                        char c[2];
                };
        union u
                {
                        struct a set;   /* set is member of struct a*/
                };
        union u st;             /*structure a is contained in union u*/
        st.set.b=45.5;
        st.set.c[0]=85;         /* 85 is ASCII code of A */
        st.set.c[1]=86;
        clrscr ();
        printf("\n%g",st.set.b);
        printf("\n%c",st.set.c[0]);
        printf("\n%c",st.set.c[1]);
}
```

OUTPUT :

45.5
A
B

Explanation :

In the above program structure a is defined. The union u contains structure member as its member variable. The variable st is an object of union u. The member variables of structure a are assigned with certain values. Using objects of structure and union with dot operator member contents of member variables are displayed.

12.15. SCOPE OPERATOR OR SCOPE RESOLUTION OPERATOR :: IN C++ :

In C the scope of local and global variables were determined by the locations where they are are first defined. Like C, C++ is also a block structured language i.e., within a block. Several statements and even variable declarations can be given and the block is indicated by a pair of curly braces ({... ; ...; ... ; }). The curly block operators limit the life of the variables declared and statements to be valid within that given block.

whereas in C++ we have a separate scope operator to determine the scope of the variables as explained in the following program.

The use of scope operator in C++ before a variable indicates its scope as global.

Program : 12.15.1

Write a program in C++ to illustrate the use of scope resolution operator

```
# include <iostream>
using namespace std;
int a=1;                        //int a is global variable
struct example
	{
		static int a;
	};
int example :: a = 9;//name scope variable or int example uses scope operator
void main ( )
{
	int a=7;//int a is local variable to main ( )
	cout<<"\n local variable a by declaration in main ( ) a="<<a;
	cout<<"\n global variable a by declaration before main ( ) a="<<a;
	cout<<"\n global variable a by scope operator a ="<< :: a;
	cout <<endl;
}
```

OUTPUT :

```
local variable a by declaration in main ( ) a= 7
global variable a by declaration before main ( ) a= 1
global variable a by scope operator a = 9
```

* * *

COMPREHENSION - 12

Note : By answering all the questions given in this comprehension one can answer any objective type of questions easily whatever be the form of the question. Answers for these questions can be obtained by going through the topics in this chapter carefully.

1. What is meant by Structure in C and C++ ?
2. In what way a Structure is different from an Array?
3. What is the difference between a Variable and a Structure?
4. What are the Features of Structures?
5. How do you declare a Structure? Explain with Syntax and examples.
6. Explain how you initialize Structures.
7. Does the declaration of a structure allocate memory for the Structure?
8. When and how the memory is allocated to a Structure?
9. Give the Block diagram of a Structure.
10. Give the different ways of defining a Structure. Explain with a block diagram.
11. Explain with example how you find the Structure elements and Structure size.
12. How are the Structure elements or Structure objects or Structure members denoted?
13. What is meant by Nested Structures or Structure within a structure? Explain with examples and syntax.
14. What is an Array of Structures? Explain with Syntax and examples.
15. Explain with examples what is Pointer to Structure.
16. How are Structure Pointers declared? Explain with examples.
17. What are the methods of passing on to a Function? Explain with examples.
18. How do you pass on a Structure as a whole to a User Defined Function? Explain.
19. What do Bit Fields do?
20. Explain the use of Bit Fields .
21. What is the advantage of using of bits instead of using integer other data types?
22. What are the restrictions in the use of Bit Fields?
23. Can a pointer be used for addressing Bit Fields directly? Is the of member access operator admissible in such cases?
24. What for unnamed Bit Fields can be used?

25. What is a Union? In what way is it different from Structure?
26. How is the memory size of the Union decided? In what way is it different from the size of a Structure?
27. What are Anonymous Union used in C++ ?
28. What is typedef ? When is it used? Give Syntax and examples.
29. What is Enumerated Data Type? When and how are they used?
30. How do you access BIOS and DOS services? Why?
31. What is Union of Structures?
32. Explain creation of Structures within a Union and a Union within a Structure?
33. What is Scope operator or Scope Resolution Operator? How and where is it used?
34. Explain REGS and SREGS Unions. List any 5 CPU registers of each Union type.
35. Explain int 86 ( ) and intdos ( ) functions. How are they used to interact with hardware?

* * *

EXERCISE - 12

Note : **By answering all the questions given in this exercise one can answer subjective type of questions easily including problems. The worked examples in the chapter may help in solving these questions.**

1. Bring out the differences clearly between a Variable, an Array, a Structure and Union as regards to declaration, initialization , size and use.
2. Explain the meaning and purpose of the following :
   i) Template ii) Tag iii) Sizeof. iv) Struct
3. Describe what is wrong in the following structure declaration:

```
struct
{
        int   number;
        float price;
}
main ()
{
        ......
        ......
}
```

4. The following code appears at the beginning of a function. Identify errors, if any, in the code

```
static int count[ ] = {
        10, 15, 20, 30;
    float value;
```

5. What is meant by the following terms?
   i) Nested structure ii) Array of structures
6. Define a structure that can describe a hotel. It should have members that include the name, address, grade, average room charge, and number of rooms.
   Write functions to perform the following operations :
   i) To print out hotels of a given grade in order of charges
   ii) To print out hotels with room charges less than a given value
7. Define a structure called **cricket** that will describe the following information:

   player name
   team name
   bating average

   using **cricket,** declare an array **player** with 50 elements and write a program to read the information about all the 50 players and print a team wise list containing names of players with their batting average.

8. Identify the most appropriate sentence to describe unions.
   a) Unions contain members of different data type which share the same storage area in memory.
   b) Unions are like structures
   c) Unions are less frequently used in the program.
   d) Unions are used for set operations

9. The member variable of structure are accessed by using:
   a) dot (.) operator b) arrow (->) operator
   c) asterisk (*) operator d) ampersand (&) operator

10. The service number is always initialized in the register
    a) AH b) AL c) BH d) AX

11. The intdos ( ) function invokes interrupt number
    a) 0 × 21 b) 0 × 17 c) 0 × 18 d) None of these

12. Interrupt 0 × 21 is a
    a) software interrupt b) hardwater interrupt
    c) both (a) and (b) d) None of the above

13. Bit fields are used only with
    a) **unsigned int data** type b) **float data**type
    c) **char data** type d) **int data**type

14. Observe the following program neatly and choose the appropriate printf( ) statement from the options.

```
        struct month
        {
        char *month;
        };
    void main ( )
    {
    struct month m={"March"};
    - - - -
    }
```

    a) printf ("\nMonth : %s",m.month);
    b) printf ("\nMonth : %s",m->month);
    c) printf ("\nMonth : %s",m.*month);
    d) printf ("\nMonth : %s",*m.month);

15. What will be the value of m displayed on execution of the following program?

```
# include <stdio.h>
# include <conio.h>
```

```
        struct bit
        {
        unsigned int m : 3;
        };
    void main ( )
    {
    struct bit b= { 8 };
    clrscr ( );
    printf ("\n m = %d",b.m);
    }
```

a) m = 0　　b) m = 8

c) m = 3　　d) None of the above

16. The size of structure in bytes occupied in the following program will be

```
        # include <stdio.h>
        # include <conio.h>
            struct bit
            {
            unsigned int m : 4;
                unsigned int x : 4;
                int k;
                float f;
                };
                struct bit b:
        void main ( )
        {
        clrscr ( );
        printf("\n Size of structure in Bytes = %d",sizeof(b));
        }
```

a) 8　　b) 10　　c) 7　　d) 4

17. Write a program to define structure with tag **state** with fields state name, number of districts and total population. Read and display the data.
18. Write the above program using pointer to structure.
19. Define a structure with tag **population** with fields Men and Women. Create structure within structure using **state** and **population** structure. Read and display the data.
20. Modify the above developed program. Create array of structure variables. Read and display the 5 records.
21. By using the data type Structure write a C or C++ Program to print Maximum marks in each subject along with the name of the student using students' records.

* * *

CHAPTER 13
FILE OPERATIONS IN C

13.1 INTRODUCTION :

Applications generally involve tremendous amount of data to be read and written to an auxiliary storage. Hence to save such information to the disk we use data files. **File is a collection of numbers, symbols & text placed on the disk. In due course of time files can be read and modified as per the user requirements. Thus, files allow us store information permanently in the disk; access and further it can be altered depending upon the needs.** This process leads to the concept of data files.

Definition of File :

File is a set of records than can be accessed through the set of library functions. There are 2 types of files. A) Text mode Files & B) Binary mode Files.

13.2. STREAMS AND FILE TYPES :

Stream means reading and writing of data. The streams are designed to allow the user to access the files efficiently. *A stream is a file or physical device like keyboard, printer and monitor. The FILE object uses these devices.*

The FILE object contains all the information about stream like current position, pointer to any buffer, error and EOF (end of file) Using this information of object, C program uses pointer, which is returned from stream function fopen ( ).

A) Text Mode Files :

There are two types of Text mode files i) Sequential file ii) Random accesses file0

i) **Sequential File :** In this type datas are kept sequentially. If we want to read the last record of the file we need to read all the records before that record. It takes more time. Or if we desire to access the 10th record then the first nine records should be read sequentially for reaching to the 10th record.

ii) **Random Access File :** In this type data can be read and modified randomly. IN this type if we want to read the last records of the file, we can read it directly. It takes less time as compared to sequential file.

13.3. STEPS FOR FILE OPERATIONS :

The following steps are the basic file operation in C.

1) Naming a file
2) Opening of file
3) Reading from or writing data into a file.
4) Closing file

C language supports many more file handling functions that are available in standard library. These functions are listed in the table given below. All the functions that support C are not listed here because all compilers do not support all the functions. One should check the C library before using them.

Table 13.1 File Functions :

Function	Operation
fopen ( )	Creates a new file for read/write operation
fclose ( )	Closes a file associated with file pointer
closeall ( )	Closes all opened files with fopen ( )
fgetc ( )	Reads the character from current pointer position and advances the pointer to the next character.
getc ( )	Same as fgetc ( ).
fprintf ( )	Writes all types of data values to the file.
fscanf ( )	Reads all types of data values from a file.
putc ( )	Writes character one by one to a file
fputc ( )	Same as putc ( )
gets ( )	Reads string from the file
puts ( )	Writes string to the file
putw ( )	Writes an integer to the file
getw ( )	Reads an integer from the file
fread 9)	Reads structured data written by fwrite ( ) function
fwrite ( )	Writes block of structured data to the file.
fseek ( )	Sets the pointer position anywhere in the file.
feof ( )	Detects the end of file.
ferror ( )	Reports error occurred while read / write operations.
perror ( )	Prints compilers error messages along with user defined messages.
ftell ( )	Returns the current pointer position
rewind ( )	Sets the record pointer at the beginning of the file
unlink ( )	Removes the specified file from the disk.
rename ( )	Changes the name of the file.

13.3.1. Opening of a File : A file has to be opened before beginning of read and write operations. Opening of file creates a link between the operating system and the file functions. We have to specify the name of file and it's mode to the operating system. This important task is carried out by the structure FILE that is defined in **stdio.h** header file. So this file must be included.

When a request is made to the operating system for opening a file, it does so by granting the request. If request is granted the operating systems points to the structure FILE. In case the request is not granted it returns NULL. That is why the following declaration before opening of the file is to be made.

FILE *fp;

Where, fp is the file pointer.

Each file that we open has its own FILE structure. The information that the file contains may be its current size, its location in memory etc.

The only one function to open a file is fopen ( );

Syntax for opening the file

FILE *fp;
fp=fopen ("data.txt","r");

Here, fp is a pointer variable that contains address of the structure FILE that has been defined in the header file "stdio.h". The function fopen () will open a file "data.txt" in read mode. The Compiler reads the contents of the file because it finds the read mode ("r"). *Here, "r" is a string and not a character. Hence it is enclosed with double quotes and no with single quotes.*

The fopen ( ) performs three important tasks

1. It searches the disk for opening the file.
2. In case the file exists, it loads the file from the disk into memory. If the file is found with huge contents then it loads the file part by part.
3. If the file is not existing this function returns a NULL . NULL is a macro defined character in the header file "stdio.h". This indicates that it is unable to open file. There may be following reasons for failure of fopen ( ) functions. i) When the file is in protected or hidden mode. ii) The file may be used by another program.
4. It locates a character pointer, which points to the first character of the file. Whenever a file is opened the character pointer points to the first character of the file.

Different modes in which a file can be opened.

A. Text Modes :

1. w (write) This mode opens a new file on the disk for writing. If the file already exists, it will be overwritten without confirmation. Here the word "write" inside parameters is for understanding and not part of the syntax.

Syntax

fp=fopen ("data.txt","w");
Here, data.txt is the file name and "w" is the write mode.

2. r (read) This mode opens a pre-existing file for reading. If the file doesn't exist, then compiler returns NULL to the file pointer. Using pointer with **if** statement we can prompt the user regarding failure of operation.

Syntax

```
fp=fopen ("data.txt","r");
if (fp==NULL)
printf ("File does not exist");
    OR
If (fp=(fopen ("data.txt""r"))==NULL)
printf ("File does not exist");
```

Here,data. dbf is opened for reading only. If the file does not exist the fopen ( ) returns NULL to file pointer 'fp'. Using the NULL value of fp with if statement we can prompt the user for failure of fopen ( ) function.

Program 13.3.1

Write a program in C to write data to text file and read it.

```
# include <stdio.h>
# include <conio.h>
# include <process.h> /*pre-processor directive for file operations*/

void main ( )
{
    FILE *fp;
    char c=' ';
    clrscr ( );
    fp=fopen("data.txt","w");
    if(fp==NULL)
    {
    printf ("Cannot open file");
    exit(1);
    }

    printf ("Write data and to stop press '.' :");
    while (c != '.')
    {
    c=getche();
      fputc(c,fp);
    }
    fclose(fp);

    printf ("\n Contents read :");
```

```
      fp=fopen("data.txt","r");
      while ( !feof(fp))
      printf ("%c",getc(fp));
      }
```

OUTPUT :

Write data and to stop press '.' : SUNIL KUMAR.

Contents read : SUNIL KUMAR.

3 a (append) **:** *Append mode opens a pre-existing file for appending data. If the file doesn't exist then a new file is opened i.e. if the file does not exist then the mode of "a" is same as "w".*

Syntax

fp=fopen ("data.txt","a");'

Here if data.txt file already exists, it will be opened and you will be allowed to append matter to the existing file. Otherwise a new file will be opened with the same name.

Program 13.3.2

Write a program in C to open a pre-existing file and add information at the end of file. Display the contents of the file before and after appending.

```
# include <stdio.h>
# include <conio.h>
# include <process.h>
void main ( )
{
FILE *fp;
char c;
clrscr ( );
printf ("Contents of the file before appending :\n");
      fp=fopen("data.txt","r");
      while ( !feof(fp))
            {
                  c=fgetc(fp);
                  printf ("%c",c);
            }
      fp=fopen("data.txt","a");
      if (fp==NULL)
```

```
          {
               printf ("File can not be appended");
               exit(1);

          }
printf ("\n Enter string to be appended :");
     while (c != '.')
          {
               c=getch();
               fputc(c,fp);
          }
     fclose(fp);
printf ("\n Contents of the file after appending :\n");
     fp=fopen("data.txt","r");
     while ( !feof(fp))
          {
               c=fgetc(fp);
               printf ("%c",c);
          }
}
```

OUTPUT :

```
"Contents of the file before appending :
String is terminated with '\0'.               .. file content before appending.

Enter string to be appended :
This character is called a NULL character.    .... appended text ....
Contents of the file after appending :
String is terminated with '\0'.               ... original content of the file ..
This character is called a NULL character     ... addl. contents after appndg.
```

4. w+ (Write + read) **While using w+ we should be careful. It searches for file, if file is found its contents are destroyed.** If the file isn't found a new file is created. Returns NULL if it fails to open the file. **In this w+ mode file can be written and read. If we do not want to delete the existing contents of file it is better to use append mode "a" instead of w+ mode. w+ mode is similar to re-writing file.**

Example :

```
fp=fopen ("data.txt","w+");
```

In the above example data.txt file is open for reading and writing operations.

Program 13.3.3

Write a program in C to use w+ mode for writing and reading of a file.

```
# include <stdio.h>
# include <conio.h>
# include <process.h>
void main ( )
{
    FILE *fp;
    char c=' ';
    clrscr ( );
    fp=fopen("data.txt","w+");
    if(fp==NULL)
        {
            printf("Cannot open file");
            exit (1);
        }
        printf ("Write data and to stop press'.' :");
    while (c != '.')
        {
        c=getche( );
        fputc(c,fp);
        }
        rewind(fp);      /*rewind () fn is to set character ptr. at beginning*/
                         /*in case read oprn. is done after write oprn.*/
        printf ("\n Contents read :");
        while ( !feof(fp))
        printf (" %c,getc(fp));
}
```

OUTPUT :

Write data and to stop press '.' : RAMA IS A GOOD BOY.
Contents read : RAMA IS A GOOD BOY.

5. a+ (append + read) *In this append + read mode file can be read and records can be added at the end of the file. This is a very useful mode.*

Example :

fp=fopen("data.txt","a+");

Here, ***data.txt*** *is opened and records are added at the end of the file without affecting the previous contents.*

Program 13.3.4

Write a program in C to use a+ mode for writing and reading of a file.

```
# include <stdio.h>
# include <conio.h>
# include <process.h>

void main ( )
{
    FILE *fp;
    char c=' ';
    clrscr ( );
    fp=fopen("data.txt","a+");
    if(fp==NULL)
        {
            printf("Cannot open file");
            exit (1);
        }
        printf ("Write data and to stop press'$':");
    while (c !='$')
        {
        c=getche( );
        fputc(c,fp);
        }
        rewind(fp);
        printf ("\n Contents read :");
        while ( !feof(fp))
        printf (" %c,getc(fp));
}
```

OUTPUT :

Write data and to stop press '$': This is append and read mode$
Contents read : This is append and read mode$

Note :

1. In case read operation is done after write operation character pointer should be set at beginning of the file using **rewind ( )**.

2. **In case write / append operation is done after read operation. It is not essential to set the character pointer at the beginning of file.**

6. r+ (read + write) This mode is used for both reading and writing. We can read and write the record in the file. If the file does not exist, the compiler returns NULL to the file pointer. It can be written as follows.

Example :

fp =fopen ("data.dat","r+");

if (fp==NULL)

printf ("File not found");

In the above example, data.dat is opened for read and write operation. If fopen () fails to open the file it returns NULL. The if statement checks the value of file pointer fp and if it contains NULL a message is printed and the program terminates.

Program 13.3.5

Write a program in C to use r+mode for writing and reading of a file.

```
# include <stdio.h>
# include <conio.h>
# include <process.h>

void main ( )
{
    FILE *fp;
    char c=' ';
    clrscr ( );
    fp=fopen("data.txt","r+");
    if(fp==NULL)
        {
            printf("Can not open file");
            exit (1);
        }
        printf ("\n Contents read :");
        while (!feof(fp))
        printf (" %c,getc(fp));
        printf ("Write data & to stop press'.':");
    while (c!='.')
        {
        c=getche( );
        fputc(c,fp);
        }
}
```

OUTPUT :

Contents read : Good morning.
Write data & to stop press '.': Welcome to C program.

B. Binary Modes for data :

For data in text mode if a command like fopen ("data.txt", "mode") is used then each bit of the data is treated as a character and it requires more bytes since each character requires one byte. On the other hand in binary mode files the arguments for data file will be ("data.dat", "mode"). In Binary files then the length of each data is of standard number of bytes depending on the type of data like int, float etc., it requires less bytes.

1. **wb (write)** This mode opens a binary file in write mode.

Example

fp=fopen ("data.dat","wb");

Here, data.dat file is opened in binary mode for writing.

2. rb (read) This mode opens a binary file in read mode.

Example

Fp=fopen ("data.dat","rb");

Here, data.dat file is opened in binary mode for reading.

3. ab (append) This mode opens a binary file in append mode i.e. data can be added at the end of file.

Example :

Fp=fopen ("data.dat","abJ;

Here, "data.dat" file is opened in append mode.

4. r+b (read+write) This mode opens a pre-existing file in read and write mode i.e. file can be read and written.

Example

Fp=fopen("data.data","r+bJ;

Here, the file "data.dat" is opened for reading and writing in binary mode.

5. w+b (read + write) This mode creates a new file in read and write mode.

Example :

Fp=fopen ("data.dat","w+b");

Here, the file "data.dat" is created for reading and writing in binary mode.

6. a+b (append + write) This mode opens a file in append mode i.e. data can be written at the end of file. If file does not exist a new file is created.

Example :

Fp=fopen ("data.dat","a+b");

Here, the file "Data.dat" is opened in append mode and data can be written at the end of file.

Program 13.3.6

Write a Program in C to open a file for read / write operation in binary mode. Read and Write new information in the file.

```
# include <stdio.h>
# include <conio.h>
# include <process.h>            /* for file operations */
void main ( )
{
    FILE *fp;
    char c=' ';
    clrscr ( );
    fp=fopen("data.dat","wb");
    if(fp==NULL)
        {
            printf("Cannot open file");
            exit (1);
        }
        printf ("Write data & to stop press'.':");
    while (c!='.')
        {
        c=getche( );
        fputc(c,fp);
        }
        fclose(fp);
        fp=fopen ("data.dat","rb");
        printf ("\n Contents read:");
        while (!feof(fp))
        printf ("%c,getc(fp));
}
```

OUTPUT :

Write data & to stop press '.': ABCDEFGHIJK.
Contents read : ABCDEFGIJK.

Explanation : This program is the same as the one explained earlier and the only difference is that the file-opening mode is binary.

b. Reading File Once the file is opened using **fopen ( ) ,** it's contents are loaded into the memory partly or wholly.) The pointer points to the very first character of the file. **The fgetc ( )** function is used to read the contents of the file.

The syntax for fgetc ( ) is as follows.

ch=fgetc (fp);

Where, fgetc ( ) reads the character from current pointer position and advances the pointer position so that the next character is pointed. The variable ch contains the character read by fgetc ( ). There are also other functions to read the contents of file, which are explained in next pages.

c. Closing a File : The file that is opened from the **fopen ( )** should be closed after the work is over i.e. we need to close the file after reading and writing operations are over.

Example :

Fclose (fp);

This statement closes the file associated with file pointer **fp.** This function closes one file at a time. To close one or more files at a time the function **fcloseall ()** is used.

Example :

Fcloseall ( )

This function closes all the open files and returns number of files closed. It does not require any argument.

13.4. FILE I/O OPERATIONS :

1. fprintf ( ) This function is used for writing characters, strings, integers, floats etc. to the file. It contains one more parameter that is file pointer, which points the opened file.

2. fscanf ( ) This function reads character, strings, integer, floats etc. from the file pointed by file pointer. A program is illustrated below based on this.

Program : 13.4.1

Write a program in C to enter data into text file and the read the same. Use 'w+" file mode. Use fscanf() to read the contents of the file and printf( ).

Also use fprintf ( ) for writing character strings.

```
# include <stdio.h>
# include <conio.h>
# include <process.h>
main ( )
{
FILE *fp;
char text [15];
int age;
fp=fopen("Text.txt","w+");
clrscr ( );
```

```
printf ("Name\t AGE\n");
scanf("%s%d",text,&age);
fprintf (fp,"%s%d",text,age);

printf ("Name\t AGE\n");
fscanf(fp,%s%d",text&age);
printf("%s\t%d\n",text,age);
printf("Enter Text Here:");
fclose(fp);
}
```

OUTPUT :

```
Name    AGE
ANIL    24

Name    AGE
ANIL    24
```

Explanation : Here printf ( ) prints the title. scanf ( ) reads data. fprintf ( ) prints data from file. Second print ( ) prints titles. fscanf ( ) reads data from file. print ( ) prints the data from file.

3. getc ( ) This function reads a single character from the opened file and moves the file pointer. It returns EOF, if end of file is reached.

4. putc ( ) This function is used to write a single character into a file. If an error occurs it returns EOF.

5. fgetc ( ) This function is similar to getc ( ) function. It also reads a character and increases the file pointer position. If any error or end of file is reached it returns EOF.

6. fputc ( ). This function writes the character to the file shown by the file pointer. It also increases the file pointer.

Syntax

Fputc (c, fp), where, fp is file pointer and c is a variable written to the file pointed by file pointer.

7. fgets ( ) This function reads string from a file pointed by file pointer. It also copies the string to a memory location referred by an array.

8. fputs ( ) This function is useful when we want to write a string into the opened file.

9. putw ( ) This function is used to write an integer value to file pointed by file pointer.

10. getw ( ) This function returns the integer value from a file and increase the file pointer.

Program 13.4.2

Write a Program in C to use putc( ) and getc( )

```
# include <stdio.h>
# include <conio.h>
# include <process.h>
void main ( )
{
char c;
FILE *fp;
clrscr ( );
printf ("\n Enter Some Words & '*' to Exit\n");
fp=fopen("words.doc","w");
while ((c=getchar() != '*')
putc(c,fp);
fp=fopen("words.doc","r");
if (fp==NULL)
    {
        printf("\nCannot open file");
        exit(1);
    }
        while ((c=getc(fp) != EOF)
        printf ("%c",c);
        fclose(fp);
}
```

OUTPUT :

Enter Some Words & '*' to Exit
This is saved into the file *
This is saved into the file *

Program 13.4.3.

Write a program in C to write text to a file using fputc () function.

```
# include <stdio.h>
# include <conio.h>
# include <process.h>
void main ( )
{
FILE *fp;
char c;
clrscr ( );
```

```
fp=fopen("lines.txt","w");
if (fp==NULL)
return;
else

      {
            while ((c=getche() != '*')
            fputc(c,fp);
      }
fclose(fp);
}
```

OUTPUT :

I love India.

Program 13.4.4

Write a program in C to write a string into a file using fputc() and fputs( ) for printing string from file.

```
# include <stdio.h>
# include <conio.h>
# include <process.h>
void main ( )
{
FILE *fp;
char file [12],text[50];
clrscr ( );
printf ("\n Enter the name of file:");
scanf("%s",file);
fp=fopen("file,"w");
if (fp==NULL)
      {
            printf("\n File can not be opened \n");
            return;
      }
            else
      {
            printf ("\n Enter Text Here :");
            scanf ("%s",text);
            fputs(textfp);
      }
            fclose(fp);
}
```

OUTPUT :

Enter the name of file : data.dat
Enter Text Here : Welcome to C

13.5. BINARY MODE - READ AND WRITE :

It is important to know how numerical data is stored on the disk by fprintf ( ) function. Text and characters require one byte for storing them with fprintf ( ). Similarly for storing numbers in memory two bytes and for floats four bytes are required.

All data types are treated as characters for example the data 3456 occupies two bytes in memory. But when it is transferred to the disk file using fprint ( ) function it would occupy four bytes. For each character one byte would be required. Even for float also each digit including dot (.) requires one byte. For example 12.34 would require five bytes. Thus, large amount of integers or float data requires large space on the disk. Hence in the text mode storing of numerical data on the disk turns out to be inefficient. **To overcome this problem the files should be read & written in binary mode, for which we use functions fread ( ) & fwrite ( ).**

1 fwrite ( ) & fread ( )

1) fwrite ( ) This function is used for writing an entire structure block to a given file.

2) fread ( ) This function is used for reading an entire block from a given file.

Below given an examples of these functions.

Program 13.5.1

Write a program in C to read the information about the structure named bike with name, make and cost from the file using fread() function.

```
# include <stdio.h>
# include <conio.h>
# include <process.h>

void main ( )
{
FILE *fp;
struct bike
{
char name [20];
int avg;
float cost;
};
```

```
struct bike e;
fp=fopen ("bk.txt","rb");
if (fp==NULL)
{
puts ("Cannot open file");
exit (1);
}
clrscr ();
while (fread(&e,sizeof(e),1,fp)==1)
printf("\n %s %d %.2f",e.name,e.avg,e.cost);
fclose(fp);
}
```

OUTPUT :

```
Model Name, Average Price : HONDA   80   45000.00
Model Name, Average Price : SUZUKI  65   43000.00
Model Name, Average Price : YAMAHA  55   48000.00
```

13.6. OTHER FILE FUNCTIONS :

a) The fseek ( ) function It is a file function. It positions file pointer on the stream. We can pass three arguments through this function.

1. File Pointer.
2. Negative or positive long integer number to reposition the file pointer towards the backward or forward direction.
3. The current position of file pointer.

The **Table 13.2** displays the various values of location of file pointer.

Table 13.2 Locations of file pointer.

Integer Value	Constant	Location in the file
0	SEEK_SET	Beginning of the file
1	SEEK_CUR	Current position of the file pointer
2	SEEK_END	End of the file

Example :

Fseek (fp,10,0) or fseek (fp,10,SEEK_SET)

The file pointer is repositioned in the forward direction by 10 bytes.

b) feof ( ) The macro **feof ( )** is used for detecting the file pointer whether it is at the end of file or not. It returns **non-zero** if the file pointer is at the end of file, otherwise it returns zero.

Program 13.6.1

Write a program in C to detect the end of file using function feof(). Display the file pointer position for detecting end of file.

```
# include <conio.h>
# include <stdio.h>
# include <process.h>

void main ( )
{
FILE *fp;

char c:
fp=fopen (*text.txt", "r");
c=feof (fp);
clrscr ( );
printf ("File pointer at the beginning of file : %d\n",c);

while (!feoff(fp))
{
printf (" %c"c);
c=getc(fp);
}

c=feof(fp);
printf ("File pointer at the end of file : %d",c);
}
```

```
File pointer at the beginning of the file : 0
INTELLIGENTIA LEAD THE WORLD
fILE POINTER AT THE END OF FILE : 32
```

13.7. SEARCHING ERRORS IN READING / WRITING FILES :

While performing read or write operations some times we do not get the result successfully. The reason may be that the attempt of reading or writing the operation may not be correct. The provision must provided for searching the error while read / write operations are carried out.

The 'C' language provides standard library function **ferror ( ).** This function is used for detecting any error that might occur during read / write operation on a file. It returns a '0' when the attempt is successful otherwise non-zero in case of failure.

c) ferror ( ) The ferror () is used to find out error when file read write operation is carried out.

d) perror ( ) It is a standard library function which prints the error messages specified by the compiler. A program is illustrated below for understanding.

Program 13.7.1

Write a program in C to detect and print the error message using ferror( ) and perror ( ) functions.

```
# include <stdio.h>
# include <conio.h>
# include <process.h>

void main ()
{
FILE *fr;
char c,file[ ]="lines.txt";
fr=fopen(file,"w");
clrscr( );

while (!feof(fr))
{
c=fgetc(fr);
if (ferror(fr))
{
perror (file);
exi (1);
}
else
printf (" %c",c);
}
fclose (fr);
}
```

OUTPUT :

lines.text : Permission Denied.

e) ftell ( ) It is a file function. It returns the current position of the file pointer. It returns the pointer from the beginning of file.

f) rewind ( ) This function resets the file pointer at the beginning of the file.

g) **UNLINK ()** and **REMOVE ()** These functions delete the given file in the directory. It is similar to del command in dos.

h) **RENAME( )** This function changes the name of the given file. It is similar to DOS command rename.

Program 13.7.2

Write a program in C to change the name of the file. Use rename( ) function.

```
# include <stdio.h>
# include <conio.h>
# include <process.h>
main ()
{
char old [12], new [12];
system("dir *.c /w");
printf ("\n Old File Name : ");
scanf("%s",old);
prinf ("New File Name :");
scanf("%s",new);
rename(old,new);
system("dir*.c/w");
}
```

OUTPUT :

```
Old File Name     : old.c
New File Name     : new.c
```

i) **fcloseall ( )** it closes all the files that have been opened.

13.8. USE OF MULTIPLE FILES :

a. Copying of one file into another file :

Program 13.8.1

Write a program in C to copy the contens of one file to another file.

```
/* File copy program */
# include <stdio.h>
# include <conio.h>
# include <process.h>
void main ()
{
/* Declaration */
FILE *ft, *fs;
int c=0;
clrscr ();
/* Opening Files */
fs=fopen("a.txt","r");
ft=fopen("a.txt","r");
```

```
ft=fopen("b.txt","w");
        if (fs==NULL)
            {
                printf("\n Source file opening error.");
                exit(1);
            }
            else
            if (ft==NULL)
            {
                printf ("\n Target file opening error.");
                esit(1);
            }
/* Reading file */
while (!feof(fs))
{
        fputc(fgetc(fs)ft);
        c++;
        }
printf ("\n %d Bytes copied from 'a.txt' to 'b.txt.'",c);
/* Closing Files */
c\fcloseall();
printf ("\n%d files closed.",c);
}
```

OUTPUT :

45 Bytes copied from 'a.txt' to 'b.txt.
2 files closed.

b) Operations using multiple files :

Program 13.8.2

Write a program in C to read the contents of three files and find the largest file.

```
# include <stdio.h>
# include <conio.h>
# include <alloc.h>
# include <process.h>
void main ()
{
FILE *f[3], *fp;
```

```
int x[3],1,y=0,k=0,t=0;
char c1;
char name [3] [11]={"1.txt","2.txt","3.txt"};
clrscr ( );
for (l=0;l<3;l++)
{
        fp=fopen(name[1],"r");
        f[1]=fp;
                if (fp==NULL)
                {
                        printf ("\n %s file not found. ",name[1]);
                        exit(1);
                        }
}
clrscr ( );
for (l=0;l<3;l++)
{
        while (!feof(f[l]))
        {
                c1=fgetc(f[1]);
                 x[l]=y++;
        }
y=0;
}
clrscr ();
fcloseal1();
for (l=0;l<=2;l++)
{
        printf ("File : %s Bytes : %d\n",name[l],x[l]);
        t=t+x[1];
}
for (l=t;l>=1;l--)
        [
                for (k=0'k<3;k++)
                [
                if (l==x[k]}
                {
                printf (" %s are the largest file.",name[k]);
```

```
                    exit (1);
                    ]
          }
}
}
```

OUTPUT :

```
File : 1.txt    Bytes  : 16
File : 2.txt    Bytes  : 20
File : 3.txt    Bytes  : 25
```

3.text is the largest file.

c. Using part of a file

Program 13.8.3

Write a program in C to copy up to 100 characters from a file to an array. Then copy the contents of an array to another file.

```
# include <stdio.h>
# include <conio.h>
# include <process.h>
# define SIZE 100
void main ( )
{
FILE *f, *f2;
static char c, ch [SIZE];
int s=0,x=0;
clrscr ( );
f=fopen("poem.txt","r");
f2=fopen("alpha.txt","w");
if (f==NULL | | f2== NULL )
{
perror("?");
exit (1);
clrscr ();
while (!feof(f))
          {
                    c=fgetc(f);
                    x++;
                    if (x==99)
          {
          fcloseall();
          exit(1);
          }
```

```
else
ch[s++]=c;
}
fclose(f);

for (s=0;s<=100;s++)
fputc(ch[s],f2);
fclose(f2);
perror("Process Completed");
}
```

OUTPUT :

Process Completed : Error 0

13.9. LOW LEVEL DISK I/O OPERATIONS :

In the low-level I/O disk operation data can not be written as character by character or with sequence of character as it is carried in the high-level disk I/O functions. In the low-level disk I/O functions, buffers are used to carry the read and write operations.

Buffer plays an important role in the low-level disk I/O program. The programmer needs to declare an appropriate buffer size. The low-level disk I/O operations are more efficient and quick than the high level disk I/O operations.

a. **Opening a file** To open a file or files **open ( )** function is used. This function is defined in **"io.h"**. The syntax of **open ( )** is as given below.

Syntax int open (const char *f_name, int access, unsigned mode)

In the low-level operation a number is assigned to the file and the number is used to refer the file. If open ( ) returns -1. it means that the file could not be opened otherwise the file is successfully opened.

The Table 13.3 describes the file opening modes in the low level disk I/O operations.

Table 13.3 File opening modes

Mode	Meaning
0_APPEND	Open a file in append mode
O_WRONGLY	Creates a file for writing only
O_RDONLY	Opens a file for writing only
O_RDWR	Opens a file for read/write operations
O_BINARY	Opens a file in binary mode
O_CREATE	Opens a new file for writing.
O_EXCEL	When used with O_CRATE, if file exists it is not overwritten.
O_TEXT	Creates a text file

When O_CREATE flag is used, it also requires one arguments described in the Table 13.4 to verify the read / write status of the file. These arguments are called as *permission argument*. The programmer need to **# include the header file "stat.h"** and **"types.h" along with "fcntl.h."**

Table 13.4

	Permission argument
S_IWRITE	Writing to the file allowed
S_IREAD	Reading from the file allowed

b. Writing a file The write ( ) function is used to **write ( )** data into the file. This function is defined in "io.h". The syntax of **write ( )** function is as given below.

Syntax : **int write (int handle, void *buf, unsigned nbyte);**

Returns the number of bytes written or -1 if an error occurs.

c. Reading a file The read ( ) function reads a file. The syntax of **read ( )** function is as given below.

Syntax int read (int handle, void *buf, unsigned len);

Upon successful end, it returns an integer specifying the number of bytes placed in the buffer, if the file was opened in the text mode, read does not count carriage returns or Ctrl-Z characters in the number of bytes read. On error, it returns -1 and sets errno.

d. Closing a file The close ( ) function closes the file. This function is defined in "io.h." The syntax of close ( ) is as given below.

Syntax int _close (int handle);

Int close (int handle);

Upon successful finish, close & _close return ( ); otherwise, they return -1 and set erno.

e. Setting Buffer The size of buffer can be set using **setbuf ( )** function. This function is defined in "stdio.h". The syntax of setbuf ( ) is as follows.

Syntax void setbuf (FILE *fp, char *buffer) ;

Program 13.9.1

Write a program in C to enter text through keyboard and store it on he disk. Use low-level disk I/O operations.

```
# include <stdio.h>
# include <conio.h>
```

```
# include <io.h>  /* used for low level disk i/o operations */
# include <fcntl.h>
void main ( )
{
char file[10];
char buff [15];
int s,c;
puts("\n Enter a file name :");
gets (file);

s=open (file, O_CREAT | O_TEXT);

if (s==-1)
puts("\n File does not exits");
else
        {
                puts("Enter text below:");
                        for (c=0;c<13;c++)
                buff[c]=getche();
                buff[c]='\0';

                write(s,buff,15);
                close (s);
        }
}
```

OUTPUT :

Enter a file name :
TEXT

Enter text below : C PROGRAMMING

13.10. COMMAND LINE ARGUMENTS :

An executable program that performs a specific task for operating system is called as command. The commands are issued from the prompt of operating system. Some arguments are to be associated with the commands hence these arguments are called as command line arguments. These associated arguments are passed to the program.

In C language every program starts with a main ( ) function and that it marks the beginning of the program. We have not provided any arguments so far in the main ( ) function. **Here, we can make arguments in the main like other functions. The main ( ) function can receive two arguments and they are 1) argc**

2) argv. The information contained in the command line is passed on to the program through these arguments when the main ( ) is called up by the system.

1. Argument argc

An argument **argc** counts total number of arguments passed from command prompt. It returns a value which is equal to total number of arguments passed through the **main ( ).**

2. Argument argv

It is a pointer to an array of character strings which contains names of arguments. Each word is an argument.

For example

Copy file 1 file2.

Here, file and file2 are arguments and copy is a command.

The first argument is always an executable program followed by associated arguments. If you do not specify argument the first program name itself is an argument but the program will not run properly and will flag an error.

Program 13.10.1

Write a Program in C to display number of arguments and their names

```
# include <stdio.h>
# include <conio.h>
main (int argc, char *argv [ ] )
{
int x;
clrscr ( );
printf ("\n Total number of arguments are %d \n",argc);
for (x=0 ; x<argc ; x++)
printf ("%s\t",argv[x]);
getch ( );
return 0;
}
```

OUTPUT :

```
Total number of arguments are 4
C\TC\C.EXE  A  B  C
```

Explanation :

To execute this program one should create its executable file and run it from the command prompt with required arguments. The above program is executed using following steps.

a) Compile the program
b) Makes its exe file (executable file);
c) Switch to the command prompt. (C:\TC>)
d) Make sure that the exe file is available in the current directory
e) Type following bold line.

C:\TC> C.EXE HELP ME

In the above example c.exe is an executable file and "HELP ME" are taken as arguments. The total number of arguments including the program file name are 3.

13.11. APPLICATION OF COMMAND LINE ARGUMENTS :

Rename can be used on command prompt similar to that of DOS command REN.

1. Rename

Program 13.11.1

Write a program in C to use command line argument to perform the task of REN command of DOS. (Save this program as change.c)

```
# include <stdio.h>
# include <conio.h>
# include <process.h>
main (int argc, char *argv[ ] )
{
FILE *fp, *sp;
        if (argc<3)
        {
        printf ("Insufficient Arguments");
        exit(1);
        }
        fp=fopen(argv[1],"r");
        if (fp==NULL)
        {
                printf ("File Not Found");
                exit(1):
        }
sp=fopen(argv[2],"r");
if (sp==NULL)
        {
                fcloseall();
                rename(argv[1]argv[2]);
        }
        else
        printf("Duplicate file name or file is in use.");
```

```
        return 0;
}
```

2. Del

unlink (argv) can be used on command prompt similar to that of DOS command DEL.

Program 13.11.2

Write a Program in C to use command line argument to perform the task of DEL command of DOS. (Save this program as cut.c)

```
# include <stdio.h>
# include <conio.h>
# include <process.h>
main (int argc, char *argv[ ] )
{
FILE  *fp;
        if (argc<2)
        {
        printf ("Insufficient Arguments");
        exit(1);
        }
fp=fopen(argv[1],"r");
        if (fp==NULL)
        {
                printf ("File Not Found");
                exit(1):
        }
unlink (argv[1])
printf ("File has been deleted");
return 0;
}
```

Explanation :

This program performs task of DEL command of disk operating system. **It deletes only one file at a time.** Create exe file of this program and execute it on the command prompt. **User should give the file name for deleting.** Opening it in read mode checks the existence of file. The file will be deleted in case it exists. In the program appropriate message are displayed if he user makes any mistake. Error messages are "Insufficient Arguments", "File not found" and "file has been deleted".

13.12. ENVIRONMENT VARIABLES :

Environment variables provide different system settings / path related to operating system. These variables are available in both MS-DOS and UNIX operating system. The output depends upon the operating system. The following program displays the output related to MS-DOS.

Program 13.12.1

Write a Program in C to use environment variable and display the various settings.

```
# include <stdio.h>
# include <conio.h>
void main (int argc, char *argv[ ], char *env [ ] )
{
int i;
clrscr ( );
for (i=0;env[i]!=NULL;++i)
}
printf (" %s\n",env[i]);
}
]
```

OUTPUT :

```
TMP=C:\WINDOWS\TEMP
TEMP=C:\WINDOWS\TEMP
PROMPT=SpSg
winbootdir=C:\WINDOWS
COMSPEC=C:\WINDOWS\COMMAND.COM
PATH=C:\WINDOWS;C:\WINDOWS\COMMAND;C:\JDK1.2.1\BIN;C;\JDK1.2.1;
CMDLINE=WIN
windir=C:\WINDOWS
```

13.13. I/O RE DIRECTION :

Consider the **dos** command dir > abc, execute it at dosprompt. Here, dir is the internal dos command and abc is the name of the file. Here, instead of displaying list of files and directories on the screen, it is redirected in a text file **abc** i.e. the files and directories would be possible to see in **abc** file. For this use *type abc command* at dos prompt.

From the above example the reader can understand that the output of command can be redirected to another file. Using redirection the output of the program instead of displaying on the screen is stored on the disk in the form of file. With this we can avoid creating separate functions for writing files to the disk or to the printer. Thus, this is an advantage and is a convenient approach for writing files to the disk. Using this redirection concept both read and write operations are possible.

* * *

COMPREHENSION - 13

Note : By answering all the questions given in this comprehension one can answer any objective type of questions easily whatever be the form of the question. Answers for these questions can be obtained by going through the topics in this chapter carefully.

1. What is a File? What does it do?
2. Define a file. How many types of files are there? Name them.
3. What is a stream? Mention some file objects. What does a file do with stream objects?
4. What does a file object consist of?
5. How does a C Program access the stream object?
6. What are the different modes of files? When are they useful?
7. What are the various types f of operations in Text Mode Files?
8. What are the various basic steps involved in a file operation?
9. Mention the different functions used in file operation and state what they do?
10. What is the structure that involves file opening and in which header is it included?
11. Give the syntax for the structure used in file opening.
12. What is the extension of the text file? How is it given?
13. Give the Syntax for opening a text file and explain.
14. What are the tasks performed by the function fopen ( ) ?
15. What are the different tasks that can be performed on a file? How are these tasks indicated in file syntax for operations on a file?
16. Give the syntax for indicating the errors at the time of opening a file. Explain.
17. What is the preprocessor directive used for file operations ?
18. What is the difference between using append mode and write and read mode in adding data to a file? Which mode is preferable? Why?
19. How do you open a file and add information at the end of the file? Explain with statements.
20. What can be done in append + read mode in a file?
21. What is the use of rewind ( ) function in file operation? How do you decide at what stage of the program it should be used?
22. Explain read + write mode.

23. What is advantage of using binary files over text files? Explain.
24. Give the alphabets used for different modes of file operations in binary file and explain.
25. Explain the use of fgetc ( ) function in file operations giving the syntax for using it.
26. How do you close a file that has been opened earlier? Give the syntax and explain.
27. Explain the functions used in file I/O operations with syntax.
28. Explain the differences between similar functions with similar actions like getc( ) , fgetc( ) etc.
29. What is done by fwrite ( ) & fread ( ) functions? When are they used?
30. How do you overcome the problem of usage of large disc space while storing numerical data in text mode?
31. What does fseek ( ) do?
32. What do the following functions do?

    i. feof( ) ii. ferror( ) iii. Ferror( ) iv. Perror( ) v.rewind( ) vi. RENAME ( ) vi. UNLINK ( ) or

    REMOVE( ) vii. Fcloseall ( )
33. Explain what functions you use to copy the contents of one file into another file.
34. Explain the use of multiple files with examples.
35. What is the problem of low level disk I/O operation? How do you overcome it?
36. In which header is open( ) used?
37. With syntax explain the use of open( ) function.
38. Describe the file opening modes in the low level disk I/O operations.
39. What are command line arguments?
40. How many command line arguments can be provided to main ( ) ? What are they?
41. What do Argument argc and t Argument argv do?
42. Name some command line arguments and their use.
43. What are environment variables? What do they do?
44. Explain with examples I/O Redirection.
45. Explain with syntax the use of additional buffered I/O functions getw( ) & putw( ). In what way they are different from getc( ) & putc( ) functions?

* * *

EXERCISE - 13

Note : By answering all the questions given in this exercise one can answer subjective type of questions easily including problems. The worked examples in the chapter may help in solving these questions.

1. What is the significance of EOF?
2. When a program is terminated, all the files used by it are automatically closed. Why is it then necessary to close a file during execution of the program?
3. Distinguish between the following functions:
   i) getc and getchar
   ii) printf and fprintf
   iii) feof and ferror
4. How does an append mode differ from a write mode?
5. What are the common uses of **rewind** and **ftell** functions?
6. Explain the general format of **fseek** function.
7. What is the difference between the statement **rewind (fp);** and **fseek (fp, 0L,0); ?**
8. Distinguish between text mode and binary mode operation of a file.
9. Distinguish between the following functions.
   i) **scanf ( )** and **fscanf( )**
   ii) **getc ( )** and **getchar ( )**
   iii) **putc ( )** and **fputc ( )**
   iv) **putw ( )** and **getw ( )**
   v) **ferror ( )** and **perror ( )**
   vi) **feof( )** and **eof( )**
10. Why the header files **stdio.h** be frequently used in C Language?
11. Compare between **printf** and **fprintf** functions
12. Distinguish between the following modes.
    i) **w** and **w+**
    ii) **r** and **r+**
    iii) **rb** and **rb+**
    iv) **a** and **a+**
13. Explain low level disk operations
14. Explain command line arguments.
15. Explain Environment Variables.
16. How re-direction of input and output is done? Explain in brief.
17. The fscanf ( ) statements reads data from
    a) File b) Keyboard c) Both (a) and (b) d) None of these

18. When fopen ( ) fails to open a file it returns
    a) NULL b) -1 c) 1 d) None of these
19. A file opened in w+ mode can be
    a) read / write b) only read c) only write d) none of these
20. Command line arguments are used to accept argument from
    a) Command prompt of operating system b) Through scanf ( ) statement
    c) Both (a) and (b) d) None of these
21. The redirection operator '>' transfers any output to
    a) text file b) console c) both (a) and (b) d) none of these
22. This function is used to detect the end of file
    a) feof ( ) b) ferror ( ) c) fputs ( ) d) fgetch ( )
23. The EOF is equivalent to
    a) -1 b) 0 c) 1 d) none of these
24. A hospital keeps a file of blood donors in which each record has the form:
    structure name : partientrec

field name	type	width
patient name	Character	25
age	integer	2
blood type	character	2 (Type A,B,AB, O)

    i) Write a program to create a data file for 100 blood donors.
    ii) use the data file to print out all blood donors whose age is below 25 and blood is of O type
25. Write a program to generate a data file containing the list of cricket players, no. innings played highest run score and no. of hatrik made by them. Use structure variable to store the cricketer's name, no. of innings played, highest run score & number of hatricks.
26. Write a program to find size of the file.
27. Write a program to combine contents of two files in a third file. Add line number at the beginning of each line.
28. Write a program to display numbers from 1 to 100. Re-direct the output of the program to text file.
29. Write a program to interchange contents of two files.
30. A file named **DATA** contains a series of integer numbers, code C program to read these numbers and then write all odd numbers to a file to be called **ODD** and all even numbers to a file called **EVEN**.

* * *

CHAPTER - 14
DYNAMIC MEMORY ALLOCATION - I
(LINKED LISTS)

14.1. INTRODUCTION :

All the items discussed under chapters 14 & 15 on dynamic memory allocation are all common to C and C++.

Overview of Data Structure :

Data structure is a method of representation of logical relationships between individual data elements related to the solution of a given problem. Data structure is the most convenient way to handle data of different data type including abstract data type for a known problem. For example the characteristics of a house can be represented by house name, house number location number of floors, number of rooms on each floor, kind of fencing to the house either with brick walls or wire, electrification either underground or open, balcony is provided or not etc. Here one can use a variety of data types to represent the data elements while solving a problem with the help of computer language such as char int Boolean type etc. For example, with the help of computer the characteristics of a house can be represented such as the number of floors of the house can be given with either int or char type. House number and number of rooms of it can also be declared with the same type provided that, the data must be in limits of the range of data type. In C/C++ the char data type perfectly works as integer data in its range from -128 to 127 and as unsigned char from 0 to 255. At some places, selection is also important to minimize the overhead. For example, suppose we are going to fence the house with bricks instead of wire. Here, the brick wall may be expensive. Likewise, if we are using signed in to store positive number of floors) instead of char i.e., we are wasting one byte of the system. Hence, here char is appropriate which occupies only one byte.

Electrification should be declared with char data type. Like the above example in practical application of data structure, to create a data structure, some components are involved directly or indirectly to build the system. In other words, data structure is a structured set of variables associated to one another in a different manner co-operatively defining components of the system.

The components of data can be organized and records maintained. Further, the record formation leads to the development of abstract data type and database system.

In data strucure, we also have to decide on the storage, retrieval and operation that should be carried ou between the logically related items. For example the data must be stored in memory in computer understandable format i.e., 0 ad 1. The data stored in the compuer must be in predictable /understandable format i.e., ASCII. In order to transform data various operations are to be performed. They are as follows:

As stated earlier, the following **activities** are **associated with data structure**.

1) **Data organization or clubbing**
2) **Accessing technique**
3) **Level of associability**
4) **Manipulating selections for information**

Data structure is the base of the programming tools and the **choice of data structure is governed by the following.**

1) **The data structure should be satisfactory to represent the relationship between data elements.**

2) **The data structure should be easy so that the programmer can easily process the data as per requirement.**

Data structures have been classified in several ways. Different authors classify them differently as given below. Besides these data structures, other types of data structures exist such as lattice, petri nets, neural nets, semantic nets, search graphs and so on.

14.1.1. Classification of Data Structures :

i) Linear : In the linear data structure values are arranged in a linear fashion. An array, linked list, stacks and queues are examples of linear data structure in which values are stored in sequence . There is a relation between the adjacent elements of a linear list.

ii) Nonlinear : This type is opposite to linear. The data values in this structure are no arranged in order. Tree, graph, table ad sets are examples of nonlinear data structure.

iii) Homogenous : In this type of data structure, values of same data types are stored. An example of it can be an array that stores similar data type elements having different locations for each element.

iv) Non-homogenous : In this type of daa strucure, data values of different types are grouped like in structure and classes.

v) Dynamic : In dynamic data structures such as reference and pointers, size and memory locations can be changed during program execution.

vi) Static : A static keyword in C/C++ is used to initialize the variable to 0 (Null). Static variable value remains in the memory throughout the program. Value of static variable persists. In C++, member function csan be declared as static and such a function can be invoked directly.

Data structure can also be broadly divided into 2 categories.

a. Linear Data Structure **b. Non-Linear Data Structure**

a) **Linear Data Structure** : i) arrays and structures ii) linked lists
iii) Stacks iv) Queues

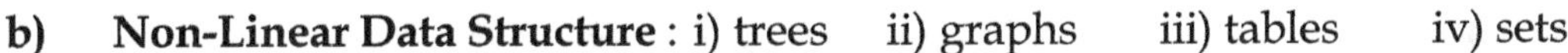

b) Non-Linear Data Structure : i) trees ii) graphs iii) tables iv) sets

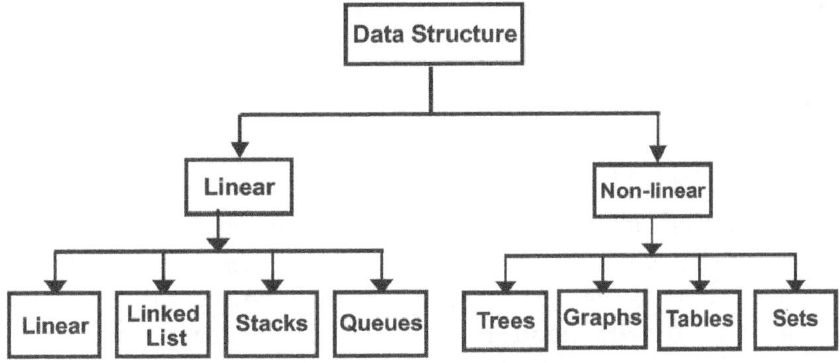

Fig.14.1. Types of Data Structure

Among Linear Data structures Arrays and structures have already been discussed earlier.

Dynamic Memory Allocation : *One of the main drawbacks encountered by array is, the size of the array cannot be increased or decreased during run time.* Consider a linear array will 100 elements and if we want to insert a new element in the middle of the list, then we have to shift all the elements one position up till the required position is reached. Similarly when we want to insert a new element in the middle of the list, then we have to shift all the elements one position up till the required position a reached. Similarly when we want to delete a particular element in the middle of the list, we have to shift all the elements one position down till the desired position is reached. *Dynamic memory allocation concept finds very much useful in cases where we do not know the exact memory required.* By using this technique it is possible to build more complex data structures like linked lists, stacks, queues and binary trees. These features of linked lists, Stacks Queues, Trees, Graphs etc., are available in both C and C++. A thorough understanding of structures and pointers is a prerequisite to understand this chapter.

This chapter deals with the concept of dynamic memory allocation using linked lists.

14.2. LINKED LIST :

A linked list not only contains a record but also the address in which the next record is located so as to avoid sequential accessing of the next record. There are three types of linked lists.

1. Single Linked List 2. Double Linked List 3. Circular Linked List

It is well known that storing information in a floppy media is not in sequential order. Suppose we want to store a file of size 10 Kilobytes, we required nearly 20 sectors (by assuming sector of size 512 bytes). Each sector has information part and address part. The first sector will have a content of 512 bytes in the information part and it also contains the subsequent sector number in the address part. The last sector will have only information part. During copying, one may notice the error 'Sector not found' if any one of the sectors gets corrupted in most MS-DOS based systems.

Linked list also employs the above technique. Linked list is further classified into singly linked list, doubly linked list and circularly linked list.

14.2.1. Singly Linked List :

A linked list is a chain of 'structs' or records called nodes. Each node has at least two members, one of which points to the next item. These are defined as Single Linked Lists because they only point to the next item. **The singly linked can be of two types. i) without header, ii) with header.** Thus, linked list having only one address filed (next) is called singly linked list Here each node has one data field and address filed. The address field contains the address of the next node in the structure. In the above pictures HEAD pointer points to the first node of a linked list. The link field of the last node has a value NULL, to indicate the end of a linked list. In linked list we can easily insert a new element and delete a element without disturbing other elements.

i) The Singly Linked List without header is given in Fig. 14.2 (a).

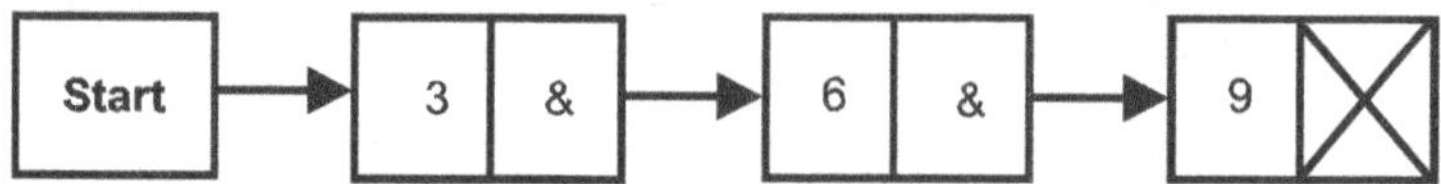

Fig. 14.2.(a) Singly Linked List (without header)

In singly linked list, two successive nodes of the linked list are linked with each other in sequential linear manner. Like a train in which two successive bogies are connected. The train is an example of singly linked list.

Recall that singly linked list is a dynamic data structure with the ability to expand the shrink as per the program requirement. the singly linked list is easy and straight forward data structure as compared to other structures. By changing the link position, other types of linked lists such as circular and doubly linked lists can be formed. For creating a linked list the structure is defined as follows.

```
struct node
{
    int number;
    struct node *p;
};
```

Here the pointer *p points to the same structure. The above structure struct node is used to implement the linked list. In it, the number is a variable to be entered and stored in memory. The second member is pointer to the same structure. The pointer *p points to the same structure. Here, though the declaration of struct node has not been completed, the pointer declaration of the same structure type is permitted by the compiler. However, the variable declaration is not allowed. This is because the pointers are dynamic in nature, whereas variables are formed by each binding. The declaration of objects inside the struct leads to preparation of a very complex data structure. This concept is called object composition and its detailed discussion is out of the scope of this book.

We are familiar with the array and we know the importance of base address. Once a base address is obtained, it is used for accessing the successive elements. In the linked list, also list can be created with or without header node. The head holds the starting address.

Program 14.2.1

Write a Program in C to create a Simple Linked List without Header for the linked list given in fig.14.1.

```
# include <stdio.h>
# include <conio.h>
# include <malloc.h>      /* header file for dynamic memory allocation */
        struct list
        {
            int n;
            int *p;
        };
void main ( )
{
        struct list elem0, elem1, elem2;
        elem2.n=3;
        elem2.p=NULL;  /* points to last element */
        elem1.n=6;
        elem1.p=elem2.n; /* points to third element */
        elem0. n=9;
        elem0.p=elem1.n;
        clrscr ();
        printf ("\n Linked list elements are : ");
        printf (" %d ", elem0.n);
        printf (" %d ", elem0.p);
        printf (" %d ", elem1.p);
        printf (" %d ", elem2.p);
}
```

OUTPUT :

Linked list elements are 3 6 9 0

ii) Singly Linked List With Header :

Sometimes it is desirable to keep an extra node at the front of a list which can store the beginning address of the linked list. Such a node does not represent an item in the list and is called header node or a list header. The info portion of such a header node might be unused. More often, the info portion of a node could be used to keep global information about the entire list. In such a data structure more work is headed to add or delete an element from the list, since the count in the header must be adjusted. However, the number of items in the list may be obtained directly from the header node without traversing the entire list.

a) Linked List with Header :

This linked list with header contains A header and a rear or tail.

The following steps are used to create a linked list with header.

1) Three pointers header, first and rear are declared. The header pointer is initially initialized with NULL. For example, header=NUL, where header is pointer to structure. If it remains NULL, it implies that the list has no element. Such a list is known as NULL list or empty list.

   The empty list would be represented by the null pointer but rather by a list with a single header node.

Fig. 14.2 (b). Singly Linked List (with header)

2) In the second step, memory is allocated for the first node of the linked list. For example, the address of the first node is 1888. An integer say 8 is stored in the variable num and value of header is assigned to pointer next.

Fig. 14.2 (c). Singly Linked List (with header)

Both the header and rear are initialized as the address of the first node.

The statement would be

```
header=first;
rear=first;
```

3) *The address of pointer first is assigned to pointers header and rear. The rear pointer is used to identify the end of the list and to detect the NULL pointer.*

4) Again, create a memory location, suppose it is 1890, for accessing the successive node.

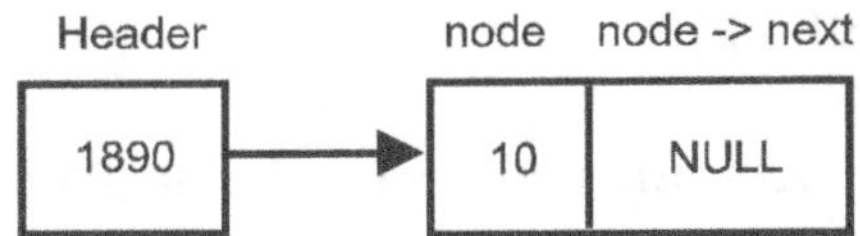

Fig. 14.2 (d). Singly Linked List (with header)

5) Join the element of 1890 by assigning the value of node rear-> next. Move the rear pointer to the last node.

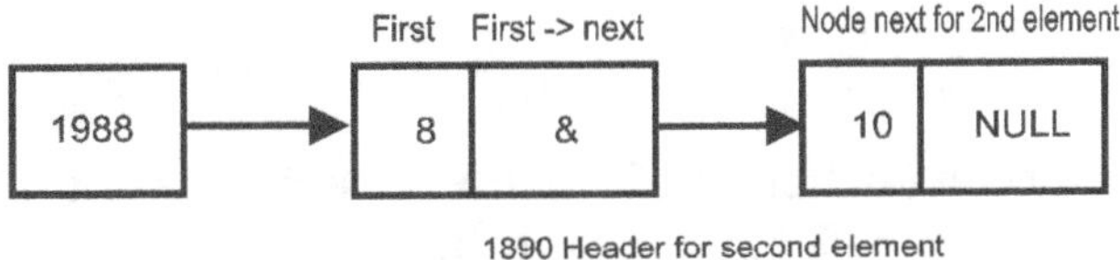

Fig. 14.2 (e). Singly Linked List (with header)

Program : 14.2.2

Write a program in C to create a linked list with header

```
# include <stdio.h>
# include <conio.h>
# include <malloc.h>        /* header for dynamic memory allocation */

struct num
{
        int num;
        struct num *next;
}       *header.*first,*rear;
int main ( )
{
        void create (void);
        clrscr ();
        create ();
        printf ("\n Linked list elements are : ");
        while (header != NULL)
        {
                printf (" #%d", header->num);
                header=header->next;
        }
return 0;
}
void create ( void )
{
        struct num *node;
        printf ("\n Enter number : ");
```

```
        if (header==NULL)
        {
                first=(struct num*) malloc(sizeof(struct num));
                scanf ("%d;&first->num);
                first->next=header;
                header=first;
                rear=first;
        }
        while (1)
        {
                node=(struct num*) malloc(sizeof(struct num));
                scanf ("%d"&node->num);
                if (node->num==0)
                break;
        node->next=NULL;
        rear->next=node;
        rear=node;
        }
    }
```

OUTPUT

Enter number : 1 3 6 9 12 15 0
Linked list elements are : 1 3 6 9 12 15

Header : *The pointer header is very useful in the formation of linked list. The address of first node (1888) is stored in pointer header. The value of header remains unchanged until it turns out to be NULL. The starting location of the list can only be determined by the pioneer header.*

14.2.2. Traversing a singly linked list :

a) Traversing singly linked list with header : The statements

```
while (header!=NULL)
        {
                printf (" #%d", header->num);
                header=header->next;
        }
```

do the traversing operation, which involves visiting all the elements of the queue. The above while () loop and associated statements are used to traverse and display the elements of the list.

b) Traversing singly linked list without header :

In the last topic we discussed how a linked list can be created using header. *The creation of a linked list without header is same as linked list with header. The difference between linked list with header and without header, is that, in the former case header list pointer contains address of the first node. In the linked list case without header list, pointer first itself points to starting of the linked list.* Consider the following program

Program 14.2.3

Write a program in C to create a linked list without header

```
#include <stdio.h>
# include <conio.h>
# include <malloc.h>

struct num
{
        int num;
        struct num *next;
        *header.*first,*rear;
}
int main ( )
{
        void create (void);
        clrscr ();
        create ();
        printf ("Linked list elements : ");
        while (first != NULL)
        {
                printf (" %d",first->num);
                first=first->next;
        }
        return 0;
}
void create (void)
{
        struct num *node;
        printf ("\n Enter number : ");
if (first==NULL)
        {
                first=(struct num*)malloc (sizeof(struct num));
                scanf (" %d",&first->num);
                first->next=first;
                rear=first;
        }
        while (1)
        {
                node=(struct num*) malloc (sizeof (struct num));
                scanf (" %d",&node->num);
```

```
            if (node->num==0) break;
            node->nex=NULL;
            rear->next=node;
            rear=node;
        }
    }
```

OUTPUT :

Enter number : 1 3 5 7 9 11 13 0

Linked list elements : 1 3 5 7 9 11 13

Traversing a list without header : The block of statements

```
        while (first != NULL)
        {
            printf (" %d",first->num);
            first=first->next;
        }
```

causes the traversal of list without header. Traversal with the first node is shown in the above code.

14.2.3. Addition and Deletion of Elements in a Singly Linked List :

In linked list we can easily insert a new element and delete a element without disturbing other elements. Addition and deletion of a single element in a Singly Linked List is done very easily by changing the value to the pointer of the element after which the new element is to be added or the existing element is to be deleted as shown in the figures given below.

The following picture depicts a linked list.

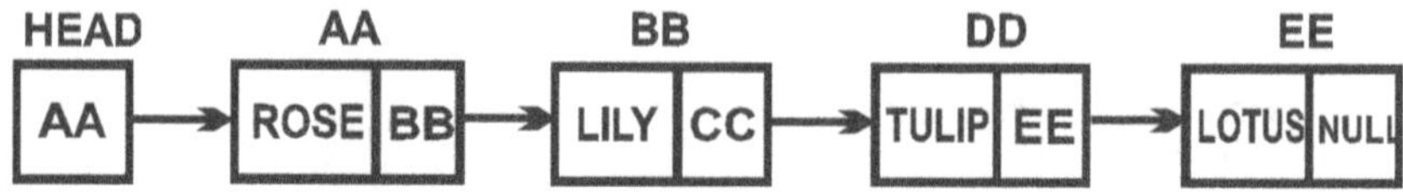

Fig. 14.3 (a) Singly Linked List

Here each node has one data field and address filed. The address field conains the address of the next node in the structure. In he above picture HEAD pointer points to the first node of a linked list. The link field of the last node has a value NULL, to indicate the end of a linked list.

The following pictures depict addition and deletion of elements in linked list.

The figures 14.3 (a) and 14.3 (b) depict the addition and deletion of an element in the middle of a linked list.

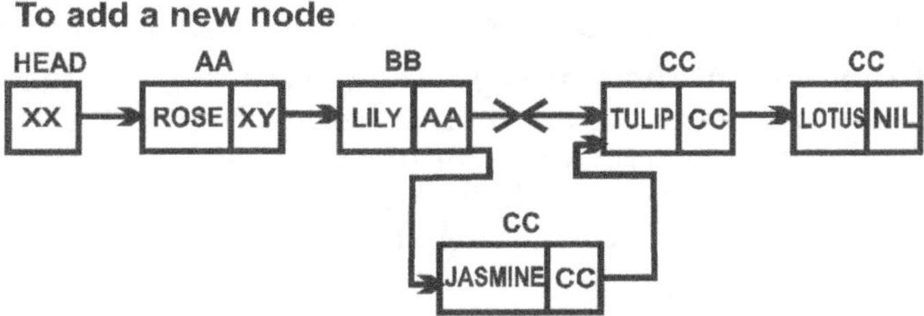

Fig. No.14.3 (b) Addition of an element JASMINE inside a linked list

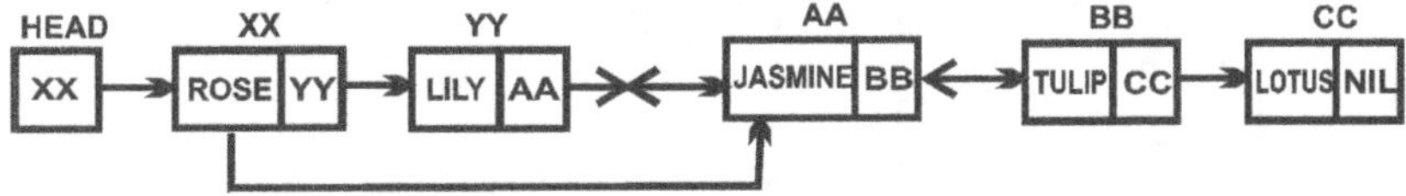

Fig. No.14.3 (c) Deletion of a node LILLY inside a linked list

Let us consider a node with the following details.

Field name	**field type**	**field width**
name	char	10
branch	char	10
examno	int	

The declaration of the above will take the following form.

```
struct info
{
        char name[10];
        char branch[10];
        int examno;
        info *next;
};
```

Note that the last field in the above structure points to the address of the same structure. **The last element of the structure here is also called as self-referential structure, since the name of the structure itself.**

14.2.4. Insertion in singly linked list :

The following steps are involved in inserting an element.

a) Creation of the node : Before insertion, the node is created. Using malloc ( ) function memory space for the node is allocated.

b) Assignment of data : Once the node is created, data values are assigned to members.

c) Adjusting pointers : The insertion operation changes the sequence. Hence , according to the sequence, the address of the next element is assigned to the inserted node. The address of the current node (inserted) is assigned to the previous node.

The insertion of the node can be done in the following position in the list.

a) **Insertion of the node at the starting :** The created node is inserted before the first element. After insertion, the newly inserted element will be first element of the linked list. In this insertion only the context of he successive node's pointer is changed. After insertion the new node will be the first node and its link field points to the second element which was earlier the first element.

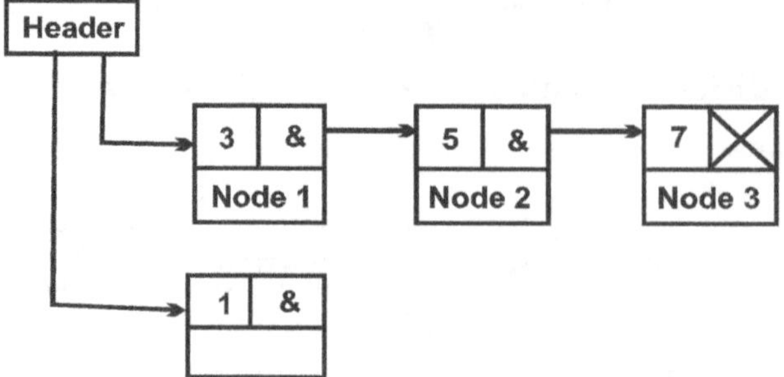

Fig. 14.4 (a) Before insertion at the beginning of a singly linked list

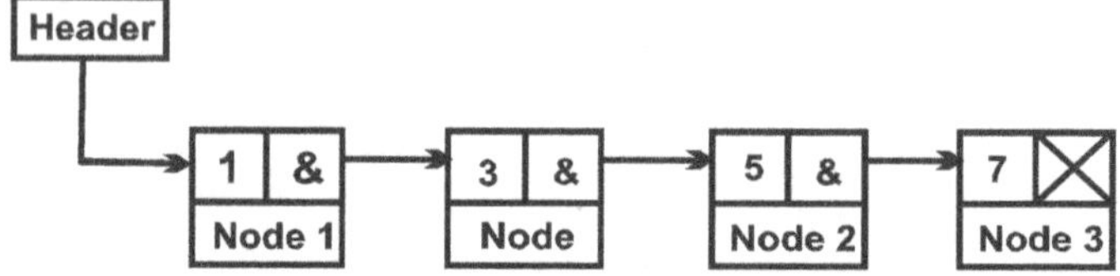

Fig.14.4 (b) After insertion at the beginning of a singly linked list

Program 14.2.4

Write a Program in C to insert an element at the beginning of a Singly Linked List.

```
#include <stdio.h>
# include <conio.h>
# include <malloc.h>

struct num
{
        int num;
        struct num *next;
        *header.*first,*rear;
}
int main ()
{
        void atbeg (void);
        void create (void);
        void show (void);
```

```
        clrscr ();
        printf ("\n Operation creation :");
        create ();
        show ();

        atbeg();
        printf ("\n The elements after insertion : ") ;
        show();
        atbeg();
        show ();
        return 0;
    }
    void create (void )
    {
        struct num *node;
        printf (*\n Enter number : *);
    if (header==NULL)
        {
            first=(struct num* malloc(sizeof (struct num));
            scanf (" %d",&first->num);
            first->next=header;
            header=first;
            rear=first;
        }
        while (1)
        {
            node=(struct num*) malloc(sizeof (struct num));
            scanf (" %d", &node->num);
            if (node->num==0) break;
            node->next=NULL;
            rear->next=node;
            rear=node;

        }
    }
void atbeg ( )
{
    struct num *node,*t;
    t=rear;
    rear=(struct num*) malloc(sizeof (struct num));
```

```
        printf ("\n Insert an element at starting : ");
        scanf (" %d",&node->num);
        t=first;
        header=node;
        header->next=t;
        first=header;
}
void show ( )
{
        printf ("\n Linked list elements are : ");
        while (header)=NULL)
        {
                printf (" %d ",header->num);
                header=header->next;
        }
}
```

OUTPUT :

Operation creation;
Enter number 5 7 9 11 0
Linked list elements are : 5 7 9 11
Insert an element at starting : 3
The elements after insertion :
Linked list elements are : 3 5 7 9 11
Insert an element at starting : 1
Linked list elements are : 1 3 5 7 9 11
Insert an element at starting : 15
Linked list elements are : 15 1 3 5 7 9 11

b) Addition of an element at the end of singly linked list :

Figures 14.5 (a) and Fig.14.5 (b) depict the addition of an element at the end of the linked list with header.

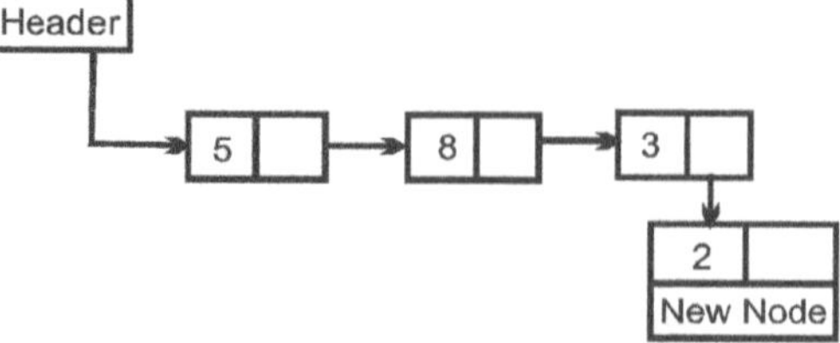

Fig.14.5 (a) Before insertion at the end of a singly linked list

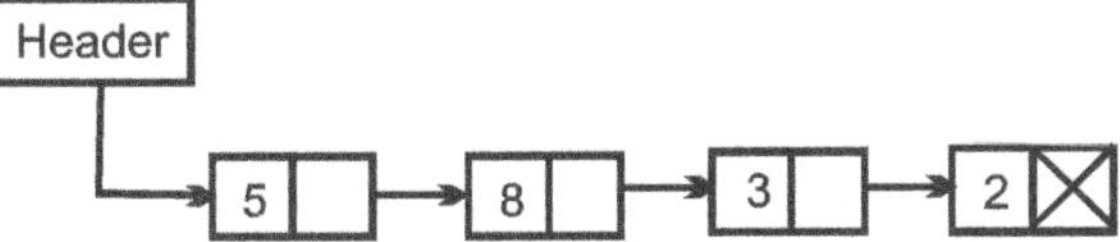

Fig.14.5 (b) After insertion at the end of a singly linked list

Program : 14.2.5

Write a program in C for insertion of an element at the end of a Linked List with header.

```
#include <stdio.h>
# include <conio.h>
# include <malloc.h>
struct num
{
	int num;
	struct num *nex t;
	*header.*first,*rear;
}
int main ( )
{
	void attend (void);
	void create (void);
	void show (void);
	clrscr ();
	printf ("\n Operation creation :");
	create ();
	show ();
	atend();
	show();
	atend();
	show ();
	return 0;
}
void create (void )
{
	struct num *node;
	printf (*\n Enter number :  *);
if (header==NULL)
	{
		first=(struct num* malloc(sizeof (struct num));
		scanf (" %d",&first->num);
		first->next=header;
```

```
            header=first;
            rear=first;
        }
        while (1)
        {
            node=(struct num*) malloc(sizeof (struct num));
            scanf ("%d", &node->num);
            if (node->num==0) break;
            node->next=NULL;
            rear->next=node;
            rear=node;
        }
    }
void atend ( )
{
    struct num *node,*t;
    t=rear;
    rear=(struct num*) malloc(sizeof (struct num));
    printf ("\n Insert an element at end : ");
    scanf ("%d",&rear->num);
    t->next=rear;
    rear->next=NULL;
}
void show ( )
{
    printf ("\n Linked Linked list elements are : ");
    while (header) != NULL)
    {
        printf (" %d ",header->num);
        header=header->next;
    }
    header=first;
}
```

OUTPUT :

Operation creation;
Enter number 2 4 6 0
Linked list elements are : 2 4 6
Insert an element at end : 8
Linked list elements are : 2 4 6 8
Insert an element at end : 10
Linked list elements are : 2 4 6 8 10

Note : *The similarity between the different modules of the two programs given above and also the subtle differences which differentiate addition of an element at the beginning and addition of an element at the end.*

c) Insertion of an element at the given position in the singly linked list :

In this operation, the user has to enter the position number. The given position is counted and the element is inserted. In this insertion contents of both previous and next node's pointers are altered.

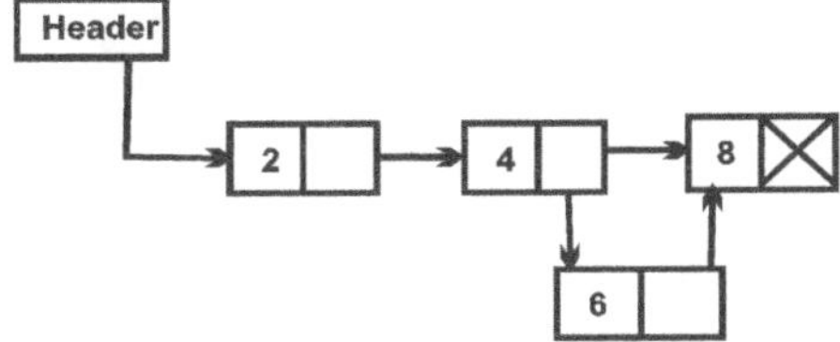

Fig.14.6 (a) Before Insertion at a specified position in a singly linked list

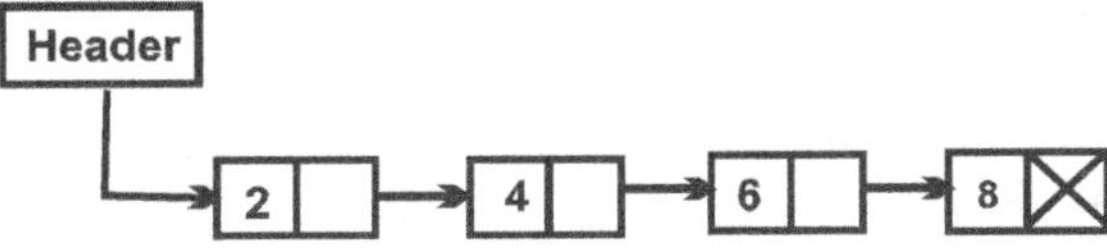

Fig.14.6 (b) After Insertion at a specified position in a singly linked list

Program : 14.2.6

Write a Program in C to insert an element at a specified position in a singly linked list with header.

```
#include <stdio.h>
# include <conio.h>
# include <malloc.h>
struct num
{
        int num;
        struct num *next;
        *header.*first,*rear;
}
        int count;
        int main ( )
{
        void atpo (int);
        void create (void);
        void show (void);
        int p;
        clrscr ();
```

```
        printf ("\n Operation creation :");
        create ();
        show ();
        printf ("\n enter position (upto %d)number (After position) ; ",count );
        scanf (" %d",&p);
        atpo (--p);
        show ( );
        return 0;
    }
    void create (void )
    {
        struct num *node;
        printf (*\n Enter number : *);
    if (header==NULL)
        {
            first=(struct num* malloc(sizeof (struct num));
            scanf (" %d",&first->num);
            first->next=header;
            header=first;
            rear=first;
        }
        while (1)
        {
            node=(struct num*) malloc(sizeof (struct num));
            scanf (" %d", &node->num);
            if (node->num==0) break;
            node->next=NULL;
            rear->next=node;
            rear=node;
        }
    }
void atpo (int k)
{
    struct num *nw, *su, *pr;
    int c=1;
    while (header !=NULL)
    {
        c++;
        header=header->next;
```

```
            if (k==1)           pr=first;
            if (c==k)           pr=header;
            if (c==(k+1))       su=header;
      }
      nw=(struct num*) malloc(sizeof (struct num));
      printf ("\n Enter a element : ");
      scanf ("%d",&nw->num);
      pr->next=nw;
      nw->next=su;
}
void show ( )
{
      printf ("\n Linked Linked list elements are : ");
      while (header)=NULL)
      {
            printf ("%d ",header->num);
            header=header->next;
      }
      header=first;
}
```

OUTPUT :

Operation creation;
Enter number 1 3 7 9 11 0
Linked list elements are : 1 3 7 9 11
Enter position (upto position 4) number (After position) : 4 2
Enter a element : 5
Linked list elements are : 1 3 5 7 9 11

Program 14.2.7

Write a function in C++ to illustrate the addition of an element in a Singly Linked List in a given position of the linked list with header.

```
void list::addrecord()
{
      info *add;
      char proceed='y';
      while (toupper(proceed)=='Y')
            {
                  add = new info;
                  cout"\n Enter name :"
```

```
            cin.getline(add->name.20); fflush(stdin);
            cout<<" Enter branch : "'
            cin.getline(add->branch,20);
            fflush(stdin);
            cout<<" Enter exam no : ";
            cin>>add>->examno;
            fflush(stdin);
            if (head==0)
                {
                        head=add;
                        add->next=0;
                        temp=add;
                }
            else
                {
                        temp->next=add;
                        add->next=0;
                        temp=add;
                }
            cout<<"\n Want to proceed y/n *;
            proceed=getchar();
            fflush(stdin);
        }
}
```

To add a new node

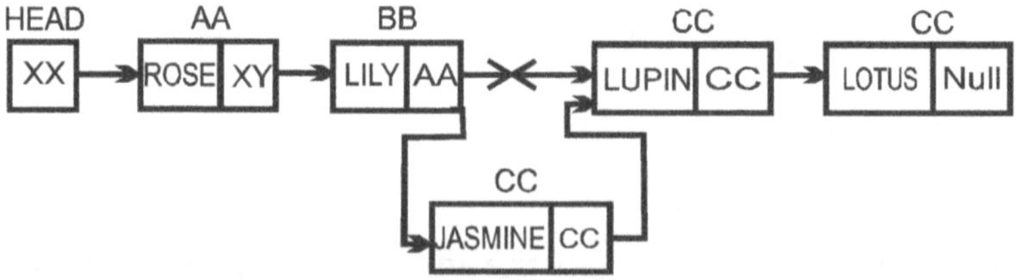

Fig. 14.7 To add an element in a given position of a singly linked list.

Program 14.2.8

Write a function in C++ to illustrate the addition of an element in a Singly Linked List in a given position of the linked list with header.

```
//Only the function for addition of an element in C++. Not full program
void list::addrecord()
{
    info *add;
    char proceed='y';
```

```
while (toupper(proceed)=='Y')
      {
            add = new info;
            cout"\n Enter name :"'
            cin.getline(add->name.20); fflush(stdin);
            cout<<" Enter branch : "'
            cin.getline(add->branch,20);
            fflush(stdin);
            cout<<" Enter exam no : ";
            cin>>add>->examno;
            fflush(stdin);
            if (head==0)
                  {
                        head=add;
                        add->next=0;
                        temp=add;
                  }
            else
                  {
                        temp->next=add;
                        add->next=0;
                        temp=add;
                  }
            cout<<"\n Want to proceed y/n *;
            proceed=getchar();
            fflush(stdin);
      }
}
```

Program : 14.2.9

Write a program in C to insert elements at the end of the linked list with header

```
#include <stdio.h>
# include <conio.h>
# include <malloc.h>

struct num
{
      int num;
      struct num *next;
      *header.*first,*rear;
}
```

```
    int main ( )
    {
        void atend (void);
        void create (void);
        void show (void);
        clrscr ( );
        printf ("\n Operation creation :");
        create ( );
        show ( );
        atend( );
        show( );
        atend( );
        show ();
        return 0;
    }
    void create (void )
    {
        struct num *node;
        printf (*\n Enter number : *);
    if (header==NULL)
        {
            first=(struct num* malloc(sizeof (struct num));
            scanf ("%d",&first->num);
            first->next=header;
            header=first;
            rear=first;
        }
        while (1)
        {
            node=(struct num*) malloc(sizeof (struct num));
            scanf ("%d", &node->num);
            if (node->num==0) break;
            node->next=NULL;
            rear->next=node;
            rear=node;
        }
    }
void atend ( )
{
    struct num *node,*t;
    t=rear;
```

```
        rear=(struct num*) malloc(sizeof (struct num));
        printf ("\n Insert an element at end : ");
        scanf ("%d",&rear->num);
        t->next=rear;
        rear->next=NULL;
}
void show ( )
{
        printf ("\n Linked Linked list elements are : ");
        while (header)=NULL)
        {
                printf ("%d ",header->num);
                header=header->next;
        }
        header=first;
}
```

OUTPUT :

Operation creation;
Enter number 21 32 43 0
Linked list elements are : 21 32 43
Insert an element at end : 4
Linked list elements are : 21 32 43 54
Insert an element at end : 5
Linked list elements are : 21 32 43 54 65

14.2.5 Counting of Nodes in a Singly Linked List :

Sometimes it may be essential to know how many nodes exists in the linked list. The linked list elements can be counted and displayed. The solution is very easy. The procedure applied previously for displaying elements can be applied here. A counter variable can be inserted there to count the nodes by simply incrementing the counter variable.

14.2.6 Deletion of nodes in a Singly linked list :

Deleting a node from the list has the following three cases

1. Deleting the first node
2. Deleting the last node
3. Deleting the specified node

While deleting a node, the node hat is to be deleted is searched first. If the first node is to be deleted then the second node is assigned to header. If the last node is to be deleted, access the last but one node and its link field is assigned a NULL value. If the node that is to be deleted is in between the linked list then access the predecessor and successor nodes of the specified node and link them.

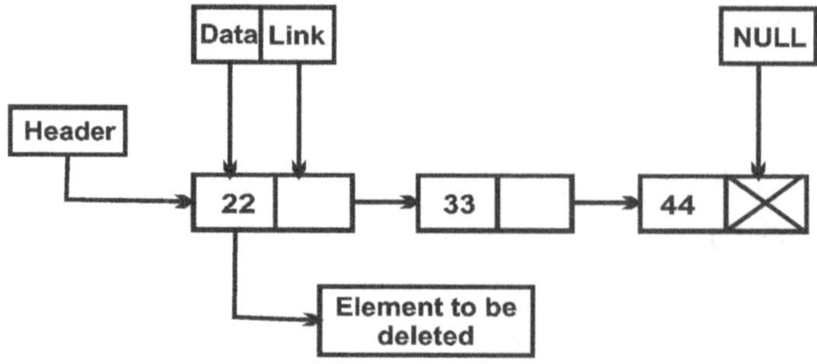

Fig.14.8 (a) Before Deletion at the beginning of a singly linked list

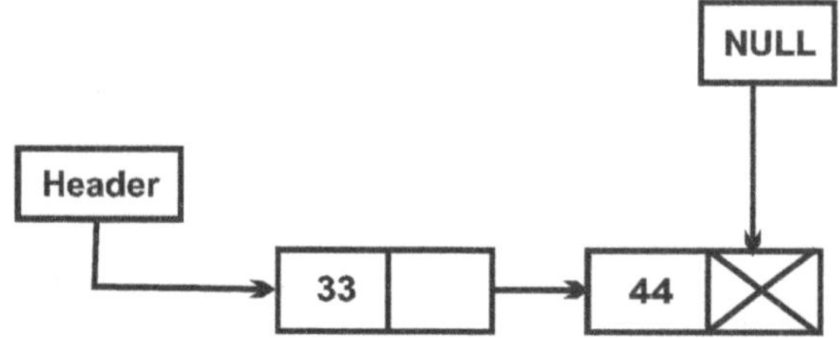

Fig.14.8 (b) After Deletion from the beginning of a singly linked list

Program 14.2.10

Write a program in C to delete three elements from the beginning of the linked list.

```
#include <stdio.h>
# include <conio.h>
# include <malloc.h>
struct num
{
        int num;
        struct num *next;
}       *header.*first,*rear; *k;
int main ()
{
        void rem (void);
        void create (void);
        void show (void);
        clrscr ();
        printf ("\n Operation creation :");
        create ();
```

```
        show ();
        printf ("\n After deletion : ") ;
        rem();
        show ();
        rem();
        show ();
        rem();
        show ();
        return 0;
    }
    void create (void )
    {
        struct num *node;
        printf (*\n Enter number : *);
    if (header==NULL)
        {
            first=(struct num* malloc(sizeof (struct num));
            scanf (" %d",&first->num);
            first->next=header;
            header=first;
            rear=first;
        }
        while (1)
        {
            node=(struct num*) malloc(sizeof (struct num));
            scanf (" %d", &node->num);
            if (node->num==0) break;
            node->next=NULL;
            rear->next=node;
            rear=node;
        }
    }
void rem ( )
{
    struct num *s;
    s=header;
    free(s);
    header=first->next;
    first=first->next;
}
void show ( )
{
    printf ("\n Linked list elements are : ");
```

```
    while (header)=NULL)
    {
        printf (" %d ",header->num);
        header=header->next;
    }
}
```

OUTPUT :

Operation creation;
Enter number 12 23 34 45 56 0
Linked list elements are : 12 23 34 45 56
After deletion :
Linked list elements are : 23 34 45 56
Linked list elements are : 34 45 56
Linked list elements are : 45 56

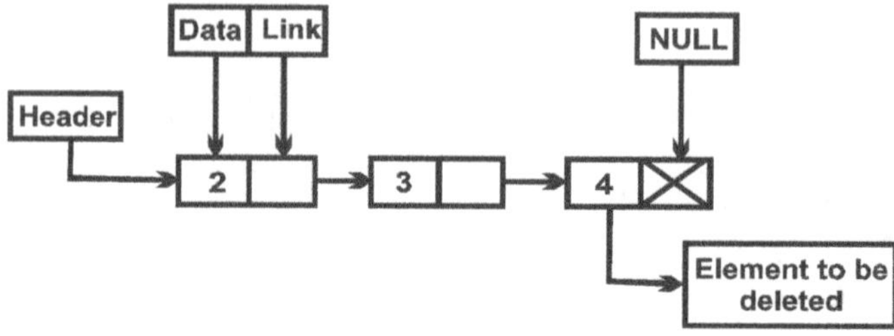

Fig.14.9 (a) Before Deletion at the end of a singly linked list

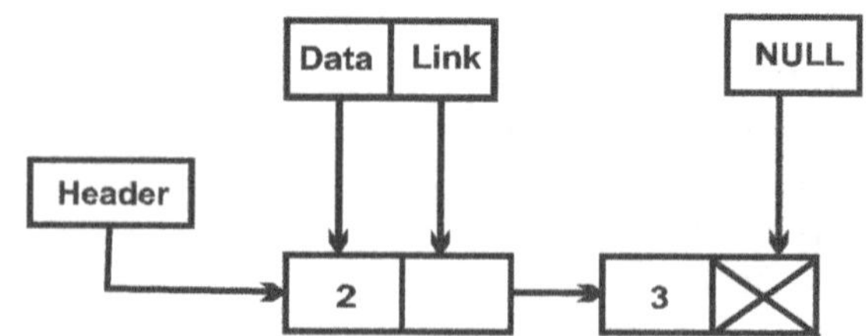

Fig.14.9 (b) After Deletion at the end of a singly linked list

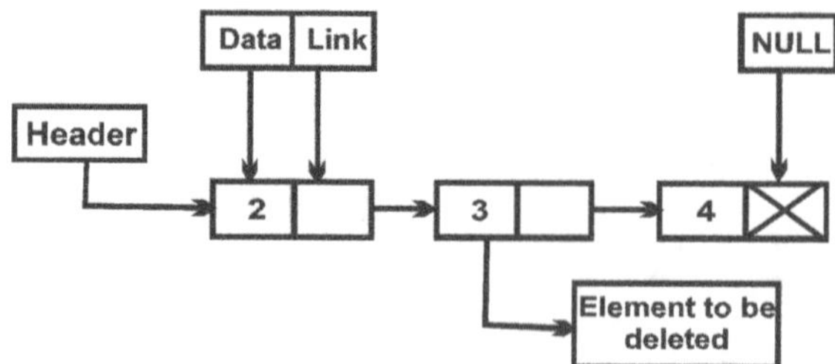

Fig.14.10 (a) Before Deletion from a specified position Inside a singly linked list

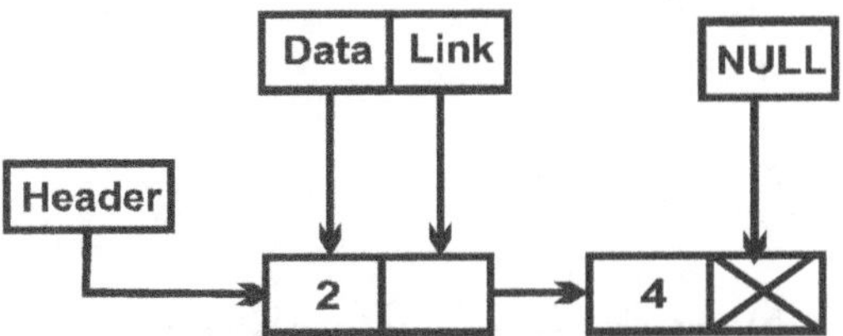

Fig.14.10 (b) After Deletion from a specified position Inside a singly linked list

A function in C++ for deleting a node is as follows.

```
//Only the function for deleting a node in C++. Not full program
void list::deleterecord ( )
{
	info *del;
	int texamno,present=0;
	if (head==0)
	{
		cout<<"\n No records to delete";
		return;
	}
		cout<<"\n Enter examno to delete";
		cin>>texamno;
		fflush(stdin);
	for(del=head;del ! =0;del=del->next)
	{
		if del->examno==texamno)
		{
			if(head->examno==texamno)
			{
				del=head;
				head=head->next;
				delete del;
				return;
			}
		else
			{
				for(disp=head;disp ! =0;disp=disp->next)
					if (disp->next==del)
					{
						disp->next=del->next;
						delete del;
```

```
                    if (disp->next ==0) temp=disp;
                }
            }
        }
    }
        if(present==0)
            cout<<"\n No such examno is present";
    }
```

Here, the user has to enter unique 'examno' to delete. In this case the record, which we want to delete, may be present in the first or in the middle or in the last. Initially address stored in the variable 'head' is assigned to the variable 'del'. If the required 'examno' is in he first record then the address stored in the 'head->next' is assigned to 'head' hereafter. After freeing the space, the control is returned to main. If the desired 'examno' is in the middle then the traversal takes place till the address stored in 'disp->next' is equal to 'del'. After anchoring the location, the address stored in 'del' is assigned to 'disp->next' and then the space occupied by 'del' is freed. In case 'disp->next' is '0' (NULL), then the current address is stored in 'temp' for further use and this situation arises only when the desired 'examno' is in the last of a list.

14.2.7. Changing the content of an element in a Singly Linked List :

There is a possibility of changing the content, here is a function to modify a record.

Most of the C++ standard libraries include the definition of NULL in order to reference to null pointers. In case that this constant is not defined we can do it our self by defining it to 0 and it takes the followig form :

```
# define NULL 0
```

The reason using the above form instead of numeric literal '0' is for greater legibility and also it is very rare that a pointer is compared or set directly to a numerical literal constant and thus thus this action is symbolically masked.

The following part of the program helps in modifying the contents of an element in the linked list.

//function for modifying the contents of an element of a linked list in C++

```
void list::modifyrecord()
{
    info *modify;
    int texamno,present=0;
    cout<<"\n Enter examno to edit";
    cin>>texamno;
    fflush(stdin);
```

```
        for (modify=head;modify!=NULL;modify=modify->next)
        {
            if (modify->examno==texamno)
            {
                    cout<<"\n Enter name to change";
                    cin.getline(modify->name,20);
                    fflush(stdin);
                    cout<<"\n Enter branch";
                    cin.getline (modify->branch,20);
                    return;
            }
        }
        if(present==0)
        cout<<"\n No such examno is present";
}
```

In the above function, the user is prompted to enter required 'examno' to modify. The traversal takes place till the required 'examno' coincide with 'modify->examno', then new values are entered for desired 'examno'. The function is designed to display the error message, if an invalid 'examno' is entered.

14.2.8. Reversing of a singly linked list :

We can also perform "reversing" operation on a singlylinked.

For example, if the inputed (read) items are

26 → 57 → 62 → 91

the elements are read until the number -99 is entered.

The reverse order of the list is

91 → 62 → 57 → 26

Program 14.2.11:

Write a program in C to obtain the reversed list of a list given above.

```
# include <stdio.h>
# include <stdlib.h>
struct list
    {
        int info;
        struct list *next ;
    };
    node *start ;
    node * reverse ( ) ;
```

```
        start = (node *) malloc (size of (node));
        create (start)
        printf ("\n linked list in the given order");
        display (start);
        start = reverse (start);
        printf ("\n linked list in reverse order");
        display (start);
}
        create (node * item)
        {
           print ("Enter Item :");
           scanf (" %d", & item →info);
           if (item →info ! = - 99)
                  {
                         item → next = (node *) malloc (size of (node));
                         create (item → next);
                  }
           else
                  item → next = NULL ;
           }
           display (node * item)
        {
           while (item ! = NULL)
                  {
                         If (item → inof ! = - 99)
                         printf ("\n %d", item → info);
                         item = item → next;
                  }
           }
           node * reverse (node * item)
           {
           node *temp1 * temp2;
           temp 1 = NULL ;
           while (item → next ! = NULL)
                  {
                         temp2 = temp1;
                         temp1 = item;
                         item = item → next;
                         temp 1 → next = temp2;
                  }
                  return (temp1);
           }
```

14.3. DOUBLY LINKED LIST (DLL) :

In this type of linked list the data structure holds two-pointer fields. In the singly linked list address of only next element is pointed. In addition, in doubly linked list address of next as well as preceding elements are linked with the current node. The singly linked list has some limitations that can be overcome by doubly linked list. Consider a case in which the access pointer is in between the linked list and we need to access the earlier elements. Due to lack of previous item link, we cannot traverse the list in reverse direction and hence, we have no option but to traverse the list from the beginning.

In a doubly linked list, each node has two link fields that hold addresses of previous and next nodes, which enables us to access not only the next element but also the previous element.

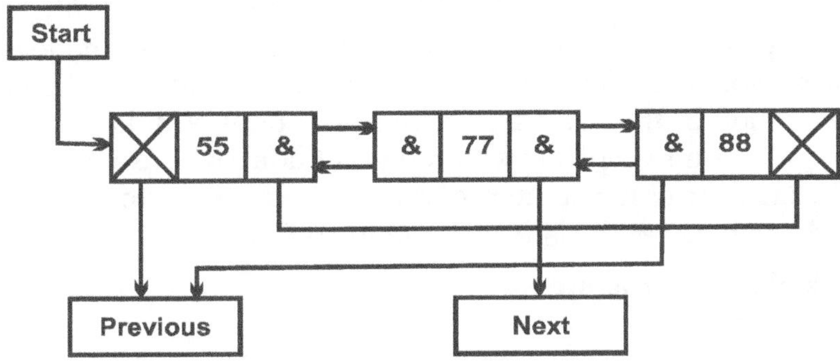

Fig.14.11 (a). A Doubly Linked List

The structure of this type of link would be as follows

```
struct node
{
        int num;
        struct node *next;
        struct node *previous;
}
```

In the above structure, the integer num is used to store data values. The pointer ***next** holds link of the next node and pointer ***previous** holds link of the previous node.

The pointer *previous of the first node is NULL because it has no previous element. The pointer *next of last element of the node will be NULL since linked list ends here. The following program explains the creation and display operation of a doubly linked list.

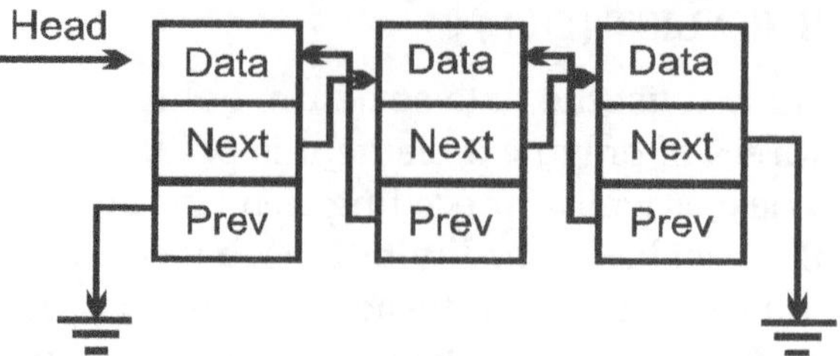

Fig. 14.11 (b) Alternative representation of doubly linked list

In a singly linked list we can move only in the forward direction, whereas in the doubly linked list allows as to move forward or backward from any node to the successor or predecessor of that node. By doubling the number of pointers, some complexity is added to the list operations, and the order of pointer manipulation is important. Doubly linked list can be represented as follows :

From the picture it is clear that, in a doubly linked list each node is provided with two link fields. The left link points to the previous node and right link points to successive node in the list. Each node in the doubly linked list consists of information part and two pointers to represent address. Also, note that in this doubly linked list one of the pointers of the first node points to the 'head' pointer and one of the pointers of the late node points to '0' (NULL).

doubly Linked List - Structure

```
struct info
{
        char name[10];
        char branch[10];
        int examno;
        info *next;
        info *prev;
};
```

Program 14.3.1

Write a program in C to create doubly linked list and display its elements.

```
#include <stdio.h>
# include <conio.h>
# include <malloc.h>
struct doubly
{
        struct doubly *p;
        int number;
        struct doubly *next;
} *first;
```

```
int main ()
{
        int create(int);
        int show (void);
        int option, nodes, n, j;
        first=NULL;
        clrscr ();
        while (1)
        {
                clrscr();
                printf ("\n 1. Create list");
                printf ("\n 2. Display list");
                printf ("\n 3. Exit");
                printf ("\n Enter Your option :  ");
                scanf ("%d", &option);
        switch (option)
                {
                        case 1;
                        printf ("\n Enter number of nodes :  ");
                        scanf ("%d"&nodes);

                        for (j=0; j<nodes;j++)
                        {
                                printf("\n Enter the element : " );
        scanf ("%d"&n);
                                create(n);
                        }
                break;
                case 2 :        show ();        break;
                case 3 :        return 0;
                }
        }
}
create (int number)
{
        struct doubly *q, *temp;
        temp=(struct doubly*)malloc(sizeof (struct doubly));
        temp->number=number;
        temp->next=NULL;
        if (first==NULL)
        {
                temp->p=NULL;
```

```
            first ->p=temp;
            first=temp;
        }
        else
        {
            q=first;

            while (q->next ! = 0)
            q=q->next;
            q->next=temp;
            temp->p=q;
        }
        return 0;
    }
int show ()
    {
        struct doubly *q;
        if (first==NULL)
        {
printf ("List is Empty ");
            return 0;
        }
            q=first;
            printf ("\n List is : \n");
            while (q !=NULL)
            {
                printf (" %d ",q->number);
                q=q->next;
            }
            printf ("\n");
            getch ();
            return 0;
        }
```

OUTPUT :

```
1. Create list
2. Display list
3. Exit
Enter Your option : 1
Enter number of nodes : 3
Enter the element 7 8 9
```

1. Create list
2. Display list
3. Exit

Enter Your option : 2

List is:

4 5 6

14.4. MODIFICATION OF DOUBLY LINKED LIST :

The functions for adding, modifying, deleting and traversing nodes in a doubly linked list are same as that for the singly linked list.

14.4.1 Insertion in a doubly linked list at the beginning :

Insertion of an element in the doubly linked list can be done in three ways

a. Insertion at the beginning
b. Insertion at a specified location
c. Insertion at the end

a) Insertion at the Beginning : The process involves creation of a new node, inputting data, and adjusting the pointers.

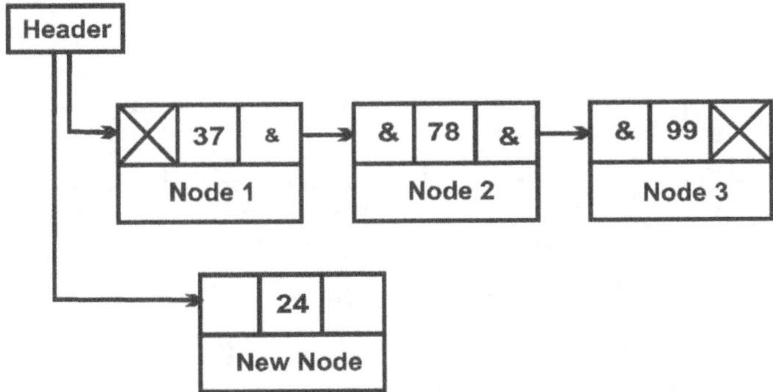

Fig. 14.12. (a) Before Insertion at the befinning of a doubly linked list

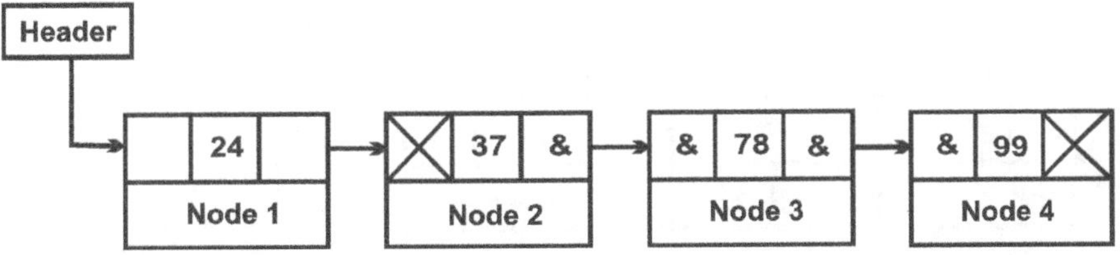

Fig 14.12 (b) After Insertion of an element at the beginning of a doubly linked list.

14.4.2 Insertion in a doubly linked list at a specified position :

An element can be inserted at a specific position in the linked list. The user has to enter the element and the position where the element is to be inserted, after searching for the require position using malloc position ( ) , function, a new node is created. A new function add after () is used incorporating the following features. The next pointer of the new node is assigned an address of the next node and previous pointer of the new node is assigned the address of previous node which is before the node that is being inserted.

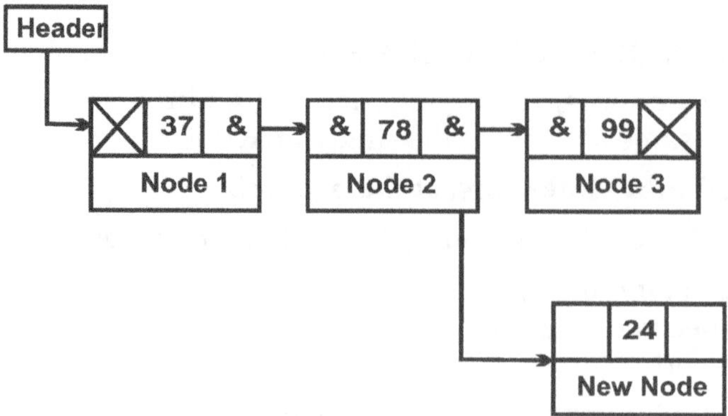

Fig. 14.13 (a) Before Insertion at a specified position of a doubly linked list

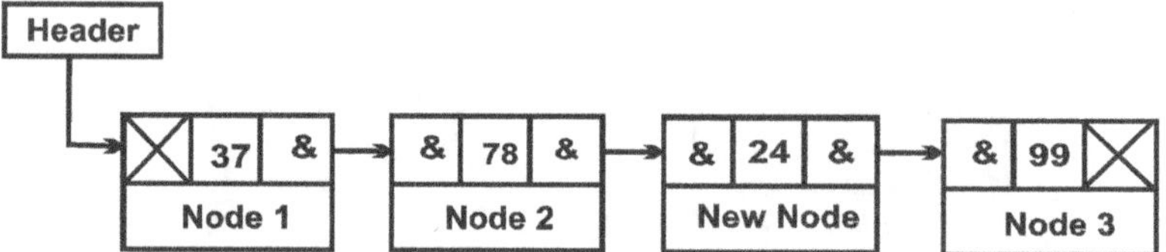

Fig. 14.13 (b) After Insertion at the specified position inside aa Doubly Linked List

a) Insertion in a doubly linked list at the end of the list :

An element can be inserted at the end of the linked list. The NULL pointer of the last node is assigned the address of the new node and NULL pointer will be the next address of the new node that is being inserted.

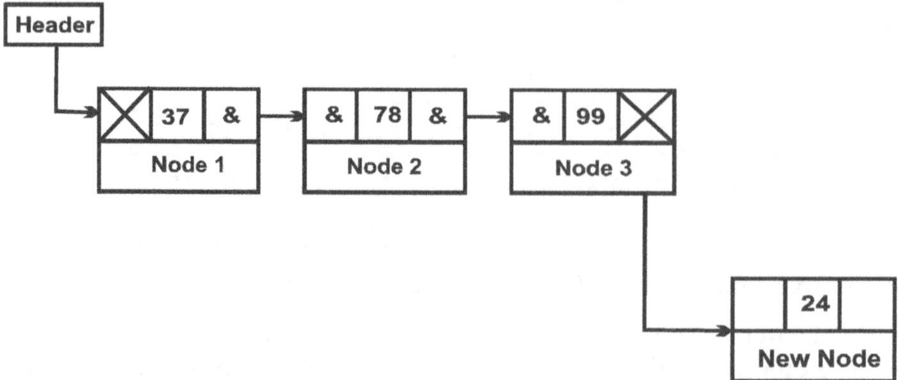

Fig.14.14 (a) Before Insertion at the end of a Doubly Linked List

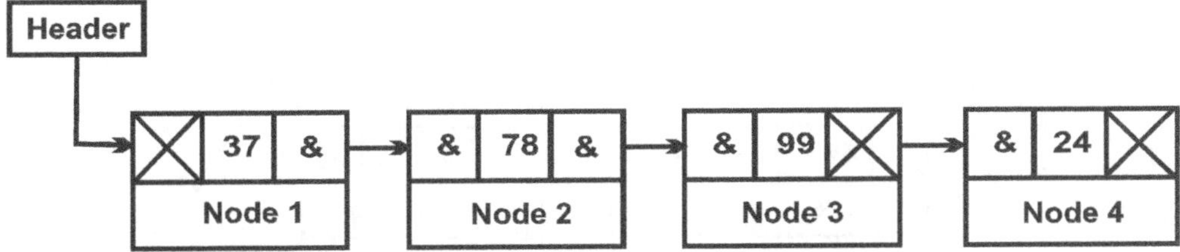

Fig.14.14 (b) After Insertion at the end of the Doubly Linked List

14.4.3. Deletion of an existing node in a doubly linked list :

An element can be removed from the linked list. Such an operation is called deletion. Deletion can be done at the beginning or a specified position or at the end of the list. In the deletion process the memory of the node to be deleted is released using a free (). The previous and next nodes are linked. If the node to be deleted is at the end of the list then the after address of he previous node is made NULL.

a) Deletion at the Beginning of a Doubly Linked List :

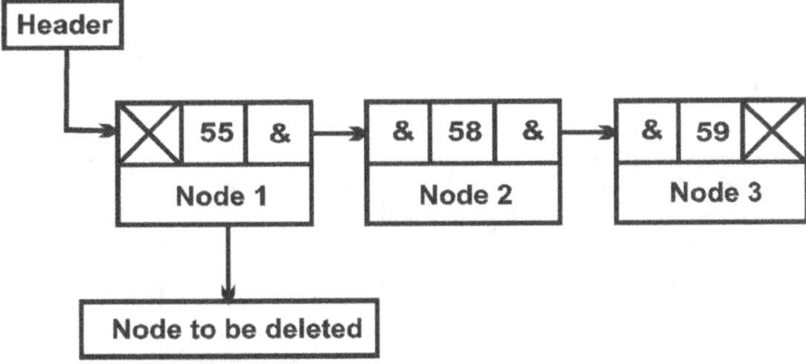

Fig. 14.15 (a) Before deletion at the beginning of a doubly linked list

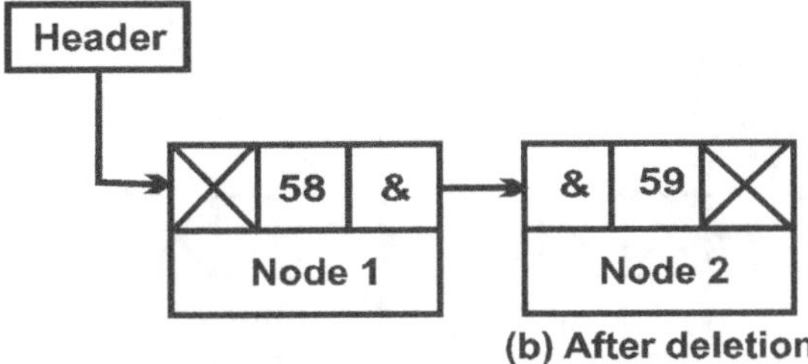

(b) After deletion

Fig.14.15 (b) Deletion from the doubly linked list at a specified position

b) Deletion at a specified position of a Doubly Linked List :

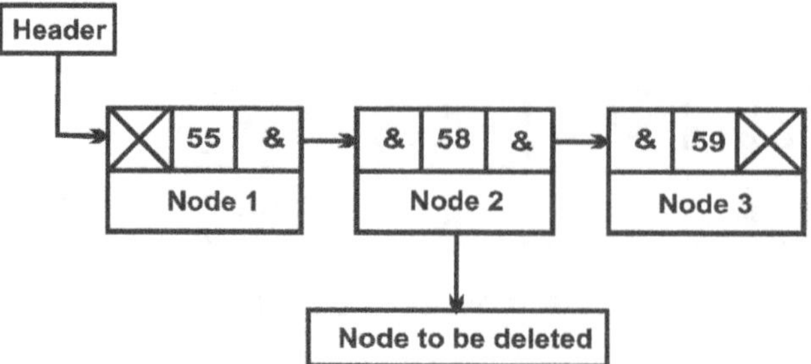

Fig. 14.16 (a) Before deletion at a specified position of a Doubly Linked List

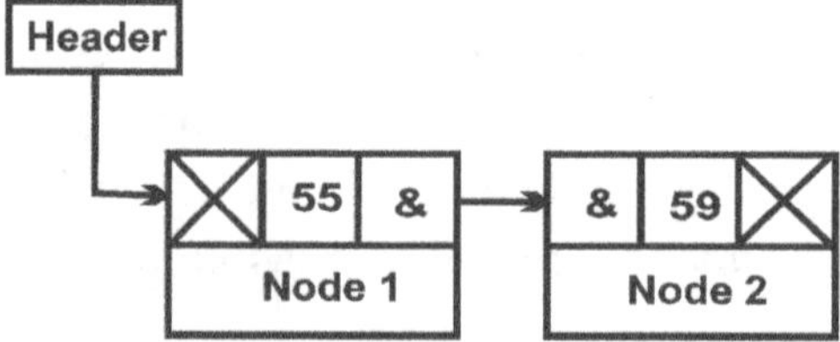

Fig.14.16 (b) After Deletion at the specified position of a doubly linked list.

c) Deletion at the end of a Doubly Linked List :

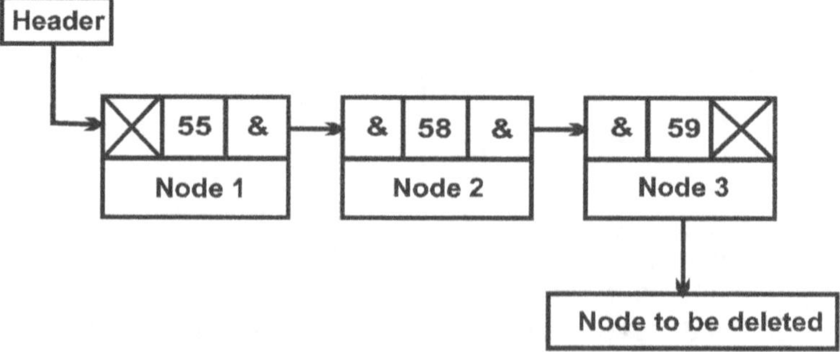

Fig. 14.17 (a) Before deletion at the end of a doubly linked list

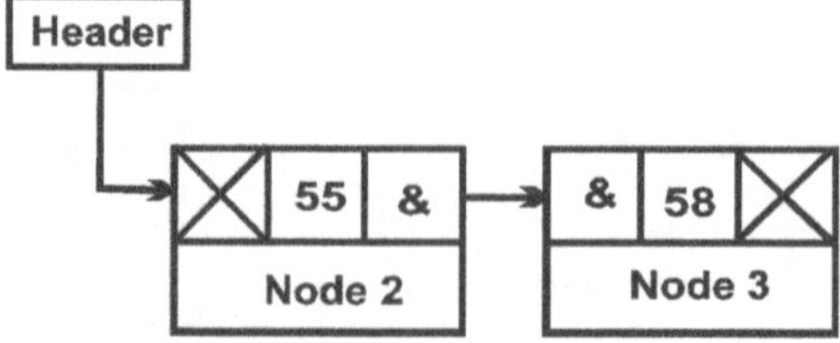

Fig. 14.17 (b) After deletion at the beginning of a doubly linked list

14.5. CIRCULARLY LINKED LIST :

The singly linked list can also be a circularly linked list instead of being open ended list.

14.5.1. Singly linked Circular List :

As we know that a singly linked list has one pointer in each node, and it refers to the next node in the list. In the case of the last item in the list, then next is set to null or nil. In such a condition operations such as counting the number of nodes cannot be performed with a reference to any node in the list. This operation requires a reference to the beginning of the list. By enhancing a linked list structure can provide the added flexibility that will allow us to reach any node in the list from anywhere else in the list.

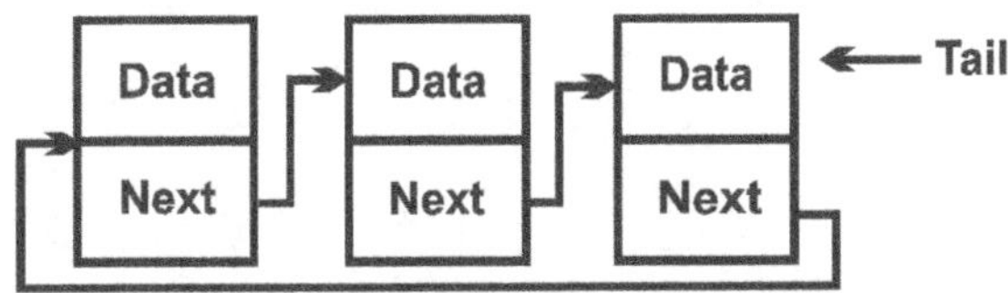

Fig. 14.18 (a) Circularly Linked List

We create a circular linked list by setting the link in the list node of the list to point to the first node in the list. We also change the external pointer to the list so that it refers to the last node rather than the first to give us a convenient way to iterate through the entire list now that there is no null link to use as a stopping case. From the figure 14.18 (a) it is known that the head of the list now points to tail link.

First and last elements of a circular list are adjacent. The circular list has neither end nor starting node. A linear single linked list can be circled by storing the address of the first node in the link field of the last node. A circular linked list appears as shown in Fig. 14.18 (b)

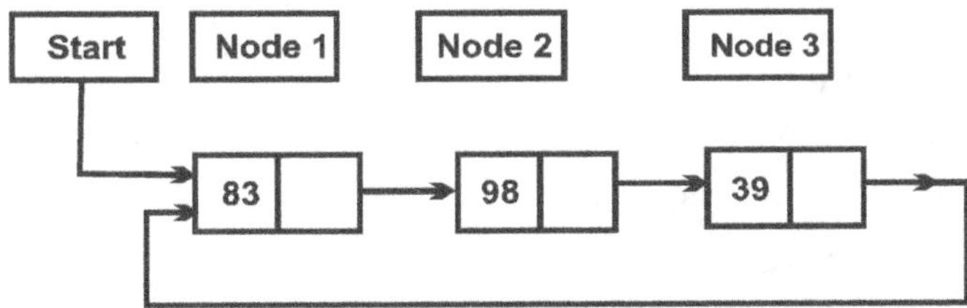

Fig.14.18 (b). Alternative representation of circular linked list

In case we are at the last node and want to access the first node, with singly or doubly linked list method we traverse the linked list from the first node. However, in the circular linked list, the first node can be accessed after the last node.

Like other list structures, insertion and deletion operations are also performed with the circular linked list. The following program illustrates the creating of a circular linked list with insert, remove and displaying element operations.

Program 14.5.1

Write a program in C to create a circular linked list. Perform the insert, delete, and display operations.

```
#include <stdio.h>
#include <conio.h>
#include<malloc.h>
#include <process.h>

struct c_list
{
        int number;
        struct c_list *next;
        } *end;

int main ( )
{

int create (int);
int insert (int, int);
int rem(int);
int show(void);
int option,num,m,pos,j=0;
end=NULL;
clrscr();
        for ( ; ; )
        {
            printf ("\n 1. Create element list ");
            printf ("\n 2. Insert an element ");
            printf ("\n 3.Delete an element ");
            printf ("\n 4. Show");
            printf ("\n 5. Exit");
            printf ("\n Enter Your option : ");
            scanf (" %d",&option);

            switch(option)
            {
                    case 1:
                    printf ("\n Enter Number of nodes : ")'
                    scanf (" %d", &num);
                    while (j<num)
            {
                    printf ("Enter the element : ");
                    scanf (" %d",&m);
```

```
                create(m);
                j++;
            }
        break;
        case 2;
            printf ("\n Enter element and position : ")'
            scanf ("%d %d",&m,&pos);
            insert (m,pos);   break;
            case 3 :
            if (end==NULL)
            {
                printf ("\n Empty List ");
                continue;
            }
            printf ("\n Enter the number for deletion : ");
            scanf ("%d", &m);
            rem(m);
            break;
            case 4 : show () ; break;
            case 5 : exit (0) ;
        }
    }
}
int create (int num)
{
    struct c_list *q, *temp;
    temp=(struct c_list*)malloc (sizeof (struct c_list));
    temp->number=num;
    if (end==NULL)
    {
        end=temp;
        temp->next=end;
    }
    else
    {
    temp->next=end->next;
    end->next=temp;
    end=temp;
    }
    return 0;
    }
```

```
int insert (int num, int pos)
{
        struct c_list *temp *q;
        int j;
        q=end->next;
        for (j=0; j<pos-1;j++)
             {
                 q=q->next;
             if (q==end->next)
             {
                 printf ("There are less than %d elements :",pos);
                 return 0;
                 }
             }
                 temp=(struct c_list*)_malloc(size of (struct c_list));
                 temp->next=q->next;
                 temp->number=num;
                 q->next=temp;
                 if (q==end) end=temp;
          return 0;
          }
             int rem ( int num)
             {
                 struct c_list *temp, *q;
             if (end->next==end && end->number==num)
             {
                 temp=end;
                 end=NULL;
                 free (temp);
                 return 0;
             }
        q=end->next,
        if (q->number==num)
        {
        temp=q;
        end->next=q->next;
        free(temp);
        return 0;
}
```

```
while (q->next !=end)
{
if (q->next->number==num)
{
temp=q->next;
q->next=temp->next;
free(temp);
printf ("%d deleted \num",num);
return 0;
}
q=q->next;
}
        if (q->next->number==num)
        {
        temp-q->next;
        q->next=end->next;
        free(temp);
        end=q;
        return 0;
        }
        printf ("\num Element %d not found\num",num);
        return 0;
}
int show ( )
{
struct c_list *q;
if (end==NULL)
{
        printf ("list is empty ");
        return 0;
}
q=end->next;
printf ("list is : ");
while (q ! = end)
{
printf ("%d",q->number);
q=q->next;
}
printf (" %d ", end->number);
return 0;
}
```

OUTPUT :

1. Create element list
2. Insert an element
3. Delete an element
4. Show
5. Exit

Enter your option : 1

Enter Number of nodes : 4
Enter the element : 101
Enter the element : 202
Enter the element : 303
Enter the element : 404
Enter your option : 4
list is : 101 202 303 404

14.5.2. Doubly linked Circular List :

Link a singly linked list, a DLL can also be a chained, or it may be circular with or without header node. If it is a chain the left link or the first node and the right link of the last node will be NULL, as shown below :

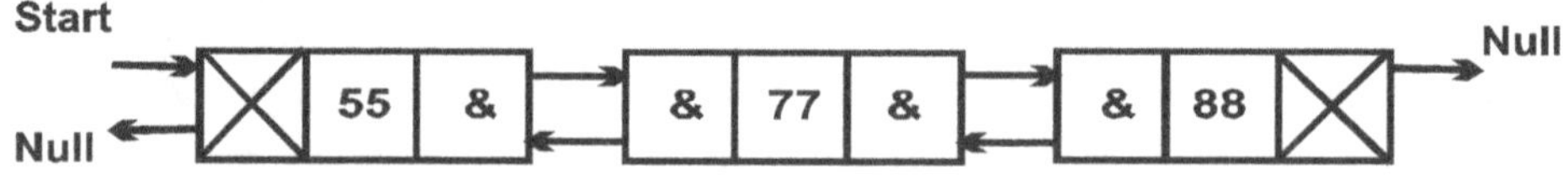

Fig.14.19 (a) A Doubly Linked List

If it is a circular list without header node then the right link of the last node will point to the first node and end left link of the first node will point to the last node as shown below :

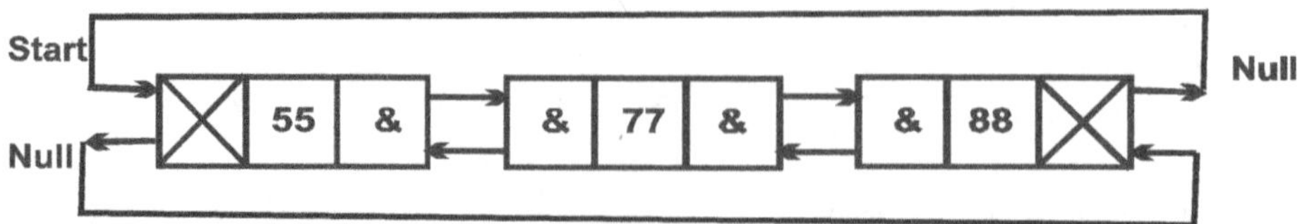

Fig. 14.19 (b) A doubly linked circular list without header

If it is a ciruclar list with header node then the list link of the first node and the right link of the last node point to the header node. The right link of the header node points to the first node and the left link of the header node points to the last node of the list as shown below.

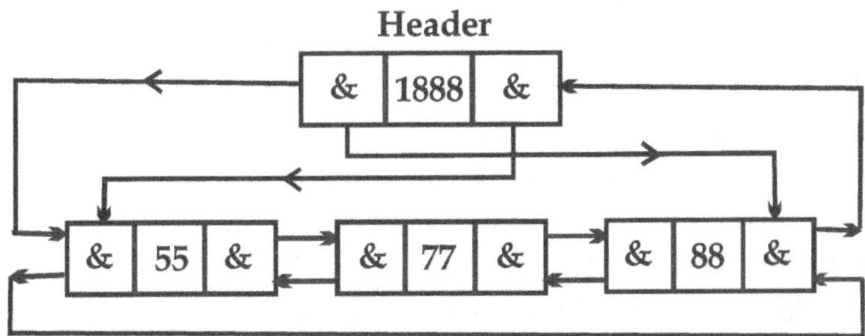

Fig. 14.19 (c) A doubly linked circular list with header

14.6. LINKED LIST AS APPLICATIONS OF LINEAR DATA STRUCTURE :

The most useful linear data structure is the linked list. This paragraph introduces you to a few applications of linear data structure useful in computer science.

14.6.1. Polynomial Operation :

The linked list is used for implementation of polynomial arithmetic operations. The operations on them include addition, multiplication, and so on. To have better proficiency in processing, each polynomial is stored in decreasing order. These arrangements of polynomials is decreasing order allow easy operation on each term. Actually, two polynomials can be added by checking each term. The prior comp[arison can easily be used to add corresponding terms in two polynomials.

14.6.2. Linked Dictionary :

The role of a computer is to create and maintain a linked dictionary that contains names. Names can be given by combination of several symbols. Names are arranged in a symbol table and the compiler keeps them in order. While designing symbol table two factors are related, access time and memory space.

The construction and the referencing of a symbol table are two important phases for preparation of a linked dictionary. Construction means insertion of symbols with their values available and referencing is obtaining or accessing their values from the table.

The ratio of estimated number of insertions to reference is a significant factor. In symbol tables, access retrieve time and insertion time are very much associated. The quick symbol table can be simply constructured if large memory space is available. Each name is stored in a unique memory location.

The easiest way to access the symbol table is linear search methods. Using a simple linked list the symbols are organized in sequence. The insertion can be easily done by adding symbols at the rear of the list. If any particular symbol is to be searched, by traversing each node the required element can be searched.

To symbol table can also be searched using binary search. All the entries in the symbol table are sorted in ascending order. A middle entry is spotted and its value is determined. A separate topic is given for search technique in this book. However, this method has some drawbacks.

* * *

COMPREHENSION - 14

Note : By answering all the questions given in this comprehension one can answer any objective type of questions easily whatever be the form of the question. Answers for these questions can be obtained by going through the topics in this chapter carefully.

1. What is a data structure? What are its features?
2. What are the activities that are associated with Data Structures?
3. What are the factors that determine the selection of data structure?
4 What are the different types of data structures?
5. What are the different classifications of linear and nonlinear data structures?
6. What is meant by Dynamic memory allocation? When do we go for it?
7. What is a linked list? Mention the different types of linked list.
8. What is meant by a linked list with Header and without Header? Explain with figures.
9. What are the different types of operation that can be performed on any linkedlist?
10. How are the operations of addition or deletion of elements made in the beginning, at the end or in the middle of a singly linked list with Header? Explain with figures.
11. How are the operations of addition or deletion of elements made in the beginning, at the end or in the middle of a singly linked list without Header? Explain with figures.
12. What is a doubly linked list? What are the advantages of it over singly linked list?
13. Explain the structure of a doubly linked list with figure.
14. How are the operations of addition or deletion of elements made in the beginning, at the end or in the middle of a doubly linked list with Header? Explain with figures.
15. How are the operations of addition or deletion of elements made in the beginning, at the end or in the middle of a doubly linked list without Header? Explain with figures.
16. How can we obtain the number of elements in a linked list?
17. What is the procedure involved in modifying the contents of an element in a linked list?
18. Explain the use of # define NULL 0 in modifying an element in a list.
19. What is a circular list? Explain with figure. What is its feature? Why do you use it?
20. What constitutes the most useful linear data structure? Why?

* * *

EXERCISE - 14

Note : By answering all the questions given in this exercise one can answer subjective type of questions easily including problems. The worked examples in the chapter may help in solving these questions.

1. Define Data Structures. Explain its requirements and the activities associated with it.
2. What is Dynamic Memory Allocation? How does it help in building complex programs?
3. Why a linked list is called a dynamic data structure? What are the advantages of using linked lists over arrays?
4. Describe different types of linked lists.
5. What is the principal difference between the functions malloc ( ) and calloc ( )
6. Define Data structure
6. Explain the classification of data structure
7. List various data types with meaning
8. Explain the term abstract data type
9. Differentiate between arrays and linked list
10 Explain with figures Singly linked list, Doubly linked list and Circular list. Enunciate the uses of the different types of lists.
11. Explain insertion and deletion operations with singly linked list at different locations of the list with and without header.
12. Explain doubly linked list
13. Explain insertion and deletion operations with doubly linked list at different locations of the list with and without header.
14. Explain the salient features of a Singly linked and Doubly linked Circular lists and their uses.
15. Explain how to get the total number of elements in a list?
16. Discuss linked list as applications of Linear Data Structure.
17. Name the functions in C to create and destroy Dynamic Variables.
18. Linked list can be implemented by

    a) Static implementation   b) Dynamic implementation

    c) Early binding   d) None of the above
19. The header is used to point

    a) First node of the list   b) Last node of the list

    c) NULL value   d) None of the above

20. Traversing means
    a) Visiting all the nodes of the list b) Shifting all the nodes as forward
    c) Randomly accessing the elements d) None of the above
21. In the linked list when an element is inserted
    a) Memory is allocated to a node
    b) Memory is deallocated from the node
    c) Memory is neither allocated nor deallocated
    d) None of the above
22. In the doubly linked list the previous pointer of the first node
    a) Has null value b) Contains address of the next node
    c) Contains address of header d) None of the above
23. In C, memory management functions which provide dynamic memory allocation are
    a) malloc ( ) only b) calloc ( ) only
    c) malloc ( ) & realloc ( ) d) malloc ( ), calloc ( ) & realloc ( )
24. Write a program in C to perform the following operations in the linear linked list data structure.
25. Write a program to create a linked list of nodes, each having two fields character field 'name' and
    pointer field, to next node and perform all the fundamental manipulations
26. Write a program to demonstrate
    i) Singly linked list ii) Doubly linked list
    iii) Singly linked circular liked list iv) Doubly linked circular list
27. Write a menu drived program to create a linked list of a class of students and perform the following operations making use of the header file :
    i) Write out the contents of the list
    ii) Edit the details of a specified student
    iii) Count the number of students above a specified age and weight
28. Write recursive and non recursive functions for reversing the elements in a linear list. Compare the relative efficiencies of them.
29. Develop a program to combine two sorted lists to produce a third sorted list which contains one occurrence of each of the elements in the original lists.

* * *

CHAPTER - 15
DYNAMIC MEMORY ALLOCATION - II
(STACKS AND QUEUES)

15.1 INTRODUCTION TO STACKS :

A stack is an important tool that is extensively used in programming languages. It is one of the most essential linear data structures. Implementation of most of the system programs is based on stack data structure. We can insert or delete an element from a list, which takes place from one end. A subclass of lists permits the same operations. A linear list belonging to this subclass is called a stack. *A stack is very useful to maintain the sequences of processing. Stack is used for solving arithmetic expressions. This application will be discussed later under different operations on representation of arithmetic expressions.* A **stack is a set of memory locations ear marked for storing and removing some data like placing and removing books in a heap of books.** The insertion operation of an element onto the stack is called as **push** and deletion operation is called **pop**. Due to the put operation from one end, elements are added in the stack, the stack is also known as pushdown list. The most and least reachable elements in he stack are known as top and bottom of the stack, respectively. A stack is an arranged collection of elements into which new elements can be inserted or from which new elements can be deleted at one end. A stack is a set of elements in a last-in-first-out technique. The end where the insertion or deletion operation is carried out is called as top. The insertion of an element (push operation) takes place at the top of the stack. The extraction of an element (pop operation) is always from the top of the stack. That means the element pushed last into the stack will be the first element to be popped. If an element is to be popped from a stack, before that operation all the other elements that are above that element have to be popped up first. **The policy, known as LIFO (Last in First Out) is the policy of the stack operation.** In the figure 15.1 (a) which depicts stack, if we want to delete element 3 it is n ecessary to delete first top elements 5 and 4. The element (5) appended lastly is deleted first.

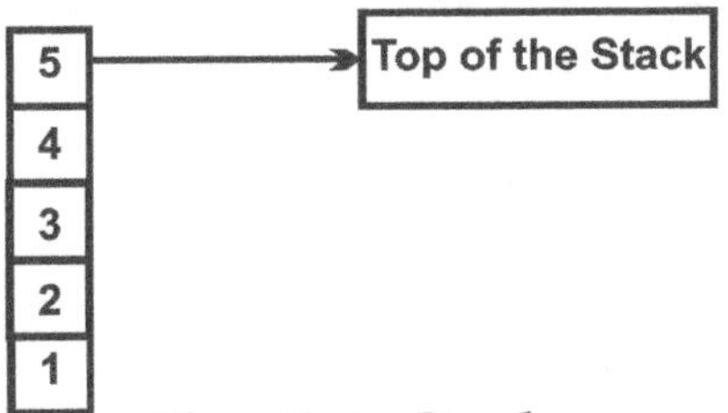

Fig. 15.1. Stack

In the beginning itself a certain amount of memory which is estimated to be sufficient for the work is earmarked for a stack. If the stack has to accommodate more elements then the stack size has to be re-adjusted.

The pointer pointing to the top of the stack is known as stack pointer or stack top.

15.2 IMPLEMENTATION OF STACKS USING LINKED LIST :

Stack, the LIFO (Last In First Out) data structure can be implemented by using linked list. In a stack, addition of a new element (pushing an element to stack) or removing an element (popping a element from stack) always takes at the same place. A stack is also called Last In First Out (LIFO) structure because here the last item added to stack, is the first one to get deleted.

In practical life, we come across many examples based on the principle of a stack. A stack of books place on a rack one over another is a good example. The placement of books is made in a sequence in the stack. The last placed book in the stack will be the first book to be removed. Figure 15.2 shows a pack of books placed on a rack one over another. Pulling of any book from inside a stack is not advisable as it disturbs the order and tumbles the books above it. If a particular book has to be picked then it has to be done carefully without disturbing the other books and a linked list will be the best way to explain that operation.

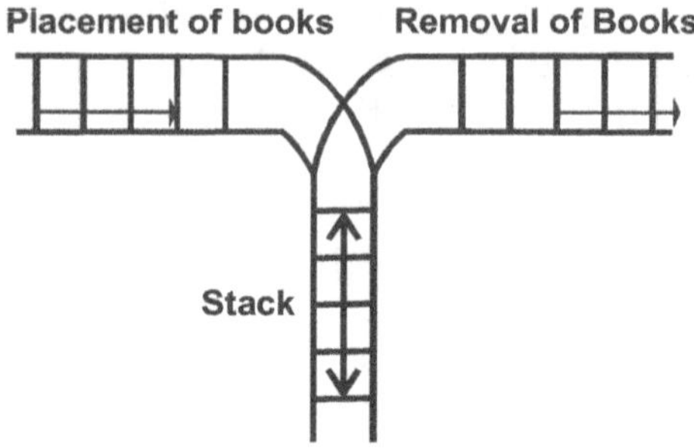

Fig.15.2. A stack of books on a rack

The following example uses two functions namely push ( ) and pop ( ). Figure 15.3 depicts the stack operation for pushing and popping operation at the top of a stack. The first one is used to add and second one is used to remove an item from stack.

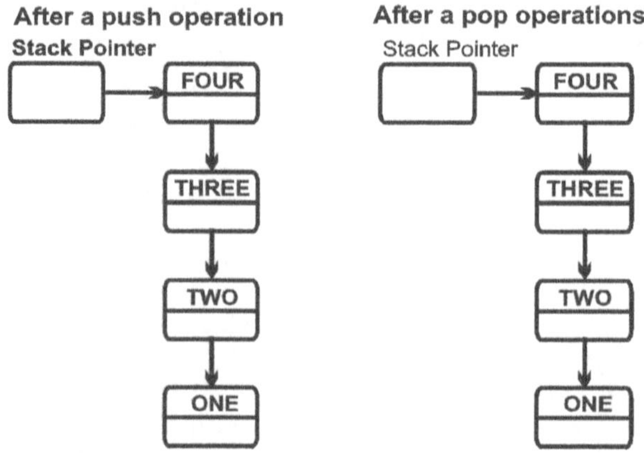

Figs.15.3. Push and Pop operations in a Stack

15.3. STACK RELATED TERMS :

i) Stack : It is an array of size N, where N is an unsigned integer.

Storage : A function contains local variables and constants. These are stored in a stack. Only global variables are stored in a stack frame

ii) Stack frames : This data structure holds all formal arguments, return address, and local variables on the stack at the time when a function is invoked.

iii) Top : The top of the stack indicates its door. The stack top is used to verify stack's current position, that is underflow or overflow. Some programmers refer an initial value of -1 to top. This is because when an element is added the top is incremented and it would become zero. It is easy to count elements in an array because the array element counting begins from zero. Hence, it is convenient to assign an initial value of -1 to top.

iv) Stack underflow : When there is no element in the stack or the stack holds elements less than its capacity, then the status of the stack is known as stack underflow. In this situation, the top is present at the bottom of the stack. when an element is pushed, it will be the first element of the stack and top will be moved up by one step.

v) Stack overflow : When the stack contains elements equal to its capacity and no more elements can be added, such status of the stack is known as stack overflow. In such a position, the top rests at the highest position. Figs. 15.4 (a), (b), (c) represent a stack under different conditions of its occupancy.

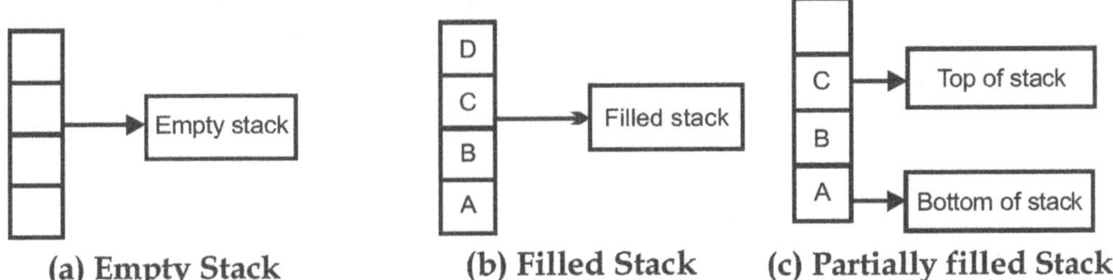

(a) Empty Stack **(b) Filled Stack** **(c) Partially filled Stack**

Fig. 15.4. Representation of a Stack with provision for 4 elements

A top pointer maintains track of the top elements as shown in Fig.15.4 (c) When a stack has no element it is called an empty stack. Fig.15.4 (a) that is, the value of top is zero. When a stack has one element the value of top is 1 and so on. Whenever an element is inserted (push operation) in the stack the value of pointer top is increased by 1. In the same manner, the value of the pointer is decremented when an element is delead from the stack (pop operation). The push operation can be applied to any stack but before applying the pop operation on the stack, it is necessary to make sure that the stack is not empty. Sometimes, to know the top element we have to perform a certain operation. Such an operation is called

stacktop(s). If a pop operation is performed on an empty stack, it results in **underflow.** An operation to insert an element more than he capacity of the stack is known as **overflow** stack In the filled stack, Fig.15.4 (b) no more elements can be inserted.

Stacks are very helpful in every ordered and chronological processing of functions. The most useful application of a stack is in recursion (explained in the previous chapter). It saves memory space. The mechanism of stack last-in-first-out is commonly useful in all applications such as manufacturing and accounting calculations. It is a well-known accounting concept.

15.4 OPERATIONS ON A STACK :

Operations on a stack is done by two ways. They are as follows.

i) **Static implementation with an array.**

ii) **Dynamic implementation with pointers.**

The following operations are normally performed on the stack.

1) **Creating a stack**
2) **Checking whether the stack is empty or full.**
3) **Initializing a stack.**
4) **Insert (push) an element in the stack.**
5) **Delete (pop) an element from the stack.**
6) **Access the top element.**
7) **Display elements of the stack.**
8) **Status - to identify the present position of the stack.**

The important operations on a stack are :

i) Push Operation : The procedure of inserting new element on the top of the stack is known as the push operation. After every push operation the top is incremented by 1, and the new element rests at the top. when the array is full (if static implementation is applied) then the status of the stack is full and this condition is called as stack overflow. In such a case, no element is inserted. Figs.15.5 (a), (b), (c) & (d) show a push operation.

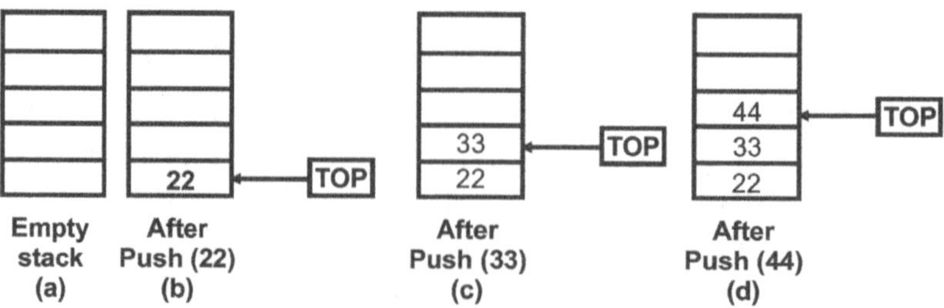

Fig.15.5. Push operations with a stack (for 5 elements)

ii) Pop Operation : The procedure of removing an element from the top of the stack is called a pop operation. After every pop operation, the top is decremented by 1. If here is no element in the stack, this status of stack is called as empty stack or stack underflow. In such a case, the pop operation cannot be applicable. Figs. 15.6 (a), (b), (c) & (d) show a pop operation.

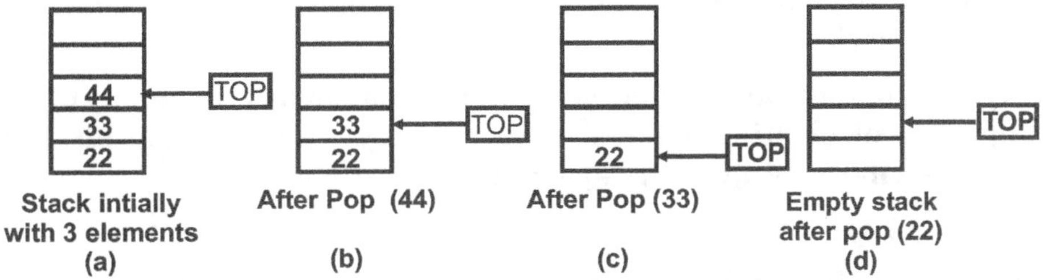

Fig.15.6. Pop operations with a stack (for 5 elements)

The stack can be represented with a one-dimensional array. The various operations listed above can be carried out with a one-dimensional array. The following programs explain he operation listed above.

As said earlier a one-dimensional array can be used as a stack. We can add elements in the one-dimensional array. Using if statement we can check whether the stack is empty or full.

15.5. IMPLEMENTATION OF A STACK :

The two ways of implementing the stack are : i) static implementation, ii) Dynamic implementation with linked list using pointers.

i) **Static implementation : Static implementation can be achieved using arrays.** It is a very simple method but has a few limitations. **Once the size of an array is declared, it cannot be altered during program execution.** While in array declaration, memory is allocated equal to array size. Thus, the program itself decides the amount of memory needed and it informs accordingly to the compiler. In static implementation, memory requirement is determined before compilation and compiler provides the required memory.

a) **The main advantage of static implementation of a stack using an array is its simplicity in programming, storing and retrieving the required stack element.**

b) **The disadvantage of a static implementation of a stack using an array is that the stack size gets fixed to the array size.** If the number of elements in the stack is less there will be a wastage of storage in the stack. If the number of elements in the stack is more then the stack declared cannot be extended to accommodate additional elements required. Hence it is useful only in case where a stack size is pre-determined.

ii) **Dynamic Implementation : Linked lists using pointers can be used for implementation of a stack, leading to dynamic memory allocation** as discussed in the previous chapter. As we used pointer implementation at run-time there is no restriction for the number of elements in the stack.

The main advantage of dynamic implementation of stack is that it is efficient in memory allocation because the program informs the compiler its memory requirement at runtime. Memory is allocated only after an element is pushed into the stack.

Eventhough the array itself is a pointer it is not as efficient as the linked list approach of creating a stack. Like an array, elements can be stored in successive memory locations using a pointer.

Program 15.5.1.

Write a program in C to demonstrate Push and Pop operations in a stack using array approach for stack.

```
#include <stdio.h>
#include <conio.h>
# include <process.h>

static int stack [10], top=-1;
void main ( )
{
   void push (int);
   void pop(void);
   void show(void);
   clrscr ();
   printf ("\n\n push operation : ");

   push (15);
   show ();
   push (28);
   show ();
   push (39);
   show ();
   printf ("\n\n pop operation :");
   show ();
   pop ();
   show ();
   pop ( );
   show ( );
}

void push (int j)
{
   top++;
   stack [top]=j;
}
```

```
void pop ( )
{
   stack [top]=0;
   top - - ;
}

void show ()
{
   int j;
   printf ("\n stack elements are : ");
   for (j=0; j<10; j++)
stack [j] 1=0 ?  printf (" %d ",stack [j] ) ; printf ("  ");
}
```

OUTPUT :

push operation:
stack elements are : 15
each elements are : 15 28
stack elements are : 15 28 39

pop operation :
stack elements are : 15 28 39
stack elements are : 15 28
stack elements are : 15

Program 15.5.2

Write a program in C to demonstrate Push and Pop operation in a stack with a pointer (dynamic memory allocation with pointers)

```
# include <stdio.h>
# include <conio.h>
# include <stdlib.h>

   struct stack
   {
         int num;
         struct stack *next;
   }     *T=0;

   typedef struct stack it ;

   void push ();
   int pop ();
```

```
        void show ( );
        main ( )
        {
              clrscr ( );
              char chr ;
              int opt.no;
        do
        {
              clrscr ();
              printf ("\n 1 : push ");
              printf ("\n 2 : pop ");
              printf ("\n 3 : show ");
              printf ("\n >3 : exit ");
              printf ("\n Enter your option : ");
              scanf (" %d", &opt);
        switch (opt)
        {
           case 1 : push ( ); break;
           case 2 : no = pop ( );
           printf ("\n The delete number was %d ", no);
           break;
           case 3 : show ( ) ; break;
           default : printf ("\n Good Bye ");
           exit ( 0 ) ;
        }
    printf ( "\n Continue (y/n ) " ) ;
    fflush (stdin);
    chr=getche ( );
    }  while (chr=='Y'  | | chr=='y');
    return 0;
}
void push ( )
{
          it *node;
          code=(it *) malloc (siteof (it));
          printf ("\n Enter the number ");
          scanf (*%d", &node->num);
          node->next=T;
          T=node;
    }
```

```
int pop ()
{
   it *temp;
   temp=T;
if (T==NULL)
   {
      puts ("\n Stack underflow ");
      getch ();
      exit ( 0 );
   }
else
   {
      T=T->next;
      free(temp);
   }
   return (temp->num);
}

   void show ( )
   {
      it *tmp;
      tmp=T;
   while (tmp=>next !=NULL)
   {
      print (" %d ", tmp->num);
      tmp=tmp->next;
   }
   printf ("%d", tmp->num);
}
```

OUTPUT :

```
1 : push
2 : pop
3 : show
>3: exit
Enter your option : 3
22 33
continue (y/n)
```

Program 15.5.3

Write a program in C++ to illustrate the operation of a stack, and also insertion and deletion of an element in the stack using dynamic memory allocation with pointers.

```
# include <iostream>
#include <iomanip>
#define NULL 0
using namespace std;
class dstack {
   private:
      struct node
      {
         int no;
         node *next;
      };
      node *head;
   public;
         dstack();
         ~dstack ();
         void push ();
         void pop ();
         void display ();
   };

dstack::dstack()
{
   head-NULL;
}
dstack::~dstack() {}
void stack::push()
{
   node *temp;
   temp=new node;
   cout<<"\n Enter No : ";
   cin>>temp->no;
   if(head==NULL)
   {
      head=temp;
      temp->next=NULL;
   }
```

```
    else
    {
      temp->next=head;
      head=temp;
    }
    cout<<"\n Element "<<temp->no<<" is pushed in to the stack";
}
    void dstack::pop()
    {
          node*p=head;
          if (head==NULL)
              cout <<"Stack is empty";
          else
          {
              head=head->next;
              cout<<"\n Element "<<p->" is popped from the stack";
              delete p;
          }
    }
    void dstack::display ()
    {
          node *p;
          if (head==NULL)
              cout <<"\n Stack empty";
          else
          {
              p=head;
              cout<<"\n The elements present in the stack :\n";
              while(p !=NULL)
          {
              cout<<setw(5)<<p->no;
              p=p->next;
          }
      }
    }
    void main ()
    {
      int choice;
      dstack dstackobj;
      while (1)
      {
          cout <"\n 1 Push ";
          cout <"\n 2 Pop ";
```

```
            cout <"\n 3 Display ";
            cout <<"\n 4 Quit";
            cout <"\n Enter your option :";
            cin>>choice;
            switch(choice)
            {
                case 1:
                    dstackobj.push();
                    break;
                case 2:
                    dstackobj.pop ();
                    break;
                case 3 :
                    dstackobj.display ();
                    break;
                default:
                    exit (0);
                }
            }
        }
```

OUTPUT :

```
1 Push
2 Pop
3 Display
4 Quit
Enter your option : 1
Enter no 108
Element 108 is pushed in to the stack
1 Push
2 Pop
3 Display
4 Quit
Enter your option : 1
Enter no 216
Element 216 is pushed in to the stack
1 Push
2 Pop
3 Display
4 Quit
```

Enter your option : 1

Enter no 332

Element 332 is pushed in to the stack
1 Push
2 Pop
3 Display
4 Quit
Enter your option : 2
Element 332 is popped from the stack
1 Push
2 Pop
3 Display
4 Quit
Enter your option : 3
The element present in the stack :
216 108
1 Push
2 Pop
3 Display
4 Quit
Enter your option : 4

15.6. INTRODUCTION TO QUEUES :

A queue is a data structure very useful in solving various real-life problems. One can simulate the real-life situations with this data structure. The theory of a queue is common to all. We come across its applications in every occupation. Queue of people in a bank and queue for tickets at a railway station are examples of queue. As such, many examples can be indicated.

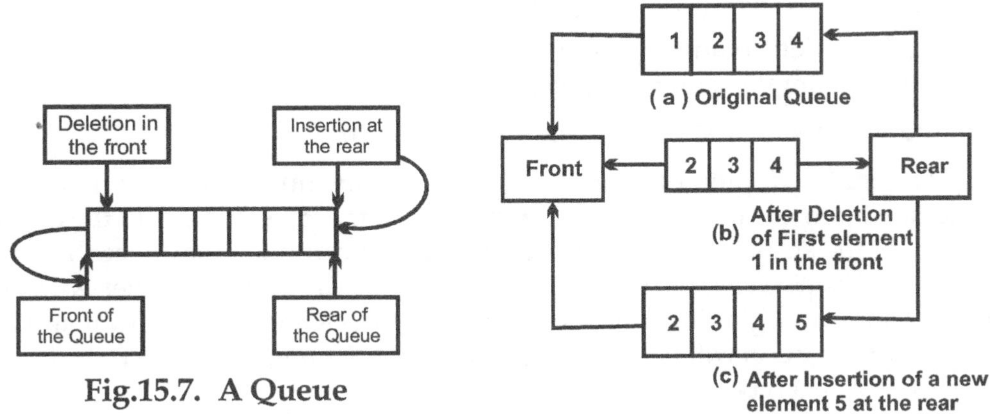

Fig.15.7. A Queue

Fig.15.8 Queue Policy

A queue is a non primitive, linear data structure, and a subclass of list data structure. Queue is an ordered, homogeneous collection of elements in which elements are appended at one end called rear end and elements are deleted at the other end called front end. The meaning of front is front (face side) and rear means back side. The information is manipulated in the same sequence as it was collected. A queue follows the rule first-in-first-out (FIFO), figure 15.7 illustrates queue.

The policy of queue can also be explained by figures 15.7 and 15.8.

Fig.15.7 illustrates the queue containing elements. The queue Fig. 15.8(a) contains original queue of four elements P, Q, R, and S. The element P is at the front end and element S is at the rear end. In 15.8 (b), the front element P of the original queue has been deleted from the queue. Now the element Q is on the front and it is the first queue element. In Fig.15.8 (c) elements S and T are inserted at the rear of the previous queue of fig. 15.8 (b). The element S is inserted before T. As far as removal operation is concerned, S is to be removed before T. Frequently, two operations are performed on a queue. They are insertion and deletion of elements. These two operations depend upon the status of the queue.

The insertion operation is possible only when the queue contains elements less than the capacity which he queue can hold as in figure 15.8 (b). The deletion operation is only possible when the queue contains at least one element as in fig 15.8 (a). The queue containing atleast one place of no elements is called underflow. The queue with a capacity of 4 elements in Fig.15.8 (a) cannot accommodate a fifth element, but it can accommodate another element if only the first element of the queue is deleted as in figure 15.8 (b). This is known as underflow. In Figure 15.8 (a) where the total queue contains 4 elements, a fifth element cannot be inserted at the rear and it is called overflow of the queue.

15.7. REPRESENTATION OF QUEUE :

The queue can be put into operation in two ways.

1) Static implementation (array)
2) Dynamic implementation (pointers)

1) Static implementation of a queue using an array :

The static implementation means an array implementation. In this implementation, we must know the number of elements to be keep in the queue. The size of the array is decided before execution at compile time. Once the array is declared, its size cannot be altered. The array at run time is neither enlarged nor shrunk. The beginning of the array, that is, 0th elements is the front and the last memory location will be the near of the queue. A queue can be declared as an array of any data type.

2) Dynamic implementation of a queue using linked list :

Dynamic implementation is carried out using pointers. By applying increment operation on pointer successive locations of memory can be accessed and an element can be stored in that location. Thus the series of elements can be continued to any number of elements. The programmer has to keep the starting address of the pointer in which the first element is stored.

Queue are FIFO data structures and they can also be implemented by using Linked list. In a stack both addition and deletion of an element takes place at the same end, on the contrary in Queue, insertion is done at the end of the Queue by means of Rear pointer and deletion is done at the beginning of the Queue by means of FRONT pointer. A queue is also called a FIFO (First in First Out) structure.

Fig.15.9. shows Insert and delete operations in a queue with queue as a singly linked list.

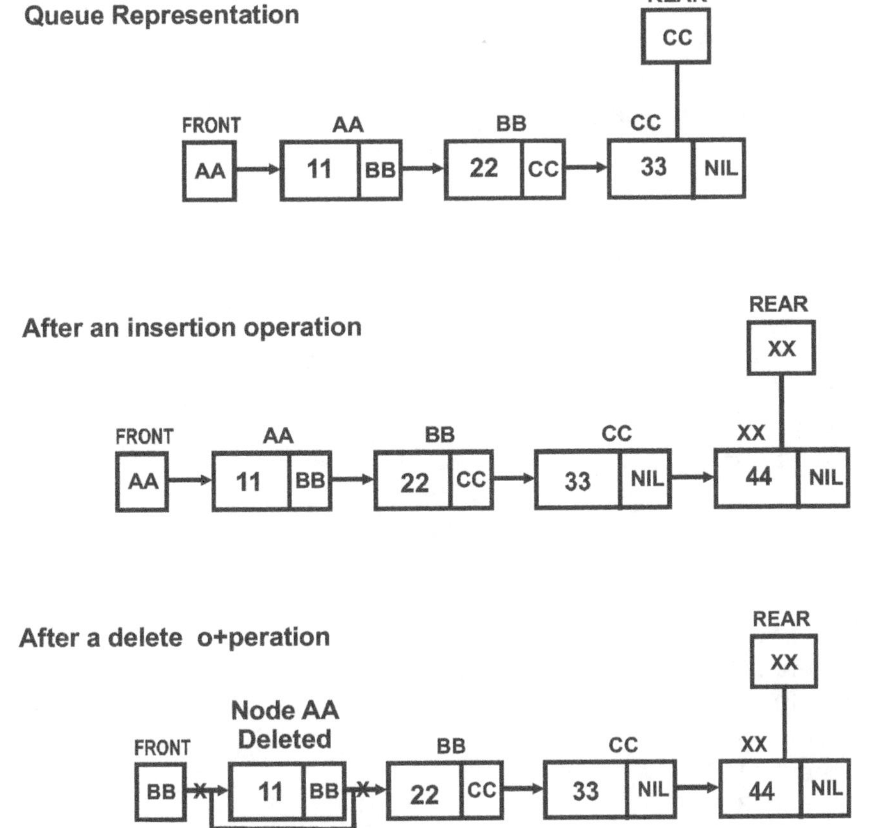

Fig. 15.9. A Queue representation with insertion and deletion of elements in the queue

Program 15.7.1

Write a program in C to implement a queue using an array.

```
# include <stdio.h>
# include <conio.h>
# include <process.h>
void main ( )
{
      int queue [8];
      int rear=0;
      clrscr ();
while (1)
{
   printf ("Enter element : ");
   scanf (" %d", &queue [rear] );
   rear ++;
   if (rear==7)
   {
      printf ("\n Queue is full ");
      break;
   }
}
printf ("\n Elements of Queue are : " );
rear=0;
while (1)
{
   printf (" %d ", queue [rear] );
   rear++;
   if (rear==7)    break;
}
}
```

OUTPUT :

```
Enter element : 707
Enter element : 606
Enter element : 666
Enter element : 554
Enter element : 447
Enter element : 345
Enter element : 588
Queue is full
Elements of Queue are : 707  606  666  554  447  345  588
```

Program 15.7.2
Write a program in C for queue implementation using pointers.

```
# include <stdio.h>
# include <conio.h>
# include <process.h>
int main ( )
{
   int *q;
   int rear=0;
   clrscr ();
while (1)
{
   printf ("Enter element : ");
   scanf (" %d",q);
   q++;
   rear++;
if (rear==7)
{
   printf ("\n Queue is full");
   break;
}
}
q=q-rear;
printf ("\n Elements of Queue are : ");
rear=0;
while (rear<7)
{
   printf ("\n Element : %d  rear=%d" *(q+rear),rear);
   rear++;
}
return 0;
}
```

OUTPUT :

```
Enter element : 707
Enter element : 606
Enter element : 666
Enter element : 554
Enter element : 447
Enter element : 345
Enter element : 588
Queue is full
```

Elements of Queue are :
Element : 707 rear=0
Element : 606 rear=1
Element : 666 rear=2
Element : 554 rear=3
Element : 447 rear=4
Element : 345 rear=5
Element : 588 rear=6

15.8. INSERTION AND DELETION OPERATIONS IN A QUEUE :

The insertion and deletion operations can also be performed on the queue. The following programs give explanation on both the insertion and deletion operations in the queue. Queue implementation is done with an array.

Program 15.8.1

Write a program in C for insertion and deletion of elements in a queue using array elements as elements of the queue..

```
# include <stdio.h>
# include <conio.h>
   void create ();
   insert ();
   erase ();
   void show ();
   int k, j=10, f=0, queue[11], r=0, e_ment crn,s;
main ()
{
      int option;
      clrscr ();
      do
      {
         puts ("\n\n QUEUE OPERATIONS\n");
         puts ("1  :  Create");
         puts ("2  :  Insertion");
         puts ("3  :  Erase");
         puts ("4  :  Show");
         puts ("5  :  Exit");
         puts ("Enter your option : ");
         scanf (" %d" &option);
         switch (option)
         {
                case 1 :  create ( ) ; continue;
                case 2 :  s=insert  ( ) ; continue;
```

```
                case 3 :  erase ( ) ; continue;
                case 4 :  show ( ) ; continue;
                case 5 :
                printf ("\n s=%d"s);
                return 0;
            }
            getche ();
            clrscr ();
        } while (option !=5);
        return 0;
    }
        void create ( )
        {
            puts ("Insert number of elements<11 in the queue : ");
            scanf ("%d" &crn);
            puts ("Enter elements : ");
            if (f ==0)
            {
                f++;
                scanf ("%d",&e_ment);
                queue [f] =e_ment;
                r=f;
            }
            do
        {
        ++r;
        if (r<crn) break;
        scanf ("%d", &e_ment);
        queue [r] =e_ment;
        } while(r<crn);
        }
        insert ()
        {
        r++;
        if (r>j)
        {
        puts ("Queue is full ") ; return (1) ; }
        puts ("Enter number to be inserted : ");
        scanf ("%d" &e_ment);
        queue [r]=e_ment;
        return 0;
        }
```

```
        erase ()
        {
        if ( f ==r)
        {
        puts ("The queue is empty "); return (0); }
        f++;
        e_ment=queue [f];
        if (f==j)
        {
            f=1;
            r=1;
        }
      return 0;
      }
        void show ()
        {
            for (k=f; k<r;++k)
            printf (" %d ", queue [k] );
        }
```

OUTPUT :

99 88 77 66 55

QUEUE OPERATIONS

1. Create
2. Insertion
3. Erase
4. Show
5. Exit

Enter your option :

4

99 88 77 66 55

Program 15.8.2

Write a Program in C++ to illustrate the use of push and pop operation in a stack. (using dynamic memory allocation with pointers)

```
# include <iomanip>
# include <iostream>
#define NULL 0
using namespace std;
```

```
class dstack
{
    private;
        struct node
        {
            int no;
            node *next;
        };
        node *head;
    public;
        dstack ();
        ~dstack();
        void push ();
        void pop ();
        void display();
    };
        dstack : dstack()
        {
            head=NULL;
        }
        dstack::dstack() { }
        void dstack :: push ()
        {
            node *temp;
            temp=new node :
            cout <<"\n Enter No : ";
            cin>>temp->no;
            if (head==NULL)
            {
               head=temp;
               temp->next=NULL;
           }
           else
           }
               temp->next=head;
               head=temp;
           }
           cout<<"\n Element "<<temp->no<<" is pushed in to the stack";
        }
        void dstack ::pop()
        {
           node *p=head;
```

```
        if (head= = NULL)
            cout<<"Stack is empty";
        else
        {
            head=head->next;
            cout <<"\n Element "<<p->no<<"is popped from the stack "
            delete p;
        }
    }
    void dstack::display()
    {
        node *p:
        if (head==NULL)
            cout<<"\n Stack empty ";
        else
        {
            p=head;
            cout<<"\n The elements present in the stack :\n";
            while(p !=NULL)
                {
                 cout<<setw(5)<<p->no;
                 p=p->next;
                }
        }
}

void main ()
{
    int choice;
    dstack dstackobj;
    while (1)
    {
        cout <<"\n 1 Push";
        cout <<"\n 2 Pop";
        cout <<"\n 3 Display";
        cout <<"\n 4 Quit";
        cout<<"\n Enter your option ;";
        cin >>choice;
```

```
                switch(choice)
                {
                case 1:
                    dstackobj.push();
                    break;
                case 2:
                    dstackobj.pop();
                    break;
                case 3 :
                    dstackobj.display();
                    break;
                default;
                    exit (0);
            }
        }
    }
```

OUTPUT :

```
1 Push
2 Pop
3 Display
4 Quit
Enter your Option : 1
Enter no.108
Element 108 is pushed in to the stack
1 Push
2 Pop
3 Display
4 Quit
Enter your option : 1
Enter no 226
Element 226 is pushed in to the stack
1 Push
2 Pop
3 Display
4 Quit
Enter your option : 1
Enter no 345
Element 345 is pushed in to the stack
1 Push
2 Pop
3 Display
4 Quit
```

Enter your option : 2

Element 108 is popped from the stack

1 Push
2 Pop
3 Display
4 Quit
Enter your option : 3

The elements present in the stack ;
226 345
1 Push
2 Pop
3 Display
4 Quit
Enter your option : 4

15.9. CIRCULAR QUEUES :

The operation of linear or straight-line queue is simple, but it has a number of limitations. Deletion of an element from a queue means creating a vacant memory location, which cannot be reutilized. Even if memory locations are available due to deletion operations at the beginning of the queue, elements cannot be inserted. This effect can be understood from Fig.15.10

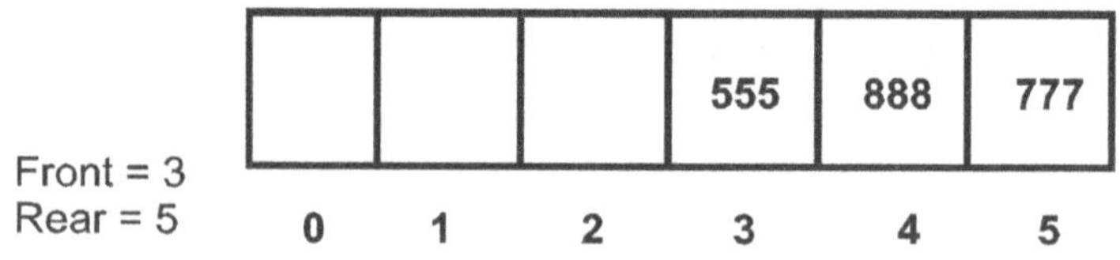

Fig. 15.10. A Simple Queue with empty spaces

The circular queue overcomes the limitations of a simple queue. A linear queue can be converted to circular from if the last node is connected to the first. Figure 15.10 is an example of a linear queue and it can be changed of circular in case the last node five is connected to the first node 0.

A circular queue is illustrated in Fig.15.11 It is like a wheel or a perfect ring. Suppose, C [4] is an array declared for the implementation of a circular queue. However, logically elements appear in circular fashion but physically, in computer memory they are stored in successive memory locations.

It is difficult to recognize the first and the last node of a circular queue. This is because, naturally we do no assign a first or last node. In a computer, the problem can be solved by setting up a first and last node by conversion.

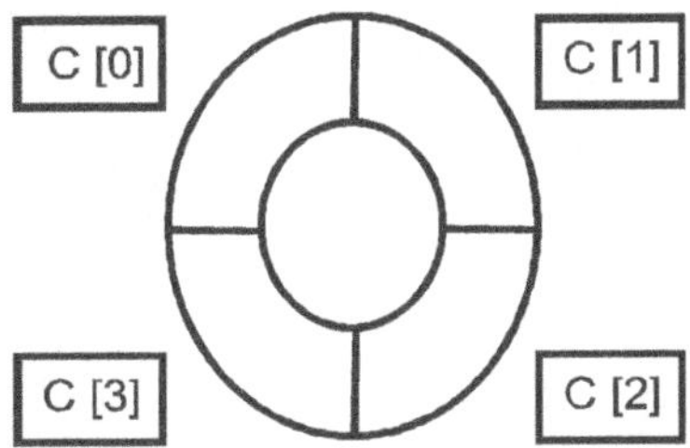

Fig. 15.11. Circular Queue with 4 elements as an array

In the circular queue the turn of the first element comes immediately after the last element. If last location of the queue is occupied then the new item / element is inserted a he first memory location of the queue, if implemented with an array (queue). For example, C [n], C is a queue of n elements. After inserting an element in the last memory location [(n-1th) **element] in an array,** the next element will be stored at the first location, if space is available. It is like a chain in which the first and last points are joined and shape of a circle can be formed. When an element is stored in he last location wrapping takes place after inserting new element. This concept can be followed from the example given below.

Recall that a pointer (stack and queue pointer) plays an important role in knowing the position of the elements in the stack and queue. Here, as soon as the last element is filled, the pointer is wrapped to he beginning of the queue by shifting the pointer value to 1.

A circular queue beats the limitation of the simple queue by utilizing the entire space of he queue. Like a simple queue the circular queue also has front and near ends. The near and front ends help us to know the status of the queue after the insertion and deletion operations. The implementation itself takes care to move a a vacant location of the queue and the element is placed at that location. In order to simulate the circular queue the following points can be noted by the programmer.

1) The front end of he queue always points to the first element of the queue.

2) If the values of from and the queue are equal, the queue will be empty. The values of front and near pointers are only increased/decreased after insertion/deletion operation.

3) Like a simple queue, the near pointer is incremented by 1 when a new element is inserted and the front pointer incremented by 1 when an element is deleted.

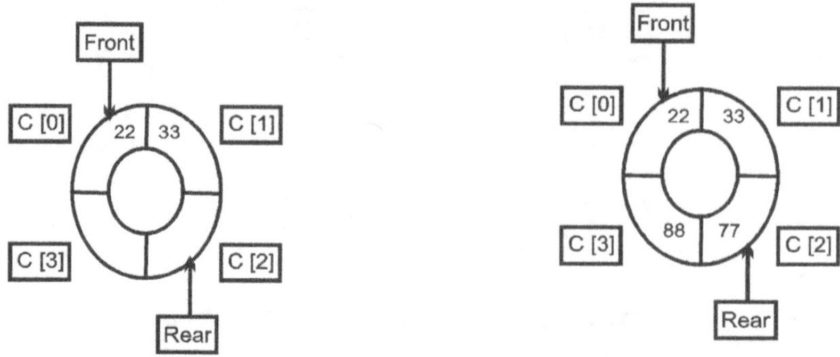

Fig.15.12. Insertion in a circular queue

Fig.15.13. Insertion of 2 more elements in the Circular Queue of 4 elements

As per Fig.15.12 the insertion of an element in a queue will be same as a linear queue. The programmer must trace the values of fron and rear variables. In Fig.15.12

only two elements are there in the queue. if we continue to add elements, the queue would be like Fig.15.13. The new element is always inserted from the rear end. The position of the next element to be placed can be calculated by the following formula.

REAR=(1+REAR) % MAXSIZE
C[REAR]=NUMBER

From the figure, the value of rear is 3 and the maximum elements storing capacity of the queue is 4. Therefore,

REAR=(1+REAR) % MAXSIZE

REAR = (1+3)%4
REAR=4%4=0

The operator % is modular divisor operator and returns a remainder. Thus, in the above equation the remainder obtained is zero. The value of front as well as rear is zero, it means the stack is full. Any attempt to insert a new element will display the 'queue full' message. Consider Fig.15.14.

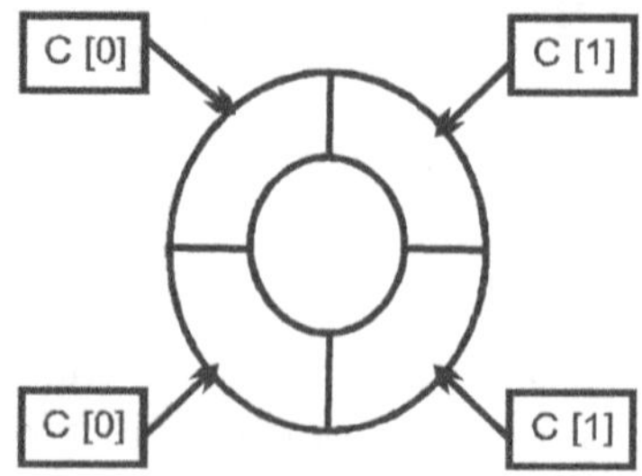

Fig.15.14. The filled-up Circular queue after insertion of 2 elements

Program 15.9.1

Write a program in C to perform insert and delete operations with a circular queue and display the elements.

```
    # include <stdio.h>
    # include <conio.h>
    # include <process.h>
    int queue [8];
    int r, f=0,x=0,j;
    void insert (void);
    void del ();
    void show (void);
    char ans='Y';
    void main ( )
{
        int c;
        clrscr ();
        printf ("\n 1] Insert Element ");
        printf ("\n 2] Delete Element ");
        printf ("\n 3] Display element ");
        printf ("\n 4] Exit ");
        printf ("\n Enter your choice : ");
        scanf (" %d",&c); switch (c)
    {
        case 1  : insert ( ) ; break ;
        case 2  : del ( ) ; show (); break ;
        case 3  : show ( ) ; break ;
        default : exit (0);
    }
        main ( ) ;
}
        void insert ()
{
        int n;
        char ch;
        if (r>=7)
        {
        while (queue [x] ==0)
          {
                prinf ("\n Enter a Number : ");
                scanf (" %d",&n);
```

```
            queue [x]=n;
            x++;
            puts ("\n Continue Y/N : ");
            ch=getch ();
            if (ch ! = 'Y')
            break;
      }
printf ("\n Queue is full \n\n\n");
main ();
{
ans= 'Y';
printf ("\n Enter elements : ")'
while (ans=='Y')
{
scanf (" %d'&queue[r] );
if (r==7)
   {
            clrscr ();
            printf ("\n Queue is Full");
            getch ( );
            break;
   }
else
r++;
printf ("\n Continue Y/N : ");
ans=getche ();
}
}
void show ()
{
int j;
   for (j=0; j<8 ; j++)
   printf (" %d ",queue[j] );
   getch ();
}
   void del ()
   {
   if (r==0)
      {
         clrscr ();
         printf ("\n Queue is empty \n\n\n");
```

```
            main ();
        }
    if (f==8) f=0;
    queue [f]=0;
    f++;
    }
```

OUTPUT :

```
1] Insert Element
2] Delete Element
3] Display element
4] Exit
    Enter your choice : 1
    Enter elements : 769

    Continue Y/N :

    1] Insert Element
    2] Delete Element
    3] Display element
    4] Exit
    Enter your choice : 3
    769 0 0 0 0 0 0 0
```

15.9.1. Deletion and insertion in a full circular queue :

Considering a Circular Queue which is full as shown in fig. 15.15 (a) suppose the elements inserted are 1, 2, 3 4, 5 and 6. Let the positions in the array be from 0th to 5th. The status of the queue is full. If we want on to remove an element, the element removed would be 1. Thus, after deletion the 0th location of the array will be empty.

If an element is inserted, support 7, it will be stored in the 0th location as in Fig.15.15 (b).

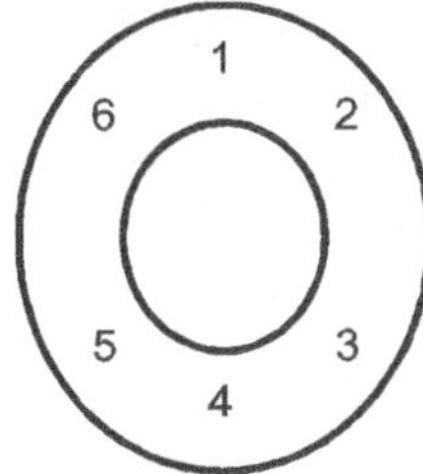

Fig.15.15 (a) Circular queue (before deletion)

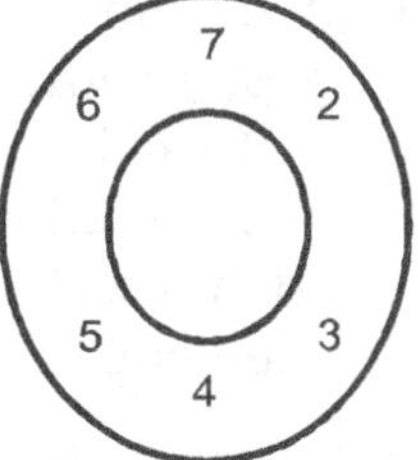

Fig.15.15 (b) Circular queue (after deletion and insertion)

Due to circular queue mechanism, if the last location is occupied and the beginning locations are empty, the element is inserted at the empty location. If we go on to remove elements continuously the elements will be removed in the order from 2, 3, 4, 5, 6 and 7. However 7 is stored at 0th location of the array but it was the last element inserted.

15.10. PRIORITY QUEUE :

A **priority queue** is an abstract data type in computer programming.

It is exactly like a regular queue or stack data structure, but additionally, each element is associated with a "priority".

* **stack:** elements are pulled in last-in first-out-order (e.g. a stack of papers)
* **queue:** elements are pulled in first-in first-out-order (e.g. a line in a cafeteria)
* **priority queue:** elements are pulled highest-priority-first (e.g. cutting in line, or VIP service).

It is a common misconception that a priority queue is a heap. A priority queue is an abstract concept like "a list" or "a map"; just as a list can be implemented with a linked list or an array, a priority queue can be implemented with a heap or a variety of other methods.

A priority queue must at least support the following operations:

* insert_with_priority: add an element to the queue with an associated priority
* pull_highest_priority_element : remove the element from the queue that has the *highest priority,* and return it (also known as "pop_element(Off)", "get_maximum_element", or "get_front(most)_element"; some conventions consider lower priorities to be higher, so this may also be known as "get_minimum_element", and is often referred to as "get-min" in the literature; the literature also sometimes implement separate "peek_at_highest_priority_element" and "delete_element" functions, which can be combined to produce "pull_highest_priority_element")

More advanced implementations may support more complicated operations, such as *pull_lowest_priority_element,* inspecting the first few highest- or lowest-priority elements (peeking at the highest priority element can be made O(1) time in nearly all implementations), clearing the queue, clearing subsets of the queue, performing a batch insert, merging two or more queues into one, incrementing priority of any element, etc.

15.10.1. Similarity to queues :

One can imagine a priority queue as a modified queue, but when one would get the next element off the queue, the highest-priority element is retrieved first.

Stacks and queues may be modeled as particular kinds of priority queues. In a stack, the priority of each inserted element is monotonically increasing; thus, the last element inserted is always the first retrieved. In a queue, the priority of each inserted element is monotonically decreasing; thus, the first element inserted is always the first retrieved.

15.10.2. Implementation of priority queue :

i) Naive implementations of priority queue:

There are a variety of simple, usually inefficient, ways to implement a priority queue. They provide an analogy to help one understand what a priority queue is:

* **Unsorted implementation:** This is perhaps the most naive implementation. Keep all the elements unsorted. Whenever the highest-priority element is requested, search through all elements for the one with the highest priority. (O(1) insertion time, O(n) pull time due to search)

* **Sorted list implementation:** Like a checkout line at the supermarket, but where important people get to "cut" in front of less important people. (if using a basic array, this takes O(n) insertion time, O(1) pullNext time (from the front), and on average O(n*log(n)) time to initialize (if using quicksort))

These implementations are almost always terribly inefficient, but are meant to illustrate the concept of a priority queue.

Note that from a computational-complexity standpoint, priority queues are equivalent to sorting algorithms. See the next section for how efficient sorting algorithms can create efficient priority queues.

ii) Usual implementation of priority queue :

To get better performance, priority queues typically use a heap as their backbone, giving $O(\log n)$ performance for inserts and removals, and $O(n)$ to build initially. Alternatively, if a self-balancing binary search tree is used, insertion and removal also take $O(\log n)$ time, although building the heap from an existing sequence of elements takes $O(n \log n)$ time; this is a popular solution where one already has access to these data structures, such as through third-party or standard libraries.

15.10.3. Effect of different data structures on priority queue :

The designer of the priority queue should take into account what sort of access pattern the priority queue will be subject to, and what computational resources are most important to the designer. The designer can then use various specialized types of heaps:

There are a number of specialized heap data structures that either supply additional operations or outperform the above approaches. The binary heap uses O(log *n*) time for both operations, but allows peeking at the element of highest priority without removing it in constant time. Binomial heaps add several more operations, but require O (log *n*) time for peeking. Fibonacci heaps can insert elements, peek at the highest priority element, and increase an element's priority in amortized constant time(deletions are still O(log *n*)).

While relying on a heap is a common way to implement priority queues, for integer data faster implementations exist (this can even apply to data types that have finite range, such as floats):

* When the set of keys is {1, 2, ..., C}, a van Emde Boas tree supports the *minimum, maximum, insert, delete, search, extract-min, extract-max, predecessor* and *successor* operations in *O*(log log *C*) time, but has a space cost for small queues of about $O(2^{m/2})$, where *m* is the number of bits in the priority value.
* The Fusion tree algorithm by Fredman and Willard implements the *minimum* operation in O(1) time and *insert* and *extract-min* operations in $O(\sqrt{\log n})$time.

For applications that do many "peek" operations for every "extract-min" operation, the time complexity for peek can be reduced to O(1) in all tree and heap implementations by caching the highest priority element after every insertion and removal. (For insertion this adds at most constant cost, since the newly inserted element need only be compared to the previously cached minimum element. For deletion, this at most adds an additional "peek" cost, which is nearly always cheaper than the deletion cost, so overall time complexity is not affected by this change).

15.10.4. Equivalence of priority queues and sorting algorithms:

i) Using a priority queue to sort

The semantics of priority queues naturally suggest a sorting method: insert all the elements to be sorted into a priority queue, and sequentially remove them; they will come out in sorted order. This is actually the procedure used by several sorting algorithms, once the layer of abstraction provided by the priority queue is removed. This sorting method is equivalent to the following sorting algorithms:

* Heapsort if the priority queue is implemented with a heap.
* Smoothsort if the priority queue is implemented with a Leonardo heap.
* Selection sort if the priority queue is implemented with an unordered array.
* Insertion sort if the priority queue is implemented with an ordered array.
* Tree sort if the priority queue is implemented with a self-balancing binary search tree.

ii) Using a sorting algorithm to make a priority queue

A sorting algorithm can also be used to implement a priority queue. Specifically, Thorup says:

We present a general deterministic linear space reduction from priority queues to sorting implying that if we can sort up to n keys in S(n) time per key, then there is a priority queue supporting *delete* and *insert* in O(S(n)) time and find-min in constant time.

That is, if there is a sorting algorithm which can sort in O(S) time per key, where S is some function of n and word size], then one can use the given procedure to create a priority queue where pulling the highest-priority element is O(1) time, and inserting new elements (and deleting elements) is O(S) time. For example if one has an O(n lg(lg(n))) sort algorithm, one can easily create a priority queue with O(1) pulling and O(lg(lg(n))) insertion.

iii) Libraries

A priority queue is often considered to be a "container data structure".

The Standard Template Library (STL), and the C++ 1998 standard, specifies priority_queue as one of the STL container adaptor class templates. It implements a max-priority-queue. Unlike actual STL containers, it does not allow iteration of its elements (it strictly adheres to its abstract data type definition). STL also has utility functions for manipulating another random-access container as a binary max-heap.

Python's heapq module implements a binary min-heap on top of a list.

Java's library contains a PriorityQueue class, which implements a min-priority-queue.

Go's library contains a container/heap module, which implements a min-heap on top of any compatible data structure.

The Standard PHP Library extension contains the class SplPriorityQueue.

Apple's Core Foundation framework contains a CF BinaryHeap structure, which implements a min-heap.

15.10.5. Applications of priority queue :

i) Bandwidth management

Priority queuing can be used to manage limited resources such as bandwidth on a transmission line from a network router. In the event of outgoing traffic queuing due to insufficient bandwidth, all other queues can be halted to send the traffic from the highest priority queue upon arrival. This ensures that the prioritized traffic (such as real-time traffic, e.g. an RTP stream of a VoIP connection) is forwarded with the least delay and the least likelihood of being rejected due to a queue reaching its maximum capacity. All other traffic can be handled when the highest priority queue is empty. Another approach used is to send disproportionately more traffic from higher priority queues.

Many modern protocols for Local Area Networks also include the concept of Priority Queues at the Media Access Control (MAC) sub-layer to ensure that high-priority applications (such as VoIP or IPTV) experience lower latency than other applications which can be served with Best effort service. Examples include IEEE 802.11e (an amendment to IEEE 802.11 which provides Quality of Service) and ITU-T G.hn (a standard for high-speed Local area network using existing home wiring (power lines, phone lines and coaxial cables).

Usually a limitation (policer) is set to limit the bandwidth that traffic from the highest priority queue can take, in order to prevent high priority packets from choking off all other traffic. This limit is usually never reached due to high level control instances such as the Cisco Call manager, which can be programmed to inhibit calls which would exceed the programmed bandwidth limit.

ii) Discrete event simulation :

Another use of a priority queue is to manage the events in a discrete event simulation. The events are added to the queue with their simulation time used as the priority. The execution of the simulation proceeds by repeatedly pulling the top of the queue and executing the event thereon.

See also: Scheduling (computing), queuing theory

iii) Dijkstra's algorithm :

When the graph is stored in the form of adjacency list or matrix, priority queue can be used to extract minimum efficiently when implementing Dijkstra's algorithm.

iv) A* and SMA* search algorithms :

The A* search algorithm finds the shortest path between two vertices or nodes of a weighted graph, trying out the most promising routes first. The priority queue (also known as the *fringe*) is used to keep track of unexplored routes; the one for which a lower bound on the total path length is smallest is given highest priority. If memory limitations make A* impractical, the SMA* algorithm can be used instead, with a double-ended priority queue to allow removal of low-priority items.

v) ROAM triangulation algorithm :

The Real-time Optimally Adapting Meshes (ROAM) algorithm computes a dynamically changing triangulation of a terrain. It works by splitting triangles where more detail is needed and merging them where less detail is needed. The algorithm assigns each triangle in the terrain a priority, usually related to the error decrease if that triangle would be split. The algorithm uses two priority queues, one for triangles that can be split and another for triangles that can be merged. In each step the triangle from the split queue with the highest priority is split, or the triangle from the merge queue with the lowest priority is merged with its neighbours.

Priority queues can be represented using HEAPS. A HEAP is a data structure with the priority that the value in every node is at least as large as the value in the children nodes.

A program to design a priority queue which is maintained as a set of queues (assume maximum of 3 queues). The elements are inserted based upon the given priority. For example (3, 34) will be inserted to 3rd queue with the elemental value 34. The deletion of an element is to be done starting from the 1st queue, if it is not empty. In case if it is empty, the elements from the 2nd queue will be deleted, and so on.

Solution :

```
# include <stdio.h>
# include <conio.h>
# define MAX_SIZE 5
main ( )
{
        int q1 [MAX_SIZE1, q2[MAX_SIZE], q3 [MAX_SIZE]
        int ele, pri, choice ;
        int f1, f2, f3, r1, r2, r3, status;
        /* Functino prototypes*/
        void display (int a [ ], int * front, int * rear);
        void pqinsert (int a [ ]; int* front, int* rear, int ele);
        int pqdelete (int a [ ], int * front, int* rear);
        f1 = r1 = f2 = r2 = f3 = r3 = 0; /* Initialize front and rear
                                          pointers of all queues to 0*/
        do
        {
                clrscr ( );
printf ((" ********** MENU ********** \n");
printf("Press 1 : Inserting an element \n");
printf("Press 2 : Deleting an element \n");
printf("Press 3 : Display contents of the Queue \n");
printf("Press 4 : Quit \n");
```

```
printf (* * * * * * * * * * * * * * * * * * * * * * * * * * * * \n");
    printf("your choice please: ")'
    Scanf (" %d", & choice);
    printf (" %d", choice)
    switch (choice)
    {
        case 1 :    printf ("\n enter the element and its priority
                        (1, 2, 3) \n");
                    scanf (" %d%d", & ele, & pri);
                    printf (" % d %d", ele, pri);
                    if (pri = = 1) pqinsert (q, f1, r1, ele);
                    if (pri = = 2) pqinsert (q2 &f2, &r2, ele);

                    if (pri = = 3) pqinsert (q3, &f3, &r3, ele);
                    printf ("\n\n\n\n element insertd - - prese any key");
                    break;

        case 2 :

                    status = pqdelete (q1, &f1, &r1);
                    if status = = 1)
                    {
                        printf ("fron the FIRST priority queue -\n");
                        getch ( );
                        break;
                    }
                    else

                        printf ("\n First priority queue is empty -
                            trying to delete from 2 queue \n");
                        status = pqdelete (q2, &f2, &r2);
                        if (status = = 1)
                    {
                        printf ("from the second priority queue -\n");
                            getch ( ) ;
                            break ;
                    }
                    else
                        printf ("\n second priority queue is also
                            empty - - trying to delete from

                                        3 queue \n");
                        status = pqdelete (q3, &f3, &r3);
```

```
                if (status = = 1)
            {
                printf ("from the thrid priority queue -\n");
                getch ( );
                break ;
            }
            else
                pritnf (|'n sorry - - - thrid priority queue is also
                                              empty - - \n");
                getch ( ):
                break ;
case 3 :
                display (q1, &f1, &r1);
                display (q2, &f2, &r2);
                display (q3, &f3, &r3);
                getch ( );
                break;
            }
        } while (choice ! = 4);
            /* END OF MAIN */
        }
        /* FUNCTION TO INSERT AN ELEMENT INTO THE
                                      APPROPRIATE QUEUE*/
            void pqinsert (int a[ ], int * front, int* rear, int ele)
            {
                if (* rear > MAX_SIZE)
                {
                    printf("Queue overflow - Try insetting into
                                              priority queue");
                    return ;
                }
                    *rear = *rear + 1;
                    a[* rear] = ele;
                    if (* front = = 0)* front = 1;
                }
        /* FUNCTION TO DELETE AN ELEMENT FROM THE
        APPROPRIATE QUEUE*/
        int pqdelete (int a [ ], int *front, int* rear)
        {
            int ele;
```

```
        if (* front = = 0);
            return 0;          /*0 means empty queue*/
    ele = a {* front);
    if (* front = = *rear)
        * front = *rear = 0;
    else
        *front = *front +1;
    printf ("\n element %d is deleted", ele);
    return (1);
}
/* FUNCTION TO DISPLAY THE CONTENTS OF ALL THE
QUEUES */
    void display (int a [ ], int * front, int* rear)
    {
        int i;
            if (* front = = 0)
            {
                printf ("Queue emptry - - - \n");
                return;
            }
            for (i = *front ; i< = *rear ; i + +)
                printf ("%d", a[i]);
                printf ("d"\n");
}
```

5.11. DEQUE or DEQUEUE (as Noun), Deque (as verb) and Double-ended queue :

Dequeue (as verb) or DQ is different from deque or dequeue (as noun). Dequeue as verb means deleting element from the queue.

Deque (as Noun) is not to be confused with Double-ended priority queue.

In computer science, a **double-ended queue** (**dequeue**, often abbreviated to **deque**, pronounced as **deck**) is an abstract data structure that implements a queue for which elements can only be added to or removed from the front (head) or back (tail).[] It is also often called a **head-tail linked list.**

5.11.1. Naming conventions of Deque :

Deque is sometimes written as *dequeue*, but this use is generally discouraged in technical literature or technical writing because *dequeue* is also a verb meaning "to remove from a queue". Nevertheless, several libraries and some writers, such as Aho, Hopcroft, and Ullman in their text book **Data Structures and Algorithms,** spell it *dequeue.* John Mitchell, author of **Concepts in Programming Languages,** also uses this terminology. DEQ and DQ are also used.

5.11.2.Distinctions and sub-types of Deque :

This differs from the queue abstract data type or First-In-First-Out List (FIFO), where elements can only be added to one end and removed from the other. This general data class has some possible sub-types:

* An input-restricted deque is one where deletion can be made from both ends, but insertion can only be made at one end.
* An output-restricted deque is one where insertion can be made at both ends, but deletion can be made from one end only.

Both the basic and most common list types in computing, queues and stacks can be considered specializations of deques, and can be implemented using deques.

5.11.3. Operations of Deque in different languages :

The following operations are possible on a deque:

Table 15.1. Operations of Deque in different languages

operation	Ada	C++	Java	Perl	PHP	Python	Ruby	JavaScript
insert element at back	Append	push_back	offer Last	push	array_push	append	push	push
insert element at front	Prepend	push_front	offer First	unshift	array_unshift	append left	unshift	unshift
remove last element	Delete_Last	pop_back	Poll Last	pop	array_pop	pop	pop	pop
remove first element	Delete_First	pop_front	Poll First	shift	array_shift	popleft	shift	shift
examine last element	Last_Element	back	peek Last	$array[-1]	end	<obj>[-1]	last	<obj>[<obj. length - 1]
examine first element	First_Element	front	peek First	$array[0]	reset	<obj>[0]	first	<obj>[0]

5.11.4. Implementations of Deque :

There are at least two common ways to efficiently implement a deque: i) with a modified dynamic array or ii) with a doubly linked list.

The dynamic array approach uses a variant of a dynamic array that can grow from both ends, sometimes called **array deques**. These array deques have all the properties of a dynamic array, such as constant time random access, good locality of reference, and inefficient insertion/removal in the middle, with the addition of amortized constant time insertion/removal at both ends, instead of just one end. Three common implementations include:

* Storing deque contents in a circular buffer, and only resizing when the buffer becomes completely full. This decreases the frequency of resizings, but requires an expensive branch instruction for indexing.

* Allocating deque contents from the center of the underlying array, and resizing the underlying array when either end is reached. This approach may require more frequent resizings and waste more space, particularly when elements are only inserted at one end.

* Storing contents in multiple smaller arrays, allocating additional arrays at the beginning or end as needed. Indexing is implemented by keeping a dynamic array containing pointers to each of the smaller arrays.

5.11.5. Language support for Deque :

Ada's containers provides the generic packages Ada. Containers. Vectors and Ada.Containers. Doubly_Linked_Lists, for the dynamic array and linked list implementations, respectively.

C++'s Standard Template Library provides the class templates std::deque and std::list, for the multiple array and linked list implementations, respectively.

As of Java 6, Java's Collections Framework provides a new Deque interface that provides the functionality of insertion and removal at both ends. It is implemented by classes such as Array Deque (also new in Java 6) and LinkedList, providing the dynamic array and linked list implementations, respectively. However, the ArrayDeque, contrary to its name, does not support random access.

Python 2.4 introduced the collections module with support for deque objects.

As of PHP 5.3, PHP's SPL extension contains the 'Spl Doubly Linked List' class that can be used to implement Deque datastructures. Previously to make a Deque structure the array functions array_shift/unshift/pop/push had to be used instead.

GHC's Data.Sequence module implements an efficient, functional deque structure in Haskell.

5.11.6. Complexity of Deque :

* In a doubly linked list implementation and assuming no allocation/deallocation overhead, the time complexity of all deque operations is O(1). Additionally, the time complexity of insertion or deletion in the middle, given an iterator, is O(1); however, the time complexity of random access by index is O(n).

* In a growing array, the amortized time complexity of all deque operations is O(1). Additionally, the time complexity of random access by index is O(1); but the time complexity of insertion or deletion in the middle is O(n).

5.11.7.Applications of Deque :

One example where a deque can be used is the *A-Steal* job scheduling algorithm.[2] This algorithm implements task scheduling for several processors. A separate deque with threads to be executed is maintained for each processor. To execute the next thread, the processor gets the first element from the deque (using the "remove first element" deque operation). If the current thread forks, it is put back to the front of the deque ("insert element at front") and a new thread is executed. When one of the processors finishes execution of its own threads (i.e. its deque is empty), it can "steal" a thread from another processor: it gets the last element from the deque of another processor ("remove last element") and executes it.

15.12. REPRESENTATION & OPERATIONS OF ARITHMETIC EXPRESSIONS USING STACK OPERATIONS :

A stack can be used to maintain sequence of processing of arithmetic expressions. An arithmetic expression contains operators and operands. Variables and constants are operands. The operators are of various kinds such as arithmetic, binary, unary and so on. For example, + (addition), - (subtraction),*(multiplication), /(division), and % (modular division) are a few operators Table 15.1 describes various types of operators which had been already discussed earlier.

Table. 15.2. Types of Operators

Types of Operators	Symbolic representation
Arithmetic operators	+ ,- * , / and %
Relational operators	>, <, =, ==, >=, <=, and !=
Logical operators	&&, | | !
Increment / decrement operators	++ , - -
Assignment operators	=
Bitwise operators	&, |, ^, >>, <<, "
Special operators	, (comma)
Conditional operators	? :

The precedence of operators also plays an important role in expression solving. the precedence of operators is given in table 15.2 which had also been discussed earlier.

Table 15.3 Arithmetic Operator and Precedence

Operators	Precedence	Priority
+ (unary), - (unary), NOT	6	----
^ (Exponentiation)	6	Right to left
* (multiplication), / (division)	5	Left to right
+ (addition), - (subtraction)	4	Left o right
<,<=, + < >,>=	3	Left to right

15.12.1. Infix, prefix, and postfix notations :

This topic illustrates an important application of different kinds of stacks. A stack has various real life applications. **A stack is very useful to maintain the sequence of processing.**

i) *In solving arithmetic expression, stacks are used.*

ii) *Various operations are applied on stacks, and compilation of infix expression is done.*

iii) *Stacks are used to convert bases of numbers.*

iv) *In a large program, various functions are invoked by the main ( ) function, all these functions are stacked in the memory.*

Most of the calculation work is on stack mechanism.

We use three kinds of notations to express arithmetic expressions. These three kinds of notations are infix, prefix, and postfix. The prefixes pre, post, and in indicate the relative location of the operators between the operands.

(a) Infix notation : Expression are generally expressed with infix notation with binary operator between the operands. The binary operator needs the two operands. In this type the operator appears in between the two operands. Following are examples of infix notation.

1) x+y
2) x+y*z
3) (x+y)*z
4) (x+y)*(p+q)

Every singe letter (A-Z) and an unsigned integer can be used as operands in an infix expression. If X and Y are two valid letters then (X+Y), (X-Y), and (X/Y) are legal infix expressions.

(b) Prefix notation : The prefix notation is also called as Polish notation. The polish mathematician Lukasiewicx invented it. In this type, he operator precedes the operands. The following are the examples of prefix notation.

1) +xy
2) +x*yz
3) *+xyz
4) *+xy+pq

(c) Postfix notation : The postfix notation is also called an reverse Polish notation.

1) xy+
2) xyz*+
3) xy+z*
4) xy+pq*+

Consider the following example.

X+Y*Z

In he above expression, we know that the multiplication has higher precedence has addition. We can write he above expression as X+(Y*Z). The results of these two expressions are the same. By applying rules of priority, we can convert the above expression to postfix notation.

X+(Y*Z)

Here, parentheses are not necessary

X+(YZ*)

Here, multiplication is converted to postfix

X(YZ*)+

Here, addition is converted to postfix

XYZ*+

The above equation is postfix form. While doing he conversion operations, the following points are to be noted.

1) When we convert an expression from prefix to postfix form, it is essential that properties such as precedence, commutability, and well-formed expressions of operators must be preserved.
2) The operations with high priority are converted first and after the remaining part of the expression is converted to postfix form. The remaining part is considered as a single operand. For example, X*Y+Z.

In this expression multiplication operation between the two operands X, Y can be converted as XY* in postfix expression. Then addition of first expression XY* with Z is expressed as XY*Z+ in postfix expression.

INFIX	POST FIX
X*Y + Z	XY*Z+

Here, XY is considered as a single operand.

3) In suffix and prefix equivalents of an infix expression, the variables must be in the relative peace. The expressions in prefix or suffix are without parentheses. The operators are set according to precedence rule of operators.

4) A fully parenthesized infix expression is converted directly to suffix form. Conversion is started from innermost parentheses to outermost parentheses. For example,

(X + Y + (P + Q + (T+Y)))

The innermost parentheses (T+Y) are solved first.

The precedence can be changed here by adding the parentheses. Consider the following example.

(X+Y)*Z

In the above example, if parentheses are not inserted then multiplication operation gets first priority. Due to parentheses the addition operation gets first priority.

(XY+)*Z

Here, the addition is converted in the postfix form.

(XY+) Z*

Here, the multiplication is converted to the postfix form.

There are five binary operations -- addition (+), subtraction (-), multiplication (*), division (/), and exponentiation. In C/C++ there is no operator exponentiation operator. Here, &^ is used to denote exponent operation.

The equation X^Y means X raised to Y 2^ 3 means 8, When any expression is without parenthesis the order of operation is left to right. Only in exponent he order is from right to left.

X+Y+Z means (X+Y)+C. On the other hand X^Y^Z means X^(Y^Z). The operation inside the parenthesis gets first priority. Consider the following examples of converting infix to postfix given in table 15.3 to make our understanding perfect.

Table : 15.4. Infix and Postfix Forms

infix	Postfix
X+Y	XY+
X+Y-Z	XY+Z-
(X+Y*(P-Q)	XY+PQ-*
L^M*N-O+P/Q(R+S)	LM^N*O-PQ/RS+/+
((L+M)*N-(O-P)^(Q+R)	LM+N*OP--QR+^
L-M/(N*O^P)	LMNOP^*/-

For converting an expression from infix to prefix the rules are the same as for conversion from infix to postfix as given in table 15.4. In the prefix conversion the operator is placed before the operand.

Table 15.5. Infix and Prefix Forms

Infix	Prefix
X+Y	+XY
X+Y-Z	+XYZ
(X+Y)*(P-Q)	-+XY-PQ
L^M*N-O+P/Q/(R+S)	+-*^LMNO//PQ+RS
((L+M)*N-(O-P)^(Q+R)	^-*+LMN-OP+QR
L-M/(N*O^P)	-L/M*N^OP

The postfix form does not require parentheses. Consider the following expressions.

X+(Y*Z) and (X+Y)*Z

Infix	Postfix
X+(Y*Z)	XYZ*+
(X+Y)*Z	XY+Z*

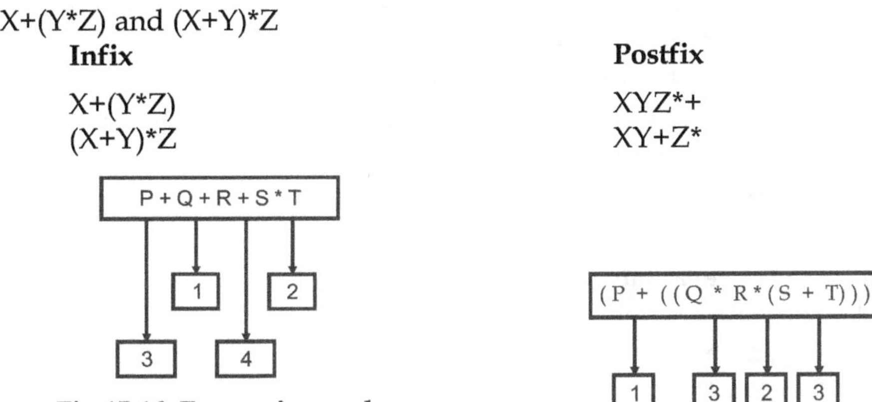

Fig.15.16. Expression and operation precedence rank

Fig.15.17. Fully parenthesized expressions

If parentheses are present in the expression, then the precedence will be changed. For example, in Fig. 15.16 the expression (P+Q)*R, first P+Q is solved and hen multiplication takes place. Actually, it is possible to declare an expression that makes he sequence of evaluation of expression independent of the priority of the operators.This can be done by putting sub-expressions in parentheses. The operators and operands are enclosed in he parentheses. Thus we have several parenthetical levels as shown in Fig.15.17. Such expressions are called fully parenthesized expressions. Consider the example in fig.15.17.

The numbers indicate parenthetical level of operators. When such an expression is solved, he subexpression having the operator with top parenthetical level is first solved. When two sets of parentheses have equal parenthetical level, the left-sided set is evaluated first. After that, parentheses 2 and 1 are solved.

In case the expression is partially parenthesized, a repetitive scanning from left to right is essential to evaluate the expressions. This is because the operators are present in conjunction with the operands within the expression. The scanning is shunned in case the infix expression is converted to suffix or prefix expression.

15.12.2. Evaluation of postfix expression :

The postfix expressions are very simple. On the other hand, finding postfix expressions with a program is complicated. This is because the numbers and characters are mixed in one string. The programmer needs initially to separate digits and symbols. After this, process of arithmetic operations is performed.

Each operator in the postfix expression is associated with the previous two operands. When we need an operand from a given expression, it is pushed onto the stack. When an operator symbol is read, the operands associated with it are the top elements of the stack. We can pop these two elements from the stack and perform the operation. The obtained result from the last operation is again pushed onto the stack. The postfix algorithm can be followed the following steps of table 15.5.

Table 15.5. Algorithm for post-fix algorithm :

1. Insert a ')' at the end of X, where X is an expression
2. Check X from left to right and go back over the next 3 and 4 steps for every element of X until ')' is found.
3. In case, operands are found and push it on the stack.

Program 15.12.1

Write a program in C to evaluate postfix expressions.

```
# include <stdio.h>
# include <conio.h>
# include <ctype.h>
# include <math.h>

        float stack [10];
        int top= -1;
        void push (char);
        float pop();
        float exp_eval (char [ ], float [ ]) ;
int main ( )
{
        int j=0;
        char s_fix [20] ;
        float number [20] , res;
        clrscr ( );
        printf ("\n Enter a postfix expression : ");
        gets (s_fix);
while (s_fix [j] !='\0')
{
                if (isalpha (s_fix [j] ) )
                {
        fflush (stdin);
```

```
        printf ("\n Enter number for %c: "s_fix [j]) ;
        scanf ("%f",&number [j] );
             }
        j ++;
}
res=exp_eval (s_fix, number);
printf ("The res of %s =%f", s_fix,res);
getch ( );
return 0;
}
float exp_eval ( char s_fix [ ], float data [ ] )
{
        int j=0;
        float opA, opB, fs;
        char ch;
while (s_fix [j] ! ='\0')
{
        ch=s_fix[j];
        if (isalpha (s_fix[j] ) )
        {
             push (data [j] );
        }
             else
             {
                  opB=pop ( );
                  opA=pop ( );
             switch (ch)
             {
             case ' + ' : push (opA+opB) ; break;
             case ' - ' : push (opA-opB) ; break;
             case ' * ' : push (opA*opB) ; break;
             case ' / ' : push (opA/opB) ; break;
             case ' ^ ' : push (pow (opA, opB ) ) ; break;
             }
        }
             j++;
        }
             fs=pop ();
             return (fs);
}
```

```
        void push (char c)
    {
        top=++top;
        stack [top]=c;
    }
        float pop ( )
        {
            float n;
            n=stack [top];
            top= --top;
            return (n);
        }
```

OUTPUT :

Enter a postfix expression : jk*
Enter number for j: 8
Enter number for k: 6
The res of jk* = 48.000000

Explanation : In the above program, before main ( ) function, the float type array stack [10] and integer variable top are defined and initialized with -1. The prototypes of function push (), pop () and exp_val () are declared. the user has to enter the expression and the gets () function activities the input stream and the entered expression is stored in the s_fix[] character array.

The expression is checked and for every alphabet the user has to enter a number. immediately after this, the function exp_eval ( ) is invoked with two arguments are array names and hold base address. This function returns result and is stored in variable res.

In the exp_eval, ( ) function the variable ch holds the arithmetic operation. The switch ( ) case structure determines the operation to be carried out. The pop ( ) function is invoked and the two popped values are stored in variables popB and popA. These variables are passed to push ( ) function in switch ( ) case structure.

15.12.3. Conversion of expression from infix to postfix :

In any expression, there are two types of components clubbed together. They are operand and operators. The operator indicates the operation to be carried out and the operand indicates the values. The operands are the variables on which the operator operates. Operators have their priority of execution. when one or more operations are clubbed together in a single expression the priority decides which operation is performed first. Suppose an expression contains two operations with high and low priority. We can force the low-priority operation to evaluate first by putting that particular operation in parentheses. When nested parentheses are present in the expression the innermost parentheses is solved first. In any expression the parentheses are solved first. The operations are generally solved from left to right.

Table 15.6. Operator and Precedence :

Operator	Precedence
Exponent	High
Multiplication (*), division (/)	Next
Addition (+), Subtraction (-)	Low

Consider the following example.

x-y/(p^q)+(u*v)

The operators are -,/^,+,* and x,y,p,q,u, and v are variables. The parentheses are used to provide higher priority to the operators (p^q) and (u*v).

Consider the following example.

Expression : X+Y*Z

The expression is scanned and when operators are found, hey are pushed on he stack. The operators are pushed according to priority of execution of the stack. When operator+ is found, it is pushed onto the stack. The precedence of * is higher than +. The symbol* is pushed onto the stack at last, when string reaches is end, the stack is popped and its content is appended to the postfix string. These postfix operations are shown in table 15.6.

Table. 15.7. Expression X+Y*Z

Character	Postfix string	Stack
X	X	
+	X	+
Y	XY	+
*	XY	+*
Z	XYZ	+*
	XYZ*	+
	XYZ*+	

Consider to Expression : (P+Q)*R

The operations for this expression is given in table 15.8

Table 15.8. Expression (P+Q)*R

Character	Postfix string	Stack
(		(
P	P	(
+	P	(+
Q	PQ	(+
)	PQ+	
*	PQ+	*
R	PQ+R	*
	PQ+R*	

In the above example, when opening parenthesis is found until the left parenthesis is not found the entire stack is popped. Here, the parentheses provide first priority to addition.

Algorithm for conversion of infix expression to postfix is given below.

1. Push to the end of X, where X is an arithmetic expression.
2. Check expression from left to right and follow the stops 3 to 6 for every element of X until the stack is vacant.
3. In case an operand is found, add it to R, where R is the equivalent postfix expression.
4. In case left '(' parenthesis is found push it onto the stack.
5. In case an operator is found, follow the following steps.
   (a) Continually pop from the stack and add each operator to R at he top of the stack. The pushed item should have the same or higher precedence than the former operator encountered.
   b) Append operator (recently encountered) onto the stack.
6. In case ')' right parenthesis is found then follow the following steps.
   (a) Continually pop from the stack and append every operator o R until left parenthesis is found.
   (b) Eliminate the left parenthesis.

Program 15.12.2

Write a program in C to convert an infix expression to postfix form.

```
# include <stdio.h>
# include <conio.h>
# include <string.h>
# include <process.h>
```

```
    char stack [20];
    int T= -1;
  void topost (char in_fix [ ] );
  void push (char);
  char pop ( );
int main ( )
  {
      char in_fix[25];
      clrscr ();
      puts ("Enter an infix expressions : ") ;
      gets (in_fix);
      puts ("\n Postfix Expression : " ) ;
      topost (in_fix);
      return 0;
  }
      void push (char s)
      {
          if (T>=19)
          {
              puts (" Stack overflow ");
              exit (0);
          }
      else
      {
          T=T+1;
          stack [T]=s;
      }
  }
  char pop ()
  {
      char num;
  if (T== -1)
  {
      puts (" Stack is Empty ") ;
      getch ();
      return (0) ;
  }
  else
  {
      num=stack [T];
      T--;
      }
```

```
return (num);
}
int prefix (char ch)
{
    if (ch=='/')      return (5) ;
    else if (ch==' * ') return (4);
    else if (ch=='+')  return (3) ;
    else return (2) ;
}
void topost (char in_fix [ ])
{
    int  len;
    static int  index=0pos=0;
    char s,t;
    char postfix [40];
    len=strlen(in_fix);
    push ('#');
while (indexlen)
{
    s=in_fix[index];
    switch (s)
{
    case ' ( ' : push (s) ; break
    case ' ) ' : t=pop ( );
    while (t !=' (')
     {
    postfix [pos]=t;
    pos++;
    t=pop();
    }
    break;
    case ' + ':
    case ' - ' :
    case ' * ' :
    case ' / ' :
    case ' ^ ' :

    while (prefix(stack[T] )>prefix (s) )
        {
        t=pop () ;
        postfix [pos]=t;
```

```
                        pos++;
                        }
                        push (s) ; break;
                        default : postfix[pos++]=s; break;
                        }
                        index++;
                        }
                        while (T>0)
                        {
                            t=pop();
                            postfix[pos++]=t;
                        }
                        postfix[pos++]='\0";
                        puts(postfix);
                        return;
                    }
```

OUTPUT :

Enter an infix expressions: a+b+c
Postfix Expression : abc++

Program 15.12.3

Write a program in C++ to illustrate the operations infix to postfix and infix to prefix on stack.

```
    #include <iostream.h>
    #define NULL 0
    class stack
    {
        private:
            struct node
            {
                char data;
                node *next;
            };
            node *head,*temp,*p;
        public:
            stack();
            ~stack();
        void push(char);
        char pop(void);
        char tos(void);
        };
```

```
        stack::stack()
        {
            head=NULL;
            temp=NULL;
            p=NULL;
        }
        stack::~stack( )
        { }
        void stack::push(char c)
        {
            temp=new node;
            temp->data=c:
            if (head==NULL)
            {
                head=temp;
                temp->next=NULL;
            }
            else
            {
                temp->next=head;
                head=temp;
            }
        }
    char stack::pop(void)
    {
        char retval=' ';
        p=new node;
        p=head;
        if(head==NULL)
        {
            cout<<"\n Stack is empty";
            return retval;
        }
        else
        {
            head=head->next;
            retval=p->data;
            delete p;
        }
            return (retval);
    }
```

```
char stack::tos(void)
{
    return head->data;
}
```

For the Infix notation A/B–C+D*E the Postfix notation will be AB/CDE*+ we have to scan from right to left in the infix notation.

Program 15.12.4
Write necessary functions in C++ to convert infix expression to postfix expression using stack operation.

```
//  program to convert infix expression to postfix
//  expression by using stack implementation.
#include <string.h>
#include <iostream.h>
#include <ctype.h>
#include "stack.h"
int weightage (char c)
{
    if (c=='+' || c==' - ')
        return 1;
    else if (c=='*' || c=='/')
        return 2;
    else
        return 3;
}
int is low (char c char d)
{
    if (weightage(c) <weightage(d))
        return 1;
    else
        return 0;
}
int isoperator (char c)
{
    switch (c)
    {
        case ' + ':
        case ' - ' :
        case ' / ' :
        case ' ^ ' :
                    return 1;
```

```
        default :
                return 0;
    }
}
void main ()
{
    char iput[20]oput[20],c;
    int len, j,k;
    stack stackobj;
    cout <"\n ENTER INFIX EXPRESSION ";
    cin.getline(iput.20);
    len=strlen(iput);
    iput[len]=')';
    iput [++len] ='\0';
    j=k=0;
    stackobj.push ('(');
    do
    {
        c=iput[j];
        if(isalpha(c))
    {
        oput[k]=c;
        k++;
    }
    else if (c=='(')
        stackobj.push (c);
    else if (isoperator(c))
    {
        while (isoperator(stackobj.tos()) &&islow(c,stackobj.tos()))
        {
            oput[k]=stackobj.pop();
            k++;
        }
        else if (c==')')
        {
            while (stackobj.tos() !='(')
            {
                oput[k]=stackobj.pop();
                k++;
                }
                stackobj.pop();
            }
```

```
            j++;
        }while (stackobj.tos() ! NULL);
        oput[k]='\0';
        cout <<"\n POSTFIX FORM IS "<<oput;
    }
```

OUTPUT :

ENTER INFIX EXPRESSION Y + Z
POSTFIX FORM IS YZ+

Note : The prefix for this expression will be +YZ using infix to prefix program.

Program 15.12.5

Write a program in C++ to convert infix to prefix a given expression using stack operation.

```
#include <iostream.h>
#include <string.h>
#include <ctype.h>
#include "stack.h"
int weightage (char c)
{
    if (c==' ')
        return 0;
    else if (c=='+' ||c=='-')
        return 1;
    else if (c=='*' ||c=='/')
        return 2;
    else if (c=='^')
        return 3;
    else
        return 4;
    }
    int is low (char c, char d)
    {
        if (weightage(c) <weightage(d))
            return 1;
        else
            return 0;
    }
    int isoperator (char c)
    {
        switch (c)
        {
            case '+';
```

```
		case '-';
		case '*';
		case '/';
		case '^';
				return 1;
		default :
				return 0;
	}
}

	void main ( )
{
		char iput[20]oput[20],c,c1;
		char rev_alp[20],oparr[20];
		int len,j,ki,op;
		stack stackobj;
		cout<"\n ENTER INFIX EXPRESSION *;
		cin.getline (iput,20);
		len=strlen(iput);
		iput[len]='\0';
		j=0;
		for (i=0;i<len;i++)
		{
			if (isoperator (iput[i]))
				stackobj.push (iput[i]);
		}
	for(i=len-1,i=0; i>=0 ; i—)
	{
		if (toupper(iput[i])>='A' &&toupper(iput[i]))<='Z')
		{
			rev_alp[j]=iput[i];
			j++;
		}
}
rev_alp[j]='\0';
j=k=0;
oput[k++]=rev_alp[j++];
oput[k++]=rev_alp[j++];
c=stackobj.pop( );
while (stackobj.tos( ) != NULL)
{
	c1=stackobj.pop( );
```

```
        if (c1==')')
        {
            op=c;
            c=' ';
        }
        if (c1=='(')
            c=op;
        if(islow(c,c1))
        {
            if(rev+alp[j]
            {
            oput[k]=rev_alp[j++};
            k++;
            }
            if (isoperator(c1))
            {
                oput[k]=c1;
                k++;
            }
        }
        else
        {
            if (isoperator(c1))
            stackobj.push(c1);
            if(isoperator(c))
            {
                oput[k]=c;
                k++;
            }
            c=' ';
        }
    }
    //while end
        oput[k++]rev_alp[j];
        oput[k]='\0';
        i=k-1;
        cout <<"\n PREFIX FORM IS : ";
        while (i>=0)
        {
            cout<<oput[i];
            i--;
        }
    }
```

OUTPUT :

ENTER INFIX EXPRESSION Y + Z
PREFIX FORM IS +YZ

15.13. RECURSION :

The recursion process is a little bit touch, but if we keep track of the execution sequence of a program, then it is easy to understand. Recursion is one of the most dominant tools used in the programming technique. There are various situations when we need to execute a block of statements for a number of times depending on the condition. Here recursion is useful. Recursion is used to solve problems that have iterations in reverse order. Data structures also support recursion. For example, tree supports recursion. Various programs are solved with recursion. A major application of recursion is game programming, where a series of steps can be solved with recursion. Recursion is a process in which a function calls to itself. Recursion is of two types.

1) **Direct recursion**
2) **Indirect recursion**

When a function calls itself this type of recursion is direct recursion. In this type, only one function is involved. In indirect recursion two functions call each other. In indirect recursion a function calls another function and then the called function calls the calling function.

Fig.15.18 describes direct and indirect recursion.

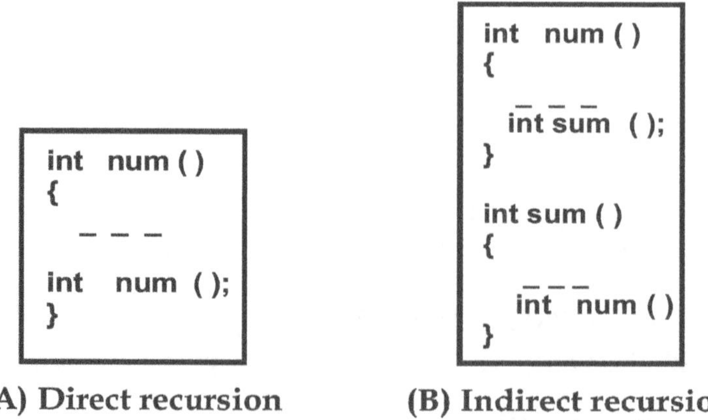

(A) Direct recursion **(B) Indirect recursion**

Fig.15.18 Types of Recursion

Recursion is one of the applications of stack. Stacks have been explained earlier in this chapter. There are several problems whose solutio would be lengthy without recursion.

The programming languages like C and C++ allow user-defined functions. Functions in the programming languages are very useful, because by using a function a separate block of statements can be defined. This block can be invoked a number of times anywhere in the program. A function obtaining a call to itself or another function and which eventually calls another function is known as a recursive function.

Two essential conditions should be satisfied by a recursive function. First, every time a function calls itself directly or indirectly, the function should have a condition to stop the recursion. Otherwise, an infinite loop is generated that will halt the system. Some people think that recursion is a needless luxury in a programming language. Using iteration one can solve the problems. However, in programming in some situations there is no substitute for recursion.

There are some kind of problems associated with a recursive function that do not present in the non-recursive function. The recursive function can be invoked by itself or any other function. **To ensure execution of recursion it is very essential for the function to save the return address in order to return at the proper location. In addition, the function has to save the formal and local variables.**

Program 15.13.1

Write a program in C to calculate the factorial of a given number using recursion.

```
# include <stdio.h>
# include <conio.h>
int fact (int);                    /*function prototype*/
void main ()
{
      int num,f;
      clrscr ();
      printf ("\n Enter a number : ");
      scanf (" %d", &num);
      f=fact (num);
      printf ("\n Factorial of (%d) is (%d)",num f);
}
int fact (int f)
{
      if (f==1) return f;
      else    return f*fact (f-1);
}
```

OUTPUT :

Enter a number : 4
Factorial of (4) is (24)

* * *

COMPREHENSION - 15

Note : By answering all the questions given in this comprehension one can answer any objective type of questions easily whatever be the form of the question. Answers for these questions can be obtained by going through the topics in this chapter carefully.

1. What is a Stack? What are its uses?
2. What is the policy of Stack?
3. Explain with a diagram the operation of a Stack.
4. Explain Stack related terms
5. What is the correspondence between a linked list and Stack?
6. Explain the terms Stack Overflow and Stack Underflow.
7. What are the normal operations performed on a Stack? Explain.
8. What are the ways of implementing a Stack?
9. Explain the static implementation of stack using arrays.
10. Explain the Dynamic implementation of stack using pointers
11. What are the relative merits and demerits in static and dynamic implementation of Stack?
12. How do you insert and delete elements in a Stack in dynamic implementation?
13. What is a Queue? When is it used?
14. What is the Queue Policy?
15. In what way a Queue is different from Stack?
16. Explain Queue and its policy with the help of diagrams.
17. What are the ways of implementing a Queue? Explain.
18. Explain the static implementation of a Queue using arrays.
19. Explain the Dynamic implementation of Queue using pointers.
20. What are the relative merits and demerits in static and dynamic implementation of a Queue?
21. Explain insertion and deletion operations in Queue.
22. What is a circular Queue? Where is it used?
23. How do you insert and delete elements in a circular Queue?
24. How do you determine whether a circular Queue is full?
25. How do you insert and delete elements in a circular Queue that is full?
26. What is priority queue?

27. What are the operations to be supported by a priority queue?
28. How is priority queue similar to a queue?
29. What are the different types of implementation of priroty queue?
30. What is the effect of different data structures on priority queue?
31. What is the difference between a priority queue and heap structure?
32. Explain the use of a priority queue for sorting.
33. Explain the use of a sorting algorithm to make a priority queue.
34. Explain the applications of priority queues.
35. How can a priority queuing can be used to manage limited resources such as bandwidth on a transmission line from a network router?
36 Explain the use of priority queue for discrete event simulation.
37. What is the use of a priority queue in Dijkstra's algorithm?
38. What is the use of a priority queue in A* and SMA* search algorithms?
39. What is difference between DEQUEUE (as Noun) or DEQUEUE (as verb) ?
40. Explain the naming conventions of deque.
41. What is the difference between a normal queue and deque?
42. What are the subtypes of deque?
43. Explain the operaton of deque in different languages.
44. Explain the two common ways to implement deque efficiently.
45. Write about the languages support for deque.
46. What is the complexity of deque?
47. Explain the applications of deque.
48. Explain representation and execution of Arithmetic expressions using Stack operations.
49. Explain infix, prefix and postfix representation of arithmetic expression.
50. What is the use of applying infix, prefix and postfix notations?
51. Explain the conversion of different fix forms like prefix, infix and postfix.
52. What are the merits and demerits of evaluation of postfix expressions?
53. Explain the conversion of infix expression to postfix expression.
54. In what way operator precedence helps in evaluating post fix expression using Stack. Explain with example.
55. Explain the evaluation of the expression (P+Q)*R in postfix using Stack.
56. What is Regression?
57. Explain the types of regression with examples.

* * *

EXERCISE - 15

Note : By answering all the questions given in this exercise one can answer subjective type of questions easily including problems. The worked examples in the chapter may help in solving these questions.

1. Explain Stack and Queue. Distinguish between them with examples.
2. Compare the advantages and disadvantages of implementing Stack as an Array and Stack as a linked list.
3. Explain the representation of Stacks and Queues.
4. Explain with real life examples in detail the Push and Pop operations of a Stack.
5. Explain Recursion and its classifications.
6. Explain Infix, Prefix and Postfix representation of expressions
7. Explain conversions between Infix, Prefix and Postfix representation of expressions.
8. Explain insertion and deletion operations with Stack and Queues.
9. What is meant by Circular Queue? How is it different from a simple Queue?
10. The stack is based on the rule

    a) First-in-last-out　　b) Last-in-first-out

    c) Both (a) and (b)　　d) First-in-first-out
11. The push ( ) operation is used

    a) To insert an element　　b) To remove an element

    c) To move an element　　d) All of the above
12. The pop operation removes

    a) The element lastly inserted　　b) First element of the stack

    c) Any element randomly　　d) None of the above
13. The top pointer is increased

    a) When push ( ) operation is done　　b) When pop ( ) operation is done

    c) Both (a) and (b)　　d) None of the above
14. A stack holds elements equal to its capacity and if push is performed then such a situation is called

    a) Stack overflow　　b) Stack underflow

    c) Illegal operation　　d) None of the above
15. The prefix notation is also called

    a) Polish notation　　b) Postfix notation

    c) Infix notation　　d) None of the above

16. From the given option which one is not a stack application?
    a) Template b) Recursion
    c) Reverse string d) Conversion of number
17. An expression containing more than one operation is solved according to
    a) Priority of operators b) Priority of operands
    c) From left to right d) Right to left
18. The following brackets change the priority
    a) ( ) b) [ ] c) { } d) &
19. The postfix notation is also called
    a) Reverse polish notation b) Polish notation
    c) Prefix notation d) Postfix notation
20. Queue follows the rule
    a) FIFO b) LIFO c) LILO d) FILO
21. The rear end of the queue is used
    a) To insert an element b) To remove an element
    c) Both (a) and (b) d) None of the above
22. When an element is inserted in a queue, the position rear
    a) Increases b) Decreases
    c) Remains constant d) None of the above
23. Explain a priority queue and its applications
24. Explain the different ways of implementation of a priority queue.
25. Explain the relationship between the priority queues and sorting algrithms
26. What is a deque? What are its naming conventions?
27. Explain the distinctions and subtypes of deque?
28 A stack is to be implemented using an array. The associated declarations are

```
int stack [100] ;
int stacktop = 0;
```

which of the statements mentioned below performs push operation
    a) stack [stacktop++]=value b) stack[+stacktop]=value
    c) stack[stacktop--]=value d) stack[-stacktop]=value
29. Assume that a stack is available for pushing and popping elements. Given an input sequence 1,2,3 (3 is the first element), which of the following output sequences is NOT possible from the input in each case the rightmost element shown is the first to be popped from the stack.
    a) 2 3 1 b) 3 2 1 c) 3 1 2 d) 1 2 3

30. State whether the following statements are true or false.
    a) Items in a stack exist in the same order in which they had entered the stack
    b) Stacks are rarely used in computer applications
    c) Writing a value to the stack is called as a pop operation, whereas reading a value from it is called as a push operation
    d) Once an item is popped from the stack, it is no longer available
    e) Pop operation increments the stack counter by one to see if the stack is empty.
    f) The stack can be implemented using the dynamic memory management techniques.
31. Write a program in C to perform the following operations in a queue as the queue is represented as a linea r linked list data structure.
32. Design a method for keeping two stacks within a single linear array S in such a way that neither stack overflows until all the array is used and an entire stack is never shifted to a different location within the array. Write C routines push1, push2, pop1 and pop2 to manipulate the two stacks. (Hint : The two stacks grow towards each other.)
33. Write a single C program to accept an input string of an arithmetic expression in infix and create and print the prefix and as well as postfix forms of that given input string of expression.
34. Write a single C program to perform each of the following
    a) Create a queue of N elements
    b) reverse the queue, so that the last element becomes the first, and so on
    c) Insert an element in between i-th and i+1 -th elements of the original queue
    d) Delete the k-th element from the original queue
    e) Print the contents of r-th element of the queue after the third and fourth operations.
35. Write a single C program by iterative and recursive procedures to evaluate a* b by using addition, where a and b are non-negative integers.
36. Write a program in C++ to demonstrate push ( ) and pop ( ) operations using class and member functions.
37. Write a program to enter an integer. Reverse the digits of the integer. Use stack mechanism.
38. Write a program to implement stack operations push and pop with a pointer.
39. Write a program to perform the following operations

    a) Push b) Pop c) Stack underflow
    d) Stack overflow e) Display all elements
40. Write a Program in C++ to convert an input expression A+B into postfix form.
41. Write a program to implement a stack with a two-dimensional array. Perform push ( ) and pop ( ) operations.

* * *

CHAPTER - 16
OPERATIONS ON DATA STRUCTURES
(SEARCHING AND SORTING)

16.1 INTRODUCTION :

From the large database of records maintained to search for a particular record and to modify its contents it becomes a difficult job, unless there is a method for quick se arching of the records. If the records are unsorted, it is more difficult to find the record. Hence this process of identifying a record and modifying in its contents becomes easier if we have two methods, one for searching and the other for sorting. Searching and sorting also helps in not only modifying a record but in creating new records at the appropriate place and also in deleting a particular record.

In short, searching is a process in which given record is searched from the set of records. Sorting is a process in which records are arranged in a particular order like ascending or descending order. *A group of fields is called a record. For example, consider the following structure.*

```
struct employee
{
int employee_id;
char *name;
int age;
float salary;
} programmer;
```

We are familiar with the above declarations and definitions. The object s contains three fields as described in the structure. A database is a collection of different fields. Each record contains the different fields, depending upon the structure defined. Sorting can be done on any one or a combination of one or more fields. Suppose, we sorted the records based on name. Then, the field name will be the key field. A record is quickly searched in a sorted database. Thus, sorting and searching are very useful concepts of data structure.

16.2. SEARCHING :

Searching is a technique of finding accurate location of an element in the given data list or set of the elements such as an array, list or trees. For example, consider an array of 10 elements. These data elements are stored in successive memory locations. We need to search an element from an array. In the searching operation, if we want to find a particular element, say n then n is compared with all the elements of an array and when the exact match is found then the search process is terminated. In case no such element exists in the array, the entire list of arrays is searched.

One of the important applications of array processing is searching. We can search a particular element present in a list or in a record. Here the element may also be referred as key. **Searching is very useful in sorting the data and presenting the data in a particular fashion like ascending order or descending order or any other order.** Before going into methods of sorting here we will discuss some of the important searching techniques namely sequential search and binary search.

If the given element is present in the collection of elements or array then the search process is said to be successful as given in Fig.16.1. It means that the given element belongs to the array. The search is said to be unsuccessful if the given element does not exist in the array as given in Fig.16.2. It means that the given element does not belong to the array or collection of the items.

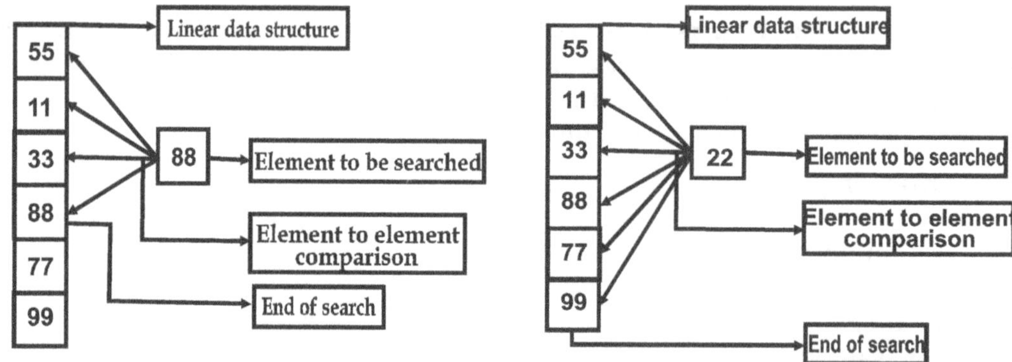

Fig.16.1. A Successful search **Fig.16.2. An unsuccessful search**

The complexity of any searching method is determined from the number of comparisons in order to find the element from the collection of the elements. The time required for the operation is dependent on the complexity of the operation or algorithm.

Searching can be classified into following two types :

1. **Linear search (sequential)**
2. **Binary search (non sequential)**

16.2.1. Linear Search or Sequential Search :

First let us explore sequential search (linear search). **In linear search process the required element is searched linearly throughout the array. The required element is found out then we can do our required operation on that. It takes a long time if the array size is large.** But this search operation is very simple.

The linear search is a method of searching an element in a list in sequence. The expected element is to be searched in the entire data structure in a sequential method from the starting to the last element. The linear search is a conventional method of searching data. Though it is straightforward, it has serious limitations. It consumes more time and reduces the retrieval rate of the system. The linear or sequential name implies that the items are stored in a systematic manner. The linear search can be applied on sorted or unsorted linear data structure.

Linear search method can be followed from Fig.16.3.

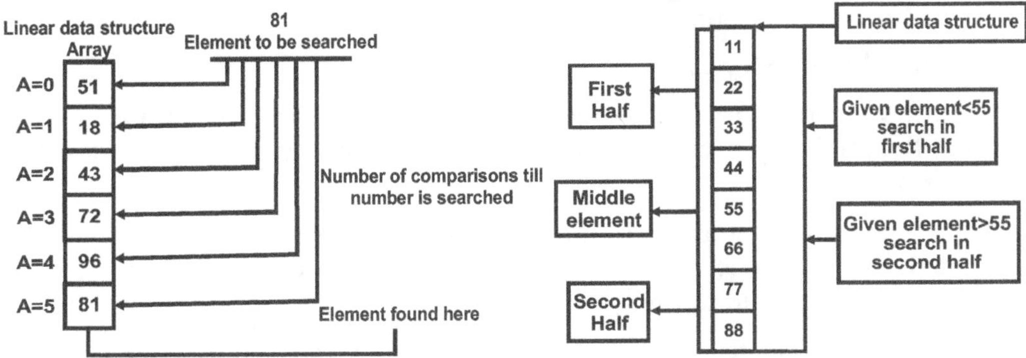

Fig.16.3 A Successful Linear Search

Fig.16.4. A Binary search to locate 77

16.2.1a. Time complexity of linear search : Time complexity of linear search is O (n)

16.2.1b. Comparison of linear search with other search techniques

i) It is easier to implement

ii) Requires more number of comparisons

16.2.2. Binary Search :

The binary search approach is different from the linear search. Here, search of an element is not passed in sequence as that of linear fashion. **In binary search two partitions of list are made and then the given element is searched in the appropriate half** Hence, it creates two parts of the lists known as binary search Fig.16.4 illustrates the operation of the binary search.

Binary search is quicker than the linear search. However, it can be applied only on sorted data structure. Before applying binary search, the linear data structure must be sorted in either ascending or descending order. The binary search is unsuccessful if the elements are unordered. **The binary search is based on the approach divide-and-conquer.** In binary search, the element is compared with the middle element. If the expected element falls before the middle element, the left portion is searched otherwise right portion is searched.

For an electrician to find out the fused bulb in a serial set normally uses the binary search technique. It is well known that if any one of the bulbs gets fused, then the whole system won't function. To find out the location of the fused bulb, after passing current the electrician arbitrarily chooses a position and he tests whether the current flow is there or not. If the current flow is there in that position, then he moves forward to some extent and he checks the current flow. If not, he looks backward to some extent and he tests the flow of current. This is the technique we employ in Binary search operation.

In this method, first of all we have to sort elements present in the array. Then the element to search is received from user. Here the terms top and bottom are used to represent first and last position of an array. **The mid position is found out by using following method.**

mid = (bottom+top)/2

Now we can compare the element present in the 'mid' position with the element to search. After comparison we can arrive at any one of the following conditions.

1. If the search element is less than the element present in the mid position, then there is no need to check elements in the upper half of array. Now we have to assign mid to top.
2. If the search element is greater than the value present in the mid position, then our search element is only in the upper half and we can eliminate elements present in the lower half. Now the value of bottom is 'mid'.
3. If the search element is equal to the value present in the mid position, then the search operation is complete.

This process is executed repeatedly on the non-executed portion of the array until the search element is found or if we eliminate all elements from search then we can say the search element is not present in the given array. Since, in this method we eliminate elements by half each time this method is fast when compared to sequential search.

Even though this method is comparatively fast enough, the input data to be sorted before search operation and this may be an overhead of this method.

16.2.2.a. Time complexity of binary search : Time complexity of binary search is O (log n / log2)

16.2.2b. Comparison of binary search with other techniques

i) It requires few comparisons compared to linear search.
ii) It works only on sorted data.
iii) It is difficult compare to linear search

Note : Binary search can be extended to number of levels like dividing entire list into two halves. The half in which required number can be located will be divided into two halves again and search is carried on. This process can be repeated any number of times.

Program 16.2.1

Write a Program in C to search an element in a given array using Linear Search

```
#include <stdio.h>
#include<conio.h>
int main ( )
{
        int j, num [6], f;
        clrscr ();
        printf ("Enter the array elements : ") ;
        for (j=0;j<6;j++)
            scanf ("%d",&num[j]);
        printf ("Enter an element to search : ");
        scanf ("%d"&f);
        for (j=0;j<6;j++)
            if (f==num[j])
                break;
            if (j<6)
                {
                    printf ("The position of element %d is        : %d"f,++j);
                    printf ("\nThe number of iterations are       : %d",j);
                    }
                else printf ("\n Number is not found ");
                    getch ();
                    return 0;
                }
```

OUTPUT :

```
Enter the array elemens : 51  18  43  72  98  81
Enter an element to search : 72
The position of element 72 is  : 4
The number of iterations are : 4
```

Program 16.2.2.

Write a Program in C++ to search an element in a given array using Linear Search

```
#include<iostream>
#include<iomanip>
using namespace std;
class linearsearch
{
    private;
        int *x;
        int items;
```

```
    public;
        linearsearch(int);
        -linearsearch();
        void input (int []);
        int search(int);
};
linearsearch::linesearch(int n)
{
    items=n;
    x=new int[items];
}
linearsearch::~linearsearch( )
{
    delete [ ]x;
}
void linearsearch::input(int a[ ])
{
    for (int i=0;i<items;++i)
        x[i]=a[i];
}
int linearsearch::search(int number)
{
    for (int i=0;i<items;++i)
        if (number==x[i])
            return i;
    return 0;
}
void main ( )
{
    int elements [20],noofitems,temp;
    cout<<"\n Enter how many elements do you want to feed \n";
    com>>noofitems;
    cout<<"\n Enter "<<noofitems<<" elements";
    for(int i=0;i<noofitems;++i)
    cin>>elements[i];
    cout<<"\n Enter search number : ";
    cin>>temp;
    linearsearch linearsearchobj(noofitems);
    linearsearchobj.input(elements);
    int position=linearsearchobj.search(temp);
```

```
        if(position ! = 0)
        cout<<"\n Search number is present and its position : "<<position;
        else
            cout<<"\n Search number is not present ";
        cout<<endl;
    }
```

OUTPUT :

Enter how many elements do you want to feed
6
Enter 5 elements 51 18 43 72 98 81
Ener search number : 43
Search number is present and is position : 3
Enter how many elements do you want to feed
6
Enter 5 elements 51 18 43 72 98 81
Enter search number : 36
Search number is not present

Program 16.2.3.

Write a program in C to sort array elements using binary search.

```
#include <stdio.h>
#include <conio.h>

int main ( )
{
    int items[10], s=0,en,j,num,mid;
    clrscr ( );

    printf ("\n Enter number of elements : ");
    scanf ("%d",&n);

    for (j=0;j<n;j++)
    {
        printf ("Enter element %d : ",1+j);
        scanf ("%d", &items[j]);
    }

    printf ("\n Enter element to be searched :");
    scanf ("%d",&num);
    e=n-1;

    mid=(s+e)/2;
```

```
while (num!=items[mid] && s<=e)
{
if (num>items[mid] ) e=mid-1;
else s=mid+1;
mid=(s+e) /2;
}
if (num==items[mid] )
printf ("\n %d found at position %d ",num,++mid);
if (s>e) printf (" %d not found ", num);
getch ();
return 0;
}
```

OUTPUT :

Enter number of elements : 8
Enter element 1 : 11
Enter element 2 : 22
Enter element 3 : 33
Enter element 4 : 44
Enter element 5 : 55
Enter element 6 : 66
Enter element 7 : 77
Enter element 8 : 88

Enter element to be searched : 44
44 found at position 4

Enter element to be searched : 27
27 not found

Explanation :

In the above program array items [10] elements are declared. The user has to enter the expected number of elements in the list. The numbers are entered through the keyboard. The variable s keeps track of the starting of list and the variable e keeps track of end. The middle point is calculated with the formula mid=(s+e) / two; if the sum of (s+e) is an odd number then the result of divide operation gives float value. However all the operands of the equation are integers, the float value is converted to the lowest integer.

Program 16.2.4.

Write a program in C++ to sort array elements using binary search.

```
#include <iostream>
#include <iomanip>
using namespace std;
class binary search

{
	private;
		int *x;
		int items;
	public;
		binarysearch (int);
		-binary search();
		void sort(int[]);
		void input(int []);
		bool search(int);
		void display ();
};
binarysearch::binarysearch (int n)
{
	items=n;
	x=new int[items];
}
binarysearch::~binarysearch ()
{
	delete [ ]x;
}
	void binarysearch::input(int a[ ])
	{
		for (int i=0;i<items;++i)
		   x[i]=a[i];
		   sort(x);
	}
	void binarysearch::display ( )
	{
		cout<<"\n Sorted numbers are :\n";
		for (int i=0;i<items;++)
		cout<<setw(5)<<x[i];
	}
```

```
void binarysearch::sort(int x[ ];
{
    int swap=1;
    for (int i=0;i<items &&swap==1;++i)
    {
        swap=0;
        for(int j=0;j<items-(i+1);++j)
            if (x[j] < x[j+1])
            {
                int temp;
                temp=x[j];
                x[i]=x[j+1];
                x[j+1]=temp;
                swap=1;
            }
        }
    }
    boot binarysearch::search(int n)
    {
        int bottom=0;
        int top=items-1;
        int mid;
        while (top !=bottom+1)
        {
            mid=(bottom+top)/2;
            if (x[mid] <=n)
                bottom=mid;
            else
                top=mid;
        }
        if (x[bottom]==n)
            return true;
        else
            return false;
    }
    void main ( )
    {
        int element [100],noofitems;
        int temp;
        bool present ;
        cout<<"\n Enter how many elements do you want to feed\n";
```

```
        cin>>noofitems;
        cout <<"\n Enter" <<noofitems<<"elements";
        for(int i=0;<noofitems;++i)
            cin>>elements[i];
        binarysearch binarysearchobj(noofitems);
        binarysearchobj.input(elements);
        //binarysearchobj.sort(elements);
        binarysearchobj.display();
        cout<<"\n Enter search element :" ;
        cin>>temp;
        present=binarysearchobj.search(temp);
        if(present)
            cout<<"\n Search number is present :" ;
        else
            cout <<"\n Search number is not present :" ;
        cout<<endl;
    }
```

OUTPUT :

Enter how many elemens do you want to feed

8

Enter 8 elements

11 44 33 22 77 55 66 88

Sorted numbers are :

11 22 33 44 55 66 77 88

Enter search element : 44

Search number is present :

Press any key to continue

Enter how many elements do you want to feed

7

Enter 7 elements

11 33 55 66 22 44 77

Sorted numbers are :

11 22 33 44 55 66 77

Enter search element : 49

Search number is not present :

16.2.3. Features of Binary Search :

1. Since in binary search method we eliminate elements by half each time this method is fast when compared to sequential search.
2. Time complexity of binary search is of the order (Logn/log2). To find a particular record in a set of n records only logn/log2 comparisons will be required.

16.2.4. Comparison of Binary Search with other Search Techniques :

a. It requires very few number of comparisons as compared to linear search.
b. It works on sorted data only.
c. It is a little hard to implement than linear search.

16.3. TREES AND GRAPHS :

Trees or graphs are used for representing data in a particular fashion making it easier to search any particular data and also the path of search leading to the goal of the identification of the data. In the process of search one of the means of finding an efficient search is the definition of a heuristic function (a relevant function) based on whose value the path of reaching the goal can be decided.

A graph is a set of nodes and arcs. Nodes representing the data location and arcs representing the correction between different data nodes. Graph is particularly useful to avoid repetition of the parts which are already searched.

16.3.1. Trees :

Trees are a data structure used to reflect a hierarchical relationship among data items. Indicative of this hierarchy is the parent-child terminology used to express the relationship between items on successive levels of the tree. Trees are by nature recursive structures, with each node of a tree being itself the root of a smaller, embedded subtree. **The difference between Trees and the data structures is that trees are non-linear data structures whereas linked lists, stacks and queues are linear data structures.** In tree data structure, the superior node is called as a **Root node** and the later are called as **child nodes.** The collection of all these nodes in the following method implies a tree structure.

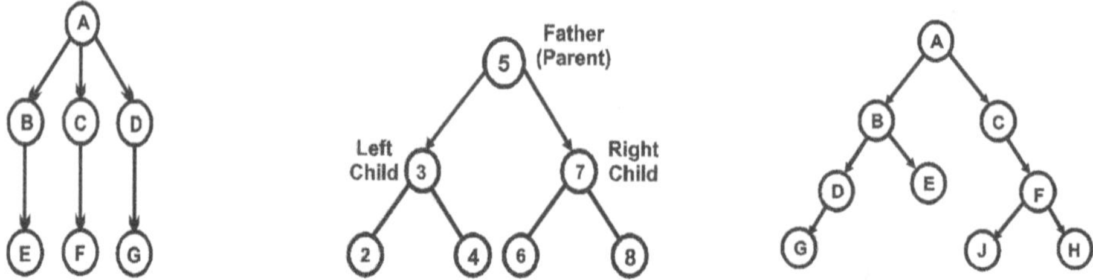

Fig.16.5. Representation of a Tree Fig. 16.6 (a) A Binary Tree with its components Fig.16.6 (b). A different form of a binary tree

Thus a tree is type of data structure in which each element is attached to one or more elements directly beneath it. The connections between elements are called branches. The elements at the very bottom of an inverted tree are called leaves. Inverted trees are the data structures used to represent hierarchical file structures. In this case, the leaves are files and the other elements above the leaves are directories. *Trees are also often called inverted trees because they are normally drawn with the root at the top.*

16.3.2. Binary Trees :

A binary tree is a fixed set of nodes. It may be empty or divided into three disjoint subsets. The first subset is called as root of the tree. It contains a single element. The other two subsets are called as right and left subtrees of the main tree. The left and right branches can be vacant as shown in figs (16.6 (a) and 16.6 (b)).

Binary trees are trees in which each parent may have at most two child nodes. Although this seems to be a major restriction, binary trees find a wide range of applications. *Three such applications are the representation of algebraic expressions, one-key tables, and priority queues.* Binary tree can be implemented by two ways and they are:

a. **Static Linear representation of binary trees using arrays :** This method uses an array and requires no pointers and it is not dynamic

b. **Dynamic Linked representation of binary trees using pointers :** This method employs pointers and able to take advantage of C++'s dynamic memory allocation.

Thus, **Binary tree is a special kind of tree, which has at least 3 elements in the structure.** The first element is called as a **root** (basically binary tree is also called as binary rooted tree). The **root or parent node will have only 2 children namely left node and right node.** The value of the left child should be less than the root while right child value is greater than the root.

Let us now examine the fig. 16.6 (a) carefully. The value of root (parent) is 5 and the values of left and right Childs are 3 and 7 respectively. Now, when we trace by keeping left child as the parent (value is 3) we have two Childs with values 2 (left child) and 4 (right child). Similar method is applied to other nodes of right child also. On inspecting above example it is understood that all the values of left child are less than the parent and the values of right child are greater than the parent. Fig. 16.6 (b) represents another form of binary tree. As shown in that figure, the tree is formed with nine nodes named with alphabets. The first node at the top is called as root that is A. The nodes B and C are its left and right subtrees, respectively. If there is no subtree indicated it means an empty subtree. For example, the node d has no right subtree and node C has no left subtree.

The next of binary is A. The node B is the root of its right and left subtrees. Hence, A is called the father of B. B is called the left or right son of A. The node without branches is called as leaf. For example E, G, I and H are leaves.

a) Hierarchy of a Binary Tree :

Also, as per Fig. 16.7 which is the same as Fig.16.6 (b) the node A is grandparent of G and H is a descendant of C. The nodes B and C are brothers because their root is same A. In computer science, the tree data structure is represented with root at top and leaves at bottom.

The direction from leaves to root is called **up** and its reverse is called **down.** Traversing from leave to the root is called as **"climbing"** and its opposite is called as **"descending".**

The root node of a binary tree has level 0. All the subsequent nodes in the tree have level one greater than its father node. Depth of a binary tree is the highest level of any leaf of the tree. Leaf of a binary tree is the node, which does not have any daughter nodes. Two nodes are called brothers if they are derived from the same father node.

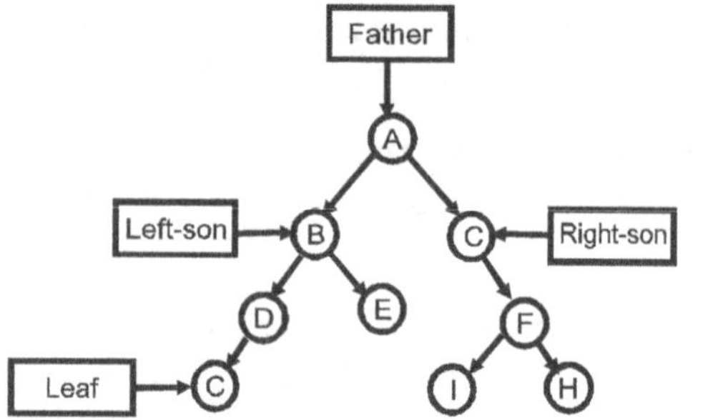

Fig.16.7. Hierarchy of a tree **Fig.16.8. Strictly binary ree**

b) Strictly binary tree :

In Fig. 16.8 a strictly binary tree is shown. **When every node with no-leaf in a binary tree has filled left and right subtrees, the tree is called a strictly binary tree.** In that figure nodes A C, and D each gave two nodes whereas Fig.16.7 does not show a strictly binary tree because the nodes C and E have one son only. The binary tree also contains levels. The root of the tree has level 0 and the level of the other nodes is always one greater than that of its father. As per the figure the node H is at level 3 and node E is at level 2. The depth of the binary tree is the highest level of leaf in the tree.

The node of a binary tree has three fields. The first field represents data and second and third fields contain information on left and right sons of the node.

c) Complete Binary Tree :

A complete binary tree given in fig. 16.9 has three fields. **In a completely binary tree all the nodes have two sons (branches) excluding the last node.**

A complete binary tree has all its leaves at the same level For a complete binary tree, the following formula is important

$N = 2^{n+1}-1$

where

N is the number of nodes; n is the depth of the tree

d) Extended binary tree : When every node of the binary tree contains zero or two (left and right) sons it is called an extended binary tree or a 2-tree. An extended binary tree is shown in figure 16.10.

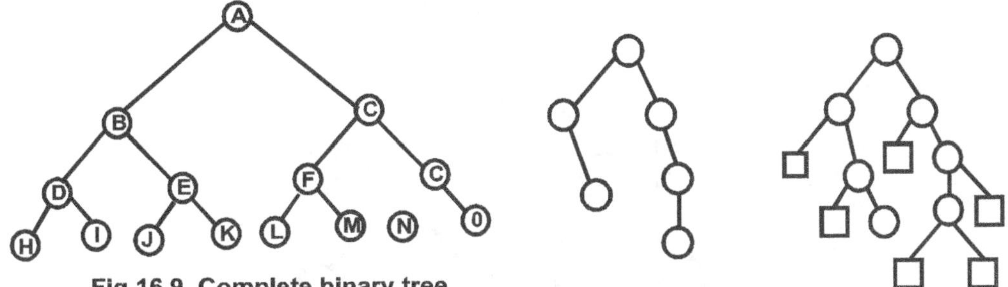

Fig.16.9. Complete binary tree

Fig.16.10. Extended binary tree

The extended nodes are indicated by a square box. Maximum nodes in a binary tree have one son either left or right. By adding one or more son, the tree can be extended. The extended binary tree is very useful for representation of algebraic expressions. The left and right sons denote operands and father indicates operators.

16.3.3. Binary Tree Representation : Like a list, a binary tree can also be implemented in two ways. They are :

1) Linear representation or Static implementation using arrays
2) Linked representation or Dynamic implementation using pointers (linked list)

Recall that the node of a binary tree has three members; one is data variable and other two are pointers. The second pointer member points to the lest son and the third pointer member points to the right son.

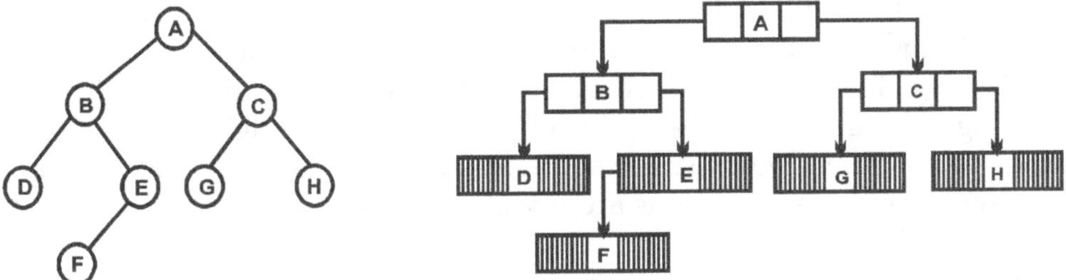

Fig. 16.10 (a) Binary Tree representation **Fig.16.10 (b) Binary Tree Using Linked representation**

The structure for a tree node using linked representation would be as follows

```
struct node
{
    int num;
    struct node *ls;        /*self referential structure*/
    struct node *rs         /* self referential structure*/
}
```

The pointers *ls and *rs point to the structure node. The pointer *ls contains the address of the left son and rs is the pointer to the right son. If there is no left son and right son then the pointers would be NULL.

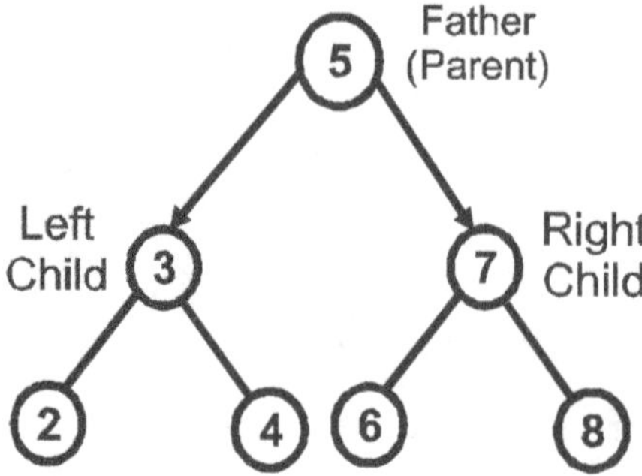

Fig. 16.11. A Binary Tree with its components

1) Insertion in a binary tree :

For insertion, it checks whether the root of the tree is empty if so make the new element as the root. Otherwise, check whether the value of the new element is greater than or less than the root. If it is greater than, then move towards the right child and apply the above step and if not do, the above proceedings through the left child.

2) Deletion from a binary tree :

To delete an element we have to anchor the element. For this we have to compare the given element with the root, if they are equal then move the rooted element and make the left child as root, if not find the path to traverse like insertion and repeat the above procedures.

16.3.4. Traversing Binary Trees :

As discusses earlier, three parameters are needed for the formation of binary tree. Passing through every node of the tree is called traversing. Therefore, traversing of the tree means traversing of the node, left and right subtrees. Assume that the root is indicated by O left subtree as I, and right subtree as R. Then, the following traverse combinations are possible. There are three types of traversal in a binary tree.

1. **Inorder :** In the inorder traversal, the nodes in the left subtree are processed first, followed by the root node, and finally the nodes in the right subtree of the root.
2. **Pre-order :** In the preorder traversal, the current root node is processed, followed by the root node, and finally the nodes in the right subtree of the root.
3. **Post-order :** In the post order traversal, all nodes in the left subtree of the current root are recursively processed. Then all nodes in the right subtree are processed, and the root itself is processed last.

Refer into fig.16.12 and 16.13 denoting root as 'O' left sub-tree as 'L' and right sub-tree as 'R' the different possible traversal tree are :

1) ORL:ROOT:RIGHT-LEFT
2) **OLR**:ROOT:LEFT-RIGHT ..... **Pre-Order**
3) **LOR:**LEFT-ROOT:RIGHT ..... **In-order**
4) **LRO**:LEFT-RIGHT-ROOT ..... **Post-Order**
5) ROL:RIGHT-ROOT-LEFT
6) RLO:RIGHT-LEFT-ROOT

From the above six methods only three are standard and are discussed as follows. **The right subtree is always traversed after the left subtree. Hence, the OLR is preorder, LOR is inorder, and LRO is postorder.**

Among the three traversals, the **inorder traversal is critical in the binary tree implementation of a one-key table because the order in which it visits nodes corresponds precisely to the ordering of items as first, second, third, within the list represented by the tree.**

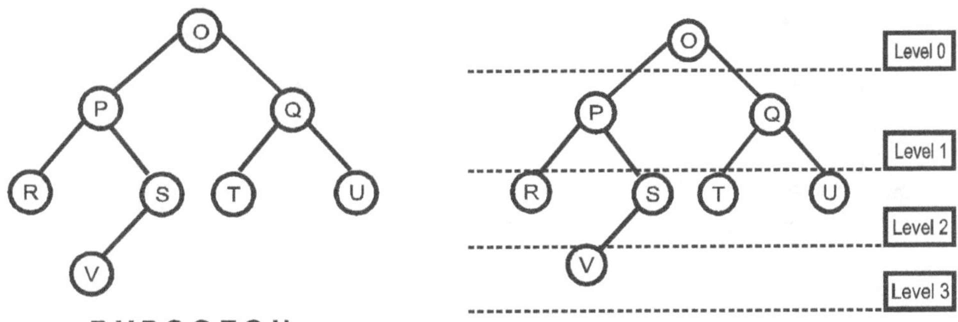

R-V-P-S-O-T-Q-U
Fig.16.12. A model tree used to explain Tree Traversal

Fig. 16.13. Level order traversal

1) OLR traversal (preorder traversal of a binary tree)

Go to the root
Traverse the left subtree
Traverse the right subtrees

As per Fig. 16.12, the nodes are traversed in preorder as **O-P-R-V-S-Q-T-U**

2) LOR (inorder traversal of a binary tree)

Traverse the left subtree
Go to the root
Traverse the right subtree

As per Fig.16.12, the nodes are traversed in inorder as **R-V-P-S-O-T-Q-U.**

3) LRO (postorder traversal of a binary tree)

Traverse the left subtree
Traverse the right-subtree
Go to the root

As per Fig.16.12 the nodes are traversed in postorder as **V-R-S-P-T-U-Q-O.**

4) Level order traversal traversal of a binary tree : In this type of level order traversal, the nodes are accessed according to their levels as shown in Fig.16.13. The traversing starts from zero to n where n is the last level number.

As per Fig.16.13 nodes are traversed in level order as **O-P-Q-R-S-T-U-V.**

Program 16.3.1

Write a program in C to create a tree structure. Perform insert, delete, and traverse the elements with different methods.

```
# include <stdio.h>
# include <malloc.h>
# include <conio.h>
# include <process.h>
struct nodes
{
     int data;
     struct nodes *ls;
     struct nodes *rs;
} *tree;
     main ( )
{
     int insert (int);
     int del (int);
     int inorder (struct nodes *);
     int preorder (struct nodes *);
     int postorder (struct nodes *);
     int show (struct nodes*,int);
     int option, number;
     tree=0;
     clrscr ();
    while (1)
       {
            printf ("\n");
            printf ("1.Insert\n");
            printf ("2.Delete\n");
            printf ("3.Inorder Traversal\n");
```

```
        printf ("4.Preorder Traversal\n");
        printf ("5.Postorder Traversal\n");
        printf ("6.Display\n");
        printf ("7.Exit\n");
        printf ("Enter your option : ");
        scanf (" %d",&option);
            switch (option)
        {
        case 1:
        printf ("Enter the number (0 to exit) : ") ;
        while (1)
            {
                scanf (" %d",&number);
                if (number==0) break;
                insert (number);
            }
            break;
        case 2:
            printf ("Enter the number to be deleted : ");
            scanf (" %d",&number);
            del (number);
            break;
        case 3 :
            inorder (tree);
            break;
        case 4:
            preorder (tree);
            break;
        case 5:
            postorder (tree);
            break;
        case 6:
            show (tree,1);
            break;
        case 7 :
            exit (0);
            default :
            printf ("Wrong option\n");
        }
    }
}
```

```
search (int ele,struct nodes **p,struct nodes **1)
    {
        struct nodes *pr,*p_s;
        if (tree==0)
            {
                *1=0;
                *p=0;
                return 0;
            }
        if (ele==tree->data)
            {
                *1=tree;
                *p=0;
                return 0;
            }
        if (ele<tree->data)
            pr=tree->ls;
        else
            pr=tree->rs;
            p_s=tree;
        while(pr !=0)
            {
                if (ele==pr->data)
                    {       *l=pr;
                            *p=p_s;
                            return 0;
                    }
                p_s=pr;
                if(ele<pr->data)
                    pr=pr->ls;
                else
                    pr=pr->rs;
            }
        *l=0;
        *p=p_s;
        return 0;
        }
        insert (int ele)
{
        struct nodes *t,*father,*m_loc;
        search (ele,&father,&m_loc);
        if (m_loc!=0)
```

```
          {
               printf ("Item already present");
               return 0;
          }
               t=(struct nodes *) malloc (sizeof (struct nodes));
               t->data=ele;
               t->ls=0;
               t->rs=0;
          if(father=0)
               tree=t;
          else
               if (ele<father->data)
                    father->ls=t;
               else
                    father->rs=t;
          return 0;
}
     del (int ele)
{
     int a (struct nodes*,struct nodes*);
     int b(struct nodes*,struct nodes*);
     int c (struct nodes*,struct nodes*);
     struct nodes *father,*m_loc;
     if (tree==0)
          {
               printf("Tree is empty");
               return 0;
          }
     search(ele,&father,m_loc);
     if (m_loc==0)
          {
               printf("Item does not exists in tree");
               return 0;
          }
               if (m_loc->ls==0 &&m_loc->rs==0)
               a(father,m_loc);
     if(m_loc->ls !=0 && m_loc->rs==0)
     b(father,m_loc);
     if (m_loc->ls==0 && m_loc->rs !=0)
     b(father,m_loc);
     if (m_loc->ls !=0 && m_loc ->rs !=0)
     c (father,m_loc);
```

```
        free(m_loc);
        return 0;
}
    a (struct nodes *p, struct nodes *1)
{
        if (p==0) tree=0;
        else
        if (l==p->ls) p->ls=0;
        else            p->rs=0;
        return 0;
}
    b (struct nodes *p,struct nodes *1)
{
        struct nodes *son;
        if (1->ls !=0) son=1->ls;
        else son=1->rs;
        if (p==0 ) tree=son;
        else
        if ( l==p->ls) p->ls=son;
        else     p->rs=son;
        return 0;
}
    c (struct nodes *p,struct nodes *1)
{
        struct nodes *pr,*p_s, *suc,*p_r;
        p_s=1;
        pr=1->rs;
        while (pr-> ls!=0)
            {
                p_s=pr;
                pr=pr->ls;
            }
        suc=pr;
        p_r=p_s;
        if (suc->ls==0 && suc->rs==0)
        a (p_r,suc);
        else
        b(p_r,suc);
        if (p==0) tree=suc;
        else
        if(l==p->ls)        p->ls=suc;
```

```
        else p->rs=suc;
        suc->ls=1->ls;
        suc->rs=l->rs;
        return 0;
}
    preorder (struct nodes *pr)
{
        if (tree==0)
        {
            printf ("Tree is empty");
            return 0;
        }
        if (pr !=0)
            {
                printf (" %d ",pr->data);
                preorder (pr->ls);
                preorder (pr->rs);
            }
        return 0;
}
    inorder (struct nodes *pr)
{
        if (tree==0)
            {
                printf ("Tree is empty")'
                return 0;
            }
        if (pr !=0)
        {
            inorder (pr->ls);
            printf (" %d ",pr->data);
            inorder (pr->rs);
        }
    return 0;
}
    postorder (struct nodes *pr)
{
    if (tree==0)
        {
            printf ("Tree is empty") ;
            return 0;
        }
```

```
    if (pr !=0)
        {
            postorder(pr->ls);
            postorder (pr->rs);
            printf(" %d ",pr->data);
        }
    return 0;
}
    show (struct nodes *pr, int lev)
{
    int i;
    if (pr !=0)
        {
            show (pr->rs, lev+1);
            printf("\n");
            for (i = 0; i < lev; i++)
                    printf ("    ");
            printf ("%d", pr->data);
            show (pr->ls, lev++);
        }
        return 0;
}
```

OUTPUT :

1. Insert
2. Delete
3. Inorder Traversal
4. Preorder Traversal
5. Postorder Traversal
6. Display
7. Exit

Enter your option : 1
Enter the number (0 to exit): 100 200 300 400 500 700 0
Enter your option : 3
100 200 300 400 500 700

Program 16.3.2

Write a program in C++ to illustrate the 3 types of tree traversal - inorder, preorder and post order.

```
# include <iostream>
# include <iomanip>
# define NULL 0
using namespace std;
```

```
class tree
{
    private:
        struct node
        {
            int data;
            node *left;
            node *right;
        };
        node *root;
    public:
        tree ();
        ~tree();
        int empty();
        int insert(int);
        void preorder (node *);
        void postorder (node *);
        void inorder(node *);
        void printtree(int);
    };
    tree::tree ( )
    {
        root = new node;
        root->data=30;
        root->left=NULL;
        root->right=NULL;
    }
    tree::~tree( )
    { }
    int tree::empty ( )
    {
        return (root==NULL);
    }
    int tree::insert(int x)
    {
        node *p,*previous*current;
        p=new node;
        if(p==NULL)
            {
                cout<<"\n Out of memory";
                return 0;
            }
```

```
p-> data=x;
p->left=NULL;
p->right=NULL;
if(root==NULL)
    {
        root=p;
        return 1;
    }
        previous=NULL;
        current=root;
        while(current !=NULL)
        {
            previous=current;
            if(p->data<current->data)
            current=current->left;
            else
            current=current->right;
        }
    if(p->data <previous->data)
            previous->left=p;
    else
            previous->right=p;
    return 1;
}
void tree::printtree(int x)
{
    if (x==1)
        preorder(root);
    else if(x==2)
        inorder (root);
    else
        postorder(root);
}
void tree::inorder(node *p)
{
    if (p !=NULL)
        {
            inorder(p->left);
            cout <<setw(5)<<p->data;
            inorder(p->right);
        }
}
```

```
void tree::preorder(node *p)
{
        if (p !=NULL)
    {
        cout <setw(5)<<p->data;
        preorder(p->left);
        preorder(p->right);
    }
}
void tree::postorder (node *p)
{
        if (p !=NULL)
    {
        postorder(p->left);
        postorder(p->right);
        cout<<sets(5)<<p->data;
    }
}
void main ( )
{
    int choice no;
    tree treeobj.
    do
        {
            cout<"Insertion [1] \n:";
            cout<"Preorder [2] \n:";
            cout<"Inorder [3] \n:";
        cout<"Postorder [4] \n:";
        cout<<"Exit    [5] \n";
        cout <<"Enter your choice --> ";
        cin>>choice;
            switch (choice)
            {
        case 1 :
                cout <<"\n Enter the element to insert \n";
                cin>>no;
                treeobj.insert (no);
                break;
        case 2 :
                cout <<"\n The preorder elements are \n";
                treeobj.printtree (1);
                cout<endl;
                break;
```

```
        case 3:
                cout <<"\n The inorder elements are \n";
                treeobj.printtree (2);
                cout<endl;
                break;
        case 4:
                cout <<"\n The Postorder elements are \n";
                treeobj.printtree (3);
                cout<endl;
                break;
        default :
                cout <<"\n Bye ...\n";
                exit (0);
            }
        } while (choice <5);
    }
```

OUTPUT :

```
Insertion [1]
Preorder [2]
Inorder   [3]
Postorder [4]
Exit      [5]
Enter your choice --> 1
Enter the element to insert
15
15 is inserted  at the left
Insertion [1]
Preorder [2]
Inorder   [3]
Postorder [4]
Exit      [5]
Enter your choice --> 1
Enter the element to insert
50
50 is inserted  at the right
Insertion [1]
Preorder [2]
Inorder   [3]
Postorder [4]
Exit      [5]
Enter your choice --> 1
Enter the element to insert
20
```

```
20 is inserted  at the right
Insertion [1]
Preorder [2]
Inorder   [3]
Postorder [4]
Exit      [5]
Enter your choice --> 1
Enter the element to insert
40
40 is inserted at the left
Insertion [1]
Preorder [2]
Inorder   [3]
Postorder [4]
Exit      [5]
Enter your choice --> 2
The pre order elements are
30 15 20 50 40
Insertion [1]
Preorder [2]
Inorder   [3]
Postorder [4]
Exit      [5]
Enter your choice --> 3
The inorder elements are
15 20 30 40 50
Insertion [1]
Preorder [2]
Inorder   [3]
Postorder [4]
Exit      [5]
Enter your choice --> 4
The Post order elements are
20 15 40 50 30
Insertion [1]
Preorder [2]
Inorder   [3]
Postorder [4]
Exit      [5]
Enter your choice --> 5
Bye ....
```

16.4. MINIMUM SPANNING TREE :

Given a connected, undirected graph, a spanning tree of that graph is a subgraph that is a tree and connects all the vertices together. A single graph can have many different spanning trees. We can also assign a *weight* to each edge, which is a number representing how unfavorable it is, and use this to assign a weight to a spanning tree by computing the sum of the weights of the edges in that spanning tree. A **minimum spanning tree (MST)** or **minimum weight spanning tree** is then a spanning tree with weight less than or equal to the weight of every other spanning tree. More generally, any undirected graph (not necessarily connected) has a **minimum spanning forest**, which is a union of minimum spanning trees for its connected components.

One example would be a cable TV company laying cable to a new neighborhood. If it is constrained to bury the cable only along certain paths, then there would be a graph representing which points are connected by those paths. Some of those paths might be more expensive, because they are longer, or require the cable to be buried deeper; these paths would be represented by edges with larger weights. A *spanning tree* for that graph would be a subset of those paths that has no cycles but still connects to every house. There might be several spanning trees possible. A *minimum spanning tree* would be one with the lowest total cost.

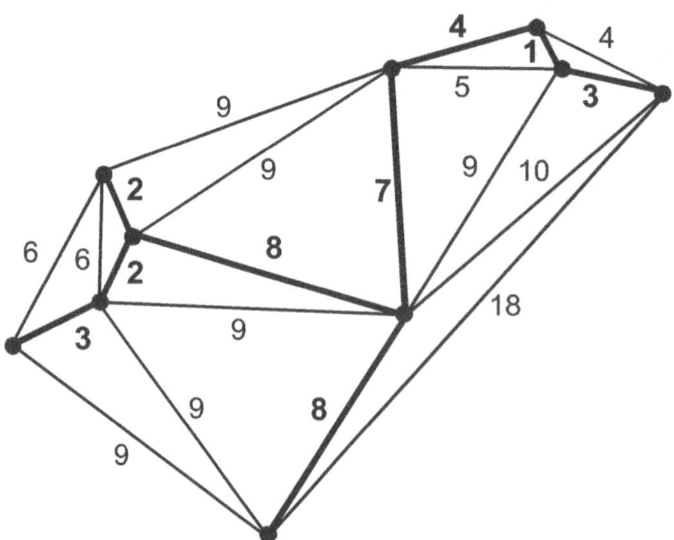

Fig.16.14. Spanning Tree

The minimum spanning tree of a planar graph. Each edge is labeled with its weight, which here is roughly proportional to its length.

Given a connected, undirected graph, a spanning tree of that graph is a subgraph that is a tree and having the following properties.

i) Possible multiplicity

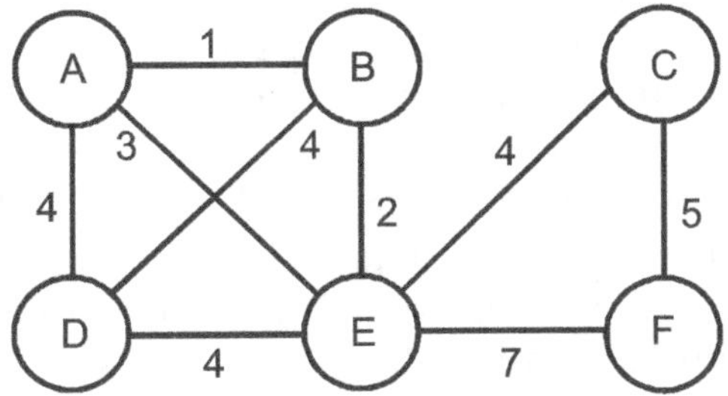

16.15 (a) Graph

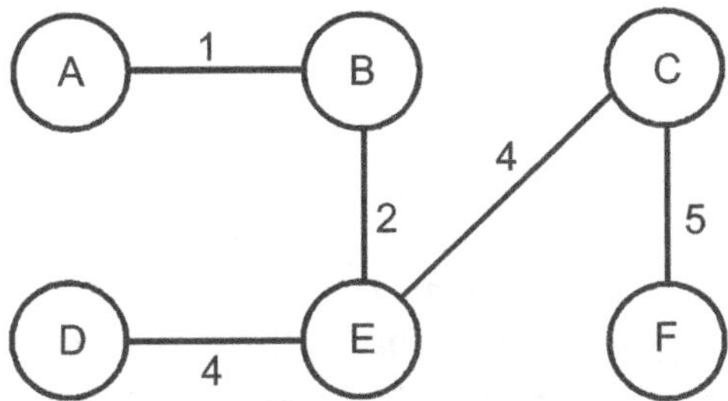

16.15 (b) One Spanning Tree

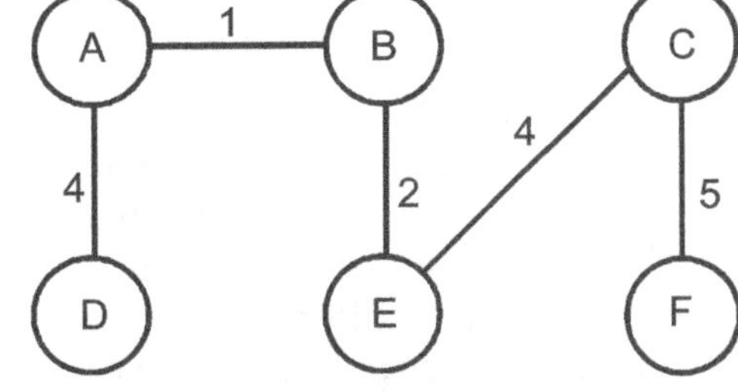

16.15 (c) Another spanning tree

This figure shows there may be more than one minimum spanning tree in a graph. In the figure, the two trees below the graph are two possibilities of minimum spanning tree of the given graph.

There may be several minimum spanning trees of the same weight having a minimum number of edges; in particular, if all the edge weights of a given graph are the same, then every spanning tree of that graph is minimum. If there are *n* vertices in the graph, then each tree has *n*-1 edges.

ii) Uniqueness :

If each edge has a distinct weight then there will be only one, unique minimum spanning tree. This can be proved by induction or contradiction. This is true in many realistic situations, such as the cable TV company example above, where it's unlikely any two paths have *exactly* the same cost. This generalizes to spanning forests as well.

A proof of uniqueness by contradiction is as follows. Say we have an algorithm that finds an MST (which we will call **A**) based on the structure of the graph and the order of the edges when ordered by weight. (Such algorithms do exist, see below.)

1. Assume MST **A** is not unique.
2. There is another spanning tree with equal weight, say MST **B**.
3. Let **e1** be an edge that is in **A** but not in **B**.

4. As **B** is a MST, **{e1}** ∪ **B** must contain a cycle **C**.
5. Then **B** should include at least one edge **e2** that is not in **A** and lies on **C**.
6. Assume the weight of **e1** is less than that of **e2**.
7. Replace **e2** with **e1** in **B** yields the spanning tree **{e1} B** - **{e2}** which has a smaller weight compared to **B**.
8. Contradiction. As we assumed **B** is a MST but it is not.

If the weight of **e1** is larger than that of **e2**, a similar argument involving tree **{e2} A** - **{e1}** also leads to a contradiction. Thus, we conclude that the assumption that there can be a second MST was false.

iii) Minimum-cost subgraph

If the weights are *positive*, then a minimum spanning tree is in fact the minimum-cost subgraph connecting all vertices, since subgraphs containing cycles necessarily have more total weight.

iv) Cycle property

For any cycle C in the graph, if the weight of an edge e *of C is larger than the weights of other edges of C, then this edge cannot belong to an MST.* Assuming the contrary, i.e. that *e* belongs to an MST T1, then deleting *e* will break T1 into two subtrees with the two ends of *e* in different subtrees. The remainder of *C* reconnects the subtrees, hence there is an edge *f* of *C* with ends in different subtrees, i.e., it reconnects the subtrees into a tree T2 with weight less than that of T1, because the weight of *f* is less than the weight of *e*.

v) Cut property

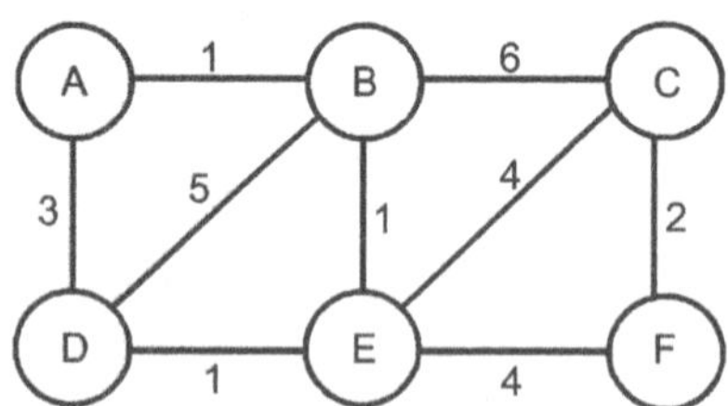

Fig. 16.16 (a) Graph

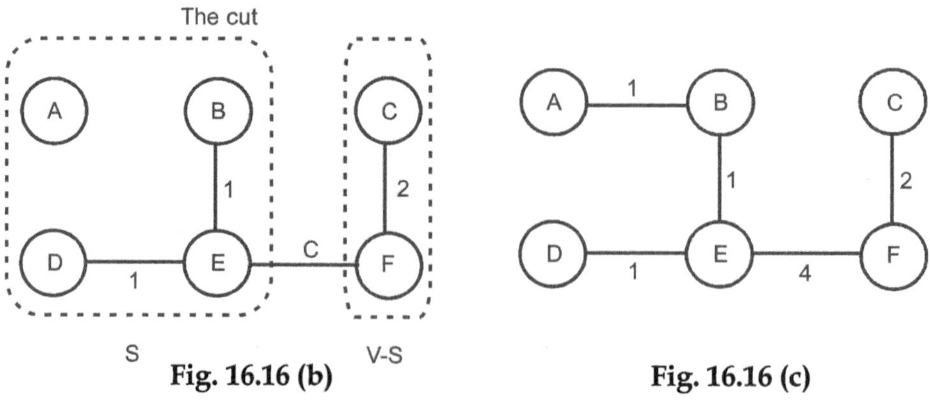

Fig. 16.16 (b) **Fig. 16.16 (c)**

This figure shows the cut property of MSP.T is the MST of the given graph. If S = {A,B,D,E}, thus V-S = {C,F},then there are 3 possibilities of the edge across the cut(S,V-S), they are edges BC, EC, EF of the original graph. Then, e is one of the minimum-weight-edge for the cut, therefore S *" {e} is part of the MST T.

For any cut C *in the graph, if the weight of an edge* e *of* C *is smaller than the weights of all other edges of* C, *then this edge belongs to all MSTs of the graph.* Indeed, assume the contrary, for example, edge BC (weighted 6) belongs to the MST T instead of edge e (weighted 4) in the left figure. Then adding e to T will produce a cycle, while replacing BC with e would produce MST of smaller weight.

vi) Minimum-cost edge

If the edge of a graph with the minimum cost *e* is unique, then this edge is included in any MST. Indeed, if *e* was not included in the MST, removing any of the (larger cost) edges in the cycle formed after adding *e* to the MST, would yield a spanning tree of smaller weight.

16.4.1. Algorithms to find a minimum spanning tree :

The first algorithm for finding a minimum spanning tree was developed by Czech scientist Otakar Borùvka in 1926 (see Borùvka's algorithm). Its purpose was an efficient electrical coverage of Moravia. There are now two algorithms commonly used, Prim's algorithm and Kruskal's algorithm. All three are greedy algorithms that run in polynomial time, so the problem of finding such trees is in **FP**, and related decision problems such as determining whether a particular edge is in the MST or determining if the minimum total weight exceeds a certain value are in **P**. Another greedy algorithm not as commonly used is the reverse-delete algorithm, which is the reverse of Kruskal's algorithm.

If the edge weights are integers, then deterministic algorithms are known that solve the problem in $O(m + n)$ integer operations. In a comparison model, in which the only allowed operations on edge weights are pairwise comparisons, Karger, Klein & Tarjan (1995) found a linear time randomized algorithm based on a combination of Borùvka's algorithm and the reverse-delete algorithm. Whether the problem can be solved deterministically in linear time by a comparison-based algorithm remains an open question, however. The fastest non-randomized comparison-based algorithm, by Bernard Chazelle, is based on the soft heap, an approximate priority queue. Its running time is $O(m$ á$(m,n))$, where m is the number of edges, n is the number of vertices and á is the classical functional inverse of the Ackermann function. The function á grows extremely slowly, so that for all practical purposes it may be considered a constant no greater than 4; thus Chazelle's algorithm takes very close to linear time. Seth Pettie and Vijaya Ramachandran have found a provably optimal deterministic comparison-based minimum spanning tree algorithm, the computational complexity of which is unknown.

Research has also considered parallel algorithms for the minimum spanning tree problem. With a linear number of processors it is possible to solve the problem in $O(\log n)$ time.[8][9] Bader & Cong (2003) demonstrate an algorithm that can compute MSTs 5 times faster on 8 processors than an optimized sequential algorithm. Typically, parallel algorithms are based on Borùvka algorithm—Prim's and especially Kruskal's algorithm do not scale as well to additional processors.

Other specialized algorithms have been designed for computing minimum spanning trees of a graph so large that most of it must be stored on disk at all times. These *external storage* algorithms, for example as described in "Engineering an External Memory Minimum Spanning Tree Algorithm" by Roman Dementiev et al., can operate, by authors' claims, as little as 2 to 5 times slower than a traditional in-memory algorithm. They rely on efficient external storage sorting algorithms and on graph contraction techniques for reducing the graph's size efficiently.

The problem can also be approached in a distributed manner. If each node is considered a computer and no node knows anything except its own connected links, one can still calculate the distributed minimum spanning tree.

16.4.2. MST on complete graphs - calculation of approximative expected size :

Alan M. Frieze showed that given a complete graph on n vertices, with edge weights that are independent identically distributed random variables with distribution function F satisfying $F'(0) > 0$, then as n approaches +" the expected weight of the MST approaches æ(3) / $F'(0)$, where æ is the Riemann zeta function. Under the additional assumption of finite variance, Alan M. Frieze also proved convergence in probability. Subsequently, J. Michael Steele showed that the variance assumption could be dropped. In later work, Svante Janson proved a central limit theorem for weight of the MST.

For uniform random weights in [0,1], the exact expected size of the minimum spanning tree has been computed for small complete graphs.

Table 16.1. MS T on complete graphs - Approximate expected size

Vertices	Expected size	Approximative expected size
2	1 / 2	0.5
3	3 / 4	0.75
4	31 / 35	0.8857143
5	893 / 924	0.9664502
6	278 / 273	1.0183151
7	30739 / 29172	1.053716
8	199462271 / 184848378	1.0790588
9	126510063932 / 115228853025	1.0979027

16.4.3. Related problems - Types of spanning trees :

i) ***k*-minimum spanning tree (*k*-MST),** which is the tree that spans some subset of *k* vertices in the graph with minimum weight.

   A set of **k-smallest spanning tree** is a subset of *k* spanning trees (out of all possible spanning trees) such that no spanning tree outside the subset has smaller weight. (Note that this problem is unrelated to the *k*-minimum spanning tree.)

ii) **The Euclidean minimum spanning tree** is a spanning tree of a graph with edge weights corresponding to the Euclidean distance between vertices which are points in the plane (or space).

iii) **The rectilinear minimum spanning tree** is a spanning tree of a graph with edge weights corresponding to the rectilinear distance between vertices which are points in the plane (or space).

iv) **Distributed minimum spanning tree :** In the distributed model, where each node is considered a computer and no node knows anything except its own connected links, one can consider distributed minimum spanning tree. Mathematical definition of the problem is the same but has different approaches for solution.

v) **The capacitated minimum spanning tree** is a tree that has a marked node (origin, or root) and each of the subtrees attached to the node contains no more than a *c* nodes. *c* is called a tree capacity. Solving CMST optimally requires exponential time, but good heuristics such as Esau-Williams and Sharma produce solutions close to optimal in polynomial time.

vi) **The degree constrained minimun spanning tree** is a minimun spanning tree in with each vertex is connected to no more than *d* other vertices, for some given number *d*. The case $d = 2$ is a special case of the traveling salesman problem, so the degree constrained minimum spanning tree is NP-hard in general.

   For directed graphs, the minimum spanning tree problem is called the Arborescence problem and can be solved in quadratic time using the Chu-Liu/Edmonds algorithm.

vii) A **maximum spanning tree** is a spanning tree with weight greater than or equal to the weight of every other spanning tree. Such a tree can be found with algorithms such as Prim's or Kruskal's after multiplying the edge weights by -1 and solving the MST problem on the new graph. A path in the maximum spanning tree is the widest path in the graph between its two endpoints: among all possible paths, it maximizes the weight of the minimum-weight edge.

viii) **The dynamic MST** problem concerns the update of a previously computed MST after an edge weight change in the original graph or the insertion/deletion of a vertex.[17][18]

ix) **Minimum bottleneck spanning tree** : bottleneck edge is the highest weighted edge in a spanning tree. A spanning tree is a **minimum bottleneck spanning tree** (or **MBST**) if the graph does not contain a spanning tree with a smaller bottleneck edge weight. A MST is necessarily a MBST (provable by the cut property), but a MBST is not necessarily a MST.

16.5. AVL TREE :

An **AVL tree** is another balanced binary search tree. Named after their inventors, **A**delson-**V**elskii and **L**andis, they were the first dynamically balanced trees to be proposed. Like red-black trees, they are not perfectly balanced, but pairs of sub-trees differ in height by at most 1, maintaining an ***O*(log*n*)** search time. Addition and deletion operations also take ***O*(log*n*)** time.

Table : 16.2. Some Trees

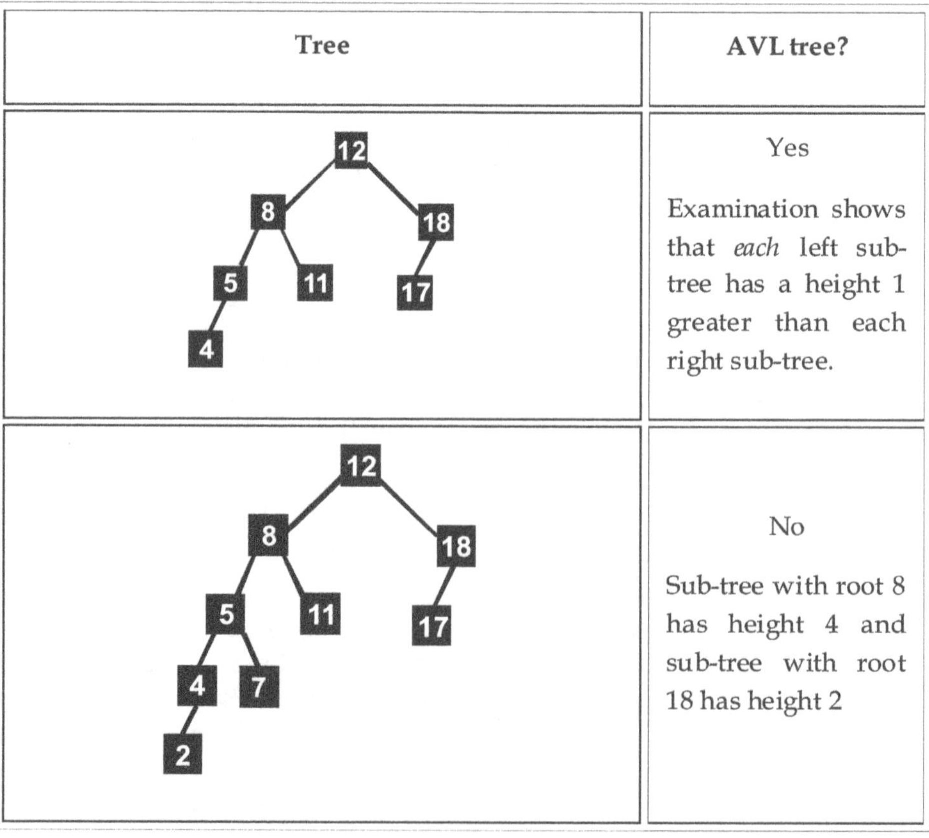

Tree	AVL tree?
12, 8, 18, 5, 11, 17, 4	Yes Examination shows that *each* left sub-tree has a height 1 greater than each right sub-tree.
12, 8, 18, 5, 11, 17, 4, 7, 2	No Sub-tree with root 8 has height 4 and sub-tree with root 18 has height 2

AVL trees Trees remain **balanced** - and thus guarantee **O(logn)** search times - in a dynamic environment. Or more importantly, since any tree can be re-balanced - but at considerable cost - can be re-balanced in **O(logn)** time.

In an AVL tree, the heights of the two child subtrees of any node differ by at most one. Lookup, insertion, and deletion all take O(log n) time in both the average and worst cases, where n is the number of nodes in the tree prior to the operation. Insertions and deletions may require the tree to be rebalanced by one or more tree rotations.

In other words AVL TREE can be defined as binary search tree which has the following properties:

1. The sub-trees of every node differ in height by at most one.
2. Every sub-tree is an AVL tree.

   Balance requirement for an AVL tree: the left and right sub-trees differ by at most 1 in height.

   We have to be to be careful with this definition: it permits some apparently unbalanced trees as shown in the table.

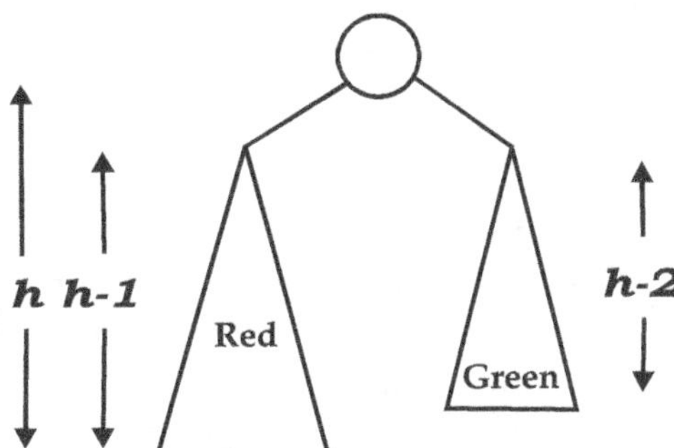

Fig.16.17. AVL Tree

16.5.1. Basic Operations on an AVL Tree :

The balance factor of a node is the height of its left subtree minus the height of its right subtree (sometimes opposite) and a node with balance factor 1, 0, or "1 is considered balanced. A node with any other balance factor is considered unbalanced and requires rebalancing the tree. The balance factor is either stored directly at each node or computed from the heights of the subtrees.

Basic operations of an AVL tree involve carrying out the same actions as would be carried out on an unbalanced binary search tree, but modifications are preceded or followed by one or more operations called tree rotations, which help to restore the height balance of the subtrees.

I) Lookup :

Lookup in an AVL tree is performed exactly as in an unbalanced binary search tree. Because of the height-balancing of the tree, a lookup takes O(log n) time. No special actions need to be taken, and the tree's structure is not modified by lookups. (This is in contrast to splay tree lookups, which do modify their tree's structure.)

If each node additionally records the size of its subtree (including itself and its descendants), then the nodes can be retrieved by index in O(log n) time as well.

Once a node has been found in a balanced tree, the *next* or *previous* nodes can be explored in amortized constant time. Some instances of exploring these "nearby" nodes require traversing up to 2×log(n) links (particularly when moving from the rightmost leaf of the root's left subtree to the leftmost leaf of the root's right subtree). However, exploring all n nodes of the tree in this manner would use each link exactly twice: one traversal to enter the subtree rooted at that node, and another to leave that node's subtree after having explored it. And since by one possible definition of trees there are exactly n"1 links in any tree, the amortized cost is found to be 2×(n"1)/n, or approximately 2.

II) Insertion :

As with the red-black tree, insertion is somewhat complex and involves a number of cases. Implementations of AVL tree insertion may be found in many textbooks: they rely on adding an extra attribute, the **balance factor** to each node. This factor indicates whether the tree is *left-heavy* (the height of the left sub-tree is 1 greater than the right sub-tree), *balanced* (both sub-trees are the same height) or *right-heavy* (the height of the right sub-tree is 1 greater than the left sub-tree). If the balance would be destroyed by an insertion, a rotation is performed to correct the balance.

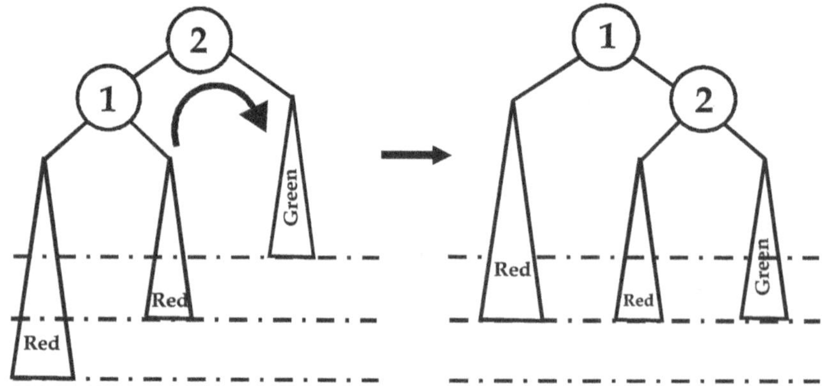

Fig.16.18. Insertion in AVL Tree

A new item has been added to the left subtree of node 1, causing its height to become 2 greater than 2's right sub-tree (shown in green). A right-rotation is performed to correct the imbalance.

i) Rotation Process for Balancing during insertion :

Pictorial description of how rotations cause rebalancing tree, and then retracing one's steps toward the root updating the balance factor of the nodes are explained in fig. 16.18. The numbered circles represent the nodes being balanced. The lettered triangles represent subtrees which are themselves balanced BSTs.

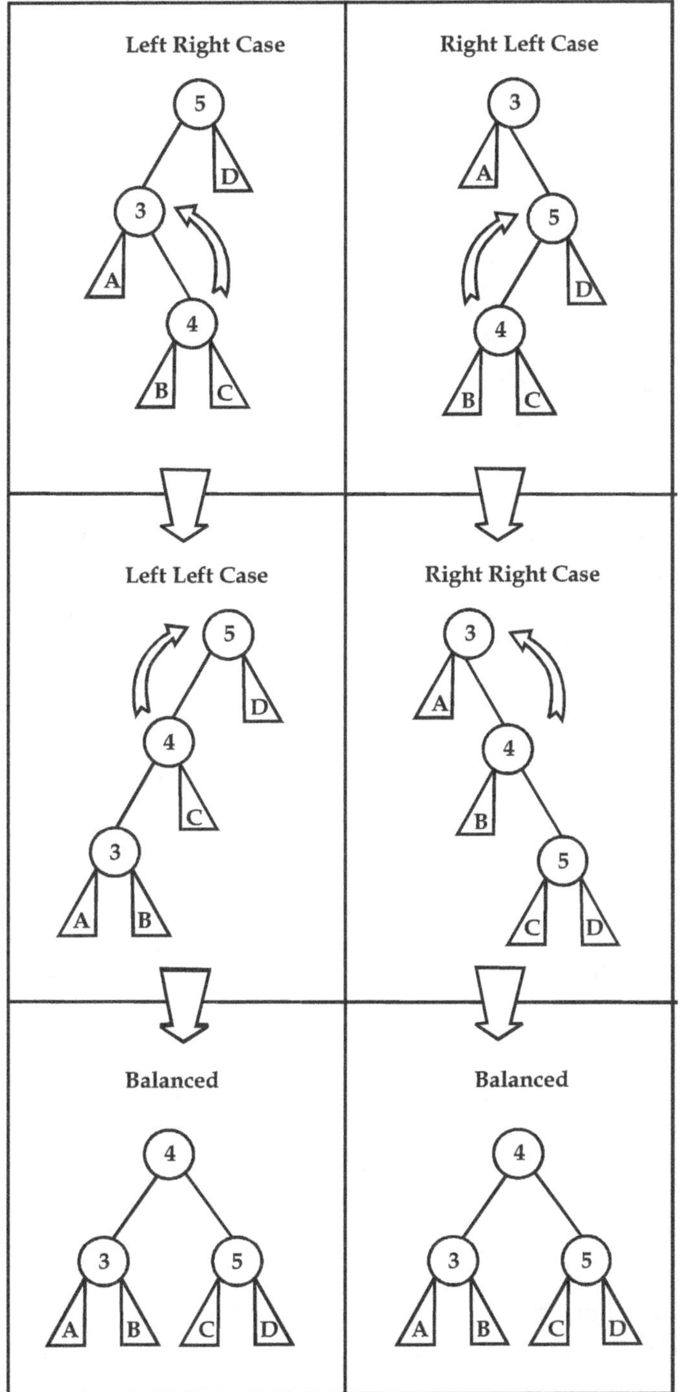

Fig.16.19. Rotation for balancing of AVL Tree during insertion

After inserting a node, it is necessary to check each of the node's ancestors for consistency with the rules of AVL. For each node checked, if the balance factor remains "1, 0, or +1 then no rotations are necessary. However, if the balance factor becomes ±2 then the subtree rooted at this node is unbalanced. If insertions are performed serially, after each insertion, at most one of the following cases needs to be resolved to restore the entire tree to the rules of AVL

There are four cases which need to be considered, of which two are symmetric to the other two. Let P be the root of the unbalanced subtree, with R and L denoting the right and left children of P respectively.

(a) **Right-Right case** and **Right-Left case**:

- If the balance factor of P is -2 then the right subtree outweights the left subtree of the given node, and the balance factor of the right child (R) must be checked. The left rotation with P as the root is necessary.
- If the balance factor of R is -1, a **double left rotation** (with respect to P and then R) is needed (Right-Right case).
- If the balance factor of R is +1, two different rotations are needed. The first rotation is a **right rotation** with R as the root. The second is a **left rotation** with P as the root (Right-Left case).

(b) **Left-Left case** and **Left-Right case**:

- If the balance factor of P is +2, then the left subtree outweighs the right subtree of the given node, and the balance factor of the left child (L) must be checked. The right rotation with P as the root is necessary.
- If the balance factor of L is +1, a **double right rotation** (with respect to P and then L) is needed (Left-Left case).
- If the balance factor of L is -1, two different rotations are needed. The first rotation is a **left rotation** with L as the root. The second is a **right rotation** with P as the root (Left-Right case).

III. Deletion :

If the node is a leaf or has only one child, remove it. Otherwise, replace it with either the largest in its left subtree (inorder predecessor) or the smallest in its right subtree (inorder successor), and remove that node. The node that was found as a replacement has at most one subtree. After deletion, retrace the path back up the tree (parent of the replacement) to the root, adjusting the balance factors as needed.

As with all binary trees, a node's in-order successor is the left-most child of its right subtree, and a node's in-order predecessor is the right-most child of its left subtree. In either case, this node will have zero or one children. Delete it according to one of the two simpler cases above.

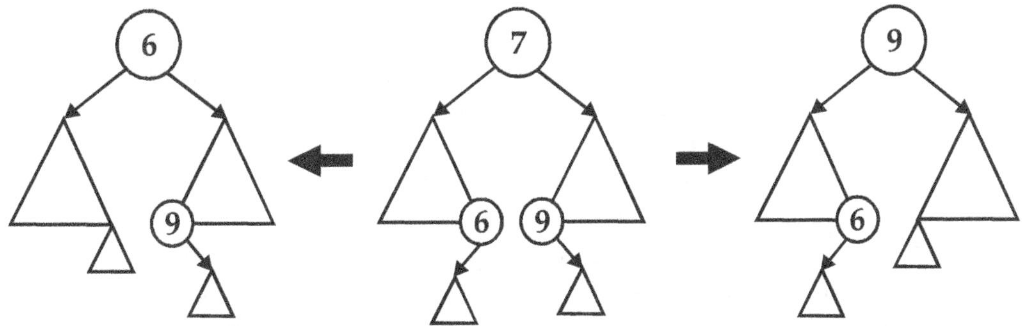

Fig.16.20. Deletion in AVL Tree

In addition to the balancing described above for insertions, if the balance factor for the tree is 2 and that of the left subtree is 0, a right rotation must be performed on P. The mirror of this case is also necessary.

The retracing can stop if the balance factor becomes "1 or +1 indicating that the height of that subtree has remained unchanged. If the balance factor becomes 0 then the height of the subtree has decreased by one and the retracing needs to continue. If the balance factor becomes "2 or +2 then the subtree is unbalanced and needs to be rotated to fix it. If the rotation leaves the subtree's balance factor at 0 then the retracing towards the root must continue since the height of this subtree has decreased by one. This is in contrast to an insertion where a rotation resulting in a balance factor of 0 indicated that the subtree's height has remained unchanged.

The time required is O(log *n*) for lookup, plus a maximum of O(log *n*) rotations on the way back to the root, so the operation can be completed in O(log *n*) time.

Table 16.3. Time complexity of a basic operations on an AVL tree.

Time complexity in big O notation		
	Average	Worst case
Space	O(n)	O(n)
Search	O(log n)	O(log n)
Insert	O(log n)	O(log n)
Delete	O(log n)	O(log n)

16.5.2. Comparison of AVL to other structures :

AVL trees are often compared with red-black trees because they support the same set of operations and because red-black trees also take O(log n) time for the basic operations. Because AVL trees are more rigidly balanced, they are faster than red-black trees for lookup intensive applications.[3] However, red-black trees are faster for insertion and removal.

Both AVL trees and red-black trees are self-balancing binary search trees, so they are very similar mathematically. The operations to balance the trees are different, but both occur in O(log n) time. The real difference between the two is the limiting height. For a tree of size n:

- An AVL tree's height is strictly less than:

$$\log_{\phi}(n+2)-1=\frac{\log_2(n+2)}{\log_2(\phi)}-1$$

$$=\log_{\phi}(2).\log_2(n+2)-1\approx 1.44\log_2(n+2)-1$$

where ϕ is the golden ratio.

- A red-black tree's height is at most $2\log_2(n+1)$

AVL trees are more rigidly balanced than red-black trees, leading to slower insertion and removal but faster retrieval.

16.6. GRAPHS :

A graph is a set of nodes and arcs. The nodes are also termed as **vertices** and **arcs** are termed as **edges. The set of nodes** as per Fig. 16.20 (a) is denoted as **{O,P,R,S,Q}. The set of arcs** is in the following graph is **{(O, P), (O,R), (O, S), (O, Q), (R, S), (Q, S)}.**

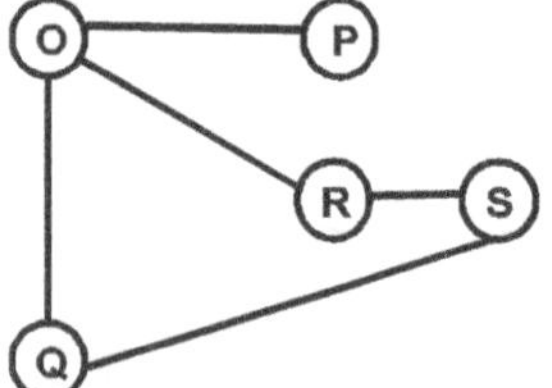

Fig.16.20 (a) Graph

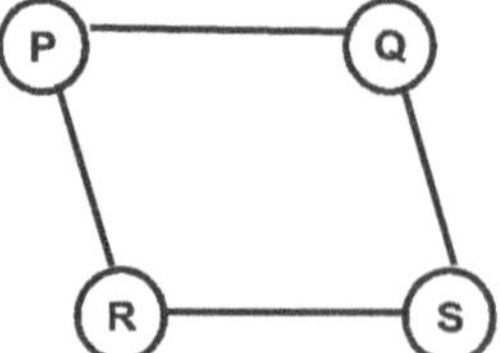

Fig.16.20 (b) Connected Graph

Fig.16.20 (c) Non-connected graph

A graph is linked if there is a pathway between any two nodes of the graph, such a graph is called a **connected graph** or else it is a **non-connected graph** as given in Fig. 16.20 (b) & 16.20 (c)

Undirected graph : A graph containing an unordered pair or nodes is termed as a **undirected graph** or **digraph** as given in Fig. 16.21 (a). The vertices are [A,B,C,D] and edges are [A B), (A,D), (A,C), (B,D), (B,C), (D,C)]. The graph has four nodes and six edges.

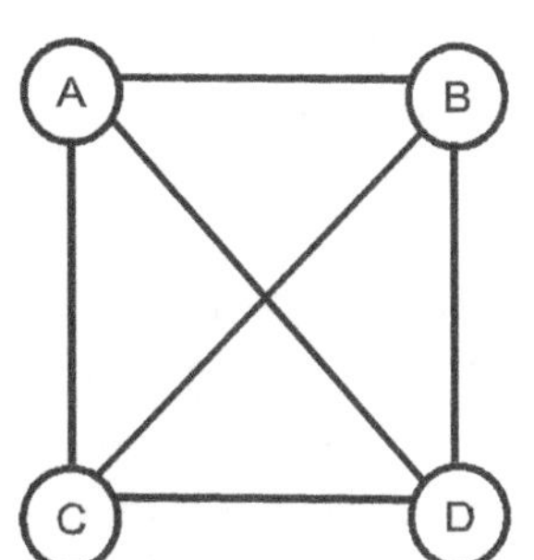

Fig.16.21 (a) Undirected graph

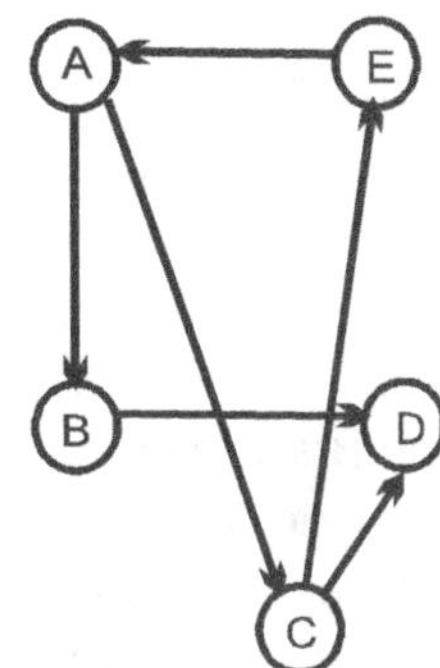

Fig.16.21.(b) Directed graph

Directed graph : This graph contains ordered pairs or vertices. For example, graph vertices are [A,B,C,D,E] and edges are [(A,B,),(B,D),(C,D) (C,A), (C,E), (E,A)]. The above directed graph has five nodes and six edges as given in figure 16.21 (b).

1) Graph Representation

The graph can be implemented by linked list or array.

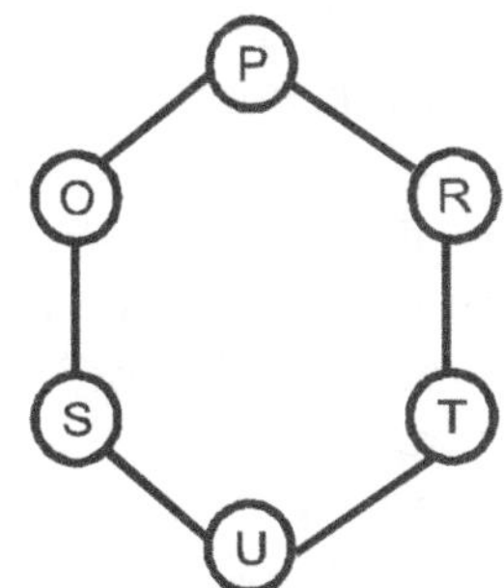

Fig.16.22 (a) Model Graph

P O

Fig.16.22 (b) nodes with no edge

Fig.16.22 (c) nodes with an edge

Different possibilities of graph representation are dependent on two cases.

i) If there is no edge between two nodes.

There is no edge between nodes P and Q. (Fig.16.22 (b))

ii) If there is an edge between any two nodes. (Fig.16.22 (c))

The nodes P and Q have an edge.

The existence of edges between different nodes can be given in the form of a table as given below. The existence is denoted by a symbol '✓' and the non-existance is denoted by a symbol 'x'

Table 16.4 : Existance of edges between different nodes of a graph.

Nodes	P	Q	R	S	T	U
P	X	✓	✓	X	X	X
Q	✓	X	X	✓	X	X
R	✓	X	X	X	✓	X
S	X	✓	X	X	X	✓
T	X	X	✓	X	X	✓
U	X	X	X	✓	✓	X

As per the above table, there is an edge in between the nodes P and Q and P and R and nodes P and S have no edge between them. The symbol '✓' indicates existence of edge and x indicates absence of edge between two nodes.

From the above table one can predict the path to reach a particular node. For example, initial node is P and the destination node is U. We have to find the path to reach node U from P.

There is no edge between P and U. Then find out the edge for the nearest node in forward direction. By observing the tables there are two edges from P, Q and R. We can select either Q or R. Suppose we selected node Q, again find out the next nearest successive node to Q by observing column Q. The next successive forward node will be S. Then refer to column S and it provides two edges Q and U. the node U is our solution. Thus, by using above table paths any between two nodes can be determined. The path should be as P-Q-S-U. The graph can be represented by sequential representation and linked list representation.

2) Adjacency matrix : The matrix can be used to represent the graph. The information of adjacent nodes can be stored in the matrix. Presence of edges from a particular node can be determined easily. The matrix can be represented by a two-dimensional array. In a two-dimensional array [ ] [ ] the first subscript indicates row and second column. For example, there are five nodes in the graph, the 0th row indicates node1 and so on. Likewise, column represents node1, node2 and so on.

For example for **nodes[j[k] the number 1** indicates the presence of edge between two nodes j and k and the number 0 indicates the absence of edge between two nodes j and k

Thus, the matrix, will contain only 0 and 1 values. The adjacency matrix x for the graph given in Fig. 16.23 is given by the side of the figure.

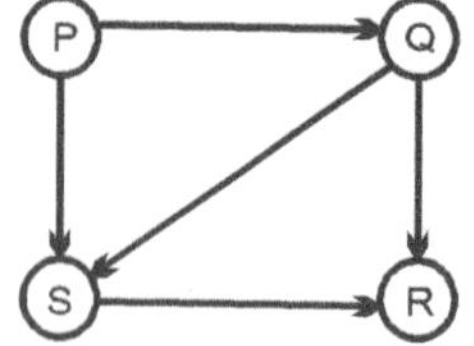

Fig.16.23. A given directed graph

The adjacency matrix X =

$$\begin{array}{c} \\ P \\ Q \\ R \\ S \end{array} \begin{array}{c} \begin{array}{cccc} P & Q & R & S \end{array} \\ \begin{bmatrix} 0 & 1 & 0 & 1 \\ 1 & 0 & 1 & 1 \\ 0 & 1 & 0 & 1 \\ 1 & 1 & 1 & 0 \end{bmatrix} \end{array}$$

Program 16.6.1.

Write a program in C to demonstrate adjacency of a given graph.

```
#include <stdio.h>
#include <conio.h>
main ()
{
        int me, j=1,k,beg,num, des;
        int adj[20] [20]= { ( 0, 0) };
        char g_type;
        clrscr ();
        printf ("\Enter number of nodes : ");
        scanf (" %d",&num);
        printf ("Enter type of graph, (d) irected or (u)ndirected: ");
        g_type=getch ();
        fflush (stdin);
    if (g_type=='u') me=num* (num-1)/2;
    else             me =num* (num-1) ;
    while (j<=me)
    {
    printf ("\n Enter edges %d ( 0 to exit ) ; ",j);
    scanf (" %d %d", &beg,&des);
    if (beg==0) && (des==0)) break;
    if (beg > num | des > num | beg<=0 | des<=0
        {
            printf ("Invalid edges !\n");
            j-;
        }
    else
        {
        adj [ beg ] [des ] = 1;
        if (g_type== 'u' )
            adj [beg] [des] =1;
            if (g_type=='u')
                adj [des] [beg]=1;
        }
                j++;
    }
        printf ("\n The adjency of matrix is : \n");
        for (j=1; j<=num; j++)
        {
            for (k=1;k<=num;k++)
            printf (" %d",adj[j] [k]) ;
            printf ("\n") ;
        }
            return 0;
}
```

OUTPUT :

Enter number of nodes : 5
Enter type of graph, (d)irected or (u)ndirected:u
Enter edges 1 (0 to exit) : 11
Enter edges 2 (0 to exit): 21
Enter edges 3 (0 to exit): 22
Enter edges 4 (0 to exit): 01
Invalid edges!
Enter edges 4 (0 to exit): 12
Enter edges 5 (0 to exit): 00
The adjency of matrix is
1 1 0 0 0
1 1 0 0 0
0 0 0 0 0
0 0 0 0 0
0 0 0 0 0

Explanation :

In the above program maximum edges are calculated by using a formula. If the graph is directed type the formula is me=num *(num-1); where, num is the total number of nodes. When the graph is undirected then the formula is me=num*(num-1)/2. After computing maximum edges, the user is prompted to enter edges. When 0, 0 are entered the while loop is terminated. When the entered edges are greater than num and less than or equal to zero, message **Invalid edges is** displayed. Otherwise, adj[beg] [des]=1.

3. Adjacency List :

Two lists are maintained for adjacency of a list. The first list is used to store information on all the nodes. The second list is used to store information on adjacent nodes.

Header node :

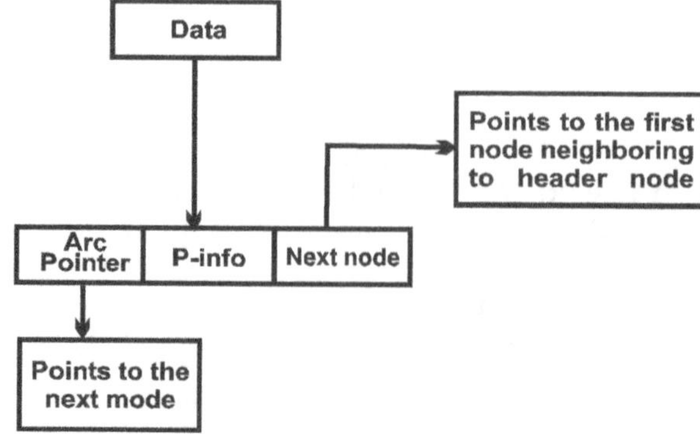

Fig.16.24. Header node

```
struct node
{
struct node *next
int num;
        struct edge *aj;   //structure within structure
}
```

Edge of a graph :

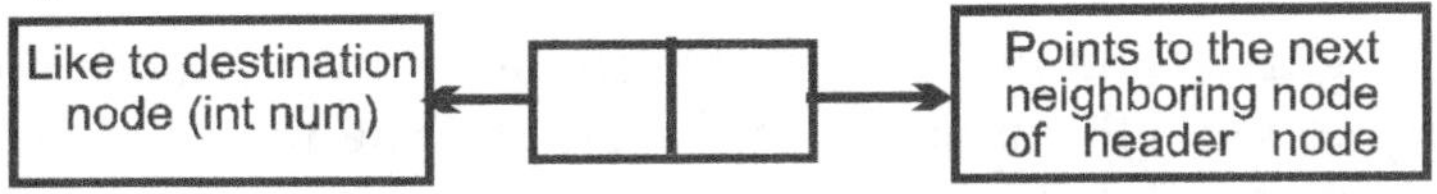

Fig.16.25. An edge of graph

```
struct edge
{
        int num;
        struct edge *ptr;
};
```

Consider the graph

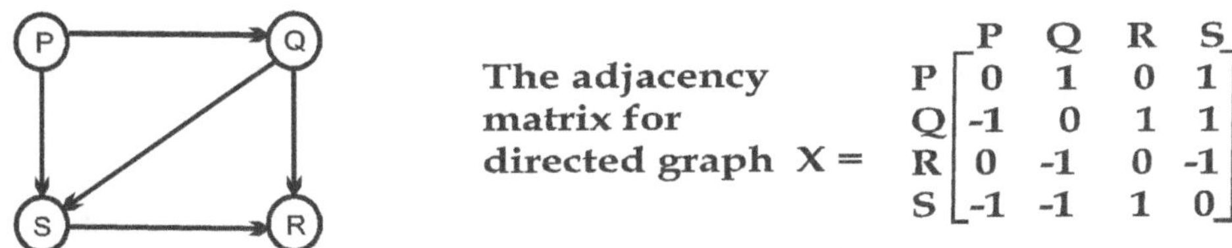

Fig.16.26. An example of directed graph

Adjacency list for the above graph would be as follows :

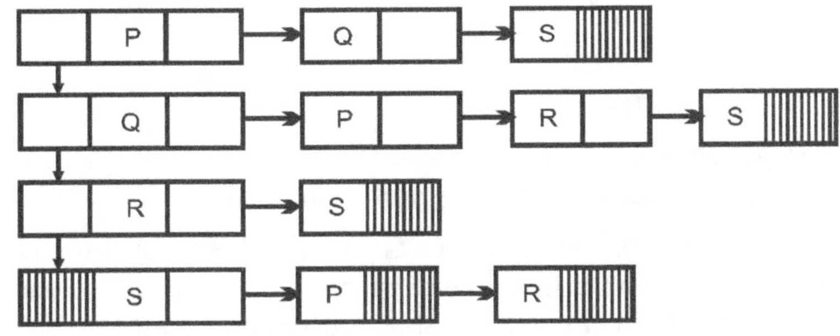

Fig.16.27. Adjacency list

4. **Rules for Traversal in a Graph :**

1) The graph has no first node or root. Therefore, the graph can be started from any node.

2) In the graph only those nodes are traversed which are accessible from the current node. For complete traversing of graph the path can be determined by traversing nodes step by step.

3) In the graph, a particular node can be visited repeatedly. Hence, the status of every node whether traversed or not is necessary to keep.

4) In the graph, to reach a particular node, more than one path is available.

5. **Spanning Trees :**

A spanning tree is an undirected tree containing only those nodes that are necessary to join all the nodes in the graph. The nodes of spanning trees have only one path between them. In spanning trees, the numbers of edges are less by one than the number of nodes.

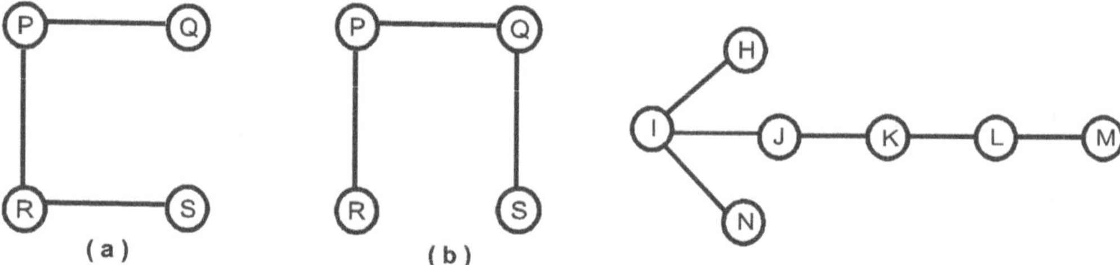

Fig16.28. Spanning trees

Fig16.29. Depth-first spanning tree

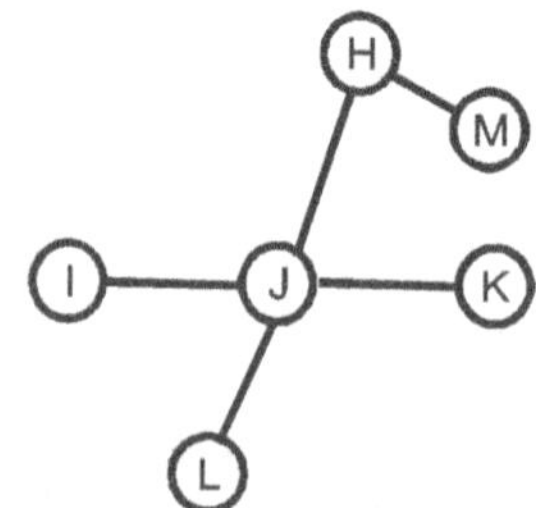

Fig.16.30. Breadth First Searching

6. **Weighted graph :** When the edges of the graph contain positive values as weight it is known as a weighted graph or a network.

16.6.1. Prim's algorithm for Traversal of a Graph : In this algorithm, the traversing can start from any node and addition can be done in spanning tree according to the weight of the edge. For example, we start with node n1, and then the next step is to check the entire connecting path to that node and find out which path has minimum weight. Thus, the nodes with minimum weight are added Prim's algorithms. Here, during program implementation it is essential to know the weight of the edge. For example, we have edges e1 and e2 with weights 3 and 5. The edge 1 has less weight than e2 and hence, e1 will be added to the spanning tree.

Program 16.6.2.

Write a program in C to create minimum spanning tree using Prim's algorithm.

```
# include<stdio.h>
# include <conio.h>
# include <process.h>
struct prim
{
        int pred_sor;
        int stat;
        int distance;
};
struct node { int x;   int w; };
int adjc [10],num;
int main ( )
{
        int y=1, wt, counter;
        struct node trees[10];
        void create (void);
        void show (void);
        int  m_tree (struct node*, int*);
        clrscr ( );
create ( );
printf ("Adjacency of Matrix : ");
show ( );
counter=m_tree(trees,&wt);
printf ("Weight of spanning trees is : %d\n", wt);
printf ("Edges to be included in spanning trees : ");
while (y<=counter)
{
        printf (" %d,trees [y] .x);
        printf (" %d\num",trees [y] .w);
        y++;
}
return 0;
}
void create ( )
{
        int y=1,m_edge,start,end,wt;
        printf ("Enter number of vertices : ");
        scanf (" %d", &num);
        m_edge=num* (num-1) /2;
```

```
        while (y<=m_edge)
        {
                printf ("Enter node %d ( 0 to Exit ) : ",y);
                scanf (" %d %d", &start,&end);
                if (start==0) && (end==0) ) break;
                printf ("Enter weight of this node : " );
                scanf (" %d", &wt);
                if (start > num || end > num || start <=0 || end<=0)
                {
                        printf ("Wrong node!\n");
                        --y;
                }
                else
                {
                        adjc [start] [end]=wt;
                        adjc [end] [start]=wt;
                }
        y++;
        }
        if (y<num-1)
        {
                printf ("Spanning tree not possible \n");
                exit (0);
        }
}
void show ( )
{
        int y=1, p;
        while (y<=num)
        {
                for (p=1; p<=num; p++)
                printf (" %3d",adjc[y] [p] );
                printf ("\n");
                y++;
        }
}
int m_tree (struct node trees [10], int *wht)
{
        struct prim p_ion[10];
        int y=1,mm, counter, cur;
        int perm (struct prim *);
        int uu, vv;
        wht=0;
```

```
        while (y<=num)
        {
                p_ion[y] .pred_sor=0;
                p_ion[y] .distance = 9999;
                p_ion[y] .stat = 0;
                y++;
        }
        p_ion[1] .pred_sor=0;
        p_ion[1] .distance = 0;
        p_ion[1] .stat = 1;
        cur=1;
        counter=0;
        while (perm (p_ion) ! = 1)
        {
                for (y=1;y<=num;y++)
                {
                        if ( adjc[cur] [y] > 0 && p_ion [y] .stat == 0 )
                        {
                                if ( adjc [cur] [y] <p_ion[y].distance)
                                {
                                        p_ion [y] .pred_sor = cur;
                                        p_ion [y] .distance = adjc[cur] [y] ;
                                }
                        }
                }
                mm=9999;
                for (y=1; y<=num; y++)
                {
                        if (p_ion [y]. stat == 0 && p_ion[y] .distance < mm)
                        {
                                mm = p_ion [y] .distance;
                                cur=y;
                        }
                }
                p_ion [cur].stat=1;
                uu=p_ion [cur].pred_scr;
                vv=cur, counter++;
                trees [counter]. x=uu;
                trees [counter]. w=vv;
                *wht=*wht+adjc[uu] [vv];
        }
        return (counter) ;
}
```

```
int perm (struct prim p_ion [10] )
{
        int y=1;
        while (y<=num)
                if (p_ion[y++]. stat == 0 )
                return 0 ;
        return 1;
}
```

OUTPUT :

Enter number of vertices : 5
Enter node 1 (0 to Exit) : 11
Enter wieght of this node : 5
Enter node 2 (0 to Exit) : 11
Enter weight of this node : 3
Enter node 3 (0 to Exit) : 0 0
Spanning tree not possible

Explanation : In the above program the structure prim is defined as follows.

```
struct prim
{
        int pred_sor;
        int stat;
        int distance;
};
struct node
{
        int x;      int w;
};
```

The function create ( ) is used to compute maximum edges. the m_tree ( ) function is used to calculate the edges. The show ( ) function is used to display the nodes.

16.7. TYPES OF TREE SEARCHES :

Searching through trees is an effective way of reaching the goal from a given starting point leading to some sort of optimization like maximization of the profits, minimization of losses, minimum distance, time minimization etc., There are different types of tree searches of which a few of the important searches will be discussed now.

16.7.1. Breadth-First Search :

This is one popular method of traversing a graph. This method uses the queue data structure for traversing nodes of the graph. Any node of the graph can act as a beginning node. Using any node as the starting node, all other nodes of the graph are traversed. To shun repeated visit to the same node an array is maintained which keeps the status of visited node.

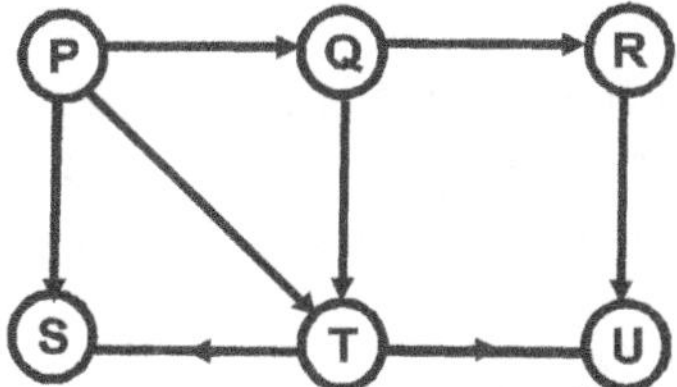

Fig.16.31. A model graph

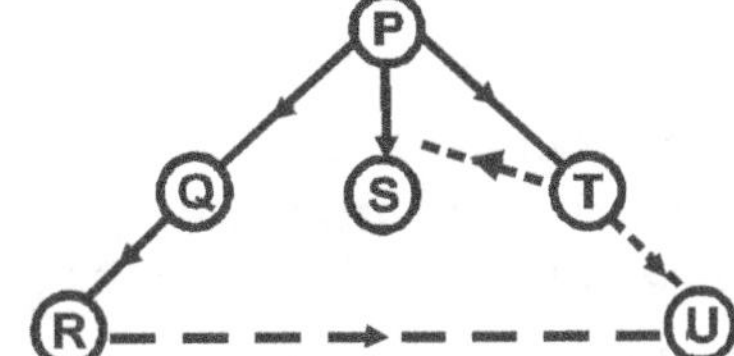

Fig.16.32. Alternate Tree model for BFS

In Fig. 16.31 the model graph of Figure 16.32 is given in an alternate form. The dotted lines are the edges that costs cycles. In tree search cycling effect has to be avoided as it leads to the same type of search again and again.

In Breadth-First Search we take the node P as a beginning node. Initially, the node P is traversed. After this, all the adjacent nodes of P are traversed, that is Q, T and S. The traversal of nodes can be carried out in any sequence. For example, the sequence of traverse of nodes is Q,S and T. The traversal will be **PQST**.

First all the nodes neighboring Q are traversed, then S, and finally T. The adjacent node of Q is R and that of T is U. The traversal now should be **PQSTRU.**

Now, the new nodes obtained, R and U are traversed and the new adjacent nodes will result previously traversed, that is, U. Hence, it must be ignored.

16.7.2. Depth-First Search :

In this method, also a node from graph is taken as a starting node. Traverse through all the possible paths of the starting node. When the last node of the graph is obtained and path is not available from the node, then control returns to the previous node. This process is implemented using a stack.

Consider the following graph

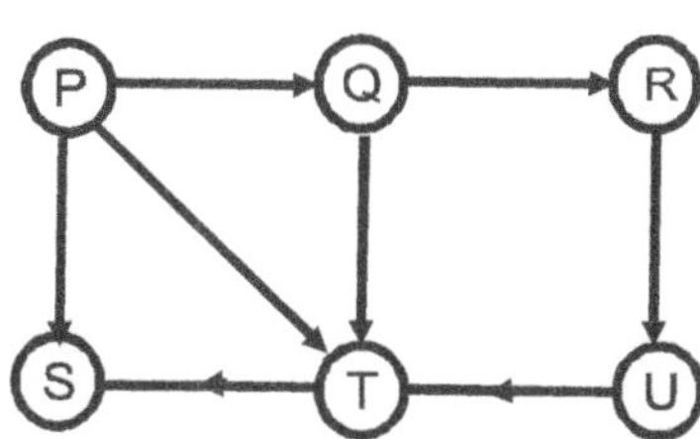

Fig.16.33. A model graph

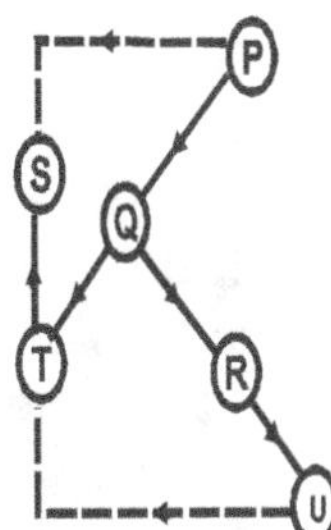

Fig.16.34. Alternate Tree model for DFS

Consider P as the starting node. Traverse the node adjacent to P and we will get Q and then R (adjacent to Q) and U (adjacent to R). The traversal will be **P Q R U.**

The search is always carried out in forward direction. After reaching U, we reach the end of the path from where we cannot go forward. Hence the control goes to the previous node and again the traverse through the available paths for non traversed nodes.

In reverse direction, we get the node R and it has an unvisited node. Hence, Q is taken and it gives T. The node T gives U, but it is already visited. Therefore, control in reverse direction checks all the nodes. It takes P and it gives node S. The sequence of traversal will be **P Q R U T S.**

The following program explains both the above procedures.

Program 16.7.1

Write a program to demonstrate breadth-first search and depth-first search.

```
        #include<stdio.h>
        #include <conio.h>
        # include <process.h>
        #define num 21
        int aj[num] [num], tra_sed[num], count;
        int main ( )
{
                int j,x,select;
                int show (void), create (void), dfs (int);
                int dfs_rsn (int), bfs (int), adj_edg (int);
                void nodes (void);
                clrscr ( );
                create ( );
        for ( ; ; )
        {
                printf ("1. Adjacency of matrix\n") ;
                printf ("2. Depth First Search with stack\n") ;
                printf ("3. Depth First Search with recursion\n") ;
                printf ("4. Breadth First Search\n") ;
                printf ("5. Adjacency vertices\n") ;
                printf ("6. printf ("1. Elements\n") ;
                printf ("7. Quit\n") ;
                printf ("Enter option : ") ;
                scanf (" %d", &select);
                switch (select)
                {
                case 1 :
                        printf ("Adjacency of Matrix\n") ;
                        show ( );
                        break;
```

```
            case 2 :
                    printf ("Enter Beginning node for Depth First Search : " ) ;
                    scanf ("%d" , &x);
                    for (j=1;j<=count;j++)
                    tra_sed[j] =0;
                    dfs(x) ;
                    break;

            case 3 :
                    printf ("Enter Beginning node for Depth First Search : " ) ;
                    scanf ("%d" , &x);
                    for (j=1;j<=count;j++)
                    tra_sed[j] =0;
                    dfs_rsn (x) ;
                    break;

            case 4 :
            printf ("Enter Beginning node for Depth First Search : " ) ;
                    scanf ("%d" , &x);
                    for (j=1;j<=count;j++)
                    tra_sed[j] =0;
                    bfs (x);
                    break ;

            case 5 :
                    printf ("Enter node to search adjacent vertices  : " ) ;
                    scanf ("%d" , &x);
                    printf ("Adjacent Vertices : " ) ;
                    adj_edg ( x );
                    break;

            case 6 :
                    nodes ( );
                    break ;

            case 7 :
                    exit (0);
            default :
                    printf ("Invalid selection\n");
                    break;
            }
    }
}
```

```
create ()
{
        int j,m_edges, start, target;

        printf ("Enter number of nodes : ");
        scanf (" %d",&count);
        m_edges=count* (count-1);
        for (j=1;j<m_edges;j++)
        {
                printf ("Enter edge %d (0 0 to quit ) : ",j);
                scanf (" %d %d",&start,&target);
                if (start==0) && (target==0) )
                        break;
                if (start > count  | | target > count | | start <=0 | | target <=0)
                {
                        printf ("Invalid edges try again !\n");
                        --j;
                }
                else aj(start) [target]=1 ;
        }
return 0 ;
}
show ()
{
        int j;
        for (j=1;j<=count;j++)
                printf (" %5d",aj [j] [j] );
        printf ("\n");
}
return 0;
}
dfs_rsn (int x)
{
        int j;
        tra_sed[x]=1;
        printf (" % d ",x);
        for (j=1;j<=count;j++)
        if (aj [x] [j] ==1 && tra_sed [j]== 0)
        dfs_rsn (j);
return 0;
}
```

```
dfs (int x)
{
        int j, stack [num], TOP=-1, popve;
        TOP++;
        stack[TOP]=x;
        while (TOP>=0)
        {
                popve=stack [TOP};
                TOP--;
                if (tra_sed [popve] = = 0)
                {
                        printf ("%d",popve);
                        tra_sed[popve] = = 1;
                }
                else
                        continue;
                for (j=count;j>=1;j--)
                {
                        if (aj [prove] [j] = = 1 && tra_sed[j] = = 0)
                        {
                                TOP ++;
                                stack [TOP]=j;
                        }
                }
        }
return 0;
}
bfs (int x)
{
        int j,fr,re;
        int queue [20];
        fr=re= -1;
        printf ("%d ",x);
        tra_sed[x]=1;
        re++;
        fr++;
        queue[re]=x;
        while (fr<=re)
        {
                x=queue[fr] ;
                fr++;
                for (j=1;j<=count;j++)
                {
                        /* Check for adjacent unvisited nodes */
```

```
                    if ( aj [x] [j] == 1 && tra_sed [j] ==0)
                    {
                            printf (" %d ",j);
                            tra_sed[j]=1;
                            re++;
                            queue[re]=j;
                    }
            }
    }

return 0;
}
```

adj_edg (int x)

```
{
        int j;
        for (j=1;j<=count;j++)
        if (aj [x] [j] ==1)
        printf (" %d ",j);
        printf ("\n");
return 0 ;
}
```

void nodes ( )

```
{
        int j;
        for (j=1;j<=count;j++)
                tra_sed[j]=0;
        for (j=1;j<=count ; j++)
        {
                if (tra_sed[j] ==0)
                        dfs_rsn (j);
        }
        printf ("\n");
}
```

OUTPUT :

Enter number of nodes : 5
Enter edge 1 (0 0 to quit) : 1 1
Enter edge 2 (0 0 to quit) : 2 2
Enter edge 3 (0 0 to quit) : 1 5
Enter edge 4 (0 0 to quit) : 0 0

1. Adjacency of matrix
2. Depth First Search with stack
3. Depth First Search with recursion
4. Breadth First Search
5. Adjacent vertices
6. Elements
7. Quit

Enter option : 1
Adjacency of Matrix
    1 1 0 0 0

Explanation :

In the above program, following user defined functions are defined to perform various tasks. Create ( ) function, when executed, prompts the user to enter the number of edges and the corresponding edge values. When the user enters edges, maximum edges are calculated. For complete details of the procedure read the topic Depth-First Search. The function adj_edg ( ) calculates the edges. The function bfs ( ) performs breadth-first search. For details, refer the topic Breadth-First Search.

16.8. SORTING :

Sorting is a process of arranging quantities in a defined manner i.e., either in ascending order or in descending order. There are so many algorithms available at present to perform the task of sorting. Let us consider some of the common sorting methods in this unit with their own merits and demerits. To start with we will take bubble sort, which is considered as an easy method among various algorithm.

As discussed above, sorting is a process in which records are arranged in ascending or descending order. In real life problems, we come across several examples of such sorted information, For example, the telephone directory contains names of the persons and the phone numbers are written according to ascending alphabets. The records of the list of these telephone holders are to be sorted by the name of the holder. By using this directory, we can find the telephone number of any person easily. Sort method has great importance in data structures.

For example, consider the five numbers 22 44 11 33 55

The above numbers can be sorted in ascending or descending order.

Ascending order (0 to n) : 11 22 33 44 55

Descending order (n to 0) : 55 44 33 22 11

Similarly, **alphabets can be sorted using ASCII code.** Consider Z K N B P

Ascending order (A to Z) : B K N P Z

Descending Order (Z to A) : Z P N K B

Sorting is classified in following types.

1. **Exchange sort or Bubble sort**
2. **Selection sort**
3. **Quick sort**
4. **Merge Sort**
5. **Heap Sort or Tree sort**
6. **Insertion sort**
7. **Shell Sort**

16.8.1. Exchange Sort (Bubble Sort) :

The bubble sort is an example of exchange sort. In this method, repetitive comparison is performed among elements and essential swapping of elements is done. Bubble sort is commonly used in sorting algorithms. It is easy to understand but time consuming. In this type, two successive elements are compared and swapping is done. Thus, step-by-step entire array elements are checked. It is different from the selection sort. Instead of searching the minimum element and then applying swapping, two records are swapped instantly upon noticing that they are not in order.

In other words the bubble sort is one of the simplest sorting methods we can use. In this algorithm, successive sweeps are made through the records to be sorted. And in each sweep, the algorithm compares the key to the data elements and swaps (exchanging values between two variables) the elements if they are not in the desired order. Since, swapping occurs only among successive elements of the data structure only one element is placed in its sorted place after each sweep. Also note that once the elements are sorted they are considered for comparison in successive sweeps.

1) Time Complexity : Time complexity of bubble sort is of the order O (n !) i.e., of the order (n!). It means that n! comparisons are required for complete bubble sort.

2) Comparison with other methods :

i) This is the easiest sorting technique to implement

ii) It requires a lot of comparisons and so takes more time than quick sort, tree sort, and the like.

Program 16.8.1

Write a program in C to sort a given array by using the Exchange or Bubble sort

```
# include<stdio.h>
# include <conio.h>
int main ()
{
    int a[5],i,j,temp;
    clrscr ( );
```

```
    printf ("Enter he elements of an array : ");
    for (i=0;i<t;i++)
        scanf ("%d",&a [i]);
    for (i=0;i<5;i++)
        {
            for (j=i;j<4;j++)
            {
                if (a[i]>a[j+1])
                    {
                        temp=a[i];
                        a[i]=a[j+1];
                        a[j+1]=temp;
                    }
            }
        }
        printf ("sorted elements in ascending order : ");
        for (i=0;i<5;i++)
        printf ("%d",a[i]);
    return 0;
    }
```

OUTPUT :

Enter the elements of an array : 22 44 11 33 55
Sorted elements in ascending order : 11 22 33 44 55

Program 16.8.2

Write a Program in C++ for writing a set of numbers in ascending order using Bubble sort.

```
# include <iostream>
# include <iomanip>
using namespace std;
class bubblesort
{
    private:
        in *x;
        int items;
    public:
        bubblesort(int);
        ~bubblesort ( );
        void input (int [ ]);
```

```
        void display ();
        void sort ();
};
bubblesort::bubblesort (int n)
{
        items=n;
        x=new int[items];
bubblesort::~bubblesort()
{
        delete []x;
}
void bubblesort::input (int a[])
{
        for (int i=0;i<items;++i)
            x[i]=a[i];
}
void bubblesort::display()
}
        cout<<"\n Sorted elements are : \n";
        for(int i=0;<items;++i)
            cout<<setw(5)<<x[i];
}
void bubblesort::sort()
{
        int swap=1;
        for (int i=0;i<items &&swap==1;++)
        {
            swap=0;
            for(int j=0;j<items-(i+1);++j)
                    if (x[j]>x[j+1])
                    {
                            int temp;
                            temp=x[j];
                            x[j]=x[j+1];
                            x[j+1]=temp;
                            swap=1;
                    }
            }
}
```

```
void main ()
{
        int elements[100],noofitems;
        cout<<"\n Enter how many elements do you want to feed \n";
        cin>>noofitems;
        cout <<"\n Enter "<<noofitems<<" elements ";
        for(int i=0;i<noofitems;++i)
           cin>>elements[i];
        bubblesort bubblesortobj(noofitems);
        bubblesortobj.input(elements);
        bubblesortobj.sort();
        bubblesortobj.display();
}
```

OUTPUT :

```
Enter how many elements do you want to feed
6
Enter 6 elements
452 236 748 335 545 647
Sorted elements are :
236 335 452 545 647 748
```

16.8.2. Selection Sort :

This selection sort is nearly the same as exchange sort. Assume that we have a list of n elements. By applying selection sort, the first element is compared with all remaining (n-1) elements. The lower element is placed at the first location. Again, the second element is compared with remaining (n-2) elements. *At the time of comparison, the smaller element is swapped with larger element.* In this type, entire array is checked for smallest element and then swapping is done.

In other words this type of sorting is also an exchange sort. In this method, as shown in Fig. 16.35 we have to find the smallest value present in the array and this number is stored in the first position. Then the second smallest number is found out and it is stored in the second position, and so on. The algorithm used in sorting is as follows. Here, the elements are stored in array X.

1. Find the position L of the smallest among the elements X(1), X(2),….., X(N). Interchange X(L) with X(1).
2. Find the position L of the smallest among X(2),X(3),…,X(N). Now interc hange X(L) with X(2).

…………….

…………….

(N-1) Find the position L of the smallest among X (N-1), X(N). Now interchange X(L) with X(N-1).

Pass \ No.	1	2	3	4	5
1	21	65	43	87	54
2	21	65	43	87	54
3	21	43	65	87	54
4	21	43	54	87	65
5	21	43	54	65	87
Sorted No.	21	43	54	65	87

Fig.16.35. Selection Sort

Since, the selection sort algorithm is based on using data elements as keys for comparison like insertion sort, only one data element is placed in its desired sort position. This algorithm is inefficient because it does not consider or fully sorted list. To sort 'n' data elements the selection sort always does (n-1) iteration, which is different in previous methods that we have seen.

1. Time complexity : The time complexity of selection sort is O (n!).

2. Comparison with other methods

i) This method require more number of comparisons than quick sort and tree sort.

ii) It is easier to implement than other methods such as quick sort and tree sort.

Program 16.8.3.

Write a program in C to write a given array elements in ascending order using selection sort

```
#include stdio.h>
#include <conio.h>
```

```
main ( )
{
      int nums [15], p=0,qr,num,t,small;
      clrscr ();
      printf ("How many elements to sort ? : ");
      scanf (" %d"&num);
      printf ("Enter %d elements : ",num);
      while (p<num)
      scanf (" %d", &nums [p++]);
      for (p=0; p<num-1;p++)
            {
               small = p;
               for(r=p+1; r<num; r++)
               if (nums [small] > nums [r] )
               small = r ;
               if (p != small )
                        {
                                t = nums [p] ;
                                nums [p] = nums [small];
                                nums [small] = t;
                        }
            printf ("\nAfter %d pass elements are : ",p+1);
            q=0;
            while (q<num)
            printf (" %d "nums[q++] );
            }
      printf ("\nSorted elements are : ");
      p=0;
      while (p<num)
      printf (" %d", nums[p++]);
return 0;
}
```

OUTPUT :

Ho many elements to sort? : 5
Enter 5 elements : 21 65 43 87 54
After 1 pass elemens are : 21 65 43 87 54
After 2 pass elemens are : 21 43 65 87 54
After 3 pass elemens are : 21 43 54 87 65
After 4 pass elemens are : 21 43 54 65 87
Sorted elemens are : 21 43 54 65 87

Program 16.8.4

Write a program in C++ to sort a given set of elements in ascending order using selection sort.

```
# include <iosream>
# include <iomanip>
using namespace std;
class selection sort
{
    private:
        int *x;
        int items;
    public :
        selectionsort (int);
        ~selectionsort();
        void input (int [ ]);
        void display ();
        void sort();
};
    selectionsort::selectionsort(int n)
{
        items=n;
        x=new int[items];
}
    selectionsort:~selectionsort ()
{
        delete [ ]x;
}
    void selectionsort::input(int a[ ])
{
        for (int i=o;i<items;++i )
            x[i]=a[i];
}
    void selectionsort ::display()
{
        cout<<"\n Sorted elements are :\n";
        for(int i=0:i<items;++i)
            cout<<setw(5)<<x[i];
}
```

```
     void selectionsort::sort()
{
     for(int j=0;j<items-1;++j)
          {
                    int lowest=j;
                    for(in k=j+1;k<items;++k)
                         {
                              if(x[k]<x[lowest])
                               lowest=k;
                         }
                    int temp;
                    temp=x[j];
                    x[j]=x[lowest];
                    x[lowest]=temp;
          }
}
          void main ()
{
     int elements[100]noofiems;
     cout<"\n Enter how many elements do you want to feed? \n";
     cin>>nofitems;
     cout <<"\n Enter " <<noofitems<"elements";
     for (int i=0;i<noofitems;++i)
     cin>>elements[i];
     selectionsort selectionsortobj(noofitems);
     selectionsortobj.input(elements);
     selectionsortobj.sort();
     selectionsortobj.display();
}
```

OUTPUT :

Enter how many elements do you want to feed?
5

Enter 5 elements
65 43 12 78 34 65 43 12 78 34

Sorted elements are :
12 34 43 65 78

16.8.3. Quick Sort :

Quick Sort follows divide and conquer technique. **Quicksort is also known as partition exchanger sort.** It was invented by Car Hoare. **It is based on partition.**

The quick sort divides the main list into two sublists. For example, suppose a list of X elements are there for sorting The quick sort technique marks an element in preferably the middle of the list. **The marked element is called pivot or key.** Consider the element J. Then it shifts all the elements less than J to left of value J. All the elements greater than J are shifted to the right side. The key element is at the middle of both the lists. It is not compulsory that the selected key element must be exactly at the middle. *Any element from the list can act as key element.* However, for best performance is given to middle elements. *Time consumption of the quick sort depends on the location of the key in the list.*

The quick sort can also be described differently in other words.

In this method, the 'n' elements to be sorted are divided into three segments and they are:

i) a left segment left,
ii) a right segment right,
iii) and a middle segment middle.

In the middle segment we will be having only one element and it is called the pivot or partitioning element. Also note that no element in left segment has a key larger than the key of the element in middle and no element in right has a key that is smaller than that of the middle element. Due to this, the elements in left and middle can be sorted independently, and no merge is needed following the sorting of left and right.

Now, let us consider the process for sorting a typical subarray A[p....r]

Step 1 :

The array A[p..r] is rearranged into two nonempty subarrays A[p..q] and A[q+1..r] such that each element of A[p..q] is less than or equal to each element of A[q+1..r]. Here the index 'q' is computed as part of this partitioning procedure. This step is divide procedure.

Step 2 : The two subarrays A[p..q] and A[q+1..r] are sorted by recursive calls to quicksort. This part is conquer procedure.

Step 3 : Since the subarrays are already sorted in place, no work is needed to combine them. This part is combine procedure.

1) Time complexity : The time complexity of quick sort is O (nlogn)

2) Comparison with other methods

i) *Quick sort is the fastest sorting method among all types of sorts.*

ii) It is a somewhat complex method of sorting so it is a little hard to implement than other sorting algorithms.

Program 16.8.5.

Write a program in C to sort in ascending order the array elements using quick sort.

```
# include <stdio.h>
# include <conio.h>
	main ()
{
	int nums[15], num,j=0;
	int q_sort (int *,int,int);
	int show (int *,int,int);
	clrscr ();
	printf ("Enter the number of elements : ");
	scanf (" %d",&num);
	prinf ("\n Enter %d elements : ",num);
	while (j<num)
	scanf (" %d",&nums[j++])
	qsort (nums0,num-1);
	prinf ("Sorted lis is :\n");
	show(nums,0,num-1);
return 0;
}
	q_sort (int items [ ], int lower, int upper)
{
	int key,temp,l,r,key_placed=0;
	int show (int *, int,int);
	l=lower;
	r=upper;
	key=lower;
	if (lower>=upper) return 0;

	while (key_placed==0)
		{
		   while (items[key]<=items[r] [ && key !=r)
		   r-;
		   if (key==r )   key_placed=1;
		   if {items [key] > items [r] )
			{
				temp=items[key];
				items [key]=items [r];
				items [r]=temp;
				key=r;
			}
```

```
            while ( items[key]>=items [1] && l != key) 1++;
            if (key==l key_pleaced=1;
            if ( items [key] <items [1] )
            {
                temp=items[key];
                iems[key]=items[1];
                iems[1]=temp;
                key=1;
            }
}
        printf (" * Key Placed is %d -> ",items[key]);
        show (items,lower,upper);
        printf ("\n");
        q_sort(iems,lower,key-1);
        q_sort (items,key+1,upper);
return 0;
}
```

show (int items [ ], int lower, int upper)

```
{
        while (lower<=upper)
        printf("%d",items[lower++]);
        return 0;
}
```

OUTPUT :

```
Enter the number of elements : 5
Enter 5 elements : 18 19 17 16 14
* Key Placed is 18 -> 14 16 17 18 19
* Key Placed is 14 -> 14 16 17
* Key Placed is 16 -> 16 17
Sorted list is : 14 16 17 18 19
```

Program 16.8.6

Write a program in C++ to write a set of array numbers in ascending order using quick sort.

```
# include <iostream>
# include <iomanip>
using namespace std;
```

```
class quicksort
{
      private:
            int *x;
            int items;
      public:
            quicksort(int);
            ~quicksort();
            void input (int [ ]);
            void display ();
            void sort (int,int);
};
      quicksort::quicksort (int n)
{
            items=n;
            x=new int[items];
}
            quicksort::~quicksort( )
{
            delete [ ]x;
}
      void quicksort::input(int a [ ] )
{
            for (int i=0;i<items;++)
               x[i]=a[i];
}
      void quicksort::display( )
{
            cout<<"\n Sorted elements are :\n";
            for (int i=0;i<items;++i)
               cout<<setw(5)<<x[i];
}
      void quicksort::sort(int first,int last)
{
            int temp;
            if (first <last)
               {
                        int pivot=x[first];
                        int i=first;
                        int j=last;
```

```
                    while (i<j)
                          {
                                  while (x[i] <=pivot && i last)
                                  i++;
                                  while (x[j] >=pivot && j>first)
                                  j–;
                                  if (i<j)
                                          {
                                                  temp=x[i];
                                                  x[i]=x[j];
                                                  x[j]=temp;
                                          }
                          }
                    temp=x[first];
                    x[first]=x[j];
                    x[j]=temp;
                    sort(first,j-1);
                    sort (j+1,last);
              }
}
        void main ( )
{
           int elements[100],noofitems;
           cout<<"\n Enter how many elements do you want to feed? \n";
           cin>>noofitems;
           cout<<"\n Enter "noofitems<<"elements";
           for (int i=0;<noofitems;++i)
           cin>>elements[i];
           quicksort quicksortobj(noofitems);
           quicksortobj.input(elements);
           quicksortobj.sort (0, noofiems-1);
           quicksortobj.display();
}
```

OUTPUT :

Enter how many elements do you want to feed?
5
Enter 5 elements
65 43 12 78 34
Sorted elements are :
12 34 43 65 78

16.8.4. Merge sort :

Merge sort also follows divide and conquer algorithm. Unlike quick sort, here the split stage is simple and merge stage is complex. In each iteration, this algorithm passes over the entire list and performs O(n) comparisons. In the very first scan, the merge sort considers only one list. In the subsequent scan, the algorithm splits the list into halves and then sorts and merges them. And in the kth iteration, the algorithm splits the list into sublists, which are 2k-1 in number. In the worst case, the merge sort has a performance on the order of nlog 2n and it is much better than most of the other methods, Now let us have a closer look at the following program.

1) **Time complexity :** The time complexity of merge sort is O(n)

2) **Comparison with other methods**

   i) In the very first scan, the merge sort considers only one list. In the subsequent scan, the algorithm splits the list into halves and then sorts and merges them. And in the kth iteration, the algorithm splits the list into sublists, which are $2^k - 1$ in number. In the worst case the merge sort has a performance on the order of $n\log^2 n$.

   ii) it is much better than most of the other methods.

Program 16.8.7

Write a program in C++ to merge sort two arrays arranging all the array elements in ascending order.

```
# include <iostream>
# include <iomanip>
using namespace std;
    class mergesort
{
    private :
        int *x,*y,*z;
        int items1, items2;
    public :
        mergesort(int,int);
        ~mergesort();
        void input1(int [ ]);
        void bsort(int[ ],int);
            void display();
            void sort();
};
```

```
    mergesort::mergesort(int p,intq)
{
    items1=p;
    items2=q;
    x=new int[items1];
    y=new int[items2];
    z=new int (items1+items2];
}
mergesort::~mergesort()
{
    delete [ ]x;
    delete [ ]y;
    delete [ ]z;
}
void mergesort::input1(int a[ ])
{
    for (int i=0;i<items1;++i)
        x[i]=a[i];
    bsort(x,iems1);
    cout <<"\n Sorted first array :\n";
    for (i=0;i<items1;++i)
        cout<<setw(5)<<x[i];
}
void mergesort::input2(int b[ ])
{
    for (int i=0;i<items2;++i)
        y[i]=b[i];
    bsort(y,iems2);
    cout <<"\n Sorted Second array :\n";
    for (i=0;i<items2;++i)
        cout<<setw(5)<<y[i];
}
void mergesort::bsort(int m[ ],int n)
{
    int swap=1;
    for (int i=0;i<n &&swap==1;++i)
    {
        swap=0;
        for(int j=0;j<n-(i+1);++j)
            if (m[j] > m[j+1])
                if (m[j] > m[j+1])
                {
                    int temp;
                    temp=m[j];
```

```
                        m[j]=m{j+1];
                        m[j+1]=temp;
                        swap=1;
                    }
    }
}
        void mergesort::display()
{
    for(int i=0;i<items 1+items2;++i)
    cout<<setw(5)<<z[i];
}
    void mergesort::sort ()
{
        int i,j,k;
        i=j=k=0;
        while ((i<items1)&& (j<items2) )
        {
            if (x[i] < y [j]
            {
                z[k]=x[i];
                i++;
                k++;
            }
            else
            {
                if(x[i]>y[j];
                z[j]=y[i];
                j++;
                k++;
            }
            else
            {
                z[k]=x[i];
                i++;
                j++;
                k++;
            }
        }
    } .
            while(i<items1)
            {
                z[k]=x[i];
                i++;
                k++;
            }
```

```
                while(j<items2)
                {
                        z[k]=y[j];
                        j++;
                        k++;
                }
}
        void main( )
{
    int elements1[100],noofitems1=3;
    int elements2[100],noofitems2=4;
    int i;
    cout<"\n Enter how many elemens do you want to feed for first array \n";
    cin>>noofitems1;
    cout<<"\n Enter "<<noofitems1<<"elements";
    for(i=0;j<noofitems1;++i)
            cin>>elements1[i];
        cout<<"\n Enter how many elements do you want to feed for second array \n";
        cin>>noofiems2;
        cout<<"\n Enter "<<noofitems2<<"elements";
        for(i=0;j<noofitems2;++i)
            cin>>elements2[i];
        mergesort mergesortobj(noofiems1,noofitems2);
        mergesortobj.input1(elements1);
        mergesortobj.input2(elements2);
        mergesortobj.sort();
        cout<<"\n Sorted merged array is :\n";
        mergesortobj.display();
}
```

OUTPUT :

Enter how many elements do you want to feed for first array
5

Enter 5 elements
12 34 21 89 76

Enter how many elements do you want to feed for second array
5

Enter 5 elements
67 98 121 6 48

Sorted first array :
12 21 34 76 89

Sorted second array :
6 48 67 98 121

Sorted merged array is :
6 12 21 34 48 67 76 89 98 121

16.8.5. K-Way Merge Sort :

It is an external sorting used to sort large data ,splitting the data into a number of chunks, keeping one chunk in RAM memory and the remaining chunks in external memory like hard disc. It is very fast sorting.

External sorting is a term for a class of sorting algorithms that can handle massive amounts of data. External sorting is required when the data being sorted do not fit into the main memory of a computing device (usually RAM) and instead they must reside in the slower external memory (usually a hard drive). External sorting typically uses a sort-merge strategy. In the sorting phase, chunks of data small enough to fit in main memory are read, sorted, and written out to a temporary file. In the merge phase, the sorted subfiles are combined into a single larger file.

An implementation of "k-Way Merging" as described in "Fundamentals of Data Structures" by Horowitz/Sahni.

The idea is to merge k sorted arrays limiting the number of comparisons. A binary tree is built containing the results of comparing the heads of each array. The top most node is always the smallest entry. Then, its corresponding leaf in the tree is refilled and the tree is processed again. It's easier to see in the following example:

Imagine 4 sorted arrays: (4 Sorted Chunks)

{5, 10, 15, 20}

{10, 13, 16, 19}

{2, 19, 26, 40}

{18, 22, 23, 24}

The initial tree looks like this:

```
        2  (Min. of first elements of all chunks)
      /   \
     2       5 (Binary Tree. So 2 elements)
   /  \    /  \
  18   2  10   5 (Heads or first elements of all chunks)
```

The '/' and '\' represent links. The bottom row are the leaves and they contain the heads of the arrays. The rows above the leaves represent the smaller of the two child nodes. Thus, the top node is the smallest. To process the next iteration, the top node gets popped and its leaf gets refilled. Then, the new leaf's associated nodes are processed. So, after the 2 is taken, it is filled with 19 (the next head of its array). After processing, the tree looks like this:

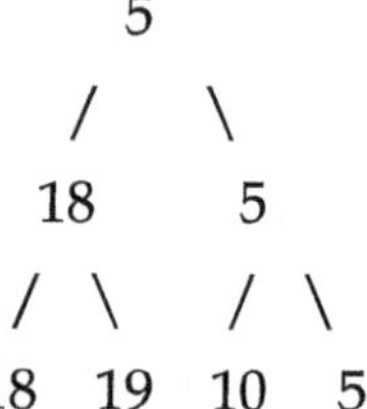

So, you can see how the number of comparisons is reduced.

A good use of this is when you have a very large array that needs to be sorted. Break it up into n small arrays and sort those. Then use this merge sort for the final sort. This can also be done with files. If you have n sorted files, you can merge them into one sorted file.

16.8.6. What differentiates a K-Way Merge sort from a regular Merge sort?

Well a normal Merge sort splits up the given data set in to two sets of data recursively. For example, in the set:

[4,6,2,8,9,1,7,5,3]

We would split it in to:

[4,6,2,8] and [9,1,7,5,3]

Then the same algorithm would be recursively ran on the left and the right pieces and then merged together:

```
merge_sort(left);
merge_sort(right);
merge(left, right);
```

Now because we ran merge_sort on the left and right pieces first we can assume they are now sorted, now it's just a matter of putting the two sorted arrays together, so this makes the actually merge_sort method pretty trivial, it's the merge() that gets interesting. And because you can see how we split it in to a left and a right you could pretty easily see how a splitting it three ways with a left, middle, and right would be pretty similar. With a K-Way we just split it up in to however many chunks we want trying to find better efficiency by reducing the chunk size much faster.

a) The Merge

The interesting piece of the algorithm, starting with the traditional two sided merge sort we have a base case of when we get down to two elements. With two elements things are pretty simple we just sort the two elements and return them, but what about when we have two sets of sorted data, what is the best way to merge them?

Well because both pieces are already individually sorted we can actually sort them together pretty quickly. We start at the beginning of each array and compare each number one by one removing the smaller and moving forward.

0For example, lets take our earlier example, sorted:

[2,4,6,8] and [1,3,5,7,9]

So compare the first numbers in each set and 1 less than 2 so we move the 1 to the result set and continue on:

Result:

[1,?,?,?,?,?,?,?,?]

[2,4,6,8] and [x,3,5,7,9]

Compare 2 and 3 together:

Result:

[1,2,?,?,?,?,?,?,?]

[x,4,6,8] and [x,3,5,7,9]

Then 4 and 3 and so forth until we get our sorted array, this should happen in no more than O(n) time.

Now there is a slight trick here, instead of passing a left and right since the left and right pieces should always be next to each other in the original array we can do some trickery to turn:

merge(left, right)

in to:

merge(data, low, high)

And find our split we can do some quick math:

(high+low)/2

Now we still have to copy over the data from low to high in to a temporary array so we can put them back in to the original one, but this does allow us to sort the original array and minimize creations to just the temp arrays.

b) So what about the K-Way merge again?

Well you can see doing a merge(data, low, high) may work better than trying to pass k number of small arrays, but the concept is pretty similar.

For the base case we have something a little less trivial since our smallest merge will have k elements in it, which for a large data set could have 10 to 50 partitions OR MORE. To solve this we can sort by putting them in to a heap real quick and pulling them back out, in the given source code below, I didn't write the heap, but it's pretty trivial to do so.

```
if (high < low + k) {

// the subarray has k or fewer elements
// just make one big heap and do deleteMins on it
Comparable[ ] subarray = new MergesortHeapNode[high - low + 1];
for (int i = 0, j = low; i < subarray.length; i++, j++) {
subarray[i] = new MergesortHeapNode(data[j], 0);
}
BinaryHeap heap = BinaryHeap.buildHeap(subarray);
for (int j = low; j <= high; j++) {
try {
data[j] = ((MergesortHeapNode) heap.deleteMin()).getKey();
}
catch (EmptyHeapException e) {
System.out.println ("Tried to delete from an empty heap.");
}
}
}
```

And for the non-base case where we have several sorted arrays we run in to a similar problem, we can no longer do a simple, is left less than right. We have to put the first index of all arrays in to a heap to figure out which array has the lowest first element. And once we figure out which array has the lowest from the heap we have to pull the element from that array and put it where it goes and then we have to refill the heap with the next element in the small array we just took from.

```
else {

// divide the array into k subarrays and do a k-way merge
final int subarrSize = high-low+1;
final int[ ] tempArray = new int[subarrSize];

// Make temp array
for (int i = low; i < high + 1; i++)
 tempArray[i-low] = data[i];
```

```
// Keep subarray index to keep track of where we are in each subarray
final int[ ] subarrayIndex = new int[k];
for (int i = 0; i < k; i++)
subarrayIndex[i] = i*(subarrSize)/k;

// Build heap
Comparable[ ] subarray = new MergesortHeapNode[k];
for (int i = 0; i < k; i++)
subarray[i] = new MergesortHeapNode(tempArray[subarrayIndex[i]++], i);

BinaryHeap heap = BinaryHeap.buildHeap(subarray);
// For each element low to high, find the lowest in each k subarray
for (int i = low; i < high + 1; i++)
{
// Take lowest element and add back in to original array
try
{

MergesortHeapNode a = ((MergesortHeapNode) heap.deleteMin());
data[i] = a.getKey();

if (subarrayIndex[a.getWhichSubarray()] <
(a.getWhichSubarray()+1)*(subarrSize)/k)
{
heap.insert(new
ergesortHeapNode(tempArray[subarrayIndex[a.getWhichSubarray()]]++,
.getWhichSubarray()));
// Increment the subarray index where the lowest element resides
subarrayIndex[a.getWhichSubarray()]++;
}

} catch (EmptyHeapException e)
{

System.out.println ("Tried to delete from an empty heap.");
}
}
}
```

16.8.7. Heap Sort or Tree Sort :

In a binary tree, we know that the elements are inserted according to the value greater or less in between mode and the root in traversing. If the value is less than the traversing node, then insertion is done at left side. If the value is greater than the traversing node, it is inserted at right side. The elements of such a tree can be sorted. This sorting involves creation of binary tree and then traversing is done in order.

Binary tree sort or heap sort is a sorting algorithm that works by first organizing the data to be sorted into a special type of binary tree called a heap. The heap itself has, by definition, the largest value at the top of the tree, so the heap sort algorithm must also reverse the order. It does this with the following steps:

When considering various sorting algorithm, the heap sort is an excellent algorithm. Like merge sort, but unlike insertion sort, heap sort's running time is O (n log n). Like insertion sort, but unlike merge sort, heap sort sorts in place. Only a constant number of array elements are stored outside the input array at any time. **Tree sort or heap sort algorithm basically rearranges the data elements in a tree so that the value at each node is greater than or equal to the values of its children.** Also note that nodes in the heap are not sorted. In this algorithm, any given parent node has a larger data element than all its child nodes, ensures that the largest data element is at the top of the heap. When we remove this top data element and swap it with the end of the array, the elements come into its proper-sorted element. Now, find the largest element among them by search through the remaining data elements. By repeating this procedure, we eventually sort the array.

In other words, the **heap sort is made up of 3 steps :**

i) Arranging the elements of the list in the form of a binary tree, which satisfies the condition of a heap.

ii) Removing the top-most element of the heap (root of the binary tree) and pushing it to the sorted list as the element before the last added element.

iii) Rearranging the remaining elemens to form a heap. This process will repeat till we get a sorted list.

Consider the list 34, 54, 12, 44 and 10 for sorting. The heap sort proceeds as follows.

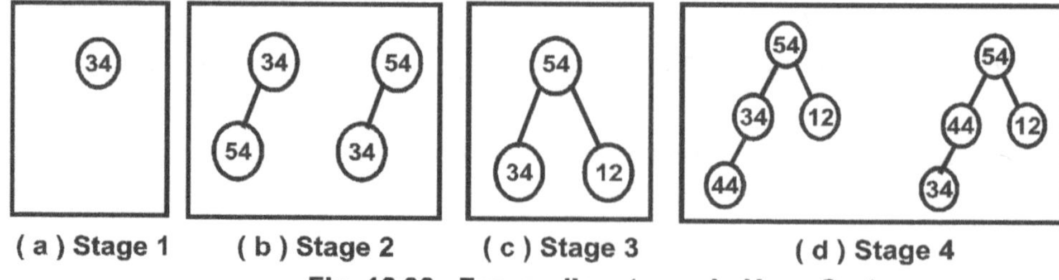

Fig. 16.36. Few earlier stages in Heap Sort

1) **Time complexity :** The time complexity of quick sort is O (mlogn), where 'm' is the number of nodes having log(n+1) levels.

2) **Comparison with other methods**

i) This is an excellent algorithm and rearranges the data elements in the form of a binary tree (which is a heap) with each node being greater than its children.

ii) It is a complex method of sorting so it is a little hard to implement than other sorting algorithms.

Program 16.8.8

Write a program in C for writing an array elements in ascending order using Heap Sort.

```
# include <stdlib.h>
# include <stdio.h>
# define MAXSIZE 500
void heapsort(int elements[ ], int maxsize);
void buildheap(int elemens[ ], int root, int leaf);
int elements [MAXSIZE] maxsize;
int main ()
{
    int i;
    printf("\n How many elements you want to sort:");
    scanf(" %d",&maxsize);
    printf("\nEnter the values one by one: %i");
    for (i=0; i <maxsize; i++)
    {
    scanf (" %d",&elements[i]);
    }
    printf("\nArray before sorting:\n");
    for (i=0; i <maxsize; i++)
        printf("[%i],",elements[i]);
    prinf ("\n");
    heapsort (elements, maxsize);
    prinf("\nArray after sorting:\n");
    for (i=0; i <maxsize; i++)
        printf("[%i],",elements[i]);
}
    void heapsort (int elemens [ ], int maxsize)
{
    int i temp; for (i= (maxsize /2) - 1; i>=0; i--)
    buildheap (elements, i, maxsize);
    for (i=maxsize - 1; i> 1; i--)
    {
    temp = elements [0];
    elements[0] = elements[i];
    elements[i] = temp;
    buildheap(elements, 0, i-1);
    }
}
```

```
        void buildheap(int elements[ ], int root, int leaf)
{
            int flag, max, temp;
            flag = 0;
            while ((root * 2 <=leaf) && (!flag))
            {
                if (root *2 == leaf)
                max = root * 2;
                else if (elements[root *2]>elements[(root *2) + 1])
                    max = root *2;
                else
                    max = root * 2 + 1;
            if (elements[root[ < elements[max])
                {
                    temp = elements [root];
                    elements[root] = elements [max];
                    elements[max] = temp;
                    root = max;
                }
            else
            flag = 1;
            }
}
```

OUTPUT :

```
How many elements you want to sort:
5
Enter the values one by one:%i
Array before sorting:
56 34 21 87 43
Array after sorting:
21 34 43 56 87
```

Program 16.8.9

Write a program in C++ for writing an array elements in ascending order using Heap Sort.

```
# include <iostream>
# include <iomanip>
using namespace std;
class heapsort
{
    private:
        int *x;
        int items;
```

```
    public :
        heapsort(int);
        ~heapsort();
        void establish_heap_property(int,int);
        void construct_heap();
        void input(int [ ]);
        void display ();
        void sort(int[ ]);
};
    heapsort::heapsort(int n)
{
        x=new int[n+1];
        items=n;
}
    heapsort::~heapsort( )
{
        delete [ ]x;
}
    void heapsort::input(int a[ ])
{
        for (int i=1;i<=5;++i)
            x[i]=a[i-1];
}
    void heapsort::display( )
{
        for (int i=1;i<=items;++i)
            cout<<setw(5)<<x[i];

}
    void heapsort::construct_heap( )
{
        for(int i=items/2;i>0;i--)
            establish_heap_property(int root,int limit)
        {
        int done=0;
        int biggest=x[root];
        int j=2*root;
        while ( (j<=limit && (done==0))
            {
                if (j<limit) && (x[j]<x[j+1]))
                    j++;
                if(biggest >=x[j])
                done=1;
```

```
            else
                {
                    x[j/2]=x[j];
                    j=2*j;
                }
            }
        x[j/2]=biggest;
}
        void heapsort::sort(int input[ ])
{
            consruct_heap ( );
            for(int i=(items-1);i>0;i—)
            {
            int temp;
            temp=x[i+1];
            x[i+1]=x[1];
            x[1]=temp;
            input[i]=x[i+1];
            establish_heap_property(1,i);
            }
        input[0]=x[1];
}
    void main ( )
{
        int noofiems=5;
        heapsort heapsortobj(5);
        static int elements [ ]=(45,34,3,2,22);
        heapsortobj.input(elements);
        out<<"\n Given elements are : \n";
            heapsortobj.display ();

        heapsortobj.sort(elements);
        cout<<"\n Sorted elements are : \n";
        heapsortobj.display ();
}
```

OUTPUT :

```
Given elements are :
    245  234  23 22  222
Sorted elements are :
    22  23  222  234  245
```

16.8.8. Insertion Sort (or Simple Insertion Sort) :

The Insertion sort is also a sort of exchange sort. The insertion sort is a very simple sorting method. Assume that we have a list of 'n' elements. By applying selection sort, the first element is compared with all remaining (n-1) elements. The lower elements is placed at the first location. Again, the second element is compared with remaining (n-2) elements. At the time of comparison, the smaller element is swapped with larger element. In this type, entire array is checked for smallest element and then swapping is done.

In other words, **the insertion sort uses data elements as keys for comparison.** The algorithm first orders x[0] and x[1] by inserting x[1] in front of x[0] if x [0] >x[1]. Using this ordered list, the rest of the data elements are iteratively inserted in the ordered list, one at a time. After performing k the iteration. X[k] is inserted in its sorted position and x[0] through x[k] are sorted.

Like bubble sort, this method also has a simple implementation. *The worst case is when the data elements are reversely ordered. The best case is when the elements are almost sorted in the correct order like bubble sort.*

An example of an insertion sort occurs while playing cards. To sort the cards in your hand you extract a card, shift the remaining cards, and then insert the extracted card in the correct place. The process is repeated until all the cards are in the correct sequence. This is illustrated with a simple example in Fig.16.37. Consider the list : 23, 17 5, 14.

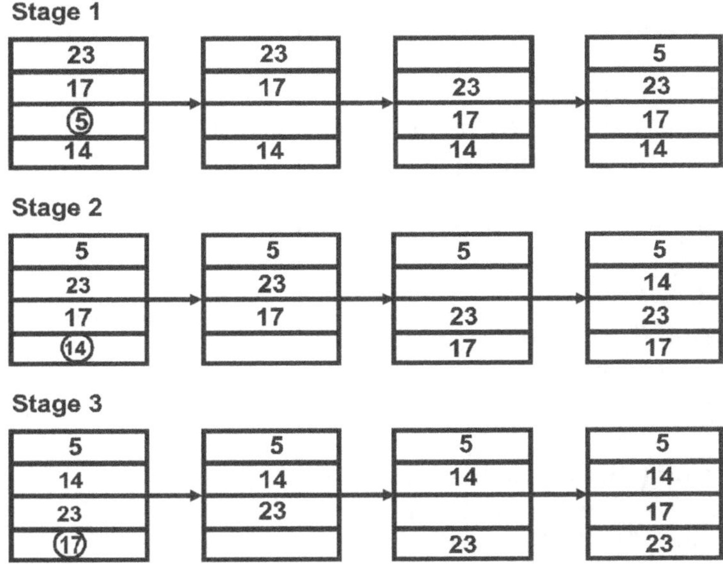

Fig. 16.37. Different stages of Insertion Sort

1) **Time complexity :** The time complexity of insertion sort is O(n!)

2) **Comparison with other methods**

   i) This requires more number of comparisons than other methods such as quick sort and tree sort.

   ii) It is easier to implement than quick sort and tree sort.

Program 16.8.10

Write a program in C to sort array elements in ascending order using Insertion sort.

```
# include <stdio.h>
# include <conio.h>
int main ( )
{
      int num [20], p=0,q=1,r,num;
      clrscr ();
      printf ("Enter number of elements : ");
      scanf (" %d"&num);
      printf ("\n Enter %d elements : ",num);
      while (p<num)
      scanf (" %d", &nums[p++]);
      while (p<num)
      scanf (" %d", &nums [p++] );
      while (q<num)
      {
            r=nums[q];
            for (p=q-1;p>=0 && r<nums [p] ; p— —)
            nums[p+1]=nums [p];
            r=nums [p+1];
         printf ("Element %d inserted in appropriate place ",r);
            p=0;
            while (p<num)
            printf (" %d", nums [p++] );
            printf ("\n");
            q++;
      }
            printf ("Sorted elements are : ");
            for (p = 0; p < num; p++)
            printf (" %d", nums [p]);
            return 0;
}
```

OUTPUT :

Enter numbers of elements : 5
Enter 5 elements : 94 96 92 91 98
Enter 96 inserted in appropriate place 94 96 92 91 98
Enter 92 inserted in appropriate place 92 94 96 91 98
Enter 91 inserted in appropriate place 91 92 94 96 98
Enter 98 inserted in appropirate place 91 92 94 96 98
Sorted elemens are : 91 92 94 96 98

Program 16.8.11

Write a program in C++ to sort array elements in ascending order using Insertion sort.

```
#include <iostream>
#include <iomanip>
using namespace std;
class insertionsort
{
    private:
        int *x;
        int items;
    public:
        insertionsort(int);
        ~insertionsort();
        void input(int [ ]);
        void display ( );
        void sort ( );
};
insertionsort::insertionsort(int n)
{
        items=n;
        x=new int[items];
}
insertionsort::~insertionsort ( )
{
        delete [ ]x;
}
void insertionsort::input(int a[ ])
{
        for (in i=0;i<items;++i)
            x[i]=a[i];
}
```

```
      void insertionsort::display ( )
{
            cout <<"\n Sorted elements are : \n";
            for (int i=0;i<items;++i)
               cout<<setw(5)<<x[i];
}
      void insertionsort::sort()
{
            int s[100];
            s[0]=x[0];
            int i;
      for (i=1;i<items;++i)
      {
            int temp=x[i];
            int j=i-1;
               while ( (s[j]>temp) && (j>=0) )
               {
                        s[j+1]=s[j];
                        j–;
               }
               s[j+1]=temp;
      }
               for (i=0;i<items;++i)
                        x[i]=s[i];
}
      void main ( )
{
            int elemens[100],noofitems;
            cout<<"\n Enter how many elements do you want to feed \n";
            cin>>noofitems;
            cout <<"\n Enter "<<noofitems<<"elements";
            for (int i=0;i<noofitems;++i)
            cin>>elements[i];
            insertionsort  insertionsortobj(noofitems);
            insertionsortobj.inut(elements);
            insertionsortobj.sort();
            insertionsorobj.display  ();
}
```

OUTPUT :

Enter how many elements do you want to feed
5

Enter 5 elements
65 43 12 78 34

Sorted elemens are :
12 34 43 65 78

16.8.9. Shell sort :

The shell sort algorithm is a variation of insertion sort. The insertion sort algorithm has the limitation that it compares the consecutive data elements and due to this a swap moves an element only one space. For elements that are far away require many passes through the sort to properly place them. **In shell sort algorithm the elements are subdivided into interleaved groups, and each group is sorted using an insertion sort algorithm.** Here, the subdivision is performed using an increment value to begin with and in our program it is 'h'. The increment values divides the original array into 'h' subarrays and these subarrays are then sorted using either insertion or bubble sort algorithm. This method is repeated using diminishing values for 'h' until the last value of 'h' is 1. In the final scan, the list is almost sorted, and the insertion sort during this scan can complete the process in linear time, resulting in a sorted list. **Shell sort method is therefore also referred to as the diminishing increment sort.**

In other words shell sort can be stated to be based on the insertion sort. The given list of elements is broken down in few smaller lists. After this, the insertion sort is applied on such smaller lists. These smaller lists are again recombined. Another partition is made and the procedure is repeated. The breaking down of the list into smaller lists is by selection elements at specific locations. This is determined by a factor called increment.

Consider the list : 23, 12, 6, 34, 13, 7 44. We may initially take the increment as 3. This would break the lis as : 23, 34, 44; 12, 13 and 6, 7. The first list is done using elements [0], elements [6] where the increment is 3. This list is sorted using insertion sort. The next list is element [1] and elements [4] where the increment is the same 3. The final list elements [2] and elements [5] with the same increment of 3. After sorting them the sublists are recombined.

As a next stage, the increment is changed (reduced by a suitable amount) and the process is repeated. The process continues till the increment is 1. The choice of increments is left to our choice. We can increments such as 7, 5 3 and or 6, 4, 1 etc.

Program 16.8.12

Write a program in C to sort an array elements in ascending order using shell sort.

```
# include <stdlib.h>
# include <stdio.h>
# define MAXSIZE 500
void shellsort (int elements [ ], int maxsize);
int elements [MAXSIZE],maxsize;
```

```
int main ()
{
    int i;
    printf(" %nHow many elemens you want to sort: ");
    scanf(" %d",&maxsize);
    printf ("\nEnter the values one by one: %i");
    for (i = 0; i <maxsize; i++)
    scanf(" %d",&elemens[i]);
    printf("\nArray before sorting:\n");
     for (i = 0; i <maxsize; i++)
     printf("[%i],",elements[i]);
     printf ("\n");
     shellsort(elements, maxsize);
     prinf("\nArray after sorting:\n");
     for (i = 0; i <maxsize; i++)
     prinf("[%i],",elements[i]);
}
void shellsort(int elements[ ], int maxsize)
{
     int i, j, increment, temp;
     increment = 7;
     while (increment>0)
     {
          for i=0; i < maxsize; i++)
          {
               j = i;
               temp = elements[i];
               while ((j >=increment) && (elements[j-increment] > temp))
               {
                    elements [j] = elements [j - increment];
                    j = j - increment;
               }
          elements[j] = temp;
          }
     if (increment/3 !=0)
          increment = increment/3;
          else if (increment ==1)
          increment = 0;
          else
          increment = 1;
     }
}
```

OUTPUT :

How many elements you want to sort:
5
Enter the values one by one:
Array before sorting:
56 34 21 87 43
Array after sorting:
21 34 43 56 87

Program 16.8.13

Write a program in C++ to sort the elements of an array in ascending order using shell sort.

```
# include <iostream>
# include <iomanip>
using namespace std;
    class shellsort
{
    private :
        int *x;
        int items ;
    public :
        shellsort(int);
        ~shellsort ();
        void input (int [ ]);
        void display ();
        void sort ();
};
    shellsort::shellsort(int n)
{
        items=n;
        x=new int[items];
}
    shellsort::~shellsort ( )
{
        delete [ ] x;
}
    void shellsort::input (int a [ ] )
{
        for (int i=0;i<items;++i)
            x[i]=a[i];
}
    void shellsort::display ()
{
        cout<<"\n Sorted elements are :\n";
        for(int i=0;i<items;++i)
        cout<<setw(5)<<x[i];}
}
```

```
      void shellsort::sort( )
{
          int temp,i,h;
          for (h=1;h<items/9;h=3*h+1);
          {
             for (;h>0;h/=3)
             {
                     int j;
                     temp=x[i];
                     for (j=i-h;j>=0;j-=h)
                     {
                             if (temp<x[j])
                             x[j+h]=x[j];
                     else
                             break;
                     }
                     x[j+h]=temp;
             }
          }
}
      void main ( )
{
      int elements[100],noofitems;
      cout<<"\n Enter how many elements do you want to feed \n";
      cin>>noofitems;
      cout <<"\n Enter "<noofitems <* elements";
      for (int i=0;i<noofitems;++i)
          cin>>elements[i];
      shellsort shellsortobj(noofitems);
      shellsortobj.input (elemens);
      shellsortobj.sort();
      shellsortobj.display ();
}
```

OUTPUT :

Enter how many elements do you want to feed
5

Enter 5 elemens
56 34 21 87 43

Sorted elements are :
21 34 43 56 87

* * *

COMPREHENSION - 16

Note : By answering all the questions given in this comprehension one can answer any objective type of questions easily whatever be the form of the question. Answers for these questions can be obtained by going through the topics in this chapter carefully.

1. In Data Base Programs how is large Data maintained?
2. What is meant by Searching? What is the need for Searching? Explain with examples.
3. What is Sorting? Explain with examples. Why is Sorting necessary?
4. What is a Field and What is a Record? Explain with examples.
5. Explain the Process of Searching in detail.
6. How is the complexity of searching determined?
7. What are the types of Search?
8. Explain with figure Linear or Sequential Search.
9. Explain with figure Binary or Sequential Search.
10. What are the Features of Binary Search?
11. Compare Linear and Binary Search.
12. What is meant by a Graph? What are the components of a Graph?
13. What is a Tree? What are the components of a Tree? What is the special feature of a Tree?
14. What is a Binary Tree? How do you represent a Binary Tree?
15. What are the methods of implementing a Binary Tree? What are their relative merits.
16. Explain the Hierarchy of a Binary Tree? What Climbing up or ascending? What is descending or going down a Tree?
17. What is meant by levels of a Tree?
18. Explain a Strictly Binary Tree.
19. Explain a Complete Binary Tree.
20. Explain an Extended Binary Tree.
21. How many Fields does a node of a Binary Tree have? What are they?
22. Explain construction of a Binary Tree using linked representation.
23. Explain insertion and deletion operations in a Binary Tree.
24. Explain the different ways of traversing a Binary Tree.
25. Explain In Order, Pre Order and Post Order Traversal of a Binary Tree.

26. Explain Level Order Traversal of a Binary Tree.
27. What is a minimum spanning tree?
28. What does a minimum spanning tree indicate regarding cost?
29. Can a spanning tree have more than one spanning tree?
30. Can there be more than one minimum spanning tree of the same weight?
31. What is a unique minimum spanning tree?
32. What should be the nature of weights if a minimum spanning tree to represent minimum costs sub-graph?
33. When does an edge does not belong to MST?
34. When does an edge belong to all MSTs of the graph?
35. When is an edge included in any MST?
36. Name the algorithms used to find a minimum spanning tree.
37. What are the other different algorithms used to find MST?
38. Explain calculation of approximate expected size for MST on complete graphs?
39. What are the different types of minimum panning trees?
40. What is an AVL Tree?
41. What is the advantage of an AVL Tree?
42. How do you decide whether a tree is an AVL Tree or not?
43. What are the basic operations of an AVL Tree?
44. Explain look-up in an AVL Tree?
45. What does look-up in AVL Tree achieve?
46. Explain insertion in an AVL tree.
47. What is meant by rotation?
48. What does rotation achieve?
49. How is rotation done?
50. What are the different types of rotation?
51. What are the different cases of deletion in an AVL tree?
52. How do you decide whether the height of the sub-tree has decreased by one? Then what do you do?
53. Discuss the complexity in big O notation for different operatoins on an AVL tree.
54. Compare AVL tree to other structures.

55. Explain with figures different types of Graphs.
56. Explain the representation of a Graph by a Table.
57. Explain Adjacency Matrix of a Directed Graph.
58. How many lists are maintained for adjacency list of a Graph? Explain.
59. Explain the Traversal in a Graph.
60. What is meant by Spanning Trees?
61. Explain the different types of Spanning Trees.
62. What is a weighted Graph? Explain.
63. Explain Prim's Algorithm for Traversal of a graph.
64. Explain Breadth First Search of a Tree.
65. Explain Depth First Search of a Tree.
66. Explain Ascending Order and Deserting Order Sorting.
67. Classify the different Sorts.
68. Explain Exchange Sort or Bubble Sort, What is its time complexity and compare it with other types of Sorts.
69. Explain Selection Sort. What is its time complexity and compare it with other types of Sorts.
70. Explain Quick Sort. What is its time complexity and compare it with other types of Sorts.
71. Explain Merge Sort. What is its time complexity and compare it with other types of Sorts?
72. What is external sorting? When do you require external sorting?
73. What is K-way merge sort? Explain with an example.
74. What is the difference between K-way merge sort and regular merge sort?
75. Explain the stages of k-way merge sort?
76. What are the advantages of k-way merge sort?
77. Explain Heap Sort or Tree Sort. What is its time complexity and compare it with other types of Sorts.
78. Explain Insertion Sort. What is its time complexity and compare it with other types of Sorts.
79. Explain Shell Sort. What is its time complexity and compare it with other types of Sorts.
80. Why is Shell Sort known as Diminishing Increment Sort?

* * *

EXERCISE - 16

Note : By answering all the questions given in this exercise one can answer subjective type of questions easily including problems. The worked examples in the chapter may help in solving these questions.

1. Discuss linear search method.
2. Explain the binary searching with a C program.
3. What is an index? How can an index speed up the search process?
4. Define a tree structure with an example.
5. Define and explain a binary tree in detail and give an example.
6. Explain the linear and linked representation of binary tree with example.
7. Write a C program to create, display and perform traversal operation on a tree.
8. Explain the construction of a tree for the given inorder and preorder traversals.
9. List the operations that can be performed on a binary tree with integer nodes.
10. Explain about binary search sort.
11. Explain the construction of a tree for the given inorder and postorder traversals.
12. Define the following terms related to tree.
    a) Root b) Leaf c) Subtree d) Degree of a node
13. Represent the following tree in array form

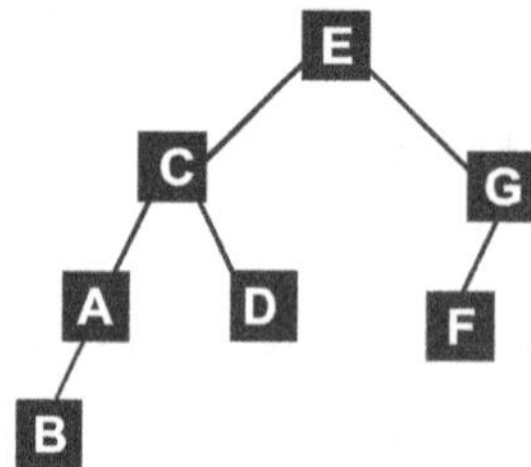

14. What is a minimum spanning tree? Explain the process of identifying a minimum spanning tree?
15. Explain the different algorithms for identifying a minimum spanning tree.
16. Explain the different types of minimum spanning trees.
17. What is an AVL Tree? Compare an AVL tree with other trees.
18. Explain the different operations performed on an AVL Tree?
19. Discuss about rotation process used in AVL Tree.
20. Discuss the insertion operation in an AVL tree.
21. Discuss the deletion operation in an AVL tree.
22. Why is an AVL tree preferred?
23. Discuss the graph representation in C in brief.

24. Discuss the various C operations that can be associated with the graph in the form of a linked list, explain this with an example.
25 Write a Program to Merge Sort two lists of 5 numbers each individually and to combine the two sorted lists into a single list and to Bubble Sort the combined list. Display all the three sorted lists at the end of the Program. Use Dynamic memory allocation and User Defined Functions for Sorting.
26. Explain K-way merge sort and itd advantages.
27. Explain the differeces between k-way merge sort and regular merge sort?
28. What does heap sort do?
29. Explain steps involved in the process of heap sort?
30. Compare heap sort with other methods of sorting.
31. What is the time complexity involved in heap sort?
32. What is Insertion sort? how is insertion sort constructed?
33. Explain the different stages involved in heap sort?
34. Compare insertion sort with bubble sort.
35. Why shell sort named as diminishing increment sort/
36. Explain shell sort? What is the relationship between shell sort and insertion sort?
37. What is the time complexity of heap sort?
38. State whether the following statements are True or False.
    a) Each data item (a through g) in a tree is called as a sub-tree.
    b) Any portion of a tree (e.g. a-b-c) is called as a node.
    c) A node that does not have any sub-tree is called as a terminal node.
    d) Accessing a tree is called as the process of tree traversal.
    e) Items of a tree must be accessed, inserted or deleted in a specific order.
    f) A tree is a recursive data structure.
    g) Set of nodes a graph can also be called as edges.
    h) A graph is **connected** if there is a path between any two nodes of the graph.
    i) If a graph is represented as a linked list then there are three types of list nodes.
    j) A header node contains the actual information of the node, a pointer to the next node, as well as a pointer to an arc.
    k) A list node contains a pointer to a node and a pointer to the previous arc.
    l) If a **depth first search** is used, the edges traversed by the search algorithm make up the tree edges, to create what is called as **depth after spanning tree.**
    m) If a **breadth first search** is used, the edges traversed by the search algorithm make up the tree edges to create what is called as **breadth first spanning tree.**

39. Explain the salient features of traversal in graph
40. What is a spanning tree?
41. Explain depth first search. What are its advantages and disadvantages?
42. Explain bradth first search. What are its advantages and disadvantages?
43. Why is depth first search considered to be similar to pre-order traversal of an ordered tree?
44. What is a cycle? Why do you say graph traversal is better than a tree traversal?
45. Explain two types of spanning trees based on the traversal.
46. Discuss bubble sort, write a C program and show its efficiency.
47. Discuss the quick sort. Derive the efficiency of the quick sort in the best and worst cases.
48. What is aheap? show how would you perform a heap sort using a heap? Work out the efficiency factor of the heap sort.
49. Show that the efficiency of quick sort in its worst case is the same as that of simple insertion sort.
50. Show that shell sort is based on the insertion sort.
51. What is sorting and searching? How are they essential for database applications?
52. Explain types of sort.
53. Distinguish between selection and exchange sort.
54. Explain search methods.
55. Make a distinction between linear and binary search.
56. State whether the following statements are true or false.
    a) Sorting and searching are always tightly interrelated.
    b) Quick sort's efficiency relies on the pivot.
    c) Bubble sort even though simple is very efficient.
    d) Selection sort is based on binary tree
    e) Shell sort is based on quick sort
    f) Quick sort uses a divide-and-conquer approach.
    g) A sorting method whose efficiency is 0 (2^n) means that the amount of time the algorithm will take to complete doubles each time you increase the input.
    h) A sorting method with O (log n) is the most efficient method.
    i) sorting method with O (log n) is the most efficient method.
    j) Binary search can be done on an ordered list only
    k) Indexed sequential search can be applied to file handling only and not to list.
    l) The choice of constructing the index by picking every third number from the main list can be changed.

* * *

CHAPTER 17
CLASSES AND OBJECTS IN C++

17.1 INTRODUCTION :

So far we have been considering the features that are common to C and C++ and we have been making a comparative study of the two languages regarding the features. Now onwards we will concentrate on the special features of C++.

As the program becomes larger and more complex the procedural languages including structured programming languages find it difficult to manage and Object Oriented Programming comes to the rescue and solves the problem. The main reason for a switch from procedural language to Object Oriented language is, the way they treat the data. **In procedural languages, program gets precedence ever the data, i.e., data is given a second-class status, whereas in the Object oriented programming data plays a vital role. In addition, code and data are considered as equal partners.**

With our knowledge of C and the common features of C++ with C which we have studied so far, it becomes easier for us to extend our study to the special features of C++.

C++ is one of the popular object oriented programming languages. The special features of C++ over C like classes and objects, inheritance, overloading, polymorphism etc., have already been introduced in the beginning of this book. Now we shall make a detailed study of these features.

Just as function is a building block in C, a class in C++ is considered as a fundamental building block of the language. Earlier we have seen 'Structures' which forms collection of different data types under a common name. **The class is just an extension to Structures where we can have both variables and functions together.** In this chapter shall discuss the definition of a class and how a Class is used on different occasions. **Classes defined can also become a part of C++ program library.** Let us start from the declaration of class.

The syntax of a Class is given below :

```
Class classname
{
    access-specifier :
    data_type variable_1;
    data_type variable_2;
    ..........
```

```
        data_type variable_n;
        return_data_type method_1(argument_list)
        {
            statements for method_1;
        }
        return_data_type method_2(argument_list)
        {
            statements for method_2;
        }
    return_data_type method_n(argument_list)
        {
            statements for method_n
        }
    }
```

In the above syntax, new term i.e., access specifier. **The access specifier can be one of the following :**

a) **Public access**
b) **Private access**
c) **Protected access**

Now, let us describe one by one.

a) **Public access :**

The function or data, which are declared with Public access specifier will be accessible i.e., accessible to other parts of the program outside of the class access specifier.

b) **Private access :**

The functions or data, which are declared with Private access specifier, can be accessed only within the class. **The data or functions without access specifier given within the class are assumed to be private by default.**

c) **Protected access :**

This protected access deals with inheritance which will be discussed later. **The data members and member functions of a protected section of a class while still unavailable to the general program, are available to the derived class.** (anything placed within a private section of the base class is available to the class itself and not to any of the derived classes).

Instances :

Data or variables within the class are called instance variables and statements within the methods are called code. The values of the instance variables at any particular instant are known as instances. An instance of a class is called an object.

17.1.1. Difference between Structures and Class :

(i) In 'struct' the members are public by default whereas, in 'class' the members are private by default.

(ii) But however, we can make our classes as public, private or protected by declaring explicitly.

(iii) Otherwise 'struct' and 'class' are functionally equivalent.

(iv) At times we may also be in need of using public variables, though it is not highly recommended as it deviates from the basic concepts of Object oriented programming (encapsulation)

(v) Like structure, data members of class are also accessed through dot operator (.)

(vi) In structure all the data of the structure can be accessed. In class, the members of a class which is declared private cannot be accessed by other classes whereas the class declared as public is accessible by other classes also.

17.1.2. Declaration and definition of a simple class :

The syntax for declaration and definition of a simple class is given below.

```
class emp
    {
        private:
            char name [20]
            int basicpay;
        public :
            void getdetail(char *tname, int tbasicpay)          //function
                {
                    strcpy(name,tname);
                    basicpay=tbasicpay;
                }
        void printdetail( )
            {
                cout << "Name   : "<<name>>"\n";
                cout <<"Basic pay  : "<<basicpay;
            }
    }
```

In the above **class** emp, data fields are 'name' as character type and 'basic pay' as integer type under private access. We have just created a new data type called class in the name of 'emp' and it is very much like 'int' data type in C. The function void getdetail(char *tname, int tbasicpay) is public and accessible from outside of the class.

To use 'area' as 'int' data type, we have following declarations in C.

int area ;

From the above statements we understand that, the variable 'area' is a instance of (type of) 'int'. Likewise we have to create an instance of 'emp', which is otherwise called an object. **An instance of a class is called an object.**

The object of the class emp is declared as follows;

emp empinfo;

Like structure, data members of class are also accessed through (.) dot operator. For example to access the method printdetail( ) in 'empinfo' object, the following method is used.

empinfo • printdetail ( );

The most important thing to point out here is we cannot access name and basic pay along with the object as they were declared as private and these two variables can be accessed through public function (here it is getdetail( )) only, which is a function defined under public.

Program 17.1.1.

Write a program in C++ to illustrate the use of public and private functions.

```
//use of public and private functions
# include <iostream>
using namespace std;
int main ( )
{
     class emp
         {
             private:
                 char name[25];
                 int basicpay;
             public:
                 void getdetail(char *tname, int  tbasicpay)
                     {
                             strcpy(name,tname);
                             basicpay=tbasicpay;
                     }
                 void printdetail ( )
                     {
                             cout <<"Name       : "<<name<<"\n";
                             cout << "Basic pay  : "<basicpay;
                     }
         }
     emp empinfo;
     empinfo.getdetail("Sridhar",9000);
     empinfo.printdetail( );
     return 0;
}
```

OUTPUT :

Name : Sridhar
Basic Pay : 9000

In the above program we have private variables namely name and basicpay. These two variables gets value through getdetail( ) method of the same class. The output of the entered data can be retrieved by using printdetail ( ) another public method of the same class. **The functions inside the class are denoted as methods.**

At times we may use all variables as public variables in a class. But this is not advisable as it deviates from the basic concepts of Object oriented programming *(encapsulation which provides access)* The following example will illustrate how to access public variables in a class.

Program 17.1.2

Write a program in C++ to illustrate the principle of use of all variables as public in a class.

```
//use of all variables as public which is not advisable generally
# include <iostream>
using namespace std;
     int main ( )
{
     class emp
     {
          public :
               char name [20];
               int basicpay;
                    void printdetail ( )        //method: function inside class
               {
                    cout <<"Name   : "<<name<<"\n";
                    cout << "Basic pay       : "<<basicpay;
               }
          };
          emp empinfo;
          strcpy (empinfo.name,"Ramesh");
          empinfo.basicpay=12000;
          empinfo.printdetail();
          return 0;
}
```

OUTPUT :

Name : Ramesh
Basic pay : 12000

In this program, we observe that the basic pay of all employees are included in public domain and hence the basic pay of any employee is accessible to all and this type of providing basic pay of all employees in public domain is not an advisable feature, since basic pay of any employee is a private data not to be known by others. **Also it violates the data abstraction property of OOP concept by assigning values directly to instance variables.**

In the following example we have a private function which is accessed by one of the public functions of the same class instead of access by all the public functions of the same class.

Program 17.1.3

Write a program in C++ to illustrate the principle of one of the public functions of a class accessing the private function in the same class.

```
//Access of a private function by one of the public functions of the same class.
    # include <iostream>
    using namespace std;
    int main( )
    {
        class emp
            {
                private:
                char name[25];
                int  basicpay;
                void prigetdetail( )            //method: private get detail
                {
                    cout <<"Enter name :";
                    cin getline (name,25);
                    cout<<"\n Enter Basic pay :";
                    cin>>basicpay;
                }
                public :
                void pubgetdetail ( )           //method: public get detail
                    {
                        prigetdetail ( );
                    }
                void printdetail ( )
                    {
                        cout <<"Name        : "<<name<<"\n";
                        cout <<"Basic pay   : "<<basicpay;
                    }
            };
        emp empinfo;
        empinfo.pubgetdetail( );
```

```
        empinfo.printdetail();
        return 0;
    }
```

OUTPUT :

```
Enter name       :   Krishna Mohan
Enter Basic pay  :   15000
Name             :   Krishna Mohan
Basic pay        :   15000
```

In the above program we see that the private function prigetdetail () accesses the objects of the public function pubgetdetail ( ), both belonging to the same class emp.

17.1.3. Inline Member Functions (Function declared inside the class or outside a class with scope operator) :

A member function that is both declared and defined in the class member list is called as an inline member function. Member functions containing a few lines of code are usually declared inline. We can also declare an inline member function outside of the class declaration by using the keyword inline and the :: (scope resolution) operator. For example

```
class sample
{
        int no;
    public;
        int getno( )
    {
        return no:
    }
};
```

The given program is equivalent to:

```
class sample
{
        int no;
    public;
        int getno ( );
};
    inline int getno( )
{
    return a;
};
```

i) **Inline member function, must be declared before it is called.** The inline member functions have internal linkage and on the other hand non-inline member functions have external linkage.

ii) The inline function can also be defined outside the class. When functions are defined outside of the class, scope resolution operator is to be used to access the function.

Though by doing so this way will cause difficulty to maintain the functions in future, in C++, we have this facility. Now let us see through other example in which function definitions are outside the class.

```
//Inline function declared outside a class
# include <iostream>
using namespace std;
class emp
{
     private :
        char name[20];
        int basicpay;
    public:
        void getdetail( );
        voidprintdetail( );
};
void emp :: getdeail( )    //inline function declared outside class using ::
{
    cout<<"Enter name ;";
        cin.getline(name,20);
    cout<<"\n Enter Basic pay :"'
        cin>>basicpay;
}
void emp :: printdetail( )
{
    cout<<"Name          :"<<name<<"\n";
    cout <<"Basic pay     : "<<basicpay;
}
    int main( )
{
    emp empinfo;
    empinfo.getdetail( );
    empinfo.printdetail( );
    return 0;
}
```

OUTPUT :

```
Enter name          :   Radhika
Enter Basic Pay         :   15000
Name                :   Madhavi
Basic pay           :   1800
```

Note : The above program reveals that the class declaration can be placed outside the main ( ) function also.

17.1.4. Array of objects :

Arrays of objects can be declared like any other fundamental data type, for example the code

emp empinfo[4];

Will create four objects of type employee.

Program 17.1.4

Write a program in C++ using array objects in Class.

```
//Use of Array objects used in a class

#include <iostream>
using namespace std;
class emp
{
    private :
        char name[20];
        int basic, allowance;
    public :
        void getpay( );
        void printtotal( );
};
    void emp :: getpay( )                //method
{
    cout <<"Enter name :";
    cin.getline(name,20);
        fflush(stdin);
    cout<<"employee basic:";
    cin>>basic;
        fflush(stdin);
    cout<<"employee allowance :";
    cin>allowance;
        fflush(stdin);
}
    void employee :: printtotal( )       //method
{
    cout<<"\n Name :"<<name;
    cout <<"\n Total Pay : "<<basic+allowance;
}
```

```
int main ( )
{
    emp empinfo[3];
    int i;
    for (i=0;i<3;++i)
    empinfo[i].getpay();
    cout<<"\n Output \n";
    for (i=0;i<3;++i)
    empinfo[i].printtotal();
    return 0;
}
```

OUTPUT :

```
Enter name : Ramu
Employee basic : 25000
Employee allowance : 15000

Enter name : Akbar
Employee basic : 30000
Employee allowance : 15000

Enter name : John
Employee basic : 40000
Employee allowance : 10000

Name : Ramu
Total Pay : 40000
Name : Akbar
Total Pay : 45000
Name : John
Total Pay : 50000
```

17.1.5. Constructor for initializing an object :

To avoid garbage value of an object stored in variables initially when an object is created in C+, a function called "*Constructor*" will be used by calling, along with the object declaration.

a) Features of a Constructor function :

(i) The constructor function has by definition the same name as the class.

(ii) Also constructor does not return any value and has no return data type specification including void while declaration.

(iii) When the class is having constructor function, the compiler will invoke this function automatically when an object of the class is created.

(iv) The purpose of the constructor function is to assign initial values to member variables.

(v) *Parameterized constructor* is used for having initial values even at the time of object declaration.

(vi) *Explicit constructor is a constructor defined with the keyword explicit.* This will be discussed later.

Program 17.1.5

Write a program in C++ for use of a constructor function inside the class.

```
//Use of constructor function
# include <iostream>
using namespace std;
class emp                       // class name and constructor fn. name
{
    private :
        char name[20];
        int no;
    public:
        emp();                           // constructor function name
        {
            strcpy(name, "Swaroop");
            no=250;
        }
        void printvalue ( );
{
    cout<<"\n Name : "<<name;
        cout<<"\n No : "<<no;
}
    int main( )
{
    emp emp1;
    cout<<"\n Values due to constructor function";
    emp1.printvalue();
    cout<<"\n";
    return 0;
}
```

OUTPUT :

Values due to constructor function
Name : Swaroop
No : 250

When we want to define the constructor function outside the class, the revised program as follows :

17.1.6. Write a program in C++ for use of a constructor function outside the class

```
//Use of constructor function outside class
# include <iostream>
using namespace std;

class emp
{
    private :
        char name[20];
        int no;
    public:
        emp( );                    //constructor fn. name inside class
        void printvalue ( );
};
    emp :: emp ( )                 //constructor fn. outside the class
{
        strcpy(name, "Swapna");
        no=283;
}
    void emp :: printvalue ( )     //constructor function output
{
    cout<<"\n Name : "<<name;
        cout<<"\n No : "<<no;
}
        int main( )
{
    emp emp1;
    cout<<"\n Values due to consructor function";
    emp1.printvalue();
    cout<<"\n";
    return 0;
}
```

OUTPUT :

Values due to consructor function
Name : Swapna
No : 283

17.1.6. Parameterized Constructors :

Parameterized constructor is used for having initial values even at the time of object declaration.

Program 17.1.7

Write a program in C++ for the use of parameterised constructor function to have initial values even at the time of object creation.

```
//Parameterized constructor
# include <iostream>
using namespace std;
class student
{
    private:
        char name[20];
        int sub,sub;
    public :
        student(char tname[ ],int tsub1,int tsub2); //parameterized constructor
        student( );        //dummy constructor without arguments
        void getdetail( );
        void printdetail( );
};
student :: student( ) { }            //parameterized constructor called
void student :: getdetail( )
{
    cout<<"Enter name :";
    cin.getline(name,20);
    fflush(stdin);
    cout<<"First Subject Marks :";
    cin>>sub1;
    fflush(stdin);
    cout<<"Second Subject Marks :";
    cin>>sub2;
    fflush(stdin);
}
    student :: student(char tname[ ], int tsub1,int tsub2)
{
    strcpy (name,tname);
    sub1=tsub1;
    sub2=tsub2;
}
void student :: printdetail()
{
    cout<<"Name : "<<name<<"\n";
    cout <<"Total :"<<sub1+sub2<<"\n";
}
```

```
    int main( )
{
    student studeninfo("Vijay",90,65);    //invoke constr.with arguments
    cout <<"\n Output Using parameterized constructor \n";
    studentinfo.printdetail();
    student studentinfo1;
    studentinfo1.getdetail();
    cout<<"\n Output Using input values \n";
    studentinfo1.printdetail();
    return 0;
}
```

OUTPUT :

```
Output Using parameterized constructor
Name : Vijay
Total : 155
Enter Name : Madhu
First Subject Marks : 78
Second Subject Marks : 95

Output Using input values
Name : Madhu
Total : 173
```

In the above example, we used two constructors one with arguments and another without arguments. When the statement

student studentinfo("Vijay",90.65);

We invoked the constructor with arguments. Also note that, we should not create objects without arguments in such cases, so, the call

student studentinfo1;

will invite compile time error when there is no constructor without arguments. **Hence, we must have dummy consructor to create objects without arguments. The dummy constructor is the one, which does not perform any actions.** The following points are kept in mind while we use constructors in our programs. (i) When an object is a local variable of a function, the constructor is called every time the function is called at the point where the variable is defined. (ii) When an object is a static variable, the constructor is called when the function in which the static variable defined is called for first time. (iii) When an object is a global variable the constructor is invoked when the program starts.

17.1.7. Explicit Constructor :

In C++, it is possible to declare constructors for a class, taking a single parameter, and use those constructors for doing type conversions. For example consider the following simple program.

Program 17.1.8

Write a program in C++ for use of single parameterized constructor to do type conversion of the data.

```
#include <iostream>
using namespace std;
class sample
{
    private :
        int a;
    public :
        sample ( ) { }          //gives scope for type conversion of data
        sample (int x)          //gives data type as integer
    {
        a=x;
    }
    void display ( )
    {
        cout<<"\n Value is "<<a;
    }
};
    void main ( )
{
    sample example=477;  //value of the data object
    example.display ( );
}
```

OUTPUT :

Value is 477

In the above the object of the public class the two highlighted statements give flexibility for declaring the type of the parameter of the objects sample and its exact value is given by the highlighted statement in the void main function.

sample example=477;

This sort of parameterized declaration of constructor gives flexibility for converting the types whereas if the constructor is declarated as explicit as given in the following program then it does not give scope for conversion of the object value. It will be rigid type and non-converting.

When we feel the first type of declaration is confusing and if we want to use conventional one then we must use a new keyword 'explicit' in the constructor declaration as given below :

Program 17.1.9

Write a program in C++ for the use of explicit constructor of non-converting type.

```
#include <iostream>
using namespace std;
class sample
{
    private:
        int a;
    public:
        sample () { }
        explicit sample (int x)     //data type has to be integer only
    {
        a=x;
    }
        void display ()
    {
        cout<<"\n Value is "<<a;
    }
};
    void main ()
{
    sample example (567);          //data given as argument
    example.display();
}
```

OUTPUT :

Value is 567

In the above program using the explicit keyword, a constructor is declared to be "non converting" and if we declare an object in the following manner.

sample example=567;

Will produce following compiler error.

'initializing' : cannot convert from 'const int' to 'class sample'

No *constructor could take the source type, or constructor overload resolution was ambiguous.*

17.2 DESTRUCTOR :

In the course of a program, if an object ceases to exist i.e., when an object is out of scope we use a special function called "Destructor function" which is the opposite of "Constructor function". **When an object ceases to exist we use destructor function with a tilde (~) preceeding the class which uses the object. While defining a destructor for a class the following points should be kept in mind.**

(i) Like constructor, the destructor function also has the same name as the class but preceded by a tilde (~).

(ii) *The destructor has no arguments and also does not return any value.*

(iii) One more difference between constructor and destructor is, *while a class can have multiple constructors, a class can have only one destructor.*

Program 17.2.1

Write a program in C++ for the use of destructor function

```
//use of destructor function
#include <iostream>
using namespace std;
class example
{
    public:
        example ( );
        ~example( );      //destructor to destruct example ( )
};
example :: example( )
{
    cout<<"\n Constructor Function is called";
}
    example :: ~ example ( )
{
    cout<<"\n Destructor Function is called";
}
    int main ( )
{
    example sample;
    return 0;
}
```

OUTPUT :

Constructor Function is called
Destructor Function is called

Destructors are called in the following ways.

(i) For objects, which are, local non-static variables, the destructor are called when the block in which the object is defined is left.

(ii) For destructors of objects, which are defined in nested blocks of functions, are called before the function itself ceases.

(iii) When the destructors of objects defined in the outer block of a function are called just before the function terminates.

(iv) The destructor function called before the program terminates for static or global variables.

(v) For programs having abnormal exit, the destructors are called only for global objects, which exists at that time, and destructors of objects defined locally are not invoked for this state.

(vi) *The constructor and destructor functions find their real application only when we deal with Dynamic Memory Allocation.*

17.3. FRIEND FUNCTIONS :

i) So far we have considered examples where only public function has a right to access private variables of the same class.

In addition C++ has one more function called "Friend function". **Friend functions access private variables of the same class even outside the class.**

ii) A keyword 'friend' is added before the function name to declare a friend function.

iii) Apart from the above usage, **friend functions are also used when two or more classes will have same function name for the same purpose.**

Program 17.3.1

Write a program in C++ for the use of friend functions.

```
//Friend function example
#include <iostream>
using namespace std;
class example
{
        private :
            int sub 1,sub2,sub3;
        public :
            friend int totalmarks(sample temp);    //friend function
            void getmarks();
};
        void sample :: getmarks( )
{
        cout<<"\n Enter 3 marks";
        cin>>sub1>>sub2>>sub3;
}
        int totalmarks(sample temp)  //To access private variables of the
                                     //same class outside the class
{
        return (temp.sub1+temp.sub2+temp.sub3);
}
```

```
        int main( )
    {
        sample example;
        example.getmarks( );
        cout<"\n Total marks: "<totalmarks(example);
        return 0;
    }
```

OUTPUT :

Enter 3 marks 70 80 90
Total marks 240

Note that, in the above program the function total marks ( ) is used in a same way as we use a function in C. That's why the function is called without the object's name. Since it is not a member function it does not qualified with an object's name. Also if we place the friend function in the private part the answer won't get changed. *As we know, one of the important paradigm of OOP is data hiding, the friend functions tends to violate this principle. Hence it should be avoided if we need to implement OOP features in our class.* Apart from the above usage, friend functions are also used when two or more classes will have same function name for the same purpose.

Program 17.3.2

Write a program in C++ to explain the use of friend function when two or more classes will have the same function name for the same purpose.

```
    //Access of classes having the same name for the same purpose.

    # include <iostream>
    using namespace std;
    class second;                 //forward declaration used since max. no ( )
                                  //uses class second before its declaration
    class first
    {
        private :
            int a;
        public :
            void agetno();
            friend int maximumno(first x, second y);
    };
        void first :: agetno()
    {
        cout <<"\n Enter number for first class :";
        cin>>a;
```

```
}
    class second
{
    private :
        int b;
    public :
        void bgetno( );
        friend int maximumno(first x,second y);
};
    void second::bgetno( )
{
    cout <"\n Enter number for first class :";
    cin >>b;
}
    int maximumno(first x,second y)
{
    if (x.a>y.b)
        return (x,a);
    else
        return (y,b);
}
    int main ( )
{
    first f1;
    second s1;
    int big;
        f1.agetno( );
        s1.bgetno( );
        big=maximumno(f1,s1);
        cout <<"Maximum number is :"<<big;
        return 0;
}
```

OUTPUT :

Enter number for first class : 89
Enter number for first class : 65
Maximum Number is : 89

In the preceding program note the forward declaration in line 4. This is necessary because the declaration of the function maximumno ( ) uses the class second before it is declared.

17.4. FRIEND CLASSES :

All members of a class can have access to all the members of another class which are declared as friend class to it. This is similar to friend function. It declares a whole class to be a friend of another class.

Program 17.4.1

Write a program in C++ to illustrate the use of friend classes.

```
#include <iostream>
using namespace std;
class second;
class first
{
        private:
              int a,b;
        public:
              int multiply()
              {
                    return (a*b);
              }
        void assign(second s1);
};
class second
{
        private:
              int c;
        public:
              void setvalue(int x)
              {
                    c=x;
              }
        friend class first;          //first class as friend to  second class
};
void first :: assign(second s1)
{
        a=s1.c;
        b=s1.c;
}
void main()
{
        first firstobj;
        second secondobj;
        secondobj.setvalue (10);
        firstobj.assign(secondobj); //first class accessing object of Second class
        cout<<"\n Result = "<<firstobj.multiply();
}
```

OUTPUT :

Result = 100

The following points should be remembered before introducing friend classes in our program.

i) Declaration of first class as a friend to second class is done inside the second class. First class has access to members of second class.

ii) **By default, friendship is not mutual. This means that on the other hand if 'second' is declared as a friend of 'first' inside first class, this does not give 'first' the right to access the private members of 'second'.**

iii) *Since, friend classes deviates the principle of data hiding, using friend classes therefore be minimized to those cases where it is absolutely essential.*

iv) **Due to above reasons, it is better to avoid friend functions or classes in our program.**

17.5. DIFFERENT METHODS OF ACCESSION OF OBJECTS :

i) Just like arithmetic assignment we can also assign one object to another provided that they belong to same type.

ii) Different objects of the same class can access each other's members even if these members are private.

17.5.1 Object Assignment :

Just like arithmetic assignment we can also assign one object to other provided that they belong to same type. An example program follows.

Program 17.5.1

Write a program in C++ to assign one object to another object both belonging to the same type.

```
# include <iostream>
using namespace std;
class example
{
    private:
        int a,bc;
    public :
        void getvalue();
        void putvalue();
    };
    void example :: getvalue( )
    {
        cout <<"\n Enter 3 values";
        cin>>a>>b>>c;
    }
```

```
void example :: putvalue( )
{
        cout <<"\n Given values are :";
        cout <<a<<" "<<b<<" "<<c;
}
void main ( )
{
        example sample1,sample2;
        sample 1.getvalue();
        sample2=sample1;
        cout <<"\n After assigning sample 1 to sample 2\n";
        sample2.putvalue();
}
```

OUTPUT :

Enter 3 values 25 35 45
After assigning sample 1 to sample 2
Given values are : 25 35 45

17.5.2. Accessing a Private data member from a different object :

Different objects of the same class can access each other's members even if these members are private.

Program 17.5.2

Write a program in C++ to illustrate the principle of accession of different objects of the same class even if these members are private.

```
# include <iostream>
using namespace std;
class sample
{
        private:
            int number;
        public:
            void assign(sample *x)
        {
            x->number=355;
        }
            void display( )
        {
            cout<<"\n Value after passing:"<<number;
        }
};
```

```
    void main( )
{
    sample example1,example2;
    example1.assign(&example2);
    example2.display();
}
```

OUTPUT :

Value after passing : 355

Unless otherwise needed this type of accessing each other's members of the same class eventhough the members are private has to be used cautiously, because that private members of an object could be changed by another object of same type.

17.6 DYNAMIC MEMORY ALLOCATION IN C++ USING KEYWORDS :

In C dynamic memory allocation is carried by 'malloc' and we use 'free' to release memory occupied by the variable. Since, the malloc ( ) function is not type-safe in C++, the dynamic memory allocation in C++ is carried out by the operator 'new'.

i) **Keyword 'new'** : For example, the address for a newly allocated block of memory suited for a certain type 'X' is returned by the operator 'new' will take the following form :

X* y = new X;

Similarly for an array memory allocation carried out by

X* y =new X [exprn];

Where 'exprn' is an integer expression that can have its value determined at either dynamically or compile time.

ii) **Keyword 'delete' :**

When we want to release the memory occupied by the variable 'y' the **keyword delete** is used 'delete' as follows

delete y;

Similarly for an array memory allocation carried out by

X* y =new X [exprn];

Where 'exprn' is an integer expression that can have its value determined at either dynamically or compile time.

An array with address 'y' must be released by

delete [ ] p;

Note that, here *memory occupied by the whole array is to be released rather than the first element, which has the same address as the array.*

17.6.1 Const. member function and const objects :

The keyword **const** is used to indicate that a member function does not change the data fields of its objects. The function usage is only to inspect the data of the object. In the following program we have three constant functions. It is better to recall the usage of 'const' once again here, whichever appears before the keyword 'const' may not be altered and does not alter its own data.

Program : 17.6.1

Write a program in C++ to illustrate the principle of use of constant function and constant objects using the keyword const.

```
#include <iostream>
#include <cstring>
using namespace std;
class stdinfo
{
private :
        char sname[20];
        char branch[10];
        int examno;
public:
        stdinfo(char *tsnamechar *tbranch,int examno)
        {
             strcpy(sname,tsname);
             strcpy(branch,tbranch);
             examno=texamno;
        }
        char const *getsname() const
        {
             return sname;
        }
        char const *getbranch() const
        {
             return branch;
        }
        int const getexamno() const
        {
             return examno;
        }
};
void main ()
{
        stdinfo student("Mahesh","M.Sc.,"200502);
        cout << "\n Student details \n";
```

```
        cout <<"\n Student Name :"<<student.getsname();
        cout <<"\n          Branch :"<<student.getbranch();
        cout <<"\n Exam number : "<<student.getexamno( );
    }
```

OUTPUT :

```
Student details
Student Name : Mahesh
        Branch : M.Sc.,
Exam number : 2005
```

17.6.2 Mutable to change const object instance :

In C++ we can have a class object instance that is constant and cannot be modified by the program, once initially set up.

A recent addition to C++, allows us to change individual data members even for a const object instance. It can be accomplished by using the keyword 'mutable'. The data member that we want to change should preceed by the keyword 'mutable'.

The format for changing the constant object is as follows :

```
class sample
{
        public;
            mutable int n;            //to change the values of const.
            sample ( );

};
const sample a;
void f( )
{
        a.x =37;
}
```

This says that "x" can be modified even though it's a member of a const object instance.

Program 17.6.2

Write a program in C++ to change individual data members for a constant object instance using the key word mutable.

```
#include <iostream>
using namespace std;
```

```
class sample
{
        private:
            mutable int x;
        public:
            sample(int t=0)
        {
        x=t;
        }
            void changevalue( ) const    //mutable changes the const. value
        {
            x++;
        }
        int getvalue() const
        {
            return x;
        }
};
void main ( )
{
        sample sampleobj(500);
        cout<<"\n Before calling change value function, the value of
        x="<<sampleobj.getvalue();
        sampleobj.changevalue();
        cout<<"\n After calling change value function the value of
        x="<<sampleobj.getvalue();
        cout<<endl;
}
```

OUTPUT :

Before calling change value function, the value of x= 500
After calling change value function, the value of x = 501

17.6.3. The size of a Class Object :

The size of an object is determined on the basis of its definition. The size of operator does not perform any conversions. If the operand operators that perform conversions, the compiler does take these conversions into consideration. The following expression causes the usual arithmetic conversions to be performed. The result of the expression x + 1 has type int (if x has type char, short, or int or any enumeration type) and is equivalent to sizeof(int);

Sizeof (x + 1);

Except in preprocessor directives, we can use a size of expression wherever an integral constant is required. One of the most common uses for the size of operator is to determine the size of objects that are referred to during storage allocation, input, and output functions.

Program 17.6.3

Write a program in C++ to use the size of class object

```
#include <iostream>
#include <cstring>
using namespace std;
class stdinfo
{
    private :
        char sname[10];
        int examno;
        char branch[10];
    public :
        stdinfo(char *tsname.char *tbranch,int texamno)
    {
        strcpy(sname,tsname);
        strcpy(branch,tbranch);
        examno=texamno;
    }
    void display( )
    {
        cout<<"\n Student details \n";
        cout <<"\n Student Name : "<<sname;
        cout << "\n    Branch : "<<branch;
        cout << "\n Exam number : "<<examno;
    }
    void individualize( )
    {
        cout <<"\n Size of sname is "<<sizeof(sname);
        cout << "\n Size of branch is "<<sizeof(branch);
        cout <<"\n Size of examno is "<<sizeof(examno);
    }
};
    void main ( )
{
        stdinfo student ("Mahesh","M.Sc.",200502);
        int objsize=sizeof(student);
```

```
            student.display( );
            cout<<"\n Size of individual fields \n";
            student.individualsize( );
            cout<<"\n Size of this object is "<<objsize;
}
```

OUTPUT :

Student details
Student Name : Mahesh
Branch : M.Sc.
Exam Number : 2005
Size of individual fields
Size of sname is 10
size of branch is 10
size of examno is 4
size of this object is 28

The size of the object is 28 and not 24 why?

17.6.4. Nested Class (Class within another class)

- **i)** A nested class is declared within the scope of another class.
- **ii)** The name of a nested class is local to its enclosing class.
- **iii)** Unless we use explicit pointers, reference, or object names, declarations in a nested class can only use visible constructs, including type names, static members, and enumerators from the enclosing class and global variables.

The following example program contains a class named 'sample1', which contains an object of another class (sample) embedded within it. When we pass four values along the method 'assign1' of object 'example1' the first two values are assigned to its own object and next two values are passed to the object 's1' through the method 'assign'. When the method 'multiply' of example1' is invoked the function 'multiply' is called and resultant gets multiply by private members 'a' and 'b' of the object 'example1'. Here is a sample illustration for he above technique.

Program 17.6.4

Write a program in C++ to illustrate the use of nested class :

```
# include <iostream>
using namespace std;
class sample
{
    private :
        int a,b;
```

```
    public :
            void assign (int p, int q)
        {
            a=p;
            b=q;
        }
        int multiply()
        {
            return a*b;
        };
};
    class sample1
    {
    private :
        int a,b;
        sample s1;
    public :
            void assign (int p, int q, int r, int s)
        {
            a=p;
            b=q;
            s1.assign(r,s);
        }
        int multiply1( )
        {
            return a*b*s1.multiply();
        };
    };
        void main ( )
    {
        sample1 example1:
        example 1.assign1(6,7,8,9);
        int z=example1.multiply1( );
        cout <<"\n The result of 6*7*8*9 is ="<<z;
        cout<<endl;
    }
```

OUTPUT :

The result of 6*7*8*9 is = 3024

17.6.5. The Copy Constructor :

In addition to providing a default constructor and destructor, the compiler provides a default copy constructor. The copy constructor is called every time a copy of an object is made. When we pass an object by value, either into a function or as a function's return value, a temporary copy of that object is made. If the object is an user-defined object, the class's copy constructor is called. All copy constructors take one parameter, a reference to an object of the same class. It is a good idea to make it a constant reference, because the constructor will not have to alter the object passed in. For example

Student (const student & x)

Here the 'student' constructor takes a constant reference to an existing 'student' object. The goal of the copy constructor is to make a copy of 'x'. The default copy constructor simply copies each member variable from the object passed as a parameter to the member variables of the new object. This is called a member-wise copy or also called 'shallow' copy, and although this is fine for most member variables, it breaks pretty quickly for member variables that are pointers to objects on the free store. Here is a sample program to illustrate the above concept.

A copy constructor is used to make a copy of one class object from another class object of the same class type. A copy constructor is called with a single argument that is a reference to its own class type. We cannot use a copy constructor with an argument of the same type as its class; we must use a reference. We can provide copy constructors with additional default arguments. If a user-defined copy constructor does not exist for a class and one is needed, the compiler creates a copy constructor, with public access, for that class. It is not created for a class if any of its members or base classes have an inaccessible copy constructor.

Program 17.6.5.

Write a program in C++ to illustrate the use of copy constructor

```
# include <cstring>
# include <iostream>
using namespace std;
class student                          //object creation without parameter passing
{
    private :
        char sname[20];
        int age;
    public :
        student( )
    {
        strcpy(sname,"Kumar");
        age=19;
    }
```

```
    student(char tname[ ],int tno)    //object creaction with parameter passing
    {
        strcpy(sname,tname);
        age=tno;
    }
    student(const student &x)    //object creaction with object as parameter
    {
        strcpy(sname,x.sname);
        age=x.age;
    }
    void display()
    {
        cout <<"\n Student name :"<<sname;
        cout <<"\n Age      : "<<age;
        cout<<endl;
    }
};
    void main ( )
{
    student studentobj;
    cout <<"\n Object creation without parameter passing :";
    studentobj.display( );

    student studentobj1("Gopal",20);
    cout <<"\n Now object creation with parameter passing :";
    studentobj1.display( );

    student studentobj2(studentobj1);
    cout <<"\n  Object creation with object as parameter : ";
    studentobj2.display( );
}
```

OUTPUT :

```
Object creation without parameter passing :
Student name : Kumar
Age      : 19

Now object creation with parameter passing :
Student name : Gopal
Age      : 20

Object creation with object as parameter :
Student name : Gopal
Age      : 20
```

17.6.6. This Pointer : (this →)

The keyword 'this' identifies a special type of pointer. **When a non-static member function is called, the 'this' pointer identifies the class object, which the member function is operating on.** We cannot declare the 'this' pointer or make assignments to it. The type of the 'this' pointer for a member function of a class type X, is X* const. If the member function is declared with the constant qualifier, the type of the 'this' pointer for that member function for class X, is const X* const. If the member function is declared with the volatile qualifier, the type of the this pointer for that member function for class X is volatile X* const. 'this' is passed as a hidden argument to all non-static member function calls and is available as a local variable within the body of all non-static functions.

For example, we can refer to the particular class object that a member function is called for by using the 'this' pointer in the body of the member function.

Program 17.6.6.

Write a program in C++ to illustrate the use of 'this pointer'

```
    # include <iostream>
    using namespace std;
    class sample
    {
        private :
            int a;
        public :
            void assignvalue(int a)
    {
        this-> a = a;          //use of this pointer referring class sample
    }
        void printvalue( )
        cout << "a = " << a << endl;
    }
};
    void main ( )
{
    sample sampleobj;
    int no = 36;
    sampleobj.assignvalue(no);
    sampleobj.printvalue ( );
}
```

OUTPUT :

a = 36

17.6.7. Static Class member, Data member & Member Function of a class :

i) Static class member :

In a class we can have both member variable and member function as static. By declaring 'static' we can make these members independent of any particular object of the class type, but is accessible by any of them. Now let us look into static data members first.

ii) Static data member

When a class variable is declared as 'static' then only one instance of that variable exists, and this variable can be shared by all instances of the class. Static members are mainly used to store constants that are specific to a class. They also store information regarding number of objects created at any point of time. To declare a static data member in a class, the keyword 'static' is placed in front of the declaration. In the following program we have a static data member 'number' and it is not a property of any specific object but of the class. **The static data member requires both declaration and definition.** In our example program we initialized the static data member outside the class. The syntax for such definition is

Storage-type class-name :: static-variable-name

Example :

Int sample :: number=0; (in program 17.6.7)

iii) Static member functions of a class

In the previous section we have seen static data member, which makes it independent of any particular object of the class. **To access static data member in a class we can declare static member functions.** Static data member functions are also declared similar to ordinary function declaration except that **they have the keyword 'static' placed before the declaration.** A static data member of a class is a member for which there is only one copy rather than one per object. The static member function can be accessed without referring to any particular object of the class.

Since, static member function is not associated with any particular object and need not be called using the special member function syntax. For example

sample :: objectcount ( ); //static function of a class

is used to call static method of objectcount(). Here we have used the class name instead of an instance name.

Program 17.6.7

Write a program in C++ to illustrate the use of static class and data members.

```
#include<iostream>
using namespace std;
```

```
class sample
{
        private :
            int x,y;
        public :
            static int number;
                void setvalue(int a, int b)
        {
            x=a; y=b;
            number++;
        }
                void putvalue( )
        {
        cout <<"\n Values of X and Y " <<x<<" "<<y;
        }
};
int sample :: number=0;               //static data member
void main ()
{
    sample sampleobj1;
    sampleobj1.setvalue(88,99);
    sampleobj1.putvalue( );
    cout <<"\n Number of objects created "<<sample :: number;
    sample sampleobj2;
    sampleobj2.setvalue(400,500);
    sampleobj2.putvalue ();
    cout<<"\n Number of objects created "<<sample :: number;
    cout<<endl;
}
```

OUTPUT :

Value of X and Y 88 99
Number of objects created 1
Values of X and Y 400 500
Number of objects created 2

Program 17.6.8

Write a program in C++ to illustrate the use of static functions of a class

```
# include <iostream>
using namespace std;
```

```
    class sample
    {
        private :
            int x,y;
        public :
            static int number;
            void setvalue(int a, int b)
        {
            x=a; y=b;
            number++;

        }
            static int objectcount ( )            //static function
        {
            return number;
        }
            void putvalue ( )
        {
            cout <<"\n Values of X and Y "<<x<<"  "<<y;
        }
    };
int sample :: number=0;
    void main ( )
(
    samle sampleobj1;
    sampleobj1.setvalue (88,99);
    sampleobj1.putvalue( );
    cout<<"\n Number of objects created "<<sample :: objctcount ( );
    sample sampleobj2;
    sampleobj2.setvalue (400,500);
    samleobj2.putvalue ( );
    cout<<"\n Number of objects crated "<<sample :: object count ( );
    cout<<endl;
}
```

OUTPUT :

```
Values of X and Y 88  99
Number of objects created 1
Values of X and Y 400  500
Number of objects created 2
```

17.6.8. Classes and Structures :

Like C, structures can be used in C++ also. **The main difference between a structure and a class is that structure members have public access by default and class members have private access by default. Also, note that we can use the keywords class or 'struct' to define equivalent classes.**

Program 17.6.9

Write a Program in C++ to illustrate the use of structures.

```
# include <iostream>
using namespace std;
struct student    //struct student is public. equivalent to class student
{
        void getdetail ( )
    {
        cout<<"\n Enter name :";
        cin.getline(name,20);
        fflush(stdin);
        cout <<"\n Enter 3 Subjects marks :" ;
        cin>.sub1>>sub2>>sub;3;
    }
        void putdetail ( )
    {
        cout<<"\n Name : "<<name;
        cout<<"\n Total : "<<sub1+sub2+sub3;
    }
        private ://class variables
        int sub1,sub2,sub3;
        char name[20];
    };
        void main ( )
    {
        student studentrec;
        studentrec.getdetail ( );
        studentrec.putdetail ( );
        cout<<endl;
    }
```

OUT PUT :

Enter name : Venkat
Enter 3 Subjects marks : 56 62 74
Name : Venkat
Total : 192

If we define a structure and then declare an object of that structure using the keyword class, the members of the object are still public by default. In the following example, main ( ) has access to the members of 'studentobj' even though 'studentobj' is declared as using the keyword class; For example

Program 17.6.10

Write a program in C++ to illustrate the declaration of keyword class for an object of 'struct student'

```
# include <iostream>
using namespace std;
struct student
{
    public :
        void getdetail ( )
    {
        cout <<"\n Enter name :" ;
        cin.getline(name,20);
        fflush(stdin);
        cout <<"\n Enter 3 Subject marks : " ;
        cin >>sub1>>sub2>>sub3;
    }
        void putdetail ( )
        {
            cout<<"\n Name : "<<name;
            cout <<"\n Total : "<<sub1+sub2+sub3;
        }
    private :
        int sub1,sub2,sub3;
        char name[20];
    };
    class student studentobj;    //object of the struct with keyword class
        void main ( )
    {
        studentobj.getdetail ( );
        studentobj.putdetail ( );
        cout <<endl;
    }
```

OUTPUT :

Enter name : Nageswara Rao
Enter 3 Subjects marks : 78 89 91

Name : Nageswara Rao
Total : 258

* * *

COMPREHENSION - 17

Note : By answering all the questions given in this comprehension one can answer any objective type of questions easily whatever be the form of the question. Answers for these questions can be obtained by going through the topics in this chapter carefully.

1. What is the need for Object Oriented Programming Languages over Procedural Languages?
2. What are the differences between Structures and Class?
3. Give the Syntax of a Class in C++.
4. How is access classified for Classes?
5. What is meant by Instance Variables, Instances and Code?
6. Give the Syntax of a Class including different access rights to data type Variables and Functions of the Class.
7. Explain with syntax and examples the principle of one of the public functions of a class accessing the private function the in the same class.
8. What is an Inline Member Function?
9. Give examples of use of Inline Member Function inside a Class.
10. Can you define inline member function outside the class it belongs to? If so how can it be done?
11. What is Scope Operator? What are its uses?
12. Explain the use of Array Objects in a Class.
13. What is a Constructor Function in C++ ? Why and where is it used?
14. What are the features of a Constructor Function?
15. Explain with example the use of Constructor Function?
16. What is a parameterized Constructor? What is its use?
17. Explain with example the use of a Parameterized Constructor Function?
18. In Parameterized Constructor use can you create Objects without arguments? What happens if you do so?
19. What is Dummy Constructor? When do you use it?
20. What are the points to be remembered when you use Constructors containing Objects like local, static and global Variables?
21. What type of Constructor can you use for type conversions.
22. What is meant by Explicit Constructor? Explain its use.
23. What is a Destructor Function?

24. What are the points to be used while using Destructor Functions?
25. Explain the use of Destructor Function.
26. What are the different ways of calling Destructors?
27. What are Friend Functions? When are they used?
28. How is a Friend function declared? Explain its use.
29. Explain the use of friend function when two or more classes have the same function name for the same purpose.
30. What is meant by Friend Classes? Explain its use.
31. What are the points to be remembered before using Friend Class?
32. Is Friendship mutual by default?
33. Explain assignment of objects in Class.
34. What is the use of malloc and free functions in C?
35. Explain the key words new and delete in Dynamic memory allocation in C++.
36. Explain the use of const member function and const objects in C++.
37. Explain the use of the key word mutable in C++.
38. How is the size of a class object determined?
39. What is meant by Nested Class?
40. What are the points to be observed in using Nested Classes?
41. What are the default access f Structures and Classes?
42. Explain the terms i) Static class member ii) Static data member and iii) static member function of a class.
43. What are the default constructors the compiler provides in C++ ?
44. What is a copy constructor? What is its use?
45. What is meant by This Pointer? How is it indicated? What does it do?

* * *

EXERCISE - 17

Note : By answering all the questions given in this comprehension one can answer any objective type of questions easily whatever be the form of the question. Answers for these questions can be obtained by going through the topics in this chapter carefully.

1. (a) How a member function of a class is defined?
   (b) How data members of a class are defined?
   (c) Write a C++ program to demonstrate various operations of complex numbers using class?
2. (a) How does a C++ structure differ from a C++ class?
   (b) What is a class? How does it accomplish the data hiding?
   (c) Write a C++ program to create a bank account which includes account number, name, account type and balance. It should include also the operations to assign initial values, to deposit, to withdraw after the balance?
3. (a) What is an abstract data type?
   (b) Are basic data types are abstract data types?
   (c) Is the user defined data type "structure" is an abstract data type?
   (d) Explain various components of space complexity?
4. (a) What do you mean by dynamic initialization of object? Why do we need to do this?
   (b) How Is dynamic initialize of objects achieved?
   (c) Write a C++ program for generating Fibonacci series?
5. (a) Describe the importance of destructors?
   (b) What is the copy constructor? What are it uses?
   (c) Write a C++ function for Tower of Hanoi?
6. (a) How does the objects are passed as arguments to the member function? Explain with an example.
   (b) Write a program to send an array object as an argument to the function? Write a program to implement the above
7. Create two classes DM and DF which store the value of distances. DM stores distances in metres and centimeters and DF in feet and inches. Write a program that can read the values for the class objects and add one object of DM with another object of DF. Use a friend function to carry out the addition operation. The object that stores the results may be a DM or DF object. The display should be in the format of feet and inches or metres and centimeters depending on the object on display.

8. (a) What is diff between malloc ( ) /free() and new/delete?
   (b) What are the access privileges in C++? What is the default access level?
   (c) What is destructor?
   (d) What is passing by reference?
9.. (a) What is a friend function? Explain the advantages and disadvantages of it?
   (b) What is static member function? Explain it's limitations.
10. (a) Can you think of a situation where your program would crash without reaching the breakpoint which you set at the beginning of main()?
   (b) When are copy constructors called?
   (c) Can a copy constructor accept an object of the same class as parameter, instead of reference of the object?
11. (a) What's the difference between public, private, and protected?
   (b) Why can't the derived class access private things from my base class?
   (c) How can we protect derived classes from breaking when we change the internal parts of the base class?
12. (a) Each class has some special member-functions, which calls can be inserted by the compiler into a code without explicit instruction of the programmer. Enumerate such functions, members and cases, when implicit calls can arise.
   (b) If when creating a variable the programmer explicitly did not initialize it, in some cases, the compiler itself would give it a certain, predefined initial value, and in some cases the initial value would be unpredictable. What does it depend on?

***

CHAPTER - 18
INHERITANCE

18.1. INTRODUCTION :

A child is said to have inherited certain characteristics of its parents if the child resembles in some characteristics of features in appearance or character of its parents. Similarly, in Object oriented programming we have the property of inheritance of objects of a class. For example, **if we have an object A and we want to declare two more objects by names B and C which contain some of the instance variables and methods that are present in the object A, then instead of declaring individual objects it is enough that we declare the first object which contains the common fields of both the objects and then the fields pertaining to object B and c alone, thus by making use of the property-inheritance.** When a class needs some of the features of the previous class we can easily inherit those features without rewriting them, thus avoiding code repetition. **In C++ the class, which feeds features to the subsequent class, is called as a base class or simply super class. A class that inherits features of base class is termed as sub class or derived class.** It is one of the properties of object-oriented programming which enhances the design and structure of the program in addition to reusability of code. As we are already familiar with the basic operations of the class it is very easy to extend it to inheritance.

Inheritance can be classified into many forms based on the level of inheritance and inter-relation between the classes involved in the inheritance process. Let us see one by one with suitable examples.

18.2. SINGLE INHERITANCE :

The derivation of a class from only one base class is called single inheritance and it is the ability of a derived class to inherit member functions and member variables of the existing base class. To illustrate the above concept, let us consider two classes of employees viz., employee and worker.

```
class employee
{
      private:
         int empno;
         char empname[20];
         char designation[20];
      public:
         void getinfo( );
         void printinfo( );
}
```

The following details are required when we want to define a worker class

```
class worker
{
    private:
        int empno;
        char empname[20];
        char designation[20];
        int bp,da,hra,pf,netpay;
    public:
        void getinfo( );
        void printinfo( );
        void getpaydetails( );
        void printpaydetails( );
}
```

when we observe closely the above two classes - **We can say that the worker class inherits the fields, empno, empname, designation and methods getinfo(), printinfo( ) which are also the features of employee class.**

So, while delcaring worker class we can inherit the features of employee class.

18.2.1. Derived Classes :

A derived class is defined by specifying its relationship with the base class in addition to its own details. The general form of defining a derived class is :

```
class derived_class : visibility_mode  base_class
{
    //Members of derived class and members to access base class
};
```

Here,

i) **derived_class** is the name of the class which we would like to add features from other class.

ii) **visibility_mode** is the access permission for the members of the derived class and it may be either private, public or protected. If it is left blank then the default access specifier is private, base_class is the name of the class from where we want to draw features.

iii) **Declaration of private and public inheritance by using a base class.**

Assume that the following class 'sample'

```
    class sample
{
    members of sample
};
```

Following examples shows how to declare private and public inheritance by using sample as a base class.

```
class example : private sample        //private derivation
{
      member of sample
};
class example : public sample         //public derivation
{
      member of sample
};
class example : sample                //private derivation by default
{
      members of sample
};
```

Now let us consider the following declaration :

```
class worker : public employee
{
      private ;
         int bp,da,hra,pf,netpay;
      public;
         void getpaydetails( );
         void printdetails ( );
};
```

Here the colon (:) indicates that we are inheriting something. It indicates the derivation of derived class (worker) from the base class (employee). Here the visibility mode is public. **The visibility mode specifies whether the members of the base class are publicly, protected or privately inherited.** *In our example case, the derived class is publicly inherited from the base class as indicated by the term 'public'*. **When a base class is publicly inherited, all public members of the base class becomes public members of the derived class.** In this case, access status of the inherited members is unchanged. **Inherited private members are private members of the derived class and they are inaccessible outside the derived class.** Also note that, *they are inaccessible to member function of the derived class, which indicates that they are purely private to the base class.*

iv) **The creation of derived object** takes the following form :

Worker labour;

Here worker is a derived class and labour is a derived object.

The following program illustrates the above concepts.

Program 18.2.1

Write a program in C++ to illustrate the concepts of class inheritance and derived objects

```
# include <iostream>
using namespace std;
class employee                              // base class, public
{
    private :
        int empno;
        char empname[20];
        char designation [20];
    public :
        void getinfo ( );
        void printinfo ( );
};
class programmer : public employee   //class : base-employee ; derived
                                      //class programmer
{
    private :
        int bp, da, hra, pf, netpay;     //These fields are different for
                                         //different programmers.
    public :
        void getpaydetails ( );        //These methods are common to all
                                       // employees
        void printpaydetails ( );
};
void employee :: getinfo ( )                // base class, public function
{
    cout << "\n Enter employee number ->" ;
    cin >> empno;
    fflush (stdin);
    cout << "\n Enter name ->";
    cin.getline (empname,20);
    fflush(stdin);
    cout<<"\n Enter designation ->";
    cin.getline (designation,20);
    fflush (stdin);
}
```

```
void employee :: printinfo ( )                // base class, public function
{
      cout << "\n Employee number : "<<empno;
      cout << "\n Name             : "<<empname;
      cout << "\n Designation      :"<<designation ;
}
void programmer :: getpaydetails ( )          //base class ; public function
{
      cout <<"\n Enter basic pay ( )
{
      cout <<"\n Enter basic pay ->";
      cin >> bp;
      cout << "\n Enter dearness allowance ->";
      cin >> da;
      cout << "\n Enter house rent allowance -->";
      cin >> hra;
      cout << "\n Enter provident fund ->";
      cin >> pf;
}
void programmer :: printpaydetails ( )        //base class ; public function
{
      printinfo ( );
      netpay = bp+da+hra-pf;
      cout << "\n Net pay             : "<<netpay<<"\n";
}
void main ( )
{
      programmer grade1progr;
      grade1progr.getinfo ( );
      grade1progr.getpaydetails ( );
      grade1progr.printpaydetails ( );
}
```

OUTPUT :

```
Enter employee number -> 2002
Enter name -> Suresh
Enter designation -> grade1progr
Enter basic pay -> 10000
Enter dearness allowance -> 2000
Enter house rent allowance -> 1000
Enter provident fund -> 500
```

Employee number : 2002
Name : Suresh
Designation : grade1progr
Net Pay : 12500

18.2.2. Access in Inheritance :

Let us first discuss the scope of members while inheriting various methods. **The relationship is base class to derived class.**

(i) Inheriting Private classes :

- private -> private
- protected -> private
- public -> private

Inheriting Public retains parent's access definitions.

(ii) Inheriting Protected classes

- private -> private
- protected -> protected
- public -> protected

In the next example we will look at how a base class is inherited privately by a derived class. **When a derived class privately inherits a base class, "public members" of the base class become 'private members' of the derived class and therefore the public members of the base class can only be accessed by the member functions of the derived class.** They are also inaccessible to the objects of the derived class and the result is that **no member of the base class is accessible to the objects of the derived class.**

Now consider the base class

```
Class employee
{
private :
    int empno;
    char empname[20];
    char designation[20];
    int bp;
public:
    void getinfo();
    void getbp();
    int putbp( );
    void printinfo ();
};
```

In the above base class we have empno, empname, designation and bp as private member variables and getinfo ( ), getbp ( ), putbp( ) and printinfo ( ) as public member functions.

Now, consider the derived class, which inherits the above class privately,

```
class worker : private employee
{
      private :
         int da,hra,pf.netpay;
      public :
         void getpaydetails ( );
         void printpaydetails ( ) ;
};
```

In the above derived class we have da,hra,pf and netpay as private member variables and getpaydetail ( ) and printpaydetails ( ) as public member functions. To access base member variables we have getpaydetails ( ) and this function also receives input for member variables for its own class. The definition of getpaydetails ( ) is follows,

```
void worker : : getpaydetails ( )
{
      getinfo ();
      getbp ( );
      cout << "\n Enter dearness allowance –>";
      cin >> da;
      cout << "\n Enter house rent allowance –>";
      cin >> hra;
      cout << "\n Enter provident fund –>";
      cin >>pf;
}
```

As we know that *in privately inheritance method, all the members of base class are inherited to derived class but they are not directly accessible by the derived object*. So, with the help of public member function of the derived class and in this case it is getpaydetails(), is used to receive input for all base class member variables.

Base class public function print pay details is used to access details by the derived class.

```
void worker : : printpaydetails ( )
{
      printinfo ( );
```

```
        netpay = putbp ( ) + da + hra - pf;
        cout << "\n Net pay          : "<< netpay <<"\n ;
    }
```

Program : 18.2.2

Write a program in C++ to illustrate the principle of inheritance

```
# include <iostream>
using namespace std;
class employee                        //base class : employee
{
    private :
        int empno;
        char empname[20];
        char designation[20];
        int bp;
    public :
        void getinfo ( );
        void getbp ( );
        int putbp ( );
        void printinfo ( );
};
class worker : private employee       // derived class : worker
{
    private :
        int da,hra,pf,netpay;
    public :
        void getpaydetails ( );
        void printpaydetails ( );
};
void employee :: getinfo ( )          //public function : base class
{
    cout << "\n Enter employee number —>";
    cin >> empno;
    fflush (stdin);
    cout << "\n Enter name —>";
    cin.getline (empname,20);
    fflush (stdin);
    cout << "\n Enter designation —>";
    cin.getline(designation,20);
    fflush(stdin);
}
```

```
void employee :: getbp ( )          //public function : base class
{
    cout <<"\n Enter Basic pay –>";
    cin >> bp;
}
int employee :: putbp ( )
{
    return bp;
}
void employee :: printinfo ( )
{
    cout << "\n Employee number : "<<empno;
    cout << "\n Name             : "<<empname;
    cout << "\n Designation : "<<designation;
}
void worker :: getpaydetails ( )
{
    getinfo ( );
    getbp ( ) ;
    cout << "\n Enter dearness allowance –>";
    cin >> da;
    cout << "\n Enter house rent allowance –>";
    cin >> hra;
    cout << "\n Enter provident fund –>";
    cin >> pf;
}
void worker :: printpaydetails ( )
{
    printinfo ( );
    netpay = putbp ( )+da+hra-pf;
    cout << "\n Net pay      : "<<netpay <<"\n";
}
void main ( )
(
    worker labour;
    labour.getpaydetails ( );
    labour.printpaydetails ( );
}
```

OUTPUT :

Enter employee number –> 2002
Enter name –> Rajendra

Enter designation —> Office Assistant
Enter Basic pay —> 5000
Enter dearness allowance —> 2000
Enter house rent allowance —> 1000
Enter provident fund —> 450

Employee number : 2002
Name : Rajendra
Designation : Office Assistant
Net pay : 7550

It should be observed that in both the cases, the private members are not inherited and therefore, **the private members of a base class will never become the members of its derived class.**

(iii) Inheriting by Base class protected Member during public inheritance : Examples that we have seen so far, does not have protected members. In this following let us see how a base class protected member changes when it is publicly inherited.

Now consider the base class declaration:

```
class employee                    //base class
{
    protected:
        int empno;
        char empname[20];
        char designation[20];
        int bp;
    public :
        void getinfo ( );
        void printinfo( );
};
```

In the above class all member variables are protected and all members functions are public. When such a class is inherited public, the protected members of base class become protected members in derived class and therefore they are easily accessible for the member functions of the derived class.

Now consider the derived class declaration and its definition.

```
class worker : public employee      //derived class
{
    private :
        int da,hra,pf,netpay;
```

```
        public:
            void getpaydetails ( );
            void printpaydetails ( );
};
void worker : : getpaydetails ( )
{
        cout << "\n Enter dearness allowance ->";
        cin >> da;
        cout << "\n Enter house rent allowance ->";
        cin >> hra;
        cout << "\n Enter provident fund ->";
        cin >> pf;
}
void worker::printpaydetails ( )
{
        printinfo ( ) ;
        netpay = bp+da+hra-pf;
        cout << "\n Net pay    : "<< netpay << "\n";
}
```

Program : 18.2.3

Write a program to illustrate inheritance of protected members of base class in public inheritance

```
# include <iostream>
using namespace std;
class employee                      //base class :
{
    protected :
        int empno;
        char emname[20];
        char designation[20];
        int bp;
    public :
        void getinfo ( );
        void printinfo ( );
};
class worker : public employee           //derived class :
{
    private :
        int da,hra,pf,netpay;
```

```
    public :
        void getpaydetails ( );
        void printpaydetails ( );
};
void employee :: getinfo ( )
{
    cout << "\n Enter employee number ->";
    cin >> empno;
    fflush (stdin);
    cout << "\n Enter name ->";
    cin.getline (empname,20);
    fflush (stdin);
    cout << "\n Enter designation ->";
    cin.getline (designation,20);
    fflush (stdin);
    cout << "\n Enter Basic pay ->";
    cin>>bp;
}
void employee :: printinfo ( )
{
    cout << "\n employee number : "<<empno;
    cout << "\n Name            :"<<empname;
    cout << "\n Designation  : "<,designation;
}
void worker :: getpaydetails ( )
{
    cout << "\n Enter dearness allowance ->";
    cin >> da;
    cout << "\n Enter house rent allowance ->";
    cin >> hra;
    cout << "\n Enter provident fund ->";
    cin >> pf;
}
void worker :: printpaydetails ( )
}
    printinfo ( );
    netpay = bp+da+hra-pf;
    cout << "\n Net pay : "<<netpay<<"\n";
}
void main ( )
{
    worker labour;
```

```
        labour.getinfo ( );
        labour.getpaydetails ( );
        labour.printpaydetails ( );
    }
```

OUTPUT :

```
Enter employee number  —> 2003
Enter name  —> Naresh
Enter designation  —> Programmer
Enter Basic pay  —> 7500
Enter dearness allowance  —> 1500
Enter house rent allowance  —> 1500
Enter provident fund  —> 500

Employee number : 2003
Name            :   Naresh
Designation     :   Programmer
Net pay         :   10000
```

18.2.3. Constructors and Destructors in inheritance :

As mentioned earlier, **a derived class inherits the functionality from its base class and also we know already that, constructors are used to initialize members variables of an object and allocating memory for it.** Thus, the objects of the derived class are usually instantiated instead of the base class in inheritance. Furthermore, it is well known that, **destructors of classes are called automatically when an object is destroyed. This rule also holds true for objects of classes that are derived from other classes.**

constructors and destructors are called in a stack-like (I.e. last in first out) fashion.

Program 18.2.4

Write a program in C++ to illustrate the effects of the inheritance on the constructor and destructor of a derived class

```
# include <iostream>
using namespace std;
class base
{
    public :
        base ()                  // Constructor
        {
            cout << "\n Calling constructor from base ";
        }
```

```
        ~ base ( )              //destructor
        {
            cout <<"\n Calling destructor from base \n";
        }
};
class derived : public base
{
        public :
            derived ( )
            {
                cout <<"\n Calling constructor from derived";
            }
            ~derived ( )
            }
                cout <<"\n Calling destructor from derived ";
            }
};
void main ( )
{
        derived  derived_object;
}
```

OUTPUT :

Calling constructor from base
Calling constructor from derived
Callig destructor from derived
Calling destructor from base
Calling constructor from base
calling constructor from derived
Calling destructor from derived
Calling destructor from base

From the output we can observe that, **constructors and destructors are called in a stack-like (I.e. last in first out) fashion. When a derived object is instantiated, the appropriate base constructor is called first, then the appropriate derived constructor is called. When derived object is destroyed, the derived destructor is called first, and then the base destructor is called for that object.** In general, a derived class destructor is called before a base class destructor is called.

18.2.4. Multilevel inheritance :

Derivation of a class from another derived class is called multilevel inheritance.

Consider the following diagram.

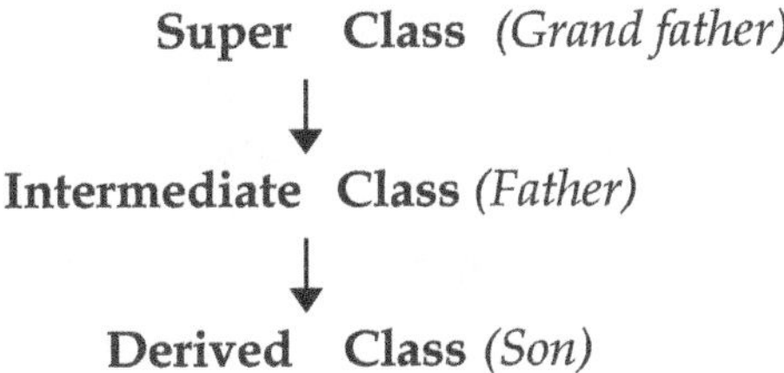

The above relationship Grandfather-Father-Son is known as inheritance path. From the above picture it is understood that *intermediate class has properties of super class besides its own. The derived class will have its own characteristics in addition to intermediate class.*

In the example that we consider here contains three classes. The base class empinfo has empname and empno as protected variables and getempinfo( ) and printempinfo( ) as public methods, The intermediate class empearn has bp, hra and cca as protected variables and getempearn( ) and printempearn( ) as public methods. The derived class empsal has lic,pf and total as protected variables and getempdedn( ), printempdedn( ) and printnetsalary( ) as public methods.

Program 18.2.5

Write a program in C++ to illustrate the properties of multi level inheritance

```
# include <iostream>
using namespace std;
class eminfo                    //super class
{
      protected :
         char empname[20];
         int empno;
         public :
                 void getinfo ( );
                 void printinfo ( );
      };
      void empinfo :: getempinfo ( )
      {
         cout <<\n Enter Employee name : ";
         cin.getline (empname,20);
         fflush(stdin);
         cout <<"\n Employee number :";
         cin >> empno;
         fflush (stdin);
      }
```

```
void empinfo :: printempinfo ( )
{
    cout << "\n Name            : "<<empname;
    cout << "\n Number          : "<empno;
}
class emp_pay : public empinfo          // intermediate class - level-1
{
    protected :
        int bp,hra,cca,tpay;
    public :
        void getempearn ( );
        void printemp_pay ( );
}
void emp_pay :: getemp_pay ( )
{
    cout <<"\n Enter Basic pay : ";
    cin >> bp;
    cout <<"\n Enter HRA       : ";
    cin >> hra;
    cout <<"\n Enter CCA       : ";
    cin >> cca;
}
void emp_pay :: printemp_pay ( )
{
    cout <<"\n Basic pay       : "<<bp;
    cout <<"\n HRA             : "<<hra;
    cout << "\n CCA            : "<<cca;
}
class empsal : public emp_pay  //multilevel inherited derived class - level-2
{
    protected :
        int glic,epf,,tpay,tdedn,total;
    public :
        void getempdedn ( );
        void printempdedn ( );
        void printnetsalary ( );
};
void empsal :: getempdedn ( )
{
    cout <<"\n Enter GLIC      :";
    cin >> glic;
```

```
        cout <<"\n Enter EPF        : ";
        cin >>epf;
    }
    void empsal :: printempdedn ( )
    {
        cout << "\n GLIC    : "<<glic;
        cout <<"\ EPF       : "<<epf;
    }
    void empsal :: printnetsalary ( )
    {
        tpay = bp+hra+cca;
        tdedn=glic+epf
        total = tpay-tdedn
        cout << "\n Total Pay : "<<tpay;
        cout << "\n Total Deduction : "<<tdedn;
        cout << "\n Net salary : "<<total;
    }
    void main ( )
    {
        empsal employee;
        employee.getempinfo ( );
        employee.getemp_pay ( );
        employee.getempdedn ( );
        employee.printempinfo ( );
        employee.printemp_pay ( );
        employee.printempdedn ( );
        employee.printempsalary ( );
    }
```

OUTPUT :

```
Enter Employee Name : Ramana
Employee Number : 2002
Enter Basic Pay : 15000
Enter HRA : 2000
Enter CCA : 500
Enter GLIC : 500
Enter EPF : 300

Name   : Ramana
Number : 2002
```

Basic pay : 15000
HRA : 2000
CCA : 500
GLIC : 500
EPF : 300
Total Pay : 17500
Total Deduction : 800
Net Salary : 16700

18.2.5. Multiple inheritance :

Multiple inheritance is different from Multilevel Inheritance.

(i) *In single inheritance we use only one base class to take features whereas, in multiple inheritance a derived class can have as many direct base classes.*

(ii) *A class can inherit the properties of two or more classes.*

(iii) *Moreover multiple inheritance allows combining features of several classes as a starting point for defining new classes.*

The general form of a derived class with multiple base classes is as follows:

```
class derived : visibility base_class1, visibility base_class2, visibility base_class 3...
{
    body of derived class
};
```

Note that commas separate the base classes and *visibility may be either public or private.*

Program 18.2.6

Write a program in C++ to illustrate the principle of multiple inheritance :

```
#include <iostream>
using namespace std;
class empinfo
{
    protected :
        char empname[20];
        int empno;
    public :
        void getempinfo( );
        void printempinfo ( );
};
```

```
void empinfo :: getempinfo ( )
{
    cout <<"\n Enter Employee name : " ;
    cin.getline(empname.20);
    fflush(stdin);
    cout<<"\n Employee number : " ;
    cin >> empno;
    fflush (stdin);
}
void empinfo :: printempinfo ( )
{
    cout << "\n Name          : "<<empname;
    cout << "\n Number        : "<<empno;
}
class empearn
{
    protected :
    int bp,hra,cca;
    public :
    void getempearn ( );
    void printempearn ( );
};
void empearn :: getempearn ( )
{
    cout <<"\n Enter Basic pay      : " ;
    cin >> bp;
    cout <<"\n Enter HRA            : " ;
    cin >> hra;
    cout <<"\n Enter CCA            : " ;
    cin >> cca;
}
void empearn :: printempearn ( )
{
    cout <<"\n Basic pay     : "<<bp;
    cout <<"\n HRA           : "<<hra;
    cout <<"\n CCA           : "<<cca;
}
class empdedn
{
    protected:
        int lic,pf;
    public :
        void getempdedn ( );
```

```
        void printempdedn ( );
};
void empdedn :: getempdedn ( )
{
    cout <<"\n Enter LIC      : " ;
    cin >> lic ;
    cout << "\n Enter PF      : " ;
    cin >> pf;
}
void empdedn :: printempdedn ( )
{
    cout <<"\n LIC            : "<<lic;
    cout <<"\n PF             : "<pf;
}
//derived class with multiple base classes
class empsal : public empinfo, public empearn, public empdedn
{
    protected :
        int totalsal;
    public :
        void calcsal ( );
};
void empsal :: calcsal ( )
{
    totalsal=bp+cca+hra-pf-lic;
    cout << "\n Net salary : "<<totalsal;
}
void main ( )
{
    empsal employee;
    employee.getempinfo ( );
    employee.getempearn ( );
    employee.getemdedn ( );
    employee.printempinfo ( );
    employee.printempearn ( );
    employee.printempdedn ( );
    employee.calcsal ( );
}
```

OUTPUT :

Enter Employee name : Radhika
Employee number : 2000

Enter Basic pay : 6000
Enter HRA : 2000
Enter CCA : 1000
Enter LIC : 500
Enter PF : 500

Name : Radhika
Employee number : 2000
Basic pay : 6000
HRA : 2000
CCA : 1000
LIC : 500
PF : 500
Net Salary : 8000

In the above example program, the class empsal derives publicly from the classes empinfo, empearn and empdedn. So the protected memberof class empinfo, empearn and empdedn become protected members of class empsal and the public members of class empinfo, empearn and empdedn become public member in class empsal.

18.2.6. Virtual base class :

i) *We can avoid duplication elements passed to derived class when multiple inheritance is involved.*

ii) Using virtual base class C++ offers a way to avoid the confusion created by multiple inheritance from the same class.

iii) We can make a virtual base class just by adding the keyword 'virtual' when declaring the base class in a class definition.

iv) A virtual base class causes a program to have only one copy of that class into a derived class.

Now let us consider the program situation where the class 'stdinfo' is inherited by two classes namely 'langmarks' and 'submarks'. The class 'totmark' then inherits from classes 'langmarks' and 'submarks'. In this process both multiple and multilevel inheritance are introduced. Now, the class 'totmark' has two base classes ie, 'langmark' and 'submark' and these two base classes have a common base class 'stdinfo'. Now, the features of 'stdinfo' are transferred to 'totmark' in two ways. One from the class 'langmark' and another from 'submarks'. In this type inheritance the class 'totmark' has all the public and protected members of 'stdinfo' twice. These duplication of inherited members should be eliminated. For that C++ offers a way to avoid the confusion created by multiple inheritance from the sameclass, by using 'virtual base class'. By doing so, a virtual base class causes a program to have only one copy of that class into a derived class, We can make a virtual base class just by adding the keyword 'virtual' when declaring the base class in a class definition.

Program 18.2.7

Write a program in C++ to illustrate the use of virtual base class to avoid confusion created in multiple inheritance from the same class.

```
#include <iostream>
using namespace std;
class stdinfo
{
        protected :
            char stdname[20];
            int rollno;
        public :
            void getstdinfo( );
            void printstdinfo ( );
};
void stdinfo :: getstdinfo ( )
{
        cout <<"\n Enter name : " ;
        cin.getline(stdname.20);
        fflush(stdin);
        cout<<"\n Enter roll no : " ;
        cin >> rollno;
        fflush (stdin);
}
void stdinfo :: printstdinfo ( )
{
        cout << "\n Name       : "<<stdname;
        cout << "\n Roll no    : "<<rollno;
}
class langmark : public virtual stdinfo                //virtual base class
{
        protected :
            int lang1,lang2;
        public :
            void getlangmarks ( );
            void printlangmarks ( );
};
void langmark :: getlangmarks ( )
{
        cout <<"\n Enter Marks for Language 1: " ;
        cin >> lang1;
```

```
        cout <<"\n Enter Marks for Language 2 : " ;
        cin >> lang2;
}
void langmark :: printlangmarks ( )
{
        cout <<"\n Lang 1  : "<<lang1;
        cout <<"\n Lang 2  : "<<lang2 ;
}
class submark : public virtual stdinfo       //virtual class
{
        protected :
           int sub1,sub2,sub3:
        public :
           void getsubmarks ( );
           void printsubmarks ( );
};
void submark : : getsubmarks ( )
{
        cout <<"\n Ener Marks for Subject 1 : ";
        cin >> sub1;
        cout <<"\n Enter Marks for Subject2 : " ;
        cin >> sub2;
        cout <<"\n Enter Marks for Subject3 : " ;
        cin >> sub3;
}
void submark :: printsubmarks ( )
{
        cout <<"\n Sub 1 : "<<sub1;
        cout <<"\n Sub 2 : "<<sub2;
        cout <<"\n Sub 3 : "<<sub3;
}
class result : public langmark, public submark
{
        protected :
           int total;
        public :
           void calctotal( ) ;
           void printall ( );
};
void result :: calctotal ( )
{
        total= lang1+lang2+sub1+sub2+sub3;
}
```

```
void result : printall ( )
{
        printstdinfo ( );
        printlangmarks ( );
        printsubmarks ( );
        cout <<"\n Total : "<<total;
}
void main ( )
{
        result student;
        student.getstdinfo ( );
        student.getlangmarks ( );
        student.getsubmarks ( );
        student.calctotal ( );
        student.printall ( );
}
```

OUTPUT :

```
Enter name   : Krishna
Enter roll no : 303
Enter Marks for Language 1 : 76
Enter Marks for Language 2 : 67
Enter Marks for Subject 1 : 87
Enter Marks for Subject 2 : 72
Enter Marks for Subject 3 : 78

Name  : Krishna
Roll no : 303
Lang 1 : 76
Lang 2 : 67
Sub 1 : 87
Sub 2 : 72
Sub 3 : 78
Total : 380
```

From the above illustration, it is evident that *when a class is made a virtual base class, the compiler will take necessary care to see that only one copy of that class is inherited, regardless of how many inheritance paths existing between the virtual base class and a derived class.*

18.2.7. Passing parameters from derived class constructor to base class constructor :

When we declare derived object with two values, the corresponding constructor for derived class is called with two arguments As this constructor uses only one argument the other argument is passed to super class constructor. So, when we want to pass arguments this way, the *derived class constructor must declare both the parameters that it requires in addition to any parameters that are required by its super class.*

The example programs that we have seen so far, does not involve any parameter communication between derived class and base class. In the following program, we have two classes namely 'sample' and 'sample 1' and each with one parameterized constructor.

Program 18.2.8

Write a program in C++ to illustrate the principle of passing of parameter from derived class constructor to base class constructor.

```
# include <iostream>
using namespace std;
class sample
{
        protected :
            int a;
        public :
                    sample(in x)
                    {
                    a=x;
                    }
};
class sample1 :public sample
{
        protected :
            int b,c;
        public :
                    sample1 (int x,int y) : sample (x)
                    {
                    b=y;
                    }
                    void sumab()
                    {
                            c=a+b;
                    }
                    void printout ( )
                    {
                            cou <<"\n Addition of a+b is : "<<c;
                    }
};
```

```
void main ()
{
        sample1 example (16,34);
        example sumab( );
        example.printout ( );
}
```

OUTPUT :

Addition of a+b is : 50

In inheritance, some of the base class data elements and member functions are 'inherited' into the derived class. By adding data and member functions the functionality of the base class can be extended. **Inheritance, when used to modify and extend the capabilities of the existing classes, becomes a very powerful tool for incremental program development.**

* * *

COMPREHENSION - 18

Note : By answering all the questions given in this comprehension one can answer any objective type of questions easily whatever be the form of the question. Answers for these questions can be obtained by going through the topics in this chapter carefully.

1. What is meant by Inheritance Property?
2. What is a Base Class or Super Class?
3. What is a Subclass or Derived Class?
4. What is Single Inheritance? Explain with Syntax and example.
5. Explain Derived Class with syntax and example.
6. What is meant by Visibility Mode?
7. What are the Visibility Modes?
8. Explain with syntax and examples Private and Public Inheritances.
9. If the Visibility Mode is not declared what will be the Default Access?
10. What is the Class from where we draw the Features?
11. Explain the creation of Derived Class and Derived Object.
12. What is the relationship between Base Class and Derived Class?
13. Explain Inheriting Private Classes.
14. Explain Inheriting Protected Classes.
15. Explain Inheriting Base class protected Member during public inheritance.
16. Explain the role of Constructors in Inheritance.
17. Explain the role of Destructors in Inheritance.
18. How are Constructors and Destructors called? What is the Policy followed?
19. Explain the sequences followed when a Derived Object is Instantiated.
20. Explain the sequences followed when a Derived Object is destroyed.
21. Explain Multilevel Inheritance with examples.
22. In Multilevel Inheritances what are the properties each participating Class will inherit?
23. Explain with example Multiple Inheritance.
24. Explain the general form of a derived class with multiple base classes.
25. What will be the nature of Visibility of Base Classes in Multiple Inheritance?
26. How can New Classes be defined combining features of different classes?
27. What is a Virtual Base Class? What purposes does it serve?
28. How is Virtual Base Class indicated in Syntax?
29. How are Parameters passed from Derived Class Constructor to Base Class Constructor?
30. How can inheritance can serve Incremental Program Development?

* * *

EXERCISE - 18

Note : By answering all the questions given in this exercise one can answer subjective type of questions easily including problems. The worked examples in the chapter may help in solving these questions.

1. (a) What does inheritance mean in C++? What are the different forms of inheritance? Give an example for each?
   (b) What is a virtual function? Why we need virtual function?
2. (a) How a member function of a class is defined?
   (b) How data members of a class are defined?
   (c) Write a C++ program to demonstrate various operations of complex numbers using class?
3. (a) What does inheritance mean in C++? What are the benefits of inheritance?
   (b) What are the different forms of inheritance? Give an example for each.
4. When do we use the protected visibility specifier to a class member and class itself? Explain them with an example.
5. (a) What is multiple inheritance? Write a program to illustrate the concept of Multiple Inheritance.
   (b) What is Hybrid inheritance? Write a program to illustrate the concept of Hybrid Inheritance.
6. (a) Explain about the C++ classes in detail and design a class for playing cards?
   (b) What are the conditions that have to be met for a condition to be an invariant of the class?
7. (a) Explain the need for "Virtual Destructor".
   (b) Can we have "Virtual Constructors"?
8. (a) What is multiple inheritance? Write a program to illustrate the concept of multiple Inheritance.
   (b) What is single inheritance? Write a program to illustrate the concept of single Inheritance.
9. (a) What's the difference between public, private, and protected?
   (b) Why can't the derived class access private things from my base class?
   (c) How can we protect derived classes from breaking when we change the internal parts of the base class?

* * *

CHAPTER - 19
DIFFERENT TYPES OF OVERLOADING IN C++

19.1. INTRODUCTION TO OVERLOADING :

Overloading is also an important paradigm in Object Oriented Programming. Overloading makes C++ more attractive than any other languages. **Overloading Improves readability by reducing namespace pollution and thus makes the language extensible.** These concepts are used in inheritance and abstraction.

19.2. TYPES OF OVERLOADING :

- **i)** Function overloading
- **ii)** Function call operator overloading
- **iii)** Constructor overloading
- **iv)** Operator overloading
- **v)** Overloading for string concatenation
- **vi)** Overloading of other items like new, delete etc.,

19.2.1 Overloading related to functions - FUNCTION OVERLOADING :

In C++ we can have the same function name but with different arguments to evaluate different functions with the same name, whereas in C, we cannot have same name for two or more functions. For example to find maximum of given three integer numbers and to find maximum of three float numbers in C we need two functions to fulfill the task. But **in C++, a function is distinguishable from other functions not only by its name but also by the number and type of its arguments.** So, the functions though having the same name have different number of arguments like

```
int max( int,int );
int max( int,int,int);
int max(int,int,int,int);
```

are all distinct and are said to be overloaded. The linker can distinguish overloaded functions because the compiler generates a symbol, which encodes both the function name and the argument type information.

In other words in C++ the number and type of arguments distinguish the different functions having the same name and the function int max *is said to be overloaded. All the arguments need not be only int. They can also be float or a combination of int and float etc.* The function is overloaded as distinguished by its arguments.

Program 19.2.1

Write a program in C++ to illustrate the use of separate functions and arguments. (without function overloading)

```
#include <iostream>
using namespace std;
float maxfloat (float,float,float);  //the two functions have different
float maxint(int,int,int);           //names and different types of
arguments
void main ()
{
    int choice;
    float x,y,z;
    int a,b,c;
    cout <<"\n Enter 1 for finding maximum number among floats \n";
    cout <<" \n Enter  2 for finding maximum number among ints \n";
    cin >>choice;
    switch (choice)
    {
            case 1 :  cout<< "\n Enter three float values ";
            cin >>x>>y>>z;
            cout << "\n Maximum number is " <<maxfloat(x,y,z);
            break;
            case 2 :  cout<< "\n Enter three integer values ";
            cin >>a>>b>>c;
            cout << "\n Maximum number is " <<maxint(a,b,c);
            break;
            default :
                    cout << "\n Invalid choice try again ";
    }
}
        float maxfloat (float p, float q, float r)
        {
            if (p>q && p>r)
                return (p);
            else if (q>r)
                return (q);
            else
                return (r);
        }
        float maxint (int p, int q, int r)
        {
            if (p>r && p>r)
```

```
                return (p);
            else if (q>r)
                return (q);
            else
                return (r);
        }
```

OUTPUT :

```
Enter 1 for finding maximum number among floats
Enter 2 for finding maximum number among ints
1
Enter three float values  45.6  78.9 12.3
Maximum number is 78.9
Enter 1 for finding maximum number among floats
Enter 2 for finding maximum number among ints
2
Enter three integer values  34  56  12
Maximum number is 56
```

Instead of writing two different function names each with different types of arguments we can as well use one function name with different types of arguments. Since, the passing parameter is different, compiler can use the types integer and float to tell the function the users want to call. Here is the example program implementing function overloading;

Program 19.2.2.

Write a program in C++ to illustrate the use of same function name but with different arguments. (example of function overloading)

```
#include <iostream>
using namespace std;
//function overloading prototypes
float max (float,float,float);  //same function name with float argument
float max (int,int,int);        //same function name with int argument
void main ()
{
    int choice;
    float x,y,z;
    int a,b,c;
    cout <<"\n Enter 1 for finding maximum number among floats \n";
    cout <<"\n Enter 2 for finding maximum number among ints \n";
    cin >>choice;
    switch (choice)
    {
            case 1 :   cout<< "\n Enter three  float values ";
```

```
                cin >>x>>y>>z;
                cout << "\n Maximum number is " <<max (x,y,z);
                break;
                case 2 :   cout<< "\n Enter three integer values ";
                cin >>a>>b>>c;
                cout << "\n Maximum number is " <<max (a,b,c);
                break;
        default :
                cout << "\n Invalid choice try again ";
            }
        }
            float max (float p, float q, float r) //same function  with float arg.
            {
                if (p>q && p>r)
                    return (p);
                else if (q>r)
                    return (q);
                else
                    return (r);
            }
            float max (int p, int q, int r)        //same function with int arg.
            {
                if (p>r && p>r)
                    return (p);
                else if (q>r)
                    return (q);
                else
                    return (r);
            }
```

OUTPUT :

```
Enter 1 for finding maximum number among floats
Enter 2 for finding maximum number among ints
1
Enter Three float values 56.8, 98.4, 33.7
Maximum number is 98.4
Enter  1 for finding maximum number among floats
Enter 2 for finding maximum number among ints
2
Enter Three integer values  87  34  56
Maximum number is 87
```

Note : *In function its signature, which is composed by its name and the type of its arguments identifies overloading each function.*

19.2.2. Over loading of Function Call Operator '( )':

Since there is no predefined meaning for operator ( ), we are free to implement any characteristics that fit appropriate. Besides, we can specify any return data type and as many arguments as we would like when we define function call operator '( )'. We can call operator ( ) the same way we specify an element of an array with the subscript operator, For example, if we define a two-dimensional array class matrix and create an object named 'addition', we can access a specific element of the array with the statement

Addition(2,1)

The syntax of the function call operator is

Data-type operator ( ) (arguments)

For example: **int operator ( ) is a function call operator**

int operator ( ) ( ) is a function call operator with arguments list for overloaded operator.

int operator ( ) ( ) declares operator ( ) to accept no arguments and returns an integer value. Here, the first set of parentheses specifies the name of the operator, and the second set specifies the argument list for the overloaded operator. For example, in our example program we use 'average' as object to average input numbers. The statement

average (20.2)

is equivalent to average.operator ( ) (20.2)

Program 19.2.3

Write a program in C++ to illustrate the principle of overloading the function call operator.

```
#include <iostream>
using namespace std;
class mean
{
    private :
        float sum;
        int n;
    public :
        mean ( )
        {
            sum=0;
            n=0;
        }
```

```
        float operator ( ) (float no)  // function call operator overloading
        {
            sum+=no;
            n++;
            cout << "\n Sum        : "<<sum;
            return sum/n;
        }
    };
    void main ( )
    {
        mean average ;
        float value = 0;
        cout << "\n Enter number, to exit enter negative number \n";
        cin >> value ;
        while (value > =0)
        {
            cout << '"\n Mean              : "<<average(value);
            cout << "\n Enter number";
            cin >> value;
        }
    }
```

OUTPUT :

```
Enter number, to exit enter negative number
18.5
sum      : 18.5
Mean     : 18.5
Enter number 12.1
sum      : 30.6
Mean     : 15.3
Enter number 33.33
sum      : 63.93
Mean     : 21.31
Enter number  -3
```

19.2.3. Constructor overloading :

In C++, when writing our own class, we do not have to provide constructors for it. The default constructor is automatically provided by the runtime system for any class that contains no constructors. The default provided by the runtime system does not do anything. So, if we want to perform some initialization, we will have to write some constructors for our class.

Like functions, constructors can also be overloaded. **The main reasons for using constructor-overloading functions are flexibility, to allow both initialized and uninitialized objects to be created and to define copy constructors.**

Program 19.2.4

Write a program in C++ to illustrate the principle of constructor overloading

```
#include <iostream>
using namespace std;
class example
{
    private :
        float p,n,r,i;
    public :
        example (float x, float y)          //two parameters constructor
        {
            p=x;
            n=y;
            r=10.5;
        }
        example (float x, float y, float z) //three parameters constructor
        {
            p=x;
            n=y;
            r=z;
        }
        float calculate ( )
        {
            i=p*n*r/100.0;
            return i;
        }
        void displayint ( )
        {
            cout <<"\n Interest amount : "<<i;
        }
};
    void main ( )
{
    example sample (30000.0,6.0); //r=10.5 is given in 2 parameter constructor
    sample.calculate ( );
    cout << "\n Interest amount using two arguments : " ;
    sample.displayint ( );
    example sample1 (50000.0, 7.0, 12.5); //r=12.5 (not 10.5) is 3rd arg.
```

```
            sample1.calculate ( );
            cout << "\n Interest amount using three arguments : " ;
            sample1.displayint ( );
        }
}
```

OUT PUT :

Interest amount using two arguments :
Interest amount : 18900

Interest amount using three arguments :
Interest amount : 43750

The above program the class 'example' has two constructors one with two parameters and another with three parameters. When we create object of this class with two arguments the constructor with two argument will be called thus rate of interest will be considered as 10.5 as given in the body of the 2 parameter constructor by default. On the other hand when we create object with three arguments the constructor with three arguments will be invoked thus by initializing p,n,r with x,y and z. The value of 'r' will be 12.5 as given in the third argument of the 3 parameter function. In both the cases the value 'i' is calculated separately by the function float calculate ( ).

Now, the programmer has more freedom to choose, initialize object with two arguments. *But when we create an object without arguments the compiler will generates an error as there is no default constructor in the class 'example' and it should be avoided* in these circumstances.

19.2.4. Operator overloading :

Operator overloading is a very powerful feature of C++.

Any C++ operator (except five) and any function can be overloaded means that it can be defined for new parameters different from any of the parameters for which it is already defined. The compiler recognizes which version of an overloaded operator to use from the types of the parameters passed to it.

Of course, without knowing its significance, we have already seen operator overloading in use with the insertion and extraction operators used for stream input and output. The symbols << and >> used for these purposes and these operators are the shift operators of C, and their use in this context suggests that the content of the input and /or output stream is shifted by the insertion or extraction of data. Using operator-overloading concept we can add functionality to these shift significance, we have already seen it in use with the insertion extraction operators operators.

For example, the arithmetic operators, which we are accustomed to, are already overloaded. *The addition operator, "+", can be applied to int or double variables.* The compiler recognizes what to do and what type to return by the types given as parameters to the operator.

In a similar fashion, *when we define new types with class declarations, we can overload existing operators of functions to work with parameters of the new type, or combinations of parameters some of which are of the new type.* Of course when we overload an operator, its function for the new parameters should be an appropriate extension of its function for the uses it already has. It is not helpful to extend an operator to an entirely new function for a new type.

Let us see what does the arithmetic operator '+' in our computing do. And it is well known that the operator '+' is used to add integer or float. *We cannot use this + operator to add two objects.* For example, if we want to add two matrices say 'a' and 'b' of order 3 by 3, certainly we need user-defined function to perform this calculation.

Consider the following statement,

c = a + b;

here a, b and c are matrices with same order and it is like a ordinary addition. The facility for doing this in C++ is called operator overloading. **In the above statement we use objects (a and b) in expressions in just the same way that we use built in data types.** The operator + is said to be overloaded because it is used for addition of corresponding elements of the two matrixes.

Operator overloading enable us to apply standard operators such as +,-,*,< and many more, to objects of our own data types. To accomplish this, we should write a function that redefines a particular operator so that it performs a particular action every time it is applied to objects of our class. **An operator overloading function is created using the keyword 'operator'.**

The general form of an operator overloading function is,

```
return-data-type class-name :: operator_to_overload(argument list)
{
    statements;
}
```

here, operator functions return an object of the class they operate on and return type may be any valid type.

Operator overloading can be classified into

i) unary operator overloading and

ii) binary operator overloading,

There should be no arguments for unary operator overloading.

There should be one parameter for binary operator overloading. In the place of operator_to_overload we can have any valid operator permitted by C++.

Exceptions in Operator Overloading :

The following rules are to be observed while writing operator overloading functions.

i) All operators except the following 5 operators mentioned in the beginning of this section.

:: scope resolution operator
sizeof operator
?: conditional operator
.*de-reference pointer to class member operator
. direct member operator

may be overloaded.

ii) At least one operand must be a class instance

iii) we cannot change precedence, operator symbols or number of operands.

iv) Overloading ++ and - - requires prefix form use by default unless special mechanism is used

v) *To overload operators =, () and [] member functions must be used and friend functions should not used.*

vi) An operator can be given multiple meanings if the data types operands differ for different meanings.

19.2.4.1. Unary Operator Overloading :

Note that, **there is no argument in unary operator overloading function. Unary operator has only one operand.** In example program we use class 'sample' in which we have two private variables and prefix auto increment operator function. This class also has constructor with two arguments and another method to display the result after incrementing. Inside the operator overloading function we increment the value of variables 'val1' and 'val2' by one.

Program 19.2.5

Write a program in C++ to illustrate the use of unary operator as prefix operator for operator overloading function.

```
#include <iostream>
using namespace std;
class sample
{
private :
    int val1, val2;
```

```
public :
    sample (int x, int y);
    void operator ++ ( );
    void display ( );
};
sample : : sample (int x, int y)
{
    val1=x;
    val2=y;
}
void sample :: operator ++ ( )
{
    val1++;
    val2++;
}
void sample :: display ( )
{
    cout <<"\n Value - 1 "<<val1;
    cout <<"\n Value - 2 "<<vl2;
}
void main ( )
{
    sample example (50,60);
    cout <<"\n Before overloading ";
    example display ( );
    ++example;
    cout <<"\n After overloading ";
    example.display ( )
}
```

OUTPUT :

Before overloading
Value -1 50
Value -2 60
After Overloading
Value -1 51
Value -2 61

In the above program the object 'example' is created with 50 and 60 as its initial values. Like, auto increment operator ++ called with 'int'; here the object example is invoked. This resulting to call operator-overloading function that matches with '++' and inside the function variables get incremented finally the method display ( ) is used to print result.

After examining the above program one may raise a question what will be the effect if we use postfix increment instead of prefix increment operator. If we substitute postfix operator the program won't compile. The compiler reports an error because when we give operator ++ ( ) it does not distinguish between pre and post operation.

To overcome this problem, we introduce one more function and it looks like this :

void operator ++ (int x);

for the prefix, the operator ++ ( ) function is called and for postfix the operator (int x) is called and x has the value zero.

Program 19.2.6

Write a program in C++ to explain the use of prefix and postfix form of auto increment operator

```
# include <iostream>
using namespace std;
class sample
{
    private :
        int val1, val2;
    public :
        sample (int x, int y);
        void operator ++ ( );              // prefix
        void operator ++ (int x);          // postfix
        void display ( );
    };
    sample :: sample (int x, int y)
    {
        val1=x;
        val2=y;
    }
    void sample :: operator ++ ( )  //prefix unary opr. overloading( )
    {
        val1 ++;
        val2 ++;
    }
    void sample :: operator ++ (int x) //postfix unary opr. overloading(intx)
    {
        val1++;
        val2++;
    }
    void sample :: display ( )
    {
        cout <<"\n Value -1 "<<val1;
```

```
        cout <<"\n Value -2 "<<val2;
    }
    void main ()
    {
        sample example (12,24);
        cout <<"\n Before overloading ";
        example.display ( );
        ++example;
        cout <<"\n After overloading - Prefix form ";
        example.display ( );
        example ++;
        cout <<"\n After overloading - Postfix form ";
        example.display ( );
    }
```

OUTPUT :

```
Before overloading
Value -1    12
Value -2    24
After overloading - Prefix form
Value -1    13
Value -2    25
After overloading - Postfix form
Value -1    14
Value -2    26
```

19.2.4.2. Binary operator overloading :

The binary operator has two operands as compared to unary operator which has only one operand.

In the previous section we have just seen how to overload an unary operator with an example. Now let us implement binary operator overloading taking matrix operation as example. Here we are overloading an operator which has two operands, also known as binary operator as opposed to a unary operator with only one operand. *In this example program we have three options such as matrix addition, matrix subtraction and matrix multiplication. Each operation is overloading binary operator.All these operations are carried out just like arithmetic operations involving basic types.* Consider a following statement.

C = multiply(A, B);

In the above case we have used user defined function 'multiply()' to multiply two numbers, *it would give more readability if we use arithmetic notation instead of functional one and it looks like as* C = A * B;

Here, the operand which is called, is the one defined in the object before the operator, and the parameter is the object after the operator. In the above statement, the operator used is A's "*" operator, and the parameter which is sent is 'B'. The same approach is adhered in the following example for all basic matrix manipulations.

In overloading of binary operators, the left-hand operand is used to invoke the operator function and the right-hand operator is passed as an argument as explicit.

Program 19.2.7

Write a program in C++ to illustrate the use of binary operator overloading in matrix manipulations.

```
#include <iostream>
#include <iomanip>
using namespace std;
class matrix
{
    private :
        int element[10][10];
        int rows,cols;
    public :
        matrix(int, int);
        void matrixinput(int,int);
        void matrixprint(void);
        matrix operator+(matrix);  //binary operator (+) overloading
        matrix operator-(matrix);  //binary operator (-) overloading
        matrix operator* (matrix); //binary operator  ( * ) overloading
};
matrix :: matrix(int r, int c)
{
    rows = r;
    cols = c;
    for (int i = 0; i <rows; i++)
    for (int j = 0; j <cols; j++) element [i][j] = 0;
}
void matrix :: matrixinput (int r, int c)
{
    cout << "\n Enter " << r*c <<"elements " <<endl;
    for (int i = 0; i <r; i++)
    for (int j = 0; c <r; j++)
    cin>>element[i][j];
}
```

```
void matrix :: matrixprint(void)
{
    for int i = 0; i <rows; i++)
    {
        for (int j = 0; j <cols; j++) cout <<element[i][j] << '\r';
        cout <<endl;
    }
        return;
}
matrix matrix :: operator+(matrix m)      //binary operator + overloaded
{
    matrix temp(rows,cols);
    for (int i = 0; i < rows; i++)
    for (int j = 0; j < cols; j++)
    temp.element[i][j] = element[i][j] + m.element[i][j];
    return temp;
}
matrix matrix :: operator-(matrix m)      //binary operator - overloaded
{

    matrix temp (rows,cols);
    for (int i = 0; i < rows; i++)
    for (int j = 0; j < cols; j++)
        temp.element[i][j] = element[i][j] - m.element[i][j];
    return temp;
}
matrix matrix :: operator*(matrix m)     //binary operator * overloaded
{
    matrix temp(rows,cols);
    for (int i = 0; i < rows; i++)
    for (int j = 0; j < cols; j++)
        temp.element[i][j] = 0;
    for (int k=0;k<rows;++k)
        temp.element[i][j] = temp element[i][ j ] + element[i][k] *m.element[k][ j ];
return temp;
}
    void main ( )
{
        matrix a(2, 2),b(2,2),c(2,2);
        int choice;
        cout<<"\n Enter 1 for  Matrix Addition"
```

```
            <<"\n   Enter 2 for Matrix Subtraction"
            <<"\n   Enter 3 for Matrix  Multiplication"
            <<"\n   Enter Your choice [1, 2 or 3]";
            cin>>choice;
            switch(choice)
            {
                case 1 :
                    a.matrixinput(2,2);
                    b.matrixinput (2,2);
                    c=a+b;
                    cout <<"\n Output - Matrix Addition \n";
                    c.matrixprint ( );
                    break;
                case 2 :
                    a.matrixinput(2,2);
                    b.matrixinput (2,2);
                    c=a-b;
                    cout <<"\n Output - Matrix Subtraction \n";
                    c.matrixprint ( );
                    break;
                case 3 :
                    a.matrixinput(2,2);
                    b.matrixinput (2,2);
                    cout <<"\n Output - Matrix Multiplication \n";
                    c=a*b;
                    c.matrixprint ( );
                    break;
                default;
                    cout<<"\n Invalid choice \n";
            }
    }
```

OUTPUT :

```
Enter 1 for Matrix Addition
Enter 2 for Matrix Subtraction
Enter  3 for Matrix Multiplication
Enter Your choice [1, 2, or 3]
1
Enter 4 elements
6 7 8 9
Enter 4 elements
10 11 12 13
```

```
Output - Matrix Addition
10    16 18
14    20 22
Enter 1 for Matrix Addition
Enter 2 for Matrix Subtraction
Enter 3 for Matrix Multiplication
Enter Your choice [1, 2 or 3]
2
Enter 4 elements
10 11 12 13

Enter 4 elements
6 7 8 9
Output - Matrix Addition
4    4
4    4

Enter 1 for Matrix Addition
Enter 2 for Matrix Subtraction
Enter 3 for Matrix Multiplication
Enter Your choice [1, 2 or 3]
3
Enter 4 elements
4 3 2 1
Enter 4 elements
1 2 3 4
Output - Matrix Multiplication
13   20
5    8
```

Points to note :

In the above program the statement, c = a + b; invokes the operator +( ) function. **Note that, only an object of same class invoke member functions.** Here, 'a' invokes the function and the object 'b' is passed as an argument to the function. So, *inside the function the data members of 'a' are directly accessible and the data members of 'b' need to be accessed through the dot operator.*

19.2.4.3. Overloading Relational Operators :

The following example illustrates, how we can overload relational operators. Here we consider equality for our test case. In the class 'String', besides two constructors we have a function to receive user input and operator overloading function to compare whether two inputted strings are equal or not. **Since, equality returns Boolean value the return data type for the operator overloading is 'bool'.**

Program 19.2.8

Write a program in C++ to explain the use of overloading the relational operator '= ='

```
#include <iostream>
#include <cstring>
using namespace std;
class String
    {
        private :
            char str[80]
        public :
            string ( )
            {
                strcpy(str, " ");
            }
            String (char s [ ] )
            {
                strcpy (str, s);
            }
            void display ( )
            {
                cout << str;
            }
            void getstr ( )
            {
                cin.getline (str, 80);
            }
            bool operator = = (String ss)
            {
                return (strcmp(str, ss.str)==0 ? true : false;
            }
            void main ( )
            {
                String s1;
                String s2;
                cout << "Enter First string : ";
                s1.getstr ( );
                cout << "Enter Second string :";
                s2.getstr ( );
                if(s2==s1)
                    cout << "\n The two strings are equal \n";
                else
                    cout << "\n The two strings are unequal \n";
            }
```

OUTPUT :

Enter First string : apple
Enter Second string : apple

The two strings are equal

Enter First string : apple
Enter Second string : orange

The two strings are unequal

19.2.4.4. Overloading Arithmetic Assignment Operators :

We can overload arithmetic assignment operators such as +=, -=, etc. Similar to previous examples, the class 'Distance' has two constructors. *When the object is created without initial values then constructor without argument is executed and initializes (feet and inches to 0 in the program given below). When the object is instantiated with parameters the second constructor will be invoked and initialize members with the given input values.* In the example program receives values (feet and inches) directly from the user. In the operator overloading function, if the inches exceed 12 then the value of 'feet' gets incremented by 1.

Program 19.2.9.

Write a program in C++ to explain the use of overloading arithmetic assignment operator.

```
#include <iostream>
using namespace std;
class Distance
{
    private :
        int feet;
        float inches;
    public:
        Distance ( )
            {
                feet=0;
                inches = 0. 0;
            }
        Distance (int ft, float in)
            {
                feet=ft;
                inches=in;
            }
        void getdistance ( )
            {
                cout << "\n Enter feet: ";
```

```
                    cin >> feet;
                    cout << "Enter inches : ";
                    cin >> inches;
                }
            void showdistance ( )
                {
                    cout << feet << "\'-" <<inches << '\";
                }
            void operator += (Distance d2);
    };
            void Distance :: operator += (Distance d2) //overloading += operator
            {
                feet += d2.feet;
                inches +=d2.inches;
                if (inches >= 12.0)
                {
                    inches -= 12.0;
                    feet++;
                }
            }
        void main ( )
        {
            Distance distance 1;
            cout << "\n Enter Feet and inch for first object \n";
            distance1.getdistance ( );
            cout << "\n distance 1 =";
            distance1.showdistance ( );
            Distance distance2;
            cout << "\n Enter Feet and inch for Second object \n";
            distance2.getdistance ( );
            cout << "\n distance 2 =";
            distance2.showdistance ( );
            distance1 += distance 2;
            cout << "\n After addition, ";
            cout << "\n distance 1 = ' ;
            distance1.showdistance ( );
        }
```

OUTPUT :

```
Enter Feet and Inch for first object
Enter feet : 15
Enter inches  : 7
```

distance 1 = 15′ -7″
Enter Feet and Inch for Second object

Enter feet : 7
Enter inches : 8

distance 2 = 7′-8″
After addition,
distance 1 = 23′ -3″

19.2.4.5. Overloading the Assignment Operator :

Usually, the compiler generates a default assignment operator (operator '=') for all classes that do not define their own. Also note that the default behavior is the same as that of member wise initialization. But, member wise assign can cause the memory leak problem and to override this default assignment, the class must define the assignment operator as shown below:

example example :: operator=(example &ss)

The above operator overloading function definition will cause the user-defined assignment operator to be used in the place of the system-defined default.

Program 19.2.10.

Write a program in C++ to explain the overloading of assignment operator using string operation.

```
#include <iostream>
# include <cstring>
using namespace std;
class example
{
    private :
        char *sname;
    public :
        example ( );
        example (char *str);
        example operator = (example & ss);
        void display ( );
};
example :: example ( )
{
        sname=0;
}
example ::example (char *str)
{
        sname=new char (strlen(str) + 1];
```

```
        strcpy (sname,str);
    }
    example example::operator=(example &ss)
    {
        delete [ ]sname;
        sname = new char [strlen (sssname)+1];
        strcpy (sname,ss,sname);
        return *this;
    }
    void example :: display ()
    {
        cout << "\n Output string is : "<<sname;
    }
    void main ( )
    {
    example firststr ("Example of").secondstr(("Operator overloading"),thirdstr;
        thirdstr=firststr;
        thirdstr.display ( );
        firststr=secondstr;
        firststr.display ( );
    }
```

OUTPUT :

Output string is : Example of
Output string is : Operator overloading

Note : Inside the definition we have used memory allocation operator 'new' and de-allocation operator 'delete'.

19.2.4.6. Overloading Special type of Operator [ ] ( )

In this section let us discuss special type of **overloading operator [ ]** and it is considered as binary operator when it involves overloading. **The general form operator [ ] ( ) is as follows to indicate array subscripting and type of data.**

```
Type class.name :: operator [ ] (int i)
{
    statements;
}
```

Since, we are dealing with array subscripting the argument should be of type "int'. In our example we use an object 'example' and the expression

Example[5]

Interpreted into this call to the operator [ ] ( ) function as:

Example. Operator[ ] (5)

Here, the value of the expression within the subscripting operators is passed to the operator [ ] ( ) function in its explicit parameter. In the example program has a constructor to initialize value of the integer array of size 10. **The overloaded operator [ ] ( ) function returns the value of the integer array as indexed by the value of its parameter.**

Program 19.2.11.

Write a program in C++ to explain the use of [ ] ( ) Operator overloading

```
#include <iostream>
using namespace std;
class sample
{
    private :
        int a[10];
        int size;
    public :
        sample ( )
        {
            for (int 1=0;i<10;++i) a[i]=i*3;
        }
        int operator [ ] (int x)        //overloading operator[ ] ( )
        {
            return a[x];
        }
};
    void main ( )
{
        sample example;
        for (int i=0;i<10;++i)
        cout << "\n location "<<i <<" value =" <<example[i];
}
```

OUTPUT :

location 0 value = 0
location 1 value = 3
location 2 value = 6
location 3 value = 9
location 4 value = 12
location 5 value = 15
location 6 value = 18
location 7 value = 21
location 8 value = 24
location 9 value = 27

19.2.4.7. Overloading conversion operators :

So, far we have seen overload operators such as + and ++ in our user defined classes. Similarly **we also overload typecasting functions such as float() and int() to convert our own classes into basic types.** And it is similar to the other operator overloaders that we have seen in the previous sections. Here is the example program:

Program 19.2.12.

Write a program in C++ to explain the overloading of conversion operator

```
#include <iostream>
using namespace std;
class sample
{
    private :
        int value1, value2;
    public :
        sample(int x, int y)
        {
            value 1=x;
            value 2 = y;
        }
        operator int ( )
        {
            return (value1+value 2);
        }
};
    void main ( )
{
        sample example (10,20);
        int a = int (example);
        cout <<"\n Value after casting " <<a;
}
```

OUTPUT :

Value after casting 30

In the above program, the class 'sample' contains an int () operator, which we can use it similarly to any other type conversion. Here, operator-overloading function is used to convert a user-defined class to a basic type.

19.2.4.8. Overloading the exponent operator ^ :

Program. 19.2.13.

Write a program in C++ to explain the use of overloading ^ operator

```
# include <iostream>
# include <cmath>
using namespace std;
```

```
class integer
{
    private :
        int ino;
    public :
        integer (int x)
        {
            ino=x;
        }
    long operator^(int n);              //overloading ^ operator
};
    long integer :: operator ^ (int n)
    {
        if (n==1)
            return 1;
        long tempno=ino;
        for (int i=1 ; i<n;++i)
            tempno*=n;
        return tempno;
    }
        class real
    {
        private :
        double dno;
        public :
        real(double d)
        {
            dno=d;
        }
        double operator^(double n);
    };
    double real :: operator ^ (double n)
{
            if (n==0 && dno==0)
        {
        cout <<"\n Invalid input";
        exit (1);
        }
        if (dno < 0 & & n!=floor (n))
        {
            cout << "\n Invalid exponent ";
            exit (1);
        }
    return pow(dno,n);
}
```

```
void main ()
{
    integer i1 (6);
    cout <<"\n Integer 6^3 is = "<<(i1^3);
    real r1(3.2);
    cout <<"\n Real 3.2^2 is = "<<(r1^2);
    real r2(2.4);
    cout <<"\n Real 2.4^4 is = "<<(r2^4);
    cout <<endl;
}
```

OUTPUT :

```
Integer 6^3 is = 216
Real 3.2 ^ 2 is = 10.24
Real 2.4 ^ 4 is = 33.1776
```

19.2.5. Overloading String Concatenation :

Similar to the matrix addition, we can also overload the + operator for string concatenation as in following example

Thirdstr = firststr + secondstr.

The class 'String' has two constructors : constructor with argument and constructor without argument. In the operator overloading function, we have temporary object in the name 'temp' to hold addition of given two strings. Before adding, the length of resultant string is checked, if it exceeds boundary then the specified concatenation does not take place and the program terminates abnormally by using exit( ) function which is defined in the header file 'stdlib.h'. If the resultant string fits the width, then the string concatenation is performed by using two string functions such as 'strcpy( )' and 'strcat( )' and the resultant object (temp) is returned to main.

Program 19.2.14.

Write a program in C++ to explain the use of concatenating of strings using the overload operator +.

```
#include <cstring>
# include <stdlib.h>
#include <iostream>
using namespace std;
class String
    {
        private :
            char str[80]
```

```
        public :
            string ()
            {
                strcpy(str, " ");
            }
            String (char s [ ])
            {
                strcpy (str, s);
            }
            void display ()
            {
                cout << str;
            }
        String operator + (String ss)//concatenating strings overloading "+"
        {
            String temp;
            if (strlen(str) + strlen (ss.str) < 80 )
            {
                strcpy (temp.str, str);
                strcat (tem.str, ss.str);
            }
            else
                cout <<"\n String width.exceeds ";
                exit (1);
            }
            return temp;
        }
    };
    void main ()
    {
        string firststr = "Mera Bharath" ;
        String secondstr = "Mahan";
        String thirdstr;
        thridstr=firstr+secondstr;
        cout << "\n Resultant string is \n";
        thirdstr.display( );
    }
```

OUTPUT :
Resultant string is
Mera Bharath Mahan

19.2.6. Overloading new and delete in memory management :

We can implement our own memory management scheme for a class by overloading the operators 'new' and 'delete'. When new and delete operate on class objects, the class member operator functions new and delete are called, if they have been declared. The return type of overloaded operator 'new' must be a void*, and its first argument must have type size_t. Like 'new', the overloaded operator delete also return a void type, and also its first argument must be void*. We can also supply the 'new' and 'delete' operator is optional and, if present, it must have type 'size_t'. Also, note that we have only one delete operator function for a class. The type size_t is an implementation dependent operator function for a class. The type size_t is an implementation dependent unsigned integral type defined in the header file "stddef.h. For new operator, the size argument is required because a class can inherit an overloaded 'new' operator. The derived class can be a different size than the base class. The size argument ensures that the correct amount of storage space is allocated or de-allocated for the object. **When 'new' and 'delete' are overloaded within a class declaration, they are static member functions invariably whether they are declared with the keyword static or not and also they cannot be virtual functions.**

Also, it should be remembered the **'delete' operator destroys an object created by the 'new' operator. The operand of 'delete' must be a pointer returned by 'new'**. If 'delete' is called for an object with a destructor, the destructor is invoked before the object is de-allocated.

The following example shows the declaration and use of the operator functions operator new ( ) and operator delete( ).

Program 19.2.15.

Write a program in C++ to explain the use of overloaded new and delete in memory management.

```
#include <stddef.h>
# include <stdio.h>
# include <iostream>
using namespace std;
class sample
{
    public :
        sample ()
        {
            printf ("sample::sample % lx \n", (unsigned long)this);
        }
        ~sample ()
```

```
        {
            printf ("sample :: ~sample % lx \n",(unsigned long)this);
        }
        void *operator new [ ](size_t sz)  //new
        {
            printf ("\n allocated size = % lu \n",(unsigned logn)sz);
            void *vp=operator new (sz);
            printf("\n allocated pointer =% lx\n",(unsiged long)vp);
            return vp;
        }
            void operator delete [ ](void *ptr)    // delete
        {
            printf ("\n returned pointer = % lx \n",(unsigned long) ptr);
            operator delete (ptr);
        }
    };
    void main ( )
    {
        sample *sampleobj=new samle[5];
        delete [ ] sampleobj;
    }
```

OUTPUT :

```
allocated size = 9

allocated pointer = 301 fe0
sample : : sample 301 fe4
sample : : sample 301 fe5
sample : : sample 301 fe6
sample : : sample 301 fe7
sample : : sample 301 fe8
sample : : ~sample 301 fe8
sample : : ~sample 301 fe7
sample : : ~sample 301 fe6
sample : : ~sample 301 fe5
sample : : ~sample 301 fe4

returned pointer = 301 fe0
```

For portability among various versions of C++, we have used C style coding in the above program. The above example program redefines operator new[ ]() and operator delete[ ] ( )and they are called when the program is executed. When the operator new [ ]( )is invoked, it is passed an argument (here it is 5) indicating how many bytes are required for the total array. Also in the above example, the actual bytes are allocated via a call to operator new ( ). That is, the non-array version is called to allocate the bytes. The operator delete[ ]() works in a similar way as the operator new [ ] ( ). When operator delete [ ]( ) is called, the system will know how many slots to iterate across to call the destructors for individual objects. Finally, the result of the above varies with the system.

19.2.7. Operator Functions as friend for overloaded operator to be commutative :

Before we use operator function as friend we must know under what situation it is required. **A non-member operator function needs to be a friend if that function must access private or protected members of that class directly. The only difference being that a friend function requires two arguments to be explicitly passed to it while a member function requires only one. We have to choose a non-member function when the overloaded operator needs to be commutative.** Now let us look at an example program.

Program 19.2.16.

Write a program in C++ to explain the use of operator function as friend

```
# include <cstring>
#include <iostream>
using namespace std;
class String
   {
        private :
            char str[80]
        public :
            string ()
            {
                strcpy (str, " ");
            }
            string (char s [])
            {
                strcpy (str, s);
            }
            void display ()
            {
                cout << str;
            }
            friend String operator + (String ss, String ss1); //opr. fn as friend
   };
        String operator + (String ss, String ss1)
        {
```

```
        string temp;
        if (strlen(ss.str) + strlen(ss1.str) < 80)
        {
            strcpy (temp.str, ss str);
            strcat(temp.str, ss1,str);
        }
        else
        {
            cout << "\n String width exceeds ";
            exit ( 1 );
        }
        return temp;
}
void main ( )
{
    string firststr = 'Mera Bharath ";
    String secondstr = "Mahan";
    String thirdstr;
    thirdstr=firstr+secondstr;
    cout << "\n Resultant string is \n";
    thirdstr.display ( );
}
```

OUTPUT :

Resultant string is
Mera Bharath Mahan

A class can specify a non-member function as a friend in order to allow a non-member function to be able to access the private data of the class.

* * *

COMPREHENSION - 19

Note : By answering all the questions given in this comprehension one can answer any objective type of questions easily whatever be the form of the question. Answers for these questions can be obtained by going through the topics in this chapter carefully.

1. How is Overloading useful?
2. What are the different types of Overloading?
3. What is the difference between C and C++ regarding Function naming and its arguments?
4. Explain with syntax and examples Function Overloading.

   [In our Book 19.2.2 after int operator ( ) ( ) add : Also add s to word return in the highlighted text.]
5. Explain Overloading of Function Call Operator.
6. In writing our own class in programs if constructors of or the class is not provided what happens?
7. Explain Constructor Overloading.

   [In our Book verify 19.2.4 Operator Overloading. There are repetitions. Refer page 253 P.R.G. C++ Book]
8. Explain Operator Overloading.
9. Explain Shift Operator Overloading. How is it recognized when used in I/O operations?
10. Explain overloading of + Operator.
11. What are the exceptions in Operator Overloading?
12. What are the rules to be followed in use of Operator Overloading functions?
13. Will there be any argument in unary operator overloading?
14. Explain unary operator overloading.
15. Explain the difference between use of Auto increment operator ++ as prefix or postfix in operator overloading functions?
16. In the above case if you want to use ++ as postfix how can you do it? What happens then?
17. Explain Binary Operator Overloading.
18. What is the restriction on an object of a class in invoking member functions?
19. Explain Relational Operators Overloading.
20. Explain overloading of Arithmetic Assignment Operators.

21. In Overloading of Assignment Operator the class must define the Assignment Operator. Why?
22. Explain Overloading the Assignment operator.
23. Explain overloading operator [ ] ( ) .
24. Explain Type Casting functions overloading or Conversion operator overloading.
25. Explain the exponent operator 6 overloading.
26. Explain Overloading String Concatenation.
27. How do you resort to memory management scheme for a class?
28. Explain overloaded new and delete.
29. When do you need operator functions as friend?
30. Explain use of operator function as friend.

* * *

EXERCISE - 19

Note : By answering all the questions given in this exercise one can answer subjective type of questions easily including problems. The worked examples in the chapter may help in solving these questions.

1 (a) What are all the restrictions and limitations in overloading operators?

(b) Write a C++ program to demonstrate overloading add (+) and compare (−) operators on strings?

2. (a) Distinguish between overloaded functions and function templates.

(b) Distinguish between class templates and templates class.

3. (a) What is the difference and what is common in specificity of constructors and destructors overloading?

(b) What is the difference between ?overloading? and "overridding"?

4. (a) What is common and what is the difference between implementations of the copy constructors, initialization and overloaded assignment operators?

(b) What is a friend function? Explain the advantages and disadvantages of it?

5. (a) Explain how we can have our own memory management for a class?

(b) Explain the concept of Operator Functions as Friend.

6. (a) Explain the concept of overloading +operator for Matrix addition and String Concatenation.

(b) Explain the default assignment operator by the compiler, its drawbacks and remedy.

7. (a) Explain the concept of overloading special ARRAY dimension operator [ ].

(b) Explain overloading of type conversion operators.

8. (a) Explain overloading of exponent operator.

(b) Explain the operation of overloading arithmetic equality operator for Boolean.

9. (a) Explain the overloading of binary Operators.

(b) Explain unary operator overloading.

10. (a) Explain overloading of Shift Operators.

(b) What are the exceptions in operator overloading?

* * *

CHAPTER - 20
POLYMORPHISM

20.1. INTRODUCTION :

C++ has a unique feature called 'polymorphism' which is an essential property of Object Oriented Programming. 'poly' means many and 'morphism' means changing of form. Thus polymorphism means the form can be changed many times depending on the requirement. There are two types of polymorphism.

i) **Compile time polymorphism :** Which means that the program is able to select the required function for a particular call during the compile time itself based on the name of the overloaded function and by matching the type and the number of parameters. **This is also called static binding or early binding or compile time binding.**

ii) **Run time polymorphism** : Which means that the program is able to select the required function for a particular call during the runtime only when the name and number of arguments of the same in parent or child class which is possible only by having appropriate pointer to point to the required function of the required class. **This is also called dynamic binding or late binding or runtime binding.**

20.2. COMPILE AND RUNTIME POLYMORPHISM :

In the previous chapter we saw function overloading and operator overloading. These **overloaded functions and operators also implement the concept of 'Polymorphism'.** We know that the overloaded functions are selected by invoking of the matching of the type and number of parameters. This information is available to the compiler at compile time and therefore is able to select required function for a particular call during compile time itself. This is called compile time binding.

On other hand if the function name and number of arguments is the same in the base class and derived class then the compiler does not know which one to select whether it is from parent class or child class. Introducing the concept of polymorphism can alleviate this problem. In this chapter let us focus a mechanism called *virtual function.* **Virtual function enables us to select the appropriate function during runtime thus achieving run time polymorphism. In runtime polymorphism the function call is linked with the appropriate function only at runtime. We call this process as 'run time polymorphism'.**

Dynamic binding or late binding requires the use of pointers to objects. Also pointers to objects of base class are type-compatible with pointers to objects of derived class.

For example let us have a base class by name 'base' and derived class by name 'derived'. The declaration of objects for these two are as follows.

```
base baseobj;            //base class object
derived derivedobj;      // derived class object
base *baseptr;           // pointer to base class base
```

Now let us consider the following assignment ;

```
baseptr = &baseobj;    // baseptr now points to base class object 'baseobj'
```

one may be surprised by the following assignment

baseptr=&derivedobj //baseptr now points to derived class object 'derivedobj'

but the above statement is a valid one as 'derivedobj' is an object derived from the class 'base'.

Program 20.2.1.

Write a program in C++ to illustrate the property of run time polymorphism to access members in the derived class which are inherited from the corresponding base class.

```
#include <iostream>
using namespace std;
class base
{
      public:
         int b;
         void show ( )
      {
         cout <<"\n From base class show :";
         cout <<"\n Value of b is : "<<b;
         cout <<endl;
      }
};
class derived : public base   //class derived is obtained from public of class base
{
      public :
         int d;
         void show ( )
      {
         cout <<"\n From derived class show : " ;"
         cout <<"\n Value of b is : "<<b;   //obtained from class base
         cout <<"\n Value of d is : "<<d;  //obtained from class derived
         cout <<endl;
      }
};
```

```
void main ( )
{
        base baseobj;
        derived derivedobj;
        base *baseptr;
        baseptr=&baseobj;
        baseptr->b=108;
        cout <<"\n The show method is calling from base and ";
        cout <<"\n baseptr now points to base object ";
        baseptr -> show ( );
        baseptr=&derivedobj;
        baseptr->b=216;
        cout <<"\n The show method is calling from derived and ";
        cout <<"\n baseptr now points to derived object ";
        baseptr->show ( );
        derived *derivedptr;
        derivedptr=&derivedobj;
        derivedpr->d=332;
        cout <<"\n The show method calling from derived ";
        derivedptr ->show ( );
}
```

OUTPUT :

```
The show method is calling from base and
baseptr now points to base object
From base class show :
Value of b is : 100
The show method is calling from derived and
baseptr now points to derived object
From base class show :
Value of b is : 200
The show method calling from derived
From derived class show :
Value of b is : 200
Value of d is : 300
```

In the above program, even though by using 'baseptr' we can access only those members in class 'derived' that inherited from class 'base' and nor members that originally from class 'derived'. Also, **if a member in class 'derived' has same name as one of the members in base class, then any reference to that member by 'baseptr' will always access the base class member.**

So, from the output it is understood that, though the 'baseptr' pointed to a derived class object 'derivedobj', it still called the base class function 'show' and not the derived class function 'show'.

20.3. VIRTUAL FUNCTIONS :

A virtual function is a function which is declared in base class and redefined by a derived class. The essential requirement of polymorphism is the ability to refer to objects without any regard to their classes. So, that by using a single pointer variable we should be able to refer to objects of all derived classes. *In the previous example program, a pointer to a base class is used to refer all derived class objects but it executes the base class function even when the pointer holds the address of the derived class object.* It depicts the compiler ignores the contents of the pointer and selects the function depending upon the type of the pointer. *To avoid this type of ignoring the contents of the pointer and soliciting the function depending upon the type of the pointer virtual functions are used* which is a topic of this section.

When the base class and derived class function both have the same function name with same type and number of arguments then declare the function in base class as virtual function by using the keyword 'virtual' before the function name. By doing so, C++ determines which function to use at runtime based on the type of the object pointed to by the base pointer instead of the type of the pointer. That is we want dynamic binding for the function in any class that's derived from this class. Also, note that we want **to describe a class as polymorphic; it should have at least one virtual function in it.** Thus we can achieve the polymorphism by making the base class pointer to point different objects and different versions of the virtual function can be executed. Now let us look at an example program.

Program 20.3.1

Write a program in C++ to illustrate the use of virtual function.

```
# include <iostream>
using namespace std;
class base
{
      public:
         virtual void show ( )
      {
         cout <<"\n From base class show (virtual void show) : " ;
         cout <<endl;
      }
};
```

```
class derived : public base
{
        public :
           void show ( )
        {
           cout <<"\n From derived class show : " ;
           cout <<endl;
        }
};
void main ( )
{
        base baseobj;
        derived derivedobj;
        base *baseptr;
        baseptr=&baseobj;
        cout <<"\n The show method is calling from base (virtual void show) and ";
        cout <<"\n baseptr now points to base object";
        baseptr->show ( );
        baseptr=&derivedobj;
        cout <<"\n The show method is calling from derived and";
        cout <<"\n baseptr now points to derived object " ;
        baseptr -> show ( );
}
```

OUTPUT :

```
The show method is calling from base (virtual void show) and
baseptr now points to base object
From base class show :

The show method is calling from derived and
baseptr now points to derived object
From derived class show :
```

20.3.1. Pure virtual functions :

The example program, which we have just seen, contains a class by name 'base' has its own implementations of the virtual function 'show' and the content of this method is also not used. **C++ permits us to declare virtual function in a base class which define them.** The **functions that are only declared but not defined in the base class are called pure virtual functions. A function is made pure virtual by preceding its declaration with the keyword 'virtual' and ending it with =0 (zero). The general form of pure virtual function is as follows :**

virtual return-type function -name (argument list) = 0

Program 20.3.2.

Write a program in C++ to illustrate the use of pure virtual function.

```
# include <iostream>
using namespace std;
class base
{
    public :
        virtual void show ( ) = 0;   //pure virtual function show prototype
};
class derived1 : public base
{
    public :
        void show ( )
        {
            cout <<"\n From derived class 1 show : " ;
            cout << endl;
        }
};
    class derived 2 : public base
    {
        public :
            void show ( )
            {
                cout <<"\n From derived class 2 show :"'
                cout << endl;
            }
    };
        void main ( )
    {
            base *baseptr;
            derived1 derivedobj1;
            baseptr=&derivedobj1;
            baseptr->show ( );
            derived2 derivedobj2;
            baseptr=&derivedobj2;
            baseptr->show ( );
    }
```

OUTPUT :

From derived class 1 show :
From derived class 2 show :

20.3.2. Abstract class :

The special feature of pure virtual function is only declaring prototype of a function in a base class and not defining them. And only in the derived class definition of virtual function takes place. *The C++ compiler will not allow the definition of an object of a class that does not define the function in question. So base class only have declaration of function and derived class must take care of the actual implementation.* Thus, such base classes acting as models to be used for the derivation of other classes are called an abstract class. **An abstract class is a class that is designed specifically to be used in a base class and It contains at least one pure virtual function.** We can declare a function to be pure by using a pure specifier in the declaration of the member function in the class declaration. The following example shows the use of an abstract class and virtual function.

Program 20.3.3

Write a program in C++ to illustrate the use of abstract class

```
# include <iostream>
# include <cmath>
# include <iomanip>
using namespace std;
const double pi=3.14159;
class shape
{
      public :
            virtual void inputvalues (void)=0;      //virtual fn. prototype
            virtual double area (void)=0;           //virtual fn. prototype
            virtual double perimeter(void)=0;       //virtual fn. prototype
};
class square : public shape                         //abstract class
{
      private :
            double side;
      public :
{           square( ) { };            //fn. square consisting stmts inside { }
            square(double s);
            void inputvalues(void);
            double area(void);
            double perimeter (void);
};
square :: square (double s)
{
      side=s;
}
```

```
void square::inputvalues(void)
{
      cout<<"\n Enter side :" ;
      cin>>side;
}
double square :: area (void)
{
      return side *side;
}
double square :: perimeter (void)
{
      return 4.0*side;
}
class triangle : public shape
{
      private :
            double x,y,z;
      public :
            triangle (double side1,double side 2,double side3);
            triangle ( ) { };           //fn. triangle consisting stmts inside { }
            void inputvalues (void);
            void area(void);
            double perimeter (void);
};
triangle :: triangle (double side1,double side2, double side3)
{
      x=side1;
      y=side2;
      z=side3;
}
void triangle :: inputvalues (void)
{
      cout <<"\n Enter first side :";
      cin >>x;
      cout <<"\n Enter second side :";
      cin >>y;
      cout <<"\n enter third side : " ;
      cin >> z;
}
double triangle :: area (void)
{
      double s=(x+y+z)/2;
```

```
        return sqrt(s*(s-x)*(s-y)*(s-z));
    }
    double triangle :: perimeter(void)
    {
        return x+y+z;
    }
    void main ()
    {
        cout<<setprecision (4);
        square squareobj;
        cout<<"\n For Square ";
        squareobj. inputvalues ( );
        cout <<"\n Area      = "<<squareobj.area ( );
        cout <<"\n Perimeter = "<<squareobj.perimeter ( );
        triangle triangleobj;
        cout<<"\n For Triangle ";
        triangleobj. inputvalues ( );
        cout <<"\n Area      = "<<triangleobj.area ( );
        cout <<"\n Perimeter = "<<triangleobj.perimeter ( );
        cout<<endl;
    }
```

OUTPUT :

```
For Square
Enter side : 8
Area      = 64
Perimeter = 32

For Triangle
Enter first side : 3
Enter second side : 4
Enter third side : 5
Area = 6
Perimeter = 12
```

The advantage of using *abstract class in program leads to a very structured way to reuse existing code.* At the same time *we require some advanced planning before we use abstract class in our program.*

20.4. TYPES OF DESTRUCTORS :

To help use of abstract class we use **i) virtual destructor, ii) explicit destructor.**

As we know already that the **virtual or explicit destructor function will be called automatically when the object is out of scope.**

We can use base class or derived class destructor without using virtual explicit destructor by having tilde or complement symbol '~'.

i) **Non-Virtual Destructor when the object is out of scope :**

The destructor function will be called automatically when the object is out of scope. Now consider the following program :

Program 20.4.1.

Write a program in C++ to explain the non-use of virtual destructor or use of destructor function

```
# include <iostream>
using namespace std;
class base
{
    public :
        base ()              //base class creation
        {
            cout <<"\n Base class - creation ";
        }
        ~ base ()            //base class destructor is not virtual
        {
            cout <<"\n Base class - destruction ";
        }
};
    class derived : public base
{
        public :
            derived ()            //derived class creation
            {
                cout <<"\n Derived class - creation " ;
            }
            ~derived ()   //derived class destructor is called
                          //since destructor in base class is not virtual
            {
                cout <<"\n Derived class - destruction";
            }
};
        void main ()
{
                base *baseobj=new derived ( );
                delete baseobj;
                cout <<endl;
}
```

OUTPUT :
Base class - creation
Derived class - creation
Base class - destruction

When observing the output of the above program we notice derived class destructor is not called. Since destructor in the base class is not virtual, the delete statement called only base :: ~base (i.e. destructor for base class) and not derived :: ~derived (i.e. destructor for derived class)as was presumably for correct operation.

20.4.1. Virtual destructor :

To call the destructor function for derived class we must make the destructor function in base class as virtual. Declaring virtual destructors in classes that have virtual functions causes the compiler to call destructors for each class from which the object inherits. That is we get the correct invocation for deleting both that part of the instance that comes from the derived class and that part at the instance that comes from the base class. The correct program implementing virtual destructor is follows:

Program 20.4.2

Write a program in C++ to explain the use of virtual destructor

```
# include <iostream>
using namespace std;
class base
{
    public :
        base ()
        {
            cout <<"\n Base class - creation ";
        }
        virtual ~ base ()           //virtual base class destruction
        {
            cout <<"\n Base class - destruction";
        }
};
    class derived : public base
{
        public :
            derived ()
        {
            cout <<"\n Derived class - creation ";
        }
```

```
                ~derived ()          //virtual derived class destruction
            {
                cout <<"\n Derived class - destruction";
            }
    };
        void main ()
    {
            base *baseobj=new derived( );
            delete baseobj;
            cout <<endl;
    }
```

OUTPUT :

Base class - creation
Derived class - creation
Derived class - destruction
Base class - destruction

From the above program it is understood that, if a class is having any virtual functions and it is intended to be used as a base class then it should have virtual destructor to guarantee that the destructor will be called when the derived object is referenced through a pointer to the base class. All the memory allocation done by 'new' operator should be released when not required failing of which will cause memory leak. **By declaring virtual destructor in base class we can also prevent memory leaks in derived classes.**

20.4.2. Explicit destructor :

Default destructor will be called when an object goes out of scope as explained in the previous program. But destructor can also be called explicitly just like using explicit constructor. **Explicit destructor can be called only when we need to place an object at a specific address.**

Program 20.4.3.

Write a program in C++ to illustrate the Explicit Destructor

```
# include <iostream>
# include <cstring>
using namespace std;
class base
{
    private :
        char *st;
        int size;
```

```
        public :
                base (char *tst)
                {
                        cout<<"\n Constructor called ";
                        st=new char[size=strlen(tst)+1];
                        strcpy (st,tst);
                }
                ~base ( )
                {
                        cout <<"\n Destructor called";
                        delete st;
                }
};
        char *base1=new char[sizeof(base)];
        void main ( )
{
        base * baseptr=new(base1) base("example program for explicit destructor");
        baseptr-> ~base ( );      //explicit destructor ~base ( )
}
```

OUTPUT :

Constructor called
Destructor called

With the concept of virtual function and polymorphism, it becomes possible to design and implement systems which are more extensive.

* * *

COMPREHENSION - 20

Note : By answering all the questions given in this comprehension one can answer any objective type of questions easily whatever be the form of the question. Answers for these questions can be obtained by going through the topics in this chapter carefully.

1. What is meant by Polymorphism?
2. How many types of Polymorphism are there? What are they? Explain.
3. What are static and dynamic bindings?
4. What feature is required for dynamic or runtime or late binding?
5. Explain with examples compile or run time Polymorphism.
6. When will any reference to a member by base pointer always refer to that base class member?
7. What is a virtual function? Explain.
8. How can you refer to all objects of the derived classes?
9. When do you declare a function as virtual and where and how do you do it?
10. What is a pure virtual function? How and where do you declare it? Explain with syntax and example.
11. What is the special of a pure virtual function?
12. What is an abstract class? Explain with example and declaration.
13. Is it necessary that an abstract class should contain at least one pure virtual function? Why?
14. What are the types of that help use of abstract class?
15. What is the benefit of using abstract class?
16. Explain virtual destructor.
17. Explain explicit destructor? When do you call it?
18. To call the destructor function for derived class what should we do with the destructor function in the base class?
19. When will be the use of virtual destructor automatically called?
20. Explicit destructor can be called only when we need to place an object at a specific address.

* * *

EXERCISE - 20

Note : By answering all the questions given in this exercise one can answer subjective type of questions easily including problems. The worked examples in the chapter may help in solving these questions.

1. (a) What are the rules for virtual functions?

   (b) Write a C++ program to demonstrate runtime polymorphism using virtual function.

2. (a) What is polymorphism? What constructions in C++ allow to say that this language supports polymorphism? What polymorphism is used for?

   (b) What is the difference and what is common in specificity of constructors and destructors overloading?

3. (a) Explain the need for "Virtual Destructor".

   (b) Can we have "Virtual Constructors"?

4. What do you mean by run time polymorphism and how to implement run time polymorphism using virtual functions in C++?

5. (a) How can we handle a constructor that fails?

   (b) How can we handle a destructor that fails?

6. (a) Write a program to illustrate the concept of virtual base class with example program.

   (b) How to implement run time polymorphism using virtual functions.

7. (a) When should my destructor be virtual?

   (b) What is a "virtual constructor"?

   (c) What's the difference between how virtual and non-virtual member functions are called?

8. (a) What are the different types of polymorphism?

   (b) What are Virtual Functions? How to implement virtual functions in "C++"

* * *

CHAPTER - 21
INPUT-OUTPUT OPERATIONS IN C++

21.1. INTRODUCTION :

C++ does not have any built in input/output (I/O) statements as a part of its syntax. In C we have used scanf ( ) and printf ( ) functions for manipulating input and output operations, which are part of a standard library "stdio.h". In the programs written in C++, we have used **cin** and **cout** for carrying out I/O operation without knowing much about "iostream". Thus in all C++ programs, the input and output functionality are provided by the standard library involving use of iostreams.

i) The term 'stream' is a flow of data between external device and main memory of our computer.

ii) Streams in C++ are objects of classes.

iii) The standard library defines an input stream **cin.** The term **cin** alongwith the stream extraction operator (>>) is used to receive data from keyboard.

iv) The stream insertion operator (<<) for output in C++ defines three-output streams viz., **'cout', 'cerr' and 'clog'** to display data on the screen.

There are a number of different kinds of streams, each represented by a class.

The following diagram is used to show the collection of such class that forms an inheritance structure.

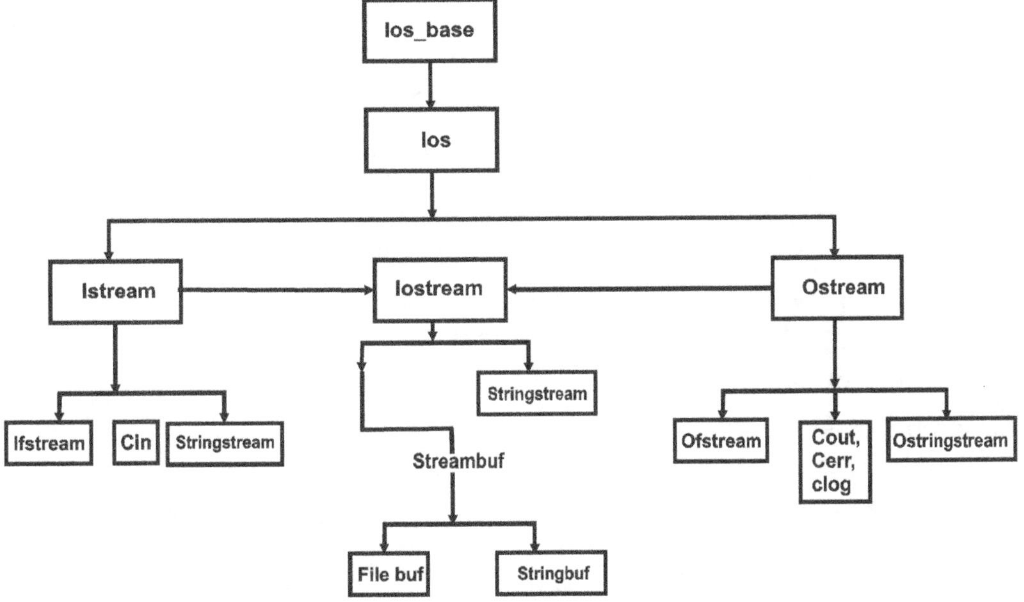

Fig.21.1. Input / Output Operations in C++

21.2. STREAM INSERTION & EXTRACTION OPERATORS (<<) & (>>)

21.2.1. Stream Insertion Operator for Output (<<) :

The program that we have seen so far use 'cout' for data output and it is used along with "<<' operator. **The stream insertion operator points to the ostream object where the information is inserted.** It is well known that the insertion, operator where the information is inserted. It is well known that **the insertion, operator (<<) takes 2 operands. The left operand is a stream expression, such as 'cout' and the right operand is an expression of simple type, or a string or a manipulator and from the diagram the operator << ( ) function is overloaded ostream class for formatted output of data values of fundamental data types. The insertion operator as defined in the class ostream is an overloaded operator having following general form :**

```
ostream & ostream::operator <<(char const *text)
```

For example consider the following output statement :

```
cout <<a<<' ' <c;
```

Now, the operator << ( ) function transforms above statement as follows :

```
operator <<(cout.operator <<(a) ' ' ).operator<<(c);
```

As said earlier, all functions return values and in this case the operator << ( ) function return a reference to the stream object for which they are called. The return value from one operator << ( ) function is used to call next operator << ( ) function. In our example code, the operator << ( ) function call to print 'a' to the stream as the first argument to the operator function call to write the blank space. The operator << ( ) function which is used to print blank space returns the stream object and it is used to call the member function that prints the value of 'c'.

21.2.2. Stream extraction Operator for Input (>>)

We use 'cin' for feeding data to our programs and it is used along with '>>' operator. **The extraction operator points to the object receiving the information obtained from the istream object. The extraction operator as defined in the class istream is an overloaded operator having following general form :**

```
istream operator>>(istream in, signed char *text)
istream operator>>(istream in,unsigned char *text)
```

Any one of the above formats is used during 'cin' operation.

The snippet code

```
cin>>a>>b;
```

is used to read two variables 'a' and 'b' from the keyboard and upon translation it takes the following form.

```
(cin.operator>>(a)).operator>>(b);
```

Like, stream insertion, the extraction operator >> ( ) function is called once for every operator and in above case it is called twice. **The extraction operator function for streams returns a reference to the stream object for which it was called and the return value is used to call the next operator function. The important point to note here is, the parameter to the extraction operator function has to be a reference, to allow the extraction function to store the data read from the stream in the variable that is passed as an argument.** The C programmers aware that the scanf ( ) function use blank space as a delimiter during inputting values. Likewise, here also white space characters are skipped and also the extraction operator does not expect pointers to variables that should be given new values, but references, which is seen from the syntax.

Program 21.2.1

Write a program in C++ to illustrate the use of extractor and inserter functions.

```
# include "iostream.h"
class student
{
      private :
            char stdname[20];
            int examno;
      public :
            friend ostream & operator <<(ostream & stream, const student&std);
            friend istream & operator >>(istream & stream, student&std);
};
//overloaded stream insertion operator
ostream & operator<<(ostream & stream,const student & std)
{
      stream <<"\n            Name : "<<std.stdname;
      stream <<"\n   Exam Number : "<<std.examno;
      stream <<endl;
      return stream;
}
//overloaded stream extraction operator
istream & operator>>(istream &input, student&std)
{
      cout <<"\n Enter Name :" ;
      input.getline (std.stdname,20);
      cout <<"\n Enter Roll No :";
      input>>std.examno;
      return input;
}
```

```
void main ( )
{
        student studentobj;
        cout <<"\n Enter input details : " ;
        cin >>studentobj;
        cout <<"\n Given details are : " ;
        cout << studentobj;
}
```

OUTPUT :

Enter input details :
Enter Name : Laxman
Enter Roll No : 416
Given details are :
Name : Laxman
Roll No : 416

Program 21.2.2

Write a program in C++ to illustrate the use of overloaded left shift and right shift operators as stream extraction and stream insertion operators.

```
#include <iostream>
#include <string.h>
int main ( )
{
string in_string;
//write literal string to user's terminal
cout << "Please enter your name:" ;
//read user's input into is_string
cin >> in_string;
if ( in_string.empty( ) )
        //generate an error message to user's terminal
        cerr << "error: input string is empty !\n";
else
    cout << "hello " << in_string << " ! \n";
}
```

OUTPUT :

i) Please enter your name :
(Input :)
error: input string is empty !
ii) Please enter your name :
hello Ramesh !

21.2.3. Formatting Output using manipulators :

So far we were not interested in the way the output was displayed.

C++ contains a large number of manipulators that allow us to control the appearance of our output. **For the use of these output manipulators, which manipulate the format of output we have to include the IOMANIP header file.**

The manipulators are classified into four different types

i) parameterized manipulators such as setw, setbase, setfill etc.,

ii) non-parameterized manipulators such as boolalpha, dec etc.,

iii) the stream manipulators which are used with the cout statement.

iv) Precautions :

a) *All manipulators except setw( ) affect the remainder of the program unless we override them by specifying new manipulators.*

b) *It should also be noted that all values are right-justified within the setw ( ) field. If the data is wider than the argument in setw( ), the setw ( ) command is ignored and the entire value is printed.*

Different types of manipulators are given in the following tables.

Table 20.1 Non Parameterized Manipulators and their Description :

Manipulator	Description
boolalpha	Represent Boolean values (bool) as alphabetic -i.e. true or false
dec	Set the default radix for integers to decimal
endl	write a newline character to the stream buffer and writes the contents of the buffer to the stream
fixed	Output floating point values in fixed point notation without an exponent
flush	Write data from the stream buffer to the stream
hex	Set the default radix for integers to hexadecimal
internal	Insert fill characters to pad the output to the field width
left	Align values left in an output field
noboolalpha	Represent Boolean values (bool) as 1 and 0
noshowbase	Omit the base indication for octal and hexadecimal integers
noshowpoint	Output integral floating point values without a decimal point
noshowpos	No + prefix for positive integers
noskipws	Do not skip whitespace on input
nouppercase	Use lower case for hexadecimal digit a to f, and e for exponent
oct	Set the default radix for integers to octal

right	Align values right in an output field
scientific	Output floating point values in fixed point notation with an exponent
showbase	Indicate the base for octal (0 prefix) and hexadecimal (ox prefix) integers
showpoint	Always output floating point values to the stream with a decimal point
showpos	Display a+ prefix for positive integers
skipws	Skip whitespace on input
uppercase	Use lower case for hexadecimal digit A to F, and E for exponent

Table 20.2 Parameterized Manipulators and their Description :

Manipulator	Description
setprecision (int)	Set the precision for floating point output to n digits and it remains in effect until we change it.
setw(int)	Set the field with for the next output value to integer characters. This will reset on each output to the default setting, which is to output value in a field width that is just Sufficient to accommodate the value
setfill (char)	Set the fill character to be used as padding within the output field to 'char'. It remains in effect until we change it since it is modal.
setbase (int)	set the output representation for integers to octal, decimal or hexadecimal, corresponding to values for the argument of 8, 10 and 16.

Program 21.2.3

Write a Program in C++ to explain the use of some of the manipulators

```
#include <iostream>
# include <iomanip>
using namespace std;
void main ( )
{
    //1. Code for boolalpha & noboolalpha
    bool b1;
    b1=false;
    cout <<"\n boolean value (in word) "<<boolalpha<<b1;
    cout <<"\n boolean value (in number) "<<noboolalpha<<b1;
    cout <<endl;
    // 2. Code for changing base
    int number = 96;
```

```
        cout <<"\n Number  (in decimal) "<<dec<<number;
        cout <<"\n Number  (in hexa decimal) "<<hex<<number;
        cout <<"\n Number  (in octal) "<<oct<<number;
        cout <<endl;
        //3. Code for float field
        float f1=567.98f;
        cout <<"\n Float value (in fixed) "<<fixed<<f1;
        cout <<"\n Float value (in scientific) "<<scientific<<f1;
        cout <<endl;
        //4. Code for adjustified
        cout.width (10);
        cout <<"\n Number (in default justification) "<<internal<<number;
        cout <<"\n Number (in left justification) "<<left<<number;
        cout <<"\n Number (in right justification) "<<right<<number;
        cout <<endl;
        //5. Code for showing base
        cout <<"\n Number (with base) "<<hex<<showbase<<number;
        cout <<"\n Number (without base) "<<hex<<noshowbase<<number;
        cout <<endl;
        //6. Code for showing positive sign
        int number1=275;
        cout <<"\n Number (with sign)"<<showpos<<number1;
        cout <<"\n Number (without sign)"<<noshowpos<<number1;
        cout <<endl;
    }
```

OUTPUT :

```
boolean value (in word) false
boolean value (in number ) 0
Number (in decimal) 96
Number (in hexa decimal ) 60
Number (in octal) 140
Float value (in fixed) 567.979980
Float value (in scientific)  5.679980e+002
Number (in default justification) 120
Number (in left justification) 120
Number (with base) 0 x 50
Number (without base) 50
Number (with sign) 113
Number (without sign) 113
```

The next example discusses he use of showpoint and noshowpoint. Unless we use I/O manipulators (or their equivalent), the default format for each floating point number depends on its value. No decimal point : 15.0 prints as 15, No trailing zeros and 1.5000 prints as 1.5. The following sample program follows will demonstrate the use of the manipulators showpoint and noshow point.

Program 21.2.4

Write a program in C++ to explain the use of show point and noshow point manipulators.

```
#include <iostream>
# include <iomanip>
using namespace std;
void main ( )
{
        float d1=98.0f;
        cout<<"\n Float value (with decimal point)" <<showpoint<<d1;
        cout<<"\n Float value (without decimal
point)"<<noshowpoint<<d1;
        cout<<endl;
}
```

OUTPUT :

Float value (with decimal point) 98.0000
Float value (without decimal point) 98

Program 21.2.5

Write a program in C++ to explain the use of Parameterized Manipulators such as setbase, setw and setfill.

```
#include <iostream>
# include <iomanip>
using namespace std;
void main ( )
{
            //code for setbase();
        int number = 80;
        cout <<number <<" in base 16 is : "<<setbase(16) <<number<<endl;
        cout <<dec <<number <<"in base 8 is : "<<setbase(8)<<number <<endl;
        cout <<setbase (10);
        cout <<endl <<endl;
            //code for setw( ), setfill( )
        float number1 = 237.65f;
```

```
        cout <<"\n Float number is : " ;
        cout <<setfill ('*');
        cout <<setw (10) <<number1 <<endl;
    }
```

OUTPUT :

80 in base 16 is : 50
80 in base 8 is : 120

Float number is : **** 237.65

21.2.4. Constructing our own manipulators :

In addition to having built in manipulators, in C++ we can also create our own manipulators. For example, if we want to create a manipulator 'set10' which will set the precision of the next field to be written to the ostream object to 10, the manipulator is constructed similar to that of a function. The 'set10' function will have to know about the ostream object in which the precision must be set. Now, consider the following code :

```
ostream &set10(osream&str)
{
        return (str<<setprecision(10));
}
```

Note that, the above manipulator function is provided with a ostream & parameter, so that the function knows about the ostream object we are referring to, can set the precision in that object. Also in the function we use the manipulator in a <<sequence. And it implies that the return value of the 'set10' manipulator must be a reference to an ostream object also. The complete program is as follows.

Program 21.2.5

Write a program in C++ to explain the construction of our own manipulator

```
# include <iostream>
# include <iomanip>
using namespace std;
ostream &set10(ostream &str)
{
        return (str<<setprecision (10));
}
void main ( )
{
        etern ostream &set10 (ostream &str);
```

```
        double phi;
        phi=22.0/7.0;
        cout <<"\n Without using manipulator, the phi value is : "<<phi;
        set10(cout);
        cout <<"\n Using our own manipulator, the phi value is : "<<phi;
        cout <<endl;
}
```

OUTPUT :

Without using manipulator, the phi value is : 3.14286
Using our own manipulator, the phi value is : 3.142857143

* * *

COMPREHENSION - 21

Note : By answering all the questions given in this comprehension one can answer any objective type of questions easily whatever be the form of the question. Answers for these questions can be obtained by going through the topics in this chapter carefully.

1. What is the difference between I/O statements in C and C++ ?
2. What is meant by Stream?
3. What does Stream in C++ constitute?
4. What are Stream insertion and stream extraction operators? How are they used?
5. What are the output streams provided by stream extraction operator?
6. Explain with the help of a diagram I/O operations in C++.
7. What are ios, istream, istream, ifstream etc. ?
8. To what class does stream insertion operator belong?
9. To what class does stream extraction operator belong?
10. What type of operator is the stream insertion operator as defined in the class ostream?
11. What type of operator is the stream extraction operator as defined in the class istream?
12. What should be the parameter to the extraction operator function? Why?
13. What is IOMANIP header file? What does it do?
14. What are the classifications of manipulators? Explain.
15. Give examples of some non-parameterized manipulators and explain what they do?
16. Give examples of some parameterized manipulators and explain what they do?
17. Explain construction of our own manipulators.
18. What are the precautions to be taken when using manipulators? Why?
19. What is a file?
20. What are the basic file operations to be performed while using file I/O operations in C++ ?
21. What is file extension?

* * *

EXERCISE - 21

Note : By answering all the questions given in this exercise one can answer subjective type of questions easily including problems. The worked examples in the chapter may help in solving these questions.

1. What is a Stream? What is I/O Stream in C++? Discuss about I/O operations in C++.
2. Discuss about Stream Extraction and Stream Insertion Operations in C++.
3. What are iostream, istream, ostream, ifstream etc. ?Explain with examples.
4. Discuss about formatting output in C++.
5. Discuss about manipulators and their functions in C++ including precautions.
6. Can you construct your own manipulators in C++? If so how?

* * *

CHAPTER - 22
FILE OPERATIONS IN C++

22.1 INTRODUCTION :

Applications generally involve tremendous amount of data to be read and written to an auxiliary storage. Hence to save such information to the disk we use data files, just as we have used in C. **File is a collection of numbers, symbols & text placed on the disk.** In due course of time files can be read and modified as per the user requirements. Thus, files allow us store information permanently in the disk; access and alteration can be made depending upon the needs. This process leads to the concept of data files.

File is a set of records than can be accessed through the set of library functions. A file is one, which will enable the user to read, write and store a group of related data, without losing them even if the program is over. To perform these functions there are several basic file operations.

22.2. FILE INPUT / OUTPUT IN C++ :

The different types of basic file operations for I/O operations in C++ are

i) **naming a file -** It is conventional and convenient to name files in relation to the data stored.
ii) **opening a file**
iii) **reading data from the file**
iv) **writing data to the file**
v) **closing a file**

To perform all the above input / output operations, we must include the header file <fstream>. It contains the classes ifstream, ofstream, and fstream, which are essential to open, close and manipulation on files. The following table gives the description of different file streams.

Table 22.1. File stream names and their descriptions :

Stream name	Description
ifstream	For input purpose, i.e. to read data from a file.
ofstream	For output purpose, i.e. to write data from a file.
fstream	For input and output, i.e. to read and write a file.

Before going to do any file operation, the concerned file should be opened. Here we have to give he external reference, which is also called physical reference to a file. The external reference is nothing but a valid file name. **The rule to be followed while naming a file (assuming MS-DOS) is that the, file name should**

not exceed more than eight characters and is called as primary file name. Usually all files come with secondary name (extension name) to give an identify to the file. The extension name should not exceed three characters. Some of the valid file names are shown below :

MARK.DA , INFORM.TXT , EMPLOYEE.FIL

It is advised not to give extension names such as .c, .for, .bas, .cob as they confuse with source code of the respective languages.

To open a file, we create a stream and then call the member function open ( ) The general form of open ( ) is

void open (const char *filename, int mode, int access=filebuf::openprot);

where 'filename' is the name of the file, 'mode' is one of the following values :

The description of different modes of data operations in the files depending on the mode values are given in table 2.2.

Table 22.2 : Different mode values in file operations and their description :

Mode Value	Description
ios :: app	In this mode data to be appended to the end of the file.
ios :: ate	seek to the end of the file. In this mode we can move the current position to elsewhere in the file subsequently.
ios :: binary	In this mode file is opened in binary mode and this mode, all characters are Unchanged when they are written to or read from the file.
ios :: in	Open the file for reading (Input)
ios :: out	Open the file for writing (Output)
ios :: nocreate	the open ( ) function will fail if the file does not exist
ios :: noreplace	the open ( ) function will fail if the file exists
ios :: trunc	truncates preexisting file to zero length

From the general form it is known that the default value for access is 'filebuf::openprot. The default mode value for 'ifstream' is 'ios::in and for 'ofstream' is 'ios::out'.

To write data to a file an ofstream object must be created. For example **to store data in the file name 'mark.dat', then the following code is used to open the file.**

```
ofstream outfile;
outfile.open ("mark.dat");
```

the above job can be done in a single statement as follows by using constructor function provided by the class ofstream

ofstream outfile ("mark.dat"); //using constructor function by class ofstream

Here, the input data will be written from the beginning of the file and this corresponds to the creation of the ofstream object in standard output mode, for which enumeration value ios::out could have been provided as well. We can also write the above statement in the following form by introducing enumeration value:

ofstream outfile ("mark.dat", ios::out); //using enumeration value

To append data instream of ios::out, the constant ios::app might have been used, in which case writing will always be done at the end of the file.

ofstream outfile ("mark.dat",ios::app); //append data using constant ios :: app

To read data from a file an ifstream object must be created. For example we want to retrieve data from he file name 'mark.dat', then the following code is used to open the file in the read mode.

ifstream infile;
infile.open("mark.dat");

We can write the above code in he following way also by using constructor function provided by the class ifstream:

ifstream infile("mark.dat");

When we want to open file for both purposes that is to perform read and write operation file a fstream object must be created.

fstream inout; //to perform read and write operation
inout.open("mark.dat",ios::in | ios::out);

By using explicit ios flag the file open for reading may take following form :

ifstream infile("mark.dat"),ios :: in); //using explicit ios flag to read

or it can be reduced into a single statement as

fstream inout ("mark.dat", ios :: in | ios :: out); //using to read and write

Here the ios constants such as ios::in and ios::out are used to indicate that the file must be opened for both for reading and writing. While using multiple constants, they are concatenated by he operator " | ". Also note that, when using fstream objects, the constant ios::out will result i the creation of he file, if the specified file does not exist and if ios::out is the only mode specification of the file. Also, if the file mode ios :: in is given, then the file is created only if it does not exist.

22.2.1. Explicit function for file Closure :

This function is not necessary because, **the close ( ) function is invoked automatically by the destructor function.** We can also use this member function to close the file explicitly and it takes the following form.

infile.close (); //to close the file explicitly

22.3. INPUT / OUTPUT OPERATIONS ON FILES :

The Input / Output operations in C++ can be done on different type of files using standard I/O functions similar to in C.

22.3.1. I/O operations on text files :

i) Writing and reading characters using put ( ) and get ( ) functions :

The put ( ) function writes characters to a disk file that was previously opened for writing through the use of the function open ( ).

The general form is :

ostream &out(char ch);

For example :

outfile.put(ch);

We can use the put(ch) function to write a single character to the output stream, where ch is the name of a variable of type char.

Similarly get( ) function is used to read characters from a file opened in read mode by open ( ).

istream & get(char &ch); //the general form to read characters

For example :

ch=infile.get( );

In the above statement we use the get ( ) function to read a character from the input stream, where ch is the name of a variable of type char.

Program 22.3.1

Write a program in C++ to explain the inputting and outputting of characters using standard functions.

```
# include <fstream>
# include <iostream>
using namespace std;
void main ( )
{
    ofstream outfile;
    char ch;
    outfile.open("abc.dat");
    if (!outfile.is_open ( ) )          //if the file cannot be opened file
    {
    cout <<"\n File open error " ;          // file open error message
    exit (1);
    }
```

```
        cout <<"\n Type characters ; to exit press $ key \n";
        cin.get(ch);
        while (ch!='$')
        {
            outfile.put(ch);
            cin.get(ch);
        }
        outfile.close ();
    }
```

OUTPUT :

Type characters ; to exit press $ key
data access object models
$

Here the data is entered through the terminal and is written character by character to the file, until the while loop encounters with '$' and then the file is closed. Now consider the following construct.

```
        if (!outfile.is_open ()
        {
        cout <<"\n File open error " ;  //if the file cannot be opened file
                                        // error message
        exit (1);
        }
```

The above code will execute only when open ( ) function fails. So, our program must have provision to exit the program if the function fails. Here the Boolean function is _open( ) is used to test he status of the file position. It returns rue if he file is opened successfully and returns false when he file does not open properly for various reasons.

Program 22.3.2

Write a program in C++ to read character from a disk file.

```
    # include <fstream>
    # include <iostream>
    using namespace std;
    void main ()
    {
        ifstream outfile;
        char ch;
        infile.open("abc.dat");
```

```
        if (!infile)
        {
            cout <<"\n File open error";
            exit (1);
        }
        cout <<"\n Characters stored in abc.dat is \n";
        while (!infile.eof())
        {
            ch=infile.get ( );
            cout<<ch;
        }
        infile.close ( );
    }
```

OUTPUT :

Characters stored in abc.dat is
data access object models

First consider the following code :

```
    if (!infile)
    {
        cout<<"\n File open error";
        exit (1);
    }
```

The above code is used to test the file status initially. Here we used the '!' Operator, which is overloaded in the ios class, is along with the file stream object. This operator returns true when the file is opened successfully. And the while loop is used to read character by character from a file until it encounters end of file. The end of file status can be found out by using another Boolean function. This eof ( ) function returns true when the file pointer has reached the end of a file character and returns false when it is not.

ii) Verifying the state of the streams in file I/O operation in C++ :

In addition to eof ( ) the following member functions are also used to verify the state of the stream and also note that all of them return a bool value.

a) **bad ( ) :** This function returns true if any failure occurs during reading or writing operation. For example, if we tried to write to a file that is not open for writing (the same with reading) or if the device (floppy / hard disk) where it is tried to write, has no space left.

b) **fail ( ) :** This function returns true in case as in bad. In addition in cases that happen to be a format error. Eg.: like if it tries to read an integer number and an alphabetical character is received.

c) **good ( ) :** This function returns false when calling any one of the previous ones it would be received true in any one.

Program 22.3.3

Write a program in C++ to count the number of vowels present in the text file.

```
# include <fstream>
# include <iostream>
using namespace std;
void main ( )
{
	ifstream infile;
	char ch;
	int noa,noe,noi,noo,nou;
	noa=noe=noi=noo=nou=0;
	infile.open("abc.dat");
	if (!infile)
	{
		cout <<"\n File open error ";
		exit (1);
	}
	while (infile.get(ch))
	{
		if (ch=='a')noa++;
		if (ch=='e') noe++;
		if (ch=='i') noi++;
		if (ch=='o') noo++;
		if (ch=='u') nou++;
	}
		cout <<"\n Number of a= "<<noa;
		cout <<"\n Number of e="<<noe;
		cout <<"\n Number of i ="<<noi;
		cout <<"\n Number of o= "<<noo;
		cout <<"\n Number of u= "<<nou;
		cout <<endl;
		infile.close ( );
}
```

OUTPUT: (For the text line "C++ programming, P. Radha Ganesan, Scitech Publications")

Number of a = 6
Number of e = 2
Number of i = 4
Number of o = 2
Number of u = 1

iii) Text file creation using overloaded insertion operator. (<<) :

In addition to the above method, the text file can be created in this way also using the overloaded insertion operator '<<'.

```
# include <fstream>
using namespace std;
void main ( )
{
        outstream testfile ("sample.txt");
        if (testfile.is_open())
        {
                testfile << "Book Name : C++ Programming \n";
                testfile << "Author                    : P. Radha Ganesan \n";
                testfile << "Publishers : Scitech Publications \n";
                testfile.close ( );
        }
}
```

iv) Text file creation using overloaded extraction operator. (>>) :

The processing file uses overloaded extraction operator '>>'

Program 22.3.4

Write a program in C++ to create a text file using over loaded extraction operator.

```
# include <iostream>
# include <fstream>
using namespace std;
void main ( )
{
        char str[80];
        ifstream testfile ("sample.txt");
        if (!testfile.is_open ( ) )
        {
                cout << "Error opening file";
                exit ( 1 );
        }
        while (! testfile.eof ( ))
        {
                testfile.getline (str,80);
                cout <<str;
                cout <<endl;
        }
}
```

OUT PUT :

Book Name : C++ Primer
Author : Stanley B.Lippman & Josee Lajoie
Publishers : Pearson Education

22.3.2. I/O operations on Binary files :

The text files can be easily modified using any text editor. In text files the stored data is accessible for others also, affecting its privacy, secrecy and security. To overcome these shortcomings we use binary files. In binary files in addition to read and write character by character we can also read and write data in terms of blocks, by using user defined data types like structures.

For binary I/O files we use **istream & read (), ostream & write ()** functions.

For example, *to open files in a binary mode for write purpose :*

ofstream outfile("mark.dat",ios :: out | ios :: binary);

To write a block of data to a binary file the function write ( ) is used and it takes the following form :

ostream &write(const char *buffer, streamsize number_of_bytes);

The write ( ) function writes *number_of_bytes* to the invoking stream from the buffer pointed to by buffer. The sizeof ( ) operator is used to find out the size of the structure which is being used.

Similarly, to read a block data from a binary file the function read ( ) is used and its syntax is

istream &read (char *buffer, r, streamsize number_of_bytes);

The read ( ) function reads *number_of_bytes* from the invoking stream and placed the data in the buffer pointed to by *buffer.*

i) Use of write ( ) in Binary functions to write data :

Program 22.3.5

Write a program in C++ to use Binary files using write ( )

```
# include <fstream>
# include <iostream>
using namespace std;
struct student
{
    char name [20];
    int rollno;
    float cpa;
};
```

```
void main ( )
{
    ofstream outfile ("mark.dat",ios :: out | ios :: binary);
    char proceed ='y';
    student studentrec;
    while (toupper(proceed)=='Y')
    {
        cout <<"\n Enter name  : ";
        cin.getline (studentrec.name,20);
        fflush(stdin);
        cout<<"\n roll no : " ;
        cin >>studentrec.rollno;
        fflush (stdin);
        cout <<"\n        cpa    : " ;
        cin>>studentrec.cpa;
        fflush(stdin);
        cout <<"\n Want to proceed?: " ;
        cin>>proceed;
        fflush(stdin);
        outfile.write ( (char*) & studentrec.sizeof(studentrec));
    }
        outfile.close ( );
}
```

OUTPUT :

```
Enter Name          :    Kiran
    roll no         :    205
    cpa             :    6.8
Want to proceed?    :    Y
Enter name          :    Vishnu
    roll no         :    304
    cpa             :    8.7
Want to proceed?    :    N
```

ii) Use of read ( ) in Binary functions to read data :

Program 22.3.6.

Write a program in C++ to use Binary files using read ( )

```
# include <fstream>
# include <iostream>
using namespace std;
struct student
{
    char name[20];
```

```
        int rollno;
        float cpa;
};
        void main ()
{
        ifstream infile ("mark.dat",ios : :in | ios :: binary);
        student studentrec;
        while(infile.read(( char *)&studentrec,sizeof(studentrec)))
            {
                cout <<"\n Name         : "<<studentrec.name;
                cout <<"\n Roll no      : "<<studentrec.rollno;
                cout <<"\n CPA          : "<<studentrec.cpa;
                cout<<endl;
            }
            infile.close ( );
}
```

OUTPUT :

```
Name    :   Narayana
Roll No :   304
CPA     :   6.2
Name    :   Ravi
Roll No :   239
CPA     :   9.8
```

iii) Use of classes in Binary functions using read ( ), write ( ) to read and write data :

We are using classes and functions to receive data and display data. For reading and writing objects we use read ( ) and write ( ) functions.

Program 22.3.7

Write a program in C++ for binary files using classes.

```
    # include <fstream>
    # include <iostream>
    using namespace std;
    struct student
        {
            private :
                char name[20];
                int rollno;
                float cpa;
            public :
                void getdata( );
                void putdata ( );
        };
```

```
void student :: getdata( )
{
        cout<<"\n Enter name
        cin.getline(name,20);
        fflush (stdin);
        cout <<"\n roll no
        cin>>rollno;
        fflush(stdin);
        cout<<"\n  cpa
        cin>>cpa;
        fflush(stdin);
}
void student :: putdata ( )
{
    cout<<"\n Name: "<<name;
    cout <<"\n Roll no       : "<<roll no;
    cout <<"\n CPA           : "<<cpa;
    cout<<endl;
}
void main ( )
{
    ofstream outfile ("mark.dat",ios :: out | ios :: binary);
    char proceed='y';
    student studentobj;
    //data entry
    while(toupper(proceed)=='Y')
        {
            studentobj.getdata ( );
            outfile.write ((char *)&studentobj.sizeof(studentobj));
            cout<<"\n Want to continue : " ;
            cin>>continue;
            fflush(stdin);
        }
    outfile.close ( );
    //data processing
    cout <<"\n Mark.dat file consists of :\n";
    ifstream infile ("mark.dat",ios :: in | ios :: binary);
    while (infileread(char *)&studentobj.sizeof(studentobj)))
    {
        studentobj.putdata ( );
    }
    infile.close ( );
}
```

OUTPUT :

Enter name : Ramu
roll no : 123
CPA : 9.1
Want to continue : Y
Enter name : Venkat
roll no : 140
CPA : 6.1
Want to continue : N
Mark.dat file consists of :
Name : Ramu
Roll no : 123
CPA : 9.1
Name : Venkat
Roll no : 140
CPA : 6.1

22.3.3. I/O Operations on Random files :

Unlike in files where sequential access method in which all the records in a file are processed one by one using FIFO (first in first out) method. **we have random files to access particular records in a file.**

In the random file organization of C++ the accessing of a particular record is based on the position of a record in a file, also binary mode for this type of organization is used.

i) **Use of seekg ( ) :** *To read a record in a file at any particular position we are using a function seekg ( ). The function seekg ( ) is used to move our file pointer either forward or backward direction.* **The amount of bytes to move is given as offset and its direction to move is given by from where.** *The complete syntax for randum files is given below.*

istream &seekg (off_type offset, fromwhere);

here from where may be any one of the following :

i) **ios :: beg** moves forward from origin

ii) **ios :: cur** moves forward or backward from current position and it is determined by the offset value. *If the offset value is given as negative then fileptr moves backward from the current position by offset amount of bytes.*

iii) **ios :: end** from the end of file.

For example,

infile.seekg (32,ios :: beg);

Will move file pointer to 32 bytes forward direction starting from origin.

In the following *after entering few records user has to enter record number to process. It is received by an identifier 'recno'. The required record position is arrived by using following code.*

```
m=sizeof(studentobj);
offset=(reco-1)*m;
```

here 'recno' is subtracted by 1, because the first record starts with 0 and it is multiplied by size of the object 'studentobj'. Once anchoring our position, we adopt usual method to read and process as we did in binary file.

Program 22.3.8

Write a program in C++ to explain I/O operations in using random files.

```
# include <fstream>
# include <iostream>
using namespace std;
class student
{
    private :
        char name [20];
        int rollno;
        float cpa;
    public :
        void getdata ( );
        void pudata ( );
    };
    void student :: getdata ( )
    {
        cout <<"\n Enter name;
        cin.getline(name20);
        fflush(stdin);
        cout<<"\n  roll no :
        cin>>rollno;
        fflush(stdin);
        cout<<"\n cpa;
        cin>>cpa;
        fflush(stdin);
    }
    void student :: putdata ( )
    {
        cout<<"\n Name: "<<name;
        cout<<"\n Roll no       : "<<rollno;
        cout<<"\n CPA           : "<<cpa;
        cout<<endl;
    }
```

```
          void main ( )
  {
          ofstream outfile (*mark.dat",ios :: out | ios :: binary);
          char proceed='y';
          int m,offset,recno;
          student studentobj;
          //data entry
          while (to upper (proceed)=='Y')
              {
                  studentobj.getdata( );
                  outfile.write( (char *)&studetobj.sizeof(studentobj));
                  cout<<"\n Want to continue? : " ;
                  cin>>continue;
                  fflush(stdin);
              }
          outfile.close( ) ; m
          ifstream infile ("mark.dat",ios :: in ios :: binary);
          cout <<"\n enter record number to process : \n";
          cin >>recno;
          m=sizeof(studentobj);
          offfset=(recno-1)*m;
          infile.seekg(offset,ios :: beg);
          infile.read((char *(&studentobj,m);
          studentobj.putdata ( );
          infile.close ( );
  }
```

OUTPUT :

```
Enter name          :   Anil
      roll no       :   101
      CPA           :   5.6
Want to continue?   :   Y
Enter name          :   Madhu
      roll no       :   115
      CPA           :   8.5
Want to continue?   :   Y
Enter name          :   Suresh
      roll no       :   148
      CPA           :   6.9
Want to continue    :   N
```

Enter record number to process :
2

Enter name : Venkat
Roll no : 158
CPA : 7.2

Here is a list of the other related function used in random file operation with its description.

ii) **Use of seekp( ) :** This function moves the associated file's current put pointer offset number of characters from the specified fromwhere.

iii) **Use of tellg ( ) :** This function is used to get the current position of the input stream

iv) **tellp ( ) :** This function is used to get the current position of the output stream

Program 22.3.9.

Write a program in C++ to explain the use of functions seekg ( ), tellg ( ) :

```
include <iostream>
# include <fstream>
using namespace std;
    void main ( )
{
    long curpos.endpos;
    char fname[20];
    cout<<"\n Enter file name :" ;
    cin.getline(fname,20);
    fflush(stdin);
    ifstream infile (fname,ios :: in | ios :: binary);
    curpos = infile.tellg( );
    cout <"\n Current position : "<<curpos;
    infile.seekg (0, ios :: end);
    endpos = infile.tellg( );
    cout <<"\n End position ' : "<<endpos;
    infile.close ( );
    cout <<"\n End position = : "<<endpos;
    infile.close ( );
    cout <<"\n Size of " <<fname;
    cout << " is " <<(endpos-curpos) << "bytes.\n";
}
```

OUTPUT :

Enter file name : example 294.cpp
Current position : 0
End position : 465
Size of example294.cpp is 465 bytes.

22.4. COMMAND LINE ARGUMENTS IN C++ :

In C++ to give input data along with command name we use command line arguments. Normally we give input data only during the execution of the program. Consider a DOS command for renaming a file.

C:\> ren abc.c def.c

here ren is an internal command to rename a file and it requires two arguments one is for source file name and another for target file name. **Here we are giving arguments along with the command hence the name command line arguments.**

So far we have seen main ( ) function without any arguments. But *it is possible to pass three arguments along with the function main ( ).*

1. **argc :** It is an integer and is the number of arguments (parameters) passed to function main ( )
2. **argv :** It is an array of strings.
3. **argenv :** It is also an array of strings. Each element of argenv [ ] holds a string and it is of the form ENVVAR = value. Here ENVVAR is the name of an environment variable, for example PATH.

assume that the following command is entered in the DOS prompt.

c:\tc>scopy abc.c def.c

here, scopy is the command to copy contents of abc.c to def.c. Upon execution of the above command argc in the main ( ) will take the value three.

argv[0] contains the file name and it is scopy.exe
argv[1] contains the first string after the name of the program being run
Here it is abc.c
argv[2] contains the second string after the name of the program and it is def.c

Program 22.4.1

Write a program in C++ to transfer the contents of one text file to another text file using command line arguments.

```
// program to implement command line arguments
// it is stored in the name of scopy.cpp

# include <fstream>
# include <iosream>
using namespace std;
void main (int argc,char *argv[ ])
{
    ifstream fp1;
    ofstream fp2;
    char ch;
```

```
        fp1.open(argv[1]);
        fp2.open(argv[2]);
        if (argc !=3)
        {
            cout <<"\n Wrong number of parameters" ;
            exit (1);
        }
        if (!fp1 | | !fp2)
        {
            cout <<"\n File read / Write error ";
            exit (1);
        }
        while (fp1.get(ch))
            fp2.put(ch);
        fp1.close ( );
        fp2.close ( );
    }
```

After making exe file for the above source code, return to DOS mode issue the following command.

C :\tcc/bin>scopy abc.c def.c

And let us verify the content of both source file (abc.c) and target file (def.c). Both will have same source code if the program works properly.

22.5. INDEXING DATABASE AND FILES :

22.5.1. Indexing Data Base :

A database index is a data structure that improves the speed of data retrieval operations on a database table at the cost of slower writes and increased storage space. Indexes can be created using one or more columns of a database table, providing the basis for both rapid random lookups and efficient access of ordered records. The disk space required to store the index is typically less than that required by the table (since indices usually contain only the key-fields according to which the table is to be arranged, and exclude all the other details in the table), yielding the possibility to store indices in memory for a table whose data is too large to store in memory.

In a relational database, an index is a copy of one part of a table. Some databases extend the power of indexing by allowing indices to be created on functions or expressions. For example, an index could be created on upper(last_name), which would only store the upper case versions of the last_name field in the index. Another option sometimes supported is the use of "filtered" indices , where index entries are created only for those records that satisfy some conditional expression. A further aspect of flexibility is to permit indexing on user-defined functions, as well as expressions formed from an assortment of built-in functions.

Indices may be defined as unique or non-unique. A unique index acts as a constraint on the table by preventing duplicate entries in the index and thus the backing table.

22.5.2. Index architecture

i) Types of Indexes

a) Non-clustered

The data is present in random order, but the **logical ordering** is specified by the index. The data rows may be randomly spread throughout the table. The non-clustered index tree contains the index keys in sorted order, with the leaf level of the index containing the pointer to the page and the row number in the data page. In non-clustered index:

- The physical order of the rows is not the same as the index order.
- Typically created on column used in JOIN, WHERE, and ORDER BY clauses.
- Good for tables whose values may be modified frequently.

Microsoft SQL Server creates non-clustered indexes by default when CREATE INDEX command is given. There can be more than one non-clustered index on a database table. There can be as many as 249 nonclustered indexes per table in SQL Server 2005 and 999 nonclustered indexes per table in SQL Server 2008. It also creates a clustered index on a primary key by default.[1]

b) Clustered

Clustering alters the data block into a certain distinct order to match the index, resulting in the row data being stored in order. Therefore, only one clustered index can be created on a given database table. Clustered indices can greatly increase overall speed of retrieval, but usually only where the data is accessed sequentially in the same or reverse order of the clustered index, or when a range of items is selected.

Since the physical records are in this sort order on disk, the next row item in the sequence is immediately before or after the last one, and so fewer data block reads are required. The primary feature of a clustered index is therefore the ordering of the physical data rows in accordance with the index blocks that point to them. Some databases separate the data and index blocks into separate files, others put two completely different data blocks within the same physical file(s). Create an object where the physical order of rows is same as the index order of the rows and the bottom(leaf) level of clustered index contains the actual data rows.

They are known as "index organized tables" under Oracle database.

c) Cluster (Oracle)

In Oracle database, multiple tables can be joined into a **cluster** (not to be confused with clustered index described above). The records for the tables sharing the value of a cluster key shall be stored together in the same or nearby data blocks. This may improve the joins of these tables on the cluster key, since the matching records are stored together and less I/O is required to locate them. The data layout in the tables which are parts of the cluster is defined by the cluster configuration. A cluster can be keyed with a B-Tree index or a hash table. The data block in which the table record will be stored is defined by the value of the cluster key.

d) Column order

The order in which columns are listed in the index definition is important. It is possible to retrieve a set of row identifiers using only the first indexed column. However, it is not possible or efficient (on most databases) to retrieve the set of row identifiers using only the second or greater indexed column.

For example, imagine a phone book that is organized by city first, then by last name, and then by first name. If you are given the city, you can easily extract the list of all phone numbers for that city. However, in this phone book it would be very tedious to find all the phone numbers for a given last name. You would have to look within each city's section for the entries with that last name. Some databases can do this, others just won't use the index.

e) Bitmap index

A bitmap index is a special kind of index that stores the bulk of its data as bit arrays (bitmaps) and answers most queries by performing bitwise logical operations on these bitmaps. The most commonly used index, such as B+trees, are most efficient if the values it indexes do not repeat or repeat a smaller number of times. In contrast, the bitmap index is designed for cases where the values of a variable repeat very frequently. For example, the gender field in a customer database usually contains two distinct values: male or female. For such variables, the bitmap index can have a significant performance advantage over the commonly used trees.

f) Dense index

A dense index in databases is a file with pairs of keys and pointers for every record in the data file. Every key in this file is associated with a particular pointer to *a record* in the sorted data file. In clustered indices with duplicate keys, the dense index points *to the first record* with that key.

g) Sparse index

A sparse index in databases is a file with pairs of keys and pointers for every block in the data file. Every key in this file is associated with a particular pointer *to the block* in the sorted data file. In clustered indices with duplicate keys, the sparse index points *to the lowest search key* in each block. primary key is a sparse index.

h) Reverse index

A reverse key index reverses the key value before entering it in the index. E.g., the value 24538 becomes 83542 in the index. Reversing the key value is particularly useful for indexing data such as sequence numbers, where new key values monotonically increase.

22.5.3. Operations on Indexing :

i) Index implementations

Indices can be implemented using a variety of data structures. Popular indices include balanced trees, B+ trees and hashes.

In Microsoft SQL Server, the leaf node of the clustered index corresponds to the actual data, not simply a pointer to data that resides elsewhere, as is the case with a non-clustered index.[5] Each relation can have a single clustered index and many unclustered indices.

ii) Index concurrency control

An index is typically being accessed concurrently by several transactions and processes, and thus needs concurrency control. While in principle indexes can utilize the common database concurrency control methods, specialized concurrency control methods for indexes exist, which are applied in conjunction with the common methods for a substantial performance gain.

iii) Covering Index

In most cases, an index is used to quickly locate the data record(s) from which the required data is read. In other words, the index is only used to locate data records in the table and not to return data.

A covering index is a special case where the index itself contains the required data field(s) and can return the data.

Consider the following table (other fields omitted):

ID	Name	Other Fields
12	Plug ...	
13	Lamp	...
14	Fuse ...	

To find the Name for ID 13, an index on (ID) will be useful, but the record must still be read to get the Name. However, an index on (ID, Name) contains the required data field and eliminates the need to look up the record.

A covering index can dramatically speed up data retrieval but may itself be large due to the additional keys, which slow down data insertion & update. To reduce such index size, some systems allow non-key fields to be included in the index. Non-key fields are not themselves part of the index ordering but only included at the leaf level, allowing for a covering index with less overall index size.

iv) Standardization

There is no standard about creating indexes because the ISO SQL Standard does not cover physical aspects. Indexes are one of the physical parts of database conception among others like storage (tablespace or filegroups). RDBMS vendors all give a CREATE INDEX syntax with some specific options which depends on functionalities they provide to customers.

22.5.4. Applications and limitations of Indexing :

Indices are useful for many applications but come with some limitations. Consider the following SQL statement: SELECT first_name FROM people WHERE last_name = 'Smith';. To process this statement without an index the database software must look at the last_name column on every row in the table (this is known as a full table scan). With an index the database simply follows the B-tree data structure until the Smith entry has been found; this is much less computationally expensive than a full table scan.

Consider this SQL statement: SELECT email_address FROM customers WHERE email_address LIKE '%@yahoo.com';. This query would yield an email address for every customer whose email address ends with "@yahoo.com", but even if the email_address column has been indexed the database must perform a full index scan. This is because the index is built with the assumption that words go from left to right. With a wildcard at the beginning of the search-term, the database software is unable to use the underlying b-tree data structure (in other words, the WHERE-clause is *not sargable*). This problem can be solved through the addition of another index created on reverse(email_address) and a SQL query like this: SELECT email_address FROM customers WHERE reverse(email_address) LIKE reverse('%@yahoo.com');. This puts the wild-card at the right-most part of the query (now moc.oohay@%) which the index on reverse(email_address) can satisfy.

22.6. FILE INDEXING :

An **indexed file** is a computer file with an index that allows easy random access to any record given its file key.

The key must be such that it uniquely identifies a record. If more than one index is present the other ones are called *alternate indexes*.

22.6.1. Indexing File Record IDs :

If you have a set of files that regularly change over time: Old files are deleted, new ones are added, or existing files are modified, you can benefit from using the *file ID* indexing methodology. Examples of this type of database might include an index of WWW resources, or a USENET news spool area. Briefly speaking, the file key methodology uses the directory paths of the individual records as a unique identifier for each record. To perform indexing of a directory with file keys, again, you specify the top-level directory after the update command. The command will recursively traverse the directories and compare each one with whatever have been indexed before in that same directory. If a file is new (not in the previous version of the directory) it is inserted into the registers; if a file was already indexed and it has been modified since the last update, the index is also modified; if a file has been removed since the last visit, it is deleted from the index.

The resulting system is easy to administrate. To delete a record you simply have to delete the corresponding file (say, with the rm command). And to add records you create new files (or directories with files). For your changes to take effect in the register you must run zebraidx update with the same directory root again. This mode of operation requires more disk space than simpler indexing methods, but it makes it easier for you to keep the index in sync with a frequently changing set of data. If you combine this system with the *safe update* facility (see below), you never have to take your server off-line for maintenance or register updating purposes.

To enable indexing with pathname IDs, you must specify file as the value of recordId in the configuration file. In addition, you should set storeKeys to 1, since the Zebra indexer must save additional information about the contents of each record in order to modify the indexes correctly at a later time.

For example, to update records of group esdd located below /data1/ records/ you should type:

```
$ zebraidx -g esdd update /data1/records
```

The corresponding configuration file includes:

```
esdd.recordId: file
esdd.recordType: grs.sgml
esdd.storeKeys: 1
```

* * *

COMPREHENSION - 22

Note : By answering all the questions given in this comprehension one can answer any objective type of questions easily whatever be the form of the question. Answers for these questions can be obtained by going through the topics in this chapter carefully.

1. What is a file?
2. What are the basic file operations to be performed while using file I/O operations in C++ ?
3. What is file extension?
4. What is the header file to be used for File I/O Operations?
5 State different File Stream names and their descriptions used for different types of File Operations
6. How do you indicate the external or physical reference to a file? Why?
7. What is a secondary or extension name to a file? Why is it used? What is its significance
8. Give the general form of file open.
9. What are the significances of different modes used in file open?
10. Give different forms of statement to write input in the beginning of a file. Explain.
11. How do you create an ifstream object? Why?
12. Explain the use of constructor function for file reading and also to perform read & write.
13. Is it necessary to explicitly file close function? Otherwise how is it done?
14. Explain use of put( ) and get ( ) functions in I/O operations on files.
15. If a file referenced is not found how is it indicated when you try to open such a file?
16. Explain eof ( ) and eol ( ) functions.
17. Explain the action of the member functions used to verify the state of the stream bad ( ) , fail ( ) and good ( ).
18. What are the advantages of using binary files over text files?
19. What is the special advantage of using binary files to read and write data?
20. How do you read and write different types of data in binary files? Give syntax and explain.
21. What is the role of buffer? How is buffer accessed?
22. Discuss about I/O operation on files with classes.
23. What is the difference between Sequential and Random files?
24. How do you access the records in Random files?
25. What is the mode used for file organization in random file organization?

26. Give the functions used in Random file operation. Explain their usage.
27. What is the purpose of using fflush(stdin) function?
28. What is meant by command line arguments?
29. What are the arguments that can be used in main () ? Explain their function.
30. What are the arguments that are contained in the Dos prompt C:\tc>scopy abc.c def.c
31. What is a Database Index?
32. How can indexes be created
33. what are the advantages of index?
34. What is an index in relational data base?
35. How is the power of indexing increased in cettain tpes of databases?
36. What are filtered indices?
37. What are the different types of indexes?
38. What are the opertions involved on indexing?
39. What are the applications of indexing?
40. What are the limitations of indexing?
41. What is an index file?
42. What are the advantages of file indexing?
43. How do you perform indexing of a directory with file keys?
44. How do you delete or create records in file indexing with file record IDs ?
45. What is Zebra indexor? What are its functions?

* * *

EXERCISE - 22

Note : By answering all the questions given in this exercise one can answer subjective type of questions easily including problems. The worked examples in the chapter may help in solving these questions.

1. Write short notes on file streams.
2. How do the following two statements differ in the operations
   i) cin >> c; ii) cin.get(c);
3. Explain the various stages of handling file operations in C++.
4. Explain the operations of insertion or deletion of data at different locations in a file.
5. Explain manipulators and formatting output in file operations.
6. Explain with the help of a program constructing our own manipulators.
7. Explain the different modes in file operations and how you indicate them for input, output and I/O operations of files.
8. Explain about the member functions used in verifying the state of the stream in file Operations.
9. What are the differences between data and binary files.
10. Explain binary I/O operations in binary files.
11. What is meant by Random Files? Explain Random File operations.
12. Explain Command line arguments.
13. Explain Database indexing.
14. Explain different types of database indexing mentioning their relative merits.
15. Explain the process of increasing the power of indexing.
16. Explain the different types of indexing, their advantages and limitations.
17. What are the operations involved in indexing?
18. Discuss about file indexing.
19. Discuss about Zebra indexor.
20. Explain the process of indexing of a directory with file keys.

* * *

CHAPTER - 23
SPECIAL FEATURES IN C++

23.1. INTRODUCTION :

In additions to the features already discussed C++ has some more additional features which are very useful in programming. The use of the such special powerful features of C++, programing in C++becomes easier reducing lot of tedious work which has to be done otherwise. The main additions to C++ are :

i) namespaces
ii) run-time type identification (RTTI)
iii) templates
iv) exceptions

23.2. NAMESPACE :

We have used the special feature 'using namespace std;' in almost all the C++ programs we have discussed so far. **Namespace permits us to group variables, functions and classes under a common name.The use of namespace standard can be done with the statement 'using namespace std; '** in the program.

According to ANSI C++ definition all the classes, objects and functions of the standard C++ library are defined within the namespace std.

23.2.1 Avoiding of namespace using scope operator :

We can also write programs without the statement **using namespace std** declaration in our programs. For example :

```
#include <iostream>
void main ( )
{
        std : :cout<<"\n Example program for namespace ";
}
```

OUTPUT :

Example program for namespace

Such program without the statement **using namespace std** requires the use of scope operator (::)

23.2.2. Use of namespace to avoid use of scope operator :

Use of scope operator : : can be avoided by using **namespace std declaration .**

Using namespace std; the above program will be as follows :

```
# include <iostream>
using namespace std;
```

```
void main ()
{
    cout<<"\n Example program for namespace";
}
```

OUTPUT :

23.2.3. Creation of separate namespaces in C++ program :

The general syntax of creating separate namespace is

```
namespace identifier_name
{
    namespace-body
}
```

where identifier is any valid identifier and namespace-body is the set of variables, functions, classes and objects that are included within the namespace.

For example consider the following code :

```
namespace example
{
    int a, b;
}
```

In the above case, a and b are normal variables integrated within the **example** *namespace.*

If we don't use namespace then to make use of these variables from outside the namespace we have to use the scope resolution operator : : .

For example, to access the previous variables we would write

```
example :: a
example :: b
```

The functionality of namespaces is especially useful in case that there is a possibility that a global object or function can have the same identifier name thus, causing a redefinition error.

Use of namespace enables us to use the same variable name for different types and values of data by using different identifier names for namespace separately.

For example :

```
# include <iostream>
using namespace std;
namespace ns1
{
    int a = 96;
}
```

```
namespace ns2
{
    double a = 31.6141;
}
    void main ()
{
    cout <<"\n Variable a in namespace No.1 is : ";
    cout <<ns1 : : a<<endl;
    cout <<"\n Variable a in namespace No. 2 is : " ;
    cout <<ns2 : : a<<endl;
}
```

OUTPUT :

Variable a in namespace No.1 is : 96
Variable a in namespace No.2 is : 31.6141

In the above program we have two namespaces namely ns1 and ns2 and same variable name is present in both the namespaces. *To avoid scope collision, in the above main program we access those variables via their namespaces.*

23.2.4. Use of namespace :

As we know already, from the previous examples we can eliminate the name of the namespace and scope resolution operator when we use namespace directive in our program. Now, let us look into the following program using namespace directive.

```
# include <iostream>
using namespace std;
namespace ns1
{
    int a = 96;
}
namespace ns2
{
    double a = 31.6141;
}
void main ()
{
    using namespace ns1;
    cout <<"\n Variable a in namespace No.1 is : " ;
    cout << a <<endl;
}
```

OUTPUT :

Variable in a namespace No.1 is : 96

In the above program it is possible to use only variables present in the namespeace'ns1'. Because of this nature we cannot access members present in the namespace 'ns2'.

23.2.5. Switching of namespaces :

We can switch from one namespace to another namespace when it is enclosed in blocks. The revised program, which follows, has two blocks, in one block we make use of namespace 'ns1' and in another block we use namespace 'ns2'.

Program 23.2.1.

Write a program in C++ to explain the switching over of namespace directives

```
#include <iostream>
using namespace std;              //using std library
namespace ns1
{
        int a = 96 ;
}
namespace ns2
{
        double a =  31.6141;
}
void main ( )
{
        {
            using namespace ns1;      //separate use of namespace ns1
            cout <<"\n Variable a in namespace No1 is :";
            cout << a << endl;
        }
        {
            using namespace ns2;      //separate use of namespace ns2
            cout <<"\n Variable a in namespace No.1 is :" ;
            cout << a << endl;
        }
}
```

OUTPUT :

Variable a in namespace No.1 is : 96
Variable a in namespace No.2 is : 31.6141

23.2.6. Run-time Type Information (RTTI) using '#include <typeinfo>' :

It is possible to determine the type of an object during run time, by including a header file type 'typeinfo'. In the following program we have included a header file 'typeinfo'. The typeid( ) produces an object of type 'typeinfo' which is described in the header file 'typeinfo'. By using member function of this type we can also get the name of a type as given in program 23.2.2.

Program 23.2.2

Write a program in C++ to explain the feature of runtime type information.

```
# include <iostream>
# include <typeinfo>          // to use runtime type information (RTTI)
using namespace std;
void main ( )
{
    int ia= 55;
    float fb=12.12 f;
    double dc=34.555;
    cout <<"\n Data type of 'ia' is : "<<typeid(ia) .name( ) <<" & value is " <<ia;
    cout <<"\n Data type of 'fb' is : "<<typeid(fb) .name( ) <<" & value is " <<fb;
    cout <<"n Data type of 'dc' is : "<<typeid(dc) .name()<<"& its value is "<dc;
    cout << endl;
}
```

OUTPUT :

Data type of 'ia' is : **int** &its value is 55
Data type of 'fb' is : **float** &its value is 12.12
Data type of 'dc' is : **double** & its value is 34.555

Note that the form of the name returned by the member function name ( ) is implementation-dependent.

23.2.7. Type Casting :

Similar to C, in C++ type casting is generally used to convert from one type to another type. For example, the standard conversions are :

i) **integral promotions :** enum to int.

ii) **the integral conversions : float to double**

iii) **Floating integral conversions : int to float.**

iv) **The arithmetic conversions : for converting operands to the type of the widest operand before evaluation.**

v) **Pointer conversion : to convert from derived class pointer to base class pointer as used in polymorphism.**

vi) **Reference conversions : To change derived class reference to base class reference.**

vii) **Pointer-to-member conversions : convert from pointer to member of a base class to pointer to member of a derived class.**

These conversions can be carried out either by the compiler or by the programmer.

*i) **implicit conversion** : conversion taking place with the help of compiler*

*ii) **explicit conversion** :.conversion taking place with the intervention of the programmer*

23.2.8. Four methods of type casting operations in C++ :

Unlike C in C++ we have four powerful castings operators as follows :

i) **static_cast :** To convert one type to another type

ii) **const_cast :** To cast away the "const-ness" or "volatile-ness" of a type

iii) **dynamic_cast :** Used for safe navigation of an inheritance hierarchy

iv) **reinterpret_cast :** Used to perform conversions on un-related types.

All the above four cast operators have same syntax. For example, to convert a static_cast of ptr to a type T we write :

T*t=static_cast<T> (ptr);

a) The static_cast operator :

The general form for static_cast operator is

static_cast <T> (exp)

To convert the expression 'exp' to type T and these conversions rely on static type information. In the following program we declare float variable 'fa' and also it initializes to 339.54.

```
float fa= 339.54f
int ia=static_cast<int>(fa);
```

The static-cast operator converts 'fa' from float to int. The complete program is illustrated in the following program.

Program 23.2.3

Write a program in C+ to explain the use of static caste operator converting from float to integer.

```
#include <iostream>
using namespace std;
void main ()
{
    float fa=339.54f;
    int ia=static_cast<int>(fa);
    cout<<"\n The value of float variable 'fa' is : "<<fa;
    cout<<"\n After conversion to int the value becomes : "<<ia;
    cout<<endl;
}
```

OUTPUT :

The value of float variable 'fa' is : 339.54
After conversion to int the value becomes : 339

b) The const_cast operator

The const_cast operator is used to cast away the "const-ness" or "volatile-ness" of a type.

In the following example program we have a class 'sample' with three functions. The constant getinput ( ) function is to return the value of 'no'. The setinput ( ) function is to assign the value of 'x' to 'no'. The another constant member function printinput ( ) has to increment the value of 'no'.

```
const_cast<sample *>(this)->no++;
```

Inside the constant member function printinput ( ), the data type of this pointer is **const sample***. This casts away the const-ness of this pointer with the const_cast. And the type of this pointer for the remainder of the statement is now **sample*** which allows the value of 'no' to be modified.

Program 23.2.4

Write a program in C++ to illustrate the use of const_cast operator :

```
#include <iostream>
using namespace std;
class sample
{
private :
    int no;
public :
    int getinput( ) const                //to return the value of 'no'
    {
        return no;
    }
void setinput (int x)                   //to assign the value of 'x' to 'no'
    {
        no=x;
    }
void printinput ( ) const
    {
        const_cast<sample *>(this)->no++; //to allow increment to 'no'
        cout<<*\n The value of 'no' after incrementation is : "<<no;
    }
}
void main ( )
{
sample sampleobj;
sampleobj.setinput (563);
```

```
    cout<<"\n Before applying cast operator the value of 'no' is :"
    <<sampleobj.getinput ( );
    cout<<"\n After applying cast operator : " ;
    sampleobj.printinput ( );
    cout<<endl;
}
```

OUTPUT :

Before applying cast operator the value of 'no' is : 563
After applying cast operator :
The value of 'no' after incrementation is : 564

c) The reinterpret_cast operator

The reinterpret_cast operator is used for both nonstandard casts such as to convert void * to int and also for standard cast such as to convert from double to int. This is illustrated in the following program.

Program 23.2.5

Write a program in C++ to illustrate the use of reinterpret_cast operator

```
#include <iostream>
using namespace std;
void main ( )
{
    unsigned a=34, *unsignedptr;                    //value of 'a' is int
    void *voidptr=&a;
    char *charptr="Welcome";
    unsignedptr=reinterpret_cast<unsigned *>(voidptr);   //non std.cast
                                                         //int with char
    cout<<"\n Value of *unsignedptr is "<<*unsignedptr;
    cout <<"\n Value of charptr is "<<charptr;
    a=reinterpret_cast<unsigned>(charptr); //std. cast char with int
    cout<<"\n char * to unsigned is : "<<a;
    charptr=reinterpret_cast<char *>(a);     //std. cast int with char
    cout<<"\n Unsigned to char *is : "<<charptr;
    cout<<endl;
}
```

OUTPUT :

Value of *unsignedptr is 76
Value of charptr is Good
char * to unsigned is : 4398583
Unsigned to char * is : Good

Here, the reinterpret_cast operator is used to cast **voidptr** to unsigned* pointer **unsignedptr.**

The next conversion

a=reinterpret_cast<unsigned>(charptr);

Here, the casting is from **chartptr to unsigned** and the result is stored in the variable a and it contains the decimal address of the string 'Good'.

The last conversion

charptr=reinterpret_cast<char *>(a);

used to cast the value of a to **char*.** The result is stored in charptr is the string 'Good'.

d) The dynamic_cast operator

The dynamic cast operator is used to cast from derived class pointer to base class pointer or from base class pointer to derived class pointer. Also, these conversions may be applied references and any pointer may also be cast to a void*. The general form of dynamic_cast operator takes the following form :

dynamic_cast<T> (expr)

For example, if we have an expression ;

dynamic_cast<T*> (p)

In the above statement the conversion takes place from p to type T*, if *p really is a T or a class derived from T; otherwise the operator returns 0.

Suppose, we have a base class pointer or reference to a base class and we want to know whether we really have a base class pointer or instead a pointer to some class object, which is derived from the base class. The following program will check for the above condition.

Program 23.2.6

Write a program in C++ to illustrate the use of the dynamic_cast operator from derived * to base *

```
# include <iostream>
# include <typeinfo>
using namespace std;
class first
{
    public :
    virtual void f ()
    {
        cout <<"\n class first :: f( ) \n";
    }
```

```
};
class second : public first
{
    public:
        void f( )
        {
                cout <<"\n class second :: f( ) \n";
        }
};
void main ( )
{
    first firstobj. *firstobjpt;
    second secondobj, *secondobjptr;
    firstobjptr=dynamic_cast<first *>(&secondobj);
    if(firstobjptr)
    {
        cout<<"\n Cast is from derived *to base *";
        firstobjptr->f ( );
    }
    else
    {
        cout<<"\n Invalid operation";
    }
}
```

OUTPUT :

Cast is from derived * to base *
class second :: f ( )

Since, dynamic_cast operator is a part of run-time type information, it has been provided for use with polymorphic classes, which contains at least one virtual function. After observing all the four cast operators, it is well understood that each operator works for different applications and this deviates C cast operator, in which the purpose is same in all applications. **By using these caste operators effectively we can make our programs more readable, less error-prone and type-safe and easier to maintain.**

23.3. TEMPLATES :

Templates are powerful recent additions to C++. **Use of template starts with the keyword template.** There are certain problems using macros either in C++. For example in C using macro the statement

define max (a, b) ((a > b) ? a : b)

which is a decision statement using the macro 'max'.

The same statement when used in C++ also will work but without type checking

Now, consider following snippet in which, one of the input parameters is integer and the other one is character as in the following form.

```
max (5,'Z');
```

upon compilation, compiler does not report any errors.

Also we know that **use of inline functions are mainly to avoid macros,** which can also lead to more insidious bugs like this :

```
int y = 24;
cout <<max(++y, 24) <<endl; //Displays 26
```

The reason is due to the macro expands in the following form :

```
cout << ((++y, 24) ? ++y ; 24) <<endl;
```

Since the preprocessor expands macros by substitution, the variable y is incremented twice. To alleviate this problem C++ is equipped with templates which is considered to be one of the powerful features added recently.

23.3.1. Types of Templates :

i. Function templates

ii. Class templates

i) Function Templates :

To start let us write template function to find maximum of given two numbers.

```
template <class T> T max (T a, T b)
{
    return (a > b) ? a : b;
}
```

Now let us dissect each unit of the above template function.

All template function starts with the keyword 'template' which helps us to identify the following code as a template. It is followed by the keyword 'class' embedded in angle brackets identifies 'T' as a type. The parameters, which we want to introduce, should be placed between angled brackets after the keyword 'template'. If there is more than one parameter then it should be separated by commas. Also, note that the type 'T' can be one of the fundamental data types such as 'int' or 'long' or it may be a user defined data type. **In function template type checking is also enforced** After creating a template like the one above, that function template can now be used for any of the following types:

```
max(210, 12);          //int
max(120.8, 12.5);      //float
max ('x' 'y');         //char
max(true, false);      //bool
```

Consider the following code :

```
int x = 76
```

cout <<max(++x, 76) << endl; // Displays 77 which is the correct answer whereas we obtained the answer 8 earlier when we used macro without using the template as explained earlier. The correct answer 77 is given since there was no macro substitution used.

Program 23.3.1

Write a program in C++ to find maximum of the two numbers by using template.

```
#include <iostream>
using namespace std;
template <class T>
T max (T a, T b)
{
        return (a>b)? a:b;
}
        void main ( )
{
        float a=3.1, b=7.1;
        cout <<"\n Maximum of "<<a<<" and "<<b<<" is "<<max(a,b);
        int c=144, d=166
        cout <<"\n Maximum of "<<c<<" and "<<d<<" is "<<max(c,d);
        cout <<endl;
}
```

OUTPUT :

Maximum of 3.1 and 7.1 is 7.1
Maximum of 144 and 166 is 166

In the above program we gave two arguments of same data type to function 'max'. Suppose, when the input to the above function is

max (60, 'b');

then, the compiler will inform error. The reason is, **in function template type checking is also enforced** and thus making the above code illegal. When a function template is first called for each type, the compiler creates an instantation, or version, of the template function specialized for that type. This instantiation will be called every time the function is used for the type. *If we have several identical instantaneous, even in different modules, only one copy of the instantiation will end up in the executable file.*

For example, when the input to 'max' function is

```
max (52, 122)
```

Causes the compiler to generate the following code :

```
int max (int a, int b)
{
        return (a > b) ? a : b;
}
```

And max('a', 'b') generates this code:

```
char max (char a, char b)
{
        return (a > b) ? a : b;
}
```

23.3.2. Faster templates using inline keywords or functions :

Use of inline keywords or functions for faster templates cause override of templates :

i) **Where macros have no overhead because the preprocessor expands them, the overhead of templates can be minimized using the inline keyword.** Also, from the chapter 'Classes', the inline keyword suggests that the compiler insert a copy of the function body into each place when the function is called. **By using inline function we can make a program faster because they eliminate the overhead associated with each function calls.**

ii) **Overriding a template function to define special behaviour for a specific type :**

Another useful feature of templates is the ability to override a template function in order to define special behaviour for a specific type. For example, if we wanted to compare the length of two strings using the same 'max' function template. The standard version generated by the compiler would compare only the pointer addresses. *The following program shows a function that overrides the compiler's default instantiation of the template in order to compare string lengths:*

Program 23.3.2

Write a program in C++ to illustrate the property of a function over riding the compiler's default instantiation of the template using inline key words.

```
# include <iostream>
# include <cstring>
using namespace std;
template <class T>
T max (T a, T b)
{
      return (a>b) ? a : b ;
}
```

```
        char *max (char *a, char *b)
    {
        return (strlen (a) > strlen(b) ? a : b) ;
    }
        void main ( )
    {
            char str1[20];
            char str2[20];
            cout <<"\n Enter first string : " ;
            cin.getline(str1, 20);
            fflush(stdin);
            cout <<"\n Enter second string : " ;
            cin.getline(str2, 20);
            cout <<"\n Template function with int data type :" ;
            cout <<"\n Maximum number is "<<max(44,88);  //overriding
                                          //char template with int template
            cout <<"\n Overriding the template function : ";
            cout <<"\n String having Maximum length is : " ;
            cout <<max(str1, str2);
            cout <<endl;
    }
```

OUTPUT :

Enter first string : class
Enter second string : college
Template function with int data type:
Maximum number is 88
Overriding the template function :
String having Maximum length is : college

iii) **Use of different functions for the same template :**

At times, we want to have function or class having two exactly equal versions with difference in data types. For example, if we want to sort integer number and double number we may need two versions to perform this task. The following program contains two templates function. First template will be used to sort given numbers in ascending order by using bubble sort algorithm. The second function is to check whether the given number is present or not in the list by using binary search technique. Here the input data may be of any data type such as int, double etc., since the templates work by generating a version of the function for each data type which we call with. Suppose, we call bubble sort with 5 different types of arrays then 5 different versions of it will be compiled, just like we had written each one of them for each of the data types. Here is an example program follows to illustrate this idea.

Program 23.3.3

Write a program in C++ to illustrate the principle of using of two different functions for two different tasks using the template.

```
#include <iostream>
# include <iomanip>
using namespace std;
template <class T>
  void bubblesort (T x[ ],int items)
{
      int swap=1;
      for (int i=0;i<items &&swap==1;++i)
      {
         swap=0;
         for (int j=0;j<items-(i+1) ;++j)
                if (x[j] > x[j+1])
                {
                       int temp;
                       temp=x[j];
                       x[j]=x[j+1];
                       x[j+1]=temp;
                       swap=1;
                }
      }
}
      template <class T>
      int binarysearch(T no, T x[ ],int items)
      {
         int bottom=0;
                int top=items-1;
                int mid;
                cout <<"\n inside search : " ;
                for (int i=0;j<5;++i)
                       cout <<" " <<x[i];
                while (bottom <=top)
                {
                       mid=(top+bottom)/2;
                       if(no==[mid])
                         return mid;
                       else if (no <x[mid])
                         top=mid-1;
                       else
                         bottom=mid+1;
                }
                return -1;
         }
```

```
void main ( )
{
    int intarray [ ] = {33, 11, 22, 777, 66};
    bubblesort(intarray,5);
    cout <<"\n Data type - Integer \n";
    cout <<"\n Given numbers \n";
    for (int i=0;i<5;++i)
    cout <<setw(5)<<intarray[i];
      int present=binarysearch(777,intarray,5);
      if(present>0)
          cout <<"\n Search number is present and its location is : "<<present;
      else
          cout <<"\n Search number is not present ";
      double doublearray [ ]={1.2, 6.2, 3.5, 72.4, 18.9}
          cout<<"\n\n Data type - double ";
          cout <<"\n Given numbers \n";
          for (i=0;i<5;++i)
              cout <<setw(5)<<doublearray[i];
          bubblesort(doublearray,5);
              cout <<"\n Sorted numbers \n";
          for(i=0);i<5;++i)
              cout<<setw(5)<<doublearray[i];
          present=binarysearch( 84.5,doublearray,5);
          if (present>0)
          cout <<"\n Search number is present and its location is : "<<present;
      else
          cout <<"\n Search number is not present ";
          cout <<endl;
}
```

OUTPUT :

Data type - Integer

Given numbers

33 11 22 777 66

Sorted numbers

11 22 33 66 777

Inside search : 11 22 33 66 777

Search number is present and its location is : 4

Data type - double

Given numbers

1.2 6.2 3.5 72.4 18.9

Sorted numbers

```
      1.2   3.5    6.2  18.9   72.4
Inside search : 1.2   3.5    6.2  18.9   72.4
Search number is not present
```

ii) Class Template:

A class template enables us to generalize an entire class so that it can work with any data type. Its definition is always preceded by a template clause. The syntax rule for class template is same as function templates. And its definition is also similar to function template except that the specified type parameters can be referred to within the definition. *The general form of a class template are given below:* **The arguments can be of same type or different types as illustrated in the programs given below.**

```
Template <class Type>
class XII
{
    private :
        Type private_members;
    public :
        ......
}
```

after declaring the template one above, we can create different types of objects of class XII as shown below :

```
XII <int> intobj;
XII <float> floatobj;
XII <double> doubleobj;
```

From the above example declarations, it is known that **template construct is useful to define a generic or an abstract type from which a hierarchy of specific or concrete types can be derived.**

Program 23.3.4.

Write a program in C++ to illustrate the class template using same data type of arguments.

```
# include <iostream>
using namespace std;
template <class T>
class sumnumbers
{
    private:
        T1 firstno;
        T2 secondno;
```

```
    public:
        sumnumbers(T1 x, T2 y)
        {
            firstno=x;
            secondno=y;
        }
        void displaysum ()
        {
            cout<<"\n First number ; "<<firstno;
            cout<<"\n Second number ; "<<secondno;

            cout <<"\n Sum of given two numbers is " <<firstno+secondno;
            cout <<endl;
        }
    };
        void main ()
{
        sumnumbers <int,float> sum numbersobj 1 (234, 45.6f);
        cout <<"\n Integer and float sum : " ;
        sumnumbersobj1,displaysum ( );
        sumnumbers <float> sumnumbersobj2 (22.8, 34.7);
        cout <<"\n Float sum : " ;
        sumnumbersobj2.displaysum ( );
}
```

OUTPUT :

Integer and float sum :
Sum of given two numbers is 279.6

Float sum :
Sum of given two numbers is 57.5

Program 23.3.5

Write a program in C++ to illustrate how to use two different data types in a class template.

```
#include <iostream>
using namespace std;
template <class T1, class T2> //two arguments are given for template.
                              //for two different data types
class sumnumbers
{
    private :
        T1 first no;
        T2 secondno;
```

```
public :
    sumnumbers (T1 x, T2 y)
    {
        firstno=x;
        secondno=y;
    }
    void displaysum ( )
    {
        cout <<"\n First number : "<<firstno;
        cout <<"\n Second number : "<<secondno;
        cout <<"\n Sum of two numbers is "<<firstno+secondno;
        cout << endl;
    }
};
void main ( )
{
    sumnumbers<int, float> sumnumbersobj1(25,10.5f);
    cout<<"\n Int and float sum : " ;
    sumnumbersobj1.displaysum ( );
    sumnumbers<int,double>sumnumbersobj2(35, 5.5f);
    cout<<"\n Int and double sum : " ;
    sumnumbersobj2.displaysum ( );
}
```

OUTPUT :

Int and float sum :
First number : 25
Second number : 10.5
Sum of two numbers is 35.5

Int and double sum :
First number : 35
Second number : 5.5
Sum of two numbers is 40.5

iii) Use of named templates

Now let us discuss how to write stack operation by using class template. For example,

template <class T>class stack

declares a class template named 'stack'. The declaration of stack template is as follows.

```
template <class T>
class stack
{
    private :
        struct node
        {
            T data;
            node *next;
        };
            node *top;
    public :
        stack( );
        ~stack ( );
        int push (T value);
        T pop ( );
    };
```

As we know that, **the class template represents a generic class from which executable implementations of the class can be generated by binding its type parameters to concrete types.** For example to work with integer stack and double stack, the declaration is as follows,

```
stack<int>intstackobj;
stack<double>doublestackobj;
```

Each of the above instantiations causes the member functions of the class to be accordingly instantiated. In the first declaration, the member function will be instantiated with Type to 'int' and in the second declaration, the member will be instantiated with Type to 'double'.

Program 23.3.6

Write a program in C++ to illustrate the use of named templates for the use of different data types.

```
# include <iostream>
# define NULL 0
using namespace std;
template <class T>
class stack
{
        private :
                struct node
                {
                        T data;
                        node *next;
                };
```

```
        node *top;
    public:
        stack ( );
        ~stack( );
        int push (T value);
        T pop ( );
    };
    template <class T> stack <T> :: stack ( )
    {
        top=NULL;
    }
    template <class T> stack <T> :: ~stack ( )
    {
    }
    template <class T> stack <T> :: push (T item)
    {
        node *p;
        p=new node;
        if (p==NULL)
    {
        cout <<"\n Error in memory allocation ";
        return 0;
    }
        p->data=item;
        p->next=top;
        top=p;
        return 1;
    }
template <class T> T stack <T> ::pop( )
{
    node *p;
    T item;
    p=top;
    if (p==NULL)
        return 0;
    item=top->data;
    top=top->next;
    delete p;
    return item;
}
 void main ( )
{
    int choice.no;
    stack<int> intstackobj;
```

```
        while (1)
        {
            cout <<"\n 1. Push " ;
            cout <<"\n 1\2. Pop " ;
            cout <<"\n 3. Quit " ;
            cout <<"\n Enter your choice : " ;
            cin>>choice;
                switch (choice)
            {
                case 1:
                cout <<"\n Enter number ";
                cin >> no;
                intstackobj.push (no);
                break;
                case 2 :
                no=instackobj.pop ( );
                if (no>0)
                     cout <<"\n Popped number "<<no;
                else
                     cout<<"\n Stack empty";
                break;
                case 3 :
                exit (0);
            }
        }
    }
```

OUTPUT :

1. Push
2. Pop
3. Quit

Enter your choice : 1

Enter number 44

1. Push
2. Pop
3. Quit

Enter your choice : 1

Enter number 88

1. Push
2. Pop
3. Quit

Enter your choice : 2
Popped number 88
1. Push
2. Pop
3. Quit
Enter your choice : 2
Popped number 44
1. Push
2. Pop
3. Quit
Enter your choice : 2
Stack empty
1. Push
2. Pop
3. Quit
Enter your choice : 3

23.3.3. Differences between Class and Function Templates :

As we know that, **the name of a template class is compound name consisting of the template name and the full template argument list enclosed in angular braces.** Any reference to a template class must use this complete name. For example:

```
template <class T, int xxx>
class example
{
        T a;
        int r;
        // ...
};
```

As, C++ requires this explicit naming convention to ensure that the appropriate class can be generated.

Following is a valid declaration

```
example<double,20>exampleobj1;
```

The following two declarations are invalid ones

```
example<double>exampleobj2;  //missing value for 'xxx'
example exampleobj3;         //no arguments along with class
```

A template function, on the other hand, has the name of its function template and the particular function chosen to resolve a given template function call is determined by the type of the calling arguments. In the following example, the call swap (x,y) is effectively a call to swap(int x, int y), and the call swap(x1, y1) is effectively a call to swap (float x1, float y1);

Program 23.3.7

Write a program in C++ to illustrate the proper use of class and function templates.

```
#include <iostream>
using namespace std;
template <class T>
swap (T *a, T *b)
{
        T temp;
        tem=*a;
        *a=*b;
        *b=temp;
}
void main ( )
{
        int x = 70;
        int y = 80;
        float x1 = 25.4f;
        float y1 = 35.6f;
        cout <<"\n Initial value - Type Integer ";
        cout <<"\n after swapping :" ;
        swap (&x, &y);
        cout <<"\n x= " <<x<<" y = "<<y;
        cout <<"\n Initial value - Type Float" ;
        cout <<"\n x1 = "<<x1<<" y1="<<y1;
        cout <<"\n after swapping : " '
        swap (&x1, &y1);
        cout <<"\n x1 = "<<x1"<<" y1= "<<y1;
        cout <<endl;
}
```

OUTPUT :

Initial value - Type Integer
x = 70 y = 80
after swapping :
x = 80 y = 70
Initial value - Type Float
x1 = 25.4 y 1 = 35.6
after swapping :
x1 = 35.6 y1 = 25.4

23.4. DEFAULT INITIALIZER IN TEMPLATE TO ONLY CLASS TEMPLATES :

Like functions, default initializers are also permitted in template arguments, under the following situations

i) They can only be applied to non-type template arguments

ii) Like functions, they can only be applied to trailing arguments.

iii) Subsequent template declarations can add default initializers but cannot redefine existing default initializers.

iv) They can only be applied to class template declarations, not to function template declarations.

Program 23.4.1

Write a program in C++ to explain the use of default initializers in template.

```
// with default initialisers applied to class template declarations only.
# include <iostream>
using namespace std;
template <class T, int i=8>   //template initializer
class example
{
    public :
        T s;
        example (int j=7);
        int getval(T&)
        {
            return i;
        }
};
    template <class T, int i> example <T, i> :: example (int j):s(i)
{
        cout <<"\n i= "<<i<<" j="<<j;
            cout<<endl;
}
     void main ( )
{
    example <int>     exampleobj(50);   //int takes default value 8
    example <int,9> exampleobj1(90); //no default initializer since
                                     //int, 9 is explicit
}
```

OUTPUT :

i = 8 j = 50
i = 9 j = 90

And, **note that a template that defines a member function of a class template is treated as a function template and such a template cannot have default initializers.**

23.5. EXCEPTION HANDLING :

A special feature of C++ is its exception handling which means that execution of C++ program can continue even if it encounters a run time error which is not anticipated by treating the error as an exception and proceed further after performing necessary action given by the programmer, which is not available in other procedure oriented languages.

In programming sometimes we should think in pessimistic ways also. The reported syntax error can always be corrected easily. But, we cannot anticipate run time errors (for example, an attempt to divide a number by zero or to find square root of a negative number). Languages such as BASIC, FORTRAN and even C on encountering run time errors come to a halt after giving an error message. **In C++, it is possible to continue to run programs even after informing run time error messages by using exception handlers.** The Exception handling provides a way for a function that encounters an unusual situation to throw an exception and pass control to a direct or indirect caller of that function. The programmer may or may not be able to handle the exception. **Code that intercepts an exception is called a handler. Regardless of whether or not the caller can handle an exception, it may rethrow the exception so that, it can be intercepted by another handler.**

23.5.1. Actions of Exception Handling :

Exception handling is used to

i. Detect errors
ii. Inform the user that an error has been encountered
iii. Receive the error message
iv. Proceed with the program after performing necessary actions given by programmer.

The general form of an exception handling is as follows.

```
try
{
        // block of code to inspect for errors
}
        catch(parameter specifying exception type_1)
        {
           //exception handler for Exception_Type_1
        }
        catch(parameter specifying exception type_2)
        {
           //exception handler for Exception_Type_2
        }
        catch(parameter specifying exception type_3)
        {
           //exception handler for Exception_Type_3
        }
```

23.5.2. Methods of Exception Handling :

i) **Try - catch** : to detect a run type error (exception) and to execute consequent action.

The statements, which might create run time error, should be placed within the **'try' block.** The error (exception) that has been produced is caught by **'catch' keyword**. Also note that, **a catch block is only executed when an exception of a matching type is thrown.**

ii) **Throw :** To detect an exception and to eliminate it.

When we want to throw out exceptions we use the **keyword throw.** To start with, let's try exceptions out in a working example, in which we will have a look at throwing exceptions of type 'int' and 'const char*'. We can also include a few statements that will help us see the flow of control.

Program 23.5.1

Write a program in C++ to explain the use of try-catch and throw blocks.

```
#include <iostream>
#include <cstring>
using namespace std;
    void main ( )
{
    int pid;
    char pwd[10];
    try                         //to detect a run type (int) error
    {
      cout <<"\n Enter login id : " ;
      cin >> pid;
      if (pid != 786)             //login id is '786'
              throw pid;
      cout <<"\n Enter password : " ;
      cin>>pwd;
      if (strcmp(pwd, "good") != 0)    //password is 'good'
              throw "Invalid Password";
    }
    catch (int)
    {
      cout <<"\n Invalid Login id \n";
    }
    catch(const char* str)
    {
      cout <<"\n Message : "<<str;
    }
}
```

OUTPUT :

Enter login id : 768
Invalid Login id
Enter login id : 786
Enter password : bad
Message : Invalid Password

23.5.3. Handling of different types of Exceptions :

i) Class objects as exceptions :

We can also throw any kind of class object as exception. So, it is appropriate to define a specific exception class designed to represent a particular kind of problem. Let us consider a simple example. Our task is to admit students to preparatory class whose age lies between 3 and 5 by assuming the year 2007 as base year for admision in 2012. The output should be under age/over age when the input year is not appropriate.

The class that just follows defines an object representing an exception that stores a message indicating that there is a problem. Within the try-catch block we receive year of birth as input value. Then we have a list of one or more exception handlers such as following one for age check.

```
try
{
        cout <<"\n Enter year of birth : " ;                cin>>yy;
        passyear (yy);
}catch(const agecheck &exc) {
        exc.displaymessage ( );
}
```

When the input value is invalid, we can throw an exception :

```
if (year > 2009)
        throw agecheck ("Under age");
```

and have it caught by one of the handlers at outer level and execution will continue at the point of the handler.

An exception may be a class object type such as 'datecheck' or a fundamental C++ type like an integer. Obviously, a class object type can store and convey more information about the nature of the exception, as illustrated in this example. Let us consider the following code .throw 87; Will indeed throw an exception, which may be caught somewhere, but this idiom is not particularly useful.

Program 23.5.2

Write a program in C++ to explain the use of class objects as exception

```
#include <iostream>
using namespace std;
```

```
class agecheck
{
        private :
                char *msg;
        public :
                agecheck (char *str)
                {
                        msg=str;
                }
                void displaymessage ( ) const
        {
                        cerr<<"\n Reason for not admitting is : "<<msg;
                        cout <<"\n";
        }
};
        void passyear(int year)
{
                if (year >2009)
                        throw agecheck ("Under age");
                if (year <2007)

                        throw agecheck ("Over age");
}
        void main ( )
{
                int yy;
        try
        {
                cout <<"\n Enter year of birth :" ;
                cin>>yy;
                passyear (yy);
        } catch (const agecheck &exc) {
                exc. displaymessage ( );
        }
        // code for processing other details
}
```

OUTPUT :

Enter year of birth : 2005
Reason for not admitting is : Over age

Enter year of birth : 2010
Reason for not admitting is : Under age

ii) Throwing an exception :

Tranasfer of control to an exception handler is known as throwing an exception. A throw transfers control to the nearest handler with the appropriate type.

Program 23.5.3.

Write a program in C++ to explain the process of throwing an exception.

```
#include <iostream>
using namespace std;
void test ()
{
    int mark;
    cout <<"\n Enter Mark ";
    cin >>mark;
    if (mark > 100)
        throw mark;
}
void main ()
{
    try
    {
        test ();
    } catch (int) {
    cout <<"\n Mark should be less than or equal to 100\n";
    }
}
```

OUTPUT :

Enter Mark 104
Mark should be less than or equal to 100

In the above example, the exception with the value 'mark' is thrown, and control passes to the handler. **A throw transfers control to the nearest handler with the appropriate type.**

iii) Catching all exceptions :

When we are not sure of what the exception is and we want to prevent our program from terminating because of an uncaught exception, we use following construct to catch all exceptions.

```
Catch(..)
{
    //code
}
```

In the following example program, we use above construct to receive exceptions of type 'int' or 'float'. Since, this catch block will handle an exception of any data type this must always be last in the sequence of handlers for a try block.

Program 23.5.4

Write a program in C++ to explain the principle of catching all exceptions.

```
#include <iostream>
using namespace std;
void main ()
{
    int mark;
    float grade;
    try
    {
        cout <<"\n Enter mark : " :
        cin>>mark;
        if (mark > 500)
            throw mark;
        cout<<"\n Enter grade ";
        cin>>grade;
        if (grade > 10)
            throw grade;
        } catch (.....)
        {
            cout <<"\n Mark should be <=500 and grade should be <=10\n";
        }
}
```

OUTPUT :

Enter mark : 504
Mark should be <=500 and grade should be <=10

Enter mark : 481
Enter grade 11
Mark should be <=500 and grade should be <=10

iv) Unhandled exceptions :

a) use of terminate ( )

If an exception thrown in a try block is not handled by any of its catch blocks, then the standard library function terminate ( ) is called in. The terminate ( ) function calls a predefined default terminate handler and subsequently it calls the standard library function abort ( ). *The difference between abort ( ) and exit. is, the abort ( ) function terminates the entire program immediately and unlike exit ( ), the abort ( ) function does not call destructors for any constructed static objects.*

```
#include <iostream>
using namespace std;
void test ()
{
        throw 100;
}
void main ()
{
        try
        {
                test ();
        }
                catch (char *msg)
                {
                        //
                }
        }
```

In the above program an exception of type 'int' is thrown, but there is no exception handler for it. And in these circumstances a special function terminate ( ) is called. This function is called whenever the exception handing mechanism cannot find a handler for a thrown exception. It calls the standard library function abort ( ). The modified program is as follows.

Program 23.5.5

Write a program in C++ to illustrate the action using terminate ( ) when we encounter unhandled exceptions.

```
#include <iostream>
using namespace std;
typedef void (*abc)(void);
abc set_terminate (abc);
void t1 ()
{
        cerr<<"\n Terminate() called \n" ;
        exit (1);
}
void test ()
{
        throw 100;
}
        void main ()
{
        set_terminate (t1);
```

```
        try
        {
               test ( ) ;
        }
        catch (char *)
        {
               //
        }
    }
```

OUTPUT :

Terminate ( ) called

Since, terminate ( ) is a binary function which by default aborts the program. Also we can override if we want.

b) Use of Unexpected ( )

The unexpected is called when a function with an exception specification throws an exception of a type not listed in the exceptions specification for the function. In the following example, test()'s exception specification is '*throw (char *)*'

A function declaration without such a specification may throw any type of exception, such as '*throw ( )* '

is not allowed to throw exceptions at all. *Here, by default unexpected ( ) calls terminate ( ).* Also, note that in certain cases where the user has defined their own versions unexpected ( ), execution may continue.

c) Use of Standard exceptions :

The standard library defines a hierarchy of exceptions that is used by many of its functions. When we design our own classes, or derive new exceptions from one of them in order to keep consistency and to have our own exception class caught by catch (exception&):

Exception

- Bad-alloc
- Bad_exception
- Bad_cast
- Bad_typeid
- Ios :: failure
- Logic_error
    - Length_error
    - Domain_error
    - Out-of_range
    - Invalid_argument

Runtime error

Range_error
Overflow_error
Underflow_error

Indentation above means derivation. Also note that all exceptions have the member function what() that returns a char * with explanations. For example consider the exception bad-alloc. This is the exception thrown by an operator new when it is not possible to allocate an object for insufficient memory. The exception ios :: failure is thrown by iostream(input output stream) classes when the input/output goes wrong.

23.5.4. Constructors and Destructors in Exception Handling :

When an exception is thrown and control passes to a catch block following a try block, destructors are called for all automatic objects constructed since the beginning of the try block is directly associated with that catch block. If an exception is thrown during construction of an object consisting of subjects or array elements, destructors are only called for those subobjects or array elements successfully constructed before the exception was thrown. A destructor for a local static object will only be called if the object was successfully constructed.

i) If a destructor detects an exception and issues a throw, the exception can be caught if the caller of the destructor was contained within a try block and an appropriate catch is coded.

ii) If an exception is thrown by a function called from an inner try block, but caught by an outer try block (because the inner try block did not have an appropriate handler), all objects constructed within both the outer and all inner try blocks are destroyed. If the thrown object has a destructor, the destructor is not called until the exception is caught and handled.

If we throw an object with a constructor, we can construct an object that contains information relevant to the catch expression.

In the following example, an object of class DivideByZero isthrown by the function divide(). The constructor copies the string "Division by zero" into the char array errname. Because DivideByZero is a derived class of class Matherr, the catch block for Matherr catches the thrown exception. The catch block can then access information provided by the thrown object, in this case the text of an error message.

Program 23.5.6

Write a program in C++ to illustrate use of constructor and destructor in exception handling.

```
# include <string.h>          //needed for strcpy
#include <iostream.h>
```

```
class Matherr
{
        public: char errname [30];
};
class Divide By Zero : public Matherr
{
        public :
                DivideByZero ( ) {strcpy (errnmae, "Division by zero") ; }
};
        double divide (double a, double b)
        {
                if (b == 0) throw DivideByZero ( );
                return a/b;
        }
        void main ( )
        {
                double a=7, b=0;
                try (divide (a,b);
        }
        catch (Matherr xx)
        {
                cout <<xx.errname <<endl;
        }
}
```

23.5.5. Other Exception Specifications :

The compiler does not prevent an exception specification from defining a more limited set of valid exceptions than the set of exceptions the function may actually throw. Such an error is detected only at run time, and only if the unspecified exception is thrown. In the following example, Name Too Short is thrown from within a function that explicitly states that it will only throw NameTooLong. This is a valid function although at run time, if NameTooShort is thrown, a call to unexpected () will be made.

```
#include <string.h>
class NameTooLong { };
class NameTooShort { };

void check(char* fname)throw (NameTooLong)
{
        if ( strlen(fname)<4) throw NameTooShort( );
}
```

* * *

COMPREHENSION - 23

Note : By answering all the questions given in this comprehension one can answer any objective type of questions easily whatever be the form of the question. Answers for these questions can be obtained by going through the topics in this chapter carefully.

1. What is namespace standard?
2. How does the use of **namespace std**; help us?
3. Explain how you can write programs using and without using namespace std;.
4. Explain creation of a namespace in C++ .
5. What is RTTI ? Why is RTTI required?
6. Explain with an example how to obtain run time type information?
7. What is meant by type casting?
8. What are the different types of type casting operators? What do they do?
9. Explain the use of different types of type casting operators.
10. What are templates? In what way they are useful?
11. Explain the different types of templates.
12. Explain the use of different functions for the same template.
13. Explain use of named templates.
14. Explain the differences between class and function templates.
15. Explain default initializers in template arguments.
16. What is meant by exception handling? Hen is it useful?
17. How is exception handling done?
18. What are the actions of exception handlers?
19. What are the methods of exception handling?
20. What are the different types of exceptions that can be handled?
21. What is throwing an exception?
22. What does a throw do?
23. Explain catching all exceptions.
24. What is meant by unhandled exceptions?
25. What methods do you follow with unhandled exceptions?
26. What does use of unexpected ( ) function do?
27. What are standard exceptions? Give standard exceptions.
28. What happens when an exception is thrown?
29. Explain the use of constructors and destructors in exception handling.
30. What happens when an exception other than specified exceptions occurs?

* * *

EXERCISE - 23

Note : By answering all the questions given in this exercise one can answer subjective type of questions easily including problems. The worked examples in the chapter may help in solving these questions.

1. Explain about namespace standard feature in C++.
2. Explain RTTI.
3. What are templates? When and how you use templates?
4. Explain use of named templates.
5. Discuss about exception handling.
6. Discuss in detail use of constructors and destructors in exception handling.

* * *

CHAPTER - 24
ABSTRACT DATA TYPE (ADT) PROGRAMS

24.1. INTRODUCTION :

So far we have gone through the features of C and C++ programming including data structures in C and C++ and also made a comparative study of data structures through C and C++. The objective so far was to write an effective program in C and C++ using various features of the two languages.

In this chapter we try to present an effective program which is common for different types of tasks of the same nature. For example if we want to have a shopping program we consider only salient structure of shopping like going to a departmental store, picking up the required items, paying the bill and finishing the shopping. These steps are common for any type of shopping program, for any type of items in any shop. Only these salient features have to be entered by the user. All other parts of the programing are immaterial for the user. This is like using a template program.

Having studied the templates and classes which can hide specified data from the users and with knowledge of abstract data types it becomes easier for us to design ADT programs (abstract data type programs) ADT programs can be withdrawn for C language also eventhou ADT and ADT programs are preferred for object oriented programming languages like C++, Java etc. This is an essential paort of design of object oriented programming.

24.2 WHAT IS ADT?

In computing, an **abstract data type** (ADT) is a mathematical model for a certain class of data structures that have similar behavior; or for certain data types of one or more programming languages that have similar semantics. An abstract data type is defined indirectly, only by the operations that may be performed on it and by mathematical constraints on the effects (and possibly cost) of those operations defining **an abstract data type (ADT)**

An abstract data type is a mathematical model, together with various operations defined on the model. Sets of integers, together with the operations of Union interjection and set difference, form a simple example of an ADT. To represent the mathematical model underlying an ADt, we use data structures, which are a collection of variables, possibly of several data types connected in various ways.

The ADT encapsulates a data type in the sense that the definition of the type and all operations on the type can be localised and are not visible to the users of the ADT. To use users, just the declaration of the ADT and its operations are important.

24.2.1 Abstract Data Structure :

An ADT is a set of elements with a collection of well defined operations.

1) The operations can take operands from not only the instances of the ADT but other types of operands or instances of other ADTs.
2) Similarly results need not be instances of the ADT.
3) At least one operand or the result is of the ADT type in question.

Object Oriented languages such as C++ and Java provide explicit support for expressing ADTs by means of Classes.

A Data Structure is an implementation of an ADT. That is it is a translation of ADT into statements of a programming language. It consists of

i) The declarations that define a variable to be of that ADT type.

ii) The operations defined on the ADT(using procedures of the programming language).

An ADT implementation chooses a data structure to represent the ADT. Each data structure is built up from the basic data types of the underlying programming language using the available data structuring facilities such as arrays, records (structures in C) , pointers, files, sets, etc.

Example :

A " Queue " is an abstract data type which can be defined as a sequence of elements with operations such as ENQUEUE(x,Q), DEQUEUE(Q) .

This can be implemented using data structures such as

1) Array
2) Singly linked list
3) Doubly linked list
4) Circular array

24.2.2 Abstract Data Type :

An Abstract Data type is defined as a mathematical model of the data objects that make up a data type as well as the functions that operate on these objects. There are no standard conventions for defining them. A broad division may be drawn between "imperative" and "functional" definition styles.

i) **Imperative abstract data type definitions :**

In the "imperative" view, which is closer to the philosophy of imperative programming languages, an abstract data structure is conceived as an entity that is *mutable* – meaning that it may be in different *states* at different times. Some operations may change the state of the ADT; therefore, the order in which operations are evaluated is important, and the same operation on the same entities may have different effects if executed at different times – just like the instructions of a computer, or the commands and procedures of an imperative language. To underscore this view, it is customary to say that the operations are *executed* or *applied*, rather than *evaluated*. The imperative style is often used when describing abstract algorithms.This is described by Donald E.Knuth and can be referenced from "The Art of Computer Programming.

ii) **Abstract variable :**

Imperative ADT definitions often depend on the concept of an *abstract variable*, which may be regarded as the simplest non-trivial ADT. An abstract variable V is a mutable entity that admits two operations:

store(V,x) where x is a *value* of unspecified nature; and

fetch(V), that yields a value;

with the constraint that fetch(V) always returns the value x used in the most recent store(V,x) operation on the same variable V.

More generally, ADT definitions often assume that any operation that changes the state of one ADT instance has no effect on the state of any other instance (including other instances of the same ADT) – unless the ADT axioms imply that the two instances are connected (aliased) in that sense. For example, when extending the definition of abstract variable to include abstract records, the operation that selects a field from a record variable R must yield a variable V that is aliased to that part of R.

iii) **Instance creation :**

Some algorithms need to create new instances of some ADT (such as new variables, or new stacks). To describe such algorithms, one usually includes in the ADT definition a create ( ) operation that yields an instance of the ADT, usually with axioms equivalent to the result of create() is distinct from any instance S in use by the algorithm.

This axiom may be strengthened to exclude also partial aliasing with other instances. On the other hand, this axiom still allows implementations of create() to yield a previously created instance that has become inaccessible to the program.

iv) Preconditions, post conditions, and invariants :

In imperative-style definitions, the axioms are often expressed by *preconditions*, that specify when an operation may be executed; *post-conditions*, that relate the states of the ADT before and after the execution of each operation; and *invariants*, that specify properties of the ADT that are *not* changed by the operations.

24.3. SALIENT FEATURES OF ABSTRACT DATA TYPES :

Before considering some of the ADT programs in C and C++ we shall recall our concepts of ADT and its advantages.

i) Abstract Data Types (ADTs):

- What is data abstraction?
  - Stack ADT
  - Abstract/algebraic specification
- Object-orientation
  - Data abstraction + code sharing through inheritance
- Object-oriented design
  - Examples (in C vs C++)

ii) Need for ADTs:

- **Advantages**
  - **Can modify the ADT implementation without affecting users of the ADT**
  - User's changes can't affect the ADT
  - Encourages modularity in programs enabling construction of larger, more complex codes by more than one programmer
- Possible disadvantages
  - Writer of ADT has to put more effort into design of a useful interface of operations.

iii) Design of ADTs :

- ADTs are usually designed with some invariant of its behavior in mind
  - E.g., Stack invariant: *top of stack is always the last element added*
- Need to initialize stack within the ADT
- Must keep some variables private (*top_of_stack*)
- May keep some operations private to prevent illegaluse (e.g., check *is Empty()* when doing a *pop*)

24.4. WHY ADT?

The purpose of a struct that people usually discuss is simply grouping heterogeneous types into a single collection, which may then be referred to collectively.

Another, and at least as important, function of a struct, which isn't usually discussed in the context of procedural languages like C or Pascal, but is a central topic in Object Based languages like Ada, or Object Oriented languages like C++ or Smalltalk or Python, is to create abstract data types (ADT's). C can do ADT's pretty well really, except for the information hiding part (which it has in common with Python, in a sense), and also C doesn't do inheritance well (C++, Smalltalk and Python do - this being the primary distinction between a mere "Object Based" language like Ada, and these "Object Oriented" languages).

The purpose of an ADT is to have a single API for a kind of data and the operations performed on that data, but implementing the data representation and operations in different ways, but with different tradeoffs insulating the dependent code from being heavily impacted when the data representation needs to change.

24.5. ADT STACK EXAMPLE :

One of the classic examples of why we might want an ADT, is implementing a stack. A stack is where you put items in at one end of a "list" (in the generic sense, not the Computer Science sense), and pull items back out from the same end. **The basic operations of a stack is the same even though the stack may be implemented using different data structures.**

Three common data representations that might be used internally by a stack ADT (abstract data type) would be an array or a linked list or both.

1. **An array :**

   The array implementation of a stack is nice because it's fast, and because it has low memory requirements when the stack is full, but it'll tend to lead to messiness if the array fills up (which C can get around with realloc, but a language like Pascal (the Niklaus Wirth definition - Borland likely extended for this) doesn't have much in the way of an equivalent).

2. **A linked list.:**

   The linked list implementation of a stack is nice because it has no fixed limit on how large the stack can grow (other than available memory, at least on non-segmented architectures), but it'll tend to be a little bit slower, and it'll use more memory than an array implementation when the two stack implementations hold a number of elements near the capacity of the array implementation.

3. **Array and Linked list (Both) :**

   If we implement both of these with identical API's, then we can very quickly and easily change our programs from using the plusses and minuses of one implementation (array) to the other (linked list - or vice versa).

As a further example of an abstract type, say we have a program that uses a singly-linked list (linked only forward, but not back again), and suddenly we find that the changing needs of the program require us to be able to quickly start at the end of the list, and work backward. We could easily approach this with a recursive algorithm (if you aren't worried about the CPU and memory requirements), but often a slight change in data representation is better.

In such a case, we have pretty much three choices:

1. If we were using a library of C functions that implements both singly-linked lists, as well as doubly-linked lists (forward and back), and the doubly-linked list API is already a superset of the singly-linked list API, then we can just switch to the doubly-linked list implementation, and all of our existing code that required only a singly-linked list should continue functioning just fine (so long as they do not violate the ADT definition by reaching inside the struct's inappropriately), so we can dive right into adding the new functionality, rather rearranging the old singly-linked code first.

2. If we are implementing our own linked list functions (seldom a good idea anymore, but a lot of CS students are required to do it, since it's a good example of ADT's/Objects), and we have carefully abstracted our singly-linked list implementation, then we can just add another ADT (possibly via inheritance in a fully object oriented language like C++ or Smalltalk or Python, but not C or Ada) that does doubly linked lists, and other than the (perhaps partially) new ADT and the new code for doubly-linked lists, our existing code doesn't need to be modified much, if at all.

3. If we weren't abstracting our code well, then we could easily end up doing a near-complete rewrite due to what may actually be a relatively small change in the program's requirements.

So by having this typedef/struct with a single element, if there is a well defined set of functions that can look inside the typedef/struct (and only they are allowed to do it – ie. the inspection/changing of the struct isn't scattered throughout our program) that opens the door to easy changes - like switching to a doubly-linked list, or adding a field that keeps a count of the members in the list, or even switching to an entirely different kind of data structure behind the scenes, while the rest of our code takes rest.

Put another way, if we have poorly abstracted code, when we need to change a data representation, we can easily get a sort of "ripple effect", where changes in the code start in one small place, and kind of "ripple outward" (a bit like a single drop into a pool of water) into ever further parts of the code. But if things are well abstracted, then most of the time (some would argue all of the time), the "ripples of change" stop at the ADT boundaries, which can be quite a time-saver in the long run.

Some common ADTs, which have proved useful in a great variety of applications, are

Container
Deque
List
Map
Multimap
Multiset
Priority queue
Queue
Set
Stack
String
Tree

Each of these ADTs may be defined in many ways and variants, not necessarily equivalent. For example, a stack ADT may or may not have a count operation that tells how many items have been pushed and not yet popped. This choice makes a difference not only for its clients but also for the implementation

24.5.1. Stack ADT :

- **Abstract Specification**
- Tells behavior of ADT; offers enough information for use of the ADT
- Operations:

– *createStack:* Stack

– *push*: Stack, element '! Stack

– *pop*: Stack '! Stack, element

– *peek:* Stack '! element

– *isEmpty*: Stack '! boolean

- Variables:

– s: Stack – x: element

- **Axioms: for Stack:**

– *isEmpty(createStack()) = true*

– *isEmpty(push(s, x)) = false*

– *peek(createStack()) = error*

– *peek(push(s, x)) = x*

– *pop(createStack()) = error*

– *pop(push(s, x)) = s*

- **Specifications of ADT Stack :**

a) one *constructor*, namely, o stack *create_stack(void) that constructs a data structure of type stack, empty for the moment, and returns a pointer to it, two *access functions*, namely,

b) boolean stack_is_empty(stack *s) that, given a pointer s to a stack, returns TRUE if the stack is empty and returns FALSE otherwise,

c) stack_object *top_of_stack(stack *s) that, given a pointer s to a nonempty stack, returns a pointer to the object on the top of the stack,

d) two *manipulator functions*, namely,

i) void push_on_stack(stack *s, stack_object *object); that, given a pointer s to a stack and given a pointer object to an object, pushes the object on the top of the stack,

f) void pop_stack(stack *s); that, given a pointer s to a nonempty stack, pops the stack.

The data type stack_object is provided by the ADT user; the data type stack is chosen by the designer of the data structure that implements the ADT. In C, the data type boolean is not provided explicitly, but may be created by the definitions

```
#define TRUE 1
#define FALSE 0
```
and the declaration
```
typedef char boolean;
```

We have already studied templates and classes which can hide certain data from the user, use of which makes creation of ADT lists (using singly linked list, stack), queue, functions etc. We are also already exposed to some ADT programs without mentioning about it, For example in an employees data only the authorised employee can view his salary details and that too only view, but cannot change with the data. Such features are taken care of in ADT programs.

Program Frame work - 1

A list ADT: implement as linked-list

A list ADT:
```
template <class C>
class list{
public:
list();                      O(1) time
bool isEmpty();              O(1) time
bool isFull();               O(1) time(just say "NO")
void insert(C x, int p);     O(n) time
C findkth(int p);            O(n) time
```

```
void delete(int p);//delete
 //the element in position                        O(n) time
int sizeof(); // how many elements in the list?
private:
.
.
};
```

Program Frame work: - 2

A modified list ADT

A list ADT:

```
template <class C>
class list{
public:
list();
bool isEmpty();
bool isFull();
void insert(C x, int p);
C findkth(int p);
void delete(int p);// delete the element in position p
int sizeof(); // how many elements in the list?
private:
.
.
};
```

Program 24.6.1

The program for ADT List in C involves the typical contents of an ADT Menu:

Append
Remove
Print
Make Null
Empty
Code:

```
//Shiela Salamat
//3ITD - UST
//EXP4_3.CPP
//August 15, 2010
```

```
#include<stdio.h>
#include<conio.h>
#include<ctype.h>
typedef struct{
char xiru[20];
int xixi;
}brand;
void append(brand *xu,char *chr)
{
if((*xu).xixi>=19)
printf("STRING IS FULL");
else
{(*xu).xixi++;
(*xu).xixi=(*xu).xixi-1;
(*xu).xiru[(*xu).xixi]=*chr;
(*xu).xixi++;
}
getch();
}
void remove(brand *xu,int *pot)
{
char xe;
printf("\nAre you sure you want to remove? ");
xe=getche();
if(xe=='y'||xe=='Y')
{
if(*pot>=((*xu).xixi+1)||*pot<=0)
printf("\nInvalid position");
   else
  {for(int xr=(*pot)-1;xr<(*xu).xixi;xr++)
  (*xu).xiru[xr]=(*xu).xiru[xr+1];
  (*xu).xixi—;
  }
}
getch();
}
void print(brand *xu)
{
if((*xu).xixi<=0)
```

```
printf("String empty");
else
{   for(int xz=0;xz<(*xu).xixi;xz++)
        printf(" %c",(*xu).xiru[xz]);
}
getche();
}
void makenull(brand *xu)
{
if((*xu).xixi>0)
  (*xu).xixi=-1;
else
  printf("Letter string already empty");
getch();
}

int empty(brand *xu)
{
if((*xu).xixi<=0)
return 1;
else
return 0;

int full(brand *xu)
{if((*xu).xixi>=19)
return 1;
else
return 0;
}
void main(){
clrscr();
int cn,po;
char y='n',xy;
brand x;
x.xixi=0;
do{
clrscr();
```

```
printf("\n\t\t\t\t-MENU-\n\n");
printf("\t\t\t1. Append\n");
printf("\t\t\t2. Remove\n");
printf("\t\t\t3. Print\n");
printf("\t\t\t4. Makenull\n");
printf("\t\t\t5. Empty\n");
printf("\t\t\t6. Full\n");

printf("\t\t\t7. Exit\n\n");
printf("Enter chosen no.: ");
scanf("%d",&cn);

if(cn==1)
{printf("\nInput a character: "); char xy=getche(); append(&x,&xy);}

else if(cn==2)
{printf("\nposition? "); scanf("%d",&po); remove(&x,&po);}

else if(cn==3)
print(&x);

else if(cn==4)
{printf("\n Are you sure you want to make null? "); char u=getche();
if(u=='y' || u=='Y') makenull(&x); else y='n';}

else if(cn==5)

{ int ru=empty(&x); if(ru==1) printf("string is empty"); else printf("string is not
empty"); getche();}

else if(cn==6)

{ int ki=full(&x); if(ki==1) printf("string is full"); else printf("string is not full");
getche(); }

else if(cn==7)

{ printf("\nAre you really sure you want to exit? "); y=getche(); if(y=='N' || y=='n')
getch(); else getch();}

else {printf("Input is invalid/not on menu"); getch(); y='n';}
}while(y=='n' || y=='N');

getch();

}
```

Program Frame work-3

A Stack ADT Program in C :

```
STACK ADT
template <class C>
class stack
public:
stack();
bool isEmpty();
bool isFull();
void push(C x);
C top();
void pop();// delete the element in position 1
int sizeof(); // how many elements in the //list?
private:
.
.
};
```

Program Frame Work - 4

Implementing Stack as a linked list

```
typedef struct stack_item
{
 stack_object content;
struct stack_item *next;
} stack_item;
typedef stack_item *stack;
stack *create_stack(void)
{
 stack *s;
 s = (stack *) malloc(sizeof(stack));
 if(s==NULL)
  {
   printf("OUT OF MEMORY!\n");
   exit(1);
  }
    *s = NULL;
     return s;
    }
    boolean stack_is_empty(stack *s)
{
     return( (*s==NULL) ? TRUE : FALSE );
}
```

```
stack_object *top_of_stack(stack *s)
{
 if(stack_is_empty(s)==TRUE)
  {
   printf("TRIED TO FIND THE TOP OF AN EMPTY STACK!\n");
   exit(1);
  }
 return &((*s)->content);
}
void push_on_stack(stack *s, stack_object *object)
 stack_item *new_item;
new_item = (stack_item *) malloc(sizeof(stack_item));
 if(new_item==NULL)
  {
   printf("OUT OF MEMORY!\n");
   exit(1);
  }
 new_item->content=*object;
 new_item->next=*s;
 *s=new_item;
      void pop_stack(stack *s)
{
 stack_item *memo;
  if(stack_is_empty(s)==TRUE)
  {
   printf("TRIED TO POP AN EMPTY STACK!\n");
   exit(1);
  }
 memo=*s;
 *s=memo->next;
 free(memo);
}
```

Program Frame Work - 5

Implementing Stack as an array

```
typedef struct stack
{
 stack_object *array;
 int capacity;
 int count;
} stack;
```

```
stack *create_stack(void)
{
 stack *s;
 stack_object *object;
 s = (stack *) malloc(sizeof(stack));
 if(s==NULL)
  {
   printf("OUT OF MEMORY!\n");
   exit(1);
  }
 object = (stack_object *) malloc(sizeof(stack_object));
 if(object==NULL)
  {
   printf("OUT OF MEMORY!\n");
   exit(1);
  }
 s->array = object;
 s->count = 0;
 s->capacity = 1;
 return s;
}
boolean stack_is_empty(stack *s)
{
 return( (s->count==0) ? TRUE : FALSE );
}
stack_object *top_of_stack(stack *s)
{
 if(stack_is_empty(s)==TRUE)
  {
   printf("TRIED TO FIND THE TOP OF AN EMPTY STACK!\n");
   exit(1);
  }
return (s->array)+((s->count)-1);
}
void push_on_stack(stack *s, stack_object *object)
{
stack_object *newarray;
 if(s->count == s->capacity)
  /* DOUBLE THE LENGTH OF THE ARRAY */
```

```
  {
   (s->capacity)*=2;
   newarray = (stack_object *)
    realloc(s->array, (s->capacity)*sizeof(stack_object));
   if(newarray==NULL)
    {
     printf("OUT OF MEMORY!\n");
     exit(1);
    }
   s->array = newarray;
  }
 (s->array)[s->count]=*object;
 (s->count)++;
void pop_stack(stack *s)
{
 if(stack_is_empty(s)==TRUE)
  {
   printf("TRIED TO POP AN EMPTY STACK!\n");
   exit(1);
  }
 (s->count)--;
```

Program Frame Work - 6

24.6. A QUEUE ADT

A stack ADT:

```
template <class C>
class list{
public:
list();
bool isEmpty();
bool isFull();

void insert(C x, int 1);
C findkth(int sizeof());
void delete(int sizeof());
int sizeof(); // how many elements in the list?
private:
.
.
};
```

```
queue<int> Q1;
Q1.enqueue(5);
Q1.enqueue(10);
Q1.enqueue(8);
cout << Q1.front();
Q1.dequeue();
cout << Q1.sizeof();
```

Program 24.7.1

Program in C++to implement the Queue ADT using an array by N.C on April 14, 2011 in C++

```
#include<iostream>
#include<conio.h>
#include<stdlib.h>
using namespace std;

class queue
{
        int queue1[5];
        int rear,front;
    public:
        queue()
         {
            rear=-1;
            front=-1;
         }
        void insert(int x)
        {
          if(rear > 4)
           {
             cout <<"queue over flow";
             front=rear=-1;
             return;
           }
           queue1[++rear]=x;
           cout <<"inserted" <<x;
        }
```

```
        void delete()
        {
          if(front==rear)
           {
             cout <<"queue under flow";
             return;
           }
           cout <<"deleted" <<queue1[++front];
        }
        void display()
        {
          if(rear==front)
           {
             cout <<" queue empty";
             return;
           }
          for(int i=front+1;i<=rear;i++)
          cout <<queue1[i]<<" ";
        }
};
main()
{
   int ch;
   queue qu;
   while(1)
    {
       cout <<"\n1.insert  2.delete  3.display  4.exit\nEnter ur choice";
       cin >> ch;
       switch(ch)
        {
         case 1:   cout <<"enter the element";
      cin >> ch;
                   qu.insert(ch);
                   break;
         case 2:  qu.delete(); break;
         case 3:  qu.display();break;
         case 4: exit(0);
        }
    }
return (0);
}
```

OUTPUT

```
1.insert 2.delet 3.display 4.exit
Enter ur choice1
enter the element21
inserted21
1.insert 2.delet 3.display 4.exit
Enter ur choice1
enter the element22
inserted22
1.insert 2.delet 3.display 4.exit
Enter ur choice1
enter the element16
inserted16
1.insert delete 3.display 4.exit
Enter ur choice3
21 22 16
1.insert 2.delet 3.display 4.exit
Enter ur choice2
deleted21
1.insert 2.delet 3.display 4.exit
Enter ur choice3
22 16
1.insert 2.delet 3.display 4.exit
Enter ur choice
S
```

24.7. ADT EMPLOYEE LIST :

Program Frame Work - 7

Implementing ADTs in C++ by Tom Kelliher, CS23, Mar. 5, 1997

ADT Example: Employee List

Members:

- first name — 20 characters
- last name — 30 characters
- department code — at most 150 departments
- Annual salary — at most $1,000,000,000 (future growth)
- Manager — pointer to manager record

- Committee codes – list of committee memberships (no limit), at most 1,000 committees

Design goals:

- Maintain all employee records
- Minimize memory usage
- Exact representation of numeric values
- Controlled modification through ADT operations only

Common implementation details

```
struct committeeList

{
  unsigned short committeeCode;
  struct committeeList* next;
};


struct employeeRecord
{
  char firstName[20];
  char lastName[30];

  unsigned char deptCode;
  long salary;
  struct employeeRecord* manager;
  struct committeeList* committees;
  struct employeeRecord* next;
};
```

ADT employee list operations?

- create
- destroy
- addEmployee
- deleteEmployee
- retrieveEmployee
- displayEmployee
- modifyEmployeeSalary
- addEmployeeToCommittee
- ...

Program Frame work in C - 8

Create:

struct employeeRecord* employees = NULL;

Where is the "wall?"

What information is hidden?

Kludge Information Hiding in C

- Separate modules (.c files)
- Static globals
- Interface in .h file
- Implementation in separate .c file

Skeleton of main module:

```
#include "list.h"
...
main(){
create();
addEmployee(...);
...
}
```

Skeleton of list.h:

```
/* definitions for committeeList, employeeRecord structs */
int create(void);
int destroy(void);
int addEmployee(<formals>);
...
```

Skeleton of list.c:

```
#include "list.h"
static struct employeeRecord* employees;

/* definitions for ADT operations */
```

Three files:

- main.c
- list.c
- list.h

Compiling:

```
cc -o database main.c list.c
```

* * *

COMPREHENSION - 24

Note : By answering all the questions given in this comprehension one can answer any objective type of questions easily whatever be the form of the question. Answers for these questions can be obtained by going through the topics in this chapter carefully.

1. Can ADT Programming be written in C Language also?
2. What is ADT?
3. What are the features of ADT?
4. What are the languages that provide explicit support for ADTs?
5. What is Data Structure in terms of ADT? What does it contain of?
6. What is a Queue? What are the operations involved in Queue?
7. What kinds of Data Structures can be used to implement Queue?
8. What is an Abstract Data Type?
9. What are the well defined operations that can be performed on the set of elements contained in ADT?
10. Define imperative Abstract Data Type.
11. Define imperative Abstract Variable.
12. Explain Instance Creation?
13. Explain Pre Conditions, Post Conditions and Invariants.
14. Why should ADT be used? What is its purpose?
15. Explain ADT Stack example.
16. What are the common Data Representations that are used in Stack ADT
17. Mention some common ADTs used in a Variety of applications.
18. Explain the concept of ADTs and their advantages. Highlight the special advantage and consequent benefits.
19. Explain Specifications of Stack ADTs.
20. Explain LIST ADT.
21. Explain modified LIST ADT.
22. Explain implementation of LIST ADT as linked list.
23. Explain implementation of STACK ADT as linked list.
24. Explain implementation of STACK ADT as linked list.
25. Explain implementation of STACK ADT as an ARRAY.
26. Describe the Frame Work of QUEUE ADT.
27. Explain implementation of QUEUE ADT as an ARRAY.

* * *

EXERCISE - 24

Note : **By answering all the questions given in this exercise one can answer subjective type of questions easily including problems. The worked examples in the chapter may help in solving these questions.**

1. (a) What is an abstract data type?
   (b) Are basic data types are abstract data types?
   (c) Is the user defined data type "structure" is an abstract data type?
2. (a) What is a Deque. Define the ADT for a Deque.
   (b) Define an abstract c++ class deque that includes methods for each function of the ADT deque.
3. Write a C ++ program using stack ADT that reads an infix expression, converts the expression to postfix form and evaluates the postfix expression.
4. Define the Abstract data type for Stack. Write a C++ program to implement Towers of Hanoi using stack ADT?
5. (a) What is a dictionary? Define the abstract data type for it? Write the abstractclass for the dictionary?
   (b) Give the applications of dictionary or dictionary with duplicates in which sequential access is desired.
6. Define the Abstract data type for Queue. Write a C ++ program to implement Queue ADT using arrays.
7. Explain ADT and ADT Programming.
8. Explain the need for ADT Programming.
9. Explain the Salient Features of Abstract Data Types.
10. Explain the Menu or Frame work of ADT for List, Stack, and Queue.
11- Explain about some common ADT applications.
12. Explain List ADT using linked list.
13. Explain Modified List ADT.
14. Write a Stack ADT program in C.
15. Explain Stack ADT Programming using Linked List.
16. Explain Stack ADT Programming using ARRAY.
17. Explain QUEUE ADT Programming using ARRAY.
18. Write ADT Employee List Program in C++.

* * *

References

1. Kemighan, B.W. and Ritchie, D.M., The C Programming Language, Prentice-Hall, 1977.
2. Data Structures Using C : Aaron M. Tenenbaum, Yedidyah Langsam, Moshe J. Augenstein, Pearson Education, 2005.
3. C Programming and Data Structures, E. Balagurusamy, - Tata McGraw-Hill Publishing Company Ltd., New Delhi.
4. C and Data Structures - Ashok N. Kamthane, Pearson Education, 2005.
5. C and Data Structures, P. Radha Ganesan, Scitech Publications (India) Pvt., Ltd.,
6. C++ Primer, Stanley B. Lippman, Josee Lajoie, Pearson Education, 2005.
7. Lafore, R., Object Oriented programming in Turbo C++, Galgotia, New Delhi, 1992.
8. Bjarne Stroustrup, The C++ Programming Language, Addison - Wesley, 1997.
9. Balagurusamy E., C++ Programming , Tata McGraw-Hill, 1997.
10. Programming with C++, P. Radha Ganesan, Scitech Publications (India) Pvt. Ltd., Chennai, 2002.
11. Wikipaedia

www.ingramcontent.com/pod-product-compliance
Lightning Source LLC
Chambersburg PA
CBHW080157170726
48282CB00005B/55

* 9 7 8 9 3 8 5 4 3 3 4 1 2 *